Published by www.ericgeorgedejong.com

ISBN 978-0-620-86455-8

Printed and bound by X Mega Digital (Pty) Ltd,
24 Kinghall Rd, Epping 2, Cape Town

In memory of Kees.

For Jenny, Gary, Veronica and Dan, with love.

Running Dogs and Rose's Children
An African memoir

Everything in my book happened – apart from the stuff that might get me into trouble. Those bits I might have made up. I hope you enjoy.

Eric de Jong
Harare – July 2019

Alas - as per the Collins Dictionary meaning - adv. 1. Unfortunately, regretfully interj 2. an expression of grief or alarm. It is a word used all too often in Zimbabwe. Alas.

Chapter One

Jenny's gynaecologist knew everything there was to know about making babies. It was his job. And to prove that he was on top of his job, the gynae kept a photo of his own personal brood in a prominent position on his busy desk. His three boys looked like three ginger peas from a ginger pod. Jenny was one of the reasons the desk was so busy. She visited her gynae a lot. She was having problems falling pregnant. Both of us were.

The doctor took up Jenny's challenge with gusto. Making women have babies was what he did best. He got busy plotting a chart of her menstrual cycle and mapping her optimum periods for ovulation. Invariably these optimum periods fell during working hours, and I had to sneak out of the office to see to Jenny's conjugal rights. It was strange. Apparently, babies were always born in the middle of the night but were always made in the middle of important business meetings. Apart from our baby, that was. After months of rushing home from the office to do my manly bit, nothing!!

The gynae was perplexed at the lack of success. He wanted to see a sperm sample. And with this in mind, he gave me a big jar that verged on huge but no proverbial dirty magazine. When I asked for one, I was told it was a family practice, and pornography was frowned upon. I found it very hard to perform on demand, especially with a room full of women outside who knew exactly where I was going and why. The gynae's waiting room was always full to overflowing with women.

But even more embarrassing was the size of my sample. As I sat considering my pathetic offerings, I remembered having read somewhere that a pig's average ejaculation was more than a tablespoon full. Mine would have been hard-pressed to fill a teaspoon. Shielding my puerile offerings from the prying eyes, I hurried them to the gynae, muttering apologies and excuses with promises to do better next time. But he said not to worry. Sperm was more a quality than a quantity issue. But once he'd peered into his microscope, he wasn't particularly happy with the quality either. Apparently, my sperm had mobility issues. He was worried they weren't reaching the eggs.

Having bunked out of more than a few biology lessons at school, I was on shaky ground here. Other than giving the little buggers swimming lessons, I didn't know what to do. But the gynae knew. For starters, he decided that I would no longer enjoy hot baths. They were now taboo. I wasn't happy with the news. Lurking in long hot baths at the end of the day with a cold beer and a book was one of my favourite pastimes, but apparently, there was every chance that the hot baths were wreaking havoc on my sperm count, frazzling my little buggers in the process. So cold baths it was. It was bearable in summer but an absolute bastard in winter. How were the little buggers expected to swim like fish when they were frozen bloody solid? Jenny kept an eagle eye on the bath temperatures. Still, no babies were made. And all the while, our friends around us were breeding like bunny rabbits, dropping babies left, right and centre.

The gynae decided to up the ante. The next level up was artificial insemination. In his rooms, the procedure was called In Vitro Fertilisation, but on a farmyard, you'd be talking artificial insemination. In Vitro was an arm and a leg expensive but the gynae was sure that it would work. I had no idea of the actual mechanics involved, and I didn't want to know, biology having not been my strong point at school. I'd gone off the subject midway through the lesson where you are taught how to dissect a sheep's eyeball. But the gynae was an acknowledged expert on In Vitro. And his reputation as a baby maker par excellence was at stake. Another interrupted business meeting and another session in the toilet with the magazines and the preposterously huge specimen jar.

Followed by the longest ever wait to see if the In Vitro had worked. Alas. The news when it came wasn't good. Still nothing. But the gynae told us not to lose heart. Often it took two or three attempts. And all the while around us, our friends and neighbours kept on breeding like bunnies.

Jenny took not being able to have kids a lot harder than I did. It didn't get to me as much. I'd just started a business with two friends and had more than enough on my plate to throw my energies at. My partners, Neil and John, were the business boffins and I was the gofer, but I enjoyed tagging along behind them, learning what I could.

Zimbabwe in the nineteen eighties was a country filled with opportunities. Our fifteen-year bitter civil war was behind us and blacks, and whites were learning how to live together. Those whites that didn't fancy living with the old enemy fled, mostly to South Africa, leaving huge vacuums and even bigger opportunities behind them. In the mould of fools rushing in where angels feared to tread, Neil, John and I did our best to take advantage of every opportunity that came our way. We staged rock and roll concerts and brought the likes of Eric Clapton, Tracy Chapman, UB40, Peter Gabriel, Sting and Bruce Springsteen out to Zimbabwe to perform. They were exciting times. I even got to drive Bruce Springsteen in an ambulance. He wasn't sick. We used the ambulance to get him away from all the fans. And I got to have a wee at the urinal right next to Sting. I even managed to resist the urge to compare willy sizes.

Neil, John and I also formed a company called Film Africa, which made movies. We did all the local production work like organising the props and extras and hunting down suitable locations. Mostly our movies were B grade movies with Italian dialogue and English subtitles. Occasionally we stepped up. We even made a Clint Eastwood movie called White Hunter, Black Heart. I tried to have a wee at the urinal next to Clint but never got the chance.

We also formed a Tourism Division and bought hotels and safari camps and timeshare resorts. They were crazy, exciting times. On the strength of a rather wobbly Diploma in Hotel and Motel Management and at age thirty, I was put in charge of the Tourism Division while my partners carried on with Rock and Roll and making movies.

While my crazy business career was roaring along, Jenny and I bought our first home. It was a ramshackle five-bedroom double story house on seventeen acres just outside Harare. It had bush for a garden and hose pipe plumbing in the roof, and the upstairs bedrooms had chipboard walls, and we loved it. Jenny set about carving a beautiful garden out of the bush while I mulled over plans to install proper plumbing in the roof. Mulling was as far as I got because like biology, DIY isn't a strong point.

I left the house repairs to Jenny while I got busy with farming.

First up, I planted a handsome crop of mostly miniature cabbages. They weren't supposed to be miniature; they just turned out that way. The mysteries of agricultural science. I went to sell my crop in Mbare Musika, the hugely bustling informal market on the outskirts of Harare. After extensive haggling with a trader who sort of looked honest, a farm gate price of $2.50 per cabbage was agreed upon. Farm gate prices were just some of the buzz words I'd picked up. And at $2.50 a cabbage, I was on my way to becoming a wealthy land baron. The trader came out to the farm early on a Saturday morning in a hired eight-ton truck to pick-up the cabbages. Embarrassingly I was still fast asleep when he arrived. I stumbled out with sleep in my eyes and pointed him in the direction of the cabbage field. Two minutes later, he was back at the door. He wanted to know where the field of ready to harvest cabbages was. Thinking he'd got lost, I threw on a t-shirt and led him to the cabbage patch.

Shaking his head sadly, he paid me $17.50 for the seven cabbages he'd managed to find that were a little bigger than miniature. He suggested I try a bit of fertiliser on my next crop. I was elated as he drove off with the seven cabbages rolling around the back of his eight-ton truck. I was almost a fully-fledged farmer. I was having the time of my life.

The only blot on our landscape was not being able to have any children. If there was ever a house built that should have had the pitter-patter of little feet running around in it, it was our house. It looked like something straight out of a nursery rhyme book. And like our house, Jenny was meant to have babies. She had trained as a primary school teacher and had read every Dr Seuss book a million times and could even teach kids how to do joined-up handwriting. She knew how to knit booties and to bake biscuits, cakes, and all the things kids loved. But even though Jenny's gynae had taken her on as his personal challenge, the In Vitro treatments were still not working.

Jenny and I were very careful to avoid playing the blame game and tried to be philosophic about having four guest rooms in our rambling house. We bought puppies, Jack Russells and a Beagle to fill the house up. And Jenny knitted booties for other people's babies while I busied myself with the hotels, the safari camps, and the farm. I planted an orchard of citrus trees, which I grew as badly as cabbages.

Then one Sunday evening, our lives changed dramatically. Pat Brown, my secretary, was visiting. She'd come for lunch and was still there for dinner. Pat and Jenny were nattering away with the television playing softly in the background, while I read up on how not to kill citrus trees. Then Jenny rushed to turn the volume on the television up. That was in the days before remote controls. One of her favourite programmes, called 'A Dream Come True' was on. It was one of those tug at your heartstring programmes about people with no legs, no wheelchairs, or about children who needed serious surgery whose parents couldn't afford it. Jenny watched it every week.

This week's programme was different, the presenter, Lawford Sutton Price, announced. He was interviewing a woman with a sad story to tell about a young mother in the last stages of cancer. The mother was looking for a couple to give her three children a loving home. The eldest child was a boy aged eleven. On television, he was described as being quiet and responsible. Apparently, he loved fishing and wildlife. The next, a girl almost six, was a chatterbox and a real live wire. The baby was a boy who was not yet two, a proper little toddler who was into everything. The mother didn't have long to live, and she was looking for a couple to take her children in and look after them and love them as though they were their own.

Jenny asked pleadingly. "Can we phone, Eric, please can we phone in?"

"Go for it," I said without a second thought. Jenny scribbled the two telephone numbers that had flashed up on the screen and started dialling. Both numbers were perpetually engaged, but Jenny stuck to her task. Eventually she got through and gave our names and contact numbers.

"I so hope that they choose us," she said.

"Me too," I said dutifully.

The conversation stopped there. Jenny and I were pros at not getting our hopes up. We'd been through too many post-In Vitro 'If Only' conversations. We'd learnt to do all our wishing and hoping silently.

On the following Wednesday, Jenny got a call from Island Hospice, a charity which provided support to terminally ill cancer patients. It was about the 'A Dream Come True' programme. They wanted us to come in the next day for a preliminary interview. Our hopes soared. We couldn't help it. Maybe, just maybe, we were going to have children. Jenny spent the whole night selecting her wardrobe for the next day. She was looking for something motherly to wear. I wore a sober jacket and tie. It wasn't the hardest choice to make because I only had one jacket and tie. I had a suit, but that was only for getting married in. On the drive into town, Jenny and I carefully avoided the 'What if' conversation.

I felt the interview went well. Two women from Island Hospice grilled us. The list of questions was exhaustive. No, we didn't have drinking problems. Or drug problems. No, we didn't routinely have sex on the kitchen table. The last wasn't actually a question, but I threw the answer in to impress on them our sense of responsibility. Yes, we had the financial means to support a family of five. I could see that I scored big points when I told them we lived on a farm and that I managed two safari camps. Apparently, the oldest boy loved wildlife and fishing. I lied and told them I was a very keen fisherman. And that I loved the outdoors; I'd been a very keen Boy Scout and knew how to tie lots of different knots and... Jenny kicked me under the table to shut me up. She scored more valuable points when she told them that she was a trained junior schoolteacher.

At the end of the interview, the hospice ladies stood up and thanked us for coming in. But I wasn't going to let them leave us hanging. I wanted to know what happened next. They explained that a shortlist of candidates would be interviewed by the mother of the children. And then an even shorter list would get to meet the eldest child, the eleven-year-old, who would play an important part in the selection process. The mother still had a few months to live, and the hospice wanted to make sure that there were no stones left unturned in the selection process. They'd also organised full medicals for both of us. They didn't want the children to be adopted by parents who'd be popping their clogs anytime soon. Any other questions, Island Hospice asked. I had plenty. What about the father? There were three. Each child had a different father. There was an extended family, a grandfather and some aunts, but we were told that none was in a position to take all three children. They could take the baby but not the older kids. The mother didn't want her children separated and so had chosen the adoption route.

When we left, Jenny and I swopped high fives silently. Then, like school kids after an important exam, we carried out an extensive post-mortem. We felt that we'd aced the interview. We were elated. We might become parents. Times three. And then a small sense of guilt slipped in amongst our happiness. We were celebrating and happy but only because a lady we didn't know was busy dying.

When we got home, we started the long wait. It was dreadful. We rushed for the phone every time it rang, hoping that it would be a summons for the interview with the mother. To keep herself busy, Jenny set about planning the conversion of our bland guestrooms into children's rooms. She stocked up our library with books on how to be better parents and read them voraciously, underlining the important bits in pencil. She ended underlining almost every sentence. She was determined to be the best mom ever. I held back. I'd been down the In Vitro road too many times. I carried on planting out my citrus trees.

After a week spent waiting on tenterhooks, Jenny and I went away for the weekend with best friends Bob and Julie Hamill. We went to Club Mazvikadei, a lakeside timeshare resort that I managed. Bob and Julie had two daughters, aged six and four. I paid particular attention to their relative sizes. Our own 'might be' daughter was almost six, and I wanted to get an idea of comparative size. Six-year-olds were bigger than I thought. On Saturday afternoon we took one of the club's pontoons out onto the lake for a booze cruise. Kelly, Bob's six-year-old, was less than complimentary about the pontoon and kept asking me over and over again if she was on the slow boat to China. I filed the information away. Six-year-olds could be bloody annoying.

We were fishing on the far side of the dam when the club's speedboat rushed towards us. The boat driver was driving like an absolute maniac, and I braced myself to give him a tongue lashing. But I didn't.

"Mr de Jong, Mr de Jong. It's an emergency, it's an emergency," the boat driver shouted.

"What is?" I shouted back. I had visions of thatched clubhouses burning down.

"The phone call, sir!!"

"What phone call?"

"The emergency one!!! At the clubhouse. For you and Mrs de Jong."

"Who's the call from?"

"I don't know. Mr Cox just told me to fetch you because of an emergency phone call," the driver said. "And he also said that I must come and get you very quickly," he said, covering his arse quite cleverly. He'd been in trouble before for driving the boats like a speed fiend.

Jenny and I clambered across into the speed boat and sped off across the dam back to the Club. We had no idea what the emergency was about. Visions of a burning clubhouse were replaced with visions of dead or dying relatives. Jonathan Cox, the Club General Manager, was waiting for us down at the jetty, with a dreadfully worried look on his face. All he could tell us was that the emergency call was from a lady called Val at Island Hospice. Jonathan rushed us up to the clubhouse. It took forever to get a call through to Harare. The club was on a telephone party line. By the time I eventually got through, half the district was listening in. Val said the children's mother had come out of remission and they didn't know how much longer she would live. The whole interview process was being fast-forwarded. Jenny and I had to get into Harare as quickly as possible.

For the first time on the hour-long drive in town, Jenny and I spoke about the very real possibility of getting three children and the changes to our lives they would make. We'd spent the last five years trying to have children, but the distant maybe had just become an almost possibly and all of a sudden, we had lots to talk about. Like cars, for instance. We were almost maybe a family of five, and we didn't have a car that five people could fit in to. Befitting my status as a wannabe farmer, I drove a pick-up truck, and Jenny drove a little VW beetle.

We drove straight to the Island Hospice offices. Val was waiting for us. The mother was very ill, and it was time to hurry things along. Val didn't know how long Rose would last. Up to then, everyone had been careful to avoid names. Up to then, the mother and her children were faceless entities, but now there was a name. Rose. Rose was too weak to travel, and so we were going to meet with her at the house where she was staying. And after meeting Rose, we would meet the children. A million thoughts jostled in my head. I might almost be a father. And I was wearing a pair of very loud Hawaiian board shorts and an even louder shirt to the most important meeting of my life.

Rose was staying in a very small house. It wasn't her home. When first she fell ill, a stranger had answered an appeal for help and had taken her and her children into his home. Jenny and I followed Val into the lounge. Rose was sitting on the couch, smoking a cigarette. She was very thin and was almost lost in the sweatshirt she was wearing and wore a bandana to cover her hair loss. Her eyes were huge in her face. Val introduced us, and Rose smiled weakly. I stuttered and stammered a greeting. The faceless entity had just become a living, breathing but soon-to-be-dead person and I didn't know what to say to her. I was at a complete loss. Clearly my standard, 'Hallo, how are you?' wasn't going to cut it. And I could hardly chat about the weather. So, I stood there like a guppy opening and closing my mouth. Thank God for Jenny. She didn't say anything. She just gave Rose a huge hug. Jenny is big on hugs, and it was exactly the right thing to do. Val left us to it and bustled off to the kitchen to make some tea.

Sitting in my very loud shorts and shirt, I braced myself for the questions I knew were coming. I had answers that shouted out responsibility down to pat. But Rose's first question floored me.

"Will you take my children?" Rose asked. Nothing came out of my mouth. She asked again. "I haven't got much time left, and I need to know if you'll take my children and look after them like they were your own."

The enormity of the moment struck me like a runaway freight train. I choked up hopelessly, tears streaming down my face. A dying woman I didn't know was asking me to take her three children. Once again, Jenny stepped into my gap. "Yes, Rose," she said. "We'll take them, and we'll look after them. And I promise you that we'll love your children as though they were our own." I nodded through my tears in complete agreement. Rose must have thought I was some sort of a dumb mute. I still hadn't spoken a word to her.

And then one of the children walked into the room, well toddled more than walked. He was the almost two-year-old and his name was Daniel. He was beautiful with blond hair and big blue eyes and a shy smile that lit up the entire room. And he was going to be my son. Wham. More tears as yet another enormity of the moment hit me like yet another freight train. After forever, I found some words.

"Hallo, Daniel," I said. "How are you?" All I got back was a shy smile. Daniel headed for the safety of his mother. But Rose was too weak to pick him up. Daniel started crying. He wanted love and attention, and he wasn't getting it. Jenny picked him up and gave him a big cuddle and a love. When Val came back into the room with the tea, it must have been like walking into Terms of Endearment times by ten. Daniel was crying. I was crying. Jenny and Rose were crying. Tears of sadness and tears of joy all mixed up. Val was an old hand at rooms full of emotion and quickly took charge. She poured the tea and got the conversation going. Daniel was the centre of attraction. He seemed comfortable on Jenny's lap. I felt so sad for Rose. I couldn't imagine the pain she was going through, watching her baby smiling and giggling on the lap of someone who was going to take her child away.

And then impossibly things got even more emotional. The other children arrived, Gary aged eleven and Veronica aged five. They'd been out for ice creams with a relative. I didn't even notice the relative. My eyes were on Gary and Veronica; my son and my daughter. Gary was short and stocky and still carried some baby fat around his face. His sandy brown hair was neatly combed, and, like Daniel, his eyes were blue. He was quietly polite and reserved, but I could feel his eyes sizing me up carefully. Especially my Hawaiian shorts and even louder shirt. Veronica stole my heart the second I saw her. She was tiny and beautiful with jet black hair and the brightest blue eyes, a doll personified. On the 'Dream Come True' programme, she'd been described as a real livewire and chatterbox. Well, they'd got that bit right as she started talking nineteen to the dozen. They'd had the best ice creams ever. She'd eaten hers without dropping even a small drop on the floor. And she wished she could always go for ice creams. And who were Jenny and I?

"They've come to be your new mummy and daddy," Rose explained.

Veronica's face lit up. Gary kept his poker face on. He didn't need his mother to tell him who we were.

"Do you want to go home with them today?" Rose asked. She directed the question at Gary.

"Okay," he said after a long pause.

Veronica gave a little jump for joy. "Can we go with them now, right now?"

"First you've got to go pack your clothes and things Veronica."

Veronica rushed out the door, followed by Gary. Rose turned to Jenny. "Do you mind if I keep Daniel one more night? With him around, you'll have your hands full and no room for Gary and Veronica."

I fled the room to escape the emotions. I had to get to grips with what had just happened. Unbelievable. We'd arrived half an hour ago, and now we were parents. Three times over. I was the head of a family of five. I went to help Gary and Veronica.

"Would you like a hand packing up your things?"

"No, thank you. I'm fine," Gary replied without looking at me as he emptied his already almost empty cupboard neatly into a battered suitcase. I was appalled at how few clothes he had. Then I noticed a birdcage in the corner with a green parrot of sorts in it.

"Hey, check out the parrot," I said, hoping to break the ice.

"He's not a parrot. He's a ring-necked parakeet. His name is Phoenix. I caught him in the garden."

"He's lovely. How did you catch him?"

"I made a bird trap." Question asked and answered.

I went through to the bedroom that Veronica shared with Daniel. She was just finishing off cramming her things into another tiny battered suitcase. Again, I was struck by another almost empty cupboard. And bare bedroom walls. Apart from Daniel's cot in the corner, there was nothing to show that the room that belonged to a six-year-old and a two-year-old. Walls that should have been papered with 'My Magic Pony' posters were empty and bland. It looked exactly like the borrowed room that it was. But there was nothing bland about Veronica's bright smile. She was packed and ready for her new life.

I carried the almost-empty suitcases and the birdcage through to the lounge.

"I'll pack these in the car, shall I?"

"What car? We're in your pick-up truck, remember?" Jenny said.

Shit. I remembered. We were a family without a family car.

"I'll borrow one. I'll borrow one from Mark Blagus." Mark was a best friend I worked with who lived nearby. He owned an old Mercedes Benz called Goebbels. There was room for ten children in the back of Goebbels. I phoned Mark and asked if I could borrow his car for a few days.

"Sure thing. When do want to collect it?"

"Now! Mark, I need it now! And can you maybe drop it off for me?"

"No problem. Daniela can follow me in her car." Mark was the sort of friend who would give me the shirt off his back. I gave him the address. We were now a family with a family car, albeit a borrowed one. Gary was very impressed when he saw the Mercedes Benz roll into the yard. "Is that going to be our car?"

"No. I've borrowed it. I've got a truck and your new mom drives a VW beetle." Gary looked slightly less impressed with the family fleet. But there had been no reaction when I referred to Jenny as mom.

"What's happening Eric?" Mark asked. "And who's the kid?" He was full of questions. I told him I would tell him all about it at work.

It was time for us to leave. Which meant it was time for Gary and Veronica to say goodbye to Rose. My face started leaking again. I didn't want to watch, so I busied myself packing the car, which didn't take long. One parrot and two small battered suitcases don't take too much packing. Gary and Veronica walked out of the house. They weren't crying but I more than made up for them. I didn't know where I was getting all these tears from. It was decided that Jenny would drive Goebbels with the children, and I would follow in my pick-up. Then Veronica asked if she could ride with me. I was elated. I was driving home with a real live daughter.

Rose struggled out the door to wave goodbye to her children. She was struggling, even more, to hold Daniel in her arms. More face leaking from me but still no tears from Veronica. She was too busy talking to look at Rose even. She was in a hurry to start her new life. I told Veronica to wave goodbye to her mommy.

"I've got a new mommy now," she told me blithely while staring out the windscreen straight in front of her. "And you're my new daddy." Impossibly I squeezed out more tears. Veronica had called me daddy. My rear-view mirror with Rose standing small was all blurred as I drove out the gate.

Veronica's questions flew ten to the dozen. Where did we live? Was it a big farm? Were there any animals on the farm? Why only chickens and dogs and cats? Why weren't there any cows? Weren't all farms supposed to have cows? And what about horses? She loved horses. Could we get cows and horses? I was over the moon happy. She prefixed every question with the word, daddy. She could ask me a million questions, and I wouldn't mind.

It was less hectic in Goebbels. Jenny was doing all of the asking. Gary answered her questions, quietly and politely. The conversation centred on more sensible issues. Gary and Veronica went to David Livingstone School. He was in grade six, and she was in grade one. He came near the top of his class, but Veronica needed lots of help with her homework. Gary liked to fish. He liked it a lot. He was a good fisherman and had a rod and a reel given to him by his grandfather. Jenny told him that he now had an extra two sets of grandparents. Oh, said Gary. He also liked wildlife and watching birds. Jenny told him that we managed two safari camps and that he'd be able to visit both with me. That would be nice, he said. And there was lots of birdlife on the farm where we were all going to live. That was also nice, he said.

Gary asked exactly one question. "What's your surname?"

"Our surname is de Jong," Jenny said.

"Oh," said Gary. They drove the rest of the way home in companionable silence.

Chapter Two

Our house was a ramshackle upstairs, downstairs farmhouse with five bedrooms and three bathrooms. The kids were thrilled that they would each have their own bedrooms. And even better, the rooms were upstairs rooms. Gary chose a bedroom with a tiny veranda. Veronica chose the purple bedroom because purple was almost pink, and the room looked like it could be in a doll's house. Jenny and I helped pack their clothes away into their cupboards, which took no time at all. Again, I was appalled at how little each child had in the way of clothes and possessions. Gary's fishing rod and tackle box had pride of place in his cupboard. Then he went downstairs to fetch Phoenix, which was when he started screaming. I rushed downstairs, fearing the worst. And I didn't even know what the worst could be. I'd only been a parent for less than an hour. And already the wheels had come off properly.

While we were busy in the house, one of the Jack Russells had broken into the parrot's cage and bitten the bird's head off in double-quick time. Gary was beyond distraught. So was I. The poor kid had not a lot left in his life, he was in the process of losing his mom, and now his parrot was gone. Killed by the bloody dog. I grabbed a broomstick and set off after the dog, screaming like a banshee. I was going to beat the crap out of the dog, which helped matters, not a jot. More violence. More tears, more raw emotion.

Eventually, Jenny settled Gary down with a hug. "I'm really sorry, Gary. And it's not Jessie's fault. She's a terrier. And her instinct is to catch things and kill them." Gary flinched but importantly didn't pull away from the contact.

I chipped in, "And how about I build an aviary, and we fill it with birds?" Jenny rolled her eyes in the background. This was Eric talking, he who was challenged by three-pin plugs, he who could not spell DIY. But I was serious. If men could land on the moon, why couldn't I build an aviary? The sobbing slowed, and the drama was over.

That first night I wanted to take the children out for a pizza. It seemed a family thing to do. Families did pizzas in the movies the whole time. But Jenny overruled me. She cooked a lasagne, and we sat around the dining room table for our first family meal. It felt good like it was meant to be. There weren't even any of those long awkward silent moments where no one said anything, mostly because of Veronica's constant chatter. And after dinner, we watched a bit of television. Jen and I had no idea how long to let that run for. So we asked Gary what time children went to bed.

"Seven o'clock for Veronica and eight o'clock for me. Unless it's not a school night, then we can stay up longer."

"Oh."

"But I'm tired. I think we both are. We had a big day. Thank you for the meal. And goodnight," he said politely. Veronica was more demonstrative and smothered us with goodnight hugs and kisses.

"Do you want a bedtime story?" I asked her as I walked her up to her room to tuck her in. I was sure this was all considered normal five-year-old protocol.

"But I haven't got a book of bedtime stories," she said in her small voice.

"No problem there, Veronica. Luckily, I've got a big book full of stories, right here in my head."

"You have?" she squealed excitedly.

'Yup. Now what to do you want me to tell you a story about?"

"I can choose?"

"Sure. How about the story about a little girl whose shoes hated each other and fought and argued with each other the whole time...or the one about the princess and a magic unicorn?"

Veronica squealed in delight. "I want the princess one, tell me the princess story."

"Okay. Here we go. Once upon a time in a kingdom just down the road and around the corner...."

"Five minutes, Eric," Jenny said from the door. She knew that my imagination let loose could draw bedtime stories out into sagas of epic proportions. And tonight was not a night for anything epic. We'd all had a big day. We'd gone from being strangers to being family in just a day.

Later I gave Jenny a congratulatory hug in bed. "Well done on your first night of mothering. You did real good."

"I did okay, didn't I?"

"But don't get too cocky. The big kids are easy. The little ones are the tough ones to handle."

"Why do you think I'm going to have problems with Daniel?"

"You gonna really struggle with the breastfeeding for starters. Kid's already got teeth on him like a hyena. Figure you either have to wear like protective gear or you gonna get ripped to shreds. Personally, I'd...."

Jenny smacked me in the mouth with a pillow.

First thing the next morning, Raphael Mutwira, the farm foreman, was at the door. He'd come to inspect our new children. He counted arms, legs, and fingers and checked their teeth. Apparently, all was in order.

"Your children are good children, sir, they are very strong ones. And this one can look after the cattle and the girl child will fetch much lobola, many heads of cattle." Veronica was five years old, and already Raphael was working out her bride price. And I decided that come the time, I'd use him as my negotiator.

After breakfast, Gary and Veronica rushed out to explore their new home, all seventeen acres of it. It was a kid's paradise, with trees to climb and bush to build forts in and whatever it was little girls played at. Veronica wanted to see the farm animals. This gave her a choice between chickens and chickens. She liked them, especially the fluffy yellow day olds. But she was still put out at the lack of cows and horses. Again, she told me that proper farms were supposed to have cows and horses.

At nine o'clock, we told Gary and Veronica that we had to go visit Mommy Rose and collect Daniel. We were taken aback by Veronica's violent reaction. She burst into a flood of angry tears and stomped her feet. Through her tears, she told us she didn't want to go back to see her old mommy. She had a new mommy now, and a new home and she did not want to go back to the old one. Eventually, Gary managed to coax her into Goebbels. Veronica grizzled halfway to town.

When we arrived, Rose was sitting in the lounge, in her bandana, baggy sweater and cigarette smoke. It was still early in the day, but already she looked tired. Gary gave Rose a gentle hug and a kiss. Veronica dutifully followed suit. Gary sat next to his mother and pulled his sister down beside him.

To give them the space they needed, Jenny headed for the kitchen to make tea. I didn't want to get caught up in the emotions, so I went off in search of my new youngest son. I found Daniel playing on the floor of his bedroom. He gave me a tentative smile. I picked him up and hugged him. No tears. I swung him in the air, rather gingerly. I wasn't sure how fragile two-year-olds were. I was instantly rewarded with peals of laughter. It was the best sound ever. It sounded especially bright in Rose's house where sickness lived. I swung Dan again. More laughter. I could have listened to him laugh all morning, but I had to get him back to his Mommy Rose. And I'd also just remembered reading somewhere that two-year-olds were sometimes prone to puking. Holding him at arm's length, just in case, I carried him through to the lounge to join the rest of his family.

Gary was in the middle of telling Rose about his new home. I handed Daniel to Gary to complete the family picture. I felt very much like a spare part, intruding on the little family time they had left, so I went into the kitchen to help Jenny with the tea. Many hands can still take forever to make a cup of tea. This was Rose's last morning with Dan. And Island Hospice had told us how important it was that the children spend quality time with their mom before she died. If they were with her through her pain and suffering, it would give them the closure they would need later in life, apparently. But taking small children to watch someone die slowly, horribly, and painfully also felt very wrong. The parent in me, who hadn't been there for very long, thought it had to be better to shield the children from watching their mother suffer. But Island Hospice were the experts. We were in their hands. We had to do what they felt was right for the children.

On that first visit, Rose had looked tired when we got there. But after an hour with her three children, she was beyond exhaustion. It was time to leave. It was time to take Daniel home for the first time. He gurgled happily on Gary's lap in the back of Goebbels. In the rear-view mirror, my new family looked happy and complete. But my heart cried for Rose. She stood small in the driveway, wracked with pain and sadness, as she watched her family drive away. Gary forced his sister and brother to look back and wave as we drove off to our new lives together.

Like the other children, Daniel had very little to unpack in his new bedroom. Jenny had put him in the downstairs bedroom next to ours. "Can't we take the kids back into town, to get them some clothes and things?" Jenny asked.

"Great idea. Let's go now."

"You get the other two ready. And I'll change Daniel. Something's a bit smelly here."

I was halfway up the stairs when I heard the violent, gut heaving, retching behind me. I rushed back down the stairs. Jenny was doubled over next to Daniel's bed.

"What's wrong? What's happened?" I cried.

"Daniel's done a pooh nappy!!" Jenny gagged.

"A what?" I wasn't up to speed on child terminology.

"He's shat in his nappy!!"

"But...but... isn't that normal? Isn't that what two-year-old kids are supposed to do?"

"Not like this!! Not huge like this!!" Jenny blurted between retches. "And what's worse, he's grabbed the crap with both hands. And he's wiped it everywhere!! He's got it all over the place!! On the blankets!! On him!!! On me!!! He's even got it on the bloody walls!!!"

"But why did you let him do that? Why didn't you just stop him?"

"I was busy trying to wipe his bum clean like you're supposed to do." More gags. More retching. "I was looking for some more of those wet wipe things, and when I looked around, he was grabbing the shit with both hands and wiping it all over the bloody place."

"Shhh!!! We said we weren't going to swear in front of the children."

"We said that before the children started grabbing fistfuls of shit and rubbing it on the walls and bedclothes and everywhere." As Jenny spoke between her heaves, Daniel reached for another handful of crap and daubed the nearest wall happily.

Jenny's stomach had a point. Daniel's shit really stank. My stomach heaved in sympathy. It didn't do foul stenches either. But a part of me was angry. Jenny was a mom now. She was supposed to have maternal instincts that could deal with this sort of stuff; she was supposed to have things under control. I rounded on her. "But surely you've changed pooh nappies before? You're supposed to know these things."

"I've done it once, maybe twice. But that was with a little baby who just lay there and gurgled and did little poohs, not huge, big stinking ones that they grab with both hands and smear it all over the walls!!"

"But...but why didn't you just stop him?"

"You come here and stop him, Mr Smart Arse." Jenny's hackles were well up. But my retching stomach forced me back to the relative safety of the doorway. I watched appalled. How could so much crap come out of one small kid?

"What do you want me to do?" I asked miserably.

Jenny answered through another gag. Vomit couldn't be far away. "I want you to come here and help me clean up all this shit!!"

"But can't we take him into the bathroom and just hose him down?"

"No, we can't take him to the bloody bathroom and just hose him down!!" Acrimony was in the air.

"Can I help you clean him up?" A small voice asked beside me. It was Gary.

"You know how to do this sort of stuff? You clean up crappy ...I mean dirty nappies?"

"Sure. I do it all the time." He stepped forward quietly and confidently. "Why'd you make such a big mess, stinky boy?" he asked. While Daniel gurgled happily, Jenny and I fled for the safety of clean air.

I watched Gary carefully in the department store. I was helping him pick out his new wardrobe while Jenny shopped for Veronica and Daniel. I was a dreadful shopper and always grabbed the first thing I saw. The quicker I got out of the shops, the better. But it looked like Gary was the complete opposite. He spent forever looking through the entire range of shirts, picking them up and checking them carefully before putting them back again. Nothing was taking his fancy. He'd been through a rack of shirts a mile long, with every style and colour imaginable, and he hadn't picked a single one. There were hundreds of them. Surely there was something there that took his fancy. And then it struck me that maybe he was looking for designer label kit. Maybe we were in the wrong shop, maybe I should have taken him somewhere more trendy.

"Haven't you seen anything you like, Gary? Do you want to go somewhere else to have a look? One of those boutique places?"

"No....no.... These shirts are all really nice, but they're all... just.... so expensive."

I thought he'd been looking at labels, but he'd been checking out price tags. Incredible!! He was just eleven years old, and he was stressing about spending too much money. Only then did I get an inkling of what the poor kid had been through. We found out afterwards that for the last year of

Rose's illness Gary had, on a very limited budget, bought all the groceries and cooked all the meals, aged ten. I'd only learnt how to spell the word budget a few years ago, and my cooking was to be avoided at all costs. I put an arm around his shoulders. He didn't pull away.

"I'll tell you what Gary, here's the deal. You choose the clothes, and you leave me to worry about the prices."

"Okay...." Gary left the sentence open-ended and hanging awkwardly. I could tell he wanted to call me something but didn't know what. I wasn't worried. There'd be plenty of time to sort out names later.

We managed to get the first shirt in the trolley. But I still had a fight on my hands to fill it. For every three items of clothing I threw in, he took two out. Eventually, and it was a long eventually, we had the makings of an eleven-year-old boy's wardrobe in the bag. We went off in search of the others.

Gary and I found three very happy shoppers. Jenny had had no problems whatsoever filling her trolley. So, she'd filled up two of them. She was in seventh heaven with a little girl and a little boy to dress up. Veronica was on a level one up from seventh heaven with an unending choice of pink My Little Pony clothing to choose from. And Daniel was happy as Larry in the bottom of the shopping trolley, rummaging through all the wrappings, with a smile on his face.

We got home just in time to turn around for the daily visit to Mommy Rose. More tears from Veronica. Eventually, she relented but only after getting dressed up in her new best dress. Gary was also resplendent in one of his new outfits.

When we got to Rose's house, Island Hospice dropped a bomb on me. They wanted to up the ante with the Rose visits. Now they thought that it was very important that Gary be there when Rose drew her last breath. It was all part and parcel of the closure thing. I couldn't believe it. To force an eleven-year-old to watch his mother die seemed wrong, horribly wrong. The poor kid had already been put through the wringer for a year, watching his mom get sick. But to force him to be there when she died seemed hugely cruel to me. But who were Jenny and I to argue, with all of two days' worth of parenting experience behind us. So that night, Jenny packed a cooked meal and sleeping bags for two and sent Gary and I off to watch and wait for Rose to die.

It was easily the longest week of my life. I hated Veronica's tears every day when we told her it was time to go and visit her mom. We had to drag her to the car every day, kicking and crying. And when we got to the house where Rose was dying, I hated each and every minute we were there. I hated watching Rose growing weaker and weaker. I hated the smell of sickness and death that filled the small house. And most of all I hated having to take my children there.

Any attempts to get all-important daily routines going were disrupted by the daily visits to Rose's sickbed. The visits were normally followed by grief counselling sessions with Island Hospice to help prepare the children for Rose's death. And then every evening, Gary and I would troop back to wait for Rose to die. Those night long vigils were the worst for me. And in between everything I managed to squeeze in a few hours at the mess that was my desk. And I found a family car fit for five. Well, actually my secretary, Pat found the car. It was a bright canary yellow Nissan Blue Bird. Veronica loved the colour and Gary semi-approved of the two-litre engine under the bonnet.

As the week dragged on, Rose slipped into a state of constant pain. The cancer was spreading rapidly through her body. She now had a permanent nurse on duty who kept her heavily sedated most of the time. Every evening Gary would sit with his mother and chat. He did all the chatting. Whether Rose heard him through her veil of medication, I never knew. Only once she'd fallen asleep, would Gary and I roll out sleeping bags on the lounge floor and watch television. I enjoyed the chance to bond with Gary. Mostly we watched American wrestling. Gary was an expert and set about teaching me who was who in the wrestling zoo. Apparently, the Undertaker was poison mean and on the top of the pile, absolutely unbeatable. And if Hulk Hogan were ever stupid enough to get in the ring with the Undertaker, he would get taken down and have his butt kicked!! Takedowns and butt-kicking!! My wrestling vocabulary came on in leaps and bounds. Apparently, even the boxing great Ali Mohammed would get a hiding from the Undertaker. His name was Mohammed Ali I told Gary politely. But he would have none of it and so Ali Mohammed it stayed. I thought it was good that the boy had a mind of his own.

I always wake up stupid early. Gary, on the other hand, was a late riser. Every morning I'd tiptoe through to Rose's bedroom to see if she had slipped away during the night. But Rose never died that long week. Every morning Gary and I would roll up our sleeping bags and head on home with the joyless prospect of another night long vigil to look forward to.

In between the madness, someone remembered that it was Veronica's sixth birthday. Island Hospice decided that she needed a birthday party. Not just for Veronica, more for Rose. Rose wasn't going to be around for any more of her children's birthday parties, so they decided to make it a good party. I didn't see how you could throw a party at such short notice. I hadn't reckoned on Island Hospice's network of goodwill. It was amazing. A very kind lady who didn't know Rose from Adam stepped up and donated her entire bonus towards the costs of the party. Others came forward with offers for riding ponies, clowns, and sweets and drinks to feed an army. But where would we find the children to eat the mountain of sweets and ride the ponies? Jenny and I only knew a handful of children. And with schools still closed for the holidays, we couldn't even begin to track down Veronica's school friends. Veronica wasn't much help. She was on first name only terms with all her best friends, and even those names changed every time I asked about them. I made another note. Memory retention skills in five-year-olds were wobbly. Jenny and I were panicked about the child shortage, but the Hospice told us to relax. They would sort it.

The party was to be held at the house where Rose was staying. With a tiny, unkempt garden, it wasn't the perfect venue. But Rose didn't have the strength to travel any distance. The festivities were to start at eleven. Veronica was up, out of bed and dressed in her new party dress by five. She was beyond excited. According to her, she'd never had a birthday party before. Her dress was a pinkish purple creation of shimmering lace and frills, fit for a princess, albeit a grumpy one. Hell hath no fury like a little girl being kept from her birthday party by dawdling adults and brothers. Veronica cracked her whip, kicked us out of bed and forced breakfast down our throats.

We got to the house early to help set up, but there was nothing left to do. The army of volunteers had laid out tables laden with sweets and chips and cakes and cool drinks of every flavour. The yard, festooned with balloons and bunting of every colour, had been transformed into a happy garden. Veronica didn't even notice the sweets and the balloons. She made a beeline straight for the riding pony, resplendent in party ribbons and tethered under a shady tree, patiently chomping away on horse cubes, waiting for the kids to arrive. Veronica told Jenny and me over and over that horses were her 'bestest' animal by a million miles. When no one was watching, I stole a handful of jelly babies. I have a weakness for jelly babies, especially the black ones.

By eleven o'clock only three kids had arrived, all carrying presents, and all dressed up in their Sunday bests, even though it was a Saturday. Veronica welcomed them from on top of the horse. She didn't know any of the children but was prepared to accept gifts from total strangers. By quarter past eleven, there were eight children, and that was counting Gary, Veronica and Daniel. It wasn't looking good. It looked like I would be called upon to deal with a lot of jelly babies.

And then Jo Jo the clown arrived, in a cloud of noise and dust in a multi-coloured VW Beetle done up to look like a technicoloured mouse complete with a huge wind-up key on the roof. Apparently, Jo Jo was a stalwart of the Harare birthday party scene. He'd offered his services for the day for free. Beneath his happy makeup, Jo Jo looked disappointed at the size of his audience. He thrived on full houses. But behind him, the floodgates opened. The children started arriving, firstly in drips and drabs, and then in ever-increasing numbers, all clutching presents, all needing to have the birthday girl pointed out to them. Finding Veronica was easy. She was the little girl on the back of a horse already starting to look tired at the prospect of the long day ahead. There were more than a hundred children. Harare had opened her heart to another plea for help. My eyes teared up every time another car full of kids pulled up.

I watched Gary shed his mantle of responsibility and join in the party games with great gusto, just like any other kid. He was surprisingly quick and won all the running races easily. It was the first time I'd seen Gary, the child. It was nice to watch. Rose came out to join the party. We carried an armchair out for her to sit on. By now, she was beyond frail and unable to walk. She was helped by two Island Hospice carers. Rose's bandana and sweatshirt were by now twenty sizes too big. Children stood and stared at the slow procession, unabashed. We prised Veronica off the back of the horse so she could open her presents in front of her mother. Veronica shredded the wrapping paper as she attacked the pile of presents with great gusto. Through her pain and medication, Rose looked happy. I wasn't the only one crying in the crowd of onlookers.

I took the call from Island Hospice very early on Sunday morning. Rose was gone. After an eighteen-month battle with cancer, she slipped away in the early hours. Rose Bull was just twenty-nine when she died. I hung up the phone and stood there for a long while, trying to compose myself. It was obvious Rose had clung to life for another week so she could see her children settle into the new home she'd chosen for them. I was glad that Gary hadn't been there to watch his mother die. Exhausted from the excitement of the birthday party, Gary and I had skipped the Saturday night vigil. It was better that his last memories were of a happy Rose, sitting on the couch at the party watching happy children at play. I stood and cried for a bit before waking up my children to tell them their mother was dead.

The Hospice told us that we should bring the children to view the body and to say goodbye to Rose for the last time. It was all to do with closure. By then I hated the word closure. The parent in me wanted to shield the children from the sight of their dead mother, but I didn't have enough faith in my instincts to stand up to Island Hospice.

Rose hadn't died in the house where she'd lived out the last months of her life. She'd been moved to a huge mansion of a house that belonged to a step relative. It was obviously felt to be a more fitting place for someone to die. The bitter part of me asked why the rich step-relatives hadn't taken Rose and the children in earlier, why did they let Rose live out the last months of her life dependent upon a stranger's charity?

When we arrived, extended members of Rose's family came pouring out of the big house to fuss over the children. There was a whole tribe of them. I'd never laid eyes on any of them before. Again, my bitterness flared up. Where had all the relatives been for that last long week of Rose's life? But I bit my tongue and repressed bitter feelings of anger and stood back to watch Rose's family grieve and fuss over her children. Jenny, Gary, Veronica, Daniel and I were the main attraction. Everyone tugged at us with questions, offering us tea and biscuits. I hated it. They were turning Rose's death into a social occasion.

After a long forever, we were called upstairs to view Rose's body. We tiptoed into the large bedroom where she lay in the centre of a large double bed that looked like it had been neatly made up with her in it. She wore a white scarf around her head. Her eyes were closed, and her alabaster hands folded over her chest. Rose looked at peace, finally free of the pain and the suffering. My tears welled up again as Gary bent over and kissed his mom for the last time. Veronica followed suit. But I still thought she was too young to be in the room. Then it was our turn to say goodbye to the lady we'd only known for a week. Jenny spoke for both of us.

"Rest in peace, Rose," she whispered. "And thank you for your children. And I promise that we'll look after them and love them."

Chapter Three.

Rose's funeral loomed large on our horizon. Mostly I was dreading it, but there was a part of me that was looking forward to it. Once she was buried, we could go forward as a proper family.

Even more of Rose's extended family came out of the woodwork to lay her to rest, all of them new faces. And again, I couldn't but be bitter that none of them had been near Rose in her last week. The person I was dreading meeting the most was Daniel's father. He'd been Rose's partner at the time of her death, and he was sure to be at the funeral. And I didn't want him anywhere near Daniel. Daniel was my son now, not his. In the end, Jenny and I decided to leave Daniel at home, not because he might see his father, but because he was too young for a long graveside ceremony.

I'd never been to a burial before. I was keen to keep to the anonymity of the back rows, but we were ushered to the graveside. Jenny stood next to Gary and held his hand throughout. I held Veronica's. I could feel curious eyes upon us throughout the long ceremony. The priest was the only person who spoke at the funeral. And it was obvious that he'd never met Rose, so he stayed on neutral ground with the usual funeral scriptures. There were a lot of people at Rose's burial. But through my veil of tears, I was able to pick out the man I thought was Daniel's father. He was grieving heavily. He looked like a normal and decent person, but I was still glad we hadn't brought Daniel.

After the burial, we were all invited back to the mansion where Rose had died for tea and snacks. I didn't want to go but had to. Jenny, I, and the children were the flavour of the month with all the aunts, uncles, nieces, and nephews who'd ventured out from the woodwork. They were all on huge guilt trips, all anxious to tell us how close and fond they were of Rose and the children. How badly they wanted to keep in close contact and visit as often as possible. I seethed silently. But you let her spend the last months of her life living off a stranger's charity. You made an eleven-year-old boy spend a year shopping, cooking, and cleaning for his dying mother and his young siblings. And where the hell were you all in that last long dark week? Not visiting your dead and dying sister for starters, I snarled silently.

On the outside, though, I stood with a polite smile on my face and almost caved into the visitation requests. Thankfully Jenny was more forthright, and she stood her ground. We'd talked this exact moment through with Rose. No aunts and uncles would be allowed to visit. Only the children's grandfather would be allowed to visit. Rose knew that the kids would have to shut the door on their old life so they could get started on their new one. Jenny told them that the no aunts and uncles decision had been made by Rose before she died. Island Hospice backed us up and told the extended family that it was the right thing for the children. The decision went down like a lead balloon. Aunts and uncles glared at Jenny and me. We fled the wake as soon as it was polite to do so.

With the funeral behind us, we were able to concentrate on living a normal family life. There were lots of changes, especially at mealtimes. Being in the hotel and restaurant business, Jenny and I were used to eating out often, and meals at home were haphazard, to say the least. But now we had fixed mealtimes befitting a young family, with balanced, nutritious meals full of broccoli, cauliflowers, and stuff. My stomach almost walked out on me in disgust, it especially hated broccoli and cauliflowers. But apparently, broccoli and cauliflower are full of iron and all manner of good stuff and should be an essential part of every growing child's diet, blah, blah, blah. And so, they ended up on the menu. And on my plate. Apparently, I was supposed to set a good example. Alas. And we also ate our meals at the dining room table instead of in front of the television. And we took turns to say Grace before every meal. I always went with the bog-standard 'Thank You For What We Are About To Receive' version but Gary and Veronica had new and interesting variations. Veronica was especially entertaining when she got her Grace and the Lord's Prayer mixed up. I couldn't but peep at her as she offered up thanks with eyes tightly closed and hands clasped in the obligatory prayer position. "Our Father, who lives in heaven, Hallo, what's your name. And thank you for our food."

Mealtimes with Daniel were a battle of wills. If he didn't like what was put in front of him, he would sit tight with pursed lips and tears on tap. But he was up against Jenny, the immovable object. She would sit next to him with his bowl of nutrition until he gave in. Often, he wouldn't. I felt sorry for the poor kid but knew better than to get involved.

Gary would offer to help cook in the kitchen. He liked cooking. Unfortunately, his signature dish was a vegetable stir fry. Aaargh!!! More vegetables!! My poor stomach threatened strike action, but I forced myself to clump my teeth through Gary's dinner manfully, and with an appreciative look on my face. And Gary's stir fry was actually very good. I was impressed. Even though I'd been to hotel school, my culinary skills didn't extend much beyond eggs boiled badly. Gary was a lot older than his eleven years.

Taking the children out to restaurant for a meal was a huge treat for them. They hadn't been out to many restaurants. Jenny decided that we'd eat out once a month as a family treat. I chose the Bamboo Inn for our first outing. It was an excellent Chinese Restaurant, complete with dimmed Chinese lanterns and Chinese elevator music in the background. Gary mastered his chopsticks in his first minute at the table. He had amazing hand-eye co-ordination. His chopstick skills irked me a bit. After years of practising with pointy sticks, more of my food ended up on the table than in my mouth.

But the next time we went back to the Bamboo Inn, Gary's chopsticks turned out to be a source of embarrassment. The restaurant was busy, and we had to wait for a table. Finally, the head waiter ushered us through to an empty table and started laying up the bowls and eating utensils. He asked Gary and Veronica if they wanted to try to eat with chopsticks. No problem, Gary told him, I've brought my own. And with a flourish, he produced the pair of chopsticks filched on his first visit from his jacket pocket. I gently slid out of sight under the table.

As a family, we had regular grief counselling sessions with Island Hospice. But the sessions weren't just to do with grief counselling. They were also a crash course in parenting. And boy did we need them. Jenny and I had already started clashing on the subject of discipline; especially when the disciplining involved Veronica. It hadn't taken Veronica long to work out that I was soft like a marshmallow on the outside and even softer on the inside. I was guaranteed to cave in almost automatically on all demands and Veronica played me like a fiddle. This left Jenny playing a lone bad-cop role. It was unfair on Jenny. Even I could see that, but I argued that the kids had been through so much, the least we could do was cut them a bit of slack on the home discipline front. Island Hospice was fair-square behind Jenny. Our children especially needed to know where their boundaries were.

At one of these counselling sessions, we were shown an amazing picture drawn by Veronica months before Rose died. The wax crayon drawing showed Veronica, Gary and Daniel holding hands in front of a house. Gary was huge in the picture, almost as tall as the house. Rose was in the background, lying down and some distance from the children. Our counsellor said the picture was full of symbolism regarding the relationships but what amazed me was the house Veronica had drawn. It was exactly our ramshackle upstairs downstairs farmhouse. I couldn't have drawn the house any better. And Veronica had drawn the picture months before she saw the house. My hair stood on end.

It was still school holidays. I spent as little time as I could at the office so I could watch the children settle into their new home. The dogs were in seventh heaven. They had kids to play with. The cats were less enamoured with the new arrivals. Veronica and Daniel loved playing with the day-old chicks the best. A new batch had just arrived, and they spent hours cuddling them and playing with them. Alas. Because of some tough loving, more than a few day olds didn't make it to two days old.

Veronica had pointed out at length the shortcomings of our farmyard in terms of animals. I set off in search of a cow. A friend ran a state-of-the-art dairy farm on the outskirts of Harare. Gary and I drove out early one morning to go cow shopping. The dairy farm boasted a massive herd of pedigree Friesland cows. They were beautiful animals with shiny bright black and white coats, grazing in the lush green paddocks with pendulous udders and soft Bambi eyes. The phrase 'soft Bambi eyes' popped into my head from nowhere. That's what happened when you hung out with six-year-olds.

I told the farmer about our noble cow quest, and minutes late, we drove off with a dairy herd of one in the back seat of the car. The herd's name was Elizabeth, and she was a day-old Friesland cow, about the size of a large dog. She was a 'vealer.' That was a cow that had been judged not good enough for the milking herd and earmarked for a one-way trip to the butcher's block. Elizabeth was a proper bargain. I paid a whole ten dollars for the cow, twenty bucks worth of fresh milk, still warm from the udder, to feed her with plus a long list of instructions on how to keep her alive. Because the instructions called for three-hourly feeds, when we got home, I handed both the cow and the instructions over to Raphael, the foreman. I didn't do three o'clock in the morning too well. Raphael examined Elizabeth carefully and pronounced her to be a very good excellent cow. He asked if I could buy another one for him. I promised him I would try.

Veronica was delighted with Elizabeth and spent hours in the back storeroom that we had converted into a barn fit for a cow, cuddling the cow and bottle feeding her. Now we had a proper farmyard, complete with the sounds of cows mooing. Unfortunately, Elizabeth's mooing grew ever fainter though. Raphael knocked on the back door of the house late at night, with a worried look on his face.

"The cow, sir, she is fucked. She has an illness that is making her shit a lot." Raphael's command of the English language was colourful, to say the least. In his vocabulary, the word fuck was reserved for use as an extreme adjective. I phoned Charles Waghorn, our aptly named vet and described the cow's symptoms. Apparently, Elizabeth had Scours, which was bovine diarrhoea. Charles told me to try to keep her liquids up and told me he'd pop around in the morning to see how she was doing. Alas. Elizabeth never made it to the morning. I was horrified. While I tried to figure out how I was going to tell Veronica that her favourite cow was no longer, I gave Raphael strict instructions not to eat Elizabeth. She was to be buried down in the bottom paddock, as far from the house as possible. Raphael looked at me like I was a complete idiot before grumbling off to waste the perfectly good meat.

Alas. Raphael wasn't the only one who thought we were wasting good meat. Just hours after I'd told Veronica that Elizabeth had gone up to heaven, her mortal and bloodied remains were dragged into the garden by Dempsey our boxer, wagging his non-existent tail ten to the dozen, overjoyed at having discovered the bone of all bones. Dempsey had already tucked into a goodly part of Elizabeth and was now looking for somewhere to bury the rest of her for a rainy day. What was left of Elizabeth looked like a prop from the Texas Chain Saw Massacre. I shouted for Raphael and told him to rebury Elizabeth's carcass quickly before Veronica saw it. "And this time make sure you dig a bloody deep hole!!" I shouted at him.

Veronica had been distraught when I told her about Elizabeth's sudden decision to head on up to heaven but calmed down quickly enough when I promised her another Elizabeth. I was amazed at how quickly kids bounce back. After another visit to Kintyre, I came back with Elizabeth the Second, Elizabeth the Third and Elizabeth the Fourth and a longer list of stricter instructions on how to care for them. Scours was caused by poor hygiene. We hadn't done our job properly with our first cow. I handed the herd of three over to Raphael and told him he could have one but only if he reared the other two successfully. He was overjoyed. As was Veronica. The only unhappy person in the story was Dempsey the boxer who spent hours looking for the remains of Elizabeth the First but never found them.

We were fast running out of school holidays, so Jenny and I had to make some school decisions quickly. Gary and Veronica both went to David Livingstone Primary, a government school, way over on the other side of town. Like most government schools, it was hopelessly overcrowded with forty plus kids per class. And David Livingstone would mean a fifty kilometre there and back commute every day. In traffic that would gobble up over two hours of every day. Jenny and I decided to look at other options. We'd been told about a small private school on a farm further out on our side of town. The school was called Lilfordia. It had been started by a member of the Lilford family, way back in 1902. Ian Campbell, the incumbent headmaster, was the grandson-in-law of the school's founder. Amazingly the position of headmaster had never passed out of the family in almost one hundred years, amazing continuity for a country as unsettled as Zimbabwe.

Ian and his wife Letitia ran the school as an extension of their home. With less than twenty children per classroom, they treated each and every child at the school as one of their own. Bad thunderstorms would see flocks of frightened five-year-olds flood the Campbell home. Children at Lilfordia were treated as people first, pupils second. Without even having seen the school, we knew it would be perfect for Gary and Veronica.

We were told that the school had a waiting-list miles long, but we drove out to the school with hope in our hearts, to meet with the Campbells. We fell in love with Lilfordia as soon as we saw it. It had a happy place feel to it. And our kids were badly in need of some happy therapy. The thatched dormitories dotted around the sprawling grounds added to the school's rustic atmosphere. We told Ian and Letitia our story, and that was that.

The kids were in. Ian said Lilfordia could always squeeze another desk in a classroom. Plus, he was short of decent batsmen for the school cricket team.

"Do you play cricket, Gary? You look like you might have an eye for the ball," Ian Campbell asked.

"I don't know sir, I've never tried."

"Well, we'll soon change that," said Ian.

Jenny and I were delighted. We knew Lilfordia would be the perfect school for Gary and Veronica, where their education would have more than a hint of healing. Lilfordia was a boarding school but had a handful of day scholars that came in from town every day. And we would be able to join a lift club, which would take the heat off the daily commute. With the new term starting in just a few days, Jenny had a mad rush to get uniforms and lift clubs organised.

In Veronica's case, though, she needn't have bothered panicking about the uniform. In the television show, Veronica had been described as a real live wire and a chatterbox. They left out the word dippy. On her first Lilfordia school morning, Veronica was dispatched with her full school uniform consisting of blue brookies, blue uniform dress, sun hat, socks x two, brown shiny shoes x two, sports shirt, sports shorts, white sports shoes x two, white sports socks x two, swimming costume and swimming towel. On top of this impressive list was a school suitcase to keep her reading book and homework book in.

I thought it was a very long list of items for a six-year-old to keep track of. Veronica was obviously in complete agreement with me because she returned after her first day with only her swimming costume. That was it. Every other thing that she'd left home with that morning had gone missing in action. Clothes, suitcase, the whole bang shoot, missing. I was amazed. I tried to help Veronica to think about where she might have left them. After some considerable thought, Veronica narrowed things down to either the day scholar's dormitory, or maybe her classroom, or maybe on the sports field, or maybe in the car she had come home in. But they were definitely at school somewhere, she announced happily unless of course, they were in the car.

We were right in our choice of schools. Both Gary and Veronica thrived at Lilfordia, especially Gary. He was drafted into every available sports team. Being a small school with a tiny player base, team selection at Lilfordia was a given. If you could pick-up a hockey stick, you were in the hockey team. Ditto the rugby team. And Gary thrived. And with amazing hand-eye co-ordination, he was a natural sportsman.

I picked up on exactly how good his hand-eye co-ordination was at the School Fun Day. It was Lilfordia's premier annual fundraising day. Each child was given a purse full of money, cunningly added onto the school fees at the end of the term and let loose on the myriad of fun stands manned by the parents and children, with strict instructions to spend every last penny. There was no shortage of different fun things for the children to spend their parents' money on. There were Toffee Apples, Candy Floss and Popcorn stalls, Tombola, and the obligatory 'Try Throw the Incredibly Small Hoop over the Incredibly Large Objects' stall.

Gary and I zeroed in on the stall where the punters were urged to 'Test Your Nerves of Steel' by negotiating an iron ring around the tricky twists and turns of an electrically charged wire maze. If you touched the wire, a loud buzzer would sound, and you'd lose your entry fee. But if impossibly, you made it all the way to the end without touching the wire, you'd win ten dollars. And ten dollars would buy a lot of candy floss and beer. My nerves of steel and I stepped up first, brim-full of confidence, but sadly blew out on the very first corner. Then it was Gary's turn. With a look of steely concentration, he whizzed his way around the maze in double-quick time. Ten dollars richer, he headed straight to the back of the short queue. The treacherous maze did away with the queue of hopefuls promptly. And then it was Gary's second turn. And again, he whizzed through the twists and turns without touching. Another ten dollars in his kitty. The stall attendant bent over to check that the maze was plugged in properly. All was in order. Gary stepped up again with the same results, but this time even quicker. Now that he knew the course, he practically flew around the twists and turns. The stall attendant took on the look of the mildly panicked.

"Don't you want to try some of the other stands? Maybe the Tombola or something?" he asked Gary.

"But I like this one."

Another thirty dollars later, the stall attendant tried to ban Gary from the stall, but I wouldn't let him. That would be like banning a fat kid from a Candy Floss stall I told him. The poor man, in every sense of the word, made some emergency adjustments to his maze, scrunching the wires up with extra viscous cutbacks and turns. No problem. Gary added a new look of boredom to his repertoire as he zipped through the new challenges with ease. Ten more dollars in the bank. Gary was officially nearly well off. By now, he had a small audience cheering him on. The stall attendant upgraded his mildly panicked look to full-on panic and slashed the prize money from ten dollars down to five.

"But you can't do that!" I protested loudly on Gary's behalf.

"Of course, I can," he retorted. "And I just did."

"But it's not fair!!" I squealed.

The stall attendant turned my tables on me. "It's the same as running a half-price special at the Candy Floss stall."

It turned out that Gary's was equally adept at winning five-dollar prizes. And if anything, he did it in half the time. Another fifty dollars in prize money later, the 'Test Your Nerves of Steel' stand went under. "Bust, bankrupt, kaput. The bank has been broken. And all thanks to your son!!!" the operator railed bitterly.

His words resonated in my head. I had a son to be proud of.

Chapter Four

Our rickety house stood testimony to my status as a non-handyman and a procrastinator par excellence. Gary's aviary joined the long list of other jobs I was currently putting off. 'Why do today what you can to do tomorrow?' was my approach to anything that needed either a hammer or a screwdriver.

Veronica decided to hurry things along. There was a busy colony of golden yellow weaver birds nesting in a tall Acacia in the garden. But not for long. Veronica climbed up the tree, risked life and limb to shimmy out along the thin branches and emptied all the nests within reach of their contents, which were mostly eggs and featherless fledglings. Back on terra firma, Veronica handed the lot over to Gary as an early birthday present; his birthday was still months away.

"Now Daddy has to build you a birdcage, Gary." I still got such a kick every time she called me daddy. Gary was less enthused at his bounty and told her she had to put them back.

"Can he keep them, Daddy, please can he keep them?" she begged.

"I don't think you should've taken the eggs, Vee," I said. Veronica's bottom lip started to tremble. "And I don't know if all the babies are going to make it. Some of them look very young."

Veronica's tears started. "Must I put the little birds back into their nests?" she sobbed.

"I don't think we can, my darling. Once we've touched them, the mommies will never take them back."

Veronica's bottom lip trembles spread up to her shoulders. She was a picture of perfect misery. I hated watching her sad. "But if Gary feeds the little birds every three hours, I'm sure they'll grow just fine," I blurted hurriedly.

The tears stopped, and she went back to being delighted. "And so he can keep them! And when they grow up, he'll have lots and lots of little Phoenixes."

Gary was clearly not thrilled at the prospect of waking up every three hours to feed the fledglings. I leant him my old alarm clock. Made in Mozambique, inspired by East German precision, it was a beast with alarm clangers the size of hubcaps and a tick-tock that made Big Ben subtle by comparison. The alarm clock was guaranteed to wake the dead, and anyone else within half a kilometre of ground zero, provided you fell asleep in the first place.

"Why didn't you just tell her to put the bloody birds back into the nest?" Jenny swore at me as the three o'clock alarm ripped us from our sleep. We'd only just fallen back asleep after the midnight alarm.

"But you can't put baby birds back in their nests. Everyone knows their mothers will reject them."

"Well, Veronica isn't everyone," Jenny hissed. "And this is all your fault anyway!!"

"How's it my fault?" I wailed.

"None of this would've happened if you'd just built Gary an aviary like you promised."

Work on the aviary started the very next day. The original design on paper was a rather grandiose walk through aviary, complete with water features and built-in rain forest. Gary looked very impressed. His aviary would be able to house a myriad of bird varieties in splendour. But he looked less than impressed when I hammered a six-inch nail through both a log and my index finger within the first five minutes of construction. After a quick visit to the emergency room at the hospital to extract the log and the nail from my finger, I decided to scale the aviary back to your basic box design with gum poles in the corners, and chicken mesh stretched over the top. Blood and pain were great reality checks.

The construction phase of the project didn't take long. By my lowly standards, the aviary was a thing of beauty. It was sort of square. And the door opened and closed. And the wire mesh was reasonably taut. It was a splendid, fully functional aviary.

"But ...." Gary started.

I cut him off. "Relax. Don't worry about how much it cost. I promised you an aviary, and that's what you're going to get."

"But I'm...."

"Shhh!!! All we have to do now is catch some birds and stick them inside."

"But..."

"Don't worry. It's not going to cost anything. I've asked Raphael to help you make some bird traps, and we'll soon have your aviary full."

"But..."

"Gary, I don't want to hear another word about how much it's costing. That's my job. And I've actually enjoyed building it. Apart from the bit where the six-inch nail went right through my finger."

"But..."

"Shhh!!!"

It didn't take long before Raphael and Gary caught their first birds. The birdlife around the house was prolific, widow finches and fire finches, bronze manikins and red bishops, blue waxbills and long-tail whydahs, all with the survival instincts of a curious lemming. Made out of the shade netting and wireframes with piles of birdseed for bait, Raphael's bird trap was simple, and it worked. They had their first cardboard box full of captured birds before lunch. It was time to put my aviary to the test. The theme song to 'Born Free' played silently in my head. But then I realised it was completely the wrong soundtrack for the occasion and axed it.

Gary and I stuck the cardboard box on the floor inside the aviary, opened the lid and stood back to watch the birds settle into their splendid new home. We watched them just briefly. This was how long it took them to squeeze out the mesh and escape back to the bush from whence they had come.

"Oh bollocks," I said. "The mesh is too big."

"That's what I was trying to tell you, Dad," Gary said.

"But why didn't you say anything."

"I tried to Dad. But you wouldn't listen. You kept telling me to keep quiet!"

"Well, you should have spoken out louder. When you see something's wrong, you've got to make yourself heard," I blustered, feeling foolish. And then it struck me. Gary had just called me dad. And he'd called me dad twice. Once might have been a slip of the tongue but not twice. Standing in the empty aviary, I was a happy man. I didn't have a single bird in my aviary, but I had a son who called me dad.

Veronica remained intent on finding a bird for Gary to replace Phoenix. We were driving the six hundred kilometres down to the South African border to pick my mother up. She was coming to inspect her new grandchildren. She was on her own because my dad couldn't get time off from work. My parents lived eighteen hundred kilometres away in Pietermaritzburg, South Africa. And that was almost a day and a half on the bus. To save her six hundred kilometres of her epic bus trip, I had offered to pick my mom up at the Beitbridge border.

Jenny decided to turn the trip into a holiday and booked us into the Lion and Elephant Hotel, a bush lodge eighty kilometres from the border, for a few nights. The children were very excited. We were going to be staying in a real hotel. With real chocolates on the pillows at night, I told them, which earned me a collective wow. The kids had never stayed at a hotel before. I got another wow from Gary when I told him, courtesy of the hotel brochure, the Lion and Elephant had a ten-thousand-acre game farm teeming with wildlife and was right on the banks of the Bubye River. Gary was so excited. He was going fishing in the bush.

A six-hour drive later, we booked in. It was a charming little hotel with thatched lodges nestled below huge Albida trees right on the banks of the Bubye River. Gary jumped out of the car, grabbed his rod and rushed off to fish. Alas. The river was miles and miles of golden sands and not a drop of bloody water anywhere. Apparently, the Bubye River was a bit of a misnomer. It only did the water thing every ten or so years, and for the rest, it was a big long sandpit. Gary was dejection personified, and his fishing rod never got further than his bedroom.

To get over the disappointment of no fishing, we all went for a bushwalk in the dry riverbed. We climbed down on to hot white sands of the Bubye while the tinder-dry Lowveld bush towered above us on both sides. Jenny and I each held Dan by the hand while Gary ran on ahead. Then I noticed that Veronica was creeping along with big eyes, like a mouse scampering from bush to bush in the riverbed.

"Why are you creeping?" I asked.

"Because I'm scared!"

"Why are you scared?"

"Because of all the lions and elephants!!"

I laughed and told her it was just a name. Veronica was relieved, then disappointed, then disgusted. The disgust was pointed at me, the High Priest of False Adverting. First up there was the river that wasn't a river, followed by no lions or elephants, even though she'd seen the pictures of lions and elephants on the hotel sign. She was slightly mollified when I showed her a shy impala, trembling in the shadows before skipping and leaping away through the bush. It looked just like Bambi. The impala was followed by some kudu bulls and then a troop of baboons that ambled passed us, out on a morning stroll.

And then Veronica hit pay dirt. She saw a nest of giant bird eggs buried in the sand of the riverbed. She ran up to them excitedly. "What are they, Daddy, what are they?"

"They're ostrich eggs."

There was a clutch of four massive eggs half-buried in the sand. I looked around the bush nervously. A vague memory nestled in the back of my head was reminding me that an ostrich could kick a man to death when provoked. And pinching a mother's eggs would surely slot in under provocative behaviour. I was ready to flee with a child tucked under each arm. Jenny and Gary would have to fend for themselves.

"Please, please can we take them home with us?" Veronica asked.

"You should never disturb nature," I told her firmly. "What you see in the bush, you should leave in the bush."

"But can't we just take one of them for Gary, to keep as a pet."

Gary stepped in with some common sense. "I don't think it's a new nest, Dad. Feel the eggs. They're all cold. And there aren't any tracks around. I'm sure the nest has been abandoned." Gary was very observant for an eleven-year-old. If I hadn't been proud, I would have been annoyed.

"So, I can't get you an ostrich, Gary?" Veronica's lower lip trembled.

"No, Vee, the eggs won't have babies inside," Gary said. "But what we can do is blow the egg, and we can keep them as souvenirs, one for you and one for me."

Veronica's tremble stopped. Even though she didn't know what a souvenir was.

When we got back to the hotel, I watched Gary blow out his egg. Using the blade on a sharp knife, he made a tiny hole in the top of the thick shell and a slightly bigger hole in the bottom. Then he blew through the top hole, forcing the egg yolk and white out through the bottom hole. It stank a bit, but Gary soon had his egg empty and washed.

"I want to try with my egg, let me have a go," Veronica said excitedly. Gary made the holes in her eggshell for her. Veronica huffed and puffed up her cheeks like a blowfish and blew hard. Nothing came out. She huffed and puffed again but still nothing.

"Let me do it for you," Gary said.

"No. I want to do it myself. I want to make the holes a bit bigger." She took a pointy stick, poked, and prodded. And poked and prodded a bit more before blowing again. A small hairline crack developed in the shell. Veronica sucked in more air, almost doubling the size of her head and blew on the hole in the egg like it was a birthday cake with a hundred candles burning. She blew and blew. The hairline cracked a bit more. Veronica gave a final, mighty blow and the hole split open and foul black toxic gunk came vomiting forth, attended by an even fouler stench. And in the middle of the foul gunk lay a blackened Ostrich chick, shrivelled, wizened and evil. Veronica screamed. And threw it all up in the air with both hands. Not a good move. Because what goes up, generally comes down. And it did, all over her. A putrid demonic ostrich chick complete with foul after- gunk rained down upon her. It was the stuff that horror movies were made of. Veronica's face was a picture of absolute panic, fear, disgust and horror. Which started Gary laughing, a good, deep belly laugh. It was the first time I'd heard Gary laugh. It was a nice sound. And it was an infectious laugh. We were all rolling on the hot sands of the Bubye River. Apart from Veronica, who carried on looking disgusted. It took three showers to get rid of that look.

Gary and I drove through to Beitbridge border post to pick my mother up. As always, the border post was an unruly logjam of hot, sweaty, ill-tempered, masses of humanity. What should have been a five-minute process was dragged out for hours and hours by fat, lazy corrupt immigration officials looking to get rich on bribes and offerings. The queues into Hell must be very like Beitbridge Border Post queues. I could see my mom from afar, gesticulating loudly with arms and broken English, no doubt her currency cache stashed away safely in the confines of her armoured bra. Eventually, she popped out of the scrum, saw me but ran straight past and latched onto her brand-new grandson with a huge hug and bigger sloppy kisses on both cheeks. With tears streaming down her cheeks, she introduced herself to Gary as Granny Bets. Gary's new family had just got bigger by one.

Back at the hotel, there was another bout of kissing and hugging and crying. And then Bets pulled me far to one side for a one on one lecture. My mom is uber big on lectures. "Eric, I think that you and Jenny have done a really good thing for these children. I'm proud you helped them."

"No, Mom. We haven't done it for the children. We did it for ourselves."

"You know what I mean," she said.

"I know what you're saying, Mom. But you're wrong. Jenny and I have adopted these children for purely selfish reasons. We couldn't have kids together. We adopted them because we wanted a family, not because we felt sorry for the children."

"Yes. But you've also done a good thing for the children. And I'm proud of you. And I love you lots." More hugs and tears all round.

When we got back to the farm, Gary's aviary had two occupants; a pair of Pied Crows, which were instantly christened Joe Crow and Mo Crow. Raphael had bought them for Gary from a kid on the road.

"They are for picanin boss Gary," Raphael announced proudly.

"That's great," Gary said. "I've heard that you can get crows really tame. You can even get them to talk and stuff."

Raphael was as pleased as punch with his efforts. But Joe Crow and Mo Crow were less than pleased. They were vicious, ill-tempered birds with cruel beaks and cruel hearts, hearts way blacker than their feathers. And that was before they'd been kidnapped and locked up in a cage. They took out all their misfortune on Gary when he went into the cage to bond with his new pets, using their beaks to inflict maximum damage, leaving Gary ripped, bleeding, and slightly less enamoured with Joe and Mo. But Gary stuck manfully to his task, determined to win them over. I thought he was on a hiding to nothing. The human body only contains seven litres of blood, so I phoned best friend John Stanton who had a tame crow. The crow had free range of his house, and it had been known not to kill people. John considered Joe and Mo from the safety of the right side of the wire mesh and gave his expert opinion. "We need to cut their flight feathers," he said.

"Will that tame them quicker?" I asked.

"Not really. But it will stop the evil bastards from dive-bombing everyone who walks into the cage."

"And then Gary will only bleed from his ankles down, cutting out most of the major blood loss," I said, looking for the positives.

Gary smiled weakly at the thought of less of the red stuff.

"No, I'm just joking," John said. "The birds will get tamer. And as soon as you've cut their flight feathers, you can let them out the cage and let them hop around the garden. They'll learn to come to you quickly enough when they're hungry."

OF BIRDS, BIRDS AND MORE BLOODY BIRDS

"Will you cut their flight feathers for me? I'll most probably cut the wrong ones," Gary asked.

"No problem," John said. "All I need is a decent pair of scissors."

"And maybe a blood transfusion for later," I said.

John laughed. But not for long.

What followed wasn't pretty. The vicious black bastard birds attacked John as a team, going for the jugular and other important blood vessels. It was straight out of an Alfred Hitchcock movie. I was horrified and enthralled. Maybe the human body contained more than just seven litres of blood. Eventually, after an epic struggle with the birds from hell, John emerged from the abattoir come aviary, clutching a fistful of flight feathers above his head victoriously. He'd triumphed over the bastard birds. "Okay, Gary, you can let them out," he said weakly.

"Are you sure they won't fly away?"

"Relax. These suckers aren't going anywhere without these things," he said as he waved the flight feathers.

Gary opened the door and gently shooed Joe Crow and Mo Crow out of the aviary. They stood there blinking at us malevolently, for a few long seconds. I thought they were going to come at us again. But then like bats out of hell, they headed for the heavens. I'd never seen birds hit high altitude so quickly.

"Damn!" John stood there ruefully, holding his handful of feathers, watching the black spots get smaller in the sky. "That wasn't supposed to happen."

As the latest of Gary's feathered pets disappeared into a cloud bank, I went to hug Gary, but there was no need. He started laughing; it was his good deep belly laugh again.

"They really shouldn't have been able to do that," John said ruefully holding a fist full of forlorn flight feathers.

Chapter Five

It didn't take long for our new life to settle down into family normality. Getting up, going to work or to school, coming home, doing homework, dinner and off to bed. It should have been boring, but it wasn't. For Jenny and me every new day was a voyage of discovery. We had lots to learn about our children. They might have had the same mother, but they were all completely different.

Jenny decided that she needed to start training Daniel in essential life skills on two fronts; on how to use the potty and on how not to drown. Not having hung out with any other two-year-olds, I didn't know if Daniel was normal in terms of skill development. I had nothing to benchmark him against. But being able to crap in a potty, as opposed to crapping in your clothes was a life skill he badly needed to take on board. And it needed to be taken on board quickly. If anything, Jenny's ability to deal with stench was waning with every crappy nappy.

Daniel hated potty training. He hated his potty even more. The fact that it was a happy sky-blue colour complete with little happy face stickers stuck all over it mattered not a jot. He hated the potty with a passion, would glare at it balefully and would hide it at every opportunity. Small wonder he hated it. Overnight it became his after meals prison. Daniel was only ever released for good behaviour in the form of either a number one or a number two. Jenny was a firm believer in positive reinforcement and both number ones, and twos were rewarded. Numbers ones received a smattering of polite applause while a number two got a boisterous round of rapturous applause and a sweetie.

Alas. Apparently, Daniel wasn't big on either applause or sweeties. His potty training turned into an epic battle of wills; Daniel the stubborn versus Jenny the immovable object. It was dreadful. I was the wimp in the middle. My pleas for an early release for Daniel fell on deaf ears. "But what if my client is constipated? What if he wants to pooh, but just can't?"

"He's not constipated," Jenny growled. "And he's not going anywhere, not until he's done either a wee or a pooh!!"

The need to drown-proof Dan was as obvious as a steaming, two kilos nappy full of number two. Dan had already breached my hurriedly erected swimming pool fence on two occasions. Swimming pools and little boys who couldn't swim weren't a good combination. I was bitterly disappointed in my fence. It looked like Stalag 13 and should have kept herds of water buffalo at bay. But Dan had gone through the bloody thing like prunes through a two-year-old. I was starting to think about modifications, like maybe electrification when Jenny intervened. She sent for the professionals who sorted out my fence's shortcomings by ripping it down and starting again. And once the new shiny and impregnable fence was up, Jenny started on the drown proofing. She'd read all about it in a book. Jenny and I got a lot of crash course parenting skills out of books and magazines.

Drown proofing was hardcore, tough love stuff, as hard on spectators as very scary horror movies. Mostly I watched, peeping through my fingers. From what little I could see, drown proofing seemed to centre on lobbing poor Dan into the pool. While he sank to the bottom, screaming blue murder, Jenny would teach him to roll on to his back, and he would bob gently to the surface and float. Drown proofing was not the faint-hearted. Thankfully swimming training was scheduled after daily potty training, so there were no ecological shallow end disasters.

The drown proofing worked. Dan would get lobbed in, twist on to his back, bob to the surface and float. It gave him a very healthy respect for the pool that would last until we could get him booked in somewhere for proper swimming lessons.

Veronica wasn't hugely keen on education. She especially hated learning how to read. And so, she developed a huge proficiency in forgetting homework books at school. Veronica knew her letters of the alphabet well enough, from Annie Apple and Bouncy Ball and Clever Cat through to Lucy Lamp and Kicking King and company. But the reading style she adopted as her own was based on a unique multiple guess approach to word formation that turned the average Janet and John book into an epic of Tolstoy proportions. She would seize on and correctly identify the first letter of the word in question and then cheerfully guess her way through all the other words in her vocabulary beginning with the same latter until she finally bumped into the right word. And if she ran out of known words, she'd start on made-up words that sort of sounded plausible. In the Veronica style of reading, Janet or John would throw Spot a bat, a bread, a bucket, a brick, a balloon, a building, a black, a brown and eventually the ball in question. Reading homework with Veronica was long and tedious stuff, but Veronica would somehow remain cheerful throughout, which is more than can be said for me.

Gary, on the other hand, approached schoolwork like he approached life, with quiet confidence and a maturity beyond his years. As shown on the day the Dempsey versus Tilden affair came to a noisy head.

Dempsey was our brindle boxer puppy. Technically he wasn't a puppy anymore but was one of those dogs that never grew up and charged through life on a perpetual adventure. And he was bloody noisy with it, barking at everything and everyone he encountered. If they ran away, he chased them. If they didn't run away, he'd lick them to death. Tilden was the huge black thoroughbred stallion, which lived on the horse stud next door. His five-star stable and paddock backed onto our garden. Tilden wasn't just any stallion. He was a stud stallion, the sire of more than one Durban July champion. He was insured for millions. But unfortunately, Tilden fell into the category of things that ran away from Dempsey's incessant barking, and there was nothing Dempsey enjoyed more than chasing the stallion all over the paddock. This pissed Tilden's owner off no end. He was a dour giant of an Afrikaner called Mr van Niekerk. I don't think his parents gave him a first name. I was petrified of Mr van Niekerk. In my books, he was up there with the taxman and dentists.

Things came to a head one day when Mr van Niekerk barged over and started thumping on our front door. Gary was doing his homework upstairs. He put his books away and answered the door politely. "Hallo, Mr van Niekerk."

"Where is your father? I want to see your father!!" Mr van Niekerk thundered, the veins in his head bulging dangerously.

"I'll go and look for him. Do you want to wait inside?" Gary asked.

"No. I'll wait here for him. But get him now!"

Gary found me hiding in the passage around the corner. Reluctantly I followed Gary back to the front door.

"Hallo, Mr van Niekerk, how nice to…"

He cut me off mid-sentence. "Your bloody dog is chasing my champion stallion again. And that stallion is worth millions I tell you, more than your whole bloody farm!!"

"Oh, dear, but …."

"And sooner than later, your bloody dog will do the horse damage!"

"I'm really sorry, Mr van Niekerk. But you've got nothing to worry about. Tilden is a racehorse, and the dog's never going to catch him. And if even he did, the dog doesn't mean any harm. He's just looking for a bit of fun."

Mr van Niekerk got all apoplectic on me. His bulging veins were by now throbbing alarmingly, threatening to pop. "Just a racehorse!!! Just a racehorse!!! And just a bit of fun you say!!!!" he roared rounding off his sentence with four exclamation marks, all blunt and subtle like a smack in the face with a shovel. "I've told you before to control that bloody dog and you've done bloody nothing!!!"

"Well, I have started training the dog," I offered up weakly. "You know like teaching him how to sit before his dinner and…."

"But you haven't stopped him from bloody chasing my stallion!!!"

"Like I said, he doesn't mean any harm. He's still just a puppy that's all."

"I want you to put up a proper fence between your place and Tilden's paddock to keep your bloody dog out of my property. Otherwise, I promise you that I will shoot the bloody animal one day!!!"

"I'll do my best, Mr van Niekerk. I'll get the fence up as quickly as I can but...."

"But what!!!" Mr van Niekerk demanded angrily. Even his questions were rounded off with the threatening exclamation marks.

"I've had a quote for the fence, and it's a bit more than I can afford at the moment and...."

"Have I told you what my stallion is worth!!!?" By now Mr van Niekerk's eyeballs were bulging alarmingly. He was either going to punch me, or he was going to have a heart attack. Please, please, God, let it be the heart attack and not the punch I begged silently.

A small voice cut through the thunder. "Why don't you put the fence up, Mr van Niekerk?" Gary asked.

The huge Afrikaner rounded on Gary. "What did you say!!!"

Gary stood his ground. "Why don't you pay for the fence, Mr van Niekerk? Tilden is your horse. And he is worth more than our whole farm."

You could have heard a pin drop in the silence that followed Gary's logic. I braced for the storm that was surely coming. But all that came from Mr van Niekerk was a loud solitary "Hmmmmpph!!!" The bull Afrikaner shook his head ponderously as he silently chewed his way through Gary's suggestion. "I suppose I'll have to put up the bloody fence." He looked at Gary as though he was looking at a piece of horseflesh. "You're a slim one, boy!!" he told Gary before stomping off heavily.

Gary's puppy fat chin quivered in the aftermath. He thought Mr Van Niekerk was poking fun at his chubbiness. "Slim means clever, Gary. In Afrikaans. Mr van Niekerk just called you clever," I told him. Mr van Niekerk was right. Gary was old beyond his eleven years.

Others noticed Gary's quiet maturity too. At the end of his first school term, the headmaster of Lilfordia chose Gary as a school prefect. I felt a massive surge of pride when his name was called out at the end of term school assembly. I was sure Ian Campbell had chosen Gary more for therapeutic reasons than for his leadership skills. And it certainly worked. The recognition and responsibility gave Gary's levels of self-confidence a massive boost.

The end of the school term marked the start of the Christmas holidays, the count-down to our first Christmas as parents. Jenny and I had made a solemn vow not to spoil the children, too much. She had me in a particularly painful headlock at the time. Now Jenny is one of those annoying people who start Christmas shopping in February and finished by June. She'd decided there would only be one big present for each child with lots of little sensible presents to fill up the gaps under the Christmas tree. I approved of the big presents she'd bought the kids, shiny new bicycles for Gary and Veronica and a shiny electric motor car complete with lots of annoying noises and flashing lights for Daniel, but the sensible gifts she bought put me to sleep. And for sure they would put the kids to sleep as well. And you wanted kids excited on Christmas Day opening presents, not nodding off. Erasers, rulers and pencils bags, protractor sets, and compasses didn't count as presents in my book; they were things for school, they were in the same league as dental braces. You got them not because you wanted them, but because you needed them.

Before the kids, Christmas in our house followed a strict ritual. Too many drinks on Christmas Eve, coincidentally also my birthday, followed by a repentant Midnight Mass during which I would nod off in the middle of the Latin bits. Jenny was a practising Catholic. I went along just for the Christmas carols, which I liked to sing loudly and badly. Once church was out the way Jenny and I would then go home for a long Christmas morning lie-in, to dilute the worst of my birthday hangover before opening our presents under the Christmas tree. Even without children in the house, Jenny always put up a Christmas tree, complete with a fairy on top and all the decorations. Once we'd opened the gifts we'd bought each other, one big present and lots of little sensible ones, we'd go to Anne and Mike Matthews for a long and liquid Christmas lunch with turkey and all the trimmings. Anne was Jenny's cousin in a long, convoluted way. Mike was excellent company and always had a fridge full of beer and a joke to tell. And this year there would be an extra special bond because two of the three Matthews children were also adopted.

The excitement in our house ramped up noticeably as Christmas approached. Gary was a bit too old for visible excitement, and Dan was still too young to appreciate Father Christmas but Veronica more than made up for the both of them.

"Are you sure Father Christmas knows that we've moved houses, Daddy? He's not going to go to our old house, is he?"

"How do you know he's coming at all? He only comes to good boys and girls," Gary pointed out, winding her up.

"But I have been a good girl," Veronica cried.

"No, you haven't. You left your clothes lying all over your bedroom floor this morning," Gary said sternly. As predicted, Veronica's bottom lip started to tremble. Gary could play his sister like a fiddle.

"But I'm going to pick all my clothes up, I promise you I am."

I stepped in quickly to nullify the trembling bottom lip. "Of course, Father Christmas knows where you live now. And of course, he's going to come and visit you and Gary and Daniel."

"Do you think he'll bring me a My Little Pony? And a Barbie doll. And a......."

"How does he know what you want if you haven't even written him a letter?" Gary asked with a smirk. He was enjoying himself.

"But I don't know how to write letters." The tears had arrived.

"I'll help you write the letter, Veronica," I said.

"But where will we send the letter? And will Father Christmas get it in time?"

"Of course, he'll get the letter. There's a special post box in town just for Father Christmas. His letters get sent straight to his house at the North Pole."

We took the children to see the Christmas lights at the Harare Gardens that night. The lights and the fairy tale themed village display looked tired to me. Nothing had changed since I was Veronica's age, not a thing. The lady who lived in the shoe still lived in her huge boot next to Red Riding Hood's Grandmother's cottage, which was just across the way from the Three Little Pigs house. It was all a bit stale and in need of more than just a coat of paint. But there was nothing stale and tired about the looks on Veronica and Daniel's faces as we posted their letters to Santa Clause. They were an absolute joy to behold. And their sense of wonderment was contagious. The Christmas carols were loud inside my head, and for weeks I was Goodwill to All Mankind personified.

Jenny's mom and dad trekked up all the way from Newcastle in South Africa to spend their first Christmas with their new grandchildren. The children had another set of grandparents to be doted on by. Hester was born to be a Nana and always had an endless supply of home-baked biscuits and cakes and a hug and a love for anyone in need. Tony a.k.a. Poppa played his role of the grumpy but loveable grandfather to perfection. Hester and Tony fell in love with Gary, Veronica and Daniel at first sight and the feeling was more than mutual. And they'd arrived with a car boot full of gaily wrapped presents. I helped smuggle the pile of presents into the house under cover of darkness lest we blew Father Christmas's cover.

My birthday that year was my best ever. Gary, Veronica and Daniel woke me up with presents, a cup of coffee, a breakfast feast of toast and a stirring out of key rendition of the Happy Birthday song. My birthday celebrations were less liquid that year, but my Christmas carolling was as loud and as bad as normal, proving my inability to hold a tune had nothing to do with alcohol intake. When we got home from church, we packed the children off to bed. Daniel had already fallen asleep in the car. Veronica tried valiantly to keep her eyes open for a peep at Father Christmas but failed. Once she'd fallen asleep, we laid out the presents around the base of the Christmas tree. The pile of brightly wrapped gifts beneath the tree was huge. Thankfully the 'Don't spoil the Children' rule had been blown out of the water. I went to bed a happy man with Come All Ye Faithful playing loudly in my head.

I was slightly less happy when the banging at our bedroom door started at four-thirty the next morning. It was Veronica, breathless with excitement. Gary was standing behind her, doing his best not to look excited. Veronica told us that she'd heard Father Christmas and his reindeers land on the roof the night before and she'd looked in the lounge this morning and under the Christmas Tree was full of presents and some of them had her name on them and there were lots of presents for everyone and if we didn't get out of bed quickly then it would all be too late and....

Jenny slowed her down. She was sure that Father Christmas might have left stockings on the mantelpiece for certain children. Those children could open their stockings no problem but would have to wait for adults to be present before the pile under the tree could be approached. I jumped out of bed and set about making a pot of coffee with an obscene amount of joie de vie. Veronica and Gary's enthusiasm was infectious and had all adults out of bed and around the Christmas tree by six.

I sat back and took a mental snapshot of my family and me under the sparkling Christmas tree. Jenny and Hester had their happy mom faces firmly fixed in position. And Tony had put his Grumpy Old Men look away. Children sitting under the Christmas tree made all the difference in the world. It was good. It was how Christmas was supposed to be.

Jenny was the designated distributor of presents. It took a while to make a dent in the pile under the tree. I sat and snapped away with the camera, capturing looks of delight and excitement whenever a present was opened plus the odd photo of my thumb. Daniel got such a huge kick out of ripping open presents. I got him to open all of mine. He was a machine. He went through wrapping paper like a chainsaw through butter. The kids all got spoiled rotten. And that was before the unveiling of the shiny bicycles and shiny electric motor car complete with lots of annoying noises and flashing lights!!

After breakfast, adorned in my brand-new underpants, socks and aftershave, we went to the Matthews house for Christmas lunch. Mike and Anne had a lovely home in Harare's leafy suburbia. Christmas lunch was always served on long tables out on the lawn, under blue skies and the spreading Msasa trees.

On the way to lunch that year we encountered a strange procession coming towards us; a long line of cars driving oh so slowly behind a live turkey legging it down the middle of the road. Someone's Christmas lunch was making a break for it. As the procession reached us, Gary jumped out and captured the turkey. And so, we arrived at Mike and Anne's with Christmas lunch on the hoof, squawking loudly. But before his head could be removed, Daniel fell in love with him. The turkey was given the name Gobble Gobble, and he became the family's designated feathered pet.

Chapter Six

We'd only just got over the excesses of Christmas when Gary's birthday hit us like a freight train. I felt ambushed. Before I had only two dates to track, Jenny's birthday and our ever-treacherous wedding anniversary. But now suddenly I had an extra three birthdays to contend with. And it wasn't good enough to just remember birthdays, you had to do something about them, like buy presents and stuff. Being in a family of five was tough going. Thank God for wives. They were worth the extra stress of having to remember wedding anniversaries.

Gary's birthday fell on January 2. Poor kid was twelve going on twenty-two. For his birthday, Jenny bought him a new fishing rod and enough tackle to land Moby Dick. I decided I'd take him and six of his new friends fishing on a small dam on a neighbouring farm as a birthday treat. The world's worst fisherman, I would be in charge of the bush breakfast while Gary and company got on with the business of fishing.

One of Gary's friends, a young Muslim kid called Shiraz Khan, arrived with a Guinea Pig as a present. While Gary looked happy with his present, I was very suspicious. I'd owned a multitude of the Guinea Pigs as a child and knew that they only come in multitudes. I looked at the gift Guinea Pig in the tummy. It was unusually fat.

"Are you sure it's not pregnant?" I demanded of Shiraz.

"No, Mr de Jong. I just fed it before I got here, that's all."

"Are you sure? Because I've seen these things breed before."

"Not if he's the only one he can't."

"Only Amoeba can breed by themselves," Gary, the twelve-year-old fountain of knowledge, told me. "They like sort of split in two. But Guinea Pigs have to mate with each other. And one of them has got to be a girl."

"Okay. You can keep him," I relented reluctantly. "But any babies that come go straight back to Shiraz."

Because the dam we were fishing at was a designated bird sanctuary, you couldn't drive there. You had to walk the last two or three kilometres. With my caravan of porters humping fishing rods, camping chairs and breakfast cooking equipment, I set off along a bush path that led towards the dam. Halfway the path split in two around a thicket of scrub acacia bushes. Gary took the left path while his friends and I took the right path. I was halfway around the thicket when Gary screamed. I couldn't see him through the thicket but boy, could I hear him. Something was obviously killing him. I dropped the camping gear I was carrying and rushed off to save Gary and, in the process, ran right over the back of the python that had scared the crap out of him. It was a massive snake, well over four metres long and thicker than my thigh. Make that thicker than other people's thighs as I am renowned for having skinny legs. The python had a lump halfway down its body about the size of a pig...or a young fisherman. I quickly did a head count, but everyone was present and accounted for. The snake wasn't at all worried about our presence. He was more interested in basking in the sun, more concerned with digesting his last meal than worrying about his next. We watched him for a few minutes before carrying on to the dam.

It was a pleasant way to spend a morning; in the bush, untangling children's fishing tackle, and hearing a multitude of birds I couldn't identify. Gary was a good fisherman, much better than his friends who spent more time casting their lines high up into trees than into the water. I was surprised no one caught any birds. Fried fresh fish fillets were supposed to take up centre stage on the menu, but I had brought bacon and eggs along for just in case. Just as well because not a lot of fish were caught, not surprising given the amount of time the fishing tackle spent in the trees.

I surprised myself by burning only a little bit of the bacon and eggs, which the kids wolfed down like um... hungry wolves I suppose. Everything was all going swimmingly well until Daniel Gould took time out to choke on his breakfast. And we weren't talking minor polite choking; we were talking major convulsions and writhing on the floor kind of choking. Daniel's father was one of my partners. I didn't know what I'd say to John at work on Monday morning if I killed his son with a bacon and egg breakfast. I grabbed Daniel and tried to perform the Heimlich manoeuvre on him but somehow that only made things worse. He started writhing like a mad man. I think he thought I was trying to finish him off by strangling him to death.

"I think he's got something stuck in his throat, Dad," Gary said calmly.

"You think?" I had gone more purple in the face than Daniel Gould as I soldiered on with the Heimlich manoeuvre. Trying to save this kid was killing me. The guy who invented this manoeuvre, Heimlich I presume, must have been strong like a Sumo wrestler.

"Why don't we just grab whatever is stuck and pull it out?" Gary asked, again calmly.

"Because this is what you're supposed to do when someone's choking," I grunted as I heaved away manfully. "I know because I've been on First Aid courses and everything. It's called the Heimlich manoeuvre, and it's what you do when people choke. You squeeze them from behind until whatever is stuck gets unstuck."

"Even bacon?"

"What do you mean bacon?"

"I think I can see a little piece of bacon sticking out of Daniel's mouth, Dad."

I stopped the Heimlich manoeuvre and dropped Daniel to the ground. Gary was right. There was a piece of bacon rasher sticking out Daniel's mouth. I grabbed it and pulled...and pulled....and pulled. The bacon rasher just kept on coming. It was like a magician pulling out a never-ending chain of handkerchiefs from his sleeve. Eventually, I yanked the last bit of rasher out of Daniel's mouth. It was about a foot and a half long.

"Jesus Daniel. Why didn't you bite it in half? Why did you try and eat all in one go?"

"Because I was hungry," Daniel said.

Even though I'd spent most of the day untangling fishing tackle from trees and bushes, I enjoyed myself hugely. I thought I was getting the hang of this being a father business. And I was keen to do more of it.

Early the next morning, as in two o'clock early in the morning, I woke Jenny up.

"What is it?" she grumped from beneath the bedclothes.

"I need to ask you something."

"No, you can't."

"Not that. I need to ask you something else."

"What time is it?"

"Two o'clock."

Jenny swore. "Can't it wait until the morning?"

"No. I need to ask you now."

"This had better be good, de Jong, real good."

"I really enjoyed my fishing trip and cooking for Gary and his friends and..."

"This is not what I want to hear at two o'clock in the morning!!"

"Wait, wait, Jenny, I'm getting there. Like I was saying I really enjoyed what I did today and..."

"And what!!!!"

"And I want to do more of it. I wanted to ask you what you thought if I sold my shares in the company. I'm sure John and Neil would buy my shares."

"And then what would we do for money?"

"I was thinking of farming. So, I could stay at home and watch the children grow up."

"Farming what? Please don't tell me you want to farm cabbages again, Eric!!!"

"I was thinking of flowers. Flower farming is really intensive. So we've got enough land. And I'm sure I could earn a living from it."

"Eric, you're talking to someone who saw your miniature cabbages!!!"

"But I'd grow the flowers properly. I'd learn. I'd get someone in to teach me, like a consultant."

"I don't know, Eric. We've got responsibilities now and school fees to pay and..."

"Maybe I can try and hang onto one of the hotels. When I sell out to John and Neil, I'll hang onto the George Hotel. I'd put a decent manager in there and just keep an eye on him, while I stay at home and farm and...."

"And let's talk about this in the morning."

"But...."

"Good night, Eric!!!"

I picked up the conversation again at the breakfast table. "So, what you think, Jenny?"

"I think I didn't get enough sleep last night."

"I mean about selling my shares in the company."

"Do it if you want to. Just make sure we get a fair deal."

"John and Neil will do right by me."

"I hope you're right. And whatever you do, make sure we can pay the bills at the end of every month."

I approached John and Neil first thing about selling my shares in the company. I figured my timing was perfect. We'd just pulled off a huge property development deal on a tract of land on the outskirts of Harare that would be called Westgate. And once the sale had gone through, we'd all be proper millionaires, not just paper ones. I was sure that John and Neil would jump at the chance to buy me out. The Dunn Gould group of companies had grown a lot in a very short space of time, and there was a lot to un-bundle. The George Hotel, Club Mazvikadei, The Hide Safari Lodge, Acacia Hotels which managed Fothergill Island and Chikwenya Safari Camp, Cassidy's Bar and Grill, Film Cater, Film Africa, Dunn Gould Communications, Dunn Gould Promotions, Gulliver's Travels and last, but not least the Red Fox Hotel. For some reason the Red Fox was the one business unit where we owned the shares in our own names and not through Dunn Gould.

Between the breakfast table and the office, I worked out a price for my shares. In my head, I'd cobbled together a plan where I would get paid a lump sum and hang onto the George Hotel. As expected, John and Neil jumped. But it was only after we did all the handshakes, John noticed that I'd left the Red Fox Hotel off the table.

"What about the Red Fox?" There was a hint of suspicion in the question.

"Shit. I forgot all about it," I said. And I genuinely had.

John rolled his eyes a bit. "Well how much for your shares in the hotel?" he asked, bracing himself for the worst.

"Tell you what. I'll swop my shares in the Red Fox for your new laptop." John had just returned from a business trip to Europe with the first laptop computer that I'd ever seen.

"You're nuts," he said.

"Take it or leave it."

John bit my hand off, and I walked out of his office, the proud owner of a brand-new laptop computer, complete with shiny black shoulder bag. I didn't even know how to switch the thing on.

To celebrate my imminent unemployment, we planned a trip to Mana Pools. On the banks of the Zambezi River, Mana Pools was still as wild as when God first made it. Two thousand square kilometres of raw African bush, hot, dry and impossibly rugged, it was easily our favourite place on Earth. What made Mana special were the animals, the Zambezi River and the fact that it was the only National Park where you could get out of your car and walk, wherever and whenever you wanted. Every season more than a few stupid tourists managed to get themselves eaten, gored, stood on or squashed by the Big Five. Make that the Big Seven because the crocodiles and hippos were also good for a few dead tourists between them. Mana Pools was wild. And more than a bit dangerous, which made it that bit more special.

Mana Pools was a six-hour drive north of Harare. The first three hours were on good tar through the small towns of Banket and Chinoyi and some of the finest farmlands in the country. Massive rolling fields of maize standing tall in deep, red, rich soils stretching away as far as the eye could see. The landscape dried out and became more rugged as you neared the small town of Karoi with its busy bazaars and its even busier petrol station, fuel stocks permitting. And then onto civilisation's last outpost; the Cloud's End Motel at Makuti, perched on the edge of the Zambezi escarpment and presided over by Duff Gifford; sometimes white hunter, mine host and purveyor of cold beer to the hot and the thirsty.

Twenty kilometres past the Cloud's End, down the winding escarpment road, was Marongora, the gateway to Zambezi Valley National Parks. Once you signed in at Marongora, it was another three hours or seventy kilometres of bone-jarring, suspension wrecking dirt road to the river. I was all in favour of the buggered road if it kept tourists in their little Volkswagens and Fiats at bay. The fewer people we had to share Mana Pools with, the better. The road got marginally better as it wound its way into the Park proper through the impossibly thick Jesse bush, the deep Mopane forests and finally out onto the lush and fertile flood plains of the mighty Zambezi River.

For the purposes of the trip, our faithful one man and a woman tent, which had served Jenny and I so well for so long, was promoted to a one-man, one woman and two children tent. We'd decided that Veronica and Daniel would share tents with us. Mana was very much on the wild side, and we were going to keep the younger children on tight leashes. We'd told Gary that he could bring a friend camping with him. He chose Shiraz Khan who arrived with his sleeping bag, his fishing rod and another Guinea Pig as a gift for Gary. I'd only met Shiraz twice, and both times he'd brought Gary a Guinea Pig s a present. I was going off Shiraz in a big way.

"Don't worry, Mr de Jong" Shiraz said when he saw my expression "This one is also a male Guinea Pig."

"What is it with this Guinea Pig thing, Shiraz? Is it like part of your culture?"

"No, Mr de Jong. It's just that I have a very lot of Guinea Pigs at home and my father said I must find homes for them."

"But you told me before you only had two. And that they were both males."

"I'm sorry. I made a mistake. But don't worry Mr de Jong, this one is definitely another male."

I harboured some serious doubts. "If they're not males Shiraz, then they're coming back to you and with all the babies too."

We packed up our brand-new Nissan Minibus, bought from the proceeds of the sale of my Dunn Gould shares, with all our camping gear. Bulging at the seams and with fishing rods tied to the roof, we squeezed everyone in. After last visits to the loo, we set off on our first family safari. Ten kilometres from home we had to make a hasty potty stop on the side of the road for Dan. A number two and a round of applause later, we were back on the road. Thirty kilometres further down the road, Veronica's bladder decided it needed urgent emptying, the sounds of which got Jenny's bladder to thinking about much the same thing but only after another thirty kilometres of road. Apparently, synchronised toilet stops are not allowed in families of five. Four hundred kilometres and a multitude of emergency toilet stops later, we turned off the tar road just past Marongora and on to the last seventy kilometres of dirt road that led to the park proper.

Following tradition, I turned the music off and opened my first beer. We were back in the bush, and it felt good. Subjecting my brand-new minibus to the rigours of the Mana road felt less good. The brand-new rear-view mirror was the first thing to fall off. Followed by both brand-new sun-visors. And then the knob from my brand-new gearstick. I opened my second beer in a futile attempt to block out thoughts of mayhem under the bonnet. Alas. Getting to Mana Pools without messing up your car was like making omelettes without breaking eggs.

Eventually, we got to the main Nyamepi campsite. It was early in the season, so we had a choice of campsites. We chose one with the obligatory incredible view of the Zambezi River and a stand of huge Natal Mahoganies that would offer up shade in the heat of the day, and the luxury of all luxuries, a flush toilet.

On a hot day, the Zambezi Valley could hit forty degrees, so I put up our one man, one woman and two children tent under a Natal Mahogany.

We tied Daniel to a leash, literally, and then Jenny and Veronica set up the kitchen area while I busied myself with the tent. I looked over to see where Gary and Shiraz were pitching their pup tent. I wanted them close by. Unbelievably they were pitching their tent out under the scorching sun. I broke out into a sweat, just looking.

"What are you guys thinking? Why don't you pitch your tent in the shade?" I asked Gary. It wasn't like him not to be practical.

Gary wasn't a happy camper. "Shiraz said Allah won't let him."

"Allah? What's Allah got to do with where you pitch your tent?"

"I don't know. Ask Shiraz."

"What's with camping out in the full sun, Shiraz?" I asked.

"Somewhere it is written in the Koran that you cannot camp under trees," Shiraz explained solemnly.

"You sure about that?"

"I think I'm sure."

"Well, okay, then. But it's going to get bloody hot in there round about your lunchtime nap."

"I think Allah will allow us to take lunchtime naps under the trees, but just not in tents that's all."

"Sounds like a pretty dumb rule if you ask me," Gary said, clearly unhappy with this divine intervention.

I left the religious debate when I heard Daniel shouting loudly from inside the toilet. I panicked. Either Jenny or Veronica had let him off the leash without checking the loo for snakes, scorpions, and spiders hiding from the midday heat. I grabbed the broomstick as I ran past and kicked the toilet door open. I hated snakes. And scorpions. And spiders.

Daniel was standing next to the toilet, his shorts and underpants pooled around his pudgy little ankles, with his arm stuck in the empty cylindrical toilet roll dispenser on the wall. Dan was in a big panic to get his arm out of the toilet roll holder. Mostly because he had a chocolate brown number two sticking out of his bum. His bum looked like Winston Churchill smoking a cigar.

"I'm skuck Dad, I'm skuck!!" Daniel wailed. And then the reason for Dan's predicament hopped out of the top of the toilet roll dispenser. It was a tiny white tree frog with delicate suckered toes and bulbous eyes. Dan must have seen the frog while seated on the loo. Tree frogs are irresistible to two-year-olds, so Dan had hopped off to grab it. Tree frogs are up to speed on the dangers posed by two-year-olds, so the frog had taken refuge in the toilet roll dispenser. Dan had gone into the dispenser after the frog, higher and higher until his arm got stuck.

If not for the perils of the falling cigar, now almost fully extended surely, it might have been funny. I jumped to help. Damn. The kid was proper stuck. I couldn't get his arm straight. And still the cigar marched on.

It was going to plop any second. And knowing my luck, it would splatter on impact. I moved to Plan B. It was a good one. Remove the toilet roll dispenser. Cut it open with a pair of tin snips. And prevent the splatter. Above all, prevent the splatter. But how to get at the screws that held the dispenser to the wall? Dan's arm was in the way. And all the while the seconds kept ticking and the poop kept on pooping. It was a perilous situation. If I hadn't been so eerily calm, I might have panicked. But how to get the screws off?

Then Jenny arrived, attracted by the hollering and the screaming. I ran her through Plan B and sent her to look in the toolbox for tin snips, a screwdriver and maybe a chisel or something.

"Let me have a look," she said.

"Hah!" I scoffed. "It's not as easy as it looks."

"Get me some soap."

"It's the angles. They're all wrong. And I can't get Dan to kneel and lower and..."

"Just get me some soap."

"There's no way I'll be able to get at the screws. I'll have to cut the dispenser while it's still on the wall. Have I even got a pair of tin snips? I'm sure I used to have some." While I rummaged around in my memory banks for the elusive tin snips, Jenny got soap and water and in two ticks, had Daniel's arm out of the dispenser. She plopped him back on the throne just in time for the sound of the not so little splash.

"My tin snip idea would also have worked."

The first night around the campfire under African stars was absolutely magic. There was nothing like it. With no competing light, the Milky Way jumped out at you with millions upon millions of stars, almost all of them bright enough to read by. And in deep, dark shadows around us, hyenas whooped and cried out to each other while a lion grunted in the middle distance.

"That last one was a lion," Gary said. "And the other sound was a hyena. Lots of them. And it sounds like they're getting closer."

Veronica jumped on to my lap and hugged me. "Is Gary right, Daddy? Were they really hyenas? And are they getting closer?"

"Yes, but you don't have to worry because...."

"What are hyenas, Daddy?"

"They're just like big dogs really," I said, trying to calm her down.

"But with much bigger teeth," Gary added helpfully. "I read somewhere that their teeth can bite right through a steel frying pan."

"I think that's enough hyena facts for tonight Gary!!"

"But ..."

"I said enough. Otherwise, Veronica can sleep in your tent tonight."

"But I want to sleep with you and Mommy," Veronica pleaded. "In case the hyena comes into camp."

"I won't let him hurt you," I reassured her. "They're actually very timid animals."

"What does timid mean?"

"It means they're more scared of us than we are of them. Enough talk of hyenas. Let's play pass the story instead." The kids had never played the game before. "Okay. Here's how it works. I'll start telling a story, and then I'll pass it on to someone. They have to carry it on for a bit before passing it to the next person." Even in the dark shadows of the campfire, I could see Gary rolling his eyes. "It's lots and lots of fun. Promise you. Let's give it a go. Who wants to go first?"

"I'll go first, Mr de Jong," Shiraz said.

"Good man."

"Okay here goes. Once upon a time, there lived a prince and a princess in a faraway kingdom." Sitting on Jenny's lap, Veronica wriggled her approval. Stories with princes and princesses in them were the best. "It was a peaceful kingdom where everyone was happy and prosperous. Until.... one day there came news of a great monster that lived in the nearby forest!!!" Veronica tensed up immediately. Monsters in stories were bad, real bad. "A band of brave woodcutters who'd gone into the forest to cut firewood told the prince and princess how they had been attacked by a monster with great shiny eyes and big sharp teeth!!!"

"I don't like this story, Daddy," Veronica wailed from the sanctuary of Jenny's lap.

"Don't worry, Veronica. Prince and princess stories always have happy endings. Even Shiraz knows that."

Shiraz carried on with his tale in his best prince voice. "Which brave villagers will ride with me into the forest to go and slay the fierce monster?" There was a long and pregnant pause. Even I could picture the villagers shuffling their feet at the thought of riding off to face the dangers of the dark forest. "And then all the brave men in the village put their hands up. They would all ride with the prince!!!" Shiraz added on the three exclamation marks before handing the story over to Gary.

Gary started, "And all the brave men rode north as they followed their prince into the dark forbidding forest looking for the monster. Only the princess, the women, and the children stayed behind. The prince and his fearless men hadn't been gone for more than ten minutes when a pack of huge hyenas with giant teeth and fierce eyes and slobbering jaws rushed out of the forest from the south!!!! The prince and his men had ridden off in completely the wrong direction leaving all the women and children unprotected!!!! The women and children screamed!!!!"

As did Veronica on Jenny's lap. Gary had upped the ante with four exclamation marks.

"And then the rabid monster hyenas...."

I jumped in quick, "...the hyenas were all slain by the princess who had a magic sword. And so, everyone lived happily ever after!!!"

Veronica wasn't entirely convinced. Her tears weren't far away. "What does slain mean, Daddy?"

"It means the princess cut their heads off. With a sword that was almost as sharp as the hyenas' teeth," Gary explained helpfully.

"And like I said everyone lived happily ever after. The End. Now who wants toasted marshmallows?"

Marshmallows toasted over an open fire, crisp on the outside and soft and gooey inside were the best. I did Daniel's and Veronica's for them as both tended towards charcoaled marshmallows. And then it was bedtime.

"Can I borrow your camera, Dad? And I need the flash?" Gary asked.

"What do you want the camera for?" I wasn't about to let Gary and Shiraz go off wandering around the campsite in the dark, taking happy snaps of things that would kill them.

"I want to try and get a photo of the hyenas. If they come into the camp."

Next to him, Shiraz shuddered at the thought of prowling hyenas in camp. The pup tent he was sleeping in just got a lot more flimsy.

"Hmmm," I pondered the request.

"Please, Dad. I'll be careful. I promise."

"Okay, then. But I also need you to promise me that you won't leave your tent. For anything. Hyenas might be timid, but they're also bloody dangerous."

"Cross my heart and hope to die," Gary said earnestly. It was an unfortunate choice of an idiom that caused Shiraz another shudder. "I promise we'll stay in the tent, Dad. I'll set up the camera by the flysheet. I'll use my boots as a rest for the camera, and I'll take all the photos from inside the tent. I promise!"

"Okay then but remember, no leaving the tent. For any reason!"

"Yes, Mr de Jong," Shiraz chorused earnestly. I relaxed. Shiraz was the perfect handbrake. Wild horses couldn't drag him out of the relative safety of the tent.

Mana Pools at night was a noisy, busy place. As I lay in my one man, one woman and two children tent, I revelled in the night sounds. Veronica and Daniel were both fast asleep. It was a pity as I wanted them to hear the lions grunting and the hyenas whooping mournfully, ever closer. The fiery necked nightjar cried out 'Good Lord Deliver Us, Good Lord Deliver Us' against a nonstop chorus from the Cicada beetles in the trees above. I lay with my head up pressed against the gauze window of the tent, peering into the darkness, watching and waiting. Before long an inquisitive Honey Badger bustled into camp and started rooting busily amongst the pots and pans.

"Do you see the badger, Gary?" I whispered loudly. The Honey Badger didn't even bother to look up at my voice.

"I see him, Dad."

"Why don't you try and get a photo of him."

"I'll try." Seconds later, the flash lit up the camp and the busy badger. "Got him, Dad, I got him! And I'm sure it will be a great photo."

Sure. A great photo of a Honey Badger butt sticking out of a dirty cooking pot. "Good man, son. I'm going to sleep now. And remember, do not leave the tent! Not for any reason!"

"Good night, Dad."

"Good night, Mr de Jong."

The early birds woke me up the next morning. Jenny, Veronica and Daniel were still fast asleep. I eased myself out of the tent and stretched luxuriously in the cool early morning sunlight. There was no sign of movement from the boys' tent either. I'd heard them whispering late into the night. I tugged on my shoes and went to coax the remnants of the campfire back into life. Once I'd got the flames going again, I put a kettle on to boil and then went for an early morning walk around the camp to see what animals had come visiting. I wasn't good at identifying animal spoor, but there was no mistaking the massive footsteps of the hippo that had ambled right through the middle of the campsite. It had passed within just two metres of our tent. And I hadn't heard a thing!

There was no shortage of hyena tracks, they were all around the kitchen area. Thankfully we'd locked all the foodstuffs in the back of the minibus. But the cast iron pots and pans used to cook the evening meal were missing. I could see where the hyena had dragged them off into the nearby riverbed for a long, leisurely chew. I headed down onto the sandy riverbank to retrieve our cooking utensils. In amongst the pots and pans, none of which were mortally damaged, I found the remains of what used to be Gary's boot. It had been a nice boot, bought brand-new for the trip. Now the only thing left was the rubber soles and a smidgeon of the leather uppers. I picked the dead boot up and headed back to camp. The intrepid photographer and his assistant were still fast asleep, with their heads poking out the tents, camera and lens ready to capture any passing hyena for posterity, but sans the makeshift tripod.

I poked the photographer through the side of the tent. "C'mon boys, time to rise and shine."

Mumbling and grumbling, Gary and Shiraz emerged.

"Get any good shots of the hyenas, son?"

"I heard them all over the place, but they never came into camp, Dad. I waited and waited, but they never showed up."

I tossed the dead shoe at him.

"What's this, Dad?"

"That's what's left of your boots, Gary."

"Jeez like!" Gary and Shiraz breathed in unison. And then scrambled to look at the spoor outside the front their tent. The closest hyena paw print was less than six inches from Gary's pillow.

After breakfast, the boy's pup tent came down. And went back up under the Mahogany, right next to our tent. It couldn't get any closer. Shiraz was in charge of site selection.

"What about that rule in the Koran, Shiraz, the one about not pitching tents under trees?" I asked.

"If there are a lot of wild animals around, then Allah is prepared to make exceptions, Mr de Jong."

Later that afternoon we watched a lion snack on a warthog. He was a small warthog so he couldn't be classed as supper. We had front row seats for the kill, with the lion using the minibus as cover for his final stalk. I had to shush everyone up.

"But can't we warn the poor little warthog?" Veronica wailed quietly.

"We can't interfere with nature, Vee."

"But he's only little."

"Lions also have to eat."

"But he's only little. And his mom and dad will be worried. And it's...it's just not fair."

"Nature's not fair, my girl."

I watched the kids watch the kill. Veronica peeked out through her fingers. The lion eased in for the final kill. And still, the little warthog rooted happily amongst the leaf litter, oblivious to his impending death. Veronica couldn't contain herself any longer.

"Run little pig, run!!" she screamed.

But the warthog didn't stand a chance. The first he knew about the lion; it was all over bar the eating. He managed just two hurried steps before the snarling lion was turning pig into pork in a cloud of dust. The lion picked his meal up, lazed over to a clump of shady bushes where he collapsed in a comfortable heap and proceeded to snack. We heard the bones crunching from the minibus. We sat and watched, all absolutely enthralled, Veronica and Daniel included. Nature might not be fair, but it made for good viewing.

Chapter Seven

We got back from the Mana trip relaxed, invigorated and ready for the start of the new school term. Jenny was in a mad panic to sort out the kids' uniforms. Socks, shoes and hats were missing in action, and the bits of uniforms she could find didn't fit anymore. Either the kids had shot up over the Christmas holidays or uniforms had shrunk.

And Jenny's panic got worse. She came back from a fruitless visit to the Lilfordia lost property office in a complete tizz. "They want me to go and teach one of the classes at school," she wailed.

"Who does?"

"Mr Campbell. He's short a teacher for the first term and wants me as a relief teacher. Someone told him that I went to Teachers Training College."

"Well, you did. You've had the training. So, I don't see what the problem is."

"The problem is I haven't taught in years. And worse still, they want me to teach Veronica's class, the Grade Twos. I've never taught children that small before."

"Don't worry about it. You'll do fine. Teaching's like falling off a bicycle. You never forget how. And the only difference between a Grade Two kid and a Grade Three kid is a couple of inches. And besides, nothing you teach them is going to sink in anyway."

"Thanks, Eric. As always, you've been a great help."

"Don't mention it."

"And what are you going to be doing while I'm out there slaving away, bringing home the bacon?"

"I've got the George Hotel to look after."

"You've just hired a manager."

"Well someone's got to manage the manager."

"So that's you busy...for three mornings a week," Jenny snorted derisively. "What else are you going to do?" She sounded very much like a hard worker talking to a couch potato.

"I told you I wanted to farm."

"Does the market need more miniature cabbages?" She just loved throwing stunted vegetables in my face.

"No. Like I said I want to grow flowers. For export. I want to do it properly, with greenhouses and everything."

"Hmmmpphh!!!" Another derisive snort. "But you just have to look at something in the garden and the poor plant dies!!! You're like a walking herbicide."

"I'll learn. I'll read books. And I'll hire a consultant to teach me."

"Hmmmpphh!!! Sounds expensive."

"Thanks. The faith you have in me means a lot."

The export flower business was just getting started in Zimbabwe in 1992. I found a consultant called Lawrence. I told him I wanted to grow roses for export. Not just any roses. I wanted to grow the best damn roses in Zimbabwe. And damn the expense I told him. And then I saw the expenses involved. They were beyond massive, verging on stupid. Once you'd built your steel greenhouse, filling it with rose bushes would cost you an arm and a leg. And the pain didn't stop there. My remaining arm and a leg would have to be sold off to pay royalties, build cold rooms and grading sheds and houses for staff to live in and...and...and. I was horrified. My start-up budget had been reduced to a bleeding torso without limbs.

"Is there nothing else I can grow?" I asked Lawrence miserably. "Something that doesn't cost as much as roses."

"Well, you could always grow summer flowers. You still need to build greenhouses and cold rooms and stuff, but you'll save a bundle on the plant material."

"That's it!! I want to be a summer flower grower. I want to grow the best damn summer flowers in Zimbabwe."

"Which type do you want to grow?"

"There's more than one?"

"There're lots of different varieties of summer flowers. Asters, Solidago, Bupleurum, there are loads of them."

"I want to grow the first one you said."

"Asters?"

"That's them, that's what I want to grow. Asters. I want to be an Aster grower."

I was thrilled and couldn't wait to get started. There was a lot to do. I had to site the greenhouses, and the cold room and grading shed. I was going to need twenty-five members of staff. I had to buy all sorts of equipment. I went through the list, bewildered. Tensiometers and thermometers, grading tables and pre-coolers, the list went on and on. And I didn't have a clue what the items on the list looked like, let alone what they did. And I'd have to buy khaki shirts and shorts and a big khaki sun hat so that I'd look the part. I was getting really excited. Lawrence promised to send me a To-Do list. He would turn me into a flower grower in double quick time, he said. As he walked away, I asked, "By the way, what do these Aster things look like?"

Jenny was thrilled with my news when she got back from her first day at school. "That's very nice dear, an Aster grower. I'm sure you'll be very good at it."

"I hope so."

"What do Asters look like?"

"From what I can make out they sort of look like little daisies."

"Sort of look like little daisies? Very professional."

"Well I haven't seen a picture yet. Or a real live one. But that's how Lawrence described them. Sort of like little daisies, he said."

"You don't feel you're rushing into this a bit?"

"Hell no!!! The early bird catches the worm and all of that."

"Not fools rushing in where angels fear to tread?"

"This flower game is just taking off in Zimbabwe, and I'm getting in on the ground floor. My timing couldn't be better."

"Well I certainly hope so." Jenny did well to hide her sigh of resignation. "You haven't even asked me how my first day at school went."

"How was your first day at school?"

"Crap. Really, really crap."

"It couldn't have been all that bad."

"Well, it was. It was as though I'd never ever taught in the classroom before. I've forgotten everything I learnt at college."

"It will all come back. Bad memories always do. What were the kids like?"

"The little girls are sweet. But the boys!!"

"Bad?"

"Worse than bad. Little bloody horrors. You wouldn't believe what they get up to."

"I'm sure that you'll get them sorted out sooner than later. And what does Veronica think of her new teacher?"

"I think she likes her. She'd bloody better."

"I'm sure she will."

"What did Daniel do all day?"

"I took the maid along to look after him. Not that she did much of that. He ran in and out of the classroom all morning."

"Won't Mr Campbell get irked?"

"I don't think Mr Campbell does irked. And one of the other teachers has got a toddler about the same age as Daniel. And he made more noise than Daniel."

"Enough school talk. Come and see where I'm going to put up my greenhouses. I'm going to put up two of them, half a hectare each and..."

"I can't Eric. I've got lessons to prepare for tomorrow. If I don't get organised, tomorrow will be worse than today."

I was very excited about my greenhouses and needed to share them with someone.

"Why don't you show Gary?" Jenny suggested. "And then you can show me on the weekend."

"Okay. I'll do that." Gary was in his bedroom, busy with his homework.

"Come, Gary, I want to show you where I'm going to put my greenhouses."

"Okay, Dad," he said with enthusiasm. Prospective greenhouse viewing stacked up well against homework. "What are the greenhouses going to be for?" he asked as we walked out the house.

"We're going to grow flowers in them."

"Flowers?"

"Cut-flowers. For export. Mostly to Holland."

"Oh. That sounds ...um...nice," said Gary excitedly.

My first hurdle was finding a standout name for my flower farm. Research indicated that every other flower farm in the world had gone with the use of the word Flora, so that was a no go for me. Ditto, Jenny's tabled suggestion of Gorgeous Flowers. Hell's bells woman, I told her, I'm a farmer, not a florist. I struggled for days to find a name for the farm. And then at three o'clock in the morning, an old Bob Hamill joke popped out of the dark recesses of my memory banks. The joke had an epic punchline involving a Red Indian and two dogs copulating. I'd found the name for my farm. But Jenny flat out refused to let me call it Two Dogs Copulating Flowers. By morning I'd diluted the name down to Running Dog Flowers, which Jenny accepted reluctantly. I went into my accountants the next morning as pleased as punch to register the company name. My accountant wasn't at all happy with my name choice. It lacked gravitas, he said, and no one would take me seriously, which suited me just fine. I firmly believe the world is full of people who take themselves far too seriously. And so, Running Dog Flowers was duly incorporated.

The next day I set to work siting my greenhouses. Bob Hamill said he would fabricate the steel structures at his factory for me. All I would have to do is bolt them together. "It'll be easy. Just like a big Meccano set," Bob said.

"Excellent," I said with a complete lack of confidence. My childhood Meccano set had been retired, largely unused. Putting three-pin plugs on to kettles was the limit of my mechanical abilities. But that was before I'd become a farmer complete with khaki shirts and khaki everything.

My greenhouses would be huge when up, each one sixty-six metres wide and seventy-five metres long. To get ready for the fabrication bit, I had to concrete anchor posts into the ground every six metres. And I had a tolerance of just fifty millimetres per anchor post, Bob told me. Otherwise, it would all be a bugger-up.

No problem I said, with not a lot of confidence. I was well out of my comfort zone.

I decided to start with the four corner posts. Once they were in, the rest would be a doddle. I bought a hundred-metre tape measure, a four-pound hammer and pegs. I was very proud of them. They were my first tools. I decided there and then that I'd buy a whole workshop of tools. I sank the first peg and sent Raphael forth with the tape measure. I knocked in the second post, sixty-six metres from the first peg. Then I sent Raphael at right angles and hammered in the third peg at the seventy-five-metre mark. I was going to have this baby in the bag before lunch. Again Raphael strode forth with the tape measure, and I banged in the last corner peg on the seventy-metre mark and stood back to admire my handiwork. Alas. It looked horribly skewed, like a parallelogram after a night out.

"It is a fuck-up, Boss." Raphael pointed out helpfully. He was born with a sailor's vocabulary. I went back to the first peg and started again. Obviously, Raphael had cocked up with the tape measure. "But Boss shouldn't we..."

"Shut up, Raphael, I know what I'm doing."

I took extra care the second time around. The second peg was exactly sixty-six metres from the first. The second and third pegs went in bang on their marks. I sank the last corner peg with the satisfaction of a job well done and turned to survey my handiwork. The bloody thing was still skwonk.

"But Boss..."

"Shut up, Raphael. I'm thinking." And then it struck me. I had to work out the diagonals first. Once I had the diagonals, I'd be able to site the corner pegs with precision.

"But Boss...."

"Shut up, Raphael, I'm still thinking." I would draw a scale version of the greenhouse on paper, which would allow me to work out the diagonals exactly. I found the biggest blank piece of paper. Alas. It wasn't a very big piece of paper so the scale was a bit smaller than I would have liked. But by using a very sharp pencil and a dose of unerring accuracy, I worked out that the diagonal was supposed to be ninety-five metres long. It was all so simple. Why hadn't I thought of it before? Using my one hundred metre tape, I measured the diagonals and in two ticks, hammered in the corner posts. Impossibly my bloody greenhouse was still skewed.

"But Boss, don't you..."

"Jesus, Raphael, can't you see I'm busy. What I need is a bigger piece of paper. This stupid little scale is no bloody use." I stapled four pieces of paper together and reduced the scale to sixty to one. My diagonal now measured ninety-seven metres instead of ninety-five metres. No wonder my poor long-suffering pegs were cockeye. But it was nothing I couldn't fix in two ticks with the right length diagonal. Several lusty hammer blows later and... My bloody corner pegs were still playing at being part of a bloody parallelogram again. I was going off flower farming in a big way. I glared at the tape measure. Made in bloody China. Well no wonder, I couldn't get the greenhouse squared up.

"But Boss ..."

I rounded on Raphael with the sledgehammer, but he stood his ground. "Pythagoras and I were thinking that you should try a three four five triangle," he said.

"Who the bloody hell is Pythagoras?" But even as I asked, there was the vaguest of murmurings in the darkest corners of my head.

"He was a very clever Greek Boss who lived a long time ago, Boss. And he worked out the three four five triangles and said that three times three plus four times four equals twenty-five and ..."

"What the hell are you mumbling about, Raphael?"

He dumbed it down for me. "The square root of twenty-five is five, which is the length of the third side of your triangle."

"It is?"

"Yes, Boss."

"But it isn't. Look here on my graph. It's clearly supposed to be ninety-seven. Or ninety-five."

With a smirk, Raphael banged the sums out on my calculator and scribbled the new diagonal down. Ninety-nine point nine metres.

"And you're sure about this, Raphael?"

"Yes, Boss." The smirk blossomed.

"Then why the bloody hell didn't you tell me about Pythagoras sooner, Raphael?"

"I tried to, Boss but...."

"No, you didn't. You stood there mumbling while I rushed around hammering pegs like a bloody idiot. Thanks to you we've wasted a whole bloody day. Next time, speak up loud, man!!!"

"Yes, Boss."

I went into the house that evening with both greenhouses pegged square and feeling very proud of my achievements. To celebrate the feel good, I took Jenny and the kids out for an early dinner and a round of miniature golf. I hadn't been near the Putt-Putt course in years. Getting to do neat kid stuff was yet another perk of being a parent. I played against Gary, Jenny with Veronica while Daniel tagged along behind, happily doing his own thing with his tiny sawn-off golf club and ball.

I started out with the noble intentions of putting my fiercely competitive streak back in the box and letting Gary beat me. That was the plan anyway, up until I found out that Gary was better at mini golf than I was. Then it was game on. Jenny and Veronica putt-putted along slowly and happily, not paying any attention to scores while Gary and I surged ahead, locked in mortal golfing combat; which was rather stupid of me really, because there are Cocker Spaniels out there with better hand-eye co-ords. I vaguely remembered being sort of good at mini golf as a child, but that had all evaporated, and I was really crap now, and Gary was thrashing me properly on every hole. I was getting flustered.

And Daniel wasn't helping my cause either. I was lining up my shot on the nasty fourteenth hole, which had a water hazard the size of the Pacific when Daniel tugged at my shirt.

"What do you want?" I snapped.

"Need the toilet, Daddy," he said.

"Just do it in the bushes," I said without taking my eyes off the treacherous fourteenth. Gary had already found the water hazard. If I could get just down in three, I'd start clawing my way back into the game. I went back to lining up my shot when I was disturbed again, this time by a gaggle of Hindus on the twelfth hole. In broad accents and in unison, the lot of them went off. "Oh, my golly gosh! Look at the little boy and what he is doing! It is very disgusting!"

"He cannot be doing that in a public place! That is very revolting!"

"You there!! That man!! That father!! You should be stopping your child! You should not be letting him do that!"

Super irritated, I looked up, just in time to see Daniel having a crap on a rose bush next to the green on the twelfth. I looked around frantically for help in dealing with the code red. But there was no one. Jenny and Veronica were poncing about way back on the tenth and Gary had plunged on to fifteen. I was on my own. It was all up to me. So, I froze. It's what I do. In pressure situations, I freeze.

Dan's imminent pooh was huge. I'd never got my head around the physics of Dan's bowel movements. The kid was the size of your average toddler, but the craps that came out of him were bigger than teenager big. And the one he was doing on the twelfth, was larger than most. It was taking him forever to get it out. And all the while, the Hindu clan and I watched on, horrified. I was utterly frozen in the moment. I wanted to sneak off and pretend I was part of another family playing on the back nine, but I couldn't move a muscle. I was stuck. And all the while, the Hindu tribe's angry invective washed over me. By now they'd ramped up big on the use of exclamation marks. "Your son there is being a health hazard!!! He is being very disgusting!!! And you should be putting a stop to him doing this in this very public place!!!"

I know I should have scooped him up on my arms and rushed him to the toilet, but I just couldn't. My legs and the rest of me kept urging me to find another more palatable family to join.

Eventually, and we're talking many long moments, Dan's pooh plopped out onto the bottom of the rose bush; where it lurked malignantly, for all to see. It utterly dominated the landscape. It wasn't a case of 'Oh look, there's a rose bush with a piece of pooh underneath it.' This more like 'Hey check out the big crap with a rose bush growing out the top of it.'

Predictably Jenny rushed across once the worst of the drama was over. "Why didn't you take him to the toilet?" she hissed angrily.

"Well, I thought he just needed a wee, so I told him to do it on the bush and..."

"You told him to!!!"

"Yes. Sort of. But...but I was busy lining up an important shot and..."

Jenny shot me a filthy look and dragged Daniel off to wipe and wash his bum.

This left me alone with the Hindus. And the turd.

If I'd had a shovel, a very long-handled shovel, I might have been man enough to remove the evidence from the scene. But alas, there weren't any shovels to hand. So, I used my trusty putter to try and scrape some soil over the top of the offending turd. It was like trying to scrape topsoil over the top of Mount Kilimanjaro. The Hindus looked on with horror and hands on mouths.

"Don't worry. It's actually very good fertiliser. This rose bush will flourish," I told them as I washed my putter in the water hazard before striding off to deal with the rigours of the fifteenth. I decided to concede the fourteenth to Gary.

Chapter Eight

Slowly my steel greenhouses emerged from the ground. They looked like the Twin Towers in New York but maybe not quite as tall. Bob Hamill said he'd done most of the hard work, bending and fabricating the greenhouses at his factory in town, ready to move to the farm in sections. Piffle is what I said. The really hard part was getting the bastard things lined up and concreted in the ground. That involved a humungous amount of swearing, cursing, and cajoling with liberal doses of hammering, digging, drilling and screwing. Raphael looked after the drilling, screwing and erecting while I attended to the swearing and cursing, especially on the numerous occasions when I hit my thumb with the four-pound hammer. Daniel always seemed to be around whenever I did myself damage and found it amusing. The ability to amuse one's children I took to be a positive parental trait. The ability not to swear in front of your children after reducing your thumb to paste with a four-pound hammer, I took to be a myth.

It was early March. It was a race against time. To get a full growing season in on my first season, I had to start planting my flowers in May. And the structure had to be up and covered with plastic. I pushed my gang of forty temporary, unskilled labourers really hard. I would select my permanent workers from their ranks. Amazingly, some thirty years on, some of those original workers still work on the farm.

One of the biggest jobs was digging the holes for the anchor posts, a half-metre square and a meter deep. With five hundred and twenty-eight anchor posts that equalled lots of digging. I took on two full-time hole-diggers, one to loosen the ground with a pickaxe and one to follow behind with a shovel, removing the soil. I told the chosen two that my absolute pet hate was one man watching while the other worked. We didn't have time for that. We were chasing deadlines. The man with the pickaxe had to stay ahead of the man with the shovel. And the job of the man with the shovel was to catch the man with the pickaxe. They both nodded their heads knowingly and set to work like Duracell bunnies. With anchor hole digging under control, I went off to look for someone else to swear at and cajole.

Not five minutes later I looked back at my hole-diggers, and they were back to one man digging, one man watching. I flew off the handle. I went over the simple instructions again. Pickaxe guy stays ahead of the shovel guy while the shovel guy tries to catch the pickaxe guy. Simple stuff. More head nodding. I was speaking in English, mainly because my Shona didn't extend much beyond asking how the other person had slept the night before, but they seemed to understand what I wanted just fine. For all of three minutes.

I looked back from where the concreting gang were pouring concrete, and the digging team were back to one man working, one man watching. I grabbed Raphael to handle translations and stormed over in a real lather, profanities flying thick in the air. I was going to give them practical instructions. I grabbed the pickaxe and Raphael grabbed the shovel. But as I lifted the pickaxe high above my shoulder, the shovel guy standing in front of me wailed, spun around and disappeared into the middle distance. Now between him and the middle distance was Charles Prince Airport complete with an eight-foot chain mesh fence. The fence didn't slow the fleeing hole-digger one iota. He was up and over the fence, quick like a prune through a child. He then disappeared down the middle of a very busy runway One Four, ignoring Beechcrafts and Cessnas with equal aplomb. I stood with mouth hanging open and watched him get smaller and smaller. I was horrified. I'd become a tyrant. Next to me, Raphael rolled on the floor with laughter. Thirty years later, I still owe the hole-digger half a month's wages.

Owning a tractor was an integral part of being a farmer. A farmer without a tractor was like a ramp model without a long pair of legs. But and it was a big but, a tractor wouldn't fit inside my greenhouses. I was in trouble. I would always be the farmer who didn't have a tractor. And then I saw an advert for a bright red, two-wheel, hand-held tractor, apparently used by millions of satisfied farmers in China who used them to till whatever crops Chinese farmers grew. The red two-wheeler was a step down from the green John Deere in my dreams, but it was a tractor. No one could deny that. And it would fit inside the greenhouses no problem. And it came with a whole array of implements that all looked jolly useful, once I'd figured out what they were used for. And it was bright red. So, I bought it.

Because the two-wheeler was brand-new out the box, I decided that I would be the only person on the farm who would use it. But this turned out to be a stupid idea. Ten minutes behind the tractor explained why your average Chinese peasant farmer always looked old beyond his years. The thing roared along like a bloody racehorse. After ten minutes of being dragged along behind the thing, I was knackered. I eyed the airport fence and the middle distance beyond wistfully. But I couldn't run away. Not only was I too knackered to be clambering over fences, but I also had an audience of workers watching on, marvelling at the wonders of eastern technology. My beads of sweat were football sized. I was seriously thinking about having a heart attack when Gary walked over.

"Let me take over, Dad."

"I don't know, son, it's not as easy as it looks."

"It doesn't look easy, Dad. You're sweating like a pig. In fact, you're sweating like two pigs."

"And you think you can do better?"

"I can do it for long enough to give you a rest."

My heart was beating in fluent Mandarin, an alarmingly quick language. "Okay, Gary. But just for a bit, just until I get my breath back."

Gary could barely look over the handles of the two-wheeler. He engaged gear and proceeded to be dragged along at a gallop. I would be amazed if the kid lasted more than a minute. But that would give me time to get my breath back. But Gary stopped after just ten metres. My heart went out to the poor kid. Shame, at least he'd done his best to help. But then as I watched, Gary bent over, fiddled with the multiple knobs that I'd been too scared to touch and fired up the tractor again, but this time at a decent walking speed.

"I found the speed controls, Dad. It's this lever with the picture of the rabbit and the tortoise on it. It's a lot easier now," he shouted with a huge smile on his face. I was too tired to kick myself.

Dan was a hazard while the building operations were going on. He was continually underfoot, attracted by the noise and the hustle and bustle. He especially loved hammers. They were his best. Veronica kept well away from the building site. Loud noises scared her properly.

Our first batch of Aster Monte Casino tissue culture cuttings arrived all the way from Israel. They were tiny, smaller than the nail on my baby finger and nothing to look at. But in my eyes, they were things of beauty and represented the promise of things to come. Raphael and I fussed over them like newly born babies. These were our mother-stock plants. We would harvest the other cuttings needed to plant out in the greenhouses from them. As we worked, Raphael pointed out a small snag he had encountered. He pointed out that we were now fully-fledged Aster growers. But neither of us had seen an actual Aster flower. Not even a picture. Was that not like a cattle rancher not knowing what a cow looked like, Raphael asked? I had to agree with him. Thankfully I had a consultant for moments just like this. I phoned Lawrence and explained my predicament. He knew another Aster grower called Noel Kent who farmed not too far away. I phoned Noel and explained my problem. I'd started planting Asters but wanted to see what they were supposed to look like when fully grown. Noel clearly thought I was mad but invited me for a walk around his farm.

To tell the truth, I was a bit disappointed with the Asters at first sight. They looked like miniature white Daisies. I was expecting something more spectacular. If I was disappointed, Raphael was positively disgusted.

"Will people buy these very stupid little flowers, Boss?" he demanded.

"I hope so, Raphael."

"But what for?"

"What do you mean what for?"

"What will they use them for, Boss? We won't get any oil out of these stupid little things."

"No, no Raphael. The flowers are just to look at."

"We're growing flowers to just look at them???" Raphael punctuated the question with multiple question marks. "So, you don't get oil from them to cook with, like sunflowers???"

I put my foot down. "We're not growing sunflowers. We're growing Asters. To look at."

"And you're sure these customers are going to pay us money, for these stupid little things?"

"I really hope so, Raphael."

Noel gave me a bunch of Asters to take home. I gave them to Jenny. Veronica rushed across to admire them. She took one look at them and rolled her eyes. Clearly, Raphael wasn't the only one who thought I was spending too much time in the midday sun with the other mad dogs and Englishmen.

Gary did a lot of the greenhouse land preparation with the two-wheel tractor. Even with the tractor set at tortoise speed, it was hard, physically exhausting work. Gary worked under Raphael's strict supervision, with emphasis on strict. Nothing escaped Raphael's eagle eyes.

"Come and do this part again, Gary. I told you I want the soil to be fine, without big fucking clods. But you have left big fucking mud clogs here. You must break them up before you knock off."

"But Raphael I'm tired. Can't I do it tomorrow?"

"No, Gary, you must finish your work today. And you have to be the hardest worker on the fucking farm because you are the Boss' son!!!"

His vocabulary might have been less than choice, but Raphael's work ethic was second to none. If only a bit of that rubbed off on Gary, it would be a good thing, something that would stand him in good stead for the rest of his life. I decided that when they were old enough, both Veronica and Daniel would also work a stint under Raphael.

I was properly scared of my tiny little Aster seedlings. I'd never grown anything in my life, other than miniature cabbages, but now I'd put myself out there as a professional flower farmer. With the world watching, there was nowhere to hide. And I'd spent a fortune building greenhouses, cold rooms and grading sheds. And then there were the million fluorescent light fittings needed to make the Asters grow. And everything hinged on these tiny little plants. I bought a textbook on how to grow greenhouse flowers, and it became my Bible. My textbook said I had to plant outside the heat of the day. So, I turned my greenhouse lights on at four in the morning, kicked my planting gang out of bed, and we started planting. I fussed over each and every seedling that went into the ground. And the fussing didn't stop there. I spent hours every day in the first week, watching them grow. My Asters were easily the most-watched plants on earth. And watching them grow was easily the most therapeutic thing I'd ever done, like watching fish in a fish tank, but way better.

Predictably my planning had gone awry. My seedlings arrived and were in the ground before I'd finished the greenhouses. The massive steel frames were up and straight, but I still had to get the plastic on top. And the sooner I got the plastic over the top of the seedlings, the better the climate inside the greenhouses. Each greenhouse measured an acre. And I was supposed to stretch plastic taut over the top of the houses, as taut as a drum-skin my textbook told me. The book was very skimpy as to how I should go about stretching the plastic over. I was super stressed because of my not so latent tendency to bugger up big jobs. Naturally, my young family elected to come and watch the fun.

I trudged out to the greenhouses at the appointed hour, with zero bounce in my step. Standing under the superstructure, looking up at the steel girders that towered above, the job looked even more daunting than it had in my head as I'd tossed and turned all night, stressing. There were twenty-four sheets of roof plastic per each greenhouse. And each sheet was sixty-six metres long, five metres wide and flapped around like a bugger in the slightest of winds. Predictably it was very windy. In fact, the word gale kept blowing into my mind. Gary kindly pointed out that it was certainly windy enough to fly his kite. Jenny, Veronica and Daniel were seated in the peanut gallery, all excited like they were about to watch a Houston space launch. I was all in favour of aborting take off but couldn't. Alas.

I walked up to Greenhouse One very slowly, with my brand-new, never used before electric drill. It was a Bosch and had a picture of a happy handyman on the box. The Bosch handyman was only happy because he didn't have to climb up into the stratosphere and drill bloody holes. Working up high where the air was rare was not a job for the fainthearted. This, unfortunately, described me to the letter. I was the epitome of faint hearts. But with Daniel and Veronica watching me, and I felt their eyes on me the whole time, there was no way I couldn't not climb up the bloody ladder. Veronica watched through her fingers, with bated breath. Daniel looked up at me like I wore my underpants on the outside and could fly faster than speeding bullets.

I went up the ladder grimly, my brand-new electric drill in hand. I didn't have a head for heights. And the rest of my body did heights even worse, especially my tummy and my bottom. When I got to the top of the ladder, I clutched on to the superstructure of the greenhouse with all my strength and stared down at terra firma seven metres below. The wind had an eerie quality as it whistled through my ears. Even the ants below looked tiny. I looked across at Jenny and kids. They looked as terrified as I felt. Apart from Daniel, who looked up with eyes huge, ready for excitement. Reluctantly I un-clutched the superstructure with my right hand, sighted the drill and pulled the trigger, just like the man on the Bosch box. I applied as much force as I could. It all went swimmingly well. Up until the part where the drill bit got stuck in the steel. I was sent whirling off even further into space like a roman candle. Through the rarefied air, I could hear Dan's excited laughter. Eventually, physics kicked in, and I thudded down to earth, seven metres below. Luckily the ground below broke my fall. My breath exploded out of me like a volcano as I landed in the flowerbeds. Daniel found it all very amusing and laughed and laughed. I was better than cartoons on television.

Raphael rushed across; concern etched all over his face. He checked the electric drill. "It looks okay, Boss. You haven't fucked the drill up. But you have fucked the plants up. Look at them. They're all squashed." Raphael scolded me with language as earthy as the mud I lay in.

I groaned. "Shhh, Raphael!!! Don't swear in front of the children, Raphael."

"Okay but let me do the drilling because you fuck things up."

I seized upon Raphael's observation with both hands. From there on Raphael was in charge of hole drilling. I'd done my bit, I told Jenny and the kids. I'd shown the workers the dangers involved in aerial drilling.

It took twenty men to pull the long pieces of plastic tight. Raphael scampered up and down the length of the superstructure, drilling holes and fixing the plastic in place beneath the wooden batons. And all the while, he bellowed out endless instructions. Where Raphael had fixed the batons down tight, the greenhouse plastic rippled in the stiff breeze, drum-skin taut, just like in the textbook. But then as I watched, the breeze upgraded to a gale and the sheet of plastic soared up in the air, like the mainsail on an ocean-going yacht.

Thankfully the men holding the plastic down had enough nous to let go of the plastic sheet, apart from two daft buggers at the end, who clung manfully to their jobs. Already seven metres above the ground, they soared even higher, like the frilly bits on a kite's tail. I closed my eyes. I didn't want to watch. Consequently, I had no idea how high they were before they eventually let go. But they must have been up very high because it took them forever to come back to earth.

Raphael rushed across to his errant cosmonauts who lay on top of the squashed, newly planted cuttings. "You are also fucking stupids!! You have also fucked up the plants!! Just like the Boss!!"

Once they were in the ground, the Asters grew quickly. Before I knew it, my plants were all grown up, looking just like the pictures in my textbook. Remarkably I hadn't killed them off. Or stunted them. Maybe I did have greenish fingers after all.

My first harvest was chaotic with not enough buckets and a plus thirty-degree heatwave. Again, Gary was drafted in, this time as a trolley pusher.

He helped non-stop, moving buckets of cut flowers from the heat of the greenhouses to the cool of the grading shed, all day long. It was back-breaking, energy-sapping work and I'm sure Gary was starting to think he was indentured labour.

In the box, packed and ready for their long-haul flight to the flower markets in Holland, the flowers looked top quality. They looked professional. Determined to soak in as much first-hand experience as possible, I decided that I'd fly to Holland with my first shipment of flowers so that I could see what happened to them on the other side. Noel Kent said he would be happy to farm-sit for me for a week. I managed to cadge free seats for Gary and I on the freight plane that the flowers would fly out on. Gary would miss a few days of school, but it would be a great experience for him. And Jenny would follow us with Veronica and Daniel on a commercial flight. While I was busying learning how flowers were sold on the auctions in Holland, Jenny would introduce our children to their multitude of new Dutch relatives. It was the middle of winter in Europe, so we had bought new winter woollies all round. Gary packed and unpacked his clothing a dozen times. He was trying to be very cool about the trip but wasn't pulling it off. He'd never flown on an aeroplane before.

Jenny dropped Gary, me and my shipment of flowers off at the airport. The plane, an old DC8, was being loaded on the apron already, with boxes of flowers. I introduced myself to the loadmaster and told him we would be flying with the flowers. He asked did I want my luggage loaded in the hold. I told him sure, and our overnight bags disappeared into the bowels of the plane. Gary and I waved at Jenny as she drove away. We'd see her in Holland the next day.

Gary had big eyes as we explored the DC8 freighter we would be flying on. There was a brass tag on the fuselage, which outlined the plane's history. Built in 1958, the plane was a year older than me. She had seen active service in the Vietnam War and was the oldest DC8 in the world still in regular service the flight engineer told us proudly, which inspired me with not a lot of confidence. To me, the plane looked rickety, especially the wings. The flight engineer explained that Gary and I would travel in the back of the plane with the flowers, with a twelve-inch wide fold-down bench for seating. And our in-flight entertainment would be limited to watching the boxes of flowers in front of us. And with a scheduled refuelling stop in Nairobi, it would be a very long flight. And to keep the flowers fresh, we would be flying at two degrees Celsius the whole way. Luckily, I'd been warned of the rigours of flying with the cargo and our bags were full of warm clothes, sleeping bags, food to eat and drink and books to read. I was already hungry and could almost smell the meat pie I was going to eat for dinner.

Our big adventure got off to a slow start as we watched the eighty tonnes of flowers being loaded. With my camera at the ready, I waited to take photos of my flowers being loaded, but I lost them in amongst the multitude of other big, brown flower boxes.

Our pilot and first officer arrived and busied themselves for take-off. The plane had a staggering array of dials to be read and knobs that had to be switched on. The last bit of essential flying equipment loaded was a collapsible aluminium ladder, which the first officer slid in between the flower boxes and the fuselage. Once all the checklists had been checked, it was time for take-off. Gary and I settled down on our twelve-inch bench seat and buckled ourselves in. I measured the distance between the end of my nose and the flower boxes directly in front of me. Less than twelve inches. Yellow roses peeked out of the breathing holes in the flower box directly in front of me. In the half-light, they looked insipid and washed out, with nothing bright or sunny about them. Gary was luckier. The box in front of him had beautiful deep dark red roses peeping out to keep him company.

It took forever to coax the old engines into life and even longer to coax the old DC8 into the air. But eventually, we were up and on our way. Unfortunately, there weren't any windows to stare out of so Gary and I stared at the flower boxes instead. Gary's eyes were closed and his knuckles white as we took off.

After ten minutes in the air, the loadmaster popped his head out the cabin door and told us he was turning on the cold air. Quickly the temperature in the back of the plane dropped down to the prescribed two degrees. Gary put on his new and warm looking jersey. After a few minutes, I decided two degrees was bloody cold. I could hear my teeth chattering above the racket from the engines. It was time to don my arctic gear. I knocked on the cockpit door and opened it. The cockpit was warm like an oven. The loadmaster looked snug and comfortable in his padded seat at the back of the cockpit.

"Sorry to hassle but can I grab my bags from the hold. It's getting a bit cold in back here."

"Sure thing," he said cheerfully. "I'll grab your bag for you, just as soon as we land in Amsterdam."

"But all our warm clothes are in the bags. And our food," I explained with teeth chattering.

"You should have kept it with you as hand luggage."

"Oh," I said and went back into the fridge and sat down on my hard bench.

We were flying to Amsterdam via Nairobi. On the world globe on my bar counter at home, Amsterdam and Harare were only twelve inches apart. With modern jet travel, the world had become a very small place. Maybe. If you were sitting on comfortable reclining seats in the warm, convivial atmosphere of the modern passenger jet, watching the latest movie and snacking on canapés, Harare, Nairobi, Amsterdam would fizz along in no time at all. But the same trip on a twelve-inch hard bench in a noisy and ponderous flying fridge with wobbly old wings took beyond forever.

There was nothing slow about the cold, though. It roared in like a freight train and took occupation of my whole body. My feet were the first to succumb to frostbite. I could feel toes turning black and rotten inside my shoes. I was too scared to have a look in case one of them fell off. I remembered reading about how Captains Scott and Oates had fended off frostbite by pissing on each other's extremities. Alas. My bladder was empty. I was going to lose my toes. Maybe Gary needed a wee. I turned to him in the gloom of the hold to ask if he would save my toes when I saw he was now also wearing a warm woollen beanie on his head and a warm woollen scarf.

"Where did you get those from??" my teeth chattered the question.

"Mom knitted them for me."

"I know that. But where did you get them from now?"

'Before we took off, the man told me I'd better get them out the bag. He said it would get very cold on the plane. Boy did he get that one right!" Gary blew warm little smoke signals into the frigid air as he laughed. Alas. I couldn't join in the humour. The face muscles that worked my laugh had frozen solid.

"Do you want to borrow either my scarf or maybe my beanie? I'm quite warm."

"No thanks," I said bravely. Either an obscure parenting instinct had kicked in, or my brain was malfunctioning in the extreme conditions.

Behind the cold, the hunger marched in on big hobnailed, steel-capped boots. With the constant shivering, my muscles were working overtime and demanded feeding. And Jenny's juicy steak pies with tender chunks of steak floating in the rich meat gravy covered in flaky golden pastry were stuck in the bloody bag, which was stuck in the bloody hold, which we could only get when we got to bloody Amsterdam. I tried eating my fingers but stopped because it was sore. To ease the pain in the massive hole that was my stomach, I turned to Gary. "Hi, Gary. You hungry?"

"I'm okay, Dad."

"That's good. I'm glad that…What do you mean you're not hungry?" I spluttered.

"I ate Mom's pies. They were real good."

My stomach wailed. "You ate your pies? When? When? When did you eat them?"

"While we were waiting for the plane to be loaded. You were busy taking photos of boxes, so I ate my pies. I was going to save one to eat on the plane, but I ate them both. Couldn't help it. They tasted real good."

"Oh."

"You should try yours."

"I will, I will." As soon as I get to bloody Amsterdam. I only half-listened to Gary as he chatted on. My mind was on other things. Like my stomach.

An eternity later, the cockpit door opened, and a burst of late afternoon sun flooded the hold, closely followed by a blast of warm air. "Do you guys want to sit inside and get warm?" the loadmaster asked.

Gary was up off the bench and in the cockpit in a flash. I followed more slowly, mostly because my joints had frozen solid. It was very cramped in the cockpit. The loadmaster crawled into a sleeping compartment tucked into the bulkhead. Gary and I sat on two tiny jump seats directly behind the pilot and the first officer while the flight engineer sat to the side of us. He was busy with the multitude of dials and levers and knobs on the bulkhead in front of him. Gary's eyes were huge. He craned his neck to stare out of the window at the unbroken landscape of dark forests and jungles that stretched away beneath. We had to be somewhere over Tanzania. On a map, Tanzania was huge. In the flesh, flying over it in an elderly DC8, it was beyond massive. And empty. There were no signs of habitation that I could see, just miles and miles of thick forest. Far in the distance ahead, Kilimanjaro rose up majestically above the clouds. Gary snapped away with my camera. And then the flight engineer did the unthinkable. He fiddled inside his flight bag on the floor next to him and pulled out a meat pie.

I sensed the pie before I saw it. It was still inside the supermarket wrapper, but I knew straight away it was a big meat pie, with crisp golden brown pastry that would flake in your mouth, a pie swimming inside with rich flavoursome gravy and big chunks of tender steak cut from a cow, not roadkill. My mouth didn't just water; there was a major cloud burst inside. It was a meat pie that you would kill for!! I eyed the back of the flight engineer's unsuspecting head, looking for the killing spots. A quick wham bam with a blunt object to the back of the head, not too hard so as to cause massive trauma or bleeding, and the meat pie would be mine to eat and savour. I aborted the plan in a hurry when I noticed the flight engineer's neck. Well it was more the absence of a neck that I noticed. The man's hulking muscular shoulders went straight up into his square, muscular head without so much as a mention of a neck. I aborted violence and sat in my jump seat and salivated like one of Pavlov's dogs instead. More like two of his dogs actually.

And then we hit some major turbulence, which flung the doddery plane and contents around. I was part of the contents, and a squawk of terror escaped my lips, like a little roller coaster panic whoop. The crew didn't do any panic. They busied themselves fiddling with settings, adjusting pitches and other things technical, all with steady hands and steady eyes. It took all hands, including both of the flight engineer's. He

GROWING FLOWERS AND MISSING MEAT PIES

had to put his steak pie down on top of his flight bag next to his chair. As we hit the next wall of violent turbulence, I watched the meat pie slip off the flight bag and under his seat. As quick as a flash and before I knew what I was doing, I stole his pie. Using my foot surreptitiously, I coaxed the pie from under the seat, slipped it under my shirt and with my best 'I need a crap real bad' face in place; I bolted into the toilet and wolfed the pie down. It took just seconds. The pie was real good. I checked in the mirror for crumbs before returning to my jump seat and sat for the rest of the flight with a poker face, watching the flight engineer fiddle under his seat for his pie. He kept looking at me suspiciously, but I gave nothing away. My only regret was that his pie didn't repeat on me.

Nairobi Airport was teeming with little aeroplanes when we landed. There was a whole flock of them on the ground, with more arriving every minute. The pilots puzzled over the traffic as they jockeyed the DC8 into its designated parking spot off the runway to wait for the fuel truck.

"Never seen it busy like this before," the pilot remarked. "Something must be going on."

Gary and I were allowed to get out of the plane and stretch our legs. The Kenyan sun was bliss on my shoulders after being stuck in the flying fridge for so long. And while we stood around waiting for the fuel tanker, still the small planes kept landing. There were at least thirty lined up on the apron, all with the same 9XR registration tags. We were joined by the flight engineer who gave me another look of suspicion before pulling the extendable aluminium ladder down from the hold. He extended the ladder and placed it up against the wing of the plane.

"Where do all those little planes come from?" I asked.

"I don't know that registration code. Somewhere around here, I guess. The guys in the cockpit are asking the control tower now." He clambered up onto the wing with a screwdriver. "Say you didn't see where my meat pie got to?" he asked while looking down at me.

"No," my poker face replied. The engineer gave me another long hard look before setting to work with the screwdriver.

I only just know which end of the screwdriver is the business end, but it looked horribly like he was tightening up screws one by one, where the wing bit of aeroplane joined the fuselage bit. I put my poker face away. And my poker voice. "Um...What you doing up there? With the um... screwdriver?" I asked conversationally.

"Just checking to see if anything up here needs tightening. This old girl gets a bit rickety after bad weather."

"Oh."

"I told you she started flying back in 1958."

"Yes."

"I told you that she flew in the Vietnam War for more than ten years before ending up in our part of the world."

"Yes."

"And now we fly her to Europe three times a week with near on a hundred tonnes flowers a trip."

"And you have to check the wings with a screwdriver after bad weather?"

He had a cruel smile. "Oh yes. Guess that's one of the reasons the old bird's kept flying for so long."

"Oh."

The old DC8 took on a lot of fuel. The old bird was a guzzler apparently. Finally, we were told to clamber back on board. It was time to hit the road to Amsterdam.

We had to wait for traffic to clear before we could take off. Still, the steady stream of small planes with 9XR registrations kept landing.

"I found out where these planes are from," the pilot said as we sat at the end of the runway, poised to roll. "They're from Rwanda. The locals there are revolting apparently. Blood in the streets and all that. The guy in the tower said there was some sort of genocide going on."

"The Hutus and the Tutsis up there are like cats in a bag. They've been hacking each other to bits for as long as I can remember," the first officer said as a medium-sized four-engine job landed in front of us, with an Air Rwanda logo on the tail.

Looking back, I remember feeling mildly sorry for the faces peeping out of windows of the Air Rwanda plane. I sort of knew where Rwanda fitted on the map. It was one of those little countries that cluttered up the middle bit of Africa. Gary and I watched the first exodus trickle in from the genocide and the madness that would soon shock the world. Over the next three months while the world stood back idly and watched, a million men, women and children were hacked to death in a bloody, frenzied orgy of long knives and tribal hatred. That Africa was still a very dark continent, complete with pangas, murder and misery, and all just a few hours flight from where we lived was a very worrying thought. But it was also one of those 'God give me the serenity to accept the things I cannot change' sort of things. I shut out the images of those worried faces, thankful that my bit of Africa didn't do murder and mayhem. Alas, I got that wrong.

Chapter Nine

Holland was everything Zimbabwe wasn't; neat, tidy, orderly and comfortably predictable. It was a country where tiny villages had four generations from the same family living in them. In Zimbabwe, you were lucky if you had two generations living on the same continent. Growing up, I'd been dragged back to the motherland every few years to see grannies, uncles and aunts. As a boy, I loved Holland and considered myself proudly Dutch. I loved chocolate on breakfast toast, salted liquorice, riding bicycles without fear of hills and gawking at the prostitutes sitting in their Amsterdam windows with not a lot on.

Gary and I arrived at Amsterdam's Schiphol Airport at three in the morning, an ungodly hour set aside for freighter planes. It was bitterly dark and beyond bitterly cold. My first reunion was with my winter woollies and my beloved meat pies. Jenny's pies were way better than the stolen pie on the plane. My second reunion was with my cousin Hanny. Family reunions in sub-arctic conditions can often be frigid. Gary got an especially warm welcome from his new Dutch second cousin. I got a warm slap around the head from her for getting her out of her bed in the middle of the night in the middle of winter.

We were staying with my Aunt Seni. My Dutch relatives have funny names. Seni lived in an extremely neat and tidy house in an extremely neat and tidy village called Sassenheim. Sassenheim was predictability personified, I thought as I looked out across the quiet Dutch suburbia. Nothing had changed in the last twenty years, not even my aunt's neighbours. The view from Seni's house was picture-postcard pretty. On the beautiful clear winter morning, crisp blue skies stretched away over the bulb fields and dog turds steamed on the pavements in the low digit temperatures.

I drove back out to Schiphol with Hanny to pick-up Jenny, Veronica and Dan. Gary stayed behind, lights out, exhausted from the long-haul freight flight. Veronica and Daniel rolled out of the airport concourse, courtesy of their many, many layers of clothing. Familiar with the saga of Captains Oates and Scott, Jenny clearly wasn't planning on losing any children to the cold. Both kids were exactly round, wearing layer upon layer of warm tracksuits and bright hand-knitted woollen jerseys, even brighter hand-knitted woollen mittens, and topped off with hand-knitted woollen tea cosy beanies on their heads. The kids' outfits were bottomed off with shiny new black Bata gumboots.

"Bata gumboots, Jenny?" the stylist within me protested. "They're plastic, tacky and not even warm."

"Those boots are very warm, I promise you. They're three sizes too big and full of sock layers."

Outside the terminal, in the cold wastelands of the car park, Veronica and Daniel squealed with delight as the cold air hit them and plumes of smoke poured out of their mouths. Their antics attracted the attentions of Dutch children nearby, all wearing name brand, designer arctic kit. Even at their young ages and in their fake fur wrappings, I saw sneers and smirks as they took in the homemade winter woollies.

Seni's house was typically Dutch, a lounge, dining room and kitchen on the ground floor with a narrow staircase climbing up to bedrooms on the three floors above, all tastefully furnished with cream furniture, deep pile carpets in white. Alas. The house clearly hadn't been exposed to little boys and girls in years. I couldn't take more than five minutes of the carnage.

"Why don't you kids go and play outside?"

"But it's freezing out there, Eric," Jenny protested.

"Relax. Cold is good. It makes children's cheeks go rosy. Which makes them more photogenic and..." They were all moot points. Gary, Veronica and Daniel had already shot out the door like bullets from a gun.

Holland is a very small country with lots of people living in it. Your average suburban garden is postage stamp big, beautifully manicured, crammed full of miniature windmills, garden gnomes and other assorted poxy ornaments. There were eight gardens in my aunt's complex, cheek to jowl, not a fence between them. Veronica fell in love with all of the ornaments, all at once. She squealed with delight. It was like a fairy garden. She spied a Bambi in the most distant garden and with Dan in tow, rushed off to hug it. Veronica was of an age where you hugged the things you most admired. My aunt's neighbours looked out their windows in amazement as two short strangers trespassed across their perfect little gardens with Daniel doing a massive amount of collateral damage as he stomped along in his shiny gumboots. When eventually Veronica reached Bambi eight gardens away, she gave it a long loving hug and turned back and bellowed,

"I just love your fairy garden, Auntie Seni. If I make some friends, can bring them here to play?"

And then Daniel saw the canal that ran along the bottom of the gardens. Or more to the point he saw the flotilla of mallard ducks complete with little yellow ducklings, just like the ones in his bathtub. He squealed in delight and rushed off to grab them. As quick as a flash, Veronica yanked his leash. In those early ambulatory days, Dan was on a permanent dog leash thing. We heard her from Seni's garden "Daniel. Don't go near rivers!!! Rivers are full of crocodiles and hippos that eat little boys!!"

I was on a working holiday, in Holland to learn all things to do with flowers. With sixty percent of the world's flowers being traded through the

Dutch Flower Auctions, Holland was the place to learn about flowers. My sales agent in Holland, a charming silver-haired fox of a man called Koos, picked Gary and I up at half-past three in the morning, which is when the flower business gets going in Holland. My body, which doesn't do cold and early too good, threatened mutiny and urged me to consider alternative employment, like eight to five plumbing.

The Auction Floors were beyond massive. "The biggest building under a single roof in the whole world," Koos told us proudly.

"Wow," Gary whistled with huge eyes. The flowers, packed in buckets on trolleys, and of every colour imaginable, stretched away into the distance, as far as the eye could see.

"There must be millions and millions and millions of them," Gary breathed.

"Over thirty million stems of flowers are sold between six and eleven every morning," Koos told us.

"And thirty thousand of them are ours, hey Dad?" We were the literal drop in the proverbial ocean, but you could hear the pride in Gary's voice.

I was more circumspect. "How the hell are we going to find my poxy little shipment in amongst all this lot?" I grumbled.

"Remember that raging torrents start from a single drop, Eric," Koos philosophised kindly. "This is your first season. Next season your shipments will be bigger. Summer Flowers are across the other side of the building. We'd better hurry to catch the Quality Inspector before he finishes with the Asters."

Gary and I followed Koos as he threaded his way through the endless trolleys. Names jumped out at me from the tags on the trolleys. Trachelium, Bupleurum, Ammi Majus, Solidago, Typha, Alstroemeria. Carthamus. Eryngium. Hypericum. Tulips, Daffodils. Lilies. Ferns. Roses. And more Roses. And yet more Roses. Millions of them of every imaginable hue and colour. Eventually we found the Asters, trolleys and trolleys of them. From Kenya, from Columbia, from Ecuador and finally from Zimbabwe. We rooted amongst the trolleys, and eventually, we found the Running Dog contingent. I eased a bunch out of a bucket. Even under the harsh fluorescent lights beneath the cavernous roof in Holland, the little white flowers looked as fresh as when last I'd seen them in the bright Zimbabwean sun. Gary snapped away proudly as I held up a bunch of my finest for posterity.

On the last few days of our first family holiday, Jenny and I were confronted with our first landmark moral decision as parents. Should we take our new family to visit Russell and Alice Stotter or not? Russell and his Dutch wife Alice were dear friends from Zimbabwe, a wonderfully quirky couple who lived in the middle of Amsterdam's vibrant Red Light District. I really liked Russell and Alice and zeroed in on the positives of a possible visit. "Their house is over seven hundred years old. It used to be a monastery and a spice warehouse. We'll be exposing the children to living history. And that's got to be good parenting."

Jenny snorted derisively. "The only thing they'll be exposed to are prostitutes in the windows, live sex shows and drug addicts in the streets."

Jenny had a point. The Cul-de-Sac was hemmed in on all sides by Amsterdam's booming and lurid sex industry. If you swung a cat out the window, you'd hit a hooker or worse. "So, we won't see Russell and Alice again until Daniel turns twenty-one?" I protested. I really liked Russell. "And better our children get exposed to the seedy side of life when we're around."

"Hmmm," said Jenny.

"And it's not like we're going to go and watch the sex shows. Amsterdam is lots more than just the Red Light District. There's loads of museums and stuff."

"I suppose you're right," said Jenny. And so, we took our young family off to Amsterdam for the weekend.

Russell and Alice were delighted to see us and hurried and scurried to find beds for our newly extended family. Well, Alice hurried and scurried while Russell dragged me to the ground floor pub to catch up on all things Zimbabwean. An avid reader, Russell kept a very close eye on his home country, especially the politics. Russell and I had debated Zimbabwe many times, over many beers in his bar. Our debates were always lively. Holland had changed Russell. Living amongst the fall-out and detritus from the liberal excesses around him, Russell had become hugely conservative and right-wing. Where I was comfortable with the easy come, easy go attitudes of the Third World and all the attendant crap that went with it, Russell was a staunch advocate of a burn and start again approach to solving Africa's woes.

The Cul-de-Sac had been a bar for hundreds of years and oozed atmosphere. It was old and smoky, dark almost bordering on dingy, with constant soft, raggedy jazz playing in the background. It was the perfect place to solve Africa's problems, preferably over Belgian beers. Belgian beer was my best. And the Cul-de-Sac was the best pub in the world to drink them in. But my recently acquired parenting instincts were suggesting prolonged exposure to Cul-de-Sac's undoubted charms was not too clever for toddlers, seven and twelve-year-olds.

"Let's go out for a walk," I suggested. "I want to show the kids the Leidseplein." The Leidseplein was Amsterdam's Time Square.

"I don't know. It looks cold out there," Russell said morosely.

"Come on. We'll wrap up warm."

Gary and Veronica raced up the steep and narrow steps to retrieve the family's arctic kit. Russell eased into an old anorak and ventured out

OF RED LIGHTS AND PROSTITUTES

reluctantly.

The Red Light District had become smaller over the years, hemmed in by Amsterdam's burgeoning commercial district. The Cul-de-Sac was on the Achterburgwal, one of the Red Light District's two main streets. We turned out of the Cul-de-Sac and headed up towards the Dam Square. The Achterburgwal was only a few hundred metres long. I figured that if we walked those hundred metres fast, as in really fast, the children wouldn't have time to notice their surroundings and we'd make it out the Red Light District unscathed.

Even on a bitterly cold day, the Achterburgwal was bustling with hordes of busy eyed tourists. Holding Veronica tightly by the hand, I set the pace up front with Gary and Russell while Jenny and Alice followed behind talking, with Daniel on his leash. Sex shops, sex shows and sex supermarkets fought for our attention with gaudy, flashing neon lights. And then, of course, there were prostitutes' windows, which lined the canal on both sides. All the windows had red lights outside burning brightly, all open for business. The scantily clad women sitting inside the windows were of all shapes, sizes and hues, some ugly and some stunningly beautiful. I ignored the lot and plunged forward at breakneck speed, dragging Veronica along next to me, popping a bead of sweat in the bitter cold in the process. Alas. The wheels came off my haste at all cost strategy within the first twenty metres.

"What is this thing, Daddy?" Veronica asked. She slipped her woollen mitten out of my grasp and turned to stare at a mannequin sitting on top of an electric bicycle outside of the Casa Rosso sex museum. The mannequin was wearing scanty sexy leathers. Every time the pedals turned around, a big dildo rose out of the saddle and disappeared into the mannequin's girly bits. Veronica stared intently as the thing went up and down.

I popped a bigger bead of sweat. "It's a bicycle, Veronica."

"No Daddy, what's this thing that's coming in and out of the saddle."

"It's um...a thing, Veronica, to um...stop the lady from falling off the bicycle."

"Oh," she said.

"Good recovery," Russell laughed.

I grabbed Veronica by the mitten again and ploughed on. Just a few hundred metres and we'd be out of the Red Light District. Another alas. Even at a near jog, the last few hundred metres dragged on like root canal work. But just more painful.

"What are those red lights for Daddy?"

"Um...They're um..."

"And why are those ladies sitting in the windows wearing no clothes, Daddy?" Veronica asked.

"Because...um...because they've got their heaters inside turned up high, and it's very hot inside so they've taken some of their clothes off and..."

"But why are they sitting in the windows in the first place, Daddy?"

"Because...um...because ... you'd better ask your mom, Veronica."

Russell laughed as Jenny shot me a withering look. "They're prostitutes, Veronica. They sell sex."

"What's sex, Mommy?"

Thankfully there is more to Amsterdam than just the Red Light District. We squeezed as much of it in as we could. The first stop was Anne Frank's museum. I'd visited the museum before and had been moved to tears by the harsh horrors of the young Jewish girl's short life. I had a personal affinity to Anne Frank's tragic story. My paternal grandfather had been sent to the concentration camps after being caught hiding Jews in secret cupboards and rooms in his house in Hilversum. He'd been hiding the Jews for years but was caught and sent to the camps just months before the German occupation ended. He was killed in January 1945. The museum moved me as much that visit as it did the first. But the rest of the family, not so much. They dragged me out and down the road to gawk at Mugabe and others in Madame Tussaud's wax museum instead.

I learnt another valuable parenting lesson in Amsterdam that day. Even the best museums can't compete with beyond giant Ferris Wheels, dodgem cars and candy floss. A massive funfair complete with all of the above had set up right on the Dam Square. And unfortunately, I also went on to learn that parents who do not have a head for heights should not go anywhere near giant Ferris Wheels, especially in the company of children of an impressionable age. It is impossible to earn the respect of your children with a set of white knuckles, a high-pitched scream and an almost wet patch in the front of your pants high above the sights of Amsterdam.

I wasn't the only person who learnt life lessons on the Amsterdam holiday. Back at school, Veronica kicked off her obligatory "What I did on my holiday" essay with a memorable opening sentence. "I went to Amsterdam on holiday, and the prostitutes in the windows are horrible, and I don't ever want to be one."

Chapter Ten

I got my first ever Father's Day present that year, a Swiss Army knife complete with toothpick, tweezers and even a device for removing stones from horse's hooves. It was the best present I'd ever received, way better than the socks and underpants my long-suffering father had received year after year. I was beyond distraught when I lost the toothpick on my knife's first outing. Alas.

Our first year as parents had passed us by in a flash and a blur. I still felt brand-new as a parent. But it also felt natural too, like it had always been. Apart from the fact that our adoption papers still hadn't been finalised. After only a million visits to the Ministry of Home Affairs, which really rankled. It made Jenny and I feel like temporary parents. We had to go to our long-suffering friendly ministry official with cap in hand to ask for temporary travel documents so we could take the children on holiday to Holland. As soon as we got back, Jenny put her boot up my bottom and kicked me into action sorting out the adoption paperwork.

I needed a good kicking because I don't do paperwork too good. As a young entrepreneur, I'd invented the 'Burst Geyser' financial filing system. It was a real winner and brought tears to the eyes of every tax official that encountered it. I would carefully file all my paperwork in the same cardboard box. Invoices, cheque book stubs, bank statements, credit notes and letters of final demand, they'd all go into the same box. And when the box was full, I'd start on the next box. And then at the end of the tax year, I'd drag all my boxes of paperwork out on to the lawn and leave them under the hosepipe for the night. After that, the wet and sodden boxes would be stored for the rest of the year, pending any tax queries resulting from my entirely fictional returns. And all queries received were met with the burst geyser story. Oh, how I yearn for those carefree days.

In terms of paperwork, adoption was even more tedious than a financial year-end. And ours was proving to be especially problematic. I didn't know Rose when she was well, but I was guessing she didn't do paperwork too good either. Her affairs were like my year-end accounts in the sodden box, as clear as mud.

Island Hospice got the ball rolling on the adoption paperwork soon after Rose's death, but a year down the road, there was still no cigar. There was no shortage of glitches. For starters, the children had different fathers. Rose had been married twice, once to Gary's father and then to another man. After splitting with her second husband, she'd had a relationship with Veronica's father, and then with Daniel's father. She was still in the relationship with Daniel's father at the time of her death. But after she'd died, we found out she'd never divorced her second husband and was buried with his surname. Which also meant that Rose's second husband was the legal guardian to all three children, even Daniel and Veronica, both born years after he'd split with Rose. This meant we needed to track Rose's second husband down to get his signature on the adoption papers. That he lived in another country helped matters, not a jot. It all hurt my head.

It took months and months of looking and lots of help from lots of people to track him down. Once we'd found him in South Africa, I asked my brother-in-law, Steve to drive hundreds of kilometres to tell him that Rose had died and to ask him to sign the adoption papers. According to Steve, Rose's second husband had lost track of her and Gary after an acrimonious bust-up and had been genuinely grieved when told that Rose had died. He signed the consent forms and wished us all of the best.

Despite all the chaos she'd left behind, my respect for Rose remained hugely intact. In life, she'd been a free spirit. And in death, she was a brave and loving mother.

Armed with Rose's second husband's million-dollar signature on the consent to adoption forms, I plunged back into the scrum that was the Ministry of Home Affairs. And still, nothing happened. Our adoption papers were thrown on to the top of a pile of papers on some civil servant's full to overflowing desk where they promptly got lost. Papers getting lost was the only thing that happened quickly in Zimbabwe's bureaucracy. Everything else moved at glacier speed, or not at all. Our papers slotted in under the 'Not At All' category.

I didn't know what to do. I pulled what little hair I had left out, ranted and raved, demanding a meeting with the minister himself. Zip. I changed tack and tried some bribery and corruption. My clumsy attempts cost me fifty dollars and almost got me locked up. So I phoned a friend who knew the minister. The minister owed him for a fireplace, installed free and gratis. He pulled some strings and got me an appointment to see the minister himself.

In Zimbabwe, the Minister of Home Affairs is a power position, the very pinnacle of government. He gets to boss up the police force, the immigration department and the all-important, electoral process. He can have you arrested, deported or struck from the voter's roll. And he also got to decide who adopted children and who didn't.

My appointment was for two o'clock sharp. Wearing my one and only best suit, I delivered myself with half an hour to spare. Like uncles and aunts, time is relative. Especially when you're waiting to see someone important. The minister's secretary interrupted her manicure session to wave me vaguely in the direction of a stuffed armchair. I sat nervously and rehearsed my impassioned plea. A multitude of fat cats with shiny suits and sunglasses came and went from the minister's office. I interrupted the manicure to ask how long before I saw the minister. The secretary looked at me blankly, as though she was seeing me for the first time and then went back to her nails. And so I sat and waited. I could feel my own fingernails growing. Three o'clock came and went. Ditto four o'clock. The clock crept towards five. I was starting to think about going home and trying again on the morrow when the secretary received an invisible signal and ushered me into the minister's inner sanctum.

At the time the Minister of Home Affairs was one Moven Mahachi. He was that fat he looked like two Moven Mahachis. In Shona, Mahachi means horse. And Moven looked like he'd eaten one for breakfast and another for lunch. He loomed large and malevolent behind his football pitch desk in the middle of his football pitch office. There was not a piece of paper in sight.

In Africa, rolls of fat down the back of a man's neck were a sign of power and wealth. Mahachi was obviously very powerful and very wealthy. From the back, his rolls of fat looked like the foothills of the Alps. From the front, he looked big and scary, and I'm talking a hundred and fifty kilos big. Mahachi looked me up and down with piggy, recessed eyes and grunted. I took the grunt as a signal to launch into my impassioned plea. I knew the impassioned plea was good, very good because I'd watched it over and over in the bathroom mirror. It was that good it moved me to tears every time. But it moved the Minister, not a jot. He just sat there like a huge fat lump with a poker face and steepled fingers and listened to my sad, sad story. Halfway through my plea, he cut me short. "Who sent you?" he demanded.

"Um...I asked ...um...Quentin Bailey if he could...um"

"I remember now. The fireplace man."

"Um...yes and ...um...I don't know if he told you about ..."

Mahachi reached into his top drawer and pulled out the adoption papers. His Rolex flashed briefly as he wielded his rubber stamp with a flourish. I could have kissed him, fat neck and all. Jenny and I were officially parents.

In celebration, we had our first family portrait photograph taken. To this day, it has pride of place on our wall. The photographer, a charming old Sicilian called Ilo the Pirate, was a master craftsman and captured the moment just perfectly. Jenny, radiantly pretty with sparkles in her eyes and a smiley Daniel perched on her lap. I'm next to her holding Veronica, who looks cute and adorable. The smug grin on my face is big and satisfied. Gary completes the happy family, standing in close behind us, beaming and peacock proud in his new three-piece suit.

When we got back from our first family photo portrait, I borrowed a family tradition from Mike and Anne Matthews. I marched the whole family off to the door of my bedroom cupboard to record their heights for posterity. Ignoring the cruel and barbed comments about the state of my cupboard, I lined Dan up against the door, made sure his feet were flat and used a ruler to make a line level with the top of his head. Jenny's handwriting was the neatest, so she recorded the date and Dan's age in years and months. Next up was Veronica. There wasn't a huge gap between her line and Daniel's. Gary tried to con a few extra centimetres by slanting his head back while I was marking, but I wasn't having any cheating. Then it was Jenny's turn. She recorded her age as being twenty-one. I went last and went into the books as being aged very old plus one month. I stood back and looked at the five lines on the inside of my cupboard door, well satisfied with the first step taken in an excellent family tradition.

My cupboard door was our first and best family tradition. And it endured. We didn't reserve any special occasion days like Christmas for the ritual measuring. We would drag out the ruler and the marking pen whenever we thought someone short in the family was making a move on the tall person in front of him.

I owned the top spot in the family by a wide margin and felt comfortable that I could preserve my lead, especially since it looked like Jenny had stopped growing. I had a nasty moment one year when my line clearly showed that I'd lost a centimetre in height. My mark on the door that year was prefixed with the comment that I was fast becoming a little old man. Down in third spot, Gary's growth spurt could only be described as glacial, but he slowly and steadily cut into Jenny's lead. My money was on Gary eventually taking over second spot. The big fight in the early years was for fourth with Dan, the biggest mover on the grid every year. From a long way out, Veronica was destined to be tiny. She tried to preserve her lead by resorting to tippy toes for the measuring ceremony, but eventually, even that stopped working for her. If only she had feet like Daniel to tippy toe on, she could have hung onto her cherished fourth spot for longer. Even when he was still small, Dan's feet were huge and chewed up most of his growth spurt. Dan's feet weren't feet, they were yards. I loved my cupboard door and spent hours in front of it over the years, watching my children grow up.

On a whim, we drove out to the cemetery where Rose was buried, to say goodbye to her, to show her how happy we were. It was a bad move. Nothing looks more forlorn than a neglected grave, in a neglected cemetery. Apart from an unmarked grave. A year after her death, Rose's relatives hadn't bothered with a headstone. The only thing to remember Rose by was a fading entry written in the caretaker's register with a cheap ballpoint and an untidy scrawl. Even the paupers buried in graves nearby were better off than Rose. They at least had their cooking pots laid out on their burial mounds for use in the afterlife. Rose had nothing.

A flood of emotions swept over me as I bundled Jenny and the kids hurriedly in the car. I told them that we'd had to leave because there was another funeral party arriving. I drove away from the cemetery angry and bitter with Rose's family. They hadn't been there for her in life, or in death. But mostly I was sad for Rose. She deserved better. I was also sad for Gary, Veronica and Daniel. But I told them that we'd come back another day, real soon.

When we did, Rose's grave was neat and tidy, with a headstone. The inscription on her black granite headstone was simple. Beneath her dates of birth and death, it read 'Here lies Rose, a loving mother.' It was one of my better, feel-good investments.

Chapter Eleven

As a parent, you get force-fed a whole new perspective on long-term. Before children, long-term was next Thursday or when the dog food ran out, whichever came first. I was in charge of pet food in the house. And invariably it ran out way before next Thursday. But with the pitter-patter of tiny and not so tiny feet in the house, suddenly you had to think about high schools and universities and careers and...bollocks, long-term could hurt your head. Especially in a place like Zimbabwe.

High schools in Zimbabwe were a challenge. Government schools were out, with horror stories of forty, fifty kids or more to a class abounding. More out of curiosity than hope, I went to look at my old school, Allan Wilson. I'd driven past it countless times since leaving but had never been in to have a look around. Alas. I should have left memories to lie. Every lock and handle on every classroom door had long since been stolen, so I was able to roam the classrooms and corridors of my childhood at will. Polished, orderly and perfect just thirteen years earlier, they were now hollow abandoned shells, long stripped of anything remotely valuable, the absolute opposite of progress. Many people credit Robert Mugabe with empowering education in Zimbabwe but standing in a classroom which had every window broken and only forty-year-old desks and chairs left to steal, it looked to me like he'd buggered things up good and proper.

On a whim, as I was leaving, I had a look in the school hall. Incredibly, the Roll of Honour was still up on the wall, detailing in gold scroll the names of the former pupils who'd been killed in action during the Rhodesian war. So many young lives lost, for not a lot as it turned out. Names of the boys that I'd known and had been friends with jumped out at me, making my tour of old memories all the sadder.

So, government schools were out. Which left us an arm and a leg expensive private schools only. We were late into the race. Other parents had paid desk deposits years in advance to secure places for their little Johnnies, but we didn't have that luxury. I was stressing, but Jenny wasn't. Because she is a Catholic and the Catholic Church took care of their own when it came to education. She was on such sure ground, there was only one name on her list of preferred high school options for Gary - St Georges College. We went to have a look. It was an inspired choice. Still run by Jesuits, the College was a hundred years old and steeped in tradition, something in short supply in Zimbabwe. The main school buildings were carved out of stone and looked like a medieval castle. It was very cool. The grounds were immaculate, and the boys were polite, almost to the point of annoyance. St Georges would be perfect for Gary, and later for Dan. But could we get Gary in?

Our spirits dropped when we heard that there were already five hundred or more names down for the hundred and twenty first form desks available. Jenny went into bat. She made an appointment with the beleaguered headmaster, and we went in to see him, armed with letters of support from her parish priest and Sunday school attendance records for Gary. To soften him up, I gave the head a harrowing and moving account of our adoption ordeal, and it worked. Gary had a place at St Georges.

Our morning logistics took on a whole new dimension. St Georges was in the middle of town and in the middle of rush hour traffic. To get Gary to school on time, we had to get him up and out of bed by six and in the car by six-thirty. Herding cats was easier. Gary just could not, would not do early in the morning. His biological clock had an impressive built-in snooze mode. To get Gary up by six, you had to start waking him up at five.

With great reluctance, we were forced to dig out my Made in Mozambique alarm clock again. Made in Mozambique, designed in East Germany, the clock worked on the basic premise that people would be easier to wake up if the people hadn't been able to fall asleep in the first place. And to keep them awake, the clock had a tick-tock that was Big Ben loud and fluorescent hands and the numbers on the clock face emitted a toxic glow that was Times Square bright. You could use the reflective light to read your Geiger counter by. And then there was the not so small matter of the alarm itself. Courtesy of two dustbin lid sized clangers perched on top of the clock, the alarm was loud enough to wake the dead. But not loud enough to wake Gary on a school morning as it turned out. Even after he'd suspended the clock from a hook in the ceiling so that it hung just centimetres above his head.

Gary's bedroom was on the top floor on the opposite side of the house to our ground floor bedroom. The clock would physically rip me from my slumbers at five every morning. I would rush through the house and up the stairs with hands over ears trying to shut out the violence of the cacophony to switch the bloody clock off before shaking Gary awake as he lay fast asleep just centimetres below.

'Morning Gary. You awake?"

"Yes, Dad, morning."

I would make sure both his feet were out of bed and on the floor before leaving the room. But invariably his snooze button would kick in, and he'd fall fast asleep again. I had to go through the shake awake routine two or three times.

With its towering battlements and stone walls, rolling green lawns and distant sports fields, St Georges was hugely impressive. Raphael shook his head in wonderment. Especially every time a schoolboy doffed his hat to him and said Good Morning, Sir. No one had ever called Raphael Sir before. Raphael had insisted on accompanying Gary on our first St George's school run so he could check the place out, to see if we had chosen a good school for Gary. He stood in front of Gary and looked him sternly in the eyes.

"Gary, your father, is giving you a wonderful opportunity to send you to this very excellent school to be educated. You must work very hard on your studies. You must not fuck it up."

"Yes, Raphael."

Gary fitted in just fine at St Georges. He made lots of good friends in his first week, some of them lifelong. His schoolbag was full to bulging with homework every evening, none of which I could help him with. Latin, French, Shona, and even his maths were beyond me. And on top of all that, he had to swot up on the school war cry, the names of all the prefects and all the members of the first team rugby. Gary's choice of sporting codes, however, was not inspired. Gary decided he'd turn out for basketball. I didn't have the heart to tell him that very short white kids can't dunk.

Gary had only one season of cricket behind him. But with his remarkable hand-eye co-ordination, he walked out as the opening batsman in the top team in his age group in the first game of the season. I marvelled at Gary's hand-eye co-ords. He could catch flies in mid-air, whereas I had the reactions of a dead cocker spaniel. During my misspent youth, I'd famously vomited on my hand while putting my finger down my throat.

There was much excitement when Gary was selected to go on his first cricket tour to Bulawayo, especially from me. The furthest I'd ever gone on tour during my illustrious school sporting career was to Lord Malvern, a school on the wrong side of Harare's railway lines. It wasn't a good tour. We lost the game, and I had my wristwatch nicked.

The St George's teams that Gary had been picked to be a part of would travel to Bulawayo overnight on the train. Jen and I would drop Gary off at the train station on our way to a Robbie Burns evening that we'd been invited to. We were running late because I couldn't find a tartan kilt anywhere in the house. The wearing of tartan was mandatory at the Burns dinner.

"Are you sure you haven't got a tartan kilt in your cupboard?" I asked Jenny for the third time while standing in front of her open wardrobe.

"Yes. I am very sure, Eric. Why did you think I might have a kilt in my cupboard?"

"Because look at how full this cupboard is. There's a lot of stuff in here. And wasn't your dad Scots?"

"My great grandfather was Scottish."

"Exactly. And you're supposed to hand down your tartan from generation to generation. But what am I going to wear?" I whined with a worried look on my face. I liked to fit in at theme evenings. "Haven't you got a checked tablecloth we can cut up?"

"You leave my tablecloths alone. But let me have a look in that suitcase of Nadine's hand me down clothes that Sue sent up for Veronica. I think I saw something tartan in there."

I kept my worried look in place. Nadine was my ten-year-old niece from Johannesburg. Jenny pulled the full to bulging suitcase out and started pulling out blue jeans and t-shirts and tops and dresses and... and then the mother lode...a red tartan kilt. Well, it was actually a mini skirt, but tartan was tartan. I kissed Jenny on the forehead. I was going to fit in no problem after all with all the Scotsmen at the Burns evening.

We dropped Gary off at the railway station before continuing on to our dinner engagement. We had to walk the full length of the busy platform to get to the train carriages booked out to the travelling St George's teams. Dan's eyes were open wide in wonderment as he dragged me along the length of the train, in a hurry to have a look at the big black diesel locomotive. My tartan mini skirt and I attracted many stares as we threaded through the masses.

We found the St George's contingent clustered at the head of the train. I looked around for familiar faces but found none. More stares. More whispered comments.

"Why are they all staring at us, Dad?" Veronica asked.

"They've never seen a Scotsman in his kilt before," I said.

"You're not a Scotsman in a kilt, Eric. You're a man in a miniskirt" Jenny corrected me snidely.

Gary seemed to be in a hurry to get the farewells out the way. "Well, goodbye then. See you on Sunday," he blurted out before bolting for the sanctuary of the train. But Jenny captured him in a hug and peppered him with kisses.

I attracted more stares when we arrived at our dinner engagement. I was the only one wearing tartan. It was very disappointing that more people hadn't made an effort. Pete and Joyce, our host and hostess, greeted us.

"Please tell me why you're wearing a tartan miniskirt, Eric?" Joyce asked.

"Robbie Burns night."

"You're late. That was two months ago. Tonight is Pete's birthday party."

Crap.

Six weeks into high school, I gave Gary his first beating, as in corporal punishment, reluctantly. Discipline is one of those fine line things, too much or too little in a family can cause all kinds of crap. And both were going on at the same time in our family. Jenny and I were horribly at opposite ends of the discipline spectrum. Other parents who go the traditional new-born route have a couple of years to work out and debate how they play the discipline card, but we weren't afforded that luxury. Our three kids arrived in a hurry and already of an age to be naughty, so the need to go on a crash course in parental discipline and set children's boundaries was obvious. Well, it was obvious to Jenny.

The problem was I'm not too big on discipline, within myself. I'd emerged from my own childhood with a leather arse and a healthy disrespect for the rules. Older brother Kees had taught me that you had to break the rules to get to do the really cool stuff in life and that discipline was a consequence only if you got caught. That was a pretty cool template for a thirteen-year-old in search of wine, women and song. You get to do all the fun bad stuff, and you learn valuable life skills on how best to construct plausible alibis. I had to take sneaky and devious to a whole other level because my mother had an arm like Arnold Schwarzenegger and a bloodhound nose that could sniff out beer breath and cigarettes from a hundred metres. And that's how you grow as a person. With sore arse ringing, you learn from mistakes made and gravitate to vodka because James Bond's breath doesn't stink. Vodka being stronger than beer can, unfortunately, lead to further infractions; which was also normally fine because when you got bust, your nether regions were normally still suitably anesthetised from the alcohol, or the pain of hanging over was such that a sore arse was a pleasant distraction.

Jenny's childhood exposure to discipline was different. With three daughters under the roof, Jenny's parents had to go the full lockdown route to keep boys like me, their hormones and their penises more than a shotgun distance away. Barbed wire sets of rules were erected and strictly enforced. To the point where even nuisance stuff like homework got done, and tests were learnt for and passed, and life experiments with hardtack were delayed.

Jenny kicked off her crash course on how to discipline by turning Dr Phil into a bestselling author. She snapped up every book the man had ever written and read them voraciously, cover to cover, including all the boring bits and made notes in the margins with a pencil. And then she handed them over to me. Unfortunately, I can't read boring. Unless someone dies in the first chapter of the book I'm reading, I have no option but to nod off. I did my manful best with Dr Phil but bailed after just seven pages in favour of Hannibal Lecter and the Silence of the Lambs. Hannibal was also good course material I told Jenny when she found I'd ditched Dr Phil. Should any of the kids display a fondness for human flesh or sweetmeats, I'd know to grab an ice hockey mask and a gum guard in a hurry. Jenny practised her discipline skills by hitting me on the head with a hockey stick and told me I was an idiot.

We had to set boundaries she said, like doing homework and keeping sock drawers tidy and build from there. I got defensive. My sock drawer is a mess and always has been, and I had turned out just fine I told her. Our children had just watched their mother die, and they didn't need to be stressing about neat sock drawers. Sure, I wanted our kids brought up so that they raised their hats to old people, but I was looking for a hiatus of maybe a couple of years on the full discipline package. When our kids were over the trauma, then maybe we could go back and revisit the sock drawers and tidy cupboards. But Dr Phil and Jenny remained unmoved by my pleas for clemency for crimes and minor infractions yet to be committed, and the lines of firm discipline were drawn in the sand. But when Jenny wasn't watching, I rubbed some of the lines out.

Island Hospice were still in the background, patiently counselling the kids on how to deal with the loss of their birth mom and keeping an eye on how Jenny and I were coping on the parenting front. Jenny's frustrations boiled over in the counselling session. She was doing all the hard yards in the house, making sure that the kids were growing up with values firmly in place while I was too busy being oversensitive to the children's emotional needs and letting them get away with murder. But I reminded her the children had lost their mom and...Island Hospice stepped in very quickly. Kids were tougher and more resilient than I was giving them credit for. They had to be tough to cope with what life had dealt them. And they had to move on. And being a parent wasn't about winning popularity contests. The truths hurt like a smack in the face with a shovel, especially the one about the popularity contest. For sure, I wanted the kids to like me as a person and as their new father.

Reluctantly, I took on board a new role for myself in the family, that of the ultimate enforcer. When the children stepped out of their boundaries, it would be my job to wield the axe. Like Veronica when she came home from school again nearly naked, having lost her school dress, her sports shirt, her vest, her hat, her school shoes, her sports shoes, her reading books, her pencil box complete with crayons and matching pencil sharpener and her homework bag. The only possessions that she hadn't managed to lose were the panties and the sports shorts she came home in. Jenny, properly at the end of her tether, pointed out that most of the stuff that Veronica had lost was nearly brand-new, having just been bought to replace items which had also gone missing in the last few weeks. Veronica was easily the most miserable little thing I'd ever seen, huddled in her skimpy shorts and vest, shivering through the cold and the flood of tears while Jenny vented her frustrations. All I really wanted to do was to give Veronica a love and a cuddle and get her into a hot bath and some warm pyjamas unless of course, she'd had lost those as well. But I steeled myself to mete out some long overdue punishment. It was time for me to wield the axe.

Well, I didn't actually go with an axe in the end because, after all, Veronica was still quite small, and she hadn't actually lost all her clothes, and her bottom lip was very wobbly. So I went with a slipper instead as my punishment weapon of choice; one of Jenny's winter slippers with a soft rubber sole, even softer leather uppers and lamb's fleece on the inside. The look of horror on Veronica's face as I advanced upon her with the deterrent in hand absolutely pierced my heart. I never spoke a truer word than when I told her that what I was about to do would hurt me more than it hurt her. I bent her over and smacked her three times on the bum. I did the job of a parent. I punished. To no avail as it turned out in the long run. Veronica carried on losing her kit like Bo Peep lost sheep. But I never raised my hand to her again. Man, but those three smacks on the bum hurt me like hell.

Gary's first punishable infraction was a biggie, in Jenny's eyes especially. It happened on a dark grey day. A brown envelope arrived from St George's College. The theme music from Jaws should have played out ominously in the background as she opened the envelope. The letter was from the College Bursar. It was a final demand for school fees, harshly worded as in pay now or don't even think about sending your child school in the morning. Way before she got to the bottom of the short, terse letter, Jenny's face went all crimson, fuelled by mortal embarrassment and by anger. But mostly anger. "But I gave Gary the cheque!!" Financially we were under pressure. My cut-flowers were eating up more money than I was making and as a result, Jenny was hard-pressed to make ends meet on the home front. It was the school fees that were doing the damage. Private schools charge like wounded buffalo. Jenny scrimped and saved to make sure she had enough set aside for the dreaded school fees at the start of the term. This term she'd been forced to unearth her cash stashes from her cupboard and deposit them in the bank, just in time to write out a cheque to cover the term's school fees. Job done for another four months. Gary was given the cheque in an envelope along with strict instructions to deliver the said envelope to the bursar as soon as he got to school.

"And he bloody lost it!!" I thundered, feeling like I had to join in. Now being a person who couldn't get to the front of a very short bank queue without losing the cash deposit on the way, you'd expect me to have been more reasonable about the missing cheque. Stop payments were easily put on lost cheques, I could have reasoned. But the boundaries and discipline lecture loomed large in my head. I wasn't going to be caught winning popularity contests again. "I'll punish him properly," I said with a steely determination.

"What did you just say, Eric?"

"I said I'll punish him."

"How?"

"I guess I'll smack him."

I had a best friend called Dave Mead. He had two children and the most level- headed approach to corporal punishment I'd ever encountered. Dave told me that he never hit his kids in the heat of the angry moment. When his kids crossed the corporal punishment line, he'd call them out about it and would table his sentence. The guilty parties were encouraged to offer up comments, apologies, and then negotiations on the punishment would begin. Dave being a hard-arsed negotiator would always kick off with six of the best, to be applied with a switch cane with some spring in it, freshly cut from the peach tree. His miscreants would usually negotiate down to two with a slipper. And once they had met somewhere in the middle, the guilty party would be sent off to their bedrooms to sweat and stew for at least half an hour, while they waited for the axe to fall. It was a good model that took the emotion out of the punishment, and I decided that I'd use it on Gary.

I summoned a very contrite Gary to the judge's chambers. I put on my best, very stern face and tabled the facts of the case. They were black, white and very stark with absolutely no grey wiggle room. The guilty party had been given the cheque, which represented a large amount of hard-earned money, in a clearly marked envelope together with equally clear instructions to deliver the same envelope to the school bursar. But the envelope was never delivered. A crime of financial impropriety had been committed. After delivering the facts of the case, I allowed Gary the opportunity to mitigate. Personally, if I'd been in his shoes, I would have presented myself as the hapless victim of either a mugging or a sleight of hand robbery. But Gary took it all on the chin and confessed to the crime. I was staggered and taken aback by his honesty and his appalling lack of guile.

Eventually, I recovered. "So, what are we going to do about it, Gary?"

"I'm going to pay it all back, dad. I'm going to work on the farm every weekend until I've got enough to pay it all back."

"No, no, Gary, there's no money missing. We put a stop order on the cheque at the bank. So, we didn't lose the money."

"We didn't?" Gary had a look of huge relief on his face.

"No. But...but that's not the point."

"It isn't?'

"No. The point is you were given a big responsibility to deliver something, and you didn't. You lost the cheque. And you didn't tell us. And so, we've got to punish you. And that's what I want you and me to talk about. How am I going to punish you?" I fixed Gary with my steely glare and let him fry.

His Adam's apple bobbed up and down as he thought hard. "I think you should give me a hiding, Dad," he said.

"Okay, we're in agreement there." I followed the Dave Mead script. "Now we just have to agree on how many and what with."

More Adam's apple bobbing. "I think you should give me six of the best, Dad," Gary quivered. "And with a cricket bat."

Holy crap!! My son had the self-preservation instincts of a lemming!! "But...but the money was never lost, Gary, we put a stop payment on the cheque!!"

"But I never delivered the envelope like I was supposed to, Dad. I lost it."

"I know but accidents happen and...and bollocks you're only a kid...and it's also our fault. We should've stuck it in a bigger envelope and...in fact one of us should have taken it to the bursar."

"No, Dad, it was my fault."

"But six of the best!! And with a cricket bat!! Are you nuts, Gary?"

"No, but..."

"How about two? With a slipper?"

"A slipper? That's for little kids. Let's do three. With a hockey stick."

"Done. But you've got to sneak on a few extra pairs of underpants first. And another pair of shorts."

The three whacks with his hockey stick resulted in a flood of choked back tears, not from pain but from the weight of having done wrong. It was wrong that he was getting this down on himself, just for losing an envelope. Gary was twelve going on thirty, with the weight of the world on his shoulders from way too much responsibility, way too early. I had a huge job on my hands. I had to teach the kid to lighten up.

Chapter Twelve

Veronica came home from school in a flood of tears. She'd been in a career debate with one of her friends, Rutendo, about what they were going to be when they grew up. Veronica had narrowed her choices to either becoming a nurse or becoming the President of Zimbabwe. Rutendo shot her down. There was no way Veronica could ever be president because she wasn't black "I can be the president one day, can't, I Daddy? The president's job's not just for black people," she sobbed.

Sitting there with my young daughter on my lap, it struck me there and then that I was bringing my children up in a country where they would be discriminated against because they were white. I was bringing them up on an Animal Farm, where all animals were born equal, just some animals were loads more equal than others. When first we got the children, I'd marvelled at how black kids and white kids in the playground were absolutely blind to colour. It was heart-warming. It made you feel like the country had a chance going forward. But the reality of it was on my lap, crying. I was torn between giving Veronica a happy answer that would make the tears dry up or an honest answer. Uncharacteristically, I went with an honest answer. "Rutendo's right, Veronica, you can't ever become the President of Zimbabwe."

"But why, Daddy, why?"

I gave her a cuddle and a hug and looked her in the eye. "You can't be the President of Zimbabwe because you're white."

"But why, Daddy, why?"

"Because of politics."

"What are politics?"

"They're a very stupid thing that adults do, Vee."

How do you explain politics to a kid? Especially when you're not too sure about what they're about either.

Growing up, politics struck me as boring grey stodge, personified by the then English Prime Minister Harold Wilson, a little grey man with a face more wrinkly than his cardigan and circles under his eyes blacker than the smoke from his pipe. From what I could see as a child, politics happened on the front pages of the newspapers and never really intruded into your life.

But that all changed in 1980 when Rhodesia became Zimbabwe, when the politics became African. African politics are more in your face. There's nothing complicated about them. The top of the pile belongs to the leader the most hungry, the one most prepared to use any and all means to get there. And once he is on top, he carries on using any and all means, including killing anyone and everyone, to stay top for as long as possible, preferably forever,

I was old enough to vote in the watershed 1980 elections at the end of the prolonged and bitter civil war but who to vote for? My choices were limited to the four blacks vying to become Zimbabwe's first leader - Joshua Nkomo, Robert Mugabe, Abel Muzorewa and Ndabaningi Sithole. Straight away, Sithole was a non-starter because how can you support a candidate when you can't even pronounce his first name. To get around the problem, we changed his name to Rubber Dingy Sithole.

Politics in Zimbabwe all comes down to what tribe you belong to. Mugabe and Muzorewa were Shonas while Nkomo was a Ndebele and Sithole a Shangaan. But I was neither Shona, Ndebele nor Shangaan, so I wasn't fettered by tribal loyalties. So, it was back to the question of who to vote for?

Nkomo and Mugabe were avowed communists, and I couldn't be voting for a communist. My father would never talk to me. And on top of being communists, Mugabe and Nkomo were both terrorists to boot. Nkomo, I especially hated. During the war, his ZIPRA forces had shot down two Air Rhodesia Viscounts with SAM Seven rockets. In the second Viscount attack, some of the passengers actually survived the crash. But not for long. The ZIPRA terrorists shot and bayonetted them in cold blood. Nkomo had defended their actions on world television, flashing a shiny gold Rolex watch on his fat podgy wrist in the process.

I actually met the members of the ZIPRA unit that shot the two Viscounts down. At the end of the war, my Police unit was tasked with kick-starting the ceasefire by escorting terrorists to assembly points or demobilisation camps around the country, where they were held under lockdown while the politicians campaigned for the elections. Mugabe's ZANLA terrorists went into their own assembly points, mostly in the east of the country, while ZIPRA were taken to assembly points in the west.

I got the call to go to an area called Hurungwe just below Kariba to try and track down a ZIPRA unit operating in the area. Once I'd made contact with them, I was supposed to talk them into the ceasefire and then to escort them all the way across to the west of the country to a ZIPRA assembly point in Lupane. I didn't want the job. Hurungwe was where the Viscounts had been shot down, and it was a scary no-go place for white Rhodesians. I sat huddled in my vehicle with my finger ready on the trigger of my rifle, sweating and stressing and jumping at every imagined noise while my black constable parlayed in the bush with the ZIPRA unit, trying to persuade them to stop fighting so that we could escort them to the assembly point. The constable was gone for hours. I was sure he'd been killed by the terrorists, and now they were coming for me. Eventually, the ZIPRA unit walked out the bush, twelve cold, hard men. One of them carried a Strela-2 surface-to-air missile launcher. I'd never seen one in the flesh but knew exactly what they looked like. I had a poster on my office wall with all the different communist weapons, including the Strela-2. And there weren't too many of those around. They had to be the terrorists who'd downed the Viscounts. I spent the next two days jammed cheek to jowl with them in a truck as we bumped our way across the back roads of Zimbabwe. They didn't speak a word to me. I was shit scared the whole time. They were longest days of my life.

As an election candidate, Mugabe was even worse, according to all the fire-side stories I'd heard about him. He might look meek, mild and bookish like the schoolteacher he'd once been, but inside he was the anti-Christ. And he hated all whites with a passion because Ian Smith hadn't let him out of prison to go to Ghana to bury his dead son.

This left me a choice between Muzorewa and Sithole. Neither of them were communists, so they were in the clear. Both were actually churchmen - Muzorewa a Methodist Bishop and Sithole a Reverend. I'd met Muzorewa just before the elections. He was a tiny man with a sparkle in his eye, and he came across as a kind person. But in the end, I voted for Sithole because his party had the coolest symbol. Like I said, African politics aren't complicated.

There might have been four candidates in those 1980 elections, but there was only ever going to be one winner, and that was Robert Mugabe. His first choice party symbol had a picture of an AK 47, entirely in keeping with his brutally simple campaign message to the people of Zimbabwe -'I am the only person who can end the war, and I'm only going to end it if I win the election.' The British were running the elections and disallowed Mugabe's party symbol- automatic weapons weren't in keeping with their quaint notion of free and fair. Instead they made him go with another symbol. Mugabe chose a chicken but already the AK 47 message had been delivered, and Mugabe won by a landslide.

When he became Zimbabwe's first Prime Minister, Mugabe endeared himself to the world when he spoke of reconciliation and peace, of turning swords into ploughshares and building a better country for all Zimbabweans. I'd already handed my notice in as a policeman, and I was trying to figure out what I was going to do with the rest of my life. Most of my friends had already decided that they would rather leave Zimbabwe than live under an avowed communist. But as I listened to his speech, I bought into what he was saying, one hundred percent. Straight up, I went from hating him on principle to quite liking him. I put him on first name terms, and he became Bob. And I decided that I would become one of his Zimbabweans. But alas, as it turned out, Mugabe was talking crap.

It didn't take long for African politics to get right in my face. One of the first bits of new legislation in Mugabe's Zimbabwe was a law that said all public areas had to display Mugabe's official portrait prominently, including all businesses. This was a red rag to the bull that lived inside my irresponsible, elder brother Kees. He was working as a mechanic at a service station in Harare at the time. Within a few days of the official portrait going up, he couldn't help himself and got busy after hours and after more than a few beers with a pot of paint and his artistic interpretation of Mugabe's inner psyche. Kees gave Bob a goatee, a pair of horn rim glasses, vampire teeth and a fine pair of devil's horns. Aggrieved at the slight to his illustrious new leader, one of his black workmates rat-finked to the cops.

Anywhere else in the free world, I'm thinking the crime would have aroused feelings of annoyance come boredom come humour in the policemen attending. It certainly would have if I'd been the policeman attending. But not in the new Zimbabwe. The cops swooped on the service station, with sirens blaring and blue lights flashing and dragged Kees away in handcuffs. Sharon, Kees's long-suffering wife, went from angry to panic when she couldn't find Kees at any of the local lockups. She'd only been married for a year, but already she was long-suffering. Heavily pregnant with their second child, she went from police station to police station. After a very long eventually, she tracked him down. Kees was in Chikurubi, Zimbabwe's maximum-security prison, locked up with robbers and murderers. Apparently defacing Mugabe's official portrait was way more than a misdemeanour.

After keeping my father waiting for hours in the corridor outside his office, the public prosecutor told him that he was going to push for a jail sentence of between five to ten years. He didn't care that Kees was young and expecting his second child. He had to face the full wrath of the law for what he'd done. Five to ten years. Surely, they had to be joking, my father asked of his new and very expensive lawyer. "No, they weren't joking" was the lawyer's answer. And we should brace for the worst, should the case end up in front of one of Mugabe's newly appointed judges.

Kees was stuck in Chikurubi for weeks awaiting trial. I was at the hotel school in Bulawayo at the time. I drove to Harare and went to visit him in prison with my dad. Set in the bush outside Harare, the prison's massive concrete façade was intimidating. Chikurubi had a reputation for being hell on earth. We drove passed spans of prisoners in their white uniforms, toiling in the fields under the harsh, midday sun and harsher guards. The prisoners looked beyond miserable. Ditto Kees. There were no smiles on him when he was led out for the visitation. Kees looked absolutely petrified and not far from tears. It had all been a joke, he said. My dad told him what the lawyer had said, and the tears came even closer. When we left him after our allotted twenty minutes were up, Kees looked small, sad and broken inside.

When eventually the case went to trial, Kees went with a Kees defence.

The evidence against him was largely circumstantial. There were no eyewitnesses, and no one could prove that he'd actually wielded the brush. So, he stood in front of the judge with hand on his heart and poker face on and lied through his teeth. He was not the one, he told the judge.

Kees was an accomplished liar. Being in the shit was a constant for Kees when growing up. He could not stay out of trouble. If he'd confessed to all his sins, the cumulative and much-deserved beatings would have taken a toll on his health. And so, he learnt to lie with the straightest of faces. He was that good that sometimes even my mom got sucked into his innocence. And the judge was a rollover. He studied Kees long and hard as he protested his innocence and with a bang of his gavel, declared Kees innocent and free to go. It was a hugely emotional moment. I was in the courtroom with my parents and Kees' wife. There were tears all round. After more than a month of being locked up in a maximum-security prison, with robbers and murders, for a minor misdemeanour, Kees's nightmare was over.

Alas. No one told that to the men from the president's office standing at the back of the courtroom in cheap suits and dark glasses. As Kees walked out of the courtroom a free man, they arrested him again, for the same crime he'd just been found innocent of and dragged him back to Chikurubi. The nightmare was back on. Mugabe did not take being slighted with bad art lightly. He wanted his pound of flesh. That night Kees' second daughter was born.

Kees' lawyer lodged a half-hearted appeal against Kees' illegal detention, but his fire had gone out, doused by a presidential disregard for the law. My parents didn't know what to do. So, my mom played the Dutch card. Kees had been born in Holland and used to travel on a Dutch passport but had allowed it to lapse, mostly because he was irresponsible. My mom went to see the Dutch ambassador and tugged on his heartstrings. I think it was the new-born baby that did the trick. Kees got his Dutch passport back, and the ambassador got busy on the phone to the Zimbabwean Minister of Foreign Affairs, talking deportation instead of prison.

Within a week, Kees was at the airport, waiting to get on a plane to South Africa. Rather than fly to Holland, Kees had opted to restart his life in South Africa. The immigration officials who'd escorted Kees from Chikurubi to the airport were human and let Kees sit with his family and hold his new daughter. A day later, I drove Sharon and my two nieces to Johannesburg. In Kees's car, it was a two-day trip. An impossibly long two-day trip. We'd been on the road for all of ten minutes when my three-year-old niece asked me if we were almost there yet. And minutes after it had started hammering down with angry rain, the windscreen wipers gave up the ghost, and I drove six hours to the border with my head out the window.

As soon as we arrived in Johannesburg, I got back in the car and drove another six hours down to Natal with Kees to help look for a job and a home. He liked the look of Pietermaritzburg. It was a pretty little town, and everyone spoke English. So, we started looking for jobs there. It was too easy. Kees's story had made the front page of all the papers, and he enjoyed minor celebrity status. Everyone was sympathetic to his plight and wanted to help him. By lunchtime, he had a job, a work permit and a house. I flew back to Harare, half happy to be home, half sad that Kees and his family could never come home again. The half happy bit didn't last long. My parents sat me down when I got back to Harare and told me they were leaving Zimbabwe. My dad had put in his notice at work, and the house was already on the market. They were going to follow Kees, Sharon and the kids to South Africa. My dad told me he couldn't see any happy endings in Zimbabwe. I had a choice. I could go with them. Or I could stay behind in Zimbabwe and finish college. I decided to stay.

Staying was an easy decision. I was at hotel school in Bulawayo, Zimbabwe's second city and after three years as a policeman, life as a college student was fun and carefree. And I'd just met a girl called Jenny. For me, life was good.

But life in Bulawayo wasn't good for everyone, especially not if you were a Ndebele. Bulawayo was full of Ndebele. It was where they came from. We had one of them on our hotel management course, the first-ever black student to be enrolled. Older than the rest of us, David had worked for years as a waiter, he had the biggest hands I'd ever seen on a man and could carry eleven soup plates at once. These are the things you notice as a hotel student. David wanted nothing more than to climb up out of the ranks and become a hotel manager and he took his studies hugely seriously, way more than me. He lived in Bulawayo's Entumbane Township. One day David came to college unshaven, wide-eyed and looking like he'd spent the night hiding in a ditch. He had. David told us the townships were on fire, full of Shona soldiers going door to door breaking heads, supposedly looking to root out Ndebele dissidents, but mostly just beating up on anyone who was Ndebele. That was the start of an operation the Army called Gukurahundi, the wind that blows away the chaff.

And with that approach to calming tribal tensions, not surprisingly there was no shortage of dissident Ndebele. The Ndebele are descended from the Zulus and are a proud, warlike people. Mostly they like fighting. They especially like fighting their benign, pastoral Shona neighbours. Tribal enmities were set aside briefly during the War of Liberation when Nkomo and Mugabe held hands to form the Patriotic Front to fight the common enemy, the Rhodesians. But as soon as the war was won, the Ndebele and the Shona went back to fighting each other like fractious cats in a sack. Tribalism is one of Africa's more enduring isms, almost as enduring as the

Shona memories of their long-ago persecution at the hands of the Ndebele. The Shona were quickly on top in the new Zimbabwe, courtesy of their massive majority in the new parliament and set about putting the boot into the minority tribe. Alas for the poor Ndebele. They should have spent more time making love, not war and got their numbers up.

Fresh from his peace and reconciliation speech at his inauguration, Mugabe focused most of his energies on wiping out the Ndebele population, and their influence within Zimbabwe. He poked and prodded at Ndebele pride and sensitivities. He demoted ZAPU's leader Joshua Nkomo from the powerful Minister of Home Affairs to the Minister of Not a Lot. He confiscated all ZAPU properties, saying they were being used to cache arms of war. Mugabe's poking and prodding got the reaction he was looking for. Demobilised ZIPRA armed forces rose up and marched on Bulawayo in a column.

Bulawayo closed down hurriedly when hostilities broke out, including the hotel school. We made the most of our unexpected day off. Our student digs were not too far from the action, and we could hear the gunfire getting closer. We hauled deckchairs and a crate of beers up on to the roof of the digs for a better view. It was like watching a real live war movie. We cheered as the Air Force Hunter jets came in live, smashing the ZIPRA column to bits.

In just a few years, Mugabe went on to murder tens of thousands of Ndebele innocents. Looking back, we should have been more horrified at the wholesale persecution of others. But we weren't. My friends and I were young, not so innocent and most importantly, it wasn't our fight.

Gukurahundi really ramped up in 1983 when Mugabe unleashed his Fifth Brigade on Matabeleland. I was unlucky enough to meet some of the Fifth Brigade just a few months before they got really busy killing. I was doing my in-service training at the plush Montclair Casino Hotel in Zimbabwe's Eastern Highlands at the time. I figured that a gig in the mountains would be the only way I'd ever be able to lay claim to having been highly trained. And while I was there, the army unit that went on to become the nucleus of the Fifth Brigade was quartered just down the road near Nyanga village. The unit was known as the Presidential Guard at the time and was led by a Colonel. They wore mustard yellow berets. All the soldiers in the unit were recruited from Mugabe's home district of Zvimba. Their instructors were North Koreans, specially imported for the job of training Mugabe's close protection unit. The North Korean connection was especially bad news because whenever the soldiers came to the hotel loud and drunk, they would leap around in Kung Fu stances, threatening to break bricks and people's heads with their bare hands. I was petrified of them. And for good reason. When three young British tourists were murdered just down the road from where I lived, their car was recovered from the Presidential Guard barracks. No arrests were made. The police were also scared of the soldiers.

Drunk soldiers beating up on hotel guests and casino punters each and every weekend was bad for business so Russell Stotter, the casino manager, phoned the colonel with a proposal. If the hotel and casino were declared an officers only facility, Russell would roll out the red carpet for the colonel and his fellow officers whenever they came to the casino. The arrangement worked well, and the colonel and his lieutenants pitched up often for free drinks and casino chips. By their standards, they were well enough behaved, and everyone was happy.

Until one long weekend when six drunken soldiers rolled into the casino on a rampage, loud and looking for a fight. The soldiers quickly captured a young sixteen-year-old white kid playing the slot machines. Gambling in Zimbabwe had an age limit of eighteen. The soldiers quickly found the terrified kid guilty of underage gambling and decided to execute him in the casino with a Tokarev pistol. When his father rushed up to plead with them, one of the soldier's pistol-whipped him and the others kicked him where he fell. None of the other guests stepped into help him. The kid lay in the corner, sobbing, petrified and forgotten about for the moment. It was all very ugly and getting out of hand. Russell phoned the colonel and asked him what had happened to the Officers Only arrangement. It took the colonel fifteen long minutes to drive from Nyanga to the Montclair. As soon he stalked into the casino foyer, the drunken soldiers snapped to attention. The colonel motioned for them to get into an open Land Rover, he apologised to Russell for their behaviour and told him they would never misbehave again.

The colonel was the master of the understatement. Minutes later, we heard six pistol shots. The drunk soldiers had been lined up against Juliasdale Post Office wall and shot, execution-style. We were later told that their bodies were dumped on the parade ground the next morning - a not so gentle reminder to the other ranks that the Montclair was for officers only and out of bounds to other ranks.

A year after I left them in Nyanga, the Presidential Guard became the Fifth Brigade and deployed into Matabeleland and murdered twenty thousand men, women and children. Such was the censorship and repression in Zimbabwe, Mugabe was able to keep the curtains closed on his excesses, the genocide that he called Gukurahundi. The Catholic Church was the first to break the news. They told the world about the mass graves happening in Matabeleland. I was horrified, but not in the least surprised. The American and British ambassadors in Harare knew all along what was happening in Matabeleland, but they chose to do nothing. Mugabe was the darling of African politics, he was their pin-up boy. They had invested heavily in him and were prepared to turn a blind eye to his excesses,

OF DIRTY POLITICS AND PRINCESSES

prepared to sweep twenty thousand dead innocents under the carpet. I suppose they didn't see it as a crime against humanity, just politics.

My next encounter with African politics was in 1987 at my wedding. When Jenny and I got married, we were running a takeaway restaurant for a living and close to penniless. I had to borrow seventy dollars from Jenny to buy her an oversized cubic zirconia engagement ring. The ring was oversized, the cubic zirconia was tiny. We were that broke we did the catering for our own wedding, which made our special day all the more hectic. We hired the municipal Mount Pleasant Hall as a wedding venue. Because Jenny hogged our one and only car to go and get her hair done, I had to hire a taxi to ferry our three cooks and a bottle washer plus all the food from the takeaway restaurant to the venue. Friends helped set up all the tables and chairs for the hundred odd guests while I rushed back home quickly to cut myself shaving and don my purpose bought shiny suit. By the time I'd made it up down the aisle and on to the top table, I was utterly exhausted. But somehow, we'd got it all done.

The wedding was a great success. Jenny looked beautiful in white, and I hadn't burnt the food. But sitting next to me on our top table, Jenny picked up on a snag. She elbowed me in the ribs viscously. "Look," she hissed, "there's not a single one of your friends in the hall. They're all in the bar getting pissed." Because the hall was too small, I'd set the bar up in the entrance foyer. I looked out, and Jenny was right. There wasn't a single man at any of the tables. And I could tell from the tone of her hissing that it was all my fault. "What am I supposed to do about it?" I whined.

"Go in the bar and kick them all out. Tell them to get back in here and to dance with their wives and girlfriends."

Because I was now married, I rushed off to do Jenny's bidding. I pushed through the swing doors into the foyer. The bar was also empty. But the car park outside was full. There were two groups gathered outside the hall, my wedding guest friends and about fifty or more belligerent black men. When I walked out, the two groups were eyeballing each other, all stiff-legged and bristling, like dogs just before a fight. I pushed through to the front.

"What's happening?" I demanded.

"These guys are from the ZANU PF Youth League and they want to come into the wedding," Dave Mead told me.

"But you can't come to the wedding because you're not invited," I wailed at the ZANU PF youth chairman.

"Ah-ha!! Exactly!!" The youth chairman seized on my point and jabbed me in my chest with a wobbly finger. He'd obviously been drinking. "And why aren't we invited? It is because we are black. This is Zimbabwe, not Rhodesia. You can't have a party with no black people enjoying it."

"Look, this my wedding. I don't know you, so I'm not going to invite you. So please just you and your friends, fuck off and let me and my guests just enjoy my wedding," I said reasonably. And then very unreasonably and when he wasn't watching, I threw the first punch of the wedding. It wasn't much of a punch because I punch like a girl, but it certainly got the brawl going. All hell broke loose. Nicodemus, my pastry cook, weighed in with a cast iron frying pan and smote the ZANU PF youth chairman in the face, dropping him like a shot giraffe.

It was a tremendous brawl in which the wedding guests plus cooks prevailed mightily. I managed to not get punched, which was a bonus. And when it was all over, we trooped back into the reception and had a hell of a party. Any ice that might have otherwise put the brakes on the party had been well and truly broken out in the car park.

Two weeks later, when we got back from honeymoon, I got arrested for public violence. To avoid court, I could admit guilt and pay a fine. I paid the fine. I didn't mind. It was the best twenty bucks I'd ever spent. While paying, I asked the policeman if the ZANU PF youth chairman had also been arrested and was told no.

"That was very unfair," I told the policeman. "There were two sides to the fight."

"Yes, it's not fair," he told me. "It's politics."

Fast forward back to Veronica and her question about why she couldn't become president because she was white. How do you explain African politics to a six-year-old kid? You don't. You change the subject to better things, like princesses. "But you don't want to be a president, Vee. You want to be something way better."

"I do?"

"Yeah. Being a president is a dumb job. It will make your hair grey. Better you become a princess instead."

"I can become a princess. Like Princess Di?" Veronica's bedroom walls were busy. And in amongst the clutter of little pony and mermaid posters, in pride of place above her bed, was a pinup picture of Princess Di. Veronica declared Princess Di to be the most beautiful lady in the whole wide world. I was with her on that and could never figure out why she'd married a big-eared Royal pillock with corgi shit on his shoes.

"Of course, yes, like Princess Di. Do you want to go and see her?"

"Me see Princess Di? For real?

"Yes for real. Mom read somewhere that she's coming to Harare. I thought we'd go and see her on the side of the road."

Veronica managed to swoon and shriek at the same time.

On the day of the Royal visitation, Veronica got dressed in her best and only tutu and plastic tiara and kicked us all out of bed when it was still dark. Veronica wanted us in position on the airport road before all the good spots were taken. The road in from the Harare airport is long on dry and dusty and short on shade. We found a good vantage point on a long straight bit of road so that Diana couldn't sneak upon us. We hurriedly set up our deck chairs and commenced waiting. And then we waited some more. And then we waited some more. We pretty much had the road to ourselves. The sandwiches were eaten in the first half-hour, and then it started to get pretty hot out. With the sandwiches out of the way, Daniel lost his humour. The word 'celebrity' wasn't in his vocabulary yet, and as far as he could make out, we were just spending the day in the sun on the side of the highway. Eventually, another car stopped down the road from us. At first we thought it was some other royal spotters, but it turned out to be a guy who needed a wee behind a tree.

I was starting to have some serious internal doubts as to whether there was room for royalty in the modern age when some other royal groupies arrived; who promptly made us feel inadequate by pulling out little Union Jacks and bits of red, white and blue bunting. Crap. We were underprepared. Diana would mistake us for stranded motorists, broken down on the side of the road. Jenny came to the rescue and produced a red ballpoint pen and a blue ballpoint pen from her handbag with a flourish. Gary got busy and transformed the car toilet roll into royal bunting fit for a not very fussy princess. It took forever, but we had all the time in the world. Princess Di was in no apparent hurry.

The tension ramped up from no tension at all to loads when a pair of motorcycle outriders roared past with sirens blaring. Veronica waved her royal toilet roll bunting at them. Then a whole procession of blurred cars roared past at huge speed, buffeting us in the process, forcing Veronica to hang onto her tiara. My efforts at royal spotting were rewarded with severe instant whiplash. And then we saw Diana, the Princess Royal.

To tell you the truth, I was bit disappointed. Sitting in the sun on the side of the road for hours, I'd built up a Disney picture in my head of a beautiful princess in an open pumpkin sort of carriage, waving at us regally, flashing us with her Colgate smile. What we actually got was a glimpse of her left hand and a blur of royal jewellery on her wrist for about a nanosecond, through the back windscreen of her speeding blue BMW.

I stood there hot and sunburned, wishing that Diana had bigger hands. I wasn't just disappointed; I was mortally wounded and felt a full-blown rant coming on. Diana was the Princess of Wales, and she didn't even have the decency to roar past us in a Rolls Royce as opposed to a bloody German car. But then I looked down at Veronica with eyes sparkling and her face an absolute picture of joy. I had the happiest child in the world, and all it had cost me was a few hours in the hot sun.

Chapter Thirteen

Farming was a means to an end, a way of working at home so I could watch my children grow up, but farming grew on me quickly, pardon the pun. Planting stuff in the ground and watching it grow into something you could sell for money was hugely satisfying, apparently. I hadn't got to the hugely satisfying bits of farming yet. But I was enjoying the long full days, rising up with the sun to face the challenges of farming head-on. It made me feel all tough and manly but with some science involved. Apparently and according to my new best friend The Farmer's Weekly, farming was no longer a way of life and was now regarded as a science, involving the three Ps – planning, precision and the third one escaped me. But I prided myself on my management skills and looked forward to putting my own spin on farming.

The old contract brickmaker knocked on my office door, again, for about the third time that morning. I ignored him out the corner of my eye. "Go away," I shouted. I was guessing the brickmaker wasn't banging on my door to tell me good news, but I was already having a bad hair day and didn't have room for more headaches. The truck was full of bloody flowers waiting to go to the airport, waiting for me to print the bloody pack list but I couldn't print because the bloody electricity had gone on the bloody fritz. I couldn't start the bloody generator, and so I was going to have to write the pack list out in bloody longhand, but one of the bloody kids had pinched my pen, and I was getting visitors from the Dutch Auctions to look at the new variety and ...there was more banging at the door. The brickmaker was back, but this time he had Raphael with him. "Tell him to come back later, Raphael. I'm too busy to see him right now. There's no electricity. The truck's waiting to go to the airport. And I haven't done the bloody pack list yet and..."

"That's why he needs to see you, sir."

"He needs to see me because I haven't done my pack list yet?"

"No. He needs to see you because there is no electricity. He fucked it up."

"He fucked up the electricity?"

"Yes. And the pickaxe."

I groaned. My bad hair day looked to be getting worse, with next stop terrible.

If my bad hair day was bad, the old brickmaker's day was panning out even worse. From behind, he looked like a bomb victim whose home address was Armageddon. I could've sworn I saw smoke coming from the peppercorns on his head. And what little was left of his overalls still looked to be smouldering. Below his knees, the overalls were in tatters, from which his skinny legs and horny bare feet stuck out like an after-thought. Not that the brickmaker had looked too good to start with.

I'd had my doubts about hiring a man who looked to be about a hundred and five, especially for a hard manual-labour job. But Raphael had shouted me down. "Very old is good, he told me. "Very old means lots of experience, and he'll give us good strong bricks to build staff houses. Plus, he's cheaper than buying bricks." I wanted to build a new compound for the staff, but the costs of bricks and other inputs were staggeringly high and off-putting. Raphael had come up with the novel idea of making our bricks on the farm. It would save us a fortune he told me. All we needed were ant heaps of which we had plenty, a mould, some coal and a brickmaker to make the bricks. I was continually staggered by this 'Can Do' approach to things. It was entirely new to me. But that was what farming was all about, you just went out and got stuff done. Even if you didn't know what you were doing, even if you didn't have the tools to do the job, you made a plan, and you got the job done.

I okayed Raphael's brick making project. "As long as you know what we're doing, Raphael. As long as we don't kill the old guy."

As we neared the calamity zone, we happened upon the remains of my pickaxe, lying next to the pathway. Raphael picked the ex-pickaxe up gingerly, shook his head sadly and pronounced it to be "Fucked, completely fucked." I remembered back to the day I'd bought the pickaxe. I'd been very proud of my first ever pickaxe when I hefted it in the hardware shop. I'd never owned anything that needed hefting. With a massively heavy solid cast iron head and a stout wooden handle, you could dig through to China with it no problem, the salesman told me. It was a definite, once in a lifetime acquisition, he said. Well apparently I was in line for a refund because my pickaxe wasn't going to be digging any more holes. The metal bits that had once been the pickaxe head were now all twisted and looked like they'd been melted in a microwave. And the stout hardwood handle that was supposed to last all the way through to China had been reduced to splinters.

I looked across to the old brickmaker with newfound respect. He weighed less than the pickaxe, but he'd fucked it up in just a day. And he'd even broken the ant-heap, which takes serious talent. What had once been an ant heap, was now a burnt and charred hole in the ground, knee deep in mud. And rearing up out of the mud in the middle of the crater like angry serpents were two end bits of electrical cable, thick like the top of my legs, all burnt and severed. Set aside neatly on the side of the crater was a five-foot-long section of the broad red cement collar that had until recently been positioned over the top of the cable to protect it from any people with pickaxes who might be digging in the vicinity. The cement collar had the words DANGER – NGOZI – CHENJERA – emblazoned large and in capital letters down its length, with lightning bolts for added emphasis. All of which had clearly been wasted on my old brickmaker who'd obviously bumped into the protective cement collar while digging his way to China. He'd humped the collar out the way, in itself an impressive physical feat, before plunging the pickaxe into the 33 KVA cable with his next blow, while standing knee deep in mud.

I was joined on the edge of the crater by the electricity repair guy who was in search of the fault that had knocked power out across the whole district.

"Damn!" he said. "I think I just found my fault. What the hell happened here?"

"The old guy over there put a pickaxe through the underground electrical cable?"

"He put a pickaxe into a 33 KVA cable, and he's still alive?"

"Ya. But he broke the pickaxe."

"He also knocked out the power halfway across the whole country. Damn but he's done a number on that cable. I don't think I've ever seen cable as burnt and buggered as that. We're going to have to replace this whole section. Do you know how expensive this stuff is? It's going to cost you an arm and a leg."

"Me? Don't look at me. I didn't stick a pickaxe in your cable. Send him the bill."

"Yeah, right."

"You are going to be able to fix it, aren't you? This morning?"

More sardonic laughter.

I'd just finished writing out the pack lists in longhand, in triplicate because my carbon paper was also missing in action when the next agricultural challenge rose up and smacked me in the face with a shovel.

"Quick, Boss, quick," Raphael wailed, all out of breath and anxious. "You must come quickly, Boss, now!!"

"Calm down, Raphael, just calm down, take a few deep breaths and tell me slowly and clearly what the problem is and how I can help."

"Ok, Boss." Raphael sat down on my visitor's chair and took a deep breath. And then another. And then another. And then another.

The suspense got to me. "Oh, for fuck's sake, Raphael, out with it, I haven't got all bloody day. C'mon, tell me what the problem is."

"OK Boss. The madam's cow has fallen down the fucking well, sir."

"What do you mean the madam's cow's fallen down the fucking well?"

Raphael spelt it out helpfully. "I mean the cow belonging to the madam has fallen down the fucking well. It was grazing next to the well, but now it has fallen inside the well, one of the black and white ones, sir." We only had black and white cows.

"What? The cow's fallen in the well? It's actually fallen inside the bloody well? How the hell did that bloody happen?"

Raphael offered up gravity as a possible cause under his breath.

"Gravity? Did you just say gravity? What the fuck has gravity got to do with it?" Already my arms and legs were rushing off in different directions at the same time. "And what the fuck are you doing there on the chair, deep breathing like you're in labour? We need to act, man, we've got a crisis on our hands. I'll phone the vet. I'll tell him it's an emergency. C'mon, c'mon, Raphael, quick, quick, quick!!!"

We had two dry, disused wells on the farm, one was nine metres deep and the other a massive, bone-shattering forty-five metres deep. Predictably, Jenny's stupid bloody cow had chosen the deepest well to fall into. A crowd from the compound had gathered around the well, easily recognisable by the cow's black and white bum sticking out of it. My vertigo kicked in viciously just thinking about the forty-five metres sheer drop down into the bowels of the earth, and my legs went all wobbly. I didn't do heights too well, or depths, so I inched up to the hole nervously, for a peek. I'd just edged my face nervously over the edge of the well when the cow let out a mournful bellow, right by my head, causing me to nearly shit in my pants. The stupid cow in the well was nowhere near the snug fit I was hoping for. There were huge gaping chasms on either side of the animal and for the life of me, I couldn't figure out why she hadn't long plummeted to her death. And then my eyes adjusted to the dark half-light and I made out the two narrow metal fencing standards, one either side of the animal's shoulders. They were W profile fencing standards, no more than an inch and a half wide, and set into the concrete collars that lined the top six feet of the well. The cow had somehow managed to nose-dive between them, and the skinny bits of metal were the only things between the cow and the bowels of the earth forty-five metres below. And as I watched, I saw the fencing standards sag and give a bit. They weren't going to hold the cow's weight forever. But what to do?

Lying next to the poor cow's backside, I racked my brains desperately looking for a scientific solution. This didn't take long because my brains were short on science. The only word that popped out was a dreadful one. Vivisection. A dreadfully harsh part of me that the rest of me didn't like grabbed hold of the word with both hands. Kill the cow up and cut it up with a chainsaw the harsh me urged, before the fencing standards give. Rump steaks in the hand were worth more than a dead cow at the bottom of a deep hole. I was about to put the 'Turn the cow into steaks' idea to Raphael and the other workers when the vet arrived, at a stroll. I stopped panicking. Charles Waghorn was one of the most relaxed, laid back men I'd ever met. He didn't do stressed. He was exactly what I needed in a crisis situation. I all but hugged and kissed him. "Thank God you're here, Charles, I've got a cow stuck in a well, and I don't know what to do."

"I see that," Charles said. "And she looks like quite a nice cow from the little bit I can see."

"What should we do, Charles?"

"I think you should get her out the well."

"But how?"

"I have no idea. But I will watch with interest." He unfolded himself up against a nearby tree.

Crap. I went back to panicking and my vivisection plan. Raphael was horrified and flat out refused to kill the cow.

"But we've got a vet here so we can kill it humanely," I argued. But to no avail. Raphael was adamant. We were going to save the cow, even if it killed us. "But how?" I wailed. "We just need to get a rope around the middle of the cow, and then we just need to lift and pull," Raphael said.

"But how?" I wailed. I was learning a lot about myself, as in don't call me when next you have a cow stuck in a well.

Getting the rope around the middle bit of the cow wasn't going to be easy, not without someone climbing down inside the well with the animal. I really did want to put my hand up for the job and lead from the front, but my vertigo shouted me down in a hurry. There was no way it was going climb down into a forty-five-metre hole. Better we have rump steak for dinner, it shouted. But before I could even go through the motions of being brave, a rush of people pushed forward to do the job. Raphael chose one of the younger workers. With a safety rope tied around his waist and a length of thick rope between his teeth, he shimmied down in between the wall of the well and the bulk of the cow until he found one of the W section fencing standards with his tippy toes. Balanced precariously on fencing standard that had to be very close to giving in, he somehow managed to thread the thick rope around the beast before scampering back out the hole, job done. All that was left was to pull the beast up out of the hole. Again, I couldn't see how that was going to be possible.

The middle of the cow that had the rope tied around it was at least six foot below the lip of the well and even if we had a hundred people tugging on the end rope, we weren't going to pull that cow out, not without pulling it through a whole chunk of Mother Earth in between. Unless...unless ... wham. Inspiration hit me like a freight train. Panama Canal. What if we dug like an inclined canal or a cow extraction chute, down one side of the well to the depth of the cow, then we'd be able to slide her up and out no problem. Obviously, we'd have to remove the concrete collars that lined the top of the well, which would be a hell of a job in itself but doable. Or we could just bash out a section of the concrete collar the width of my cow extraction chute, again hard work but doable.

While I worked through the ramifications of the massive engineering task at hand, Raphael erected a simple tripod of gum poles up above the well and pulled the cow out, no problem. Because there were no shortage of difficult calculations to make, not least of all the upward angle of the incline of my escape chute, I wasn't able to pay much attention to proceedings and consequently got a hell of a fright when the stupid cow popped out the well and landed back on terra firma, mooing loudly, right next to where I was working on my calculations. It looked around and within seconds, resumed grazing, utterly nonplussed at having just spent an hour in a deep dark hole, suspended forty-five metres above certain death. I, on the other hand, was utterly shattered and needed a rest. And it wasn't even nine o'clock in the morning yet. Charles Waghorn, the vet, gave both the cow and me a quick examination and pronounced us none the worse for wear for our ordeal.

I'd only been back in my office for ten minutes, all of them spent power drinking strong coffee to settle frayed nerves when Raphael came to tell me that my Dutch visitors had arrived. The leader of the tour party was Jaap, a representative of the flower breeder whose varieties I grew. Jaap was my flower guru, a frequent visitor and fast becoming a friend. The others in his group were from the Dutch auction where I sold my flowers. They were in Zimbabwe to visit old growers and to vet the new one. They were all intrigued by my farming pedigree, from hotelier to flower grower in a year and one of them, a crusty farmer type with a weathered face and hard hands, was candid enough to express his concerns as to whether I would make the grade in the world's toughest market. Where they came from, he told me, farming was a generational occupation, a bloodline thing where farmers followed the footsteps of their parents and their grandparents before them. I lied through my teeth and told him I'd been born with green fingers and was descended from a long line of Dutch horticulturalists. As far as I knew, the only thing my grandparents on either side grew were weeds. But my visitors seem to buy my bullshit. Emboldened, I went on to inform them that farming was no longer a way of life, it was now a science, underpinned by planning, precision and the other P whose name continued to escape me. Using those principals and my considerable management skills, I would uplift and empower my workers and instil in them a sense of pride in their work and in the flowers that they grew, blah, blah, blah. I could have listened to me talk all day I was that good, but my visitors couldn't. They were on a tight schedule they said and asked if we could do the farm tour.

I headed for the Hypericum, a new variety, grown for its berries rather than its flowers. I didn't know much about Hypericum, but the numbers were very exciting, and I'd taken a bold punt on a hectare, planted into new purpose-built tunnels that I'd only just finished building. The tunnels were my very own design. There were eighteen of them in a line, all things of beauty. As we walked up to them, the crusty Dutch farmer in the group picked up on my unique flat roof design. I was rather pleased he'd noticed. The design was my very own. I bumped into it entirely by accident. My attempts to bend the 40 mm metal tubing into uniform curves had failed spectacularly over and over again. Over a very long and disappointing day, I discovered that it was much easier to bend steel tubing in straight angles, rather than treacherous curves and so I'd invented the angular design tunnel, which I called the Eric 2000. The angular approach gave my tunnels a very clean, sharp, almost aerodynamic look. "They look good, don't they?" I said to my visitors while patting myself on the back.

"But how will the water drain off when it rains, and your roof is flat on top?"

I stopped patting myself on the back. "Good point ...um... These are just prototypes, though and..."

"Eighteen prototypes?"

"But you haven't flown all this way just to look at tunnels. Why don't we go inside and a look at the Hypericum instead?"

"Why are you growing Hypericum under plastic?" the crusty old bastard Dutch farmer asked. He was a real twenty questions man. "Aren't you worried about rust?"

"Rust? I don't think we'll find any leaves with rust on them." Rust was a leaf disease that I'd picked up on for the first time just the day before. According to my textbook, rust was bad news, especially if it got out of hand. But I was on safe ground. I knew there was no rust on my Hypericum because I'd sent staff into to the tunnels to pick off the infected leaves before the Dutch got there.

It was one of the more embarrassing 'Voila' moments of my life. As soon as I stepped into the first tunnel with my Dutch visitors, I could tell straight away that my staff had done an extremely thorough job on rust removal. There were thousands of plants in the tunnel, each of them over a metre tall, and not one of them had a single leaf on it. Not a single leaf. On the plus side, there was no rust either.

"Very clean crop," the crusty old bastard Dutch farmer commented. "In Holland we like to leave some of the leaves on, for photosynthesis."

Mindful of their tight schedule, I whistled my visitors through the bald Hypericum at pace. I slowed down only when we got to a block of ready to harvest Asters. As per planning, Raphael and the harvesting team were already in place. With Asters, I was on safer ground. Asters aren't prone to rust, so mine had all their leaves on. And fortuitously, the tour block of Asters was easily the best I'd ever grown. Standing with my back to the crop, I elaborated at length on the crop's strong points; good length, good weight, good colour, no rust, no other diseases, no pests, etc., etc."

"What about your cut stage?" the crusty old bastard Dutch farmer had his hand up in the air again.

"Cut stage? I'm glad you asked about that. Because we have to fly the flowers to the other side of the world, we take extra care to harvest the flowers when the first bud is just starting to show colour. If we leave them any longer, in our heat the flowers will get to Holland overblown."

"Then why haven't you started picking these ones?"

"No, we have started picking them," I replied firmly.

"No, you haven't," he replied, equally firmly.

I spun around and crap, the old crusty bastard Dutch farmer, was right. There was Raphael with twenty harvesters complete with buckets and bloody secateurs just standing there, not picking a single bloody flower. As I watched, I could actually see the bloody Asters bursting into bloom. Calmly and collectedly and with a broad false smile fixed in position, I rushed across to Raphael. "Why aren't you harvesting the fucking flowers, Raphael?" I hissed under my breath.

"Because there is a big fucking snake in the flowers, Boss, a fucking big green one!!" Raphael smiled back at me.

Snakes in Africa are a showstopper, especially fucking big ones. Fucking was an excellent adjective to denote the length of a reptile and Raphael used it often because every snake he ever saw happened to be a fucking big one. And along with all the other workers on the farm, Raphael was absolutely petrified of snakes. I peered into the dense foliage but saw nothing. "Are you sure you saw a snake, Raphael?"

"Yes, I'm sure, Boss. It was a fucking big one."

I stepped up to the flowers for a closer look, rather reluctantly because I'm not too keen on snakes either.

"Be careful Boss. I think it was fucking poisonous too," Raphael pointed out helpfully.

With my heart hammering in my chest, I forced myself down on my haunches to see what I could see. Still nothing. "Where did it go in Raphael?"

"There, right there where you're kneeling, Boss."

I gave a quick involuntary bunny-hop backwards. But mindful of the Dutch spectators watching, I hurried another closer look. Still nothing. I was starting to feel foolish. "If your big fucking snake slithered in here, then why can't I see it, Raphael?"

"Because the snake was green, Boss, the same colour as the flowers."

Crap. Another involuntary bunny-hop backwards and I was next to Raphael again. Behind me, the Dutch were looking on with great interest. I shouted over my shoulder to fill them in on what was happening. "Stand well back there. We've got a bit of a situation here with a poisonous snake in the flowers, a rather large poisonous snake. But don't worry. Raphael and

I are going to have to go into the harvest area to kill the snake because it's interfering with the harvest..."

"We are?" Raphael asked in a small voice. Going in after the snake and not away from it was the most stupid idea he'd ever heard. Away was the direction God invented right after he made snakes.

I had to put loads of steel into my voice to anchor him next to me. "Yes!! Raphael and I are going to walk into the flowers and kill the serpent!!" I don't know where the word serpent came from, but it was epic and entirely in keeping with the moment. In the movies, the word would've been punctuated with a drum roll. In real life, for sure it would have been punctuated by the pitter-patter of Raphael's large feet as he fled for distant hills, but for my vice-like grip on his shoulders. I flashed a quick look over my shoulder. The Dutch in amongst the harvesting team were all eyes and had cameras rolling. I could hear their collective heartbeats hammering. I used the vice like grip to pull Raphael in close. "Go and get two sticks, one for you and one for me" I hissed. "And if you don't come back, I'll kill you worse than any fucking snake!!"

"Yes, Boss," he gulped, all big eyes, bobbing Adam's apple and beads of sweat.

The twig that Raphael brought back for me to wield was pathetic. I'd be hard-pressed dealing with a blind worm let alone fucking big snakes. For himself, Raphael had gone with a gum pole that big he could hardly pick it up, let alone wield it. It was fully deserving of the adjective fucking big. Raphael's fucking big gum pole entered the killing field of blooming Asters, eventually followed by him and then me, prodding him from behind with my pathetic twig. The silence was deafening, apart from Raphael's laboured breathing. Raphael stopped, he was wilting fast under the weight of the big fucking pole and the suspense of the moment. I jabbed him viciously with the pathetic twig, and we took another step into the killing field. A drop of sweat larger than my nose rolled down it. And then there was a sudden flash of movement beneath the foliage right in front of us. Raphael screamed something that sounded like Banzai, I nearly shat in my pants and Raphael's fucking big gum pole scythed through a huge swathe of Asters. But there was nothing, apart from the huge swathe of buggered Asters. "Thought I saw something," Raphael breathed.

"Me too."

"We took another step forward.

"There."

"Where?"

"There." Raphael's fucking big gum pole came thundering down, again and again, and again, smiting everything and anything beneath it. Eventually, Raphael stopped, only because he didn't possess superhuman strength, and we peered down into destruction. More silence. Abruptly broken by Raphael's triumphant cries. "I got it, I got it, I got it, I got it!!"

Behind him, Dutch cameras clicked furiously, and the watching workers ululated loudly. And next to him, I grumped silently and bitterly. I, I, I, not a single fucking we anywhere. And then we saw the snake, or what was left of it, in amongst the destruction of the flower crop. The snake was all of six inches long. It was pathetic, even more pathetic than my twig. But that didn't stop Raphael from picking it up and holding it aloft, in triumph. I was horrified. "That's it? That's all of it? You destroyed a whole field of flowers to kill a fucking worm?"

Raphael smiled for the cameras. But I couldn't let it go. "I thought you said it was fucking big?"

"It would have grown up to be fucking big," Raphael told me out the side of his mouth. "If I hadn't killed it now!!"

I like to go to bed, dwelling on the positives from the day, rather than the negatives. It was tough going that night, but eventually, I found one. I woke Jenny up. "You know what Jaap told me today before he left."

"He told you that you were an idiot?"

"Yes, but what else?"

"It's too late for twenty questions Eric, so I give up."

"He said I was lucky.

"Lucky to still be alive?"

"No lucky to be living and farming in Zimbabwe. He wants to come live here when he retires."

"Must be all those dodgy marijuana coffee shops they have in Holland."

"No seriously, Jen, that's what he said. Zimbabwe is Jaap's retirement destination of choice. You know he travels the world. North America, South America, the Caribbean, you name it, and he's been there, but Zimbabwe is where he wants to live when he retires."

"Like I said, I think smoking in all the dodgy coffee shops has addled him."

Chapter Fourteen

I stopped reading the Sunday Mail in 1995, which was a bugger. Without a big fat Sunday paper to read, you had a big hole in your Sunday between getting up and having lunch. And no Sunday paper meant you missed out on which team had beaten Liverpool on the Saturday and all manner of other interesting news. But I had no choice but to give up on all of that when I saw my first racist Affirmative Action Group advert.

Abhorrent is a very strong word, it is right up there with hate. It means repugnant, loathsome, and detestable. Used in the context of the Sunday Mail adverts, abhorrent was an understatement. The first advert I saw, and the one that still sticks out in my mind these many years later, was a full-page advert showing a photo of a black man being squeezed to death by the biggest anaconda in the world. The snake was beyond huge, and the poor guy caught up in its coils didn't stand a chance. According to the not so small print at the bottom, the snake depicted how the white community in Zimbabwe feasted on poor black people, squeezing the crap out of them in the process. The advert and its message were that disgusting and that disturbing, I trashed the paper before Jenny, and the kids saw it. Goebbels would have been proud of the advert, designed to stoke the fires of racial hatred. The advert had been paid for by the Affirmative Action Group, a bunch of black millionaires feasting at the national trough looking to become billionaires, by punting an indigenisation drive. That was the last Sunday Mail I allowed in the house.

A footnote in the middle of the page on the founding members of the Affirmative Action Group. It was headed up by a racist called Boka who made headlines when he became the first black Zimbabwean to own a bank and then made more headlines shortly after that when he broke his brand-new bank. He was also on the record for his point-blank refusal to be interviewed by white journalists. One of his AAG lieutenants was Phillip Chiyangwa, Mugabe's chameleon nephew, who had been a proud and enthusiastic British South African Police reservist right up until his uncle Robert won the elections. Boka's other lieutenant, Peter Pamire, died when his rough, tough Mitsubishi Pajero hit a shallow pothole in one of Harare's most affluent streets. Unfortunately, they never got to the bottom of the actual cause of death because both car and body were removed by the CIO before post-mortems and investigations were carried out. Pamire was rumoured to be the First Boyfriend at the time. A friend of mine who had business dealings with Pamire showed me the logbook of the soft-top go faster BMW sports car he'd bought from Pamire just before his death.

The sports car was registered in the name of Grace Marufu, who went onto becoming the Second First Lady a short while later. My friend took Gary and Dan for a spin in the open-top BMW, and they held their arms up in the air as if they were on a roller coaster and squealed the whole way excitedly. Grace sure must have hated giving that car up.

Back to the Sunday Mail adverts. They threw a massively disturbing shadow across the quiet, happy waters of my life. But what to do about them? Looking back now, I should've uprooted my family there and then move to greener pastures in Australia or similar. But I didn't. Like Anne Frank's dad, I ignored the shit storms gathering on the horizons and bumbled on in the hope that things would get better. Mostly it was all Enoch Dumbutshena's fault.

Enoch Dumbutshena was Zimbabwe's first black Chief Justice. I knew the man's name from the newspapers but would've walked past him in the street without knowing it. The first time I saw Dumbutshena was when Jen and I were invited to some fundraising function at the Holiday Inn, and the Chief Justice was the after-dinner speaker. Tall and scholarly looking, he looked like a Chief Justice, and I started yawning before he even stood up. But then he spoke. He started with a humorous anecdote that got the whole room smiling. But the smiles fell away quickly as he got into the meat of his subject- Zimbabwean politics and everything that was wrong with it, namely Mugabe. He spoke about the rampant corruption and the blatant disregard for the laws of the land, the stupidity of cult politics and the sycophantic adoration and equally stupid policies it spawned.

Dumbutshena came across as humble, intelligent and insightful. And brave. You had to be brave to stand up in public and speak the way he did about Mugabe. Dumbutshena went onto say he could no longer stand by and watch as the country was run into the ground by stupid politicians and their stupid policies and had decided to form a political party called the Forum Party and contest the forthcoming general elections. Up until then, I didn't even know there were going to be elections. Dumbutshena's announcement wasn't greeted by wild cheers and ululation because it wasn't that kind of crowd, it was a bunch of mostly stodgy whites with stiff upper lips, but in my heart of hearts, I was up on my feet, going crazy.

I rushed home and dared to hope. All night long, I tossed and turned, daring to hope of a Zimbabwe where all were equal, where my children and their children's children could have a happy and prosperous future. As soon as I woke up, and before my euphoria wore off, I tracked Raphael down to infect him with Dumbutshena's enthusiasm for the future. The night before Dumbutshena had spoken for about twenty minutes, max. With Raphael, I must have gone on for more than an hour. Looking back, that was the first of a million political discussions I would have with Raphael in the years ahead.

On the strength of my feel good about the future, I went out and bought another farm. Mostly because Dan couldn't fly kites on Running Dog, and because three into two doesn't go.

Daniel first brought up the subject of farm shopping when I took him kite flying. In the absence of wind, kite flying requires lots and lots of forward momentum, which in turn requires lots and lots of room to run, especially if I've had anything to do with the aerodynamic design of the kite. I've met bricks that fly better than my kites. Lots of open spaces and lots of room to run was now a problem on Running Dog because I'd filled the place up with tunnels and greenhouses. Every time Daniel and I tried to launch the kite, we ended up all tangled in greenhouse stay wires. And so, I took Dan across to the Homefield Centre to fly his kite.

The Homefield Centre, a home for mentally challenged adults, was just down the road from Running Dog. They had a hundred-hectare field with a gentle slope, perfect for kite launching. But we encountered a problem. Daniel couldn't run fast enough to get our kite airborne. He was supposed to run behind me holding the kite while I ran out in front with the ball of string. One of the Homefield residents, a very happy young man called Billy, volunteered his services. Billy was certainly fleet of foot. If anything, he was too fleet. On our first two launch attempts, he kept overtaking me with the kite in hand, which was a problem. And a source of amusement for Daniel.

And so, we switched roles. I made the fleet of foot Billy the lead-out man while I brought up the rear with the kite. It all went swimmingly well to start. My lead-out man shot off down the hill like a bunny rabbit, and I followed as best I could with the kite. Small wonder I could feel the winds buffeting the kite. We were running at a hell of a lick. Until my lead-out man reached the one and only tree in the field. Predictably, it was a thorn tree. And unpredictably, Billy felt compelled to run around the tree as if he was on a merry go round. Disaster. Which again Dan found fairly amusing. We untangled the kite eventually and trudged back up the slope to try again, but this time with me as the lead-out man. Same results. As soon as we got to the tree, again Billy insisted on running around and round the trunk with the kite. Daniel found it all most amusing and didn't want us to stop. But after flight attempt thirteen, I had to stop because total exhaustion had set in.

"That was fun, Dad. But it would have also been fun if we got the kite to fly. If only we had a bigger farm."

Despite my sock and underpants drawer suggesting otherwise, I am quite an orderly person. I like it when things match up. Maybe I was a sheepdog in a previous life. The night of the many aborted kite flights, I lay in bed and pondered. The thought of leaving Gary a farm, Veronica a hotel and Daniel nothing when I die hit me like a shovel in the face at two in

THE NEW FARM

the morning. And it was even worse than that, the George Hotel was only leased. What would happen if they didn't renew the lease? Crap. Then it would be even worse, Veronica would be out her inheritance, and it would be three into one. And the one was a very small farm. I had to get busy. I woke Jenny up. "We have to buy another farm."

"You've woke me up in the middle of the night to tell me that you have to buy another farm?"

"Yes. I'm stupid. It's been staring me in the face. I should've started looking earlier."

"I'm not arguing with you on the stupid."

"You're not?"

"No. I'm in agreement there. But tell me what's been staring you in the face?"

"We've got three kids. And we've only got two businesses."

"So?"

"So what are we going to leave the third kid when we die?"

"Daniel's not even six yet, and you're starting a business for him. This is nothing about inheritance. You're bored, and you like starting new businesses. Now shut up and go back to sleep."

"And plus Running Dog is too small to fly kites on," I added. Jenny hit me in the ribs hard with her elbow. She can be quite crabby. Like her Granny Fulton. I lay awake next to her and carried on pondering.

Farms were more expensive than I thought so I had to cobble together a consortium to buy the new farm. First up was an Irish friend called Brian Whelan with an appetite for life larger than himself. There was nothing he wasn't keen to try. And he especially loved Zimbabwe and jumped at the chance of owning a farm in Africa. The others on my list of potential partners were my agronomists, Steve and JC, clever young men with agricultural degrees and heads full of long words that were hard to spell.

With a consortium in place, Brian and I made an appointment to see Murray Dawson who lived down the road. Murray had lots of spare land. Maybe he could sell me some. I took Brian along to head up negotiations because he was big business personified and had driven multimillion-dollar projects the world over.

Murray lived in a big rambling house perched on top of a hill with his brother Terry who was wheelchair bound after a parachute accident in the war. I told Murray that we were looking to buy some farming land for a new project. He sat and listened impassively. If you were meeting Murray for the first time, he came across slow. But his farm told a different story. It was vertically integrated to the nth degree. Murray sold the vegetables he grew through his own vegetable wholesale company, the cattle from his feedlot were slaughtered in his abattoir and the meat sold in his butcheries. The bread that was baked in the on-farm bakery was made with flour that was milled from the winter wheat grown under Murray's centre pivots. I primed Brian there was more to Murray than met the eye, but he laughed. Brian was a hardball negotiator who'd cut his teeth doing seven-figure dollar deals on the oil fields of Libya whereas Murray only ever wore khaki clothes, morning, noon and night.

Going into the first meeting, I felt sorry for Murray. I'd sat him down at the table with a hungry shark. As it turned out, I shouldn't have worried. There might have been a few flies on Murray but there were none on his lawyers, or his accountants, or his real estate agent or his tax consultant.

The first meeting was very short. Brian did all the talking, using lots of long buzzwords and phrases. I kept quiet on strict instruction from Brian on account of the fact I have a poker face like a beagle puppy. Murray sat and listened. He only asked two questions. How much land were we looking to buy and how much were we prepared to pay? And then he sent us away. He needed time to think. And time to talk to the lawyers, the accountants, the real estate people and the tax consultant without flies on them. Murray knew what he didn't know and hired the best people who did.

Long story short, Brian and I came away with the land we wanted, but we paid top dollar and then some. Our new farm was a thousand hectares of undeveloped land, with good soils and good water and nice trees. And most importantly for me, it was just eight kilometres from Running Dog, if I took the short cut through the rest of Murray's farm. I had a grand plan for the farm that the others bought into. We'd cut the farm up into twenty sections of fifty hectares each, each member of the consortium would keep a section, and we'd sell the rest to people who wanted to grow cut-flowers for export. We would make a handsome profit selling off the land and would use some of that to put in central cold rooms and start up marketing companies and the like. The project was called Quality Flowers. It read really well on paper, and we got lots of interest. One of my selling points was that the project when finished, by weight of the value of the improvements, would be land-grab proof if ever the government went ahead with the land redistribution program people were talking about. At the time, there was a quaint belief that the government would compensate farmers whose land was taken for their improvements. Alas. As it turned out, I got that a tad wrong.

While Brian the architect got busy with the big picture subdivision plan, we all set to planting out crops and putting in infrastructure on our fifty-hectare sections. Brian, JC and Steve put up greenhouses for roses while I went the field flower route. They spent more on their pack-shed roof than I spent on my whole project. It all went swimmingly well. I was able to spend enough time on the new farm without losing control of Running Dog. Until the rains kicked in. Murray's farm had deep red soils and his farm roads were graded with pronounced cambers, and my eight-kilometre short cut became an impenetrable bog. The long way around to the new farm was thirty minutes through town and traffic. I don't do traffic to good, so I persevered with the mud. I got to know the mud well. Every time it rained. Murray's deep red soils and I'm talking beyond knee deep, sucked me in like the Bermuda Triangle every time it drizzled.

On Christmas Eve, which also happens to be my birthday, Murray's fields took my entire fleet hostage. I was the first to slide off into a field of potatoes in my pick-up truck. It was almost dark, and a gentle rain had started falling. And as it did, I slid gently off the camber and into the potatoes. At the time, I had an annoying Christmas carol playing in my head, like elevator music, going on and on about joy to the world. Bollocks. And then as I watched in the rear-view mirror, my three-ton truck, full of flowers destined for my cold room, hit the same treacherous bit of road and also slipped gently down into the mud next to me. Double bollocks. Murray was away in Mozambique for the holidays, so I couldn't ask him for help. This was in the days before cell phones, so my driver had to hump the three kilometres in the wet to Running Dog, while I sat in the bog, guarding flowers, cursing and feeling decidedly un-Christmassy.

Forty minutes later, headlights in the distance cheered me up no end as the driver came barrelling along the road in my tractor. Salvation at last. But then another alas. The driver duly hit the camber at speed, ploughed off deep into the field and as I watched in horror, the two front wheels of the tractor disappeared from view completely. Yet more bollocks. And another extended bout of cursing while the driver tramped off to fetch Jenny in our last remaining vehicle. Forever later, another set of headlights breached the dark depths of my misery. Jenny had come to rescue me in her car. By then, I'd decided against any rescue heroics. The vehicles and the flowers could spend the night in mud, and I'd make a plan in the morning. All I wanted to do was get into a hot bath and a beer. I badly needed a beer. This time the headlights crept along at snail speed. Until they hit the camber. At which point they sped up briefly as they slid off to join the rest of the fleet in the mud and spuds. Joy to the world. What a load of bollocks.

January was a wet month. I seemed to spend all of it commuting to the new farm, Quality Flowers. I was starting to hate the new farm, not a good thing for a new venture. In February, the farm right next door to Running Dog came onto the market. It was a big commercial chicken farm. It had good soils, lots of water, two nice houses, a big warehouse, a big office block and most importantly, no mud to get stuck in and no commute. I had to buy it. Brian, Steve and JC paid me out for my shares in Quality Flowers, but not enough to buy the chicken farm. I threw all my creative letter-writing skills at the bank and got the loan. I was thrilled. I was up to my neck in debt for the foreseeable future, but I also had room to grow; from my current two hectares up to thirty-five.

I loved my new farm. It would be perfect for flowers with lands that were long and wide. But to open up the lands, I had to pull the chicken houses down first. There were twenty of them, forty metres wide and a hundred metres long. They were rickety gum pole structures with roofing sheet walls and more roofing sheets on top. They'd been up for over thirty years and were in a hurry to come down. I was standing with the dogs, watching the labour rip off the sheets on the first chicken house. As the corrugated iron sidewall came off with a screech, a sea of rats came pouring out. There were millions of them. The rats were leaving the sinking ship they'd lived in for the last thirty years. The dogs and I stood back and gawped. Well, I gawped right up and until one of the rats ran up my leg. After that, I screamed, panicked and added to the general confusion. The three Jack Russells were the first to dive in and get busy. They were awesome ratters and would grab the rat by the back of the neck with pinpoint precision, two quick shakes, and it was dead, and they were onto the next one. No noise, no fuss. The Beagle, the Boxer and Saint Bernard, on the other hand, were all noise and all fuss but didn't even come close to catching a single rat. In minutes, the multitude of rats, bar the ones the Jack Russells had dispatched, had disappeared into thin air.

Alas. The compound bore the brunt of the rat plague that we'd unleashed. Small children were bitten in their cots and beds at night. And we still had another nineteen chicken houses to pull down. I couldn't picture the plague I'd seen times twenty. My head couldn't do sums that big. We had to kill the rats before they got out of the chicken houses.

We pulled the next house down at night. Half the compound was there, armed with badzas and pick handles. And golf clubs. Gary chose a three iron while I went with a Big Bertha one wood. It was dark inside the chicken house and not a sound to be heard. We'd rigged up floodlights and I flicked the switch and lit the chicken house and surrounds up bright like a football stadium. Let the games begin. The deep chicken litter was piled thirty centimetres deep with not a rat in sight. Maybe they'd already moved on. The dogs suggested otherwise, whimpering and straining against their leashes. We hooked up one of the tractors to one of the internal walls. The tractor took up the strain and then ripped out the flimsy partition and half the roof with it. And suddenly the floor of the chicken house was swimming in a sea of disgusting, filthy rats. About a hundred of them broke towards me. As per standard emergency procedure, I closed my eyes tight but felt one of the disgusting rodents brush up against my leg. I let go the dog leashes, squealed loud like a girl and beat the earth in front of me to a pulp, managing to emasculate Big Bertha, my rodent weapon of mass destruction, by snapping her head off on my first frenzied swing.

Thankfully, the three Jack Russells were infinitely more effective. They were lightning quick, killing rats left, right and centre with vicious shakes of their heads. The terriers didn't have it all their own way. George, the smallest Jack Russell, got bitten on the end of his nose by a rat that was nearly the same size as him. The rat bit in and hung on for dear life. It was a classic Mexican standoff, for about thirty seconds, until one of the other Jack Russells jumped in with jaws flashing.

The other breeds though were not so good at ratting. Like me, they made lots of noise but little impact. Mackenzie the Beagle looked like he'd been gripped by St Vitus Dance. His legs, alerted by his hunting nose to live targets to the front, the rear and both sides, tried to run off in all directions at once. And every now and then he'd break off his seizure to lift his head in a long, loud, mournful howl. Dempsey the Boxer's genetics failed him time and again. He'd corner a rat nicely and snap away like a blender on full speed, but with little or no effect, courtesy of his massively overshot bottom jaw. It's hard to kill something with your bare teeth when the said bare teeth don't even come close to gnashing. Joshua, the Saint Bernard, was easily the most enthusiastic dog in the hunt, and easily the most useless. It is very hard to chase down scampering rodents while dragging seventy kilograms of hugely excited, uncoordinated body mass. After five minutes of frenzied hunt, the massive dog collapsed, knackered and completely exhausted when the rat he'd most recently been chasing nimbly hopped up onto a narrow shelf fixed to the wall some four foot off the floor. Safe and out of harm's way, the rat lingered to laugh and taunt the distraught slobbering Saint Bernard below. Hah. The rat should have paid more attention to the Jack Russell who'd hopped up onto the shelf behind him. But rats, like cats, obviously have more than one allotted life. George pounced. The rat should have been dead meat. But George's teeth slammed shut.... on where the rat had just been, just milliseconds earlier. It was a remarkable escape. But alas for the rat, it was very much a case of out of the pot and into the fire. Well more like into the mouth of the Saint Bernard. Who could not believe his luck. He'd spent the last five minutes sweating blood, chasing rodents left, right and centre and getting nowhere. He takes his first time out to grab some badly needed oxygen, and a kamikaze rat throws itself down his throat. While I watched, Joshua bit down and swallowed, in one fluid movement. God and rats moved in mysterious ways. Joshua spent the rest of the rat hunt, lolling about with his mouth open and his eyes fixed above, waiting for his next bit of largesse.

It was a hell of a rat hunt. Out of the thousands of rats we put up, we killed one hundred and ninety. I say 'we' but I'm not sure if I actually killed any rats personally, on account of having lost the club part of my golf club in the opening salvo. And having my eyes closed for big chunks of the hunt didn't help my kill stats either. I think the Jack Russells were easily on top of the leader board. Gary and his three iron were deadly though. As were the workers with their badzas and pick handles. The workers got to take home the spoils, filling up empty sacks with the dead rodents, which got me to thinking about pots full of rattails, which then got me to retching and heaving.

The main house on the chicken farm was a beautiful house with four bedrooms and a bar and high ceilings and terrazzo floors and a huge swimming pool and a kitchen with a separate laundry and an en suite bathroom with a bidet...and I was the only one who wanted to move into it. The rest of the family were dead set on staying in our old double storey with the funny little loft bedrooms and the cosy little lounge and the bathrooms with the hosepipe plumbing and no bidets. I couldn't believe that no one else wanted to move. It was like buying a new pair of shoes and not wearing them. I set out on an aggressive marketing campaign to win over other influential family members.

"And it's got a bidet in the bathroom, Dan, a proper bidet."

"What's a bidet?"

"It's... um...it's a good thing to have, Dan. Even the Pope's got one."

"Who's the Pope?"

Gary shot my sales spiel down in flames. "A bidet's like a toilet thing that you wash your bum in, Dan."

In the end the only way I got to move into my new house was by inviting Jenny's mom and dad to come and live with us in Zimbabwe. Like his father before him, Tony had been a thirty-year man on the Rhodesian Railways. He'd worked every day of those thirty years as a fitter and turner in the locomotive sheds in Bulawayo, rebuilding Garratt locomotives from scratch. He loved his life's routine and counted down daily to his retirement. But then the transformation from Rhodesia to Zimbabwe came along. Everyone in the know predicted the worst. The wheels were going to come off everything, the Railways included. And so, Tony, along with so many others, felt he had to cash in his pension, sell up house and home and everything else he owned and move on in search of greener pastures.

They settled in Newcastle, a dreary little coal town in Northern Natal and started up from scratch. Tony nearly broke himself, working twelve-hour days and then some, snagging every bit of overtime he could. He put the hard-earned money to good use when the company he worked for sold off all the staff housing. The company was restructuring and refocusing on core business, Tony told me. Things were looking up. Once again, Tony was the proud owner of a roof. But alas, not for long. As it turned out, the real estate clearance sale was just a precursor to the whole bang shoot going bust. Within a month of signing the mortgage documents, the company went under, and Tony was out of a job. And worse than that, he now also had a mortgage to worry about. Tony's former company was one of the biggest in Newcastle, and the local economy went into a tailspin when it closed down. Jobs were hard to find, especially for middle-aged Englishmen who couldn't speak Afrikaans. After a long month of stressing, Tony was eventually able to find work, for longer hours and a smaller pay packet. But at least it was a job. It wasn't long after when Hester suffered her first mini stroke.

Jenny was beside herself with worry. It was eating her up. Even when they were far away, her parents were very close to her. The solution to the problem was obvious to all. Tony and Hester should come and live with us on the farm. That would take away all the stress in their lives. They would have a home and income, and most importantly, Tony would have a job to get up to go to in the morning. And it wasn't just a job, it was a job that would centre on tinkering and fixing and making things. Tinkering and fixing and making things wasn't work for Tony, it was what he did for pleasure and enjoyment. And Hester would have grandchildren nearby to love and bake biscuits and cake for. It was the perfect solution, but Jenny needed me to put the idea up. She didn't want to foist her parents on me.

The idea of Tony coming to help me on the farm struck me as a good idea just seconds after hitting my thumb with a hammer for the third time in a day. The first time is bloody sore, but the third time makes your eyes water properly. With a posse of quietly snickering staff watching on, I hopped and skipped and sucked my thumb like a baby while swearing loudly like a trooper. Which was when I noticed that the row of light masts that I was busy erecting badly was horribly cockeye and out of sync. Even with the most vicious squint and a cricked neck, I couldn't get the poles already in the ground to line up neatly in the row. Crap.

Don't get me wrong. I'm not a perfectionist. For me perfect is a pain in the arse, especially if good enough works out just fine and does the job. But unfortunately, that rule doesn't apply to lines of light masts that your friends and neighbours will drive past and judge every time they come on to the farm. The friends and neighbours would feast upon the cockeye poles until the cows came home. I can't spell DIY to save my life, my right angles are never right and my already very low pain threshold decamped and fled every time I went anywhere near a hammer. And with me wielding the hammer, my new farm would lean horribly before falling apart prematurely, and my friends would get fat from all the nonstop feasting. Unless....unless...I found someone to come and do all the DIY stuff and the hammering and the fixing and the...what about Tony? Tony would be perfect.

Jenny was hugely relieved and hugely thankful when I suggested that we offer her parents a home and a job on the farm. She agreed that it was a great idea. I like being the purveyor of good news, so I made the phone call to Newcastle. Tony choked up a bit on the phone before accepting the offer of a job and a home, again with thanks and lots of relief. I assured him that my motives were entirely selfish. My very low pain threshold couldn't take much more hammering. And Jenny and the kids would have no option but to move into the new house, complete with bidet.

I didn't have too much moving experience. Before marriage, moves didn't really count. They used to take me all of twenty minutes, and half of that was spent trying to get Fred, the dog in the car. Jenny and I had only moved twice after the wedding, once from a garden flat into another garden flat and then again when we moved onto the farm. Both episodes had largely been erased from my memory banks although I still had faint scars on my upper thighs; souvenirs from when Basil the cat from hell had done his damndest to emasculate me after I conned him into the front seat of the car. And after ripping me into bloody bits, he'd shat on my lap. Unfortunately, memories centred on the stench of cat crap are largely un-erasable. Alas.

The distance from the old house to the new house was less than five hundred metres. The move would be a doddle. Trying to get the rest of the family involved was like root canal work. They still had their hand brakes fully on, determined to drag out their stay in the old ramshackle upstairs downstairs house for as long as possible. It had been a very happy home for all of our family life. And so the move was left up to me. I decided to approach it room by room, using the farm truck and farm labour. Given the distances involved, I decided to eschew the use of packing boxes. I purposely invented the Eric carpet and curtain method of moving. It was genius. You walked into the room to be moved. You pushed the furniture in the room aside. First, you took down the curtains and laid them on top of the carpet. Then you wrap up the entire contents of the room, clothing, lights, ornaments and all the bric-a-brac crap that your wife won't let you throw out, into the curtains, making sure not to heap it too much. And then you roll up the curtains and their contents up in the carpets, and you're packed and ready to move. And when you get to the new house, you roll out the carpet, unpack the curtains, hang them up and hey presto, you are done. Bar a whole lot of broken bric-a-brac and ornaments, a lot of which was crap that Jenny should have let me throw out, it was all too easy. As it happened, we got to practice a variation on the Eric carpet and curtain method of moving often in later years, but under less happy circumstances.

The new house was perfect. It had high ceilings and rooms with lots of light and Italian crafted stone floors. It had bedrooms to burn. The main bedroom was huge, with massive built-in cupboards. Veronica and Dan were next to us, each with their own bedroom. Jenny converted the fourth bedroom into her office come sewing room while I turned the last one into a pub, overlooking the pool table and the Jacuzzi on the back veranda. And then there were two outside bedrooms with bathrooms in the garden. Gary appropriated the one furthest from the main house, so he could make lots of noise and do stuff he wasn't allowed to do. The other bedroom we turned into a guest suite. And then, of course, there was the bidet, which I had to hurriedly ban Dan from trying because he got hold of entirely the wrong end of the stick.

Tony and Hester arrived safe and sound and very eager to get on with their new lives. As expected, the kids revelled in having grandparents on tap, especially grandparents with a bottomless jar of homemade cookies, and spent more time at the old house than the new house. And they weren't the only ones. Dempsey, the Boxer, had already defected. He flat out refused to move. And as soon as Tony and Hester moved in, Dempsey became Tony's constant shadow and companion and would follow him around the farm all day. I have to admit the sight of the two grumpy old men trudging across to the farm workshops in the early morning wounded me deeply. Dempsey had never shown the slightest urge to accompany me around the farm, not even when I whistled. Ratfink dog.

The workshop staff were in two minds about their new boss. Tony insisted in speaking Chilapalapa to them, a bastardised language originally invented by South Africa's gold miners to talk to the African labour they'd hired in from across the continent. It was a simple language but was now largely considered demeaning and was now seldom used. Until Tony got on to the farm. "Hamba tata lo sando kamina chop chop," he told Clever, the workshop foreman and farm electrician.

Clever sidled across to me and whispered: "What does he want?"

"I think he wants you to fetch his hammer, chop chop."

As soon as he'd settled in his new house and new job, Tony told me we had to cut out all the dead meat. He said we were doing far too many favours, too many free jobs for others and the unauthorised and unbudgeted expenditure had to go. The workshop staff were bleak. Jobs on the side were how they made their beer money and how they curried favour in the compound. But Tony put a stop to them. Farming was a business he told us and put in a job card system with room for a million signatures, detailing inputs and time spent on the jobs to the nth degree.

About a week into the new system, I walked past the workshops and saw one of the free jobs, standing watching Tony work on his bicycle. The free job's name was Kuda. He was a black kid with polio with callipers that outweighed his wasted legs ten to one. He lived in a sprawling compound in the nearby brickfields but attended school kilometres away on Murray Dawson's Rainham Farm. Unable to walk, Kuda sort of rode to school on an old buggered bicycle, sort of on account of the fact his bike was always falling apart. I'd long given Kuda a free pass to the workshops, and we'd practically rebuilt his bike, many times over, over the years, replacing small broken frames with larger new ones, keeping Kuda on the road. "I hope you've filled out a job card for that bike, Pop."

"Hmmph!!!" Tony snorted, red-faced and embarrassed at having been caught red-handed being kind. "I can hardly charge the poor little bugger!! Not for a come-back job like this, that was done so piss poor badly before!!" By the time Tony finished, Kuda's bike was better than brand-new. Not surprising, given the cost of the new spares that went into it.

But Tony soon won the farm staff over. He was an old school artisan, and when Tony fixed things, they stayed fixed. He and Dempsey trudged around the farm, looking for things that were broken and then fixed them. Cutback after harvest was one of the worst jobs on the farm, especially with blunt secateurs. Tony ran them across his grinding wheel, and they were sharp enough to shave with. Harvesters' trolleys were greased and easy to push. I bought Tony a small lathe to potter on and then we were properly cooking with gas. There was nothing Tony couldn't make on that lathe. For the first time ever, I was able to look across Running Dog and admire things that were straight and not broken. It felt good and more than made up for the pain of losing a dog.

When the elections came around, I decided to get off my arse and vote, mostly because of the Enoch Dumbutshena feel good that still lingered but also because I'd now invested so heavily in my Zimbabwean future. There was a polling station not far from the farm at the government youth training centre. I joined the long queue of voters on polling day and stood patiently, practising putting my cross next to the Forum party candidate. Then eventually, I got to the front of the queue. After showing my ID, I was asked to ink my forefinger. I stepped into the voting booth with pen at the ready, ready to do my bit to change the fortunes of the country. But there was only one box on my polling paper with only the one name next to it, Sabina Mugabe, the ZANU PF candidate and the president's sister. I turned my paper to look on the back, maybe they'd stuck the Forum Party there but still no luck. I stuck my head out the voting booth and called one of the polling officials over. "I've got a problem. I want to vote for the Forum Party, but I can't see their little box anywhere."

"That is because the Forum Party did not put up a candidate for this constituency" he explained. "So, there is only the ZANU PF candidate that you can vote for, Ms Sabina Mugabe."

"But I don't want to vote for her."

"Then don't put a cross on your paper."

I was getting heated under the collar. "But that's a load of bollocks. What sort of bullshit stupid democracy is it where you can only vote for the person you don't want to vote for?" Stupid is a red rag to a bull word, and the polling official's hackles went up. I was starting to attract the attention of the other voters. And the policemen on duty outside the voting station who poked his head in to see what the raised voices were about.

"If you don't want to vote, then you should leave now," the polling official said. "Before I call the police."

"I'll do that. I'll just drive into town and vote there. For the Forum Party, not for bloody Sabina Mugabe!!"

I drove into town. I knew there was a polling station in Avondale, so I headed for that. The queues were long and slow, but I waited patiently, again practising my Forum Party X in my head. At the front of the queue, the polling station officials got excited when they saw my already inked forefinger. I told them that I'd walked away in Mount Hampden without voting because I'd been given a choice between Sabina Mugabe and Sabina Mugabe. "And so I drove into town to come and vote here because at least here the Forum party have fielded a candidate."

The polling station official thought my story was quite amusing. "But I'm afraid you've wasted your time. You can't vote here because your name isn't on the Voter's Roll."

"But...but..."

"It is a constituency-based Voter's Roll. You can only vote in Mt Hampden."

For the second time that day, I almost got arrested for creating a public disturbance in a polling station.

Chapter Fifteen

At my first Running Dog staff Christmas party, there were just four people; me, Raphael, a worker called Joseph, and another called Taffy who ate all the chips. Just a few years later, impossibly there were a hundred and forty workers in the Running Dog time book. And with an average family size of five, that worked out to a staggering seven hundred mouths all feeding off the one small farm, just thirty-five hectares big. It was a huge number that kept me awake at night, worrying. And when I wasn't awake stressing about how I was going to pay all the workers, it seemed I was awake delivering pregnant mothers to the clinic to have their babies. Unfortunately, it is a fact of life that most babies get born at two in the morning.

The very first time Raphael came banging on my bedroom window to tell me that a worker's wife had gone into labour and needed to get to the clinic in a hurry, I told him no problem, I'd phone for an ambulance. He fell over laughing. Apparently, ambulances didn't go onto the farms anymore and hadn't since Rhodesia became Zimbabwe. And so I was the designated driver. Other than it being bitterly cold, the two o'clock trip into town was uneventful. The mom-to-be and her midwife, one of the grading shed supervisors, sat in the back of the pick-up, quiet and stoic, nothing at all like pregnant mothers in the movies. I dropped them off at Harare Hospital and rushed back to my warm bed. The mother and child were back on the farm by eight o'clock the next morning and were paraded in front of my office by the very proud father. To compensate me for a disturbed night's sleep, he'd decided to call his son Eric.

Naming your child after the emergency driver became a Running Dog tradition and before long, there were a dozen Erics and Ericas in the compound. And the one poor kid called Peugeot, named after best friend Mike Matthews's pick-up truck. Mike was visiting the farm one afternoon and got roped in as an emergency driver when a very worried worker came banging on my office door with his wife who looked to be eleven months pregnant and in lots of pain. She was that big I was sure she'd give birth to a teenager. We only just managed to load her and her midwife volunteer into the back of Mike's pick-up truck. She was making lots of very loud 'I'm having a child' noises, so Mike put his foot down flat on the accelerator. Unfortunately, he forgot about the speed humps on our road. Just before he ramped the first one, there were two faces in his rear-view mirror. When he landed, and the dust had settled, there were three.

Mother and child were back on the farm within the hour. Those ladies were so tough and got over childbirth like it was a thorn in the foot. The father was apologetic when he told me that he'd gone with neither Mike nor Matthew as naming options, but he quite liked Peugeot. Hopefully, his son would grow up strong, he told me, just like the pick-up truck.

I wish Peugeot had grown up to work at Running Dog. His name would have been a welcome addition to my time book. I had a competition going with best friend Noel Kent to see whose time book had the best workers' names in it.

Peugeot's mom and dad aside, the Shona put a lot of effort into naming their children, often picking a name that they hoped would have a bearing on the way the kid went in life. The time book was full of Lovemores and Learnmores, there was a Blessing and a Happiness, a God Knows, a Clever Sixpence and even a Typewriter. But sometimes the parents' thought process at the time of birth was less altruistic; I had a Killer on the books, and a Punishment and even a Disaster. But none of them came close to Noel's winning entry. Noel's right-hand man went by the name of Black Face. Noel was a top flower grower and received an endless stream of Dutch visitors on his farm, many of whom would arrive with preconceived ideas about the ills of colonialism. Noel would oblige by shouting for Black Face out his office window and achieved great shock value each and every time. I offered to swop Clever Sixpence and Typewriter for Black Face, but Noel wasn't having any of it. Alas.

HIV Aids has wreaked havoc amongst the Running Dog workforce over the years, and I've lost so many good people to the scourge. Zimbabwe had one of the highest prevalence rates in the world, but the numbers were kept under wraps by a government obsessed with projecting healthy statistics. A doctor friend told me that rate was as high as 50% amongst the sexually active, which was just a roll in the hay away from 100%, scary stuff!

I lost my first farm worker to AIDS in 1994. He was a hardworking sprayer called Maxwell. I watched him go from hale and hearty to skin and bone in weeks; Maxwell had a very fast case of what the cynics called slow puncture disease. The worst were his eyes, they grew suddenly huge and sunken in his skeletal face, and so sad. Maxwell knew he was dying, but he didn't know why. Back then, none of us knew much about AIDS. Government clinics and hospitals mostly sent AIDS patients home to die. I heard about a newly opened palliative care centre at St Anne's Hospital. It was horribly oversubscribed, but I bullied the nuns into giving up one of their precious beds to Maxwell, and he died there a few days later. The palliative care centre at St Anne's didn't last long, utterly overwhelmed and unable to cope with the flood of AIDS patients looking for hope or somewhere decent to die.

We lost our next AIDS victim a short while later. Her name was Memory. She was married to a farm supervisor called Killer, and they had a five-year-old daughter called Fortunate. Killer, Memory and Fortunate; if it weren't so sad, it would be funny.

Unfortunately, Memory died in the compound. Using my brand-new cell phone, I phoned the police from outside Killer's house. I had to shout over the wailing and ululating. In Africa, death and grief are very noisy emotions to be shared with anyone and everyone in earshot. No stiff upper lips and sobbing quietly behind demure handkerchiefs.

"Are you sure the deceased is dead?" the policeman asked.

"Yes, I'm sure the deceased is dead," I shouted. "And if she weren't deceased, then she wouldn't really be one. A deceased that is."

"Huh?" said the policeman. "What did you say?"

"I said I am sure the dead person is really dead, officer."

"And what is the deceased's name?"

"Her name was Memory."

"And her next of kin?"

"Her husband's name is Killer."

"Aha!! It is always the husband!!"

"No, no, no!!" I said hurriedly. "He didn't do anything. She died of AIDS. His name is just Killer."

"Are you sure there isn't any foul play?" The policeman sounded disappointed that murder hadn't been committed.

I'd stepped into the small cramped single room that was home to the small family, and everything looked to be very tidy and orderly, and very sad. "I'm sure there wasn't any foul play, officer. Look, can't you just come and take the body away?"

"Ah!!" the policeman said. I could almost hear him shaking his head on the other end of the conversation. "Transport is a big problem these days."

"I could send a truck to the station to come and collect you."

"Ah no!! I am alone at the station. The other details are on roadblock duty."

"Or we could bring the body in if you like."

"Ah no!!" Another shake of the head. "You are not allowed to move the body. Just in case there are suspicious circumstances."

"But we've got a dead body just lying here. We need to get her buried."

"First, we must do our investigations. Then you need a death certificate."

"Do we get that from the police station?"

"Ah no!! The next of kin must get it. From the Births and Deaths Registry."

"And then can we get her buried?"

"Ah no!! In case there are suspicious circumstances."

"So we have to wait for you to attend?"

"Yes."

OF WORKERS AND MEMORY LOSS

"But you can't attend. Because transport is a problem." I was starting to get

déjà vu dizzy.

"Transport is a big problem," the policeman agreed.

"And we can't pick you up because you are alone at the station."

"I'm alone at the station. But I will report the matter to my officer-in-charge. When he comes back from the meeting."

Okay. Thanks. I'll hear from you later then," I said to no one in particular. The policeman had already hung up.

I stepped back out into the sunlight and the fresh air. Raphael was waiting for me. He cut to the chase. "Are the police coming to get Memory, Boss? Before she starts to stink the compound out."

"She's not going to stink, Raphael. Have some respect for the dead, Raphael. But no, the police aren't going to come. They haven't got transport."

"Then she will stink, Boss. It is very hot. And when it's very hot, dead people can stink a lot."

"She's not going to stink. And we'll get her buried. We just have to make sure Killer gets a death certificate, and then we can bury her."

"No!" Raphael said emphatically.

"What do you mean no?? That's what the policeman told me on the phone."

"Killer is not the relative of Memory, Boss. They were never married in the church. Killer hadn't finished paying the lobola or bride price. They won't give him the death certificate."

"Well, then we'll just have to get Memory's relatives here so they can get the death certificate. And then we'll bury her."

"Ha!! It will be a big fuck up, Boss!!"

"You're just being negative, Raphael. Have some faith. It will work out fine. We'll get Memory's relatives here, and we'll get her buried."

The relatives arrived three days later. And it had been a very long three days, mostly spent camped at the Births and Deaths Registry, sucking up to bored bureaucrats, to no avail. Memory's body was still in her little house in the compound, but now with an armada of huge blue blowflies buzzing in attendance, at half-mast. It was hot like hell and Raphael had called it right, she was starting to stink. And worse than that, an owl had taken up residence in a large tree in the middle of the compound. In African culture where superstitions rule, owls were the worst possible omen. The other workers were way past just unhappy. But at least now the relatives were here and we could get Memory in the ground and buried. I hurried to meet them in the compound.

I wasn't expecting quite so many relatives. I'd been expecting the mother and the father and maybe a brother and an aunt or two, but it looked like the whole clan had descended down from the hills. There were more than twenty of Memory's relatives, seated in a cluster outside the house where Memory lay dead, all seemingly unaffected by the smell of death and the swarm of busy flies.

"Raphael, please can you tell all of them that I'm very sorry at the untimely loss of their daughter, Memory. Tell that I was extremely fond of Memory and that I share their grief and..."

"But Boss...."

"Look Raphael just tell them what I told you to say. And also tell them that I am sure that they also want to make sure that she receives a decent burial as quickly as possible. For the sake of their granddaughter. And for the sake of all the other people living in the compound."

Raphael rolled his eyes and duly jabbered away in Shona at the gathering of the clan. He directed his comments at the old Sekuru who seemed to be the head of the Memory clan. Looking at the old man, the name Beelzebub came to mind. I tried my hardest to ignore the flies while I waited for Raphael to finish translating but flinched every time one of the disgusting things landed on me. I shuddered to think what Memory looked like inside. Maybe I should bring down a mosquito net to cover her body. It took Raphael forever to finish the translation. Beelzebub sat cross-legged and ruminated on my commiserations. And then he blurted out a quickfire response.

"Well, what did he say, Raphael?"

"He said he wants his lobola first. And then we can bury Memory."

"But didn't you tell him the bit about his granddaughter and the health hazard and..."

"I told him all of that, Boss. But he just wants his lobola paid."

"Okay, okay," I grumped. "Just ask the old bastard how much then."

"But..."

"Just do as I say Raphael and ask him how much." I slipped my best poker face on. The old goat squatted with his skinny knees around his ancient ears and stared back at me through unblinking, rheumy eyes. And then he replied with a question of his own. "He wants to know if you are related to the groom, Boss."

"Of course, I'm not related to Killer. Just tell....". I broke off to take half a dozen deep calm down breaths. The old goat was getting to me.

"Like I was saying Raphael, tell the old man that I'm Killer's employer and all I'm trying to do is help sort things out."

The old goat looked as old as the hills as he ruminated on my latest offering. "He says that the lobola is strictly a matter between the bridegroom and his family on the one hand and the father-in-law and his relatives, on the other hand," Raphael translated.

"Tell he's just being plain bloody unreasonable..." My poker face slipped. I was getting annoyed. "Okay, Raphael, you can tell the old bastard that for the purposes of this meeting he can take it that I am now part of Killer's family and…"

"Are you sure you want to be telling that, Boss. I am thinking…"

"Of course, I'm bloody sure Raphael. Just tell him what I said," I snapped, poker face hanging by the merest of threads. I cut to the chase. "And also ask him how much we're talking about to make all of this go away." I glared at my watch. The day was getting away from me. And the ground was fucking hard, and my backside was aching. The old fucking goat had to be double fucking jointed, the way he sat there squatting as he mulled the question over. I watched in fascination as a fly crawled around the old goat's face, exploring the crinkled crevices. The old goat ignored the fly as he jabbered off his quick-fire answer. "He says it will cost thirty thousand dollars, Boss. Excluding interest."

My poker face hit the dirt. "Thirty thousand?" I spluttered. "Thirty fucking thousand. Excluding interest. But…But …But that's more than Killer earns in a fucking year. It's more than he earns in two fucking years. He can't afford that and…look how much was the lobola in the first fucking place?"

"The bride price agreed upon before the marriage was set at two beasts."

"Two beasts…Two beasts…" I spluttered. "How does the old fucking goat get from two fucking cows to thirty fucking thousand dollars?"

Another jabbered answer. "Apparently he has a very good bull at his kraal."

"What the hell had that got to do with anything? Just because he's got a good fucking bull, now he wants thirty thousand fucking dollars?"

"Plus interest. What he is saying is that his bull would have sired many calves with the two beasts, Boss."

"But that's simply bloody preposterous, Raphael. He can't just sit here and put a nonsensical value on calves that weren't even bloody born in the first place. And tell him I can't afford thirty thousand bloody dollars. And… and ask the old fucking goat what happens now?"

More deliberation. I watched as the fly disappeared right up into the old bastard's nostril. Either the man had lost all feeling in his face. Or he had amazing powers of concentration and a will of steel.

"The Sekuru says that the dispute over the lobola will have to be referred to the village courts. They will deliberate."

"But…but… what happens in the meantime?" I realised I was spluttering a lot but couldn't help it. "Look surely the old fucking goat realises that we can't just let Memory lie here bloody decomposing."

"He says that the village court will have to decide." More jabbering. "And he also says that he is not an old fucking goat, Boss."

"You didn't go and tell him that I called him an old goat?"

"Of course not, Boss."

"But...how..."

"I am thinking that maybe he can speak English, Boss."

"He can speak English? But..."

In the end, I paid the thirty thousand dollars I didn't have, plus the six thousand in interest the old goat was asking for. The old bastard knew his ten-figure bank account number off by heart. And then before they took the body away for the burial, the clan stripped Killer's little house absolutely clean. It was the most cold-hearted thing I'd ever seen. They took anything and everything of value, bickering and fighting amongst themselves as to who got what. They even took all the kid's clothes, leaving her with not a stitch. And then they went back and took all the other stuff, the stuff that had no value, just to make sure.

I sent instructions to the security guard at the main gate not to let them leave the farm, not until I'd spoken to them for the last time. Raphael told me I was wasting my time, but I made them come to me in my office anyway. The leaders of clan shuffled into the office behind the old goat. I made them stand in front of my desk and then blasted them with both barrels. I spoke from my heart.

"You are the most disgusting people that I have ever met." The old goat stared me down. "Before, my wife and I used to admire the Shona culture and your approach to family. My wife and I recently adopted another mother's three children because she was dying and we brought them to live here as though they were our own children and gave them our name. But in your culture that would never happen. In your culture, you would never allow others to take away the children of a dead daughter. But then I met you people. That man out there, Killer, is your son-in-law, and the little girl is your granddaughter. He is a hard-working young man and did his best to provide for your daughter and granddaughter. Today you have taken away everything in the world they own, even her bloody clothes. Like locusts, you have left them with nothing. And she is your granddaughter."

In response, Beelzebub hawked up a huge glob of phlegm and ruminated upon it as he considered my words. He glared at me, looking for all the world like a malignant turkey buzzard. And then before he jabbered his reply, he spat the phlegm out onto my office floor between his horny feet. Raphael translated. "Daughters are an investment for when a man gets old like me. The lobola is a return on that investment. The husband should have paid me my lobola. He didn't. And so, I've have taken back what is mine." And then he stalked out the office haughtily, with the rest of his clan following closely.

That afternoon I decided to hammer home a harsh non-fraternisation policy. I was determined that Memory and Killer would be the last people to die of AIDS on Running Dog. For sure Killer would be HIV positive and it would be a matter of time before that turned into full-blown AIDS. If I didn't slow it up, I was going to end up with no staff sooner than later. And central to the AIDS epidemic on Running Dog was the grading shed. It was big, with more than fifty girls working in there at the height of the season, mostly young and single. Young girls had the sharpest eyes and nimble fingers and could pluck out problem leaves and flowers in a flash. The grading shed girls were accommodated on the farm, two to a room, in single dormitories. But, unfortunately, not too much attention was paid to the word 'single', and the girls' dormitories were very popular after hours. Very mindful of the fact that my graders were someone else's daughters, I wanted to physically fence the dormitories off, but the word prison was bandied about, and I had to abandon my plans for Stalag Virtue.

After the Memory loss, I decided to have another go at building walls around the grading shed, in the form of ultra-harsh and punitive anti-fraternisation regulations. I decreed that with immediate effect, any female members of staff who consorted with any senior male members of staff, other than their husbands, would be dismissed summarily. There was an immediate uproar. How come only the females would be dismissed, why not the men? Mostly because I didn't want to be losing any more of my supervisors, I told Raphael. We'd lost too many supervisors to AIDS; I couldn't afford to fire any for promiscuity. I told him drastic measures were called for and we had to take the grading shed girls out of play. Raphael shook his head sadly. My intervention wasn't a good plan he said and wouldn't work. But I was determined and called a meeting in the grading shed with all the supervisors and female staff. There was a deathly hush as I read out my decree. The female members of staff hung on my every word, the male supervisors, almost all of them married, stared up at the ceilings, at the floor, anywhere but at the women seated in front of them. Any questions, I asked? Just the one hand went up. It was a woman seated in the middle. Raphael translated her question. "Your rule say we can't sleep with supervisors and foremen. But what about with drivers?" she asked. At the time we employed just one driver. A quiet, well-mannered man, he was stood in amongst the supervisors, near the back, squirming with every pair of eyes in the room on him, his wife's included.

Later that night, I went through to tuck the kids into bed. Veronica asked me a question before we started on her prayers.

"Where is Memory, Dad?"

"Did you know Memory?"

"Sure. She's Killer's wife."

"Well, she's ...um... she's still in the compound...but... I'm afraid that Memory is not very well and..."

"You mean she's not dead, Dad? Because Killer told me she was dead days ago."

"No, Vee, she is dead. It's just that I didn't know how to tell you..."

"Look, Dad, I just need to know where she's gone."

"You do?"

"I need to know if she's still in the compound or if she's already gone to Heaven. Because if she's already gone to Heaven, then I don't need to ask God to carry on looking after her because she's already there with Him."

"You asked God to look after Memory?"

"Sure. Killer asked me to."

"Killer asked you to pray to God to look after Memory?"

"Sure. And I did. All last week. I promise you I did. But I don't think God heard me. Because she went and died anyway."

"Sometimes God is really, really busy, Vee and He can't look after everyone."

"I know He's busy, Dad. That's why I don't want to waste His time by asking Him to look after someone that He's already got up there with Him."

"That's very um...considerate of you, Veronica."

"I don't know what that means, Dad."

"It means um...that you um...think of others. It's a good thing to be."

"Sure. So anyway, I'll just ask God to look after Killer and Fortunate. And you and Mom and everyone else that I normally ask him to look after. I just hope that He's listening tonight."

Chapter Sixteen

The Governor of the Reserve Bank of Zimbabwe phoned me up out of the blue one morning and introduced himself by name. I didn't recognise the name because who reads the scrawled signatures on banknotes. So, he had to point out to me that he was not only the Governor of the Reserve Bank but also a doctor and very important to boot. He needed my help; he told me. He'd been given my name by the freight forwarder at the airport. Could I come out to his farm to look at his cut-flowers? I told him no problem. Putting the phone down on him, I felt very clever. The Governor of the Reserve Bank and a doctor to boot was asking me for help and farming advice.

He had a beautiful farm on the outskirts of Harare with deep red soils, water to burn and lands that stretched as far as the eye could see. There was nothing you couldn't grow on those soils. The Governor was wearing his landed gentry outfit, complete with cravat and shiny shoes. He'd thrown millions at his farm he told me but was having quality issues that he couldn't get to the bottom of. As we walked down to the fields, we talked flower grower talk and compared notes on markets and sales agents. He slipped on his inscrutable poker face and told me his sales agents were based in the British Virgin Islands. They made all his marketing decisions, nudge nudge, wink, wink! At first, I thought he'd got something stuck in his eye until he did the wink-wink thing again but more slowly. Then I got it. The Governor of the Reserve Bank was telling me how to duck and dive foreign currency regulations.

That the good Governor couldn't get to the bottom of his quality problems in his greenhouses wasn't surprising, given the fact he couldn't tell the difference between bird shit on his rose bushes and powdery mildew. He bollocked all over his rose manager in front of me. If anything, the powdery mildew on the roses was worse than on the Governor's last visit.

"Look at it on top of this bush, wet and fresh and not even powdery yet," the Governor said as he used his banknote counting finger to poke and prod at a recently deposited lump of bird shit. The expensive chemicals he told the manager to use weren't working, which meant the manager must be applying them wrong. "What would you use to treat the powdery mildew, Eric?" he asked.

"I'd use a pellet gun. To shoot the birds nesting in your greenhouses. This is bird shit, not powdery mildew."

The Governor nodded knowingly and told his manager to make notes.

The Governor's outdoor field flower beds were six hundred metres long and stretched as far as my eye could see. My long-distance vision sucks. A spray operator who was skinny like a greyhound with a fifteen-litre knapsack on his back was busy spraying the field when we got there. I was exhausted after just five minutes of watching the poor chap. With refills, he had to be running three kilometres for every bed sprayed. And there were hundreds of beds. That might have something to do with the Governor's pest problems, I ventured. Maybe the Governor would do better if his beds were no longer than fifty metres. The Governor stood at the edge of the monster land and pondered the problem and the advice given carefully while his manager made notes.

The Governor had the attention span of a cocker spaniel puppy and soon grew bored with his horticultural problems. He dragged me off to show me his pride and joy - his still under construction three-storey mansion. He ignored an army of builders as he gave me the guided tour of his almost finished house. He dragged me up and down staircases and whisked me in and out of a multitude of en-suite bedrooms, complete with bidets. The Governor's pride and joy though was his grand fireplace in the main lounge. It was a monster, big enough to parallel park his Range Rover in he told me proudly. Wow, I said politely. We went out onto the soon-to-be rolling lawns to marvel at the edifice from the outside. Looking up, I asked him where his chimney was. On the roof, of course, he told me. But it wasn't. And the builders who were placing the last of roof tiles hadn't seen the chimney anywhere either. Not since the second floor, one of the young bricklayers hazarded a guess. I withdrew politely while the governor ranted and raved. He told his workforce he wanted his chimney found by the next afternoon or else. As we walked away, the builders started removing the roof tiles above where the chimney should have been.

Walking with the Reserve Bank Governor around his farm gave me a valuable insight into the reasons behind silly inflation and the Zimbabwe dollar's not so slow slide into junk currency status. I quite liked the Governor. He was bombastic and full of himself, but he was also quite likeable. But in the great filing cabinet of life, you'd find him filed under idiot. And would I trust him to manage the national coffers? Hell no. I wouldn't have him in charge of my Post Office Savings Book, and that had a zero balance.

When I got home, Jenny had Daniel seated in front of his piggy bank and was forcing him to feed his precious pocket money into the slot. It was a fierce battle of wills and one that happened at the end of every week. Daniel wanted to invest in sweets and chocolates, but Jenny was determined to teach him the benefits of saving. When his pig was full, then Daniel could break it open and spend on something big and meaningful, she told him. What, like lots of sweets and chocolates he asked? Normally, I was very supportive of Jenny's home economics lessons, but not today, not after having spent the morning with the custodian of the national currency. I butted in. Better Dan spends his pocket money now because, by the time he's filled his piggy bank, his sweets and chocolates will be double or treble the price. Dan was overjoyed at my intervention, Jenny uber bleak. And it brought on the hugest case of the Zimbabwe blues.

Later that night, she asked me, "What the hell are we doing living in a country where you're supposed to encourage your children to not save their pocket money?"

And then just as Jenny asked the question, the lights went out. Yet another bloody power cut. Power cuts before clever things like generators and inverters came along were the bane of our lives. They happened frequently and with impeccably bad timing, like when your wife is in the middle cooking dinner, or even worse in the last five minutes of a France versus the Springboks World Cup Rugby semi-final.

As it turned out, that particular power cut was epically bad, a seven-day marathon; our first long haul power outage. Seven days without power in a house without a generator translates into a lot of candles, a lot of no talking and early to bed evenings, no talking mostly because I cheat at monopoly and early to bed because my monopoly games end quickly, again mostly because I cheat. There is a myth out there that power cuts are the root cause of much procreation. This is a complete fallacy. Power cuts are actually the most powerful anti-aphrodisiac known to womankind, especially if the man has also just been busted cheating at monopoly. And if the power cuts drag on for seven long days and even longer nights, then you're into the realms of cold showers, followed by no showers on account of the fact our water on the farm came from boreholes and needed to be pumped. And way worse than all of that, we're talking no cold rooms for my cut-flowers, no irrigation to water the crop, which all makes for Mr Grumpy Pants deluxe. So why the hell were we still living in Zimbabwe?

For me, it was a question easily answered. We lived in Zimbabwe because our children could run around barefoot and with the sun on their backs, growing up innocent. Veronica aged ten didn't have a clue as to how to cross a busy street but knew all about not going near rivers and dams for fear of crocodiles and hippos. We lived in Zimbabwe because one day, three young bull elephants bust through the wall of our wall of a Garden Centre business we owned on the edge of town. The elephants walked around sampling the shrubs and bushes on sale - they especially liked the seedling section - before considerately exiting via the same hole in the wall. The security guard's report in the morning was a classic.

"The elephants fucked up the wall and damaged the plants with their feet and also by eating. And then they left through the same hole in the wall," he told me. I told him he was a liar and that he'd slept through some drunken lout driving his car through the Garden Centre and that he was blaming it on elephants was testimony to the strength of the alcohol he'd been quaffing. He was able to save his job by producing a still steaming piece of elephant shit. Alas. Later that morning, National Parks had to shoot all three elephants when they went walkabout in the suburbs. It was a crazy day that would loom large in my memories for the rest of my life. And at the end of the day, memories are the difference between a boring life and a life well-lived.

So many of my family's stand-out memories, both good and bad, have been made in Mana Pools. Like the time we went camping in Mana with Brian and Kerry Wehlburg. Brian was a hunting, fishing, shooting type farmer from Chegutu. Also on the trip were Reinier Pronk from Holland, all wide-eyed excited on his first trip to Africa, Gary's best friend Mike Mullins and Raphael, there to guard camp against marauding baboons and hyenas and to clean the fish we caught. Or rather the fish that other people caught.

Because there were so many of us in the party, I'd taken the farm three-ton truck on the trip. Slightly elevated with lots of clearance and plenty of room on the back for deck chairs and cooler boxes, it was the perfect game viewing vehicle. We were out on an early morning game drive when Brian noticed a sky full of vultures. The vultures were circling lower and lower above a clearing a kilometre off the road.

"They're coming down on a kill," Brian told us. "Looks like an impala. Most probably a leopard kill. Let's stop and go have a look." Brian was very knowledgeable about the bush. All I could see was a bunch of birds in the sky and a bunch of bush.

The best thing about Mana was that you could get out of your car and walk whenever and wherever. There were no rules to keep you safe. Through the binoculars, I nervously eyed the thick clump of trees and bushes that formed the backdrop to the clearing. It was properly thick. Lots of room for lots of carnivores in there. I was glad Brian was with us. He knew his way around the bush better than I did. Through the binoculars and melee of scrummaging vultures, I could make out what was left of the impala carcass "Wow. Those vultures sure have been busy. Those bones are clean."

"Dad, Dad, please can I come with. I want to see the dead impala's bones, Dad." Daniel was about five at the time, not at school yet, but fully mobile and fully into blood, guts and dead bones.

"I don't think so, Dan. I think you'd better stay on the truck with the girls." The girls - Jenny, Kerry and Veronica - heaved not so little sighs of relief.

We set off towards the clearing and the vultures in single file, with Brian leading the way, followed by Gary, Mike, Reiner and me. Impossibly, the bush around the clearing grew thicker as we walked towards it. I clutched my not nearly stout enough walking stick tightly and nervously and stared at undergrowth so hard that my eyes hurt, looking for the first sign of movement. I have a very vivid imagination, which is not a good thing to have in the bush. Reiner picked his way through the bush in front of me. He was older than me by about ten years but looked fit and trim. As we walked, I wondered if I could run faster than him. Then I remembered Gary and Mike and felt guilty for a bit. But not for long. They were fourteen and in their prime and for sure, would be able to run faster than Reiner.

There must have thirty or more vultures scrapping and fighting over what was left of the ex-impala. They were mixing it up so much it was hard to tell them apart. Up close, the birds were huge with vicious beaks and muscled necks all bloodied and gory from the carcass. The vultures closest to us turned and glared with beady eyes, angry at our intrusion. I could almost hear them ripping at what little flesh was left on the carcass. I picked up a flicker of movement through the bush ahead, and my bowels gave a not so little hop and a skip. Through the binoculars and the thick bush, I could see a herd of impala grazing a hundred metres or more beyond the kill. Must be the dead guy's buddies. Things move on quickly at the bottom end of the food chain. I took it to be a good thing that the herd of impala were there. Surely, they wouldn't be there if whatever had eaten their friend was still around.

Brian stopped us in our tracks twenty metres short of the kill and sank down to his haunches to scan the thick bush around the clearing carefully. I couldn't hear what he was saying. The blood pounding in my head was too loud. And I was standing too far back. Reluctantly I crept forward so I could hear his whispering. "I'm sure it was a leopard. Just want to make sure he's not up one of these trees before we get any closer."

I quickly shifted the focus of binoculars into the branches above. I could see nothing. Which was good, real good. I was shit scared of leopards. I turned to look back at the truck and did my best to wave nonchalantly. Crap. I wish I'd stayed at the truck, to look after Daniel and the girls. But I hadn't. Crap. My mouth was over dry. I wish I'd brought some water. But I hadn't. Crap. I....

"No sign of him." Brian's whisper dragged me back to the edge of the clearing. "I think he's gone. Let's get rid of these birds, and we'll have a look at what's left of his dinner." Brian rose to his feet and strode towards the clearing, waving and clapping his hands, shouting loudly. "C'mon, voetsak, voetsak, voetsak you ugly birds!!"

Voetsak was Africa's 'go to' command when you wanted something, anything to bugger off. It worked it's wonders on the wake of vultures on the kill. One second the clearing was full of squabbling vultures, and the next second they were out of there, scrambling on ungainly legs, flapping massive, ponderous wings, clawing, fighting for altitude. Gary and Mike joined in, laughing and shouting, with arms waving wildly. "Voetsak, voetsak, voetsak!!" Even Reiner gave it a go. I was too busy scanning the trees for the leopard. We walked into the clearing to examine the carcass. It was amazing. From the neck down it was stripped clean to the bone, from neck up it was intact, bar the eyes. The vultures had enjoyed those. One of the horns had a small nick out of it. I touched the impala's neck. It wasn't cold and stiff.

"It wasn't killed too long ago," Brian confirmed my thoughts. He was on his haunches, looking for the leopard's pugmarks. "I'd say an hour back, no more. Can't find his spoor anywhere. It's all been messed up. But here's a bit of his fur". Reiner, Gary and Mike leaned in to look at the bit of fluff that Brian had found. Again, I was too busy scanning the trees looking for the rest of the fluff still on the leopard. A couple of the vultures glared down at me malevolently. I shivered. The place was really starting to give me the shits.

"Dad, Dad, I want to see the bones." Dan hollered from the truck.

'Don't disturb the bush' was a big rule and one that I was keen to drum into Gary. But it was also the perfect out I was looking for. The clearing was creeping me out properly. "C'mon, Gary, you grab one horn, and I'll grab the other. Let's go."

Gary and I led the way back to the truck, dragging the picked clean carcass behind us. Brian and Mike were behind us, deep in leopard conversation while Reiner brought up the rear. We were just thirty metres short of the truck when I heard another vehicle. It was a Land Rover station wagon with camera lenses protruding from every window.

"Drop the impala, Gary. I don't want this car to see us dragging dead animals around the bush." We gathered in front of the carcass, shielding it from view and waved happily at the passing tourists. Once they were gone, Gary and I bent down to pick the impala up again.

As we did, Reiner piped up conversationally, "Hey. Isn't that a lion?"

I spun around so quickly I put my neck out. Reiner was right. It was a lion, low to the ground, looking pissed off and bearing down on us, impossibly fast. I'd never seen anything move so quick in my life. The lion's eyes burnt out the back of my head.

"Run. Run. Run for the truck!!" I shouted as I dropped the impala. Mostly I was shouting at Reiner, still gawking at the lion. Brian, Gary and Mike, already legging at full speed, were more than halfway back to the truck. It was a no-contest, though. I was the first one to get to the truck by a country mile. Fear is the best propellant.

I leapt behind the steering wheel and fumbled for the keys. I was all thumbs and all shakes. Where was the bloody lion? More fumbles. Then I got the key to turn in the ignition. Crap. The engine turned but never fired. The truck had a dodgy starter motor. The seconds dragged on forever. And all the while I was wondering where the bloody lion was and waiting for screams and blood and guts from the back of the truck. Turn the key again. Eventually, the engine fired. A quick headcount in the rear-view mirror to make sure I wasn't leaving anyone behind to be eaten before letting the clutch out.

"It's okay, Dad, he's stopped on his kill. But he sure is angry." Gary's voice was calm. I turned to look at him. He was on his haunches in the back of the truck, snapping away with his camera, his long lens stone steady.

"I'm going to move off a bit anyway. I've seen how fast that bloody lion can run."

The lion glared at us from behind his kill. We could see his tail flicking from side to side. Eventually, he picked up his impala carcass and dragged it back to the bush. Which dropped Dan into the sulks. "But I wanted to see the bones, Dad."

"I don't think he's going to let you, Dan. They're his bones."

My hands were still shaking as I eased out the clutch and headed back to camp. I reached for my secret stash of cigarettes and gave up not smoking. My first drag was a long one, burning back half the cigarette. I sucked the acrid smoke down deep. It felt good. Smoking was a disgusting habit that would kill me, unless of course I got eaten by a lion first. As I drove back to camp, trying to secretly direct my exhaled smoke down into the floor well of the truck which was full of holes, heart still hammering twenty to the dozen, it struck that there was nowhere else in the world that I would rather be. You never feel so alive as when you're almost not alive.

Chapter Seventeen

1998 was a watershed year for our family. It saw Dan's first schoolboy cricket match and Gary's last. And Veronica started high school. And I ignored worrying signs that should have had me scrambling my family off to the safety of another land. The signs were big for me to read, but I missed them completely. Alas.

Test cricket has been described as the world's most noble sporting endeavour, a five-day competitive tapestry, etched with courage and resilience, strength and ability, and failure. Under-eight cricket is much the same but without the noble bits and they use wax crayons instead of etching.

The Lilfordia bowler measured out his run-up carefully and made his mark. He tossed the shiny new red cricket ball from hand to hand as he eyed out the opening batsman quivering at the far end of the pitch. There was a big difference between eyeing out and gawking. The bowler was very good at eyeing out. He'd practised eyeing out for hours in front of the mirror. And the long hours of practice had paid off. The batsman certainly looked nervous as his bat tap-tapped the pitch in front of him. The bowler tossed his shiny red ball up again, but this time with some Shane Warne spin. He hadn't made up his mind yet whether he was going to be pace bowler or a spin bowler. He dropped the ball by accident. It wasn't easy catching a ball when it was spinning like crazy. Thankfully the batsman didn't notice the fumble. He was too busy fiddling down the front of his shorts, adjusting his cricket box, for the umpteenth time. The bowler decided to switch back to being a pace bowler.

"Stop poncing about, Kekana and get on with it!" the umpire, who was also the bowler's headmaster barked.

"Sorry, sir!" the fast bowler said. He checked his field placements one last time. His fielders in the close catching positions were ready in their crouching, ready to pounce positions. Two slips, a gully and a silly mid-off. And then the bowler noticed something untoward in the outfield.

"Third man's practising his handstands again, sir!"

The umpire cupped his hands together and bellowed in his headmaster's voice. "Stop doing handstands, de Jong!"

"Thank you, sir."

"Pleasure, Kekana. Now can we get on with the game?"

Kekana's stock delivery was a donkey drop that soared heavenwards before dropping on a length as gravity reasserted itself. But Kekana also knew how to mix them up. Some deliveries fell upon the hapless batsman like bolts from heaven. Others were pitched much shorter and bounced once, twice, three times before reaching the batsman... or the wicketkeeper... or the slip fielder. It was exactly the type of penetrative bowling that would expose the soft underbelly of the opposing team's entire batting line up.

I was watching Daniel's first competitive cricket match, and it was certainly living up to its billing. It was going to be a cracker. I looked across at the opposition team bickering and squabbling behind the scorers' desk. They were fighting over the batting pads, the possession of which determined the batting line up. They'd better sort things out quickly because their opening pair didn't look comfortable against Kekana's aerial onslaught.

The opposing team were from the Hellenic School in Harare. The opening batsman was the only Greek on the team. The school had an excellent academic record and attracted pupils of all nationalities. The opening batsman looked especially rattled by Kekana's bowling. Daniel's best friend, Sean Doorly, was fielding at silly mid-off. He was fiercely competitive, and if he had his way, he'd bowl every ball of the match, and also keep wicket and also open the batting and also field up close in kamikaze positions, mostly because you got to wear a batting helmet all the time. I liked Sean and hoped that some of his competitiveness would rub off on Daniel. Even from the side lines, I could see Sean was wound up tight like a watch spring. He watched the flight of Kekana's next delivery like a hawk. He leapt up and took the catch clean and without fuss or fumbles. He flung the ball up in the sky in triumph, and his celebratory cries of 'Howzat' rang through the air. Kekana, the bowler, joined in the celebrations, running around with arms outstretched like an Allan Donald. The rest of the team rushed in to congratulate all and sundry - apart from Daniel at third man who'd gone back to practising his handstands and had been upside down facing the wrong way at the time the catch was taken. The batsman, looking bewildered as befitted his Greek heritage, stood his ground resolutely and waited for the umpire's decision.

"Not out!" the headmaster said in his umpire's voice.

"But sir, I caught it cleanly, sir, I did sir!! I promise you I did, sir!" Sean Doorly wailed, absolutely distraught at the shocking umpiring.

"I know you did, Doorly but, unfortunately, you caught the ball before it got to the batsman."

"Ah, but sir!"

"Cricket's a funny old game, Doorly, it's a funny old game."

Sean shrugged off his disappointment as the field shuffled around at the end of the over. "Please, can I bowl, sir? Please, can I bowl?"

A gritty eighth wicket stand of eleven helped nudge the Hellenics score up towards the daunting forty run total set by Lilfordia. Daniel's mis-fielding helped turn ones and twos into threes or fours. It looked like Lilfordia were going to snatch defeat from the jaws of victory. But then Sean Doorly got stuck into the Greek tail. He'd taken a sharp catch at first slip, this one legitimate. And then he'd bagged the ninth wicket with a deceptive coolie creeper. The dismissed batsman stood his ground. He couldn't be out to a coolie creeper because it was an illegal delivery. The umpire's outstretched finger had, however, remained resolute. But the batsman said in a shrill voice that reached the boundary that his dad had told him that coolie creepers weren't allowed anymore because they were racist. Alas. In the end, the batsman had to walk.

Unbelievably though it was Daniel's sterling efforts though that brought the Greek innings to a close when his wildly enthusiastic shy at the stumps careened off the back of first slip's head and hit the stumps. First slip had retired hurt and in tears, but the dismissal had stood. Hellenics all out for thirty-nine and Lilfordia were worthy winners by a single run.

Gary had excelled at St Georges College both academically and on the sports field, especially the cricket field. Blessed with extraordinary hand-eye co-ordination he'd made the opening batsman slot in the College First Eleven his own. Which unfortunately meant that that he wasn't the only de Jong to stride out on to the field in the annual and prestigious First Eleven vs The Fathers cricket fixture.

While I quite like the intensity of Test cricket, my attention span is more suited to the wham-bam one day form of the game. I especially like the bright strip and the festival atmosphere. And so, I purposely chose my loudest board shorts and t-shirt for the Fathers versus Sons game. Unfortunately, the other fathers in the team went with test whites. As did the School First Team. I did stick out a bit.

The rules of the tournament were simple. Fifty overs a side and all the players had to take it in turns to bowl two over stints. The First Eleven won the toss and opted to field. While the fathers bickered over the batting order, I watched the First Eleven's opening bowler warm up. I watched him overheat more like. The veins in his neck were already popping out alarmingly even before his first delivery thundered down the pitch. The keeper winced as the ball thudded into his gloves. Holy crap.

I sidled across to Gary. "Who is the kid bowling?" I'm not entirely sure why I used the word kid. The bowler was well over six foot, and strong with it. And it wasn't even ten in the morning yet, and already he had a five o'clock shadow.

"That's Steyn, Dad." Gary laughed at the panic in my eyes. "And wait till you see him when he really gets going." It struck me that the bowler's name rhymed with pain as I made my way miserably back to the huddle of fathers as they stood around joking and practising their strokes. Poor fools. They had no idea what was coming.

"Where do you want to bat?" I was asked.

"Eleven."

"Are you a bowler?"

"No. I just want to bat at number eleven."

Steyn was wild like a runaway train. His first ball that he put down was a vicious bouncer that almost removed the batsman's head. His second delivery was a wide that raced away to the boundary, and his third sent all three stumps crashing out the ground. I mostly watched through cracks in my fingers. It wasn't pretty watching. The fathers' top-order collapse inspired the middle order to follow suit at regular intervals. There was no way we were going to bat through our allotted fifty overs. Our bottom order showed some resistance, mostly because the non-bowlers in the First Team were bowling, but not enough resistance for the number eleven, i.e. Yours truly to not bat. Then the second but last wicket fell, and I was up. Crap. I wasn't ready. I didn't even have the pads on. My fingers fumbled and fought with the unfamiliar buckles. A slow clap started. I grabbed a bat and ran out on to the field with just the one pad on.

Walking out into the middle, several things struck me all at once, and I'm not talking glancing blows, I'm talking struck like a shovel in the face. Steyn was warming up with the ball. Everyone had bowled their two obligatory overs, and Steyn was up again. Steyn's name also rhymed with maim. It was so hot inside my helmet that I couldn't breathe. I was only wearing one glove. And worst of all, I wasn't wearing a cricket box. My man bits were going to be exposed to cannonball cricket balls without any protection. And apparently, I was doing all of this because it was fun. I turned to go back and hide in the pavilion, but slow clap started again.

I was a sight of abject misery as I huddled in front of the stumps in my stupidly loud clothes, with only one pad and one glove on and an unprotected groin. Steyn frazzled me with his glare from the end of his impossibly long run-up. It also struck me that the rules of cricket were stupid. Twenty-two yards wasn't nearly long enough. I didn't see Steyn's first ball. I was too busy trying to hide my willy and my unprotected hand behind the cricket bat. The ball hit the shoulder of the bat and sped across the outfield like a startled bunny. Four runs.

Steyn frazzled me with an even more venomous glare before stalking back to the start of his impossibly long run-up. I took up my preferred Quasimodo stance behind the bat and waited for the second ball like a bunny in headlights. Again, the first I saw of the ball was after it had nicked the bat and was off racing to the boundary. Another four runs. The veins in Steyn's neck took on a life of their own. And then I heard the umpire say "Well, that's over, gents." I was swamped by a tsunami of relief and thanked God and everyone else who was listening for bringing my ordeal to an end. I ripped my hot, sweaty helmet off and shot off back to the pavilion before the umpire changed his mind. Gary headed me off, halfway across the outfield. "Where are you going, Dad?"

"Back to the pavilion."

"But why, Dad?"

"Because that umpire guy said it was over. I heard him."

"He was just calling the end of the over. You got to go and bat some more."

"Crap."

Thankfully the batsman at the other end was out caught behind in the very next over, and I was able to retire, eight not out. After the game, Gary ran up to me. "Hey Dad, you did real good. Two fours off Steyn. And my friends said they've never seen a fielder run so much." Gary's heady praise made my ears blush.

The biggest hurdle in 1998 for Veronica was high school. I couldn't be putting my daughter into a government school with forty or more kids per classroom, so we had no option but to go to the private school option. Private schools are big business in Zim with massive desk fees the norm. A desk for your kid at one of the elite schools could cost tens of thousands of dollars. And the kid had to pass a stiff entrance exam first. Thankfully and because Jenny was a Catholic, we didn't have to deal with all those dramas. Veronica would go to the Convent. We'd done the hard yards of Sunday school and confirmation classes. And Veronica even had a picture of the Pope on her bedroom wall, just below Britney Spears. Catholic schools were a great safety net. Gary had thrived at St George's College. And Veronica would do just as well at the Convent. After she passed the entrance exam.

Come the day of her entrance exam, Veronica was falling apart at the seams nervous. For good reason. She'd never done exam pressure too good. During term time she got the job done just fine but come exams she always had a major wobble and jettisoned large chunks of the knowledge in her head. And the fact that the convent exams were supposed to be tough, with so many girls from so many schools vying for so few places didn't help. Don't sweat it, I told her. You've got a secret weapon. Sneak into your answer somewhere that you've got a picture of the Pope on your bedroom wall. And that you also know your rosaries. And you're in. And don't forget you're good at English and Geography and stuff. "Focus on what you know, and you'll be fine," I told her. Alas. Apparently, within the female branch of the Catholic Church, great importance is placed on mathematical ability and not a lot on English and Geography and stuff. As a result, the entrance exam was very maths top-heavy. Which was not so good for us. Not only was Veronica properly crap at mathematics, but she was going to struggle to broach the subject of the Papal content of her bedroom décor while trying to answer X+5 x Y-2 equals what?

Predictably Veronica came out of the exam room in a flood of tears with bottom lip trembling. "Relax." I gave her a reassuring hug. "You're a Catholic, and this is a Catholic Convent School. They're not allowed to not let you in. It's in the small print in the Bible."

Alas. The old bat of a nun in charge of entrance exams obviously didn't bother with small print. She failed Veronica. It was a big load of bollocks. They could not deny my daughter a place. I demanded an audience with the Boss Nun and put my case to her with passion and verve. Waving letters of support from her parish priest, I pointed out that not only was Veronica a sweet kid and a good practicing Catholic with a picture of the Pope on her bedroom wall, she was a special case who'd been through a lot of trauma in her short life, losing her birth mom when she was not yet six, then being adopted and if anyone deserved a break it was her. And she was okay academically, maybe not too hot at maths but she'd pay attention in class, and in time she'd learn what $X+5$ x $Y-2$ equalled.

My impassioned plea moved the Boss Nun not a jot. Evidently, the woman had been breastfed on battery acid and enjoyed kneeling on pencils. I would have got more reaction telling the sob story to a watermelon. The convent is an academic school, she told me. We only take the brightest girls. I told her that was the biggest load of crap I'd ever heard. Since when did God differentiate between clever kids and dumb kids who didn't know maths? Had God sent the nuns on a mission to only teach clever kids? And which kids were more in need of good teachers, the clever ones or the dumb ones who couldn't figure out what letters of the alphabet were doing in the middle of a sum anyway? Good day, Mr de Jong, she told me. And that was that, interview over.

We were screwed. We were that confident that Veronica would be accepted by the Convent, we hadn't sat entrance exams for any other schools. Things on the home front were not good. Veronica was in a perpetual flood of tears. Jenny was properly pissed off with Veronica, the Catholic Church, the state of education in Zimbabwe and me, for some reason. Jenny and I wrote out a list of other private school options open to us and set off with caps in hand and our sad, sorry story to beg for a desk for Veronica. We started with Arundel, the Anglican version of the Convent.

Arundel enjoyed an incredibly pretty setting with the pastel pink campus buildings set in amongst a massive, sprawling, leafy park-like campus. Known as the Pink Prison, Arundel had a reputation for academic excellence, so Jenny and I didn't hold out much hope for our chances. We joined a short queue of other dejected parents and waited to see the headmaster. We were eventually ushered into the headmaster's office. He looked like he'd been picked straight out of a headmaster's catalogue with grey suit and scholarly horn-rimmed glasses. It was only nine o'clock in the morning, and already he looked like he'd had a long day, so we launched straight into our tale of woe, starting with all the trauma of our adoption process. I'd prepared a nice monologue about Veronica's sunny disposition, thriftiness, enquiring mind, willingness to go the extra mile to make up for any problems she might encounter in the maths classroom, blah, blah, blah but the headmaster cut me short. Veronica was in. They would find a desk at the school for her. But she would have to work hard academically to keep up. Jenny and I did a little dance in the car park and heaved the hugest sigh of relief. Veronica had a good school to go to.

I went back to the Convent the next day to share our happy news with the Iron Nun. I got the same reaction you get when you poke a big granite rock with a stick.

With Veronica safely ensconced at a good high school, everything was all good in our world. Our businesses were doing fine despite the Zimbabwean economy, our children were doing fine, life for Jenny and I just couldn't be better. Nothing was pinging on my radar, life was good. Alas. As it turned out, there were lots of loud pings, but I just didn't pay them any attention.

The loud pings came in the form of little blue Chinese tractors, thousands and thousands of them, all lined up in an obscure government vehicle yard on the backstreets of Kuwadzana Township. I only bumped into them because I got lost on a short cut to best friend Bob Hamill's factory. There were that many of them I stopped to take a better look. They were cheap and nasty and cried out 'Made in China'- the sort of tractors Chinese peasants might use. And there was a multitude of them, row upon row, all dirty and dusty from a long time in storage. Bob knew about the tractors. They'd been imported by Chenjerai Hitler Hunzvi, the erstwhile leader of the Zimbabwe War Veterans Association.

"What does he want with so many tractors?" I asked.

"Maybe he wants to go farming," Bob said.

Chenjerai Hitler Hunzvi was infamous for having killed the Zimbabwe dollar. He was also the recently elected Chairman of the War Veterans Association, even though he'd spent the war in Poland botching and re-botching his medical degree. Hitler was his chimurenga name or Nome de Guerre, but I'm guessing he kept it a secret while heroically studying in suburban Warsaw and trotted it out only when he got back to a free Zimbabwe fully ten years after the war had finished. Once there, Doctor Hunzvi hung out his shingle and made a living mostly as a pox doctor, treating erstwhile comrades for diseases of the willy.

Hunzvi hit the big time though when the government set up a commission in the mid-nineties to peg compensations for former war veterans based on the injuries they'd suffered during the struggle. Hunzvi made headlines when he notched up a massive $650000 settlement for one of his clients whose persistent headaches, ear and stomach aches, hallucinations, congested throat and the occasional cough all dated back to traumas suffered during the struggle. According to the good doctor's arithmetic, his client's ailments added up to a 98% disability.

The headlines made for great advertising. War veterans beat a path to Dr Hunzvi's surgery, all looking for jackpot settlements, all prepared to cut the good doctor in for a percentage of any compensation awards for services rendered. Feeling left out, and obviously, rather poorly, Hunzvi gave himself a thorough examination, discovered that his various ailments, when added up totalled a whopping 117% disability and negotiated a $500,000 pay-out for himself. Alas. If it weren't so disgusting and sad, it would have been funny.

Not happy with having made lots and lots of money, Hunzvi used his newfound popularity with his erstwhile patients and comrades to snag the top job in the War Veteran's Association. With that in the bag, he set about looking for new and more lucrative fields to plough on their behalf, for a fee of course. Hitler Hunzvi wanted the big time.

He set his targets very high. At a press conference, he declared his war veterans to be deserving of a fifty-thousand dollar lump sum pay-out, plus monthly stipends of two thousand dollars, plus subsidised schooling for their children, plus etcetera etceteras too numerous mention. He'd called for a meeting with President Mugabe to table his demands.

Fifty thousand dollars at the time could buy you a house in a high-density suburb. Or seven hundred and sixty thousand bottles of beer. (Having survived the war myself, I got mildly excited. Silly me. Apparently, the financial pat on the back was reserved for war veterans from the winning side only.) The sums were huge. Multiplied by the fifty thousand war veterans supposedly on the books got you to 2.5 billion, an impossibly large petty cash withdrawal for a country with a well-knackered economy. It was obvious that Mugabe would have no option but to kick Hunzvi's demands into touch. Alas. As it turned out, Hunzvi played hard-ball poker better than Mugabe, who gave in to the war veteran's demands immediately.

The news of Mugabe's collapse in the face of Hunzvi's intransigent demands broke on the Friday, a Friday that would go down in the history books as Black. The sycophantic Herald's headlines announced the good news about the war veterans' bountiful payday jubilantly but hid the bad bits about the dollar's subsequent freefall and the attendant collapse of the Stock Market in the small print on the back pages, appropriately next to the obituaries. The currency black-market leapt into overdrive as street traders and coffee shop dealers clamoured and fought for US dollars, euros and pounds, anything but Zimbabwe dollars. People emptied their bank accounts looking for a currency port in the storm ahead. The black-market rate levelled for a breather at an impossible sixteen hundred to one, thirty times higher than the official bank rate.

Overnight long multiplication and division became the order of the day. Very quickly, my head hurt. I am the sort of person who has to stop walking to chew my bubble-gum to avoid lacerating my gums. The sixteen hundred times table was way beyond me.

As an exporter, my hard currency earnings would protect me against the massive deflation to come. But I was still Mr Grumpy Pants with a hangover. On the morning of Black Friday, I got into a huge argument with the counter salesman at an irrigation supply company. He was very happy the war veterans were getting their just rewards. The war veterans were his heroes, he told me. They'd won the liberation war, why shouldn't they get the lion's share of the spoils. I told him that he was stupid and would soon be a millionaire. He smirked at the thought. But I pointed out that being a millionaire sucks when a loaf of bread costs two million bucks. The counter salesman burst out laughing. Alas. Annoyingly for all, it turned out my crystal ball was in good working order.

I had two war veterans working for me on the farm at the time. They were husband and wife. She worked in the grading shed and he sort of worked in the general gang, where he did not do a lot. I was surprised when I found out they were war veterans because both were so nondescript. They didn't stand out at all. I treated them no different from any of my other workers.

When Mr and Mrs War Vet both got their fifty- thousand dollar pay-outs, there were raucous celebrations in the compound that went on late into the early morning. Shona people are nice people and are always very genuinely happy with other people's good fortunes. Both Mr and Mrs War Vet struggled into my office the next day with epic hangovers to ask for their annual leave, starting immediately. They told me they needed time off to spend their windfall money. They came back on the first day with his and her television sets. He got a twenty-four inch, and she got a twenty-one inch.

Notwithstanding the complete crap they showed on ZTV, two television sets for a family of two was strange, especially when they didn't have electricity. It took them just a month to blow their lump sum pay-outs. He invested heavily in new friendships, beer and strong stuff at the local bottle store and she bought shiny clothes and wigs. As soon as their money was gone, they tendered their resignations. The monthly stipends they'd get as war vets were ten times more than what they earned on the farm.

I waved goodbye to them as they trundled down the farm road in a hired truck, piled high with cheap electronic acquisitions. I wished good luck to them both and felt sorry for them. They'd been given enough money to make a difference to their lives but received zero support and zero guidance. There was no benevolence in the government gesture to compensate their former fighters. It was politics. Mugabe sold the country to buy Hunzvi and his war veterans going forward.

And now Hunzvi had gone out and bought a shit load of cheap Chinese peasant tractors. What the hell for, I wondered? But life was busy though and good, and it didn't take me long to forget about the little blue tractors. Alas. As it turned out, I should have packed up my family and worldly possessions and scurried for the safety of far, far away.

Chapter Eighteen

1999 was a helter-skelter busy year for the family de Jong. With the threat of Y2K hanging over us, it was a year to tick bucket list stuff off and get things done. Apparently, according to a friend who knew, all the electronic devices in the world could cease to function on the 1st of January 2000. Their motherboard brains would bump into a whole lot of unexpected noughts on the day and jetliners would fall out of skies, computers would stop computing, microwaves would stop microwaving, and my toaster would serve raw toast. Alas. My computer was only three years old, and I hated raw toast.

Gary's birthday falls on the second of January. Jenny had her old VW Beetle souped-up and finished off with a killer spray job, and we gave it to Gary for his birthday. The look of absolute excitement on his face was worth the money we'd spent on it and more.

As part of the same birthday present, we also took him to the Victoria Falls to shit in his pants while white-water rafting on the Zambezi. Jenny and I had done the white-water rafting trip a few years back. It was the most exciting thing I'd ever done, and I couldn't wait to share the experience with Gary. The Vic Falls was up there with the best white-water in the world with rapids called Stairway to Heaven, The Terminator, The Washing Machine, Judgement Day, Devils Toilet Bowl, Oblivion and Commercial Suicide. Jenny's memories were less than fond, however, and she opted to sit out a bob down memory lane. Furthermore, she threatened me with certain death if Gary got lost, maimed, drowned or eaten.

Jenny told me that my certain death would be upgraded to a slow one if I took Gary on either of the last two rafts of the excursion. Each raft had six rafters plus a professional oarsman on it, and there were normally ten or more rafts per excursion. Cameramen in kayaks accompanied the flotilla through the rapids, capturing memories on film. And to make sure the memories were memorable, traditionally the last two rafts were the designated hairy rafts, full of nutcase tourists keen on extra excitement a.k.a. flipping for the benefit of the cameramen. Jenny and I had found out about the quaint tradition on our last excursion. She'd spent the day on the last raft in the line, mostly screaming "Oh my God, we're going to die!!!!" With Jenny's death threats still ringing in my ear, Gary and I had no option but to sign up to bring up the rear in raft number ten.

It was a low water year, so the rapids were quicker, more angry, more exciting. Our excursion started at rapid three, which gave rafters a more than rude Zambezi welcome. HMS Raft Number Ten was last in line, and we waited forever, nervous in our high buoyancy vests and safety helmets, watching rafts one through to nine disappear into the swirling maelstrom that was the river. And then it was our turn, and everything got wet, upside down and crazy. It was like sticking your head into a washing machine. After forever, I emerged from the vicious froth and foam, still on the raft, exhilarated and ready for the next rapid. I turned to high five Gary next to me and crap, he wasn't there. Oh my God, I was so going to die. We hadn't been on the river for more than three minutes, and already Gary was missing in action, on the first bloody rapid. Our guide, a young black guy with a very old head on his shoulders, told me not to panic as his busy eyes searched the surging froth of the river around us. Bugger not panicking. The only thing that went through my head was crocodiles, crocodiles and more crocodiles. And then after forever one of the safety kayaks downstream gave a loud shout as Gary came popping up out of the swirling waters like a champagne cork, 50 metres downstream of the raft.

"Don't do that again, Gary!!" I hissed angrily at him as he was hauled back into the raft, grinning like a wet Cheshire Cat.

"Yes, Dad," he promised me solemnly. And then promptly proceeded to fall out of the raft again, and again, and again. The kid was hopeless. He spent so little time in the raft I was thinking about changing his name to Bob and asking the rafting company for my money back. But Gary was having the time of his life.

Our most spectacular flip of the day happened on the Three Sisters, three wild rapids one straight after the other, and then the next without a break. Our raft flipped on the First Sister, and we had no time to right it before the Second Sister, and so we went through the Sisters Two and Three clinging for dear life to the safety ropes on the bottom of our upside-down raft.

The oldest guy on our raft was an Australian merchant seaman in his late fifties called Mick. Rapid number nine was a murderous vortex of angry water called Commercial Suicide. It was a no-go zone for the rafts, and we had to porter around it. Mick's land legs weren't too clever, and he slipped on the wet rocks and fell in at the water's edge. The angry water grabbed him immediately. Looking on horrified, I thought that was the end of Mick. Not so Gary. As quick as a flash, he dived full length on the jagged rocks and grabbed Mick by his fast disappearing ankle. It was an incredibly brave thing to do. Alas. Mick outweighed Gary two to one and Gary also started to disappear into threshing white waters. I dived and grabbed Gary's leg. And someone grabbed my leg, and everyone else heave hoed and Mick and Gary re-appeared, soaking wet but otherwise all good. I was hugely proud when Mick told me that Gary was a good bloke.

Young Dan set himself lofty goals for the other side of 1999. He told me he wanted to be a test cricketer when he left school. But not a farmer, definitely not a farmer. I could understand a dustbin man encountering that sort of occupational resistance from his son, but I had to say I was hurt by Dan's career stance. Plus, I had doubts about the test cricket option. Dan's talents with both bat and ball were well masked. Dan decided the problem was he wasn't given enough match practice out in the middle, not surprising given the fact that he hadn't made the school team. And so, he formed his own cricket team on the farm.

Daniel drafted his picanin friends from the farm compound into a Running Dog Eleven and set about teaching them the rudiments of the game, plus what a cricket bat and ball looked like. They must have been naturals because that didn't take more than ten minutes. Pleased with how his team was shaping, Dan felt they were more than ready for their first test challenge. He threw the down the gauntlet to the picanins from the Ministry of Roads camp next door. Who picked the gauntlet up gladly. And so, the Mount Hampden Five Day Test was on, although they would have to cram it all into just the one day on account of the fact it wasn't school holidays. The test match promised to be a real humdinger, even though none of the Ministry of Roads kids had even heard of the game cricket, let alone picked up a bat or ball,

On the morning of the test, Daniel was very not quietly confident. Like the English Coach David Lloyd, Daniel was predicting a murdering. Alas, as it happened, he was on the money. The Ministry of Road's raw talent in the bowling department scythed through soft underbellies of Dan's top, middle and lower batting orders, dispatching the entire team for single figures. Dan played a captain's knock and top-scored with two. But still, there was nothing quiet about Dan's confidence as he rallied his troops. With his fiercest grimace in place, he told his not very gallant men that all they had to do to win was to bowl the other team for less than twelve. It was a hell of a game to win, and the famous victory would be talked about for days to come. And because captains were supposed to lead from the front, Daniel decided he'd open the bowling himself, with a beguiling mix of either spin and or pace. It was all wonderfully stirring stuff. If Dan had asked his men to walk on broken glass, they would have cut their feet to ribbons for him. It was just a pity that he didn't get around to asking them to field well and take their catches. The Ministry of Roads opening batsmen bludgeoned the winning runs off Dan's first over. Alas.

Easily the biggest thing on the family's To-Do list that year was a trip to Euro Disney. We tacked a visit to Paris on to my annual flower business trip to Holland. We set off early in the morning from Amsterdam by bus in the general direction of Paris. Our bus driver got horribly and repeatedly lost and stuck in several obscure quaint little backwater villages whose streets weren't wide enough for double-decker buses. A trip that should have taken a few hours dragged out into a twenty-four-hour epic.

Gary and I shared the upstairs front of the bus with a 280-pound Hindu traveller. Breath, flatulence and his amplified body odour aside, he seemed a delightful chap. But unfortunately, we never really got the chance to get to know him well over the next twenty fours because he spent the entire time farting, belching, snoring and breathing all over us from close range, rendering small talk impossible. The only thing we learnt about him was that garlic, chillies and some kind of powerful smelling onion featured prominently in his diet. It must have been real bad inside that Hindu, because the garlic, chillies and powerful onion toxic stench flowed out him in a nonstop hurry, like a stream of rats from a sinking ship.

Mickey Mouse had never done much for me as a kid, I'd found him saccharine sweet and boring. Ditto Cinderella and Peter Pan and pretty much the whole Walt Disney tribe, bar maybe the cast from the Jungle Book. Accordingly, I was fully prepared to be underwhelmed by Disneyland Paris as I hobbled off the bus, contorted like Quasimodo and gagging on my first fresh air in twenty-four hours. But I was absolutely blown away by the place as soon as we'd navigated the 4-kilometre queue to get in. The feel-good was that infectious it grabbed hold of you as soon as you stepped onto the cobblestones and into Walt's fantasy. Coming from the dirty Third World, what struck us was that the Park was so clean and on such a large scale and the detail that went into themes of rides was amazing.

We rode on every ride, most more than once. Each of us had our favourite rides. Jenny and Veronica went with the nice but wimpy 'It's a Small World' and Aladdin, Gary declared Indiana Jones and the Temple of Peril the best ever and I couldn't get enough of Star Wars while Daniel favoured everything. Every ride he went on was better than the last one but not as good as the next. He was beyond hyper and determined to not miss out on anything to the point where Dan pushed the limits of his bladder way past the outer edges of the envelope. At times he was that contorted standing in the queue for his next ride, I was pretty sure he'd fashioned a knot in his willy. Eventually, Gary and I would have to physically him drag out of queues and into the toilet screaming and fighting.

We upgraded our Nikon camera in Paris, especially for the Disney trip. The new camera was a thing of beauty with long lenses and wide lenses and far too many buttons for me to ever get my head around. Because of my propensity for taking photos of my thumb, I was relegated to humping the old camera around while Jenny was the designated new camera snapper. She put it through its paces and snapped 14 million photos of our Disney holiday.

There must have been some super photos in amongst them, but alas, we never go to see any because Jenny, unfortunately, left her camera bag behind on the Metro the next day. Manfully, I grumped, sulked, cried and stomped around the Paris Underground swearing and cursing. In the absence of any cats to kick, I took it all out on poor Jenny. Shame. She got all excited every time she saw a blue train pull into the station. It had to be the train with the camera bag on it. The train she'd left the camera on had definitely also been blue. I took perverse pleasure in pointing out to Jenny that every one of the thousand freaking trains on the French Underground was blue.

We set out to find the Lost and Found. With years of high school French under his belt, Gary was in charge of communicating with the locals. Alas. Apparently, the French as spoken by Frenchmen in France was not the same French as taught in Zimbabwean schools. Either that or the Underground was lousy with foreigners who didn't speak proper French. Eventually, Gary was able to get some hippy guy with a ponytail, a rucksack and a smattering of English to stop and listen. Excellent. At long last, someone we could ask questions of. Alas. He turned out to be a tourist from Ecuador. He was lost and could we point him in the direction of the Louvre? And no, he hadn't seen our lost Nikon. And no, he didn't know where the Lost and Found was. Well, could he do us a favour and ask for directions to the Lost and Found? No. His French was worse than Gary's.

When we got back to Zim, Jenny wrote to a very nice English family that we'd met at Euro Disney and told them about our camera disaster. They were kind enough to send us copies of all their Euro Disney photos but looking at other people's happy holiday snaps didn't quite cut it. I promised Jenny and the kids I'd take us back to Euro Disney for another photo session as soon as possible.

Running businesses in Zimbabwe wasn't easy though with the currency in free fall, and prices gathered noughts with alarming alacrity. But I threw myself into work and read Donald Trump books cover-to-cover and went on an efficiency binge. Nick Dickens and I opened an Irish themed pub in the George Hotel, which we called the Freckle and Phart. We acquired the lease on the Feathers Hotel with seventeen bedrooms, a nice carvery restaurant and three bars. The Feathers was in the neighbourhood that I'd grown up in. I'd enjoyed my first illicit beers at age thirteen there and vomited them out in the hotel's flower beds shortly after that. The farm was flying. We exported twenty tons of cut-flowers to Holland in a single week. Our Garden Centre on the outskirts of town was busy, ditto our Wholesale Garden Plant Nursery on the farm. I was flat out busy and enjoying it hugely.

December that year was particularly crazy busy. First up was my fortieth birthday party. Gary suggested a medieval theme might be appropriate, given my age. For the big event, the grading shed was transformed into the Royal Court of King Eric the Flatulent and Queen Jenny the Also Flatulent, complete with dungeons and cardboard crenulations, royal squires, royal pages and serving wenches (Gary, Daniel and Veronica) singing bards complete with electric guitar and amplifiers, punishment stocks and a royal abundance of meads, ales and other stuff to quaff. The turnout was epic with best friends that I hadn't seen forever, including Cousin Hanny who flew in from Holland.

Stand-out memories that survived the alcoholic assault on my memory banks included Ben Mundangepfupfu, my best Shona buddy, being thrown into stocks for coming dressed like a shiny Nigerian pimp. The George Hotel did the bar. Raphael and Clever were drafted in as extra bar hands come security guards, and both got legless drinking to my health. I didn't really mind. They'd been with me on the farm from the beginning, and I counted them as friends. I have very vague memories of it being a great night. According to hearsay, my behaviour was less than kingly. I drank, danced and behaved badly like a teenager and woke up with parts of me feeling seventy, especially my head.

We only just finished hanging over from my fortieth, when the farm hosted a family wedding when Jenny's sister Michelle married new brother-in-law, Kevin Maher, from Johannesburg. The wedding reception was held in a marquee in Tony and Hester's garden. A massive contingent of South African friends and family, including the new Maher branch of the family, braved Beitbridge border post to celebrate the nuptials. The festivities went on until dawn, apparently. I say apparently because now that I was forty, all-night parties were beyond me. Gary, cousin Hanny and new cousin by marriage Tom, tried to drive the five hundred metres home, three up on the farm four-wheeler. Unfortunately, they were blinded by the rising sun, took a wrong turning and ploughed their way across fields and fields of flowers. Raphael was enraged when he saw the damage and gave Gary a tongue lashing that woke the neighbourhood up.

We only just finished hanging over from the wedding when it was onward and upward to a bigger and better party; an epic Millennium New Year's Eve Beach Party in Beira, Mozambique. It was a massive undertaking, and Jenny worked on the logistics for months. All our best friends signed up for the trip, and their best friends, and their best friends plus honeymooners Kevin and Michelle, and cousin Hanny from Holland. We were forty strong and called ourselves Le Grande Group, which sounded sort of Portuguese.

Rio Savane was on a tiny island across a lagoon, just north of Beira. It took the army of porters hours to get Le Grande Group and all our kit across the lagoon in little pontoon rafts. Our accommodations were barracas, little more than reed huts, tucked in behind the dunes on the middle of the narrow island. A two hundred metre walk one way brought you onto the long golden rolling beaches and the open sea and two hundred metres the other way brought you to the still waters of the lagoon. With no shops or other distractions on the island, there was nothing to do other than lie on the beach, swim in the sea or loll in the warm waters of the lagoon. Or get up to mischief. Dan and Sean Doorly captured a sack full of mangrove crabs and released them in the ladies showers, causing loud screams and consternation. Dan and Veronica tanned to the deepest darkest brown. Gary and best friend Matt spent long days on the beach pumping out their chests and biceps whenever they thought girls might be watching. Rio Savane was the perfect family holiday destination. At sea level, my rubber duck with its 25 horsepower outboard flew across the lagoon, dragging laughing kids behind on a tractor tube. Gary wanted me to pull him and Matt out into the open sea, and the rolling surf but the power of the ocean petrified me.

We planned a trip into the city of Beira to buy prawns and crabs for a seafood dinner. The last time I'd been in Beira was 1975 just before the Portuguese colonial lords and masters woke up one morning and left Mozambique, all three hundred and fifty thousand of them, gone almost literally overnight. And from what I could see, in the intervening twenty-five years, the new lords and masters of Mozambique had been busy doing not a lot. Driving around Beira was surreal. Rusted trains stood parked on the rusted tracks, not having moved a metre in a quarter-century. The harbour was still clogged up and unusable, because of a half dozen sunken ships had been scuttled by their fleeing Portuguese skippers. The ruin of the luxury Dom Carlos Hotel loomed large above the beach, completed in 1975 but never opened and now home to thousands of people living in filth and squalor. On the fifth floor, a massive mango tree, obviously well fertilised with human waste had burst out through the walls and roof. Beira International Airport was the most surreal. It boasted two runways, but one was still closed, obstructed by the wreckage of a MIG jet shot down by the Rhodesians in the late seventies. Removing the wreckage would have been half an hour's work with a tractor, but the Mozambiqueans had soldiered on manfully with just the one runway for over twenty-five years. And inside the arrivals hall, the digital information board still showed the details of the last flight to Lourenço Marques, twenty-five years earlier. Mozambiqueans took laid back to another level. Beira's pavement restaurant menus offered up a choice between peri-peri prawns or peri-peri chicken. Both dishes took more than an hour, but the wait spent drinking Laurentina beer added to the meal experience.

After lunch we went to the fish market. On the way there we encountered the only thing in Beira that works, the traffic cops. They lurked behind every bush, waiting to pounce on foreign number plates in search of beer money fines. The first cop that pulled us over came up against my Portuguese-English phrasebook. It was a non-contest. Phrasebooks are ridiculous things and allow you to come across fluent in a language that you cannot speak. The cop wanted to fine us a lot of money for ignoring the missing speed limit signs, I think. I say I think because his English was very broken. Enter the phrasebook. I asked the cop, in near-perfect Portuguese, if he thought there might be a frost tonight. It was easily forty degrees out in the midday sun, so he replied "Huh?" I pressed on with the next question. "Is there are a hairdressing salon nearby?" Another "Huh?" Again, in fluent Portuguese, I asked: "Is this the road to Lisbon?" The cop broke and waved us on.

Walking around the Beira fish market, it struck me that the word hygiene didn't translate into Mozambiquean Portuguese. The market was heaving, full of people, flies and smells, all clamouring for our attention. Eventually, in amongst the crowded stalls, we found some prawns and crabs that sort of looked fresh and didn't smell too dodgy. Negotiations dragged out by my phrasebook were eventually concluded and we left with cold boxes bulging. The New Year's Eve seafood dinner on the beach complete with fireworks and dancing was epic. And then more of the same the next night for Gary's black tie and swimwear birthday party.

Rested and recharged after a great holiday, I was ready to go home to take on the challenges of the new century ahead. Lying on the beach on that last day of the holiday, hanging over and soaking up the last of the sun and the crashing waves, it suddenly struck me that I was utterly content with my lot in life. I loved my life, I loved my family, and I loved what I did for a living. There was nowhere else in the world I'd rather be. Which is a pretty huge thing. Not too many people get to tick the utterly content box.

Jenny was sitting next to me, lathering Daniel in his daily blanket of sunscreen. The sunscreen hadn't worked too well. By the end of the holiday, Daniel had tanned dark brown, verging on black. Jenny called me to look at something on the back of Dan's leg. I didn't have to ask what she was looking at. There was a patch of white skin the size of my fist, tucked in behind his knee joint. It was shockingly white against the rest of his dark brown tan, almost albino like, without any pigment at all. It hadn't been there a few days before.

"What is it, Eric?" There was worry in Jenny's voice.

"You've smeared the sunscreen on so hard, you've rubbed some of his tan off," I joked.

"But what if it spreads?"

"It won't spread. Put some extra cream on today, and it will go away. Everything will be just fine." All was well in my world; everything would work out just fine.

Alas. As it turned out, I got that all a tad wrong. Within four short years, Dan would lose ninety percent of his skin pigmentation to the autoimmune disorder, Vitiligo. And the rest of my happy little world didn't do too good either.

Chapter Nineteen

What do you get the dictator who has everything for Christmas? It's the sort of question that will keep you awake at night if you're a Mugabe sycophant. The answer was simple. More power, for longer, wrapped up in a shiny new constitution.

The constitution bit was important these days. A dictator couldn't go out of a morning to oppress his peasants any old how anymore, not like Joe Stalin and Chairman Mao used to. The world was a different place now, full of bloody human rights, with too many people watching, like CNN and the accursed BBC. If you oppressed the downtrodden, the televisions would be full of it and then the International Criminal Court would start banging on their drums about tribunals in The Hague and sanctions. And what was a Dictator to do if he couldn't take his wife shopping in Paris or Milan? God, he'd never hear the end of it. And it wasn't like you could take Grace shopping in North Korea instead. All you could buy there were little red books and cheap, grey suits with the collars missing. And how unfair was that? How come all the good shops were in the west? It was enough to make any reasonable dictator see red and...which brought you back to the bloody constitution again. Which meant holding a bloody referendum. And giving the bloody peasants a bloody choice.

But where there was a will, there was a way. And the old adage, you can fool all the people, all the time, provided you threw enough money and enough press at it.

At the end of 1999 going into 2000, Mugabe's ministers set about crafting a new constitution with loads more power for the President hidden in the screeds and screeds of small print that nobody read anyway. They set a date for a rushed referendum in January and rolled out a massive Vote Yes campaign, monopolising headlines, radio, television and billboards countrywide, urging the people to vote Yes to the new constitution.

I broached the subject of the referendum with my farmworkers and was horrified to find out that they were all buying into the bullshit of the Yes campaign. With no free press or independent media, the only opinions they were exposed to were Mugabe's and his propaganda machine.

Eventually a Vote No campaign got slowly out the starting blocks. They didn't have the big buck budget of the Yes campaign and had to rely more on teams of young volunteers going door to door, stripping away the small print, exposing the new constitution's flaws. I tracked the Vote No campaign offices down and organised some activists to come and talk to my workers. The only time slot they could offer me was nine o'clock on a workday. It wasn't ideal. We were right in the middle of the early build-up to Valentine's Day exports. And it would clash with another visit from a Dutch Auction delegation. But it was nine o'clock or not at all, so I rushed into town to collect the Vote No activists. There were two of them, both second-year university students taking time out from their studies to get involved. They impressed me hugely. When we got back to the farm, we interrupted the harvest so that all the workers could listen to the Vote No campaigners. The Dutch visitors arrived in the middle of the meeting. I took them on the guided tour but winced when we got out in the fields. It was a hot morning, and we were losing the cut stage in the field quickly.

"Why aren't you picking?" the sales director of the auction asked.

I told them about the referendum and the need to educate the workers about their democratic choices and...they looked back at the fields of ready for harvest flowers and shook their heads. They clearly thought I was mad for letting politics come before business.

I wanted to get involved in the No Vote campaign but couldn't. We had to take Gary down to South Africa to deliver him to university. He was booked in to do a Fine Arts degree, majoring in photography. Gary going to university was a big deal for both Jenny and me. He was the first member from either side of the family to go to university. Not to put any pressure on Gary, we pointed this fact out to him ad infinitum on the 2500- kilometre drive down to Grahamstown. We'd picked Rhodes University mostly because it was in such a small town. There was nothing to Grahamstown outside of the university campus, and there was no need for Gary to have a car down there. He could walk home from all the pubs in town no problem. And South Africa's big cities like Pretoria, Johannesburg or Cape Town scared us as parents. They were such violent cities, and Gary was a softy.

Grahamstown eventually appeared on the horizon after an endless bum and brain-numbing drive through the Karoo. The town and the university were small, charming and everything we expected them to be. I tested all the pubs rigorously and approved of them thoroughly, especially the Rat and Parrot. What I wouldn't have given to be young again and embarking on a university adventure like Gary's. Alas.

We got back to Harare just in time to vote in the referendum. After not being able to vote in all the previous elections where my choices were limited to a Mugabe or a Mugabe, it felt real good putting my emphatic X in the Vote No box. I felt even better later when the news came through on the car radio days later that the No Vote had won, overwhelmingly. I was driving back from the airport at the time, gridlocked in heavy traffic right outside ZANU PF headquarters. As one, the traffic jam around me hit their hooters in elation when the news broke on the radio. The guy next to me pressed both hands flat on his hooter and cried tears of joy. I joined in the cacophony. It was a huge feel-good moment. That I was looking up at Mugabe's ugly grey monstrosity of a building at the time, added to the feel good. I just hoped the old bastard was inside, hearing all the joyous hooting.

Mugabe came across as almost presidential when he conceded defeat in a live address on television that night. He was stone-cold expressionless as he congratulated the people of Zimbabwe for exercising their democratic rights quietly and peacefully. But beneath the camera façade, you could sense that the veins in his head were throbbing with rage. He told the watching world that the referendum had shown that contrary to belief, democracy was alive and living in Zimbabwe. He and his government would accept the will of the people as expressed in the referendum results. And given the results of the referendum, Mugabe felt he had no choice but to set a date for presidential elections. He was sure that those elections would be as peaceful, dignified and orderly.

In closing and with a poker face from hell, Mugabe singled out the white population for 'sloughing off their apathy' and getting involved in the poll. It was a chilling moment and gave me goose bumps. It was like watching a snake telling a rat well done for sticking his head out.

Mugabe the snake, played his cards almost immediately. Within a week, the first white commercial farms were invaded by landless peasants delivered in government vehicles. Chenjerai Hitler Hunzvi and his war veterans led the invasions. War veterans was a term very loosely applied to anyone between the ages of eighteen and sixty. The invasions happened countrywide. They were well organised by the military. Landless peasants and war veterans fuelled on government-issued marijuana and cheap booze and delivered in army and air force trucks told the waiting ZTV cameras that they were sick and tired of waiting for the land that had been promised them after the war. And because white farmers had joined with anti-ZANU PF supporters to reject the constitution that would have given Mugabe the powers to give them the land, the war veterans were taking back forcibly the land of their forefathers, with machetes, clubs and burning torches.

Some of the most productive farms in the country went up in flames. But bollocks was it about the land. It was nothing other than a huge smokescreen to divert electoral attentions away from real bread and butter issues like unemployment and a knackered economy come the general elections.

I went to my first political meeting a week after the first farm invasion. It was a meeting held by a newly formed party, the Movement for Democratic Change. Most pundits gave the MDC less than a year before they disappeared from sight beneath Mugabe's boot, like the other opposition parties before them. But I decided to go and hear them out anyway.

The MDC was formed by a mishmash of trade unionists and academics.

THE START OF THE MADNESS

They looked to be extremely organised. The main speakers at the meeting were Morgan Tsvangirai, formerly the leader of the Zimbabwe Congress of Trade Unions and a young lawyer called Tendai Biti. First up they taught us the party slogans. Apparently, African politics have to have slogans. The main MDC responsorial chant 'Chinja Maitiro' was used as a greeting and meant Change Your Ways. It took a few attempts, but the stodgy white element in the audience eventually caught on. I loved it. The chanting was my best bit. Tsvangirai wasn't the most polished of speakers, but he said everything that I wanted to hear from a black politician. Tendai Biti spoke well and with infectious enthusiasm, like a lawyer out of a John Grisham novel. Come question time the mostly white audience put the former trade union leader through the wringer, but he acquitted himself well. Most white Zimbabweans view trade unions with suspicion.

A question from an old black guy in front of me was a stark reminder of what opposition politics in Zimbabwe was all about. What was he supposed to do when ZANU PF came to his house late at night, kicked his door in and beat him for supporting the MDC? Morgan told him he needed to have courage. He told us the story of how the secret police or CIO had kicked down his office door the previous year and hung him out of his tenth-floor window and gave him a good view of the pavement below. The CIO operatives told him that unless he gave up on politics, the next time they would drop him to his death. In his place, I would have been on the very next plane to London. Instead, Morgan reaffirmed his commitment to challenge Mugabe in the 2000 elections.

The last speaker at the meeting was a white industrialist called Bill Searle. He introduced himself as a white war veteran. He likened his involvement with the MDC to another stint of national service. He asked us to be generous with our donations. After the meeting finished, the queues that formed in front of the pledge desks went out the door. I wasn't the only one in the room to be filled with hope. The next day I went to the MDC offices, met with a burly rancher come volunteer called Hendrik O'Neill and offered up my services. I also offered up the George Hotel free of charge, as a venue for all MDC meetings and to accommodate out of towners. Hendrik pencilled me in for my home constituency, Zvimba South.

"The old man's constituency," Hendrik told me. "Good luck with that."
"Which old man?"
"Mugabe. You're going up against Mugabe in his home constituency."

Things moved very quickly. That evening I went to the first MDC Support meeting, held at the George Hotel and attended by volunteers, mostly farmers from what I could see, from all over the country. Hendrik chaired the meeting and seemed to know most of the people in the room, including one Roy Bennett from Chimanimani. Hendrik split us into provincial groups and constituencies. Our roles as members of the MDC Support would be to provide logistical support for our constituency candidates. There were lots of questions. I eyed out the provincial groups. The rural provinces were well subscribed, but Harare Province was very thin on the ground with just one support member. At the end of the meeting, I was properly enthused. This thing that I'd just become a part of was going to make such a huge difference to Zimbabwe. It would right all the wrongs and drag the country out of the morass. I couldn't contain my excitement and had to share. I phoned Bob Hamill and duly infected him with the democracy disease that I would later christen the 'Chinja' Virus. The next day Bob volunteered for the Harare Support.

My MDC boss was a giant of a man called John Brown. John was a very successful farmer and engineer. His office wasn't far from Running Dog. When I arrived, he was putting up one in fifty thousand maps of Zimbabwe on the main wall of his office, with all the constituencies marked out on it. John had been tasked with setting up MDC Support teams in the north of the country. It was a huge job, but then John was a huge man. Well over six foot four with a deep gravelly voice, John had a massive presence about him. He told me that my job would be to provide logistical support for my MDC candidate and help him organise his meetings and rallies. Didn't sound too daunting. I went back to the farm and handed over the reins to my farm manager Brian Masona.

"You run the farm, Brian. I'm going to play politician full time right through to the elections."

I met my candidate the next day. His name was Titus Nheya. He was an elderly trade unionist with absolutely zero fire and brimstone about him. I congratulated him on his brave decision to contest Zvimba South against Mugabe's sister, Sabina. Titus's brave face wobbled at his prospects. He had all the conviction of St George going up against the dragon whilst wearing inflammable underwear. We looked at the constituency map, and Titus wobbled some more. Kutama Mission in the Zvimba Communal Lands, Mugabe's birthplace, lurked large and malignant in the middle of the map like a real-life Mordor, surrounded by huge swathes of commercial farmland. It was an area that stretched at least a hundred and fifty kilometres from top to bottom.

Titus explained the task at hand. Our first job was to organise a series of rallies and meetings to mobilise MDC party structures at cell level across the length and breadth of the constituency. Each party cell had a chairman and a treasurer and a secretary with similar structures for women and youth. I was very impressed and asked for a list of phone numbers so I could start phoning. Alas. There wasn't a database. Mostly because there weren't any party structures in place, at any level. Titus was starting from scratch. And me along with him.

"We've got lots do, Titus so see you tomorrow, bright and early."

Unfortunately, Titus couldn't do bright and early, mostly because he lived in Chinoyi, a town a hundred kilometres away, and Titus didn't have a car, and the public transport was badly affected by the fuel shortage and... I told him that I'd send a truck to collect him first thing in the morning. I tossed and turned all night, stressing about missing chairmen and non-existent party structures. What the hell was I doing? My sock drawer in my cupboard was an official disaster zone, and here I was trying to organise a political party.

The next day Titus moved into a house on the farm. The fuel shortage was crippling, and we couldn't afford to send a truck to Chinoyi twice a day to collect Titus and drop him off. And by the end of the first day, he had held his first rally, on Running Dog Farm. It was a good turnout of more than three hundred. I watched the rally from the fringes. Titus was the most wooden of speakers but was still able to get the crowd up on their feet and all excited. When he hit them with the opening CHINJA MAITIRO the response that came back from the crowd was beyond deafening. The people's excited enthusiasm was out in the open for all to see. I knew that what I was watching wasn't a flash in the pan, the people of Zimbabwe wanted political change, badly. Titus spoke about the basics that the MDC would target, creating jobs, putting an end to corruption, improving health delivery etc. The crowd roared their approval every time he said something. And when at the end of the rally he asked for volunteers for the party structures, there was a veritable stampede and minutes later, Titus had his first Party cell structure in the bag. Raphael emerged as the duly elected district chairman. Running Dog was going to be short another member of management for the duration.

Over the coming days and weeks, we repeated the rally over and over again across the district and were always met with the same excited enthusiasm. Wooden Titus pulled crowds everywhere he went and was welcomed with the emphatic open hand and loud cries of Chinja. I loved it. It was like hanging out with Father Christmas.

I roped in friends to help me get things organised. There was lots to do. Every meeting held required written requests in triplicate to be submitted to the police station. And there was lots of begging to do with farmers; asking them if we could have access to their workforces and hold meetings on their farms, and most importantly, for donations. I was starting to find out very quickly that politics was an expensive indulgence, especially African politics. To win the hearts and minds of the African electorate, all you needed to do was to give them free Party t-shirts and caps. But free t-shirts and caps were actually bloody expensive. Neighbours Phil and Tony were my right-hand men while Terry Dawson did loads of the organising from the confines of his wheelchair.

At our first Provincial Support meeting held in Banket, Phil and I were able to report huge progress in Zvimba South. What was the reaction from ZANU PF we were asked? So far absolutely zero we reported back. ZANU PF hadn't held a single rally in Zvimba South yet, and we'd held dozens. It was as though they'd been caught flat-footed. The other constituencies reported much the same. Phil and I drove back in high spirits and chinjaed all and sundry on the road home.

Our first major fundraising meeting was held in John Brown's engineering shed and attended by more than a hundred prominent farmers and others from the district. Phil and I wore MDC T-shirts and were in charge of welcoming the farmers to the event. Before handing over to the main speakers, I urged the farmers to dig deep to help give Mugabe a bloody nose in his own backyard come elections. The main speakers drawn from the MDC leadership were Trudi Stephenson, a prominent human rights activist and Tendai Biti, the young firebrand lawyer. In his opening remarks, Biti extended a warm welcome to all the secret policemen from the CIO that were with us in the audience. Crap. And I'd just stood up in the front of the crowd and prattled on about giving Mugabe a bloody nose. Biti was a punchy speaker and worked his magic on the crowd. He spoke about his own aspirations, and what he wanted out of life and they weren't much different to anyone else's in the room. Peace, prosperity, children and grandchildren who would grow up and grow old in Zimbabwe. He loosened the purse strings effectively and donations flooded in at the end of the meeting.

My own fundraising skills were slightly more suspect, though. I memorised big chunks of Tendai's speech and used them on a prominent farmer in the district a few days later. The farmer told me I was a troublemaker and kicked me off his farm. Alas.

The highlight of our electoral campaign was a series of Star Rallies to be organised in which the local candidate would share the stage with a headline speaker from the Party leadership. I managed to snag Tendai Biti for the Zvimba South Star Rallies. In front of a bigger crowd, Tendai was a hundred percent electric and our first two Star Rallies we held were hugely successful. The third promised to be even bigger. We were holding it at Nyabira, a small high-density suburb with a thousand or more residents about twenty kilometres from Running Dog. But our real target audience for the rally were the soldiers from the nearby Nkomo Army barracks.

The Nyabira rally was only due to start at two o'clock but the crowd starting building at ten in the morning. Our farm security company had its headquarters not far from the rally venue, and they sent me hourly updates. At eleven o'clock, the boss of the security company phoned me up with bad news. His undercover details had reported back that a large contingent of war veterans had been bussed in to disrupt the rally. And also to beat de

Jong...badly.

I almost vomited there and then as fear grabbed hold of me with both hands. I have the worst possible combination, a vivid imagination and the world's lowest pain threshold, and they teamed up on me. I could almost feel the fists and boots, and whips and clubs, thudding into me, targeting mostly my balls, I just knew my balls would be in for a good kicking.

"What am I supposed to do?" I asked the security company manager.

"Cancel the rally," he told me.

"But...but I've got police permission."

"Hah. The police," he snorted derisively. "As soon as the war veterans arrived, the police ran away."

I phoned Tendai in a complete panic and told him what was happening. I could have kissed him when he told me to pull the plug on the rally. Panic averted. My balls were overjoyed. They weren't going to be booted.

The panic was back on when the security company phoned at three o'clock. A mob of war veterans fifty strong and all properly liquored up had started marching down the main road to Running Dog. The beating for de Jong was back on apparently. I got hold of Hamish Turner on the short-wave radio to tell him what was happening and to ask him what to do. Hamish was both our district Commercial Farmer's Union rep and the leader of our neighbourhood watch team. He was everyone's 'Go to Guy' for farm invasion hassles.

"What do I do, Hamish?"

He gave me the CFU's stance. "You meet them at the gate, and you listen to their demands. Keep your gates locked. Don't provoke them, don't start the war."

"But this is nothing to do about my land, this all about politics," I wailed. Hamish said he would try and get the police involved and told me to keep him posted.

I went to go and tell Jenny what was happening but not before digging Daniel's cricket box out his kit bag and jamming my man bits inside it. It was tiny, and it hurt as I waddled through to the lounge to tell Jenny what was coming. I wanted her to take the kids into town. She flat out refused. Just then, Veronica walked through and asked what was going on. Jenny told her. Veronica burst into tears, her eyes were huge with fear, and with anger. She rounded on me.

"Why are you doing this to us, Dad, why are you getting involved in politics?"

My heart broke into little bits. "I can't not do it. I can't not get involved, " I told her and Jenny. "This thing isn't about just politics. It's about good versus evil. And evil flourishes when good men do nothing." It sounded lame as it came out, but it came from the bottom of my heart. I told them about my paternal grandfather who died in the Second World War because he got caught hiding Jews. "He stood up to evil. And this is the same sort of evil. And I can't not stand up to it. I can't just sit back and hope that it goes away." My voice quavered. Mostly because my balls were screaming out about the hopeless inadequacies of Daniel's cricket box. Jenny gave me a hug. I asked her again to take the kids into town, and again, she flat out refused.

And all the while I kept getting phone calls and radio messages of warning from people who had seen the mob on the road. Five kilometres down and just fifteen to go. At this rate, the mob would get to Running Dog at about five. John Brown arrived. He had heard what was happening and he'd come to sit with me and help me through the shit storm coming. My esteem for John, already high, jumped through the roof. He was one of the finest men I've ever met. John wasn't the only person who came to spend the day with us. Gayle Arnold, a widowed mother of three and one of our dearest friends, pitched up unannounced. She'd heard the stories and had invited herself for tea. It was surreal, sitting in the garden, trying to indulge in small talk and tea while waiting for a beating or worse. And all the while I argued with myself. This wasn't about land; it was about politics and confrontation. And if I weren't on the farm when the war veterans arrived, they'd have no option but to leave. It sounded like a very good idea in my head, so I bounced it off Hamish Turner again on the radio. Again, he told me I had to stay on the farm to meet the war veterans. If I didn't, it would be game over. I would never be able to walk onto my farm again, and I'd lose everything I owned. Crap. What Hamish said also made sense. But mostly, I just wanted to run away.

Jenny could see I was losing grip and doped me with Sulpiride. It worked a treat and allowed me to sit calmly, my thoughts wrapped up in a gentle cotton wool blur. John Brown filled the awkward silence with his take on a man's priorities. As he saw it, a man had obligations first and foremost to his family and friends, secondly to those who worked for him and thirdly to his country and community. Through the warm fuzz from the Sulpiride, it sounded all very deep and meaningful. And it made what I was doing feel right. Right there and then I would have followed John Brown across fields of broken glass.

There was a commotion at the main gate. It had to be the war veterans. My promised beating had arrived. John Brown was lighting his pipe at the time, and his hand remained steady throughout. He had balls of steel. I, on the other hand, had balls of plasticine, sweating and cramped within the confines of Daniel's cricket box. I had to go and take a peek at the gate. I walked the three hundred metres to the gate alone and on wobbly legs. The gates were locked, and there was no one to be seen, apart from the security guard. False alarm. Then I saw movement in the long grass around the gate. My sphincter puckered. There was a black face in the long grass. And it was

THE START OF THE MADNESS

holding an axe. But it was a happy black face, creased with a huge white grin. It belonged to Edgar, one of the farm supervisors. And behind him lay was another worker, and another and...the patch of long grass was full of my workers, all lying hidden, holding axes and badzas. Edgar greeted me cheerfully.

"Hallo, Boss."

"What are you doing hiding in the bush, Edgar?"

"I am waiting, Boss, for the war veterans."

I mumbled a repeat of Hamish's warning, telling Edgar he mustn't be confrontational. Lying in the grass, cradling axes and clubs, Edgar and his workmates thought that was pretty funny. "Don't worry Boss. We won't confront the war veterans. We can just fuck them up when they want to beat you."

That worked better than the Sulpiride. I told John Brown when I got back to the garden. He nodded his approval. "It's good that your workers are standing with you, it's a very good thing."

The afternoon dragged on and on interminably, interrupted only by regular updates on the progress of the mob. They were fifteen kilometres from the farm, then just ten, then just five. They were going to get to the farm a little after dark. I didn't know if that was a good thing or a bad thing.

Then from out of nowhere, God intervened and dumped a violent and unseasonal hailstorm on the war veterans as they marched. The storm blew in from absolutely nowhere. We went from blue sky to dark and angry. And then hailstones the size of eggs hammered down on the unruly mob unmercifully. It had to be divine intervention. We got hail on the farm infrequently, maybe one season in five and never in February that I could remember. And never hailstones big like chicken eggs, big enough to disrupt an angry mob. The mob was on a stretch of open road just three kilometres from the farm when the storm smashed into them. By then they'd marched more than fifteen kilometres. Their feet were sore, and the effects of the liquor had long worn off. The war veterans broke under the fury of the storm and fled for shelter. And that was that. Panic over. I thanked God quietly, over and over.

It was all very anti-climactic, but I wasn't complaining. I couldn't thank John Brown and Gayle enough for spending the day with us. I would never have made it without them. And then it was just me, Jenny, Veronica and Daniel. Which was dreadful. We tried to do normal family stuff that evening like watching television, but that didn't work. We jumped up at every little sound. We called it quits and went to bed way too early. But that was even worse. The wind rustling in the leaves in the dark outside was for sure a mob of war veterans sneaking up on the house. Veronica and Daniel came through to our bedroom and asked if they could sleep on camping mattresses at the foot of our bed. In the end, I phoned best friend and neighbour Marlowe Ellis and asked if he would come and spend the night. Marlowe and Helen arrived complete with shotgun and mattresses, and we all camped on the lounge floor. Jenny doped me up with more medication, and somehow, I managed to get some sleep, bringing an end to a long and crappy day, a day when I was supposed to be beaten and killed.

Chapter Twenty

CFU Farm Invasions update ⊙

At the time of writing, ⊙⊙⊙ properties have been a⊙ected by farm invasions, ⊙⊙⊙ of which are currently occupied. Since the Court Hearing on the ⊙⊙th March ⊙⊙⊙⊙, just over ⊙⊙⊙ properties have been invaded. The application for an urgent hearing of the case of the Commissioner of Police versus CFU was granted in the High Court this morning, and the set down is for Monday ⊙⊙ April in the open court. Advocate de Bourbon will present CFU⊙s case, and either the Attorney General or his deputy will argue for the Commissioner.

Mash East

On Marwe Farm, Tim Swanson was assaulted by invaders on his farm while trying to assist his tractor driver. Mr Swanson has been taken to Borrowdale Hospital for treatment, and we gather the invaders dispersed.

In the Bromley⊙Ruwa area substantial huts continue to go up, farmers have been told to remove cattle from the invaded paddocks, and in the Epworth and Airport area, residential plots are being pegged and sold for between ⊙⊙⊙⊙ to ⊙⊙⊙⊙.

The Ruzawi area under self⊙styled warlord Wilfred Marimo is continuously volatile.

Beatrice ⊙ Maasplein Farm has been evacuated, the farmer and his family moved to Harare. A death threat has been given on a farmer, his wife, and his son⊙s family in the area, and they have also evacuated their farms.

Featherstone ⊙ There is intelligence gleaned at Rosarum Store near the Dunn⊙s Farm that some farmers are targeted by a hit squad. Those involved have been informed and may evacuate for their safety.

Matabeleland

A meeting was held yesterday in Nyamandhlovu at Red Bank School between war vets and farmers. This morning when farmers went out to the Nyamandhlovu area some ⊙⊙ ⊙⊙⊙ acres had been pegged between Ulundei farm and Pontnydd and Red Leaf farm. There were ⊙ or ⊙ war veterans present, no aggression took place. There were ⊙ vehicles, a Land Rover, Datsun and blue Mazda, which had been used to transport the vets. No sign of any weapons. Most other areas quiet.

Springs Ranch, Umzingwane ⊙Bi⊙en⊙. Mr Bi⊙en went into the bush this morning and came across ⊙⊙ war vets ⊙ all holding war vets cards. No ⊙rearms were visible, and the attitude was non⊙aggressive, but they wanted land. A meeting has been agreed between Mr Bi⊙en⊙s Manager, and the war vets at ⊙⊙.⊙⊙am on Wednesday.

Mash West

On Grand Parade Farm in Karoi, tractors and a motorbike have been smashed with demos, in particular, the fuel tanks.

In Karoi death threats were received by four farmers and one security agent. ◎ farms have had work stoppages today. There was a total of ◎ assaults on labourers. Again, more details are unknown at this stage.

Idaho Farm, Norton, a gang of ZANU◎PF Youths threatening to burn down the homestead. Police have reacted.

Norton ◎ The owner of Parklands has received a letter telling him that no farming operations can continue and that he must leave the country. His labourers were told that the war vets will be doing land prep with the Parklands tractors and drivers on Kintyre Estate. Last night the labour were shown that the invaders◎ weapons work and shots were ◎red. A tractor driver was abducted for some time, but he is unharmed.

Chegutu ◎ Bosury Farm ◎◎◎ people pegging on fringes of the farm which border the town. Pegging out plots for homes. Told by a War Veteran that they have been instructed to occupy all farms if possible ◎ including black◎ owned farms.

Harare West◎Nyabira ◎ PGS Farm and Stapleford Farm were visited yesterday, and a group of about ◎◎◎ has returned to Stapleford today. Haydon Farm was invaded and pegged yesterday. ◎ people visited the National Sheep ◎ Goat Abattoir asking who owners are and if they could have free meat. They forced workers◎ families to go to PGS where they were made to sing.

Mash Central

Centenary: The situation at Vuka Farm is now quiet, but at Aranbira Farm the owners have been told that it is a waste of time to plant new crops as the farm will be acquired before they can harvest.

Horseshoe: Farmers are being pressured to donate funds to the ruling party.

Glendale: There was a hostile new invasion by a group of ◎◎◎ at Thorncreek Farm this morning. There was a temporary work stoppage and over half the workforce were required to go to a ZANU PF rally.

Brecon Farm was revisited yesterday. Some war vets in a white Mercedes visited Mazowe Citrus and were demanding that the owner hand over part of the land to them. It is suspected that it was the same group that visited Chirobi yesterday and advised the owner that they would return to peg his farm.

Harare West ◎ Komani Estate ◎ Howard Norman ◎ rose vehicle stopped, windows smashed, tyres punctured. Driver assaulted and missing.

Lowdale ◎ Mick Townsend ◎ ◎◎◎ war vets demonstrating within the homestead fence yesterday ◎ now defused.

Masvingo

Mwenezi ◉ Tom Ackerman◉s truck stopped by war vets at a roadblock between Rutenga and Zvishavane. War veterans wanted to burn the vehicle. Windows of vehicle smashed by war vets. A driver carrying farm wages managed to escape to farm but two other employees from the vehicle still missing. It is believed that the leader of the war vets on Sango Ranch is unbalanced.

Invaders on Ngwane Ranch, Chiredzi have indicated that they are going to peg out the whole ranch. They have said that if the police come to arrest someone, they will all be arrested. There is extensive cattle movement, as well as tree◉cutting going on in the Region. The environment is severely damaged.

Manicaland

Quiet. Invaders in the Juliasdale area have been issued with uniforms similar to the Frelimo type.

OTHER◉

STRESS MANAGEMENT SEMINAR FREE FOR C.F.U. MEMBERS AND THEIR FAMILIES◉ How to cope with personal stress, family stress and the immense problems of employees. Contact Alison on ◉◉◉◉◉◉

Pet Evacuations: Tracy, of the Wet Nose Society, sends best wishes to all and expresses solidarity with all farmers who are being a◉ected by invasions. She will make special arrangements for anybody wanting to take domestic pets to South Africa. She is in liaison with the Zimbabwe SPCA. Anybody wishing to contact her directly can do so on ◉◉◉◉◉◉◉◉◉◉◉◉◉◉

Large house in Strathaven for sale Tel: ◉◉◉◉◉◉

Meikles Hotel has very kindly o◉ered commercial farmers who need to get o◉ their farms two free nights ◉Bed and Breakfast only◉ at Meikles Hotel. They have asked the CFU to co◉ordinate this, and anyone wishing to avail themselves of this o◉er should contact Nicky or Jan who will put arrangements in hand.

Rob Wilson, family and friends would be happy to o◉er accommodation to farmers and their families.

I hated the daily CFU Farm Invasion sit-reps. Read out over the security radio by Hamish Turner, they were badly written, stiff, dry and stilted; and sans emotion, as though they'd been penned by someone far removed and uninvolved. But sit-reps sans emotion were good, sans emotion helped you not hear the crowd at the farm gate baying for blood, drunk and stoned; dry and stilted helped you not feel the pain of the beatings or smell the acrid, choking smell of burning tobacco barns and dreams going up in smoke. But as much as I hated the sit-reps, I couldn't not listen in to them. The sit-reps were like gory roadside accidents that you didn't want to slow down to gawk at but had to.

Listening to Hamish labour through the CFU sit-reps after evening roll-call had become a dreaded part of our daily ritual. Every evening Hamish would struggle to keep the emotion out of his voice and fail. Every evening Jenny and I would listen for news of friends, and without fail, someone else we knew had been sucked into the maelstrom and the chaos of the ongoing farm invasions. That was the downside of living in the small village that was Zimbabwe. Everyone knew everyone.

"God. When is it ever going to end, Eric?" Jenny asked after listening to Hamish sign off. "I don't know why they read it out every night. Listening to the misery, day in and day out, just makes you want to pack up and go."

"We can always move to Manicaland. Apart from war vets in Frelimo uniforms, it's all nice and quiet there."

"I'm being serious, Eric. You don't think we should pack up and go?"

"Sell to who? Who's going to buy a farm in Zimbabwe, Jenny? And we don't want to leave. Where else in the world are you going to get a stress management seminar and two nights at a five-star hotel for free, just for being a farmer?"

"I wish you'd be serious. And I'm not talking about selling, I'm talking about just packing up and leaving."

Jenny and I had had the pack up and go debate more than once. I gave her a hug of reassurance. "Hey, don't talk like that. It'll all work out just fine." But even to my own ears, I didn't sound too convincing.

In the beginning, the land-grab had been carefully co-ordinated with military precision, targeting farms centrally located and farmers of influence. But it rapidly denigrated into a free for all. And it was all about the forthcoming elections and nothing to do with restoring historic imbalances in land ownership, righting colonial wrongs, blah, blah, blah. The land-grab was a cunning two bird with one stone strategy; to disrupt the MDC's support base in the farming areas and secondly to lock the recipients of the stolen land into a Mugabe vote come election time. And we weren't just talking the 2000 elections. If Mugabe gave you a farm for free plus tractors and cattle and whatever else you could grab, you would carry on voting for him in every election until the cows come home. You were locked in forever.

Collectively, white commercial farmers were the largest employers in the country, with well over a million workers on their books, or more importantly, a million voters. And with a population of around twelve million, most of them under eighteen, a million voters was an important chunk of the vote. And the government was about to displace most of them. And displaced people can't vote. That the economy would go down the toilet in the process was a bugger, but hey, you can't have your cake and eat it.

To give some semblance of order to the chaos that was the land-grab, the government gave it a fancy title. Now when the stoned and drunken mob were delivered to the farm gate, baying for white blood, they were the Fast Track Land Reform Program in action. And to make it official, they drafted a whole bunch of supporting bullshit official paperwork, either a Section Five notice or a Section Seven giving notice to expropriate the land in the national interest, blah, blah, blah. The paperwork was supposed to arrive at the farm before the mob but normally didn't. I guess procedures went out the window when there was just so many fat, juicy farms out there waiting to be pinched, cut up and parcelled out to Mugabe's sycophants. And there was no shortage of sycophants once word got out that there were free farms to be had. Generally, the shinier the farm, the more likely you were to have a general or a judge or maybe even a police chief at the farm gate, urging the mob on, whipping them up into a frenzy. Flower farms were especially popular because of the foreign currency they earned. Or sometimes the land thieves would drive past the big, fancy gates to zero in on the weakest and the most vulnerable and grab their farms.

There was no rhyme nor reason, no thought to the greater consequences to the country and the economy at large, the whole land-grab had a dreadful 'That's Africa Baby' feel to it. 'That's Africa Baby' was the punchline to a philosophic story about a hippo and a scorpion. The scorpion was trying to hitchhike across the Zambezi River. The only way he was going to get to the other side of the swollen river was if he was able to persuade the hippo to give him a lift in his mouth. The hippo thought about it long and hard but in the end, he told the scorpion sorry, but no way. "I've heard stories about you", he told the scorpion "people tell me you're crazy and you're poisonous with it. I let you climb up into my mouth, and on to my tongue, you'll sting me and kill me just because you can." "It's obvious I won't do that," said the scorpion. "I sting you and you'll die, and then I'll also drown. So, there's no way I'm going to sting you."

The hippo was a genial chap who liked to help others. And so, he relented and opened his mouth up wide and let the scorpion climb up onto his soft pink tongue and set off for the other side of the river. They were just halfway across the mighty Zambezi when the scorpion flexed his murderous tail and drove his poisonous venom deep down into the hippo's tongue. He hated genial chaps. The poison was very strong, and death was quick. In lots of pain, the hippo croaked his last words "Why, why did you kill me, scorpion? You're also going to drown." The scorpion replied "T.A.B. That's Africa, Baby. I did it just because."

I'd been on the fringe of two of the farm invasions that featured on that day's sit-rep- PGS Farm and Haydon Park. They were the first invasions in our district. Nothing too scary happened on either, but my sphincter had puckered, nonetheless.

PGS Farm was owned by an old Indian guy called Florian Ferrao. Business-wise, Florian started out with a corner store selling fruit and veg. A natural trader, Florian, was highly successful, and he sold lots of fruit and veg. And so he had bought a farm to grow the fruit and veg on. Florian didn't look like a farmer. Short, with a sparkle in his eye, a natty dresser who would give you the shirt off his back if you asked for it, Florian was at his happiest when bargaining on the price of potatoes or tomatoes. He had only just finished building a monstrously big supermarket on his farm when all the troubles had started.

Florian was anything but happy when he phoned to ask me to come and negotiate with a war veteran who had pitched up on his farm for the second day running. I dropped what I was doing and rushed to PGS with a dry mouth and clenched bottom. The war veteran I met was actually quite disappointing. I had braced myself for a burly, black Fidel Castro. What I got was a short black guy in a white Toyota Corolla, neatly dressed in a pair of tight designer denims and a crisp white lounge shirt and wearing what looked suspiciously like a bit of a ponytail. I walked across with my heart in my mouth and introduced myself. The war veteran all but ignored me. His eyes were flicking everywhere as we spoke, sizing up the buildings, sizing up the lands, weighing up the equipment insight. I knew exactly what the bastard was doing, he was measuring up for curtains. He was like a bloody house hunter looking for the bargain of the century. Straight away, he got right up my nose, which gave me balls enough to accost him with a strangely steady voice. "What do you want here?"

"Who are you?" he demanded.

"Who I am doesn't matter. What do you want here?"

"I want this land. It belonged to my ancestors." All the while, his eyes stayed busy, weighing, appraising, making decisions.

"Crap. It's not your land, and you know it." Straight away, his eyes flashed back to me. I was cocking this up properly. So I changed tack. "The farm belongs to Mr Ferrao and...and look at him, he's an old guy, old enough to be your father..."

We both turned to look at Florian who was standing at the window of the shop watching. "And if you take his farm, he's got nowhere else to go." It was like appealing to a snake to spare a rat on account of the fact the rat was fat, cute and furry. Alas.

"How did it go? How did it go?" Florian asked when I went back into the shop after the war veteran had driven off. "Not so good, Florian, not so good."

Alas. From PGS, I went down the road and back towards town to watch Haydon Park Farm being pegged by an army of people from the nearby townships. Haydon Park was a large farm, about 1000 hectares and hugely valuable in that it butted right up against the City of Harare boundary. It was a matter of time before the farm got swallowed up by the march of progress, and when that happened, Haydon Park would go from being hugely valuable to ten times that. In anticipation of a change of use to come, the owner, a Greek property developer, had built two warehouses a few years earlier, which he leased out, to an agricultural supply company.

"And more, lots, lots more to follow," the developer had told me at the time. He had very big dreams for Haydon Park. Alas.

I stood with Raphael on the side of the main road and watched the Greek developer's dreams turn into a nightmare. A line of crude, ugly huts had been built in full view of the road, they would serve as home base for the war veterans operating in our district. And in front of the huts, an excited gaggle of soon-to-be not so landless peasants swarmed like kids on an Easter Egg hunt, carving Haydon Park's large open pastures up into 500 square metre plots with pegs and string. The process was being managed a group of war veterans, who Raphael told me were actually soldiers.

"This farm has been taken by General Zvinavashe, the head of the army," Raphael told me. "And he has told the people that they can buy bits of land on which to build their houses. But first, they have to pay a deposit."

Stupidly, I was horrified. "But how can he do that? He hasn't even got change of use or planning permission or...and it's not even his land in the first place."

"But he is just doing it, Boss. Some of our workers are there now, pegging land for houses."

"Workers from Running Dog?'

"Yes. I told them they are stupid, but they rushed here anyway to give the General their money."

It was all too depressing to watch, so I went home and phoned the Greek property developer. Normally he was brash and aggressive on the phone, today he was subdued; all his brashness had been sucked out. I urged him to get busy with a court order, challenging the invasion and seeking an immediate eviction. The developer had an army of aggressive in-house lawyers who dined out on serving eviction orders on defaulting tenants. And with Haydon Park right on the city boundary, surely the courts had to uphold the rule of law I told him. Alas. It was like trying to urge a jellyfish to stand up tall. It wasn't going to happen.

Once the war veterans had their base set up on Haydon Park, they quickly shifted the ZANU PF election campaign up into top gear. Drums pounded on farms all around us as all night long political meetings called pungwes became the order of the day. Attendance at the pungwes was mandatory, roll calls were taken, and if you were absent, you got beaten. In the beginning, there were many, many beatings.

Within the district, Running Dog quickly became an MDC island. Titus Nheya was still living on Running Dog. We carried on with his election campaign as best we could, but quickly ran out of farms to hold rallies on. Before, driving around the district with the MDC open hand salute, I called it chinjaering, had been lots of fun but now not so much. Now any responses I got were hurried and furtive. And then one of my supervisors came home beaten and bloody. The war veterans had smashed all Mike's front teeth out with an iron bar. Apparently working for de Jong on Running Dog was now a beatable offence. The policeman at our local charge office listened to Mike's report with a wooden face. He didn't even bother writing down a single word. Hell, he didn't even take his pen out of his pocket. I was incensed.

Impossibly the pressure ramped up a notch. Peter, our cook, and Ngoni, our housemaid, were forced to all the ZANU PF rallies in our district and were made to open proceedings with the ritual chants 'Pamberi ne ZANU PF, Pasi ne MDC, Pasi ne de Jong. Forward with ZANU PF, down with MDC, down with de Jong.' Crap. I had become the local MDC poster boy. I wanted to crawl off and hide in a black hole until it was all over but couldn't. There was stuff to do.

Apparently, I had to recruit six polling agents for each of the seventy-odd polling stations in the constituency. Their job would be to guard the ballot box and the votes in them over the weekend of the election. We were told that if the polling agents took their eyes off those boxes for just a minute, the ballot boxes would get stuffed full of ZANU PF votes in a heartbeat. And I had to figure out how I was going to deliver the polling agents to their polling stations, how to feed them, how to train them and to keep them motivated and strong in the face of mounting intimidation. Because we couldn't put posters up anymore or hold any more rallies - posters got ripped down and going to rallies got people beaten or worse - we had to resort to printing flyers in their tens of thousands on secret Risograph machines hidden away in people's back storerooms, flyers that told the people that their vote was secret, that their vote gave them the power to choose their leaders, urging them to use the votes wisely in the upcoming election, to stand up against intimidation. Once printed, we had to get the flyers out to people, under cover of darkness. At the time, I was driving an old beat up 4-wheel-drive, bottle green Mercedes Benz G Wagon. It was renamed the Chinja mobile and together with the farm pick-up, went out on flyer runs most nights. There was lots to do and not enough time to do them.

Brian kept the farm going as best he could, which pained me to say was actually better than I did. Like a herbicide, I could kill flowers, whereas Brian had green fingers and made stuff grow. Every day he'd write me up a brief report of what had happened, quality challenges, how the markets in

Europe were behaving, what fertilisers and chemicals he wanted to order, etcetera, etcetera but for the most part, I didn't even read them. I didn't have room in my head to worry about business stuff and just signed all the cheques. The George Hotel was much the same. Now the only time I went anywhere near the hotel was for MDC meetings, of which there were plenty.

On the home front, things weren't so good either. Conversation in our house died a dismal death. Jenny had sensibly banned politics as a permitted subject around the dinner table. And consequently, we spoke about not a lot. I had very little interest in anything other than politics. On television, the sitcoms weren't funny anymore, not even Friends. Sports like rugby and cricket were a rude kick in the nuts reminder to me that people out in the real world didn't give a rat's arse about the struggle in Zimbabwe and were more intent on normal stuff, like enjoying. The only time my ears would prick up was when BBC or Sky infrequently ran with a snippet of information on Zimbabwe, but for the rest, television was just white noise. When the struggle was done and dusted, when Mugabe was an unemployed ex-dictator properly worried about being strung up on the nearest lamppost or living the rest of his life out in a desert somewhere, I decided I would sue him for a season of Super Rugby and a season of Friends. That was the least he owed me.

They were crappy days and a big, indelible blot on my copybook as a family man. Alas. But perversely, I was also having the time of my life. Enmeshed in the suffering of my country, I'd never felt more like a Zimbabwean. Like something out of Desiderata, I felt I belonged. And more than just belonging, I was making a difference. I was fighting evil, and I was making a difference. I felt like Luke Skywalker. And around me were standout people, black ones and white ones, some rich but mostly poor, some important but mostly not, but all brave. Before I got involved in the struggle, most of them I wouldn't have even noticed, but now I was lucky enough to call them friends.

And then one Sunday morning, I was rudely reminded that just when you think that things can't possibly get worse, they do. I got a phone call from Ian Campbell at Lilfordia School. "I am sitting at a ZANU PF rally that I've been forced to attend." Ian was having to talk above the crowd sounds behind him.

"Lucky you," I said.

"Indeed. Anyway, I'm sitting here listening to Sabina Mugabe, and she has just told the whole rally that you have an arms cache buried on your farm and that you are an enemy of the state."

I all but collapsed. "Sabina Mugabe said that I had an arms cache buried on my farm?" I parroted weakly. "President Mugabe's sister?"

"Yes. She mentioned you by name. And I thought I should just give you a head's up."

I hung up the phone completely ashen-faced and told Jenny what Ian had just told me.

"But that's all lies."

"I know it's bullshit. And you know it's bullshit. Even Sabina fucking Mugabe knows it's bullshit. But that's not going to stop police from coming here and finding AKs in every hole they dig.'

"But what are we going to do?"

"I tell you what we are going to do. We're going to pack up, and we're going to get the fuck out of here. Now!!"

"But..."

"No buts, Jenny. Christ, when the president's fucking sister stands up at a rally and brands you an enemy of the state that means they don't want you in this God-forsaken country anymore. It means it's time to fucking leave."

What followed was dreadful. Veronica and Daniel were in tears. I kept shouting at them that they had five minutes to pack up their most important belongings, which in Daniel's case meant his hamster. Jenny kept shouting at me as she pulled photos off the wall that it was all my fault for getting involved in politics. And I couldn't stop crying. It was all so unfair. I tried my boy on the burning deck speech again about how evil flourishes when good men do nothing, but Jenny shouted me down quickly. Evil also flourished when good men got hung by the neck for being enemies of the state, she told me. Which got everyone crying even more, but mostly me.

John Brown wasn't answering his phone. In the end, I got through to Bill Searle at MDC Support. Bill was the white war vet who had spoken at my first MDC meeting. Sobbing, I told him what was happening. Bill was calmness personified. He told me to pull myself together and to sit tight. He would have a lawyer with me in the hour. Which wasn't what I wanted to hear. I didn't want a lawyer. I wanted to get the hell away. Like the Italian tank, my preservation strategy mostly centred on the use of reverse gears. Forward gears were for when you get attacked from the rear.

"You can't run away from this," Bill told me. "If you do, the cops will get there, and they will uncover an arms cache." Bill was right. I had to stay. If I didn't, I would lose everything. Suddenly an hour seemed like an awful long time for a lawyer to get out to me. "Can't you hurry the lawyer up, Bill?"

While I waited, I played my ace card. I had a police friend in a very senior position. Our friendship dated back to when I was in the police. I'd gone to see him when the troubles first started to find out if I could count on him when it mattered. He'd told me, of course, I could count on him but told me better to save my phone call for when I really needed help. With hands trembling, I made the phone call. When Caleb answered, I told him what was going on. Caleb said he would check it out. He came back to me in five minutes. Police Mabelreign were on standby to come out and search my farm for weapons of war. They had a search warrant and everything. Apparently, they were having transport issues and were waiting for another truck to arrive. Crap.

"What should I do?" I asked. He told me good luck. He couldn't help me any further.

My human rights lawyer arrived. The lawyer seemed awfully young. I had my heart set on an older, grizzly lawyer, someone who'd been there and done that. But he was razor-sharp and all business. He sat me down and extracted the whole sorry story. I finished off by telling him what Caleb had told me on the phone.

"Excellent, Eric. Here's what we are going to do. Have you a truck big enough to go and collect the cops?"

My jaw dropped. "I've got a three tonner for my airport deliveries. You want me to go and fetch the police to bring them back here so they can find an arms cache?"

"Exactly. Is your truck branded? Has it got the name of the farm painted on the side?"

"No."

"Even better. I need to talk to your driver. When he arrives at the police station, he mustn't tell them where he is from. He must just say he has been sent to take them to Running Dog Farm."

It took an hour for the truck to get back from town, fully laden with cops in their riot blues. My lawyer went out to meet them. He introduced himself as my attorney and asked to see the search warrant. The policeman in charge, an inspector from the infamous Law and Order Maintenance Section, was taken aback that a) my lawyer was there waiting for them and that b) he knew that the police were there to search for an arms cache. And he was more than just taken aback when the lawyer pointed out to him that the police had been ferried to my farm on my truck.

"Sending a truck to help the police in their search for illegal weapons is hardly the actions of a guilty man," the lawyer told him. "I am sure the judge will agree with me on that. And I'm sure that he will also agree that any arms you might find in your search were hidden by your good selves." And that was game over. With a face like thunder, the inspector ordered his men back into the truck. He wasn't even going to go through the motions. I couldn't thank my lawyer enough for all his help.

We unpacked our clothes and our most important belongings and in Daniel's case, his hamster, almost as quickly as we'd packed them. But Jenny left the family photos in the cardboard box. She said she would hang them later. We were late for lunch at a friend's house in town. It felt strange doing normal stuff. At lunch, we were the centre of attention and had to tell our stories over and over. Running Dog was only twenty kilometres from the city centre, but it was in a different country. Harare's suburbs were so quiet and peaceful and normal.

The lunch was a great release although the laughter was all a bit loud and brittle and everyone drank a bit too much, especially me. Jenny had to drive home. When we got to Homefield Road turnoff, the ladies who sold tomatoes and the vegetables at the little informal market on the corner jumped into the road to wave us down. I knew all the ladies well. I had built the thatched shelter they sold their vegetables under for them a few years earlier. That the ladies were still at the market after dark was strange. Normally they went home before last light. But they were all still there and very excited about something. Jenny wouldn't stop, though.

"They most probably want to ask you to build them another shelter. But they'll have to wait until tomorrow. I've had more than enough of today already."

About ten minutes later and just as I'd settled down in front of the television, there was some timid ringing of the cowbells at the main gate. I went out to see who it was. It was one of the ladies from the market. Without saying a word, she handed me a note and then hurried away into the night. I took it inside the house to read. Because I was still a bit pissed from lunch, it took me a while to unscramble the scrawl. But when I did, I sobered up in an instant. "You must not stay, Mr de Jong. The war veterans can come and kill you tonight." Less than five minutes and a lot of sobbing later, we were back in the car and on our way back into town with our clothes, photos and hamster.

We stayed with friends Pete and Trudy that night. First thing the next day, I found pressing flower business in Holland and booked tickets for Jenny, Veronica, Dan and me on the first available plane out of Harare. I had hurried meetings in town with Brian to talk about the farm, and with Tony to talk about preparations for the elections. I wanted Tony to check out all the polling stations that had been used in the referendum and more. Terry Dawson from Rainham Farm would also be able to help. And here I was running away. But I told him I would back in plenty of time for the elections. To help with transport, I lent him my beloved Chinja mobile.

My last meeting was with Hendrik at the MDC Support Office. Hendrik was tough like teak. I could tell that he wasn't buying into my story about the pressing business in Holland. He knew I was running away. Which made me feel really bad. I felt like a coward. But hours later, sitting in the plane staring down at the sprawl of Harare's lights as we climbed up into the night sky, I had never felt so relieved and so happy to be leaving a place in all my life.

Chapter Twenty-One

Holland was everything Zimbabwe wasn't. It was clean, neat and tidy, and things worked. Things were normal, slightly boring and utterly predictable. After the last few months in Zimbabwe, slightly boring and utterly predictable were good, real good. When in Holland, mostly I stayed with my aunt in a little village called Sassenheim. My aunt wasn't at all put out to see us. She'd been following the news on television, and I'm sure had been half expecting us. She asked us to walk into the village to stock up on groceries, like salted liquorice for me, and hagelslag for the kids. Hagelslag were little chocolate hundreds and thousands that you spread on your breakfast toast. Weird but nice, especially if you were a kid.

In the twenty years that I'd been visiting, Sassenheim hadn't changed. The tulip fields behind my aunt's house still stretched away as far as the eye could see, and I'd swear they were still planted to same coloured tulips. It was a five-minute walk to the High Street. The shoe shop was still next to the cheese shop was still next to the camera shop, which was still full of gadgets that I wanted to buy but couldn't afford. And incredibly the guy who owned the coffee shop in the middle of the village still also owned a silver Suzuki Jeep that he parked on the street, just a newer model.

Compared to Zimbabwe, Holland was in an 'oh so comfortable' time warp. "Why don't we come and live here, Eric?" Jenny asked as we walked past the coffee shop guy's new silver Suzuki jeep.

"What, us come and live here in Holland?"

"Yes, Dad, why don't we live here?" Dan was quick to seize on the benefits of living in a country where it was legal for kids to put chocolate on their bread for breakfast. For a few seconds, the idea of living in Holland felt comfortable. Until reality smacked me in the face with his shovel. "But what would I do for a living?"

'I don't know. Get a job, I suppose."

"As what? I'm not qualified to do anything?"

"You're a flower farmer, Eric."

"Not in Holland, I'm not. Here they farm flowers properly. Here the only thing I could do is weed."

"Ya, Dad, you could weed. I bet you would be a really good weeder." Dan badly wanted chocolate on his breakfast toast instead of peanut butter.

But once I was in Holland, away from Zimbabwe and safe, suddenly all I wanted was to be back there. I was dreadful. I camped in front of the television from morning to night, waiting for snippets of news from home. Jenny bit my head off. So, I dragged my sorry bottom off to the flower auctions to have a look at my flowers. A shipment had just arrived and was being unpacked. The supervisor complimented me on my quality, especially over the last three months he said. I picked up a bunch of my flowers out of the box. The supervisor was right. Brian's flowers were really good. And it suddenly struck me how crazy things had become. I was standing in Holland holding the first bunch of my flowers I'd held in three months.

The manager of the Import Department at the Auctions was a frequent visitor to Zimbabwe. He asked me if I'd speak to the unpacking staff in the canteen and tell them what was happening back home. I jumped at the chance. There were more than forty people in the canteen, some Dutch but mostly foreigners, including a handful of Africans from West and Central Africa.

There were no soapboxes in the canteen, so I stood on a chair instead. I told them about Zimbabwe. I lived in a country where few made it to forty. Zimbabwe's life expectancy had fallen to just thirty-seven, the lowest in the world. I told them about Zimbabweans' amazing hunger to learn, even though they were sometimes crammed fifty or more into classrooms that didn't have desks or books. Not that many of them would find jobs in the formal sector after leaving school, unemployment stats were well on their way to ninety percent plus. I told them about how my president went to work every day in a motorcade of more than forty cars and motorbikes. And if you were on the road when he was travelling, you had to pull over or be arrested, beaten or maybe even shot. The Dutch workers in the room shook their heads at that, but those from Africa didn't. To them, that was normal. I told them about trying to run a business in a country where you sometimes had to queue for days to buy forty litres of petrol for your truck so you could get your flowers to the airport. I told them how much fun a seven-day power cut was, bathing in buckets, not looking at television or your e-mails for a week. I especially told them about the farm invasions, where homes and livelihoods were forcibly taken away from people, just because they were white. I told them that the same farms would be given away free to people who didn't know how to farm but who knew how to put an X next to Mugabe's name on the ballot paper. The import manager gave a polite cough. I'd overshot the tea break, and there were flowers in hot boxes to unpack. "Were there any questions?"

One of the Dutch workers asked, "Why do you stay? Why don't you leave?"

"Because it's my home. Zimbabwe's my country and I love it. But mostly because we have sunshine for more than three hundred days a year." Which earned a few smiles from the audience.

On the way back to my aunt's house, I got a rebuke from Jenny. She accused me of stupidly tilting at windmills. I told her it was good that people in Holland knew what was really happening in Zimbabwe.

"Why bother? It's not like the Dutch are going to do anything? Mugabe can do what he likes, and no one will lift a finger to stop him."

When we got home, I turned the television on, hoping to catch some news of Zimbabwe. Unfortunately, there was lots of news, and all of it bad. There were images of burning tobacco barns, and the Dutch headlines scrolling across the bottom of the screen said something about a white Zimbabwean farmer having been murdered. My Dutch didn't extend much beyond asking for beers and directions to the toilet, so I hurriedly scrambled through the channel options in search of an English news station. CNN was running the same story with the same backdrop of images of burning tobacco barns. The details of the story were stark and shocking. David Stevens, a white farmer and an MDC activist from Arizona Farm had been dragged out of a police station in Murehwa where he had taken refuge. He was dragged out by war veterans who accused him of supporting the MDC and then they shot him in the face with a shotgun. His black foreman had also been murdered. Five other white farmers had been savagely beaten and were in hospital in a serious condition. The murderers had not been brought to book.

I didn't know David Stevens, but I knew who he was. I had seen him at the MDC Support meetings. His murder shocked me to my core, to the point where I had to rush out of the warm apartment into the cold air outside to vomit. I stood over a flower bed; my body racked with dry heaves. Some kids nearby watched me curiously.

I was absolutely gutted by David Stevens' murder. Sure, people around the world got murdered every day, the world over. Shit happens. But Stevens was dragged out of a police station in broad daylight, and shot because of his politics, and because he was a white Zimbabwean. He'd fled into the police station looking for help, looking for the protection of the law. But the policemen on duty hadn't lifted a hand to save him, they had all stood there, watching and listening in their clean starched uniforms, while Stevens was dragged outside and driven away to be shot because he was white and because he supported the MDC. His black foreman, who was also shot, had his lips hacked off with a knife. His lips were later paraded around Stevens' farm to show the workers what happened to MDC supporters.

The Stevens' murders were a blunt message from Mugabe to white farmers and black voters - 'Don't Do Opposition Politics'. It was all so wrong, and so close to home.

I couldn't stop watching the Stevens' report over and over. I watched it on BBC, I watched it on Sky, even on Al Jazeera. Mostly, I was waiting for a reaction from the world, the same free world that waffled on loud and proud about the importance of democracy. And bollocks to just standing on the lawn outside the White House looking stern, I wanted Bush and Blair to send their soldiers into Zimbabwe to arrest Mugabe and drag him off to the International Court in The Hague to be tried and hanged for being the murderer he was.

But it quickly became apparent that wasn't going to happen. Just like the police in Murehwa, Bush and Blair and all the other pontificators were just going to stand back and do nothing, again. Just like they had when Mugabe murdered twenty thousand men, women and children in the eighties. Suddenly, I hated Bush and Blair almost as much as I hated Mugabe. And I lay in bed that night, tossing, turning, with the David Stevens' murder playing over and over in my head, agonising about what to do next. I had absolutely no idea.

The next day, we ran away some more, this time to Berlin. While I'd been trapped in front of the television, Jenny had been busy booking flights and hotel rooms. She chose Berlin because it was close to the front of the alphabet, close to Holland and most importantly because the news on the television would be in German and I wouldn't listen to it, twenty-four seven. My family, me included, badly needed a break from me and my depression, and Zimbabwe.

I was happy with Berlin as a destination choice. It had long been on my bucket list. World War Two had impacted so hugely on the lives of my father's family, and Berlin was where it had all started and ended. Dan's ears pricked up when he heard 'war'. He was fully into war movies and fully keen to go on holiday to a place with tanks and rockets and explosions and...Shame. I didn't put him right and left him to leopard crawl happily amongst foxholes in his imagination. Veronica was less happy with Berlin as a destination choice. She had a picture of a grey, staid, stodgy city straight out of the pages of her history book and full of grey, staid, stern and stodgy people. But that couldn't have been further from the truth. Berlin might have been steeped in history, but it was a colourful, vibrant city, busting with roadside terrace cafes with buskers and street magicians and heaving with people. Jenny had booked us into a funny, old fashioned hotel right on the Kurfustendamn, right in the middle of all the buskers, mimes, street musicians and all the other action.

Sitting on a terrace in the weak spring sun, drinking delicious beer - it took me just two sips to fall in love with German beer - watching the street mimes and the world walk by, I absolutely loved it and could feel all the Zimbabwe tension falling away from me. Dan quickly grew bored with buskers. We'd been in Berlin for hours and so far not one tank, not one explosion, nothing. He was starting to figure me for a liar. But his ears pricked up again when I suggested we go for a walk in Berlin's famous Tiergarten. I told him I thought Tier meant tiger in German and tigers were good.

The gardens were beautiful. My travel book and I pointed out famous landmarks to Veronica and Jenny while Dan scouted the foliage ahead for predators. But there was a not a single tiger to be seen and again Dan was starting to look at me like I was a liar. We were halfway through the park when point man Dan spotted something of interest. "Hey Dad, check out that guy's big balls!"

As one, Veronica and Jenny's heads swung around. I was slower off the mark because surely Dan was wrong. But he wasn't. Unbelievable. A guy was lying down on a towel, just metres away, tanning his bountiful man bits. And Veronica was standing there, rubbernecking them. I grabbed her, spun her around away from the prone streaker... and pointed her in the direction of a far greater selection of naked men and their penises. Big ones, small one, floppy ones, penises playing Frisbee, we were surrounded. Dan revelled, in his guide duties and pointed them all out in a loud voice. "Wow, check at that guy's huge willy."

Somehow, we'd blundered into a nudist colony, right in the middle of the city, a nudist colony without a single naked woman in it. Feeling more than just a bit inadequate, I hurriedly dragged my gawking wife, my daughter and my son in the general direction of away.

I decided we'd all had more than enough of the Tiergarten and we should go look at Hitler's bunker instead. Dan was happy with underground bunkers. With my guidebook open on the map page and my thumb on the spot where the bunker had been, we traipsed up and down Wilhelmstraße for bloody miles looking for the bunker.

"Of course, the bunker's still there," I told Jenny after we'd passed a kid's playground for the third time. "Hitler's bunker was a big part of history. You can't just erase it and pretend it didn't happen."

Well, I got that one wrong. Eventually, the thirteenth person we stopped and asked, pointed out the playground that had been built on top of where Hitler's bunker had once been.

Dan was fast running out of patience. No war, no tigers and now no bunkers. Pretty soon he was going to kick me in the kneecap. Luckily, I found an advert for a tour of the Berlin Dungeons nearby, apparently offering a gruesome tour of Berlin's horrible history, including torture and plague. Dan's eyes lit up when I told him what gruesome meant. Torture and plague are practically in the same movie as tanks and explosions. Jenny and Veronica were keen to veto the dungeon. It really is quite difficult going on holiday with family from the opposite ends of the spectrum. In the end, I used my casting vote, and we headed down into the depths of Berlin's dark underbelly. As it got darker, I saw Dan edge closer to Jenny. He might have been rough and tough on the outside, but inside he was still only ten.

The first exhibit was a gloomy mock-up of a medieval surgery with a waxwork doctor/ butcher hacking away at some unfortunate's leg. It was all very subtle with flickering lights, buckets of blood and a soundtrack of screams. Dan edged in past the barrier ropes for a closer look at the gory bits. Just then, the lights faltered. Dan edged in even closer. Then as the lights failed completely, plunging us all into complete darkness, the blood-stained wax work surgeon leant over and grabbed at Dan. Who screamed lustily. Closely followed by Veronica and Jenny. Fittingly, I was the last to scream. Unfittingly, my screams were screams of pain. In trying to flee, I'd run straight into the nearest wall. The lights came back on. The waxwork surgeon was back in position at the operating table. We looked around at each other sheepishly.

"What the hell just happened?" Jenny asked. "And where were you going?"

"I was going for help. And I could've have sworn that thing came to life and grabbed Dan."

"It did. It grabbed me. I swear it grabbed me. I think it wanted to cut my arm off."

We all turned to look at the waxwork surgeon again, who stood there motionless and unblinking, like he was made out of wax. And then, after forever, the surgeon turned his head and leered at us horribly. More screams, especially from me after smacking my head again on the wall in another headlong rush to fetch help.

We regrouped in the tunnel outside the surgery, wide-eyed and with hearts racing. Keystone Cops had just met Friday the Thirteenth in a medieval surgery. Jenny was the first to start laughing, closely followed by the rest of us. It was deep, cleansing belly laughter. And damn, but it felt good. I couldn't even remember the last time I'd laughed, let alone my wife and kids.

The rest of the dungeon tour was just as epic. Torture chambers with wax mass murderers who came to life and scared the crap out of you when you were least expecting, even though you were expecting, had us screaming and laughing till we couldn't laugh anymore. In the cafeteria, at the end of the tour, we stocked up on memorabilia like scream masks and worse. Dan stuck his mask on and plunged back into the dark tunnels and scared the crap out of other tourists.

The Berlin Dungeons set the tone for the rest of our tour. We so enjoyed everything the city had to offer. Checkpoint Charlie and the last crumbling bits of the Berlin wall were fascinating, eating monstrously big white disgusting German sausages and drinking delicious beer in pavement restaurants followed by a stroll through old grey East Berlin where there was no advertising and where blue jeans had been banned and where citizens lived in brand-new, crumbling grey tenement blocks, closely watched by Big Brother. The same Big Brother now lived in Zimbabwe, still busy watching citizens. Mugabe had modelled his CIO secret police closely on the East German Stasi.

But it was nice to know that human spirit had won through in the end and beaten the system and ripped down the Wall. It gave me hope for Zimbabwe. Back home, people were celebrating Independence Day. But no one was independent. They were more under the boot than ever. But standing in a new Berlin, I knew for sure that one day the small guy at home would also stand up and win. The feel-good lasted all the way back to the hotel, right up to point where I switched on the television in our room to find out that another white farmer in Zimbabwe had been shot, beaten and murdered. I went straight to an internet café to get the details. I wish I hadn't.

I didn't know Martin Olds but knew his brother who fixed my boreholes. Martin farmed in Nyamandhlovu near Bulawayo. He was described by those who knew him as a giant of a man. Olds was murdered on Independence Day by a mixed group of forty soldiers and war veterans, purposely bussed in from the other side of the country. The group was led by a notorious war veteran called Black Jesus. The attack on Olds went on for hours. Olds fought bravely. He spoke to his mother and his neighbours by phone and told them what was happening. His mother phoned the Nyamandhlovu police station nonstop, but they never answered. They were all too busy manning roadblocks around the Olds farm, set up to stop neighbours from coming to his rescue. Eventually, the soldiers and the war veterans flushed the badly wounded Olds from his house by setting fire to it. They beat him senseless with a spanner and then they killed him with a shot to the head. And then they beat him some more. Martin Olds was a decorated hero, decorated by Mugabe ten years earlier for saving another man's life. And all the while, his friends and neighbours were gathered helpless at the armed police roadblocks. The police on the roadblock allowed an ambulance to pass, not for Martin Olds but for the attackers that he'd shot. Another two hours later, after looting the farmhouse and sanitising the scene, removing all the spent cartridges, the convoy of trucks and buses bearing the heavily armed murderers, singing and celebrating, were waved through by the police.

Two days after Martin Olds was murdered, wild horses had to drag us on to the plane that was taking us back to our real world in Zimbabwe. I have never wanted to not go somewhere quite so much in all my life. Alas.

Chapter Twenty-Two

Even though we weren't happy that we were home, others were. The farm road down to the house was lined with farmworkers smiling, waving and ululating, welcoming us home as though we'd been away for years. They brought tears to my eyes, literally. But Jenny was more cynical. She said the workers were just happy to see me because I signed the salary cheques at the end of the month. But there was nothing ambiguous about the welcome from the cats and dogs who bowled us over in a tsunami of wagging tails and slobber. Most of the slobber came courtesy of Joshua, the Saint Bernard. Dan did a quick headcount of the cats to make sure all were present and correct while I went off to inspect the farm. Brian had everything more than under control with nice flushes building for the Mother's Day peak.

But, walking around the farm, something didn't seem quite right. Up close, the happy workers weren't so happy and were nervous to look me in the eye. It was almost like they weren't keen to be seen talking to me. Raphael filled me in. With the elections just weeks away, the pressure in the district was huge. Titus Nheya was still living on the farm, but his MDC election campaign had ground to a halt. He hadn't held a meeting since the disrupted Nyabira rally. The war vets on Hayden Park Farm were holding all night pungwes most nights. Saturdays were ZANU PF rally days. Peter, our cook and Ngoni, our maid, were still being forced to lead the opening anti de Jong chants at each rally. Some of Running Dog workers had burnt their MDC membership cards, but most were holding firm. But now that I was back, Raphael told me that we could get the MDC campaign back on track. Crap. I could have climbed back on the plane quite happily.

I phoned Tony to get my car back and to find out how he was getting on with election preparations. He wasn't, he told me. And he'd hidden the Chinja mobile at our town Garden Centre. Tony had called time on his short political career after the war vets had phoned him the day after I'd left and told him that they would cut both his fucking ears off if they saw him driving in around in the Chinja mobile. Tony was badly rattled.

Jenny drove me to fetch my car. Amazingly, it started first time. I drove to the MDC headquarters. On the way, I got to thinking about having my ears cut off. I decided I quite liked my ears. Along with my eyes, nose, mouth and chin, my ears were my favourite facial feature. I was as attached to them as they were to me. Driving through town, I couldn't but notice how normal everything looked, people hustling and bustling, busy with their normal daily routines, not worrying about the pain of imminent ear removal. Not worrying about ear removal had to be the pinnacle of normalness. There and then, I decided that I wanted normal. I decided that I'd also pull the plug on politics and go back to humdrum boring and restrict my worrying to overdrafts and the onset of pattern baldness. It was a huge decision, but I was glad I'd made it. And Jenny would be even gladder.

The MDC headquarters were on the eighth floor of a high rise in the middle of town. Which gave me time to practice my resignation speech in the elevator mirror on the way up. It was a good speech, apologetic and earnest. I stepped from the elevators into a maelstrom of frenzied enthusiasm. There were stacks of paper piled everywhere and droves of volunteers, men, women and even some children, running around, all frantically busy, all on a mission. Lots of the faces I knew, but there were lots of new ones I didn't know. I dithered on the edge of the organised chaos with my prepared speech ready. Then Hendrik saw me. "Ah, the prodigal son from Zvimba has returned!! Welcome back, Eric. And don't just stand there, get busy. We've got an election to win!!" Alas. My zero will power kicked in, and I was back at the coal face.

Hours later, I headed back to the farm, the Chinja mobile loaded with hundreds of Titus Nheya's election posters. Titus was like a kid with a new bike when he saw the posters. His poker face cracked into a huge beaming grin as he ran his fingers over his unsmiling face in the poster, over and over. It wasn't a very good photo of him. The photographer had managed to capture all of Titus's awkwardness. He looked more like a shoplifter than someone you would vote for.

"Can we send the truck out tonight to put them up, Eric?" he asked. All MDC campaigning now only happened under cover of darkness.

"Sure we can Titus. We'll send Raphael out as soon as it gets dark. He can do the whole district."

Alas. By lunchtime, the next day, every one of Titus's posters had been torn down by ZANU youth and ripped up. Titus and Raphael trooped off to the police station to make a report. The policeman didn't even bother to take his pen out of his pocket.

Big picture-wise, things were even worse. Countrywide, the violence spiralled as ZANU ramped up their terror campaign in the final weeks leading up the election. In Mount Darwin, 400 panga wielding ZANU thugs hacked retired policeman, Matthew Pfebve, to death mistaking him for his brother Elliot, who was running for parliament on the MDC ticket. A week later another ZANU mob beat Allan Dunn, a white farmer and MDC activist, to death on his farm in Beatrice. I'd seen Allan at MDC meetings. On the same day, two hundred war veterans invaded a fertiliser factory on the outskirts of Harare, rampaging from house to house, dragging people out to beat for being MDC supporters. Four days later, Beatrice farmer John

Weeks was murdered by ZANU PF thugs.

The police reacted to the massive surge in violence by sending a directive out to all white police reservists telling them their gun licenses had been revoked and that all weapons had to be handed in forthwith. To his credit, our local officer in charge looked sickened when he read out the directive at our neighbourhood watch meeting. I ignored the directive, and my shotgun stayed in my gun cabinet.

I developed a healthy paranoia and saw bad guys behind every bush and in every twin-cab. I was like a rhino that had just heard about the extent of rhino poaching. The slightest sounds at night amplified and had me scrambling for gun cabinet keys. To get any chance of sleep, I had to take a second sleeping tablet in the early hours and woke up wooden headed like a zombie. I stressed that there was only one entrance to the farm. If the bad guys barricaded the main gate, we'd be trapped like fish in a barrel. And so on a Sunday when no one was watching, I cut a secret car-sized bolt-hole in the bottom security fence, for just in case. On my way home from town, I took to driving round the Westgate traffic circle twice every time, to catch out any bad guys following. And just because I didn't see any bad guys, didn't mean they weren't there.

At a support meeting at the George Hotel, the MDC Director of Elections asked us to report on our election preparedness. His name was Paul Themba Nyathi. To stop the rigging, Paul told us we needed six trained polling agents per polling station and one backup vehicle to follow the ballot boxes back to the counting centres. Come my turn to report on Zvimba South, I told them that we'd lined up three hundred polling agents plus spares and were busy with training. But I'd hit a brick wall on the support vehicles. So far, I had just five support vehicles lined up, two of which were mine. I had no clue as to how I was going to deploy three hundred people, let alone follow ballot boxes around the countryside. And if the intimidation, violence and threats carried on, chances come election I'd be down to just my two vehicles. Most farmers in my district didn't want to be seen talking to me, for fear of losing ears. Paul told me to try harder and moved on to the next constituency.

And just when you think things cannot possibly get worse, they do. Jenny and I were called into Lilfordia by the new headmistress. Ian Campbell had decided to retire. Formerly, the Grade four teacher, the new headmistress had known Daniel since he was a toddler and had become a family friend. She sat us down with her calamity face on and hit us with the bad news. Daniel was slipping further and further out of his academic comfort zone, to a point where she felt he could no longer cope with mainstream education. Dan's high school entrance exams were only two years away, and there was no way he was going to pass. She felt Dan should be assessed by a child psychologist and depending on the results, it might be better if he left Lilfordia and went to a remedial school instead. Daniel's learning problems were complex. She wasn't happy with her decision but knew in her heart of hearts, that it was the right thing for Dan.

I sat there, stunned. Lilfordia turning away a kid with learning problems was akin to the Catholic Church kicking out sinners. It would never have happened had Ian Campbell still been the headmaster. Ian did things differently. His approach was a cut and paste out of Desiderata. According to Ian, even the slowest of kids had a right to be there. Slow kids might not do well in the classroom, but there was always something that they would be good at, and it was his job to find that something and nurture and develop it. He'd always told us that Dan would struggle with the academic stuff throughout his school career, but as long as he picked up some of the basic concepts, he would survive and be happy. Kids being happy in themselves was the most important thing, according to Ian. But alas, Ian had retired. But I could also see where the new head was coming from. Just being happy wasn't going to be enough to get Dan into a decent high school. She gave us contact details for a child psychologist.

Jenny and I hardly spoke on the way home. I was bleak with the punishment life was giving me. Farm invasions, dirty politics where people got killed and now my son was all of a sudden damaged goods. What the hell had I done wrong to deserve all this crap in my life? Just two months ago, the beer glass that was my life had been full to overflowing. Now it was empty, dirty, cracked and broken.

Daniel's psychologist wore a tweed jacket, horn-rimmed glasses and an earnest expression on his clean-cut, pleasant face. He summed up the brief he'd received from the school and outlined the regime of tests and assessments that Dan would be undergoing. Dan would do Wechsler tests and Bender Gestalt tests, Raven's Progressive Matrices and Visual Motor Integration and Motor Free Visual Perception tests and blah blah blah. As the psychologist went on and on, I hated him. He sounded like he was talking about Hannibal Lecter, not my beautiful little boy who might be quirky but was always sweet and quick to smile. Jenny read me like a book and stood on my foot.

And so it began, Daniel's endless barrage of tests and interviews. The poor kid jumped through hoops as the psychologist and other clever people who could all spell very long words queued up to get inside Daniel's ten-year-old head to find out why he couldn't spell even simple words. Over and above all the tests, there were endless interviews with clinical psychologists and neuropsychologists and occupational therapists. So many specialists, for one poor, scared kid.

Dan hated all the attention and the poking and prodding. He wanted to be back at school with his friends, doing normal stuff. He didn't really care that he always came last in class. But every night when he got home after a psychologist session, I'd ask him how it'd gone and he'd always give me the same stock answer. It went fine Dad, he'd tell me, it went fine. But when the thick sheath of test results came back, they told a different story. Dan was anything but fine.

First up was Dan's Psychological Assessment, based on his Wechsler test score. His Full-Scale score was just 72, well below the average IQ of between 90 and 109. According to Wechsler, Dan's general knowledge, which he gained through experience and education, was mildly below average, but for his similarities, which measured memory and concept formation, Dan scored a test age of just 7 years and 2 months well below his actual age of 10. Arithmetic, vocabulary and whatever the hell digit span was, Dan was significantly below in terms of test age. I went through the report with a heavy heart, looking for the smallest of positives. At the bottom of the page, comprehension, which measured understanding of general concepts jumped out at me. Dan had scored 8 years and 10 months.

"That's not too bad," I said to Jen, "he's almost his own age." She pushed the rest of the results across the table at me. "Read on. There's more. And it gets worse."

I stumbled through the rest of Wechsler's findings. Picture completion, measuring alertness, visual perception and ability to identify essential from non-essential and isolate, Dan scored low. For picture arrangement, which apparently measured cause and effects relationships, Dan tested at just 6 years and 6 months. And on block design, which gave an indication of planning ability and motor skills, Dan lacked a clear strategy for completing tasks. I was going off Wechsler in a big way. But the man wasn't finished. Object assembly, which measures perceptual-motor skills, Dan was more than two years off the mark. Ditto coding which according to Wechsler measured visual-motor dexterity, whatever the hell that was. In his summary, the psychologist opened the door to the possibility of Attention Deficit Disorder compounding Dan's problems and then rounded things off with a cheerful one-liner that there was a need to evaluate through therapy, the possibility of Dan suffering from depression.

Next up was the Occupational Therapy Assessment Report. Alas. More of the same. Or worse. On his 'Draw a Man' test, Dan scored a mental age of just 6 years and 1 month. He hit rock bottom of 5 years and 10 months on his motor free visual perception test.

The clinical psychologist was given the responsibility for the wrap-up assessment. For the most part, her report was written in the cold, unfeeling medical speak, full of harsh, blunt phrases like errors of distortion and perception, below-average cognitive ability and generalised slowness in intellectual ability. Only twice in four pages, the doctor allowed her medical mask to slip. In the one narrative, she described Dan as a pleasant, polite boy and in another as a quiet, gentle child.

But easily the saddest bit in the whole report was Dan's one-liner description of himself, given to his panel of interviewers at the outset of all their poking and prodding –"I'm stupid and I normally come last in class." When I read that, all I wanted to do was cry. And all along, I'd thought Dan was the happiest kid in the world.

Having told us what was wrong with Dan, the psychologist went on to tell us how we could possibly fix the problem. We had to give careful consideration to the long-term goals of remedial work, but Dan had to be given opportunity and encouragement to develop his thinking skills. She felt it would be more appropriate for Dan to attend a school where classes were streamed and where he wasn't in competition with more academically able kids. The goals set for Dan's academic attainment had to be realistic. If there was an overemphasis placed on extra tuition, Dan's low self-image would be reaffirmed. And finally, she suggested that we encourage Dan to develop interests and activities outside the academic area that were non-competitive, like wildlife and nature interests.

Reading the reports left me confused and angry. Mostly I was angry with God. Why Dan? After giving him the shittiest start to life, why had God had dumped another whole bucket full of woe on the poor kid? But I was also angry at the clever people who had done the poking and the prodding. Their reports told us what was wrong, but no mention of why? To fix something, especially something you couldn't see, surely the start point had to be finding out why the something had broken in the first place. Surely you had to know the why before you could start the fix.

Later we were allowed to ask questions. I tried to nail the experts down as to why Dan was like he was. Only the occupational therapist ventured a theory. She used a building analogy. She told us the human brain was a complicated thing with a left side that controlled certain emotions and functions and a right side that controlled others. The building blocks on the opposing sides of the brains were fused together during infancy, to form sound foundations underpinning the continued building of the brain through ongoing education and life experiences. Possibly a lack of stimulation during Dan's infancy, possibly caused by his mother's illness, had prevented Dan's building blocks from fusing together properly. And now that we were layering education on top of them, the foundations beneath were cracking.

It sort of made sense. We'd got Dan just before he turned two. Because Rose was sick and busy dying for most of his short life, often she wasn't able to pick him up and love him and hug him when he was looking for attention. And chances were that Dan's crib never had one of those three-dimensional mobiles hanging above, stimulating him, developing his visual perception. Maybe, just maybe, it could be fixed through ongoing occupational therapy, she opinioned. But she sounded anything but confident

And so we went remedial school shopping. We decided the biggest speedhump on our near horizon was getting Dan into a decent high school. Once we'd crossed that bridge, we could start Dan's catch up by trying to fix some of the many other problems like low self-esteem etcetera, etcetera. There weren't too many remedial school options open to us. One of them happened to be run by the psychologist's mother-in-law. He pointed us towards her. He said she was very good, so we made an appointment to meet her. She was an old school no-nonsense teacher who ran her school from her home. Getting slow and troubled kids ready for high school entrance exams was her speciality. She believed that all problems academic were best solved through reading, writing and arithmetic, and lots of it, as in from eight o'clock to five o'clock every day. Poor Dan's face dropped at the prospect.

Dan's tearful departure from Lilfordia was made a bit more bearable by the fact that his best friend Sean, dyslexic and also not coping in the classroom, had also been enrolled at the remedial sweat academy. As it turned out, there were a lot of farming kids enrolled at the remedial school whose lives had been severely disrupted by the ongoing land invasions. Alas.

In amongst all the doom and gloom, Gary blew into town like a breath of fresh air, on his first university vacation. Befitting his status as a Fine Arts student, Gary wore the obligatory earring and long hair dyed a funny colour. Jenny had been suffering from worst-case empty nest syndrome and clucked over him like a mother hen. And Gary loved it. The best though was when Dan came home from school. We had kept Gary's holiday plans under wraps and Dan had absolutely no clue that his big brother was coming home. And Gary was way bigger than just a big brother in Dan's eyes, he was superhero big. I sent Dan to his bedroom to dump his school things. Gary was hiding behind the bedroom door and ambushed him. Watching the look of utter joy on Dan's face when he saw and hugged Gary brought tears to my eyes. I have never ever seen a person that happy to see another, before or since. Jenny captured the moment on her camera, and we still have the photo of the happiest little boy in the world hanging on our wall.

That evening Gary laid out some of his university artwork on the dining room table for us to look at. He was very proud of his work and rightly so. He'd come a long way as an artist in just a few short months. His paintings and drawings were excellent, but it was his photographs that were stand-out. Gary was majoring in photography, and it was obviously a good fit. His compositions were simple but so effective. He presented Jenny with a framed black and white photo of a coffee mug overflowing, with a scribble inscription below. 'Mom-may your cup always runneth over.' It still has

DAN'S MEDICAL PROBLEMS BEGIN

pride of place on the wall in Jenny's kitchen.

But Dan had eyes for one piece of art only, a charcoal drawing of a topless girl. The girl wasn't too pretty, but her bosoms were spectacular. The art critic in Dan was drawn to the girl's chest like Borat to Pamela Anderson. His eyes were absolutely riveted.

Eventually, he breathed, "Wow. Who is she, Gary?"

"I don't know Dan. Just some model the university brought into class for us to draw."

"You mean she's a real person, Gary?"

"Yeah."

"Your teacher brings real-live naked girls to the classroom for you to draw? You promise?"

"He's not a teacher, Dan, he's a professor. And yeah, he brings real-live naked girls for us to draw."

Dan made a career choice there and then. "I also want to become an artist, Dad, and I also want to go to university."

Chapter Twenty-Three

My rule of thumb was I didn't like politicians. Most were both grey and wrinkled like Harold Wilson, or they were cast from the plastic mould that spawned Ken, Barbie and Tony Blair. Apart from maybe Bill Clinton. He'd clearly enjoyed his time in the Oval Office and on top of that, he played the saxophone. Bill was cool. But there was no way that Morgan Tsvangirai could ever be described as cool. And I was pretty sure that he couldn't play sax. So, it was strange how in just a few months Morgan Tsvangirai had become such a big thing in my life, and also my family's. Six months earlier and I would have walked past him in the street. I'd never been within fifty metres of the man. Even now, I struggle to spell his surname properly.

Jenny and I were watching television one night, long after the kids had gone to bed when Dan came through to the lounge. Something was bugging him, and he couldn't sleep.

"Can you take me to meet Morgan Tsvangirai?" he asked with a Dan sense of urgency.

"You want me to take you to meet Morgan, Dan?"

"Yes, Dad. I want to say hallo to him, and I want to tell him Chinja Maitiro." Chinja Maitiro was easily Dan's best thing. He loved hanging out the car window shouting out MDC chant to all and sundry, all the while keeping score of the Good Guy versus the Bad Guy responses. It was like having a Gallup poll on tap in the car. Tracking people's political affiliations by their responses was easy. MDC supporters would respond enthusiastically with the open-handed salute while ZANU PF supporters would scowl and shake their fists. For the most part, the MDC won by a handsome margin. "Can you take me to meet him, Dad?"

Because I was soft on the outside and even softer on the inside, I said: "Sure I can, Dan, no problem."

"Thanks, Dad," Dan said and went back to bed, weight lifted. More like weight transferred, fair and square on to me. I had a slight dilemma in that I'd never actually met Morgan before. I'd seen him at a distance a few times, but his security was such that it was near impossible to get up close. Crap. I was going to have figure a way to get Dan into meet Morgan.

"So you going make Dan an appointment to meet Morgan?" Jenny snorted derisively.

"Well, um..."

"I guess it helps that you've got Morgan's number on speed dial."

"I never said anything about having Morgan on speed dial," I mumbled defensively.

More snorts of derision. "The way you carry on about Morgan this and Morgan that, Dan thinks you're part of his inner circle."

"But..." It wasn't the most convincing of buts. Jenny was right. There was an outside chance that I might erroneously, without intent, have created an impression that Morgan and I appeared closer that we actually were.

"You shouldn't have told him yes for sure. Now you're just going to disappoint him again."

I hated disappointing Dan but had a spectacular track record on the subject. Like the time I told him we were going to see Jurassic Park.

Jurassic Park the title meant nothing to Dan who was five at the time, but when I told him it was about a bunch of dinosaurs eating a bunch of people, he commenced to obsess. Dan always could obsess on something from a long way out. Dan could start obsessing on next year's birthday present the day after his last birthday. At first I thought Dan's ability to focus on something so intently, to the point of excluding all else, and for such long periods was a good thing, signs of a hitherto well hidden, inner mental strength but alas, the inner mental strength remained well hidden and Dan conversations were Déjà vu and predictable when he was in obsessed mode.

Jurassic Park smashed box office records the world over. Small surprise given the storyline. A bunch of people stuck on an island get eaten by a bunch of dinosaurs. And what a stellar cast. Tyrannosaurus Rex, velociraptors, stegosauruses and the guy from The Fly. The movie had Dan written all over it. Amazingly, especially given the blood and guts, it had no age restrictions.

Even before he saw it, Dan was a fan. And straight up, Jurassic Park became the biggest thing in his life. And when I told him the movie was coming to Zimbabwe soon and that we were going to see it on the opening weekend, wham, bam, he had died and gone to heaven. For a solid month before, all we talked, morning, noon and night, were dinosaurs and their dietary habits. Would dinosaurs kill you before they ate you or would you still be conscious on your way down to the dinosaur's stomach? Did dinosaur breath stink? Did dinosaurs eat the whole body, or did they sometimes leave just the head behind, likes cats and rats? How fast could dinosaurs run? Did I think that Dan could run faster than, say, a T-Rex? What about vegetables? Didn't dinosaurs have to also eat vegetables?

After forever, Jurassic Park D Day arrived. Predictably Dan woke me up before first light and started nagging me to hurry up otherwise we would be late. And equally predictably, we were late because I had a bunch of stuff to do on the farm before we left. By the time we got to the cinema, the queue was out the door and around the block. And by the time I found parking, the queue was even longer. Dan was getting very edgy. Relax, I told him, it's a big movie house, and of course, we would get seats. Dan and I revisited the dietary habits of your average dinosaur while standing in the queue. We were in the queue for a long time. Dan got more and more hyper, and I got more and more panicked. What the hell was I going to do if we didn't get tickets? I sent Dan off to the loo as we neared the front.

While he was in the loo the last Jurassic Park tickets sold. The only movie we could get tickets for was The Secret Garden. Crap. I had no idea what The Secret Garden was about, but the poster screamed unrequited love, inner turmoil and no blood and guts. It looked like Enid Blyton meets Wuthering Heights but more artsy-fartsy and without any of the gripping parts. What to do, what to do? God, I hated executive decisions. Did I give it to Dan on the chin, admit failure and come back to Jurassic Park another day or did I take Dan to The Secret Garden, numb him with popcorn and junk food and then blame the wrong movie with no blood and guts on an inept projectionist. I bought tickets for The Secret Garden.

Impossibly Dan's excitement ramped up as we filed into the cinema, fully laden with popcorn, to find our seats. And then when the movie flickered into life, Dan, in anticipation of what was to come, sat up on the edge of his seat. To his credit, Dan stayed on the edge of his seat for at least the first hour of the movie. In keeping with the warm milk and cookies theme to the movie, the foreground of The Secret Garden, where none of the action took place, was full of pastel-coloured petunias, pansies and the like. But in the background lurked some fairly promising and ominous foliage, large enough to conceal a ready to pounce mid-sized dinosaur, like say a velociraptor. From his edge of the seat vantage point, Dan ignored all the inane dialogue, mostly about love and instead, focused all his attention on the foliage, just waiting for the velociraptor to burst forth and rip the pretty little girls in their pretty little frocks, limb from limb. The tension in Dan mounted, and mounted, and mounted. Until after an endless hour of inane romantic babble, Dan rounded on me and demanded loudly and angrily, "But where are the dinosaurs, Dad? You told me there were going to be lots of dinosaurs? But where are they? When are they going to jump out of the bushes and eat this stupid girl?"

And there was the time I promised him a tenth birthday trip to the amusement park at Gold Reef City in Johannesburg, the home of the dreaded Anaconda, the scariest roller coast ride in the whole of Africa. On a previous visit, even on tippy-toes, Dan hadn't made the minimum height marker at the entrance to the ride and had to stand back disgusted and watch his brother and sister scream as they rushed around at breakneck speeds, mostly upside down. But a full year had passed and Dan, by his reckoning and mine, had stretched and strained and grown enough to make it on to the Anaconda. After endless begging, I promised Dan that I would find a reason for a business trip to Joburg during the school holidays, with a bolt-on visit to Gold Reef City. For a solid month before our departure date, Dan flogged the Anaconda to death, dissecting each and every twist, turn, climb and drop and the G-Force implications endlessly, over and over. The hot and dusty drive from Harare to Johannesburg would take twelve or thirteen hours, depending on how we went at the border. With Dan in Gold Reef City mode, the trip seemed to take at least twice that.

"So Veronica, how many Gs do you think I'll pull in that last corkscrew?" And "I'm going to do all the upside-down bits with both hands up in the air. I bet you didn't do that, Veronica. I bet you held on tight the whole way, with your eyes closed." After forever and like a Godsend, eventually Joburg's skyscrapers appeared, minuscule on the distant horizon.

"I bet you that tallest skyscraper, that one over there almost in the clouds, I bet you that's Gold Reef City, Isn't it, Dad, isn't it?"

We stayed with my brother Kees in Joburg. He almost got us a good one when he told us, with a deadpan straight face, that Gold Reef City was closed for a month, for annual maintenance. Hah! What to do with an uncle who is always joking? We got up first thing in the morning so we could rush off and get hopelessly entangled in Joburg's nightmare early morning rush hour traffic, which gave me the next three hours to refine my theory that everyone who lives in the South of Joburg, works in the North and vice versa. I then spent another hour getting lost, which added hugely to all the fun we were having as a family in the car. It also gave me all the time I needed to ponder how it was possible to spend millions and millions of dollars on a resort and then hide it in the arse end of Johannesburg and skimp on the signage. Oh, how the family laughed. Especially every five minutes when Dan asked why I was taking so long to get to Gold Reef City. Eventually, I bumped into a Gold Reef City sign. And then another. And another. And then there it was, dominating the skyline, Gold Reef City and the dreaded Anaconda! We could see the Anaconda from a mile away as its tracks twisted and turned and climbed and clawed their way high into the sky only to drop away alarmingly. Even from a great distance, my stomach lurched. Dan was speechless for the first time in hours. Eventually, he squeezed out a breathless Wow! Followed by whoops of joy and triumph. Which died the most dismal of deaths when we got to the entrance to find the tall gates locked. Gold Reef City was closed for a month for annual maintenance. Alas.

With that track record behind me, I just had to find a way for Dan to meet Morgan Tsvangirai. And then providence shone upon me. The very next day, Hendrik phoned. Did I have a three-ton truck? And could I spare it for a few days? He needed to move a fridge and a lounge suite and some other household stuff to Morgan Tsvangirai's rural home. By bolstering his roots in the community, Morgan would send an important message to his constituents, apparently. My ears pricked up at the mention of Morgan's name. I told Hendrik no problem, I could spare my farm truck for a few days.

"You sure? Your truck is going to have to go all the way to Buhera."

Now I had no idea where Buhera was, but I would have sent the truck to Timbuktu for Morgan.

There was much excitement of the farm when the news got out that the truck would be transporting Morgan's furniture. The driver preened and strutted, stopping just short of offering autographs. Raphael rushed in to see me straight away, miffed. As the senior man on the farm, it would only be fitting for him to escort Morgan's furniture to Buhera, just to make sure the driver didn't get lost and to make sure the driver drove carefully and didn't fuck up the furniture. Or fuck up the truck. Raphael added on the afterthought for my benefit. I didn't have the heart to say no, and so Raphael drove off, the happiest man in Zimbabwe.

Buhera must be close to Timbuktu because the truck only came back four days later. Raphael was exhausted but had a satisfied smile on his face. He had travelled well, he told me. "But did you meet Morgan?" I asked.

"Yes. The president was at his home."

It threw me every time Morgan was referred to as the president. It was like Morgan was trespassing onto Mugabe's hallowed turf. Which was what Morgan was all about, I suppose.

'Did you get to talk to him?"

"Yes. After the president killed a chicken for us to eat, he and I discussed late into the night. We discussed and discussed. I gave him my opinions about the current situation." I winced for Morgan. Raphael and his discussions were deadly, rather like when Dan obsessed. And Raphael's opinions took forever. Dan walked past in time to catch the end of the story.

"You got to meet with Morgan?" he demanded of Raphael.

"Yes. Your father sent me to meet with him and to discuss."

"But Dad, why did you send Raphael when I asked you first? Why didn't you send me to meet with Morgan?" Dan stormed off, pissed off that I was messing with his head again, just like with the Anaconda and Jurassic Park.

The phrase 'when it rains, it pours' certainly applied to Morgan Tsvangirai and me. Two days later, I got another phone call from Hendrik. He had another problem. Morgan was having a meeting in Harare's Northern Suburbs that night, and Hendrik was worried the audience would be mostly white, which would open the door to more attacks from Mugabe and The Herald that the MDC was a white man's party, that Morgan was a stooge for the Western governments, blah blah blah. Hendrik needed more blacks in the audience. Could I send some farmworkers in for the meeting? Politics in Zimbabwe was such a dirty game and hurt my head. But I could

DAN MEETS MORGAN BUT NO DINOSAURS

see where Hendrik was coming from. The Herald had long stopped being a national newspaper and was now a full-time propaganda club that Mugabe used to keep his people cowed and in the dark. I put the word about the meeting to the farmworkers, and there was a veritable stampede to get on the truck, led by Raphael. He was just back from a four-day pilgrimage to see Morgan Tsvangirai, and still, Raphael wanted more. My mind boggled.

I followed the truck full of workers in. Morgan's meeting went well. The Running Dog workers helped balance out what would have been a mostly white audience. And my workers were good value and gave the meeting some badly needed loud and oomph. Whites in Zimbabwe approach their politics like one would the Queen of England, oh so politely and reservedly with stiff upper lips to the fore, with the odd "Hear, hear!!" being as loud as it got. The black electorate, on the other hand, let it all hang out, with loud ululations, laughter, cheers and cries, all with an emphasis on loud. It was sort of like a black Baptist congregation sitting in on the same service as a bunch of stiff upper lipped white Presbyterians.

Come question time, Raphael's arm shot up into the air. He waved it around frantically, like a kid with a small and full to bursting bladder trying to attract his teacher's attention. But Morgan steadfastly ignored Raphael for as long as he could, fielding every other question in the room first, his recent marathon Q&A session with Raphael still obviously fresh in his memory. I think he was hoping Raphael would tire and drop his arm, but he didn't. And so eventually, Morgan had no option but to turn to Raphael with a wince fixed firmly on his face and a groan not far away.

"Ah, Mr Raphael Mutwira. Nice to see you again. What is it that you want to ask me now?"

Straight away Morgan shot way up in my esteem with the way he accorded Raphael dignity and acknowledged him by name. It was a big deal and allowed Raphael to puff his chest out proud like a bantam rooster. And all the next day, Raphael flogged to death the fact that he and Morgan were practically on first name terms with anyone and everyone who stood still for long enough. Including, unfortunately, Daniel. Who was horrified that again I'd taken Raphael off to meet with Morgan Tsvangirai instead of himself.

"But I told you, Dad, I told you that I want to meet Morgan. But you just keep taking Raphael with instead. And it's just not fair."

Dan and I were on our way home after picking him up from his weekly Saturday morning karate lesson. I asked him how the lesson had gone, but Dan quickly changed the subject to Morgan Tsvangirai. Had I made an appointment for him to see Morgan yet? Dan wasn't enjoying karate. He'd signed up to learn how to smash bricks with his bare hands, but after weeks and weeks, the only thing he'd been taught was how to bow and how to count halfway to ten in Japanese. He was supposed to have learnt all the way to ten, but the numbers beyond six in Japanese weren't easy. Dan was getting very irked with my continued reluctance to introduce him to Morgan. I told him Morgan Tsvangirai was a busy man and that I couldn't just phone him up and make an appointment, but Dan shot me down in flames.

"You got Raphael in to see him, Dad, two times this week! And I asked you first, Dad!"

"I'll try to see what I can organise, Dan."

Dan took a leaf out of my standard education lecture that he'd heard so many times. "Well you just have to try harder Dad, just try harder."

It worked. I jammed on brakes and did a U-turn in traffic.

"Where are we going. Dad?"

"To the MDC offices. Let's see if we can see Morgan."

With just weeks to go to the elections, the MDC offices were crazy hectic. With Dan in tow, I eased through the crowded offices in search of Hendrik. Wearing his white karate suit and his 'I can break bricks with my bare hands' frown, Dan attracted more than a few comments. As soon as I found Hendrik. I was going to ask him straight out if we could gate crash Morgan's inner sanctum so that Dan could meet the boss. Someone upstairs must have been listening to me because just then Hendrik stepped out of the back offices in deep conversation with Morgan. One of the unwritten laws of physics clearly states that all politicians, while electioneering, shall be drawn to babies and children like moths to a flame. And so it was with Morgan. He looked up and straight away zeroed in on Dan in amongst the multitude. With a broad smile on his face, Morgan bent over to shake hands with Dan.

"Hallo, young man, who are you then?"

Dan frowned up at him, thrust out his open palm and shouted, "Chinja Maitiro" right in Morgan's face. Who almost shat himself. I think he thought Dan was pulling some sort of a Kung Fu move.

Chapter Twenty-Four

Like Nigerian prostitutes, elections in Zimbabwe are neither fair nor free. Take our list of invited international election observers for instance. Instead of Jimmy Carter, we got some guy called Abdul Salaam Abubakar. Instead of the US or Europe, our international observers were drawn from bastions of democracy like Russia, Nigeria, and Equatorial Guinea. Apart from staffers from the local US embassy, the only American who made it on the invite list of observers was the leader of some obscure Black Consciousness movement, a modern-day Malcolm X but not as moderate.

The inside of my head in the run-up to the 2000 elections was even busier than normal. There was no shortage of things to toss and turnabout at night. How were we going to get Dan into high school? What the hell was that noise at the gate? Where to buy diesel? How low could the Zim dollar go? How to stop the hair on my head from migrating down to my ear lobes. And now added to that list was how to stop the election from being rigged. What an utterly bizarre thing for a flower farmer to stress about. Only in Zimbabwe. And maybe in Russia. And Equatorial Guinea and Nigeria. How the hell was I going to stop Mugabe from rigging my bit of election? What happened inside the polling stations was sort of under control with six polling agents taking it in turns to keep their eagle eyes on the ballot box. But it was what came after that was giving me my biggest headache.

Apparently, all the ballot boxes from all the polling stations in Zvimba would be uplifted by government vehicles and transported the hundred-odd kilometres to the counting centre in Murombedzi. And of course, being government vehicles and because rules were rules, opposition party polling agents would unfortunately not be permitted to accompany the ballot boxes. Bummer. Which meant no eyes on the ballot boxes. Which meant I was supposed to find fifty-plus vehicles to follow the ballot boxes around the countryside. Alas. Given the threats of death and ear removal that had been prevalent in Zvimba South, I was going to fall a bit short of my fifty-vehicle target, like about forty-five- vehicles short. What to do, what to do, what to do? I chewed down on yet another sleeping pill and tossed and turned some more.

Like children, my ideas mostly get born at three in the morning. I sat bolt upright in bed. I would make each polling station an anti-rigging kit, complete with sealing wax and I'd ask Tony to make me individualised seals, like little branding irons with a ZS for Zvimba South and a number for each polling station to stamp into the wax. And in each kit, I'd also put in a pot of specially tinted paint to clearly mark each ballot box. And some duct tape to seal the sides with and an indelible marking pen to sign over the masking tape so you could see if someone had messed with it. My idea was that good I celebrated with a Eureka, which, unfortunately, woke Jenny up and earned me a crack on the head.

Hendrik also thought my idea was a good one. Which was a bummer. Because he asked me if I could do anti-rigging kits for the whole country. Crap. More stuff to stress about. There were one hundred and twenty constituencies times fifty polling stations in each meant I had to find sixty thousand paintbrushes on a budget of zero. And sixty thousand little pots of paint and sixty thousand blobs of sealing wax and...It was clearly an impossible task. I had no choice but to delegate it to best friend, Sean Cairns. Sean invented the phrase 'Can Do'.

He took over the flower grading shed and in two ticks, turned it into an election anti-rigging kit production line. Move over Henry Ford. Sixty thousand paintbrushes? No problem. He cut pencil thickness twigs from a bougainvillaea bush and hammered the one side out into bristles and job done. Sean took my idea and fleshed it out into a big fat guy like Billy Bunter. A prominent paint company donated different colour paints for each province and sixty thousand little sample pots. It's amazing how generous people got when the good cause they were supporting centred on no more Mugabe. The 6mm round bar for the seals for each constituency also cost us nothing. Watching the anti-Mugabe anti-rigging election kits roll off the production line was good therapy, like watching fish in a fish tank. I loved it.

Alas. My anti-Mugabe anti-rigging kits were the merest of farts against the rolling thunder of politically inspired rapes, beatings and murders unleashed by Mugabe on the country in the run-up to the elections. It was a planned, systematic attack on the MDC codenamed Operation Tsuro which means rabbit in Shona, with MDC supporters countrywide the designated bunnies in the headlights to be beaten, raped and or killed. ZANU PF supporters selected as Operation Tsuro operatives were rushed through a seven-day training and indoctrination course held at Harare's KGVI barracks where they were taught all manner of useful things like how to dispose of a knife after stabbing someone or how to burn an opposition member's hut down. Tadius Rukini from Bikita was an Operation Tsuro target and became the first MDC parliamentary candidate to be murdered.

As part of the Operation Tsuro roll out, war vet leader Dr Hitler Hunzvi converted his surgery in Harare's Budiriro Township into a torture centre. ZANU PF gangs roamed Harare, abducting hundreds of suspected MDC members and dragging them off to the torture centre to have the soles of their feet beaten and their genitals wired into the national grid. The police knew exactly what was going on in the surgery but did nothing. In the farming districts, where there were fewer prying eyes, Hunzvi operated on a much larger scale. He converted recently seized commercial farms into political re-education centres and herded men, women and children in their hundreds and thousands to attend pungwes or all-night attitude readjustment sessions in which they were beaten with whips and clubs and forced to chant ZANU slogans. Again, the police knew what was happening on the farms but did nothing. Operation Tsuro hit the remote Mberengwa district like a runaway freight train, with gangs of ZANU PF thugs, scores strong, raping, pillaging, burning and beating anyone remotely suspected of being an MDC supporter. The police turned a blind eye to row upon row of blackened, charred villages and the mounting death toll and did nothing.

The police weren't the only ones who did nothing. When the horrific details of Operation Tsuro were leaked to the world press, along with the news that Mugabe himself had presided over a graduation ceremony of Op Tsuro operatives, I sat back and waited for a swift and emphatic response from the West. I grew up on James Bond movies and Tom Clancy novels, so I knew the response was coming. When, just weeks before the elections, Mugabe announced that 85,000 white Zimbabweans, most of them born and bred, were to be removed from the voter's roll for not having renounced their rights through the descent to British citizenship, I sat back with bated breath and waited some more. And then waited some more. And then, at long last with drums rolling, the response came. With sycophant Tony Blair hovering in the background, George W Bush frowned mightily for all the world's cameras to see and appointed South African President Thabo Mbeki his point man on the Zimbabwean crisis. Job done and buck passed. George W had watched Black Hawk Down more than three times and knew exactly what happened when a president sent the marines into Africa to play the good guy. Never on his watch would the world watch dead marines being dragged around the streets of an African city.

Thabo Mbeki was delighted at the opportunity to shine in the world spotlight. When asked how he would respond to the humanitarian crisis unfolding on his borders, the newly appointed point man trotted out his own statesmanlike frown and sternly announced that he would tackle the unfolding humanitarian crisis on his northern border with quiet diplomacy. Which translated into exactly doing nothing... other than flying up to Harare periodically to hold pinkies with Mugabe at the airport. Strong stuff indeed. I was so beyond fucking cross, I burnt all my Tom Clancy books for being bullshit fiction.

A week out from the elections, the electoral playing fields in Zimbabwe looked horribly skew. No, Jimmy Carter, a Zimbabwean Electoral Commission headed up by a Mugabe lickspittle and twenty-five MDC corpses and counting. But apparently, there was nothing to panic about. According to George W's point man Thabo, stick all of those things into a pot, stir vigorously, and you get conditions conducive to free and fair elections. The MDC wasn't as sure. Rocked by the viciousness of the ongoing violence, they said they were considering boycotting the election. The coward in me rooted hard for a boycott. It didn't make sense to go into a brawl with a bully with both hands tied behind your back. The MDC hummed and hawed about the boycott. And then decided to stay the course and contest. Crap. That was not what I wanted to hear, but Raphael and the MDC supporters on the farm cheered the decision. Of course, we would win the election. I wish I shared the power of their convictions.

The elections were to be held on the last Saturday and Sunday in June. Our Jimmy Carter replacement, former Nigerian President General Abdul Salaam Abubakar jetted in on the Tuesday with the Commonwealth Observer team and set up five-star base camps at the Meikles and Sheraton hotels. Amazingly, some of the observers actually left their hotels to do some observing on the ground. On the Wednesday, a contingent of us from the MDC Electoral Support team met Abubakar in the field. We met him on Duke du Coudray's farm in Banket. It was a surreal setting. A former Nigerian head of state sitting down with a bunch of mostly white political activists mostly wearing khaki on a white farm in Zimbabwe talking democracy or lack thereof.

I'd never met a real live former head of state before. Apart from Abel Muzorewa but then he didn't really count. I had an Idi Amin caricature stuck in my head, but Abubakar was actually quite impressive. There was a lot of him, all very big, very black and very loud, in voice and in dress. His voice was Louis Armstrong gravelly. And I loved his oh so loud shirt and wanted one badly. But easily the most impressive thing about him was that he wasn't puffed up with self-importance, and he listened. And he listened. And then he listened some more. Mostly to Duke du Coudray. In fairness to Duke, it wasn't so much that Duke can't spell succinct, which he can't, but it was more a case of ZANU PF doing lots and lots of bad. Like for instance declaring the whole of Hurungwe West a no-go zone for the MDC. And sticking up roadblocks on the national highway to enforce it. And this just two days before the election, and on the morning a former Nigerian head of state pops in to check that things on the ground are hunky-dory and free and fair.

For those not familiar with rural Zimbabwe, I need to put Hurungwe West into perspective. It's big, ten thousand square kilometres big, like half of Wales. ZANU PF imposing a no-go zone on the district was like Tony Blair saying no Tories allowed past Swansea or they'd all get a good kicking.

General Abubakar tut-tutted his displeasure over and over, especially at the no go zone and made sure his minion scribe spelt Hurungwe West correctly. And then he did bugger all. He wished us luck and climbed into his big shiny motorcade and headed off in the direction of Harare. Which really sucked. Oh, how I yearned for Jimmy Carter. But it wasn't all bad, Duke told us. At least we had reported the infraction to the observers. And that was what we had to do over the weekend whenever we saw bad stuff going down. Phone the observers observing in our constituency, report the infraction and get the report in the record books for the world to see after the elections.

When I got back into town, I drove straight to Observer HQ at the Meikles Hotel to get phone numbers for the Zvimba observers. The place was a madhouse with armies of observers rushing about, all pumped up with self-importance, all wearing their little khaki photographer vests with Observer tags on the back, all far too busy to talk to me. Eventually, I cornered one who looked at me like I was mad when I said I needed phone numbers for my observer, for just in case. For just in case what he asked? He rolled his eyes like I was a drama queen when I told him for just in case of violence and intimidation on the weekend. Luckily, he believed in humouring madmen and told me that Zvimba had been assigned to the South Africans who were based at the Sheraton.

As it happened, I didn't have to wait for the weekend to call out my observers. On the Thursday before the elections, one of my polling agents got captured by ZANU PF in broad daylight. The polling agent's name was Jericho, and he worked as a labourer on a nearby brickfield. Jericho had been sent by Raphael to round up some polling agents for last-minute re-training. An off-duty farm guard had watched the abduction happen. Thugs had jumped on Jericho and bundled him into a twin-cab with no number plates and had taken him to the Mt Hampden Youth Training Centre. The training centre was just around the corner from Running Dog and had recently been commandeered by ZANU militia to use as their base camp for the duration of the elections. And to show exactly how fucked up and far from free and fair things were, the training centre was also one of the weekend's designated polling stations.

I sent two guys down to the training centre to listen and look. One of them reported back promptly. They had crept up to the eight-foot wall surrounding the training centre and heard screaming, lots of screaming. It had to be Jericho. I positioned Raphael in the farm pick-up truck to watch the front of the training centre, in case they moved Jericho and then hot-footed it to the Sheraton Hotel to find our South African observers. The coffee shop in the hotel foyer was full of them in their natty khaki waistcoats with many pockets, all busy observing menus and cocktail lists. Eventually, I tracked the boss observer down. He was sitting at one of the tables with the rolls of fat down the back of his neck like a Brahman bull that came with being important. He looked irked that I was interrupting his pre-lunch lunch. I told him what had happened. Not even halfway through my story, he started looking bored. I begged and pleaded for an observer to accompany me back to the training centre. He wasn't keen but relented when I told him I'd go tell my story to the television news crews camped outside the hotel. He called a woman across, told her my story and asked her to go with me and check it out. While he was talking, I checked out her name tag. Her name was Patricia de Lille, and she was a member of the Pan African Congress. That was great, just great. The PAC was like the black Klu Klux Klan party of South African politics, fringe lunatics whose rallying calls of 'One Settler, One Bullet' and 'Kill the Boer, Kill the Farmer' had resonated around the world loudly in 1994, taking the shine off Mandela's calls for reconciliation. Mrs de Lille had a mean look in her eyes, and I could picture her squeezing the trigger of a rifle. But at least, she appeared to listen carefully while the fat man gave her a much-condensed version of my story. And she looked keen to get out of the hotel and into the field. I offered her a lift, but she said she would follow in her issue 4 X 4.

At the training centre, she told me to wait outside while she went in with her driver to investigate. She came out ten minutes later and shook her head. She had found nothing. Which wasn't surprising. The training centre had been a motel in a previous life and was a sprawling complex with dozens of outrooms. There was no way she could have searched the whole place in ten minutes. Raphael wanted her to go back in and search again, but she said she couldn't. She left me with her cell phone number and told me to call her if there were any further developments. I left Raphael staking out the training centre while I went back to the farm, frustrated and angry.

Not two minutes later, I got a phone call from Raphael. The twin-cab with no number plates had just left with Jericho trussed up like a chicken in the back. Raphael, following at a distance, said it looked like they were headed for the Marlborough police station. Straight away, I phoned Mrs de Lille and told her what had happened. She sounded angry and turned around and headed to Marlborough police station. I was waiting outside when she arrived. Again, she told me to wait while she went inside. And again, she came out minutes later, shaking her head. No Jericho to be found. Or at least, according to the cops anyway. But short of calling them liars there wasn't much else that she could do to help us. Mrs de Lille wished me luck for the elections before driving off back into town. And that was that, I thought. But it wasn't.

Late that night, or more like early Friday morning, I got woken up by the guards. Jericho had just staggered up to farm gate in a bad way. He'd been beaten so badly I hardly recognised him. But easily, the worst were the wounds on his back. The letters MDC had been carved across his back, twelve inches high and deep into his flesh. The letters had been carved with an Okapi knife, a marker to show MDC supporters what they had coming to them. Jericho had been tortured in the training centre and again, at the police station. Jericho said the police had been badly rattled when the

South African observer pitched up looking for him by name and so they waited until it was dark and then they drove him deep into the bush in the middle of nowhere and kicked him out. Jericho had walked more than thirty kilometres to get to the farm so that he could report for his polling agent duties.

"You still want to be a polling agent?" I asked, feeling more than a bit inadequate. With his wounds, I would have lurked on my death bed for a week.

"Yes," was his unwavering answer.

"And you actually saw the South African observer?" I asked.

"Yes. At the training centre and again at the police station." At the police station, de Lille had actually come into his holding cell, and the police had lied to her, telling her that Jericho was a suspect in an armed robbery. I poured some antiseptic into the wounds on Jericho's back, and he didn't even squeal, again making me feel inadequate. And then I drove Jericho to the George Hotel to meet Patricia de Lille. I'd phoned her earlier to tell her that we'd found our man.

"He was being beaten badly at the training centre you went to, Mrs de Lille. They carved the initials MDC across his back with a knife. The letters cut into his back are about twelve inches high and very deep. And he'll tell you that he was also at the police station when you got there. He heard the police tell you that he was an armed robber."

"When can I see this man?" Mrs de Lille asked.

"In the next half an hour. I'm bringing him into town to see a doctor before taking him out to his polling station. He's one of our polling agents."

"He still wants to do the election?"

"More than ever, Mrs de Lille, more than ever."

Patricia de Lille will go down in my books as one of the good people. She looked at me sideways when she saw the South African television crew waiting at the George Hotel but said nothing. I'd phoned them and told them what was happening. Jericho was waiting inside a small conference room that I'd commandeered. Even though Jericho was just a labourer, Mrs de Lille treated him with dignity, his horrific wounds with empathy and his courage with respect. She questioned him closely about his experiences the previous day. Deep down, I think she was an angry person inside. And her anger came very close to boiling over when it became very apparent that ZANU PF and the police had hidden Jericho away from her at the training centre and again at the police station. And then she did a very good thing. Once she finished interviewing Jericho, she invited the South African television crew to set up inside the conference room and then went through the whole interview with Jericho again. She let the whole world see the letters MDC carved deep into Jericho's back with a knife, carved by Mugabe's thugs in a government building that would also double as a polling station the next day. Free and fair elections bollocks my arse. She left that bit unsaid, but it came across strength five.

The next twenty-four hours were a big schlep. We deployed the polling agents from Running Dog. Raphael pulled Titus Nheya up on to the back of the pick-up truck so he could inspire the troops with a rousing speech. Titus made a wooden one instead and urged the polling agents to be vigilant and brave. It might have been stirring stuff, had it lasted for more than thirty seconds. Raphael filled in the awkward silence and dragged Jericho up on to the back of the truck, lifted his shirt and showed-cased his wounds as a not so gentle reminder of the evil we were all up against. He applauded Jericho's courage and told the polling agents they had to be just like him. Finally, some strong, stirring stuff and everyone left tall, proud, and all fired up.

The deployment took all night and then some. We had nowhere near enough vehicles to deploy the more than three hundred polling agents to the more than fifty polling stations spread out over a huge chunk of the countryside. The polling stations were mostly at government schools or clinics, on farms and in the communal lands, and all heavily manned by police and government agents. There were no friendly faces to be seen when we drove up, all we got were scowls. It felt like we were dropping the polling agents deep behind enemy lines and I felt sorry for them. The deployment dragged on all through the night and into the morning. The roads in the communal lands were knackered, and we got horribly lost more than once. The sun was well up by the time we did the last drop off, and a long queue of voters had already formed. The sense of the excitement amongst the voters was palpable though, and I took heart. This was the part in the movie where the good guys fucked up the bad guys.

I went home, showered, ate some breakfast and then divided the polling stations amongst Raphael, Titus, Sean Cairns and some other volunteers. Raphael and Titus set off in the farm pick-up, I jumped back into the Chinja mobile with a farm supervisor called Shepherd, and we hit our polling stations, one by one, checking on polling agents and geeing them up, making sure there was no skulduggery going on. Alas. I drew the short stick with the Zvimba communal land polling stations, including the birthplace of evil, Kutama. Driving to Kutama, I felt like Frodo Baggins on his way to Mordor.

Just a hundred metres before Kutama Mission, I had to pull off the road for flashing lights and screaming sirens. Crap. Mugabe's motorcade. Evil was going home to cast its vote. There were a million cars and motorbikes in the motorcade giving me plenty of time to observe the reactions of the throng of men, women and children standing on the side of the road watching. I was looking for signs of affection towards Mugabe, waving and cheering but saw absolutely zero. The villagers just stood and stared woodenly at the mad rush of vehicles. Mugabe might have been born amongst them, but he was that far removed from his people, he might as well have come from a different planet. I decided to try an experiment. I waited until the motorcade was long gone before hitting the clump of villagers with the open-handed Chinja salute. Straight up, I got the open-handed response I was looking for. And plenty of broad smiles. And right outside Kutama Mission where Mugabe had grown up. For the first time, I felt as though we could win this thing.

The polling station at Kutama was full to overflowing with Mugabe and his security detail, so I decided to give checking on our polling agents inside a miss. Which got Shepherd to sulking and nagging but the coward in me wouldn't budge. A white farmer walking in to do democracy checks while Mugabe was voting would have been a big red rag to his bull.

I picked Jenny up later in the day to go and vote. We cast our votes at the training centre, the same place where Jericho had been tortured two days before. The queue was long and out of the gate. I felt that the people in the queue had a quiet sense of purpose to them. There was a pair of thuggish policemen bossing the front of the line up like night club bouncers. They didn't say anything, they just stood there looking menacing, Fear Factor personified. And it worked. There were more than a few of my farmworkers in the queue, but they were guarded in their greetings and all Jenny, and I got were the smallest of nods. The queue moved quickly enough, and before long I was in the voting booth with a purple stain on my fingers, a pen in hand and a huge feel good inside as I stuck a big emphatic X next to Morgan Tsvangirai's box. Sticking it to the bad guy felt oh so good. And I felt a small bit of personal pride when I pushed the slip into the ballot box that had already been indelibly marked by my top-secret anti-rigging paint. Mugabe wasn't going to be able to switch this box out in a hurry.

The rest of the weekend passed in a slow, weary blur. Two days of voting was cruel, but the MDC polling agents stuck to their tasks manfully. Even the women polling agents. I was completely knackered. It must have been worse for the polling agents who also had the mind-numbing boredom to contend with. Some of the polling stations had finished their voting by the afternoon on the first day and then sat around doing nothing for another whole day. After finishing my rounds, I managed to grab a few hours of sleep, which was more than most, before hitting the polling stations again. By Sunday lunchtime, voting had slowed to a non-existent trickle, and it was time to move the ballot boxes to the counting centre at Murombedzi.

A mishmash of government vehicles, from air force trucks to ambulances, came out to move the ballot boxes to the counting centre. Having struggled to move 300 people, I was struck by the enormity of the logistical feat. And that it was happening countrywide, boggled my mind. If only the government put the same amount of effort into running the country as they put into stealing the election. Alas. Predictably, MDC polling agents weren't allowed onto the trucks to accompany the boxes, and so they had to stand and wave goodbye to the boxes they'd guarded around the clock for the last two days. Free and fair, just like a Nigerian hooker. And suddenly my anti-rigging devices looked woefully inadequate.

I trailed an animal health inspector truck full of ballot boxes to the district counting centre. Murombedzi was just twenty kilometres from Mugabe's rural homestead at Kutama where it was rumoured, he would spend the night, waiting for the results of the countrywide count to come in. And judging by the number of Ministerial Benzes cluttering up the bottle store car parks, it looked like half the ZANU PF hierarchy were in Murombedzi to wait things out with their beloved supreme leader. I wasn't allowed to join Titus Nheya in the counting centre. Rather than hang out with the sycophantic fat cats, I went back to the farm and slept the sleep of the dead. I was glad I wasn't going to be there for the count. While my heart was saying we could win Zvimba, my head was saying no way. And I was going to have to go with my head. The Fear Factor in the district was too deeply embedded. And after all the hard work we'd put in, I didn't want to be there in person when we came in second. Second in a two-horse race is pretty much the same as last.

Chapter Twenty-Five

I set up a television in the office so the staff could watch the election results live. I hadn't watched local television in years. Normally the only stuff that ZTV showed was bad propaganda, made badly. But the election result show was good, spectacularly good. And watching the results being read out live in the crowded office was like watching good rugby in a crowded stadium. I stood next to Titus and Raphael and was deafened every time the MDC won a seat.

The MDC dominated in all the cities and towns. They smashed ZANU in the Matabeleland constituencies and also took a big chunk of Manicaland, including Roy Bennett's seat in Chimanimani. For a white farmer to win in an overwhelmingly black constituency was massive. I started thinking landslide. But then a whole swathe of ZANU results came in, one after the other, from the three Mashonalands. Including Zvimba South. Shame. Poor Titus came in a very distant very second, polling just four thousand votes against Sabina Mugabe's sixteen thousand plus. As his results were announced, Titus put on his stoic face, which wasn't too different from his ecstatically happy one. Poor Titus would have made a better poker player than a politician. And maybe if he played poker for a living, the adjective poor wouldn't have been a permanent fixture. Titus might have been a crappy politician, but he had a big pair of balls. To go up against Sabina Mugabe and brother Bob in their hometown of Zvimba, I had nothing but respect for him. And more than that, I liked the guy and would be sorry to see him go. It felt as if he'd been on the farm forever.

A few short months later in December 2000, Titus was murdered by ZANU thugs. They beat him to death, cracked open his skull and scooped his brains out and smeared them about to show people what happened to MDC supporters. Alas.

In the end, the MDC won fifty-seven seats of one hundred and twenty up for grabs. ZANU PF won sixty-two, and ZANU Ndonga won the remaining seat in Chipinge where Shangaans take tribalism very seriously. The Shangaan are a tribe of 5 million people, mostly living in Southern Mozambique, South Africa and a very few in Zimbabwe, in and around Mt Selinda.

Raphael was so distraught the MDC had come second by just three seats I thought he'd slit his wrists. But I was happy enough. When you run a marathon just finishing feels real good and finishing a close second is a bonus. And because the elections were over, my life could go back to normal. Ditto the country. And with an opposition party in parliament for the first time ever, the checks and balances would muzzle Mugabe. He would have to start worrying about the economy, and obviously, the land-grab would stop, and everyone could go back farming.

We were all summoned to a post-mortem wrap held at the George Hotel, to look at all the stuff we'd done right and all the stuff we'd done badly. So, we could build on our performance next time, they said. Next time. Haha!! How I laughed. We had to stand up, one by one, and tell everyone who we were, what we'd done and review our results. Best friend Bob Hamill sitting next to me got big applause. As the head of Support for Harare and Chitungwiza provinces, he'd delivered nineteen seats. And then it was my turn. Alas. Bob's was a hard act to follow, especially if you're from Zvimba South. I stood up and told people I'd come second. Before I could sit down, Bill Searle acknowledged me for donating the George Hotel and for the anti-rigging kits. I was chuffed with the gesture. Afterwards, I bumped into Morgan and asked him to autograph an election poster for me, as a memento of my brief career in politics. Morgan thought that was very funny.

The next day Jenny and I took the kids to South Africa for a long-overdue holiday. As we crossed the border, I literally felt the pressures and the stress and strain fall away. I'd been wound up tight but didn't know. South Africa has always been a stark contrast to Zimbabwe, the grass not only greener but also neat, tidy and well mown, like a well-manicured putting green up against the roughest of rough. But this time, the contrast hit me even harder. The shop shelves were full to overflowing with unlimited choices. Coming from a place where you could choose either Colgate or Colgate, the toothpaste section in the South African supermarket hurt my head. More of the same in the sweetie section. Fruit Pastilles, Toblerones, Maltesers and endless more. Dan went into sensory overload. In the car, he whooped and hollered every time he saw a Porsche or a Ferrari. But the biggest difference was the people we met. They were all so normal, mostly talking about the weather and about business and about the plight of the Springboks. I was jealous. Oh to be able to get seriously down in the dumps about a rugby team. I did my best to shut Zimbabwe out but jumped on the internet whenever I could, looking for news of home.

And none of the news was good. Impossibly, the land-grab had ramped up since the elections with five new invasions per day and no end in sight. Hitler Hunzvi, the king of the war veterans, was more vocal than ever. Mugabe had let him and his war veterans off the leash, and he was no hurry to get back on. The lesson to white farmers about what happened when you interfered in opposition politics was ongoing.

There was a backlash in the cities as well. Newly elected Member of Parliament, Edwin Mushoriwa was beaten up and hospitalised by thirty soldiers in uniform who gate-crashed his victory celebrations. The police declined to investigate and said arresting soldiers was a job for the military police. Three other brand-new MDC MPs had to go into hiding for fear of their lives after receiving death threats.

And while all of this was going on, Bush's point man, Thabo 'See No Evil, Hear No Evil' Mbeki gave Mugabe a pat on the back for conducting free and fair elections in which only thirty people were beaten to death.

Our week in South Africa, mostly spent in retail therapy and restaurants, absolutely flew by, and before we knew it, it was time to go home. We were all down in the dumps when we crossed back over the Limpopo River into Zimbabwe, into a sea of litter, trash and crap washed up against the buggered road verges, back to dreadful roads with deadly potholes, dead donkeys, buggered tarmac and pirate taxis. But way worse than all of that was the dreadful uncertainty that hung over us. Driving back to Harare through empty farms that should have been busy, we had no idea where we would be living in six months.

Once back at home, I tried to get busy farming again for the first time in months, but it was tough to focus. There were lots of distractions. All our farming friends were being hassled, and many were leaving for greener and more peaceful pastures. Farewell parties were the order of the day. Best friends Kerry and Brian Wehlburg of the leopard in the tree that actually turned out to be a lion fame were going to Australia. But there were also plenty of farming friends who made the decision to stay. Best friends Eric and Fiona Dawson got busy with renovations to their farmhouse and started up a game section on their model Marondera farm. Another flower grower, Jack Callow, threw caution to the window investing everything he owned and more into greenhouses on his Mazoe farm. Ditto best friends Noel and Jackie Kent who started a cut flower farm in Borrowdale. Noel had the greenest fingers I knew and could get anything to grow.

Because of their foreign currency earning potential, flower farms became prime targets with the army top brass grabbing the choicest. The sudden focus on flower farms was especially a bummer if you lived on a flower farm. The thought of fat cats in uniform getting fatter on flowers they hadn't planted was irksome to a few of us, so we put our heads together to figure out a way of shutting down the export markets to stolen flowers. Holland was the obvious starting point. We met with representatives from the Dutch auction floors and presented them with the problem. I was worried about the reaction we'd get. The Dutch are born traders. Selling flowers is what they get up for in the morning and to ask them to not sell flowers on moral grounds was a big ask. But in the end, I had nothing to worry about. The Dutch came up with a simple solution. Most cut flower varieties are royalty protected. Rose royalties especially are an arm and a leg expensive, at close to a hundred thousand dollars a hectare. By law, the auctions were obligated to check on royalty compliance. And if the grower couldn't prove that he'd paid his royalties, then they wouldn't be able to market the flowers from the farm. We patted ourselves on the back. By cutting off the access to the Dutch auctions, we thought that was Europe closed and job done.

But very quickly the flow of stolen flowers was diverted to South Africa via the auctions in Johannesburg. I followed the flowers down to Joburg and asked for a meeting with the auction floor's board of directors. The auction floors are grower-owned, so I was hopeful of a sympathetic ear. For about the first hour spent in their reception. After that, I grew less hopeful. Eventually, one of the directors deigned to meet with me. The flower business in Joburg must have been good because he dripped wealth with a chunky Rolex and more gold chains than a West Indian fast bowler. I told him how the flow of stolen flowers from Zimbabwe had shifted to his auction floor. He all but yawned. I showed him letters from the Dutch flower breeders confirming the royalties on the stolen flowers being sold on his auction were indeed outstanding. He looked at the letters for all of thirty seconds and then asked me what it was that I expected the auction to do. Stop selling stolen flowers, I told him. He laughed. And then he got all huffy and puffy and pissed off with me. How dare I tell him how to conduct his business? How dare I ask him to get involved in land disputes in another country? Who was he to judge whether or not the blacks had rights to take Zimbabwean farms? I tried to placate him. That was exactly why we were coming in from a royalty perspective, I told him. No moral decisions required, just yes or no, have you paid your royalties? Alas. I should have paid more attention to the Rolex and the bling. He all but threw me out of his offices, but not before telling me that he would continue to do his job and sell any and all flowers that came in from Zimbabwe, without prejudice. I kept my calm and thanked him for the meeting. And then I told him he was a greedy knob who would suck blood from a dirty stone and that I hoped that sometime in the future, he got kicked off his own flower farm so that he knew what it felt like. Way to go, Eric, how to win friends and influence people. I kicked myself all the way out of his office, wondering how long before I attracted the attentions of the fat cats.

Not long as it turned out. Just a week later, I got another middle of night warning from the friendly policeman that I'd once served with, telling me it would be a real good idea if I left the farm in a hurry. Waking Veronica and Daniel up out of the deepest of sleeps and telling them they had ten minutes to pack was déjà vu from nightmares past.

"But I thought the elections were finished," Veronica mumbled.

"They are," I told her.

"But then why are they doing this to us?"

"Just because", I told her.

I left out the bit about it being all because we were white farmers. The kid was stressed out enough as it was. I also left out the bit about it being because I was helping shut down markets for stolen flowers. I hadn't got around to telling Jenny about my latest project. She would kill me quicker than the war vets if she found out. It sort of went against promises that I would curb my subversive activities.

Alas. As it happened, over the next two years, we ran away from the farm in the middle of the night seventeen times in all. We got real good at grabbing the stuff that mattered in a hurry. Like hamsters, an abundance of guinea pigs and BB guns as opposed to stuff like homework and toothbrushes. Things like photographs that had come off the wall in the first hurried evacuation never went back up again. They now lived in a box with a friend in town. Sometimes we stayed away from home for just a few days, other times for much longer periods. Sometimes it was a false alarm, but there were more than a few occasions where for sure I would have been killed had the warnings been ignored. It was all extremely unsettling. But every time the decision to run away felt right. I was sure getting killed would hurt like hell, and I didn't do pain well. But I also didn't have it in me to bury my head in the sand while evil flourished around me. I had to carry on meddling. Alas.

Not surprisingly, Jenny and I started talking about where we would live if we were to move away from Zimbabwe. But what happens to my parents if we move away, Jenny asked? Tony and Hester had been back in Zimbabwe for five years. After the stresses and strains of multiple retrenchments in South Africa, they loved the comparatively slow pace of farm life in Zimbabwe. Hester worked at Mr Mole, our retail garden centre in town and loved it like it was her own. Tony was in seventh heaven on the farm with an endless list of buggered things to tinker with and fix. It would be cruel to uproot them. And starting over in a new country would be difficult enough with two kids, let alone with a set of grandparents in tow. Better to leave them in Zimbabwe, I told Jenny. If anything ever happened to the farm, we'd resolved to buy Tony and Hester a garden flat in town, and they could earn their livings from Mr Mole. They would be just fine, I told them.

With that resolved, we started thinking about where else we could live, if ever push comes to shove. Working off a blank canvas when choosing a new place to live should have been a liberating experience, but for me, it wasn't. Even just thinking about moving made me feel like a rat fink abandoning ship.

Officially, we now had more friends living in Australia than we had in Zimbabwe, so Australia was an obvious choice first up. We had holidayed there twelve years earlier and had enjoyed it. We found an expensive immigration agent and battle commenced. And a battle it was. The Aussies did not endear themselves to me by making me fill out a rain forest's worth of forms, full of never-ending, intrusive questions. And then came the medical tests. I was subjected to the humiliation of having a woman doctor examine my balls to see if they bounced up and down when I coughed. In keeping with Einstein's theory of relativity, time slowed down as though it was trudging through thick porridge while the woman peered at my nether regions for what felt like hours. Small talk was out of the question, so I was left with just my thoughts for company. Why were Australians so hung up on fully functional balls? What did it matter if your balls didn't bounce? If you were born Australian and your balls malfunctioned, did they make you emigrate? And why pick such a pretty woman doctor?

Rather than tell you there and then whether you were in or not, the Australians preferred to leave you hanging. And because I wasn't a hundred percent convinced that I'd passed the testicle test, we decided to add a couple of fall-back options. I told Jenny I was keen on either Vanuatu or Belize. She hit me and told me I wasn't allowed to make countries up. I showed her them in the atlas, but she hit me again anyway and told me I had to pick countries that we could afford to get to. Alas. With a stroke of the pen, Belize and Vanuatu were consigned to the scrap heap.

I quite liked Zambia. By all accounts, it was a lot like Zimbabwe with lots of big land, lots of opportunities and scant regards for whether or not a man's balls bounced when he coughed. Jenny, on the other hand, didn't like Zambia because it was a lot like Zimbabwe. Zambia got parked, pending further investigation. And so it was back to the atlas.

Uncertainty is a dreadful thing, especially on a farm. It affects everything you do. The first things put back on the shelf were the long-term projects, like our staff housing project. I wanted Running Dog to be a model farm with all workers living in three or four-roomed houses, each with its own toilet and vegetable garden. I'd started an upgrade project a few years ago, knocking down an eyesore single quarters block we called Baghdad, replacing it with better housing. Alas. The upgrade got put on hold, and those workers still living in the remnants of Baghdad were told they would have to share a crapper until things improved. Even short-term work on the farm suffered. Now when something broke, rather than replace it, I told Tony to make a plan and tie the thing back together with rubber and or wire. Tony was the consummate artisan, and it pained him to work like that. I was always careful not to talk about plans for the future in front of Tony for fear of unsettling him. But looking back on things, I think not talking about the future was a mistake and made it worse. Without meaning to, I'd stuck Tony back in a place where he worried about tomorrow. So, he had a stroke.

It happened in the afternoon. I was at home talking with Rod Dawson, a friend visiting from SA. Tony rushed into the garden, wild-eyed, hugely agitated and worked up about something. I asked him what the problem was and he told me a lot of different crap, all jumbled and all at once. It was like he was trying to say three different sentences all at the same time. At first, I thought he was being funny, pulling my piss for pulling in different directions as is my want. But Rod called it straight away. I think your dad has had a stroke, he told me. I didn't know what to do. By the time we got him home, Tony's left side had already gone numb, and the one side of his face had started drooping. I don't do medical emergencies and sick people too good. I fall to pieces. Thank God for Rod. We rushed Tony into hospital, but the damage was already done. The doctor confirmed that Tony had suffered a massive stroke. The doctor couldn't tell us to what extent he would recover, if at all. I took it all very personally. And rightly so. I should never have left Tony and Hester on the farm. I should have moved them into town away from the 'in your face shit' on the farm.

Tony came out of hospital after a week. He was very weak and talked with a slur that made him near impossible to understand. I decided that I would make a point to pop in after work every day and visit with Tony, to tell him what was happening on the farm, but only the good stuff, to try and cheer him up. Embarrassingly, I missed the first four days through the pressure of work. On the fifth day, I got to Tony's house just after four in the afternoon, and I found Philemon, my gardener, sitting on the veranda next to Tony, chatting away while massaging the muscles in Tony's left arm gently, over and over. I watched him start at the shoulder and then slowly work his way down to Tony's hands and fingers, gently but firmly massaging and kneading away at the muscle structure in the damaged arm. Philemon worked oh so slowly as though he had all the time in the world. And when he finished with the hand and the fingers, he started all over at the top again. Over and over. It was a proper labour of love. How long has been doing this for, I asked Hester. Philemon comes every day, she told me, as soon as he finishes work at your house. He talks to Tony and massages until it gets dark.

I got a big lump in my throat watching a black domestic servant helping the grumpiest old white man, in his own time and out of the goodness of his heart. It was one of the kindest and most pure acts I'd ever seen. And it made me happy that I lived in Zimbabwe, despite all the crap that was going on around me. Mugabe talked complete crap when he shouted off about there being problems between white men and black men in Zimbabwe, complete and utter crap.

Chapter Twenty-Six

Zimbabwean farmers were told to turn their other cheeks every time war veterans arrived at the gate, either baying for blood and or demanding diesel, booze, money or food. Second nature for most farmers would've been to stand up to the demands and tell the war vets to bugger off, followed with a backhander if there were any arguments. But the CFU script called on farmers to avoid confrontation, to not let the next war start at their gates. But to constantly turn the other cheek gives you a pain in the arse, a pain in the neck and invariably you end up hurting on both sides of your face. Inevitably some farmers hit back.

In Chinoyi, when a farm gate confrontation turned ugly, nearby farmers responded to desperate radio calls for help and a punch up started. Instead of meek and mild, this time the farmers hit back, and the war veterans got a hiding before fleeing in the general direction of away. The police in Chinoyi reacted straight away. They swooped in and arrested all the farmers. The thugs who'd been smashing up property, brandishing pangas and long knives, threatening men, women and kids with murder and worse, they ignored. Instead, they arrested the victims and dragged them off to the cells where they were treated like convicted criminals. Shackled and cuffed and with heads shaved and in filthy lice-ridden prison kit, the farmers were paraded in public and in front of the ZBC cameras, proof that law and order were alive and living in Zimbabwe.

Law and order were not doing so well on the streets of downtown Chinoyi though. To be white and out on the streets in Chinoyi that day after the farmers fought back, got you beaten. Young or old, man or woman, it didn't matter, the ZANU thugs beat anyone who was white with absolute impunity, secure in the knowledge the police would not react.

Alas. Things didn't stop with the random beatings in Chinoyi. Two days after the farmers retaliated, the commercial farming district of Doma 60 kilometres to the north of Chinoyi got trashed. Doma was a hugely productive district, a hundred plus farms carved out of the harsh bush, turned into some of the country's most productive and progressive farms. The farmers opened up Doma after the Second World War. Before then, there was nothing but bush. Tobacco, horticulture, cereals and grains thrived in the fertile soils and under the hot burning sun. As did the farmers. Along with the dams and farming infrastructure, they built the tightest and most caring of communities, complete with country club, cricket pitches and enthusiastic but verging on bad amateur theatricals. Best friends Dave and Sue Mead moved to Doma to farm tobacco on a leased farm, and it very quickly became home. Their neighbours could not have done more to help them settle. We went to visit the Meads on their new farm, and I remember being very envious of their sense of community spirit. It was like watching one of those impossible American sitcoms with neighbourhoods full of apple pie and bonhomie. I'm not saying that my own neighbours weren't nice, but they didn't make apple pie good like Sue and Dave's.

The mob that started the Doma trashing was state-sponsored. They started on a farm called Two Tree Hill before first light which was always a bad sign. Mobs are spontaneous things. They don't set their alarm clocks for five in the morning so they can get a full day of rioting in, especially in the middle of winter. That's more a disciplined soldier sort of thing to do.

The mob of thirty or forty strong arrived at the farm gate and softened up the farmer and his young family locked inside with abuse and death threats. Then they turned their attention to the sheds and the farm buildings, stealing and looting everything and anything they could find. Fertilisers, the graded tobacco crop, tools and workshop equipment, there was lots to loot. Two Tree Hill was a successful farm. Watching his life's work being carted off by the truckload, the hapless farmer phoned the police but no luck there. And after what had happened in Chinoyi just two days earlier, the farmer couldn't phone his neighbours for help either. He was on his own, with his wife and his two young kids, up shit creek and with no paddles. It doesn't get much worse than that. During the war, when you got attacked, you could at least fight back. And you knew that help was just a radio call away.

Once the farm sheds and outbuildings had been stripped, the mob turned its attention back to the homestead. The security gates were forced open, and the mob poured into the garden and shot one of the dogs. Not long after, a gaggle of politicians including Provincial Governor, the Minister of Local Government and the local Member of Parliament arrived on the scene, with television cameras in tow. By now, the farmer, his wife and his young children had been under siege for more than eight hours. He must have thought that with the arrival of the politicians, some semblance of order would be restored and that at long last his family's ordeal was over. Alas. No such luck. In front of the cameras and perched on stolen sacks of fertiliser yet to be carted off, the Minister accused the farmer of having instigated the violence, even shooting his own dog. And then he left. The mob got back to work, targeting the house. The farmer bundled his wife and kids into the family car and managed to escape. They took nothing with them. Everything they owned, they left behind. And everything was stolen. Clothing, bedding, furniture, every single thing, got ripped out and carted off. Even the door frames and the window frames.

And once Two Tree Hill Farm had been reduced to ruins, the mob turned its attention to the next farm. And then the next. And then the next. The free looting with no reprisals had been shown on prime-time national television, and very quickly the mob doubled and then trebled in size, and the sky above Doma turned black as the district burned. Eventually, even the farmworkers joined in. I'm guessing it was one of those if you can't beat them, join them sort of things. And the way the workers saw it, there wasn't going to be any work to go to come Monday morning. And all the while, the police stood by and did nothing. Farmers and their families evacuated the district. And that wasn't easy. The mobs had chopped down trees to block off the main escape routes. In the end, the farmers had to put a light aircraft up into the sky above to guide fleeing farmers to safety.

Fifty-four farms later and fully sated from their orgy of destruction, the mobs broke up and went home. Job done. Doma had been trashed and a message sent out to all other white farmers- don't fight back. From above, the district must have looked like the biggest army of locusts had passed through, destroying and reducing everything in their path to nothing. Alas. Dave and Suzie Mead stayed with us when they got into town, wide-eyed and absolutely shell shocked. Their farm had been one of the fifty-four. I didn't know what to say to them. Where do you begin to console a couple who've just lost everything?

The Doma trashings did for what residual feel good had built up inside me after the election results. I took them far worse than even Dave and Suzie, who'd incredibly elected to go back out to their farm to pick up the shattered pieces of their lives and start over. After the trashings, Zimbabwe closed in on me terribly. I wanted to take my family away, to somewhere orderly, where property and life were protected, somewhere a farmer could plant trees and know that he would still be around to reap the fruit.

Jenny and I put together a Zimbabwe bucket list, places that we had to see again before we left. First up was a road trip to the back end of Kariba. Normally you'd get there by houseboat, this time we thought we'd drive. We loaded up the Chinja mobile and threw the rubber duck on to the roof rack and set sail for Gokwe. There was that much play in the Chinja mobile's steering, driving it felt exactly like sailing a small boat on choppy waters.

Gokwe was the massive, oft-forgotten chunk of Zimbabwe right in the middle, directly below the length of Lake Kariba. With dramatic escarpments and breath-taking views that stretched out for as far as you could see and beyond, Gokwe just went on and on and on; especially in the Chinja mobile which could do nought to sixty, but only just. The last time I'd driven through Gokwe was as a gawky policeman in the war, and I'd forgotten how big it was, and how good. And in the twenty years since I'd left, there'd been zero work done on the roads. They were tatty beyond belief, and I was glad the rubber duck was on the roof rack above and not on a trailer behind.

Jenny had booked us into Tiger Bay, a thatched resort on the banks of the upper reaches of the Ume River. The place was nearly empty, just a few other farming families who'd come across the Lake in their boats to fish and relax, but mostly to get away from the harsh realities of being a farmer. Dan eyed the array of big shiny power boats pulled up on the grassy embankment outside the thatched rooms with envy, as we took turns to pump up the rubber duck. In the forty degrees heat, it was hard work and took forever, especially with Dan doing more gawking than pumping.

"Why can't we get a boat like that, Dad?" he asked, pointing to an eighteen-footer with monstrous twin outboards.

"Shut up and pump."

Twenty minutes and a million calories later, the Duck was pumped up and good to go. We loaded up with Jenny and Veronica, fishing rods and worm boxes plus cold boxes and beers and set off to explore.

The Ume River was a maze of nooks and crannies, twists and turns, all absolutely lousy with crocodiles and hippos. I'd never seen so many crocodiles since my life. And skimming along in the rubber duck, alarmingly close to the green waters, most of them looked to be bigger than our boat. We were ten minutes out when Veronica asked why the sidewalls of the rubber duck she was sitting on were getting softer. Straight away, all eyes flashed across to Daniel.

"It's not me, I didn't do anything this time, I promise, I didn't," he protested loudly, with both hands held up high.

A year earlier on the Zambezi River on the rubber duck at speed, Dan had asked me what the main air outlet valve cap was for, just seconds before unscrewing it. The rubber duck went from flat out to just plain flat... in seconds flat. Oh, what fun!!

And now the same thing was happening all over. But this time round, Dan wasn't to blame. The valve cap was still in place. Which could only mean a puncture! I cut the motor, so we could also listen for the leak.

"I found it," Veronica shouted.

"Me also," shouted Jenny, "I've also found the leak."

"And me also. I found a leak too," wailed Daniel.

Crap. Multiple leaks. Almost as many leaks as there were crocodiles in the water outside. Keeping a cool head, I screamed: "Put your fingers on top of the holes. Where the hell is the foot pump? There it is, grab it, grab it, grab it! Stick it in, stick it in, stick it in and pump, pump, pump! Pump faster Daniel, pump, pump, pump! If you don't pump, the boat will go flat, and we'll sink, and we'll all die! Pump, pump, pump!"

Not my finest moment. When we eventually made it to the nearest piece of dry land, we found a multitude of little puncture holes in the top wall of the rubber duck. It was as though someone had got busy on the boat with a pin.

"How the hell did they get there?" I asked.

Jenny helped me out very helpfully. "Maybe, just maybe, they've got something to do with the thorn tree I told you not to drive under when you've got a rubber boat on top of your roof rack!!"

Oh, what fun we had as we pumped and pumped and pumped as we limped back through the crocodile-infested waters to Tiger Bay and the puncture repair kit in the car. And how we would miss Kariba when we got to Australia. And the rubber duck.

Back on Running Dog, things stayed the same. Just a few days after getting back from Kariba, another scribbled warning from the ladies at the musika on the corner that they were coming to get me, had the family scrambling for clothes and treasured possessions at three in the morning. With no photos to take down and with lots of practice under our belts, we could pack and go in minutes.

We were away for a week, spent at best friends Bob and Julie before we got the all-clear from Brian and moved back home. While we were away, Jenny's dairy cows came down with mastitis. She was livid and gave Philemon, the gardener-come-cowherd hell. Jenny loved her cows and fussed over the small herd like children. And Jenny's herd was getting smaller all the time. She started off with black and white Friesland cows, but she had introduced Dexters into the mix a few years earlier. Dexters were a tiny miniature breed of cow, black squat and in perfect proportion. Apparently, they were very cute. So I was told over and over, by Veronica and Jenny. I didn't mind the little Dexters so much. Six of them in a flower field didn't do nearly as much damage as the big black and white cows did.

The latest outbreak of mastitis was severe and stressed Jenny out. She decided that enough was enough and the Dexters like our photos, would be packed up and put away for the duration. She asked Murray Dawson if he could look after her cows on Rainham Farm. As was his wont, Murray said no problem, he'd stick them in with the few milk cows that he kept for the house.

Alas. A week after Jenny's Dexters moved on to Rainham, so did the war vets. Their ugly huts, made of wooden poles and bits of scrap plastic, sprung up overnight, all over Rainham.

Rainham Farm was a huge model farm with fattening pens, an abattoir and a butchery. It had large massively productive lands under centre pivots producing soya beans, golden wheat and more. There was a huge vegetable section, and export rose section. All of that plus the fact that it was right on the outskirts of Harare made it a prime target for a fat cat to grab. That there well over a thousand workers and their families living and dependent on the farm mattered not a jot. Ditto the fact that the Dawsons were pillars of the community and had been for over forty years. What the fat cats saw and coveted, they just took. And damn the consequences.

The fat cat with his eyes on Rainham was Enos Chikowore, a former Minister of Energy and Transport. He sent a war vet by the name of Kambanje on to Rainham to kick the Dawsons off. Kambanje was at least old enough to have seen the war, unlike the mob of young louts and thugs beneath him who'd been recruited from the street corners to make up the numbers.

The war veteran's huts went up overnight. Made out of sticks and sheets and plastic and bits of sheet metal, they were ugly like scabs and in your face. They put up lots of huts because the Dawsons would be tough nuts to crack. They built the huts right up alongside the main road that ran past the farm so that passing motorists couldn't but see them. They built them right outside the main house, right outside the workshops and right next to the main vegetable lands. They were going to get under Murray's skin, come what may.

I felt especially sorry for Rob Dawson, Murray's older brother. Rob and his wife had just moved back home after years in South Africa to help run the family farm. Rob had built his dream house, a rambling thatched home and picture-postcard pretty, overlooking Rainham Dam and the adjoining bird sanctuary. The war vets built eight huts right up against Rob's security fence that ran around his garden. First thing every morning, the war vets would pull their pants down and squat in full view of the house and then throw their shit over the fence on to the lawn. And the war vets would get pissed every night on government-issued booze and bang away on drums non-stop, all night long. Predictably, the cops did nothing when reports were made.

I would have packed up my belongings and moved out after a day. But the Dawsons were made of sterner stuff and dug in for the long haul. Murray hired the best lawyers in town and initiated legal proceedings in the High Court to have the farm invaders kicked off. I called in to see Murray and Terry to offer up my support. Murray said he was determined to carry on farming and to prove it, had ordered in another 40-hectare centre pivot. Terry quoted the new family dictum from his wheelchair "Illegtimi Non Carborundum" Latin for 'Don't let the bastards grind you down.'

To counter the weekend war veteran activities, Murray hosted an extended dragged-out farmworker football tournament. On most weekends, as many four different teams were playing, including Running Dog FC. Who were easily the worst team on show, even though I'd bought them new strip.

I'd started the team a few years earlier as a way of building staff morale and team spirit. Hah! There is nothing like a never-ending losing streak to kick staff morale and team spirit in the balls, pardon the pun. In a word, the team's problem was Raphael. He was the team tactician. He was also the team manager, head coach and selector and was crap at all those jobs. But his main job was tactics and he was especially crap at tactics. Raphael's game plan centred on a ten-man attack. He thought it would be prudent to leave the goalie in defence, for just in case. Given the appalling lack of footballing skills, vision and physical fitness within Running Dog F.C., the just in case scenario was pretty much a constant. When his ten-man attack had come to nothing, Raphael would switch to an eleven-man defence strategy that proved equally ineffective. Raphael's pitch side coaching soundtrack went something like this. Attack, attack, attack, attackkkk! Fuck. Fuck, fuck, fuckkk! Defend, defend, defendddd! Fuck, fuck, fuckkkk! One nil. Running Dog would trudge back to the centre spot and then more of the same. As the game slogged on relentlessly, the word fuck would come more and more to the fore. And invariably the poor goalie would cop all the blame, and he'd get switched before the end of the game. And then the carnage would really begin.

Murray's football tournaments did their job though and raised worker morale on Rainham. But as the invasions dragged on, and as Kambanje became more confrontational, Murray's workers' spirits started to flag. Then Kambanje drew a line in the sand. He told Murray and his workers that they weren't allowed to plant soya beans under the new pivot. If they did, there would be trouble. Ever the diplomat, Murray told Kambanje to fuck off and went ahead with the preparations to plant. But his workers were properly scared and didn't report for duty. The war vets had been busy in the Rainham compound, and the workers had been thoroughly intimidated. It looked like Kambanje had won. Murray was determined to get his crop in but what to do? He couldn't plant forty hectares of soya on his own. I had a hurried meeting with the staff on Running Dog, told them what was happening on Rainham and asked for volunteers to go help Murray plant. Forty hands shot up in the air. We dressed the Running Dog workers in Rainham overalls, and they trooped off with their badzas to plant soya. Kambanje was furious and rushed over with twenty thugs to stop the planting. Murray was in the lands behind the tractor. Kambanje ordered Murray to stop. Murray told him to fuck off. Kambanje and his thugs rushed Murray and started beating him with sticks and clubs. At which point, the Battle of Rainham Farm commenced.

It was a short battle. Wielding badzas and frustrated by a year of kowtowing, the Running Dog contingent tore into Kambanje and his war veterans. Having fought in the armed struggle, Kambanje knew all there was to know about tactical withdrawals and headed for the safety of distant hills. But twenty years spent in beer halls and shebeens had taken the edge off his ability to withdraw at pace, and Kambanje only made it as far as the first barbed wire fence. His more fleet of foot flunkies left him snagged on the top strand where one of the Running Dog foremen gave him a thorough beating with his badza. Unfortunately, the foreman didn't use the sharp end of the badza, and Kambanje only ended up in hospital.

Alas. We might have won the battle, but not the war. It wasn't long after before the Dawsons got chased off their farm for good. A group of armed men pitched up just after dark on a Friday night and drove around Rainham, shooting the place up. Murray's nephew Andrew was trapped in the house. A couple of us went there in my car to get him out. The house was all dark when we got there. I could hear the crack and thump of bullets whistling over the roof above. They sounded like they were coming from the compound. I wanted to run away but couldn't because I was there with others. Where the fuck was Andrew? The sooner we got him out of there, the better. I tried the front door. It wasn't locked, so I went in. Andrew was hiding behind the door and almost took my head off with a giant shifting spanner. We emptied Murray and Terry's cupboards in minutes, grabbing what we could so we could get the hell out. Toothbrushes, toiletries and not a lot else. Alas. The little that we grabbed were the only things the Dawsons got off their farm. They were never able to go back home and lost everything.

A few days later we heard that the war veterans butchered Jenny's herd of little Dexter cows to death in an orgy of bloodlust on Murray's front lawn, hacking steaks off the poor animals while they were still living. Murray's front lawn was less than twenty kilometres from Harare city centre. Hate is a very strong word and should never be used loosely. God but I hated those people. Alas.

Chapter Twenty-Seven

In amongst all the trauma, angst and near death, we still had to do normal stuff in Zimbabwe, like teaching sixteen-year-old daughters how to drive; which translates into more trauma, angst and near death.

I'm guessing teaching kids how to drive is traumatic the world over. In Zimbabwe, it's trauma times ten. Rules of the road are optional, every second traffic light is either buggered or out because of a power cut, roads have more potholes than road, road markings have long since faded and are guesswork, and one in three other motorists on the road bought their license. When Gary turned sixteen, Jenny taught him. So, it was my turn with Veronica. But Jenny was lucky. Gary knew his left from his right and his brake from his accelerator. He was a good driver and only failed three times before passing.

I'm sure Veronica was an American motorist in a previous life because no matter what I did, I couldn't get her to drive on the left side of the road. Every time we got in the car with the L plates on and her behind the wheel, a huge unseen vortex sucked us across the middle line and onto the wrong side, the side of the road where unsuspecting pedestrians with the survival instincts of lemmings in free fall strolled along happily. And upon being presented with the prospect of a pedestrian popping into the car via the windscreen, we would commence panic procedures. I'd get the ball rolling by telling Veronica in my loud, shaky voice to stay calm. As soon as she heard the word calm, Veronica would commence screaming, so as to set the tone for what was to come. And to avoid unsettling eye contact with the rapidly approaching pedestrian, she'd look down at her feet to consider her pedal options. Clutch. Brake. Accelerator. Or Brake Clutch Accelerator. Eeny meeny miny moe. With impact just seconds away, Vee would make an executive decision and stab down viciously on the accelerator. Galvanised into the action by the brutal forward surge, I'd grab at the steering wheel and just miss the poor pedestrian busy with final prayers and emergency bowel evacuations. I would break the Do Not Swear at Children rule, tears would commence, we'd practice our seventeen-point turns and go home again to practice in the driveway behind locked gates and high walls. But only after locking away dogs, cats and lawn furniture. Oh, what fun we had.

Once she sort of knew how to drive a car without destroying the gearbox, I handed Veronica over to a nerves of-steel driving instructor who got paid not nearly enough to take her out on to the carnage that is Harare's traffic. What happened out on the road had to be real bad. When asked, Veronica would describe her driving lesson as fine. Fine is teenage speak for not fine. But I was happy with zero detail.

After his nerves were thoroughly shot and after he'd earned enough danger money to buy a tropical island, the driving instructor adjudged Veronica to be ready for her test. And so I made a booking at the VID testing centre. Veronica failed. So, I made another booking. Veronica failed again. And again. And yet again. After which I moved the show to Kadoma, the nearest small town with a testing centre. And a single traffic light. And a cost of living low enough that driving examiners could get by on salaries alone, without needing to top up on bribes.

When I drive, Kadoma is a one hour plus drive. With Veronica behind the wheel, the trip turned into a four-hour epic complete with tears et al. But it was all good practice before her driving test. Just thirty seconds into that driving test and before getting out of the testing centre, Veronica drove into the wall of black and white 44-gallon parking drums. And so it was back to Harare but with me driving while Veronica grumped. A week later, back behind the wheel in Kadoma, Veronica celebrated her safe passage through the treacherous drums by driving out the in-gate, ignoring the massive Strictly Entrance Only sign hanging above it. And so, it was back to Harare again. And so it went.

Once we were on first name terms with all the Kadoma examiners, we moved on to KweKwe, an even smaller town with zero traffic lights and hopefully less discerning examiners. To save commute time, I took the precaution of making a double booking. And I left the bribe money in the cubbyhole, apparently the prescribed place for just in case. Incredibly we didn't need either. Veronica passed on her first attempt, well her first KweKwe attempt at least. Sufficiently numbed, I let her drive back to Harare but spent the hours hunkering down, reflecting on the importance of avoiding short straws when Daniel turned sixteen.

To calm my nerves after Veronica's driving licence chronicles, I went to my first ever CFU Congress. I'd been a member of the Commercial Farmer's Union since I started farming but had always given the annual Congress a miss. I don't do stodge and boring. And a big room full of serious farmers, all dressed up in their best khaki, discussing important stuff like export beef quotas, government tariffs on imported fertilisers and the minutes from the last congress took stodge and boring to a whole other level. But after Veronica's driving, boring was what I needed in my life, so I went to Congress.

As it turned out, Congress was anything but boring. This was a Special Congress, convened to find a positive solution to the farm invasion problem. It was held at ART Farm on the outskirts of Harare. I got there late as is my want. The room was full to overflowing, but I was able to find a seat right at the back. I couldn't see the podium because there was a big, fat black farmer in front of me.

The mood in the room around me was half angry, half scared. To a man though, the farmers were confused and uncertain as to the way forward. Their lives and their communities around them were being ripped asunder, and they didn't know what to do.

To set the tone, proceedings kicked off with an overview of the farm invasions to date. The total number of farms invaded was shockingly high and rising daily. Just now there wouldn't be any farmers left on the land. The shock statistics were followed by a presentation by the CFU's young deputy director, out of the box bright and very young, apart from the big black circles under his eyes. The deputy director was proposing a positive response to the farm invasions. He told us that as commercial farmers, we had to get more involved in the communities around us, we had to reach out to our black neighbours and help them become better farmers. There was plenty enough land out there for everyone. Commercial farmers in Zimbabwe were amongst the best in the world and had plenty of skills they could transfer. It was good positive stuff, but cynics in the room muttered too little, too late. The deputy director opened up the discussion to the floor.

The big black guy in front of me stood up and introduced himself. He told us that he was a commercial farmer and a paid-up member of the Union. He spoke very slowly and very ponderously, following every sentence with a long, pregnant pause during which you could hear the proverbial pin drop. He went on to tell the room that he was also there in his capacity as a member of the ZANU PF politburo. Another even more pregnant pause, filled with even more absolute silence. He'd come to Congress to tell us that the land redistribution was irreversible and that it would not end until all white farms had been taken. Yet more silence. Apart from a very few white farmers, who would be allowed to continue farming. At which point the politburo member took time to glare around the room and then he walked out, his steps as ponderous and as measured as his speech. The whole room stayed silent and watched him leave. Only once he was gone was the silence broken. I was absolutely shattered. It was a chilling display of personal power that made my skin crawl. I'd never seen one man put the mockers on a whole room like that, a whole room full of rough, tough farmers, plus me.

An expert in negotiations who'd been retained by the CFU to help them shadow box with the government was asked to comment on what had just happened. His analysis was short, to the point. How the hell are you supposed to negotiate with a stone wall like that? Analysis over. The debate then raged, between hawks and doves. A hawk stood up. As farmers, we had to shut the economy down, he thundered. Don't deliver a pint of milk, not a bag of maize, not a kilo of tobacco to the market, not a single cut flower to the airport, nothing must come off the farms, not until law and order were restored and property rights were respected. It sounded good to me. And to lots of others in the room. But not to the doves. Negotiations had to continue. But as I listened to the arguments rage around me, not one person called it like it was. Everyone was talking about land, and no one was talking about politics. And the land-grab was all to do with politics. Mugabe was kicking us off the farms because he'd fucked the country up so much, he had nothing left to give his supporters. He couldn't give them jobs or free education or free healthcare, the only thing he could give them was our farms. And he wasn't going to stop until we were all gone unless we all did something to make him gone. With my MDC hat on and my heart in my mouth, I stood up and pointed out to all present that the land invasions were a political problem and as such, required a political solution. The only solution to our problem was to get rid of ZANU PF, period. Alas. My two cents worth went down like a lead balloon.

Shame. I had nothing but the utmost respect for all the CFU Presidents I met over the years that followed. Without exception, they were all good men, all brave enough to stick their hands up when called upon and all of them tried to do the best for their farmers in the face of insurmountable odds. But none of them were equipped to deal with the problem. They were honourable men trying to play poker by the rules against a dirty thieving, lying murdering cheat who cared nothing about rules and even less about the people that got hurt, killed, raped or worse in the process. In the years ahead, we found out that you can't win a dirty poker game, playing clean. Looking back, we should've listened to the hawk and shut the whole place down. Or better still, we should've hired a hitman and fixed things with a bullet. Alas.

After Congress, the farm invasions gathered pace. There was no way Hitler Hunzvi could keep up with his workload, and he was joined centre stage by a murderer called Black Jesus, the same Black Jesus who'd bossed up the murder of Martin Olds and a gap-toothed buffoon in a grass hat called Chinotimba. Black Jesus had recently made the headlines again when he beat five MDC supporters to death in front of a crowd in a township in Kariba and walked away scot-free. In his previous life, Chinotimba had been a municipal policeman. With a penchant for violence, Chinotimba and his grass hat and gap teeth soon became a poster boy for the farm invasions. When he pitched up at the farm gates with a mob behind him, for sure things would get out of hand.

The farm invasions were stupidly short-sighted. Over the course of some months, I watched a massively productive one hundred hectare, citrus orchard north of Harare slowly wither and die under the harsh summer sun because the war vet who'd grabbed the farm blew a big hole in the irrigation dam wall so he could harvest the fish from the bottom of the dam once all the water had buggered off downstream. He harvested lots of fish because it was a huge dam that backed up some kilometres. Bummer about the soon-to-be-dead citrus orchard though, but that's how it goes in Africa.

Chapter Twenty-Eight

Lots of noughts and reasons why Thabo said nothing, saw nothing and did nothing

I replaced the Chinja mobile in 2002 with a car that cost me a million dollars. A million-dollar transaction should have been a standout milestone, but it wasn't. My new car was a second-hand Land Rover Defender with a hundred thousand kilometres on the clock and engine noises that the car radio couldn't quite drown out. Mugabe had managed to reduce millionaire status to a pinnacle with a view as good as a car park puddle. Zimbabwe became the land of noughts. Things that had cost ten cents when I was a kid cost a dollar, then ten dollars, then a hundred, and then onward and upward to a thousand and beyond. And it was all because of the farm invasions.

Commercial agriculture was the cornerstone of the Zimbabwean economy. Farmers generated more than half the GDP and employed more than half the country's workers. A big chunk of Zimbabwe's downstream industries processed crops grown on the farms. Zimbabwean agriculture was the goose that laid the golden egg, but Mugabe remained hell-bent intent on murdering it. As the land-grab intensified, supermarket shelves emptied, and fuel pumps ran dry as people bought up foreign currency, for just-in-case. The exchange rate ran and ran and ran like a Kenyan jogger.

When I started growing flowers, just eight years earlier, an American dollar cost three Zimbabwean dollars. Fast forward to 2001, and the same American dollar cost you a hundred Zimbabwe dollars. I told everyone and anyone who would listen, mostly Daniel, that it meant things were coming to a head, the Zim dollar couldn't possibly sink any lower, that we had finally hit rock bottom. Alas. I rolled out the same speech a couple of times every month whenever the Zim dollar exchange rate reached yet another psychological barrier. Come 2002, the black-market rate was a thousand to one, and Daniel knew my rock bottom speech word for word. Eventually, eight years later, the Zim dollar US dollar exchange rate would peak at thirty-five quadrillion to one. For those not in the know, a quadrillion has fifteen noughts.

Trying to run a business in Zim was like sticking your head in a washing machine every morning, just more muddled and with less clarity. Harvard business school rules did not apply.

But if you took your blinkers off, Zimbabwe was pregnant with opportunities. A friend from Holland, Goos Bartels said he was looking for someone to buy Shona stone sculptures for him, by the container load. Even though I have zero artistic appreciation I told Goos no problem and look no further, I'd buy the artwork for him. Because I have zero artistic appreciation, I drafted in best friends Sean Cairns and Nick Dickens to help. Sean and Nick were obvious selections. Sean had actually visited the Louvre in Paris, and the furniture in Nick's house went with the curtains. The Goos deal was win-win for both parties. We would buy the sculptures, and Goos would set up a gallery at his home in Aalsmeer and sell them.

We bought our first Shona sculptures from a roadside tourist trap gallery. My cutthroat bargaining skills were cruelly exposed on our first purchase when I managed to snap it up for about fifty percent more than the salesman's start out asking price.

"You're supposed to bargain them down, not up," Nick pointed out, helpfully.

"Sorry, Nick but I really, really liked the piece. It sort of looks like a mermaid, if you turn your head sideways and squint. Plus, I felt sorry for the guy. He looks like he hasn't eaten in a week." I said this of a man who picked up the seventy-kilo sculpture effortlessly to load it onto Nick's pick-up truck.

After that, I was demoted to the buyer's assistant's assistant. Nick and Sean used my artistic tastes as a foil. If I liked a sculpture, that meant it was really shit. We couldn't build a business buying at silly tourist prices and were told that the serious artists worked out of Chitungwiza, the massive, sprawling satellite township to the south of Harare. So I asked newly elected MDC MP for the area, Fidelis Mashu, to introduce me to the sculptors in his community. I quite liked having Members of Parliament on speed dial and phoned them often, especially when others were watching. Fidelis took us to Unit O Chitungwiza where all the artists lived.

We went in my Land Rover because it didn't have hubcaps that could be stolen. I'd driven through Chitungwiza only a few times but had never stopped for fear of being robbed. To get out of your car and actually meet the people who lived there was a new experience. And a good one. The people lived cheek by jowl in tiny houses, but they were hugely proud, but also very polite and friendly. Every house on the crowded streets of Unit O was home to a sculptor, each tiny garden packed with stone sculptures. Mostly the artists used springstone, grey on the outside but with intricate hues of light brown through to black on the inside. They would start out with a massive chunk of raw stone and set about coaxing out the unseen, hidden shapes within, using chisels, chipping hammers, brute strength and patience. Springstone was incredibly hard rock, and the sculptors all had bulging arm muscles like Schwarzenegger.

Each guy had his own style and would have ten or more pieces on display in his garden, each with a name and a story behind it that you had to listen to. The one Rasta artist had a sculpture of a broken bloodied corpse which he'd named 'Bomb blast victim', but Nick wouldn't let me buy it. Nick was in charge of art selection and price negotiations. If he saw a piece he liked, he'd walk around it a few times, ask the price and then walk away quickly with an expression of sincere regret on his face. The artist would coax him back with a discount and negotiations would begin in earnest. When a price was agreed upon, Nick would take a digital photo and record the price on his clipboard and then move onto the next garden. My job was to carry the camera and clipboard. Apart from dropping the camera a few times, I was damn good at my job.

We attracted a lot of interest as we made our way from house to house through the crowded township. White visitors weren't common. I expected to feel intimidated but never did. If anything, it was therapeutic. Some people even smiled when they saw us, especially the kids who would shout out murungu, murungu, white man, white man, and follow us for a bit to gawk at our every move. As we progressed, we got further and further away from my car, so I went back to retrieve it. I found an old man with a headful of grey hair looking at the 'No farmers, No Future' bumper sticker on the back of the Land Rover.

"What is happening to you farmers out, there is being done by a very few evil people. Please, you must know that we don't hate you," he said.

Straight up, he put a smile on my heart. Back at the farm that evening after a particularly grim sit-rep on the security radio, I tried to raise community spirits by sharing what the old man had said to me, but it didn't really work. What one old black guy said in a distant township doesn't mean much when the mob at your gate is baying for your blood.

As the economy haemorrhaged, and currency became short like a dwarf, supermarket shelves started running empty. Best friend Bob Hamill pointed out to me that empty shelves meant huge gaps and even bigger opportunities. I am economically challenged and didn't get where he was going with his line of thinking. And so he reminded me that as an exporter, the Reserve Bank let me keep half my export receipts in hard currency to fund imports while they stole the rest at the paltry official exchange rate. And so with Bob's help, Running Dog registered as an importer. We made more money importing tampons and toothpaste than we did exporting flowers.

Tampons and toothpaste weren't the only things we imported. We also brought in a twenty-foot container of spray paint canisters for the MDC which they used to paint Harare red. And fluorescent pink. And fluorescent green. And fluorescent yellow. I brought cases and cases of paint canisters back to the farm and handed them over to Raphael and his team. Every night they went out in the farm pick-up and got busy. I need to use this opportunity to offer up belated apologies to every wall owner within a fifty-kilometre radius of Mt Hampden for Raphael's fluorescent political graffiti.

The MDC asked me if I'd talk to an undercover American journalist for Newsweek magazine who'd snuck into the country to do a story on Zimbabwean politics. The American asked me if I could hook him up with some of the political graffitists. I gave him directions to the farm and told him to get there just after dark. He pitched up on time wearing cameras and cargo pants and was allocated space in the back of the farm pick-up already fully laden with cartons of spray canisters. Because he had a real live journalist on board, Raphael told the driver to set sail for Mugabe's rural home at Kutama. From Running Dog to Kutama is seventy kilometres or more, with many, many walls en route. Raphael stopped to paint them all, with MDC slogans or 'Mugabe Must Go'. Every wall was treated as a work of art. When it came to political graffiti, Raphael was a neat freak and didn't tolerate sloppy stroke work or missing punctuation. And invariably, halfway through a wall, a vehicle would happen along, and everyone would have to take cover in the bushes until it passed.

After an hour, the journalist said he was done. Raphael looked at him blankly. The journalist told Raphael that he had more than enough photos for his story. More blank looks. The journalist cut to the chase and asked if he could be taken back to his car.

Raphael spoke to him slowly, like he would to a child. "But we haven't finished our paint yet." They were two cartons down, with six unopened to go. "And we haven't painted Kutama yet."

They only got to Kutama at three in the morning. By then the journalist had long put down his camera in favour of a paint canister. He knew he would only get to go home when the last carton of paint on the truck was done.

When I was a kid growing up in suburban Harare, roof-rattling was the ultimate adrenalin rush. It was a fairly sophisticated pastime. A group of us young yobs would roam the neighbourhood at night, dressed up like Tom Cruise in black kit and balaclavas, choose some poor unfortunate's house, either at random or to settle a grudge, and then we would all commence lobbing large rocks onto his roof, causing chaos and pandemonium within. And if the guy who lived in the house was big as a gorilla, even better still. And because I had a throwing arm like a girl, I would add even more excitement as often my missiles would fall short of the roof and crash through the windows instead. Roof-rattling was the most exciting thing I'd ever done.

Fast forward thirty years and spray-painting political graffiti was the new roof-rattling, but even more exciting. If you got caught spray-painting, depending on who caught you, you would be in proper shit and worse. Before going out, I'd muddy up the Land Rover number plates front and back so they couldn't be read. I'd wear dark overalls and a balaclava and end up drenched in sweat just minutes out. But not just from overheating either. With hearts hammering louder than the Land Rover's engine knock,

LOTS OF NOUGHTS AND REASONS WHY THABO SAID NOTHING, SAW NOTHING AND DID NOTHING

we'd sneak out the farm with lights off, looking for walls. One person would be the lookout/get-away driver while others in the car were the artists. Any and every set of headlights had the artists scurrying for the sanctuary of the nearest ditch or hedge and the driver ready to pop the clutch.

My whole family joined in, even Veronica's current boyfriend. Normally we'd go out in the small hours of the morning. I was a pretty crappy artist and would invariably run out of wall halfway through my slogan and be forced to scrunch up the last letters to make them fit. Having been a schoolteacher, Jenny's letters were always well-formed, neat and annoying. Gary was the best, though. His slogans were works of art, especially when viewed next to my scrappy offerings. Apart from the once when he fell down a hole halfway through a long anti-ZANU PF diatribe. He'd kept his finger on the nozzle as he fell and the paint tracked his descent to the bottom of the hole. It was too funny, and I asked him to do it again so I could get it on video but he wouldn't.

The family de Jong got more and more daring, targeting high profile walls and busy roads, even in broad daylight. The walls of the Harare Sports Club were my finest moment. Harare Sports Club was the home of Zimbabwean Test Cricket and right next door to the heavily guarded State House. You couldn't get much more high profile. I struck like a stealthy Ninja during a one-day game against Sri Lanka, targeting the expanse of wall right next to the main entrance into the cricket grounds. The world and his cousin, including Mugabe and his entourage hopefully, would read my offerings. For maximum impact, I went with a can of shocking fluorescent pink and a message that focused on the economic mess that Zimbabwe was - We Want Jobs!! Complete with punctuation and in four-foot letters. Short, sharp and brutally to the point.

Jenny drove while I sat in the front passenger seat, practising my air strokes, over and over. She pulled over right outside the cricket grounds. There were a million people, including security guards milling around. And fifty metres down the road I could see the armed storm troopers outside Mugabe's house, with AK bayonets fixed and fingers on triggers. I leapt out the car and with sphincter tightly clenched, heart in mouth and my spray canister held to my side and my finger on the nozzle, I walked up to the queue at the gate nonchalantly. And then I swooped, lightning-fast and with my tongue protruding from the corner of my mouth. My spray hand was a blur of practised motion. It took just seconds to get my message up on the wall and then I was back in the car.

"Go, go, go!" I shouted to Jenny. But my getaway driver just sat there, replaced by a bloody teacher. "You spelt want wrong," she told me.

"What?"

"You spelt want wrong. Look. You spelt it with an M. You've written WE WAMT JOBS!!" By now, Jenny was laughing. "How the hell do you expect to get a job if you can't even spell want properly? No wonder you're unemployed."

Alas. Normally officialdom came and painted over political graffiti within the week. But they left my fluorescent pink spelling mistake up for well over a year, a stark reminder to all the illiterates of the world that unemployment lurked if they didn't brush up on their ABCs.

Unemployment stats in Zimbabwe soared as farms were stolen and downstream industries spluttered. The percentage of formally unemployed roared past the fifty percent mark, then through sixty, next stop a whopping ninety percent! Outside of a war zone, it was unprecedented.

Braving the grey, green, greasy crocodile-infested waters of Rudyard Kipling's Limpopo River, Zimbabweans started flocking across the porous border and into South Africa in their tens of thousands in search of work. Educated, well-spoken, beyond desperate and willing to do anything for next to nothing, South African employers snapped them up.

The South African government had the power to rein Mugabe in at any time. Ninety percent of Zimbabwe's imports came in through South Africa. Most of our lights went on at night only because of South African largesse. Mbeki could close the taps whenever he wanted, bringing Zimbabwe to a grinding halt and Mugabe to heel. The precedent had already been set when Henry Kissinger told John Vorster to reign Ian Smith in in the seventies with the threat of border closure. Ian Smith had jumped as per Vorster's instructions. Mbeki could have followed suit whenever he wanted, but he didn't.

Someone lent me three theories to explain away why Thabo Mbeki did absolutely nothing to stop the neighbourhood from going up in flames.

The first theory was born in 1980 when the ANC took advantage of Zimbabwean independence to push the front lines of their armed struggle up from the back of beyond in Zambia to Zimbabwe. One of the first commanders sent to Zimbabwe to establish the foothold was a young, bright-eyed Thabo Mbeki who was roaring up through the ANC ranks, more because his daddy Govan was locked away on Robben Island with Mandela than because of any natural leadership skills.

As commander of the newly opened ANC base camp in Matabeleland, Thabo was called upon to pass judgement on the accused in a routine rape case involving two Umkonto we Sizwe cadres. Umkonto we Sizwe was the military wing of the ANC. He duly found the accused guilty and following ANC disciplinary procedure, executed him with a single shot to the back of the head. Unfortunately for Mbeki though, back in those days the Zimbabwean police still investigated political murders. The police heard about the incident, rushed in and found Mbeki holding the smoking gun, and he was duly arrested. But because his dad was who he was, Thabo's murder docket was sent straight to Mugabe's office. Mugabe sprang Mbeki but locked his murder docket away in his top drawer where he kept all his rainy-day dirt on important people. Fast forward twenty years and that rainy day came along when George W Bush appointed Thabo as his point-man on the Zimbabwe crisis. Loving the world's attention, Thabo thought he'd quickly solve the crisis by reining, thus cementing his position as Africa's premier statesman. Bob pissed all over that parade. He sent Thabo a copy of his very own murder docket, together with strict instructions on how to tackle the Zimbabwean crisis using silent diplomacy, a.k.a. say nothing and do even less.

The second theory is less dramatic but equally believable. In it, Thabo the sycophant sleeps in Bob Mugabe pyjamas under a Bob Mugabe poster on his bedroom wall.

But how to force Mbeki into taking the action that he didn't want to take? As always, my Eureka moment arrived at three in the morning, causing me to sit bolt upright, and also causing me intense pain courtesy of a violent elbow to the sternum from Jenny. The next morning, I rushed into town to place an advert in the Herald and the Daily News classifieds. I wore dark glasses and a cap in the queue in case there was close circuit television. I was advertising tens of thousands of jobs, all in South Africa, and in all sectors, including mining, agriculture, industry and tourism. For assistance with immigration and employment permits, applicants had to report with copies of their qualifications to a Mr Khumalo at Number One, Elcombe Avenue, Belgravia. The address belonged to the South African Embassy and Mr Khumalo was the incumbent ambassador. Using a false name and number, I paid cash for the adverts to run for three consecutive Thursdays. Mbeki and more importantly the South African Congress of Trade Unions were about to get a sneak preview of what was coming their way if Mbeki carried on doing nothing.

The results were spectacular. I drove past the Embassy at nine o'clock on Thursday morning for a look-see. There must have been well over ten thousand angry people crammed into the carpark, waving copies of their O Level certificates at the guards, demanding to see Mr Khumalo. The riot police were there in force, waiting for the first signs of trouble. I felt a bit sorry for the ten thousand desperate people but not too sorry. Better they also get a sneak preview of what they and their children's children could expect more of if they didn't get rid of Mugabe and ZANU PF. I got the South Africans again, the very next Thursday but my third advert got pulled.

The South Africans never took heed of my warnings, though. By 2008, there were upwards of one and a half million Zimbabweans in South Africa illegally, looking for work, looking to steal jobs from South Africans, looking to do whatever they had to do to feed their families back home. More Zimbabweans were working in South Africa than Zimbabweans were working in Zimbabwe. Crazy numbers.

Which brings me to the third theory as to why Thabo Mbeki did nothing. He scored a million and a half of the best worker bees in Africa. He got waiters working in his restaurants that could speak good English and actually knew how to smile. And besides the waiters and workers, there were accountants and lawyers, engineers and bankers, all working hard, all building up the South African economy. And every month end, they all sent home groceries made in South Africa to their desperate relatives in Zimbabwe. South African tills rang loudly while the Zimbabwean economy, formerly the second largest in the region, curled up and died. Leaving South Africa to fill the vacuum. Alas.

Chapter Twenty- Nine

Looking back, our decision to take Dan out of mainstream schooling was wrong. Too late, we learnt that schools are about way more than just learning to read and write, they are where kids learn to get on with other kids and where they develop friendships, often lifelong. We took Dan out of school for all the right reasons, but that didn't make it right. Alas. But it's also okay to make mistakes as a parent. As long as you thought you were doing right.

To compensate, we set about helping Dan develop hobbies and interests that would build self-esteem and help him meet people. At the time, I sent all my vehicles to a deaf mechanic called Fred. Stone-deaf, Fred was a genius mechanic. He would listen to my Land Rover's running engine with his hands on the engine block and hear the multitude of problems that I'd been hiding with the volume button on the radio. One day while watching Fred working on the Land Rover, I noticed a model aeroplane in the corner of the workshop. It was a big white biplane with German crosses on the wings. Apparently, it was a Fokker. And yes, the Fokker was for sale. And yes, Fred would be happy to teach Dan how to fly the thing. And how to work on the engines.

We bought the Fokker for Dan as an early birthday present. Apparently, the biplane was Dan's best present ever, or so he told us, over and over and over. Sure, he liked the plane, but mostly I think he liked being able to say the word Fokker out loud, around the house. It didn't take Jenny long to ban the word.

With impeccable timing, the model aircraft club moved their aerodrome a week after we bought the Fokker, from just down the road to Ruwa, way out on the other side of town, more than an hour's schlep. On the day of our maiden flight, Dan all but wrapped the plane up in cotton wool before packing it in the back of the Land Rover. Fred was waiting for us at the aerodrome. He put the plane up into the air and through its paces. Dan watched intently as Fred showed him how to control the plane's speed, altitude and direction by using the twin toggles on the radio controls. Fred had the patience of Job with Daniel but got flustered whenever Daniel turned his head away to follow the plane's progress in the sky.

"Remember I can't hear you, Dan, if I can't see your lips," said Fred.

"Yeah, yeah, yeah, Fred," Dan said to the distant clouds.

I had told Dan over and over how lip reading worked, but I don't think he listened very carefully.

Fred circled the biplane overhead our position and then handed the controls over to Dan. "You fly it now, Dan."

Dan was a bundle of nerves, and the plane jiggled in the sky as he took over the controls.

"But what do I do when I want to land it, Fred?" There was no reply from Fred because he couldn't see Dan's lips. "Fred, Fred, what do I do when I want to land it?" Still no reply. The plane continued on its way to the distant horizon. Dan thumbed the toggle. And still, the plane flew on. "Fred, Fred, the plane won't turn!! I'm telling it to turn Fred, but it's not listening to me!!"

And neither was Fred. I could hear Dan getting frazzled. "Remember Fred can't hear you, Dan, if he can't see your lips."

At which point Fred stepped in with his calm, measured tone. "Okay, Dan, work the toggle like I showed you. Bring the plane around." Dan thumbed the toggle with renewed vigour. "Turn the plane around, Dan, turn it round," said Fred in a not so calm and measured tone.

By now, Dan was screaming. "I am turning it, Fred, just like you showed me Fred, but it's not turning, it's not listening to me!!" Dan was close to ripping the toggle off the control box.

I stepped directly in front of Fred. "Dan's controls aren't responding Fred," I said, enunciating clearly and calmly.

But Fred had eyes only for the by now rapidly disappearing biplane. "Turn the plane, Dan, turn the plane, now!! Like I showed you. You're flying out of range."

"I'm telling you, Fred, I'm turning it like you showed me. But it's not turning, Fred, it's not turning" Dan screamed up at the clouds, all thumbs and desperation.

I grabbed Fred by the shoulders and forced him to look at me. "Dan's controls aren't responding, Fred."

"Huh?"

"I said Dan's controls aren't responding, Fred."

"Damn. Why didn't he say? "

"He did but..."

Dan's strangled scream brought the debate to an end. I turned around just in time to watch the distant speck that was the biplane fall out of the sky like a brick. Dan yanked back on both toggles mightily, just in case, but to no avail. His maiden flight ended with a thud that we all heard from afar, even Fred.

"Don't worry, Dan, we'll fix it."

The MDC was also crashing and burning. They might have owned half the seats in parliament, but in Zimbabwe, that didn't mean a lot. And just because you were now a Member of Parliament, didn't mean the police had to step in to stop ZANU thugs from beating up on you. Every second day there was a photo of a beaten and bloodied MDC MP on the front page of the paper. Anything and everything that had MDC written on it was a target.

I got a phone call from Welshman Ncube, the MDC General Secretary at the time. He asked me to report to his offices at Harvest House, the MDC's new multi-storied headquarters in the city centre. I enjoyed brief delusions of importance before I figured out that my summons was more a reflection of exactly how bare the MDC cupboards were when it came to supporters with cheque books.

It was my first visit to Harvest House. The pavements around the building were teeming with busy commuters pushing through the throngs of the party faithful loitering outside; either party faithful or CIO. I could feel the eyes on me as I threaded through the throng. I should have worn a false nose and sunglasses. It suddenly struck me this was the last place on earth that I wanted to be. Ah, paranoia, it really does give you that wanted feeling.

There was a seriously enthusiastic security team on the ground floor headed up by an activist I knew called Joel. Just because I knew Joel, didn't exempt me from lots of body patting and questions. The lifts weren't working, so I had to walk up to the third floor. The first two floors of the building were deserted and empty, the commercial tenants having decided that the eye of the storm wasn't a good place to do business.

Welshman greeted me warmly. After just thirty seconds of pleasantries, he cut to the chase. The MDC's provincial office in Chinoyi had been torched over the weekend, by CIO and ZANU thugs. And Welshman wanted to reopen it. And he had a wish list a mile long - new furniture, new computers, vehicles, new everything, because all the old stuff had been burnt, apart from the old computers and the filing cabinets. Those had been carried off by CIO before the place got torched. I knew all about the Chinoyi attack. Artwell Tax, one of the guys who ran the office had pitched up at Running Dog late Saturday night, wide-eyed, bloodied and petrified, looking for a place to hide.

"Why?" I asked Welshman.

"Why what?"

"Why do you want to open another office in Chinoyi? You're just going to make the place a target, and every single person who visits the office. I won't go there anymore because CIO watches the place all day, every day. So why not run it underground?"

"Because we are the official opposition party. And you can't run an official opposition from the boot of your car?"

"Well, you can't run it from an office that keeps getting burnt out either, Welshman. Because they'll attack it again. And any money you put into the place is good money after bad." That was the end of the meeting. It was the first time I'd ever said no to the MDC.

I don't know whether it was related or not, but a couple of days later I received a phone call from Roy Bennett, the white MP for Chimanimani. He wanted to know if it was all right if he came out to the farm to talk with me. I'd seen Roy at lots of meetings at the George but had never met him. I told him sure he could come and talk to me. Roy was the stuff of legends. I'd hero worshipped him from afar as a kid when he'd boxed for Zimbabwe. We'd briefly been members of the same boxing club, but I'd been too scared of him to talk to him. Roy spoke Shona beyond fluently and had been accepted by the blacks in his rural Chimanimani community as one of their own. They called him Pachedu which meant together in Shona. Roy arrived on the farm with another MP, Edwin Mushoriwa.

I offered them tea or coffee, but Roy said no thanks, they were already running late for other meetings. Roy said he'd heard I was disaffected with the MDC. He told me to hang in there and to chin up and that things were always darkest before the dawn. From anyone else that would have come across as cheesy but not from Roy Bennett. I told Roy thanks for coming and waved him and Edwin off. They'd come in separate cars. About thirty minutes later, Roy drove back on the farm. He said he'd driven all the way back into town and realised he'd forgotten to tell me something. He asked me if I kept a weapon in the house. I told him I had a shotgun.

"If war vets ever come for you, especially at night, Eric, use it. Shoot them. Kill them. They're not coming to talk to you about politics, or about land, they're coming to kill you. Because of who you are and what you've done for us. So you need to be ready to kill first."

"But..."

"No buts. If they come, get your shotgun out. And use it if you have to."

For the second time that day, I waved goodbye to Roy. That he'd driven all the way into town and then turned around and driven all the way back because he'd forgotten to warn me meant the world. He could just have easily phoned me or warned me in a text, but he'd turned around and came all the way back. I was more scared now than before, but right then I would have followed Roy Bennett over broken glass if he asked me to.

I don't know why Welshman got his knickers in such a knot when I'd suggested the MDC go underground because they were pretty much there already. Most of their political message was delivered via flyers, printed on Risograph machines hidden away in backyard garages and storerooms, delivered and distributed in the dead of night, dead also being a description of how you'd end up if caught. Embracing the football theme, MDC had also churned out red cards by the millions, which people would use to give Mugabe the send-off. The MDC branded red cards were wildly popular, and almost everyone had one secreted away in the depths of their wallet, ready to be flourished, but only when no one was watching.

As was our wont, the de Jong family fully embraced the red card campaign. We fully stocked the Land Rover with hundreds of thousands of cards and flyers for a road trip to Kariba. Best friends, the Hamills had invited us on a houseboat trip. I drove behind Bob in the Land Rover. Ever the brave, I favoured the high-speed approach to flyer delivery. We would roar past every cluster of war veteran huts on every invaded farm with hand on the hooter, while Dan and Jenny shovelled out thousands of flyers and cards. Taking daring to another level, Jenny's preferred drop zones were the many police roadblocks we encountered. While I kept the cop busy at the driver's window, Jenny and Dan would dump hundreds of red cards surreptitiously out the passenger window, for the cops to find after we'd driven off.

Our road trip went swimmingly well, up until Karoi where the Land Rover started making alarming noises. We limped into the Twin Rivers Hotel, steam billowing from the radiator. While Bob laughed, I crawled under the car with my Leatherman at the ready, in the forlorn hope that the problem was something that even I could fix. While I was under the car, a pair of feet sidled up and called me in a loud and urgent whisper, causing me to hit my head viciously on the sump. I rolled out. The feet belonged to the hotel manager. His name was Talkmore. He'd worked for me as a barman long ago at Club Mazvikadei. Talkmore and I caught up every time I passed through Karoi. But he wasn't keen on small talk this time round. He ducked down behind the car, thrust a scribbled note at me and disappeared. The note got my sphincter muscle going. It read, 'Can't talk. People watching you. Wait three minutes and follow me behind the hotel.'

Crap. My mouth dried up, and my heart started hammering. The three minutes took forever before I made my way around the back of the hotel. Talkmore was waiting for me, agitated and on edge. He pulled me into a storeroom quickly and pulled the door closed.

"Hallo, Mr de Jong. You are in trouble. I overheard a group of men talking about you at a table on the veranda. They are very rough men, war veterans from Harare. They came in a pick-up truck. They followed you all the way from Harare, watching you distribute MDC propaganda. And I overheard them on the phone to Black Jesus who said he would come and capture you."

My sphincter wobbled alarmingly when I heard the name Black Jesus, the notorious war vet who'd led the gang that murdered Martin Olds. And he'd infamously beaten five MDC supporters to death in front of a crowd in a Kariba township.

"They are very rough men, Mr de Jong, very, very rough." Talkmore threw in very three times, just in case I wasn't taking him seriously.

I snuck a furtive peep at the war veterans around the corner. There were eight or more of them at the table, drinking beer, talking on their phones and glaring at the table where Jenny and the Hamills were sitting.

The words big and angry all jumped out at me, along with pain, pain and more pain. I took a deep breath, forcing myself to stay calm and collected while I thought about what to do. After three seconds of calm and collected, I still hadn't come up with a plan, so I slipped into panic mode and commenced to wail pitifully, while I blamed all and sundry for my predicament. Damn Land Rover, damn Jenny, damn surreptitious and above all, damn the MDC.

Bob heard my snivelling and came to see what was happening. Talkmore brought him up to speed. While I carried on with my wail, Bob and Talkmore came up with a plan. Bob phoned a friend who lived in Karoi called Calvin and told him the problem. Calvin said no problem. Five minutes later, a tow truck rolled up, closely followed by a Toyota Venture. Amazingly, someone I didn't know was lending me his car to carry on to Kariba in. And another someone was going to fix the Land Rover. While the tow truck quickly hitched up the Land Rover, Talkmore and an army of porters transferred our luggage across to the Venture. The boxes of MDC flyers and red cards stayed behind in the Land Rover. Talkmore said he'd make a plan to hide those until someone from the local MDC branch collected them. The tow truck started to pull out of the hotel car park with the wounded Land Rover as we started to pile into our borrowed car. The war veterans were in a quandary. They quickly figured what was going on but with only one car and still no sign of Black Jesus, they didn't know what to do. Follow us or follow the Land Rover with all the MDC paraphernalia. They decided to follow us. But not for long. As soon as I pulled on to the road, I put my foot down and heaved a sigh of relief as I watched the old, knackered pick-up truck get smaller in the rear-view mirror. It was like driving away from my problems.

All houseboat trips on Kariba are memorable, but this one was especially so. We enjoyed spectacular game viewing, spectacular sunsets and scenery, spectacular fishing for some, and good company with lots of laughter. But before we even got on the houseboat, Julie pulled me to one side and gave me a good bollocking for taking the red cards and flyers on holiday and exposing her family to danger.

But the stand-out memory of that house trip was of Bob's brother Sparky giving Dan his very own Dan song, specially imported from Belfast.

"Dan, Dan, the funny wee man
He washed his face with a frying pan
And combed his hair
With the leg of a chair
Dan, Dan, the funny wee man."

Dan loved his song and sang it over and over the whole weekend.

Chapter Thirty

Time is especially relative when you have children. Impossibly, ten years had passed since we'd adopted the children, and it was time for Daniel to go to high school. Which presented a huge problem. Sure, Dan was big enough and old enough for high school, but there was no way he was ready, even with over a year of frantic cramming behind him. Jenny and I got advice from lots of people, and the consensus was to get him into a high school, with kids his own age, so that Dan could find his way. We would gain nothing by holding him back for another year of remedial cramming. Chances were that he would still struggle but being left behind by kids all a year younger than him would hurt him even more.

With that difficult decision behind us, all we had to do was to find a high school that would take Daniel. High schools in Zimbabwe remained a bottleneck with too many kids feeding into not enough classrooms. Entrance exams for their form one wannabees were the norm, but unfortunately, Daniel couldn't spell the word exam, let alone pass one.

The only school on Daniel's list was St Georges College, where his brother had done so well. He had his heart set on following in Gary's footsteps.

"And we've already got a St Georges blazer. I can wear Gary's old one, so you won't even have to buy me a new one," Dan told us.

Dan absolutely swam in Gary's blazer. But his cost-cutting suggestions tugged on our heartstrings and Jenny and I made an appointment to see the headmaster.

Mr Tiernan reluctantly saw us and only because he had fond memories of Gary. After about fifteen seconds of small talk, Tiernan made us cut to the chase. He was a busy man. Stammering and stuttering, Jenny and I told him that we wanted him to find a desk for Dan, even though Dan didn't stand a hope in hell of passing the entrance exams. Tiernan raised an eyebrow. He wasn't used to parents begging in advance of their children failing. Jenny and I hit him with our full arsenal. We reminded him about the adoption. We presented him with a letter of support from the parish priest who confirmed that Dan had been confirmed and reminded Tiernan unsubtly that St Georges had been built by the Catholics to educate Catholic children. Tiernan was teetering so I hit with my sob story about being a farmer, with all the attendant woes and worries.

Tiernan shook his head sadly as he read Daniel's assessment. "With some reluctance, I will allow Daniel to attend college. He will still be required to sit the entrance exam for streaming purposes."

After thanking him profusely, Jenny and I escaped Tiernan's office happy, but in a very hollow way. There was nothing hollow about Dan's happiness, though. When he got the news that he was in, he whooped and hollered like all his Christmases had come at once.

To celebrate we decided to go to the Friday night social at the Mazoe Rowing Club pub. I invited Ian and Neryl. Their two boys, Ryan and Roo, aged between Veronica and Daniel, also went to St Georges. Ian was the general manager of Glenara Estates which was down the road from the Rowing Club. Glenara Estates was an iconic farm formerly owned by the Anglo-American Oppenheimer family. When I was a kid, we used to drink Glenara milk. But big business doesn't do sentiment, and the Oppenheimers sold Glenara as soon as the farm invasions started. Glenara was one of the first farms in the district to be invaded. A large group of war veterans commandeered one of the manager's houses on Glenara and commenced operations, politicising and terrorising the farming district around them, starting with Ian. But Ian was tougher than most and took everything the war veterans threw at him in his stride.

Ian agreed to meet us at the Rowing Club pub. On my way to Mazoe, Ian phoned to say that he would be late. His war veterans had kindly cut a hole in his security fence and herded two hundred cattle into Neryl's pristine garden. It was malicious nuisance shit, designed to mess with people's heads and it went on all the time at Glenara. Ian told me he'd be an hour getting the cattle out the garden and fixing the fence and they'd see us in the pub later. I offered to help, but he told me no. On our way past Glenara, Jenny and I stopped to pick Ryan and Roo up.

The Rowing Club pub was busy, mostly full of people like me who thought rowing was why God created the outboard motor, there for the booze, looking to take the edge off another crappy week. Simon Silcox was playing his guitar, and it had all the makings for a festive evening. Embarrassingly, I was a secret smoker at the time, and I snuck out the pub for a quick puff in the carpark behind the Land Rover when I heard Neryl on the security radio. She was sobbing, beyond frantic. Ian had just been abducted at gunpoint by the war veterans, along with the farm owner and his son. She had locked herself in the house. And she was watching a war veteran on the veranda outside, trying to set fire to the house. He couldn't get his lighter to work. I ran back inside the pub and told Jenny what was happening and told her that I was going to go and help Neryl. The pub was very noisy, and I had to repeat myself, mostly because I had my hand over my mouth to hide the smell of cigarette. I was hugely relieved when best friend Sean Cairns said he would come with. Unlike me, Sean was one of those people who always kept calm and didn't do panic.

I told Neryl on the radio that we were on our way. The Rowing Club to Glenara was just ten kilometres, so we were just minutes out, even in the Land Rover. She told us to hurry. The thug was still outside trying to set fire to the roof. The radio network got busy as the district mobilised. Thankfully, I wasn't the only one rushing to help. Unflappable Hamish Turner took charge and got onto the member in charge of the nearest police station, asking him to go out to the scene and negotiate with the war veterans for Ian's release. Ordinarily in Zimbabwe phoning the police would mean squat but that particular member in charge was a good man and about the only policeman left in Zimbabwe for whom I had any respect for. He told Hamish that he would go out to Glenara to speak with the war veterans. While Sean kept Hamish informed on the radio as to our progress, I was panicking internally about how to take out the war veteran who was trying to burn Neryl's house down. Because I packed a punch like a girl, I carried a length of inch thick armoured cable under the driver's seat. I decided I would go in with the cable and maximum aggression and take the fucker's head right off and damn the consequences. But with my luck, the war veteran would be a giant with a helmet for a head. Or he'd be North Korean trained and would break my head like a brick with a Kung Fu bicycle kick. By the time we got to Glenara, my heart was racing flat out.

Luckily, I wasn't the first vehicle on the scene. A pick-up truck arrived seconds in front us, and a young white farmer called Manuel got out and walked up to the house, calm like he was on his way to tea. The war veteran, aged all of eighteen, just stood there with wobbly legs and unseeing eyes, messed up badly on stuff he'd smoked and drunk, trying over and over to get his cigarette lighter to work as he held it up to the thatch. Crap. I'd missed my chance. The war veteran was a skinny little runt, skinnier than even me. For sure I could have taken him with my armoured cable. The young farmer didn't need violence. He just walked up to the thug and scolded him in fluent Shona. The thug all but stood to attention and called him Boss. Manuel scolded him some more, and then the thug slunk off with his tail between his legs. I stared at him menacingly, but he never even looked at me. I replaced my menacing look with my practised devil may care hero look as Neryl, all full of trembles, tears and pent up emotions, struggled to unlock the door to rush out and thank us.

About an hour later, Ian, his boss and his son were released, unharmed but shaken. While on his knees with hands tied behind his back, Ian said his captors had threatened to cut his balls off. But he'd told them they didn't have a knife sharp enough. But for the good cop, it could have all gone horribly pear-shaped.

With an all's well that ends well mentality, we retired to the Rowing Club pub and drank too much and laughed too loud. Jenny drove home. Brave on too much beer, we went home via the war veterans' base camp on Glenara. We snuck up to the house they'd commandeered, and red carded it, dumping tens of thousands of red cards and MDC flyers around their base camp.

Zimbabwe's economy was all but dead, killed by the farm invasions. There were so many downsides to being one of the last men standing, not least of all the attentions of a tax man left with a choice of far fewer stones to squeeze blood from. With immediate effect, exporters had to withhold a ten percent tax on all sales commissions and royalties levied on Zimbabwean flowers sold in Europe. Sales commissions were deducted at source. How the hell was I supposed to recover ten percent from my agents in Holland for the Zimbabwean taxman? And the breeders whose varieties I grew would be equally charmed to contribute ten percent of the royalties to the cause.

For me, tax had become a four-letter word to be avoided at all costs. It would be a different story if taxes were used to fix roads and build stuff but not when the taxes disappeared into Mugabe's coffers to fund more farm invasions. Come year-end, I told the taxman that I'd sent a final demand to my sales agents and the breeders, but they'd told me to bugger off, quote unquote. The taxman told me in a letter tough luck and said the onus was on me to withhold and collect the taxes. After ten seconds of careful consideration, I wrote back and told the taxman to bugger off, again quote unquote.

Desperate for foreign currency and to break the logjam impasse, the Reserve Bank invited defaulting exporters to a one-off round table meeting at the Monomatapa Hotel to resolve outstanding issues. I pitched up to find only one other exporter waiting, Dave from one of the flower marketing companies. Armed with bulging files of outstanding queries, Dave looked nervous and was chain-smoking hard. Crap. I'd forgotten my skinny correspondence file on my desk. Dave lit up another cigarette. He was properly nervous and for good reason. For exporters, the Reserve Bank was like the Gestapo. To buoy his spirits, I told Dave we needed to hang tough and tell the Reserve Bank to stick their stupid new tax laws up their collective arses. Dave quickly used his stompie to fire up a new cigarette.

No one else pitched up, so Dave and I were the only ones to file into the meeting room at the allotted time. The Reserve Bank team were already in place, twenty or more sharply dressed, earnest banker types seated on the one side of a very long conference table, all with pens and legal pads poised at the ready. It was going to be more like an inquisition than a meeting. Dave and I sat in the middle on the opposite side of the table. Dave smiled weakly at the enemy and got another cigarette on the go. The leader of the Reserve Bank delegation suggested we wait another five minutes for any latecomers. Dave dived into his files and puffed away frantically while I practised my lame speech in my head, over and over. It got lamer and lamer. I really should have brought some paperwork with.

After five long minutes, no one else had pitched. The boss Reserve Bank guy stood up and coughed, by now there really was quite a lot of smoke in the room and suggested we get started. He spoke well, outlining clearly and concisely the reasons for the meeting. He had brought his team along, all twenty or more of them, to resolve any outstanding issues that we the exporters might have, blah, blah, blah. He used a lot of long words, half of which I didn't understand. Eventually, he wrapped up and handed the floor over to our side. I looked at Dave, by now only barely visible within his cloud of smoke with what looked to be as many as four cigarettes on the go. But he showed no signs of wanting to go first, so I got up reluctantly, promptly forgetting my lame presentation in the process. I steeled myself by glaring up and down the length of the table at the bankers one by one, and all my hate came bubbling forth.

Along with broccoli and Mugabe, I hated each and every one of the Reserve Bank officials. "I stand here now, looking at all of you with your soft hands and your French suits and Swiss watches that cost what I make in a year, and you're here to squeeze bullshit taxes out of me, taxes that I haven't got, taxes that your bosses will spend on further persecuting white farmers. Taxes are supposed to be spent on fixing roads, and building schools and clinics for poor people, but your bosses use that money to buy drugs and alcohol to give to hired thugs to rape, pillage and murder. You've used our tax money to burn down our houses and farms, the farms that are the cornerstone of the country's economy, just so you can keep one old bastard and his evil henchmen in power until he dies. Which makes all of you agents of evil. And when you die, all of you are going to go to hell, because of the evil that you are here to perpetrate today!!!" I wrapped up my stirring speech with three exclamation marks, burnt all the Reserve Bankers with a final glare and stalked out of the conference room, leaving poor Dave behind, sitting with a full ashtray in his cloud of smoke.

On the drive home, I stressed as the enormity of what I'd just done sank in. Maybe it wasn't such a good plan to label the collective management of the Reserve Bank of Zimbabwe as agents of evil. But then I thought bollocks. It needed to be said. And besides, what could they do to me for telling the truth? The very next day, all my bank accounts were garnisheed. Alas.

Chapter Thirty-One

The Presidential Elections of 2002 were like the worst Christmas ever, the Christmas where you behave yourself properly for the whole twelve months, forsaking wine, women and all the other stuff that will get you into trouble, only to sit under the Christmas tree on Christmas morning, opening presents containing only underpants and socks. Put another way, it was a bad return for a lot of effort.

The elections got off to a rollicking free and fair start when with just two weeks to go, my farm Mazda pick-up got rammed in the middle of the night by a Police Land Rover. The farm Mazda had been busy dishing out Vote Morgan flyers when the Police Land Rover rammed it after a frenetic car chase. Apparently somewhere along the way, dishing out electoral material had become illegal, punishable by repeat ramming.

My poor pick-up, brand-new just a few years earlier, was completely stuffed. When I went into Harare to recover the Mazda's corpse, the MDC activist who'd been driving it told me that when the police Land Rover rammed him for the last time, both vehicles crashed, and he duly ran off and hid in the bush. According to him, the back of the police vehicle was full of ballot boxes, one of which burst open in the accident. From his hiding place, he'd watched the policemen gather up the already completed ballot papers.

Despite a million other similar stories, I wasn't unduly worried about the outcome of these elections. In my heart of hearts, I knew that Morgan Tsvangirai would win. We'd almost won in 2000. And this time round, we were far better prepared. And Morgan was the good guy with the white hat on. And in the movies, the good guy with the white hat always wins. Apart from the odd Star Wars episode. And the odd presidential election.

For Zvimba, I pulled out all the stops. I was determined that I wouldn't be under-resourced like last time. Again, I handed over the farm reins to Brian and set up shop at the George Hotel for the duration. Best friend Sean Cairns came on board full-time and brought with him his best friend, Andy. We set up an ops centre in one of the hotel function rooms, covered the wall with 1:50,000 maps, marked out all the polling stations and divvied up the jobs. I focused in on recruiting the polling agents, training them and feeding them. Sean ran with the anti-rigging kits, again for the whole country. I threw the transport portfolio at Andy. It was his job to figure out how we were going to follow each and every ballot box to the counting centre at Murombedzi. Like the last elections, we figured that switching boxes between the polling station and the counting centre were where they were going to rig it.

As the MDC district chairman for Zvimba, Raphael had spent the last year setting up MDC cell structures throughout the constituency. He had them all mapped out in his long spidery hand in school exercise books. I was super impressed with the degree of organisation. Every ward had an MDC chairman, an organising secretary, a secretary for youth affairs, one for security and another one for women's affairs. It made the job of recruiting the polling agents easy. The only area where we again struggled for volunteers was in the Zvimba communal lands where Mugabe had been born and where the Fear Factor was particularly strong. While there were MDC cell structures in place even in Zvimba, none of the office-bearers wanted to stick their heads up above the parapets for fear of having them hacked off with pangas. Any chances we might have had were dealt a death blow when ZANU PF sniffed out a poor unfortunate MDC ward chairman the week before the election and beat him within an inch of his life and burnt down all he owned. After that, we had to change tactics and made plans to ship in the polling agents from afar.

Come the day, somehow we were ready with six polling agents per polling station trained, motivated and fully provisioned, ready for a Friday deployment ahead of the Saturday/Sunday elections. We assembled the three hundred polling agents at John Brown's factory in Mount Hampden for their final briefing. John's yard was jam-packed with the polling agents and an army of volunteers to deploy them, plus a Swedish television news crew. While we were milling around, waiting for stragglers to arrive, Sean fielded a phone call from his wife, Monique. Fearing the worst, Sean had shipped Monique to her parents in Cape Town for the elections.

"You promised me you weren't going to get involved in the elections, Sean."

"Yes, my darling, I'm not."

"Then why am I watching you live on television, standing behind Eric?" Just then, he lost the signal.

I lined up all the agents, six per polling station, in front of their anti-rigging kits and ration packs for the last briefing before deployment. But because I had a captive audience and a television camera hovering over my shoulder, instead of a final briefing, I gave the polling agents a stirring speech. I told them it was their job to go out and be brave and that the future of democracy in Zimbabwe rested entirely upon them remaining resolute in the face of terror and intimidation and that...Sean kicked me hard on the ankle. We would be deploying agents at midnight if I didn't shut up. With the camera in close attendance, I moved down the line of polling teams, handing each team their polling agent paperwork, offering up last words of encouragement. I came to a grinding halt in front of Raphael.

"What the fuck are you wearing, Raphael?" I asked. It was a nonsense question. I knew exactly what he was wearing. A ridiculous, full length shocking pink dressing gown, once Jenny's, topped off with an enormous pair of welding goggles with the visor flipped up.

Raphael gave me a huge beaming grin. "Ah, these are my monitoring goggles, sir!!!"

Raphael's wardrobe was the last bit of humour that weekend.

Deployment was chaotic, with too many agents and not enough vehicles. It went on into the small hours of the morning. I did three deployments in the Land Rover. It was a tight squeeze with six polling agents, their paperwork and their rations for the weekend. There was no way they were going to starve to death. I dropped off my last lot of agents well after three in the morning at an obscure primary school, deep in the middle of nowhere in the Zvimba communal land. The polling agents, including one of my foremen called Petros Dzoma, looked less than happy to be there and extremely jumpy. To bolster them, I gave them my 'The only thing you have to fear is fear itself' speech. Alas. I left out the most important bit about the need to fear ZANU PF. Within thirty minutes of deploying them, Petros and his team were captured by the local ZANU militia, trussed up with barbed wire, thrown into the bottom of a disused dip tank nearby and threatened with death by being cut up into small pieces and being fed to the dogs, should Mugabe lose. As it happened, they lay in that dip tank for five long days before being released.

There was no election that weekend, instead what happened was a brutal mugging from the word go. Volunteers Alex and Clarry, sent in to keep an eye on free and fair at a polling station right next door to Nkomo army barracks, got locked up almost immediately. But I feared the worst was happening in the communal lands. Hardly any of the more remote teams had reported in. I was keen to put non-communications down to no signal or dead cell phones but had to send someone into check. I didn't want to go myself, mostly because I was shit scared of Zvimba.

Thankfully two of my volunteers, Elisha and Cleopas, had bigger balls than me and put their hands up. They'd go into Zvimba they said, they just needed a car. The only vehicle I had spare was my neighbour's brand spanking new and shiny Mazda 626. Not exactly the right vehicle for Zvimba's knackered dirt roads, but it was all I had.

As it turned out, the only thing worse than not knowing what was going on, was knowing. Elisha's and Cleopas's report back out of Zvimba wasn't pretty. The polling stations all had long lines of voters, but at most, there was no sign whatsoever of any of the MDC polling teams at any of the polling stations. Our agents had been disappeared. Eventually, they found a few forlorn MDC polling agents watching voting procedures from afar. Apparently, before the voting commenced, a car full of supposed election officials had driven from polling station to polling station with a piece of official paper that said partisan polling officials were not allowed within thirty metres of the polling stations. Which was a load of bullshit and completely against the rules governing the elections. It was a complete disaster. Of the fifty polling stations in the constituency, in fifteen of them only God and Zanu PF knew what was going on inside. I phoned the incidents through to the International observer team but got no reaction. The Norwegian who took the call sounded a tad overwhelmed. It looked like Morgan would have to win the elections without the benefit of those fifteen Zvimba polling stations.

I have never worked such long hours as we did that weekend. I commandeered a bedroom in the George Hotel but only managed to pinch a few hours of sleep, here and there. Andy grew a pair of hugely impressive black rings under his eyes, trying to grapple with the problem of how to follow all the ballot boxes in from the polling stations. Against all the odds, he managed to get enough vehicles in place to get the job done.

I threw my beloved Land Rover into the pot. It would be driven by one of my neighbours, Marlowe Ellis, while I teamed up with Nick Dickens in his Land Cruiser. The polling station that Nick and I had been assigned to was deep in the heart of Zvimba and was one of the polling stations where the MDC support had been chased away before voting even started. Following the ballot box into the counting centre was akin to slamming the stable door shut long after the horse had been dragged off to the glue factory, but it was written into the job description. So, we followed the government pick-up truck that loaded up the ballot boxes all the way back to Murombedzi.

It all went swimmingly well up until the part where Nick looked into his rear-view mirror and said "Oh shit." I put my neck out swivelling round. Shit was an understatement. There was another Land Cruiser, a military green one, right up our arse, the bench seat on the back bristling with Mugabe's Presidential Guard storm troopers all carrying AK 47s. As soon as I saw the mustard coloured berets, I all but fouled Nick's passenger seat. Mugabe's guards were all completely mental and would sooner shoot you than look at you.

"What do we do?" Nick asked.

"I dunno," I replied incisively.

"How about I speed up, try and lose them?" Nick put his foot down. As did the Presidential Guard pick-up. If anything, it got even closer.

"What now?" Nick asked.

"I dunno." I was too panicked to think.

"There's a dirt road to the left up ahead. How about I turn in there and maybe he'll carry on straight?"

"I dunno." Obviously inspired by my leadership, Nick careered off the highway onto the narrow dirt road. Closely followed by the Presidential Guard storm troopers behind us. Crap. Our escape route petered out immediately. We'd turned into a large, ploughed field. "What now?" Nick asked.

"I dunno." By now, my voice had cracked, and my eyes had welled up. What a crappy ending. I was going to die in a field in Zvimba. While I sat there waiting for the worst feeling uber sorry for myself, thankfully Nick took charge, rammed his Cruiser in reverse and backed up around the truck full of Presidential Guards behind us. As he pulled level with the driver, granite-faced behind his cheap sunglasses, Nick apologised out his window. "Sorry about that. Took a bit of a wrong turning. Bye." He gave them a cheery wave and set off down the highway after our ballot boxes.

Murombedzi used to be just another dusty communal land business centre on the road to nowhere, with more bottle stores and bars than business. But because Mugabe had been spawned just down the road, Murombedzi got promoted to growth point status. Which, on the ground translated into more bottle stores, more bars plus a big and ugly government administration building complete with two whole floors full of civil servants to administrate. The government admin building was the designated counting centre where the ballot boxes would be opened up and counted, under the watchful eye of Mugabe's election officials, a handful of Norwegian observers and the one extremely nervous MDC election agent. Who had every reason to be nervous. Murombedzi had filled up with bad people - ranking ZANU PF sycophants - in town for the night because their beloved leader and boss was spending the night of the count at his rural home just down the road.

The streets outside the bottle stores and bars were lined with their Benzs, double cabs and burning braais, while the heavies inside drank heavily, already celebrating the victory to come. The whole town had a menacing feeling about, it felt like a barroom brawl just waiting for the first punch to be thrown. Some of the heavies came out with beers in hand to glare at us as we drove past, following our ballot box to the counting centre. I studiously avoided gawking, but from the corner of my eye, I saw Phillip Chiyangwa, the Mugabe nephew who'd made millions because of his uncle, and Joseph Chinotimba who'd led the farm invasions from under his grass hat. As soon as our ballot box had been offloaded at the counting centre, Nick and I got the hell out of town. On our way out, we passed Marlowe Ellis driving into Murombedzi in my Land Rover. And right behind were Andy and his friend Shane. I waved them down to tell them that Murombedzi wasn't a nice place to be and once they'd followed their boxes in, they should turn around and get out as quickly as possible.

But Marlowe is a big and burly man with legs too long to fit in the front of the Land Rover. When he got to the counting centre, he decided his legs needed stretching, so he took them off to look for a cold coke. Marlowe turned heads as he strolled down the main street of Murombedzi, unfazed by the hostile glares and catcalls from the bars and bottle stores. And then in front of one of the bars, he saw a body in the back of a twin-cab, lying in the full sun, hogtied with barbed wire. He took a closer look. The body was very much alive. From the tag on his bloodied shirt, he was one of our missing MDC polling agents, gagged, bleeding from his barbed-wire bonds, exhausted and wide-eyed terrified.

Marlowe rushed off to the counting centre for help and returned, dragging a rather reluctant young, skinny Norwegian election observer with him, plus Shane and Andy. Marlowe was giving the Norwegian observer a close-up view of what free and fair elections looked like when they were all trussed up and hog-tied with barbed wire when the twin-cab's owner stormed out of the bar with a mob in tow. He was a ZANU fat cat, wearing a cowboy hat, a Mugabe t-shirt and a fat belly beneath. Clearly outraged at Marlowe's show and tell, he wanted to know what the hell they were doing messing with his trophy. Marlowe, Andy and Shane backed away and headed for their cars, leaving the Norwegian observer to do his job.

But on their way out of town, Shane had second thoughts. He jammed on his brakes and reversed back to the bottle store drama. He got out, walked up to the Fat Cat and his twenty or more cronies and told them he was going to pray to God for them, on account of the fact they were evil. Fat Cat and company couldn't believe their eyes and ears and stood simmering in disbelief while Shane said his simple prayer. He wrapped it up with an amen, climbed back in his car, looked them all in the eye and then gave them his middle finger.

The moment froze in time like someone had pressed pause... and then all hell broke loose. Fat Cat screamed his anger and scrambled for his twin-cab, ditto his mob of flunkies. Shane and Andy lit out of town in a cloud of burnt rubber, with the mob right up their bottoms in hot pursuit. They flew past Marlowe trundling along in my Land Rover at not a lot of miles per hour, blissfully unaware of the shit storm breaking behind him.

Unfortunately, in the ensuing chase and with legendary Land Rover efficiency, one of the fan belts that ran the water pump came off and the Land Rover's temperature gauge jumped through the roof alarmingly. Rather than stop and fix it, Marlowe went with the 'carry on fleeing for his life' option and in the process, cooked the engine. Completely. To the point where the alternator melted. Shane and Andy ended up towing Marlowe out of Zvimba. Alas. I loved that Land Rover. But at least it had perished for a good cause, and hopefully a winning one.

Lo and behold, the mugging that happened in the Zvimba polling stations was small potatoes compared to what went down in rural districts countrywide where-ever MDC polling agents could be made to disappear without the eyes of the world watching, giving ZANU all the room in the world to rig. ZANU PF knew they would have to rig hard to negate the urban vote and they did just that.

In the infamous Uzamba-Maramba-Pfungwe, a district in ZANU's heartland and a permanent no go zone for the MDC, ZANU garnered an unprecedented and impressive one hundred and twenty percent of the vote. They're big on party doctrine in the Uzamba-Maramba-Pfungwe, but not so big on arithmetic.

In Gokwe where the distances are huge and the roads are knackered, ZANU PF used Air Force of Zimbabwe helicopters to get the rigging job done. A former Zimbabwe national rugby captain and friends who'd volunteered to provide electoral support for the MDC, watched them do it and even took a video of a chopper moving ballot boxes on the first morning. But they were observed observing and spent the rest of the weekend hiding for their lives. It was like something out of a Vietnam movie, with the former rugger buggers group chopping bushes and vegetation to camouflage their vehicles hidden in ravines, so they couldn't be seen by the helicopters hunting them from above.

But we only heard about all the bad stuff afterwards. Right up until the final count, I carried on gazing myopically out of rose-tinted glasses, knowing in my heart that Morgan would win, that all the shit would be behind us, so that we could carry on with our lives and fix everything in Zimbabwe that had been broken, including my beloved Land Rover. Crap. When the final results were announced and Mugabe was still the President, I was absolutely gutted. All the hard work for the last two years, all those many sacrifices, including my Land Rover, all for nothing. It was 'The Empire Strikes Back' but in real life.

I needed to grieve with kindred spirits, so I went to fellow MDC supporter Duke du Coudray's town flat where we cried into our beers, literally. A reporter for the Guardian newspaper in England pitched up and recorded our tears for posterity. Duke explained how he'd lost his farm and would now have to pack up his family and start all over with nothing in his native Mauritius. There was a brief surge of hope when Duke fielded a phone call. Morgan wasn't going to accept the results, and he was going to lead a march of millions to State House to rip down all that was rotten and claim what was rightfully his. I would have joined Morgan in a heartbeat. We waited and waited and waited with bated breath in Duke's little flat, but Morgan never pressed the button. "He'll never become president," the reporter opinioned. "This was Morgan's golden moment, and he's missed it." The reporter looked well-seasoned like he'd been around the block a few times, and unfortunately, I believed him. With all my heart, I didn't want to believe him, but I did. The good guys in the white hat had lost and the evil fucker had won.

Chapter Thirty-Two

After the elections, I moped hard, like a kid who'd lost his puppy, the cute Labrador puppy from the toilet paper adverts, and not just lost but clubbed to death on the carpet in the lounge in front of the television.

In the aftermath of Mugabe's stolen election, Zimbabwe closed in on me. As did the fact that the next elections were only going to be in 2005!! Another three impossibly long years before we got another chance to fix things.

On the farms, impossibly the feeding frenzy ramped up as the victors rushed to grab their spoils, including a certain Gowrie Farm. Mugabe's sister Sabina had been wanting to upgrade farms for some time, her own was not very well run, nor productive. She'd walked around Gowrie Farm and really liked it. Prior to the commencement of negotiations, Sabina decided that God's Commandments that frowned upon killing and coveting thou neighbour's goods including his farm were piffle and did not apply to Presidential relatives. ZANU thugs played hardball negotiations with the farm owner, Terry Ford. They beat him and punched him around, dragged him out into the garden, tied him to a tree and then shot him in the head. And that was the end of the negotiations. Gowrie Farm had a new owner.

The world was moved by the poignant images of Terry Ford's body, lying under a blue blanket, fiercely protected by his loyal Jack Russell, Squeak. But as was their wont, they did nothing. A short while later, Sabina took possession of her new farm.

No doubt inspired by his President's sister; the Head of Security at Harare International Airport decided it would be rather quaint if he also had a farm to farm on weekends. He kicked my best friend Eric Dawson off his. Eric was a top farmer. He'd just won the prestigious Tobacco Grower of the Year award, paid a gazillion in taxes and employed hundreds, yet government decided it was in the national interest to give Eric's home and business away. The new owner used his agricultural nous to very quickly reduce one of the country's most productive farms to a wasteland, where not a lot grew.

And even closer to home, just a kilometre down the road, our nearest and dearest friends and neighbours the Lowe family lost their one hundred-hectare Fairfield Farm, complete with tractors and trucks, fridges and stoves, even the blankets and sheets on their beds. They lost it to a successful black gymnasium owner who pitched up at the Lowes' front gate wearing muscles and a designer tracksuit with a letter from the government saying that everything now belonged to him.

Losing friends and neighbours like the Lowes and the Dawsons hit me hard. No man is an island, and my neighbour's hurts and pains were also mine. I had no idea how to go forward. I don't think Morgan Tsvangirai was too clued up on the way forward either. I got a thank you letter from Morgan shortly after the elections, peppered with words and phrases like anguish, insurmountable obstacles, evil machinations and tyranny. Morgan signed his letter off with a bold statement that justice would prevail, and that victory was ours, however long and hard the road may be, for, without victory, there is no survival blah, blah, blah. I'm afraid it all rang a tad hollow.

There was more of the same in another letter received from Welshman Ncube, the General Secretary of the MDC. In it, Welshman told me that I was a winner and that the power was in our hands, stirring stuff but somewhat diluted by his sign off phrase, 'Yours in the struggle.' But I was moved by their letters, and to this day both have pride of place on the wall in my bar.

Less than a week after receiving Morgan's letter, the evil he'd touched upon in his letter came knocking on my door, literally. It was late in the afternoon. Jenny and I were in town picking up kids on the school run when Brian phoned.

He spoke in a whisper, badly rattled. "You mustn't come home, Eric, they're here on the farm, six of them, looking for you."

"Who, Brian, who's there looking for me?'

"There's six of them Eric, they've got guns, and they're in your house looking for you. I told them that you weren't here, but they've gone into your house to check anyway. I think they've come here to kill you."

My mouth dried up instantly and I all but peed my pants. "What do you mean they're in the house? Who are they, Brian, do you know who they are?"

"They're bad, Eric, bad men. And they're real serious. One of them told me that he killed that farmer the other day, Terry Ford and ...I got to go, Eric, they're coming back." I'd pulled off the road and out of the traffic and just sat there, ashen-faced and trembling.

"What's happening, what did Brian say?" Jenny asked.

"Brian said we must stay in town, that we mustn't come home."

A veteran of countless run away and hides, Jenny was more angry than scared. "How long did Brian say we had to stay away this time?"

"I don't think we can go home, Jenny, ever."

We spent that night with Bob and Julie Hamill in their guest cottage. Seasoned refugees, Jenny, Veronica and Daniel, busied themselves with homework and routines while I sat in the garden and stressed. Bob did his best to cheer me up but failed. I was completely useless, freaked out that there were people out there who wanted to kill me, just because. And there was nothing I could do and no one I could call upon to help. No police, no neighbours, no one. Just me. Better to run away and not fight another day.

I packed the house up the next day by remote control, using farm labour and the farm three-ton truck. Jenny wanted to go out to supervise, but I wouldn't let her. Brian said that the man who'd pulled the trigger on Ford had moved on to a farm next to where the Lowes had once lived, just a kilometre down the road and was waiting for me to show up. Our household crap - precious possessions, unfortunately, get reduced to crap when hurriedly thrown in the bottom of a truck - filled the farm truck four times, way too much for Bob and Julie's cottage so another friend, Tony Vass, allowed us to clutter his house up with the overflow. I was horrified that in all the chaos and confusion, I clean forgot about the dogs and the cats. Dan was beside himself. I phoned the SPCA, and they went in after-hours to recover the animals and put them into kennels

That first night at Bob and Julie's, Jenny couldn't sleep. She went through to the kitchen in search of a cup of tea and bumped into Julie, who also couldn't sleep. After the day she'd had, cups of tea somehow seemed inadequate, so Jenny broke open the boxes that housed our booze collection and found the liqueurs. Julie, being the loyal and supportive friend that she was, joined Jenny in an Irish Cream. And then another. And another. And another. And then the Bailey's ran out. But no problem, Jenny and Julie went onward and upward to Kahluas, Amarulas and beyond.

I owned two hotels at the time, so my booze collection was boxes and boxes big. Peach schnapps came and went, followed by a whiskey liqueur called Cock of North which at three in the morning was apparently very, very funny. By now Julie had gone from being a supportive friend to a friend badly in need of support, and so the party moved to our bed where, thanks to a bucketful of sleeping tablets, I was soundly sleeping.

To fit three on the bed, Jenny rolled me over, waking me up in the process. She offered me a Cock of North, more hilarity, but because it was four in the morning and because one of us was going to have to take kids to school in just a few hours, I declined. Which earned me rambling lectures from Jenny and Julie on the need to lighten up and the risks associated with stress. Jenny told me that a Cock of North was actually very good for me, although some cocks could make you pregnant. More hilarity. Eventually, and after lots and lots of hilarity, a bottle of Jägermeister slammed the door shut on the fun and frivolity with Teutonic efficiency.

Just before five o'clock, Julie thanked Jenny for her hospitality, exchanged teary hugs and declarations of undying friendship and snuck into bed next to Bob. The school run wasn't far away, so Julie tried to fall asleep quickly but couldn't. For reasons unknown, her bed was intent on spinning violently. Julie was forced to seek urgent pharmaceutical assistance and prescribed herself an anti-nausea pill, a motion sickness pill, a headache pill, and because time was not on her side, a sleeping pill. Julie kept her medicine in a recess under the seat of her dressing table stool which folded up rather cleverly, like a toilet seat. Unfortunately, the dressing table was located on the far side of the bedroom. It took her a while to get there because whatever it was that was making the bed spin, had also taken a grip on the bedroom carpet. Eventually, she made it to the dressing table stool, unfortunately, without her reading glasses which were back next to the spinning bed and the writing on the phials was in stupidly small print and how the hell were you supposed to be able to figure what was in the bottles if you couldn't read the stupid small print. Next problem up was the bloody lids on the bloody bottles, they were all bloody child proofed. How were you supposed to fix your bloody headache when trying to figure out how to open the bloody bottle using brute force because nothing else worked without spilling the bloody pills all over the bloody wobbly carpet which gave you an even bigger headache than the one you'd started out with in the first bloody place. Strewth!! It was enough to drive a person to drink. But she'd had enough of that, and she had a school run to do.

Having spent five minutes emptying medicine bottles from the recess of her dressing table stool and wrestling unsuccessfully with childproof lids and obviously inspired by the seat of the dresser which folded up rather like a toilet seat, that which had gone down duly came back up, mostly into the recess of the seat. And then, because she had to do the school run just now, Julie quickly fell asleep, in amongst the debris of strewn pills, childproofed bottles and dietary detritus.

Thirty minutes later a still sleepy Kelly walked into her mom's bedroom in search of a hairbrush, looked down on her comatose mother, lying amongst the pile of pills, put two and two together and came up with suicide, and screamed, waking Bob up in the process. Bob was totally confused. He and Julie had gone to bed early and had fallen asleep watching a riveting episode of E.R. on television. Fast forward to early the next morning, and a real-life medical drama had played out on his bedroom carpet.

Unsurprisingly, Bob and I did our respective school runs that day while Jenny and Julie slept through the morning and hungover through the afternoon.

Although Bob and Julie said we could stay in their cottage for as long as we needed to, instead of going to the office that day, I went hunting for houses to rent, mostly because I was worried about my wife's liver, my booze collection and my friendship with the Hamills. As was my wont, I snapped up the first house I saw. It belonged to a business acquaintance. The cottage was entirely unsuitable, small, pokey with just two bedrooms, meaning that either Daniel or Veronica had to sleep in a laundry room-come-storeroom with impressive rising damp outback. And the cottage was way out of town, miles from the nearest shops and a hell of a commute to anywhere. But it was perched on the side of a huge hill and looked out over valleys and hills below that stretched away forever. As soon as I got there, I collapsed on the edge of the lawn and just drank in the sight of Africa. From up top, you couldn't see the chaos, mayhem and destruction on the ground below, just the good stuff like the wild hills, trees and kopjes. The view was exactly the therapy I needed, a timely reminder of how much I loved Zimbabwe. And maybe, just maybe, on a clear day and with a fully functional imagination, I reckoned you'd be able to see girls in bikinis on the beach in Beira. So I snapped it up, on a month to month basis.

I went back to Bob and Julie's to tell the family we now had a home from home. But for a lingering hangover, Julie would have thrown a party at the news. I took my family to see our new home, making sure to show them the view before I showed them the pokey little dwelling. Thankfully everyone fell in love with it, even Daniel, who drew the short straw for the laundry storeroom bedroom with the rising damp.

The very next day, I sprang the dogs from the SPCA, but not the cats. Not knowing what our future held, I'd told the SPCA staff to let the cats go to a deserving home should one come along. Daniel was absolutely heartbroken. His cats were his best friends, and he loved them dearly. I wanted to tell him no problem, we'd get him another kitten but couldn't. Our Saint Bernard Joshua had aged years in the short time he'd been in kennels, the weight had literally fallen off him, reducing him to skin and bones. But even though he was in obvious pain, he scampered around his new home, overjoyed at his reunion. Charlie Waghorn, the vet, did a house call and told us Joshua had terminal, inoperable cancer. He died a few short weeks after coming home. I cried my heart out.

The rest of the family settled into new routines in our new home but I couldn't. Shit scared of the man down the road who shot Terry Ford, I moved my office from the farm to the George Hotel. I tried hard to put on a brave face for the workers when I visited the farm infrequently but failed. My visits were random and never more than fifteen minutes long. I dreaded every single minute there. I was jumpy with my heart in my mouth, waiting for a man with a gun to come through the gate.

I so badly missed my farm, I missed walking around the fields with the dogs, I missed watching things grow, I missed being busy. The little cottage, already small when we moved, got smaller thanks to Dan having the urinary aim of a blind man with the shakes. The cottage's one and only toilet bathroom became a battleground where family wars were waged, and discontent festered. I put effort into teaching Dan how to piss straight but failed.

Dan, Vee and I played a lot of five-day test cricket on the tiny patch of lawn in front of the cottage, losing a multitude balls over the side of the hill mountain. Vee also taught me French, and after just a few months, I could say cheese, potatoes, first floor and 'My name is Eric' fluent like a Frenchman. If ever I got lost in France, I would be able to find my way to the first floor no problem. Any floors above or below the first floor, not so much.

But outside of French lessons and test cricket, mostly I stressed about where we were going to live and about what I was going to do to earn a living - not good things to be stressing about aged forty-three. Normally for me, long-term was next Tuesday but now all of a sudden, I needed to know where I was going to be, not just next year but also in ten years. I couldn't see how I was going to park off in my pokey rented cottage through to the next elections in 2005.

Increasingly, I turned my thoughts and efforts to political activism, to do what I could to help raise the profile of Zimbabwe's downtrodden and oppressed, hopefully prompting international intervention and hastening Mugabe's fall. How I did not end up with my genitals wired into the national grid, I do not know.

I offered up my help to a shadowy group called Zvakwana, Shona for Enough, whose aim was to ferment civil disobedience. They were secretive, for good reason. I never did find out who the brains were behind the organisation. Some impossibly young Serbians with wispy beards and furtive looks flew into town to teach Zvakwana the lessons they'd learnt overthrowing Milosevic. The Serbians were organised with PowerPoint presentations and a set of training manuals on 'How to Get Rid of Dictators', including my favourite, entitled 'How to Find Your Dictator's Achilles Heel.'

I had no idea how a bunch of Serbian experts on subversion happened to end up in Zimbabwe but having read every Tom Clancy novel out there, I put my money on CIA involvement, but then again, I am the proud owner of a vivid imagination. For the 'How to Get Rid of Your Dictator' series of lectures, I organised a conference room at the Feathers Hotel, rather than the George. The George was too high profile and big on the CIO radar. On the day, working on a gut feeling, I set up the lecture room in the manager's flat, which was situated at the back of the Hotel. Just as well, because the seminar got raided and the lecture participants got arrested. But luckily the cops stormed the Hotel's conference room on the ground floor first, giving us time to hide the subversive material.

One of the things we were trying to achieve through Activism was to force the international community to intervene in Zimbabwe. Exactly how unsuccessful we were at that was thrown in our face when the International Cricket Council rewarded Zimbabwe's non-existent human rights records by allowing them to host some of the games in the upcoming Cricket World

Cup tournament in South Africa. It really sucked. The world had united to force apartheid South Africa into sporting isolation but fast forward twenty years to Mugabe's reign of terror, and he gets asked to host a part of the cricket World Cup, one of the biggest showcases of world sport. Now all of a sudden, sport was a great healer. Well, tell that to the white farmer whose barns had been burnt down and his animals slaughtered and his home and everything he owned taken from him because he was white. Tell that to the poor black villager with the broken balls and broken feet, broken by the policeman's baton, broken because he supported the opposition. And to rub more salt in the wounds, the ICC announced a preparatory tour of Zimbabwe by Pakistan. Mugabe's propaganda machine crowed long and loud.

Not long after the Pakistani tour announcement, I had another three o'clock in the morning bolt upright Eureka moment. The first game of the tour was to be played at Harare Sports Club. How about we sneak into the grounds the night before the game, dig holes down the length of the pitch and plant mealies a.k.a. maize in them? And then we invite the world's press to come at first light to marvel at the only maize left growing in Zimbabwe. It would be huge, and the photos of our maize would make it onto the front page of every paper in the world, a stark reminder to the fuckwits who ran the ICC that supporting dictators and sweeping crimes committed against humanity under the carpet just wasn't cricket.

Hippos and whales hang out in pods, activists hang out in cells. Our cell met once a week, under the guise of being a book club. I had to wait three long days before I could bounce my 'mealies planted in the cricket pitch' idea off them. They loved it and gave it the thumbs up. With just six weeks to go, I planted a row of mealies in black bags on the farm and showered them with love, compost and fertilisers. The results were spectacular, and my mealies would have done Jack of the beanstalk fame proud. With the mealies in the ground and growing, I had to recruit the party youth who would actually go over the Sports Club wall, dig the holes and plant the mealies. Mugabe had long labelled the MDC as a puppet party controlled by whites and the West and us white activists were supposed to stay well in the background. But also not a bad thing, given the fact that I wield a shovel with the power and authority of a girl guide. Without telling him what we were planning, I asked Roland, a senior Party member, to recruit two fleet of foot and daring members of the MDC youth for a job two nights hence. Roland said he knew just the man to head up the insertion team, an MDC youth member who worked in the security department called Joel. I knew Joel. He often stood guard outside Morgan's office.

I went over the plan with Joel, and he loved it but had never seen a game of cricket before and had no idea what a pitch was or what it looked like. I took him to Harare Sports Club, the scene of the crime to come, on the Thursday night for a good look-see. Joel and I sat on the wide veranda at the Harare Sports Club, enjoyed a beer and spied out the lay of the land. All the preparations for Saturday's big game, advertising boards and catering tents were up and in place. With beers in hand, Joel and I ambled across the outfield to do a pitch inspection. The pitch had a rope around it to stop foot traffic, but Joel was able to reach through and gauge how hard the ground was that he was going to have dig holes into. It was bloody hard, so we added a pickaxe to the menu. Back on the clubhouse veranda we nursed a beer and watched the security guards and their routines. There wasn't a lot to watch. All three guards on duty, from a well- known security company, were old and comatose in the dark shadows on the other side of the field. We could almost hear their snores from the veranda. If any of the guards woke up during the maize planting season, my money was on the MDC youth. From what I could see, Joel's muscles had muscles. It was game on.

I got pulled out of a Friday morning hotel management meeting by a nervous receptionist. He said there was an urgent phone call for me, from the Office of the President. It turned out to be Morgan Tsvangirai's office, not Mugabe's but the receptionist was hellish impressed none the less. Tsvangirai's chief aide de camp was on the phone, and he sounded none too happy. He wanted to see me urgently. I'd never actually been summoned to Tsvangirai's office before. I was guessing it had to be about the cricket pitch raid, planned for later that night so I phoned my activist boss for advice. His read was that somehow Tsvangirai's top brass had heard about our planned stunt and were obviously unhappy with the potential for negative press if we got caught and they were calling me in to tell me to pull the plug. I hated going to MDC Headquarters at Harvest House- the pavements outside as always were teeming, mostly with CIO- keeping track of MDC visitors. I especially hated that I was going to see the man I was going to see. There were all sorts of rumours that Morgan's right-hand man was actually a CIO plant, infiltrated in early start-up days of the party to worm his way right up to the very top.

I was ushered up to Morgan's floor and into the aide de camp's office. He was an ugly man who had always made it very plain that he didn't like the other white MDC support members or me. In keeping with his personality, he gave the normal pleasantries like offering me a seat a complete miss and went straight for my jugular. "I've heard about your cockamamie cricket stunt, and I want to know why you want to put President Tsvangirai at risk?"

I got right back in his face. "What are you talking about?"

"You want to use Joel. You know that he is a member of the President's close security team and if caught, will cause the President and the Party huge embarrassment."

"I didn't ask for Joel. I asked for volunteers to do a job that will cause ZANU PF huge embarrassment and massively bad press in the world's newspapers. And they sent me Joel. And he volunteered to do the job."

"Who? Who sent you Joel? Who did you approach for volunteers?" He was hunting for Roland's name. "I won't tell you that."

"Why? Why won't you tell me?" he spat viciously.

"Because it's confidential, that's why. And confidential means you don't blab."

He got a poison mean look in his eyes like he wanted to plug my balls into the mains and beat the soles of my feet. But then in a blink, he put his poison mean look away, replacing it with his version of warm and sincere. "Sit, sit, Eric." He smiled warmly, warm like a snake about to bite a bunny. "I have studied your planned operation carefully, and I've done a thorough risk assessment, and I am happy for you to proceed. Good luck."

The best I could come up with was "Huh??"

"I said you can go ahead. So you can leave now."

I went straight back to my activist boss. He was as confused as I was. "What do I do?" I asked.

"You've got to press the button. He told you to go ahead so you can't back out now."

I spent the rest of the day stressing, with a bad feeling in my stomach, trying to make sense of my Harvest House meeting but failing.

Friday night was D Day. With no moon to speak of, it was nice and dark, perfect for skulduggery. I told Jenny I had a business meeting in town and would be late. I hotfooted out to the farm to collect the maize plants, five foot tall and near to tasselling in their planting pockets, plus a shovel and pickaxe and then back into town to meet Joel and his colleague, a hard as nails looking guy called Ishmael. On an earlier recon, I'd found a place to stash the mealies and the tools in an alleyway just a block down from the Harare Sports Club. I issued Joel and Ishmael purpose-bought black overalls, balaclavas and running shoes and dropped them off at the nearby Bronte Hotel. They were going to climb the wall at three o'clock in the morning and rather than have them milling around, looking suspicious, I'd bought them a double room. I went home and tossed, turned and stewed, waiting for Joel's thumbs up phone call. We had a gaggle of journalists, reporters and cameramen on standby to tour the cricket pitch/ maize field at first light.

Joel's call came at half past three in the morning. I went through to the lounge to talk to him. He was stuttering, stammering and out of breath. I could hear him shaking over the phone. When I eventually got his story out of him, it wasn't a happy one. He and Ishmael went over the wall dead at three o'clock, with the mealies and the tools. They were halfway to the pitch when the ground was lit up by floodlights and a hundred or more security guards charged at them out of the shadows.

"And they weren't from the normal security company, they were all like paramilitary, and they were lying in ambush, waiting for us."

He gave me the name of an elite security company, mostly ex-military who mostly worked offshore jobs in war zones. They didn't do normal security guard jobs. Both Joel and Ishmael managed to escape, but only just.

"But I'm very sorry. I dropped your shovel and your pickaxe and couldn't go back to fetch them. I'm very, very sorry. I know that they were brand-new."

I spent what was left of the night, sitting in the dark, waiting to be arrested and deeply depressed. As far as I was concerned, any suspicions I had about Morgan's aide de camp had just been put to bed. I had no doubt that the ugly son of a bitch had set up the Harare Sports Club ambush, designed to cause maximum embarrassment to Morgan and the MDC. And what hope was there for Morgan, or for any of us, if his right-hand man and one of his closest advisors was a CIO mole.

At five o'clock, I stood the journalists down. Unfortunately, there would be nothing for them to take photos of. Rather than hang around waiting on tenterhooks for the axe to fall, watching a game of fucking cricket that was so fucking wrong, I went out to Marondera to help evacuate best friends Eric and Fiona Dawson's farm. Today was the day that the Head of Airport Security come Fat Cat Land Thief had decided to take possession of Warwick Farm, lock, stock and barrel.

Eric wasn't able to pack up his life on his own. One of the strongest men I knew, and one of the most focused, Eric was struggling to cope with the thought of losing everything he'd built and everything he owned, and he needed help. Me and a few of his other friends went out to help him and Fiona strip the houses of light fittings, plumbing fittings, anything and everything. It was a hugely depressing task. Eric and Fiona had spent the last five years on a labour of love, renovating and building, converting what had once been a squat little farm cottage into a beautiful family home. There wasn't any time to unscrew fittings and fixtures and remove them gently, the Land Thief and his greedy family had already gathered to take what was not theirs, so we ripped stuff out in a hurry. A friend of Eric's ran a transport company and loaded the Eric's prize-winning tobacco crop on to 30-ton rigs while the Land Thief watched, wringing his hands as he watched the fortune he'd hoped to steal being carted off. The Land Thief said nothing because Eric's friend was built like two shit houses.

Before leaving Warwick Farm, our last job was to cut Eric and Fiona's game fence and shoo the animals out. Better they fend for themselves in the bush than to be hacked to death behind the fence for the Fat Cat's Sunday lunch. The last animal out the hole in the fence was Eric's pride and joy Zebra stallion that he'd named Sarge. We had to throw rocks at the poor animal to get him to run away into the bush. I had no idea how long Sarge would last out there, but it would be a lot longer than the twenty minutes he would last with the Fat Cat Land Thief.

Progress is a precarious and precious thing. It doesn't just happen by accident. It only happens through someone's perseverance, through their slog and hard work, through their tears and dreams. And spending a day ripping down my best friend's dreams and aspirations was one of the most depressing things I'd ever done. I drove back to my little rented cottage feeling lower than rock bottom. There were still no police waiting to arrest me. Which made sense because, in the end, no crime had been committed. The cricket pitch hadn't been dug up, and the mealies hadn't been planted, and the world had been able to tune in and watch and enjoy a stupid fucking game of cricket, played in a country where there were no fucking rules. Alas.

Chapter Thirty-Three

The old adage 'it never rains but pours' was one that Zimbabwe flogged to death. Mixing metaphors, the last two straws that broke my camel's back were humdingers.

I came back from work to find Dan, still in his school uniform, sitting in front of the cottage, just staring out into the view, broken and dejected, sporting black eyes and worse. Hopelessly out of his depth with academics, Dan had struggled at St Georges from the start. But recently things had taken a turn for the worse.

Not long into his first term, Dan got into a fight with a black kid in his class who was talking it up big that his dad, a prominent and successful doctor around town, had just been given a farm by the government. This in the month where Dan had been forced from his own home. Dan didn't have a violent bone in his body but saw no way forward other than to punch the black kid. Which alas, did not go terribly well for him. And that was just the start of it.

When Gary was at St George's, race wasn't an issue at all. Some of his best mates were black. But things had changed. By the time Dan started at the school, there was an ugly racial and political undertone. Chief culprits in Dan's Form One year was a group of Government ministers' sons whose favourite pastime was to hunt Dan down in the corridors so they could bully and humiliate him and punch him around a bit. I wanted to go to the headmaster, but Dan begged me not to. He said that would just make things worse. Instead, I phoned a friend's son who was a prefect at the school and asked if he could keep an eye out for Dan. That seemed to work. But when I came home and saw Dan bloodied and beaten again, I thought the bullying had flared up again. But I got that wrong. What had happened to Dan was worse, much worse.

It took me a while to get the story out of him. He hadn't been beaten by the usual bullies; he'd ended up on the wrong side of a Mob Justice session in his Religious Education class. The RE teacher had given Dan a thumbs down. What the hell was Mob Justice, I asked? And what was thumbs down all about? Instead of talking about religion and stuff, Dan said the RE teacher would often hold Mob Justice sessions to punish behaviour he wasn't happy with. I was still none the clearer. What the hell was Mob Justice? "If the teacher thinks you've done something wrong, he gives you the thumbs down, and the rest of the class have to punish you."

"Punish you how?"

"Mostly by punching you and kicking you."

"And that's what happened to you?"

"Yes, Dad."

"And what did you do wrong, Dan, for the teacher to give you a thumb's down."

"It's not what I did Dad, it's what you did."

"Me! What did I do?"

"The teacher gave me the thumbs down because you're an MDC supporter, Dad."

It was a twenty-minute drive from the cottage to St Georges. I got there in ten. I didn't know where to look for the Religious Education teacher so stormed into the Headmaster's office instead. The headmaster always looked under pressure, a man with a world of worries on his shoulders. But as he sat and listened to me rant and rave about Dan's attack, he visibly buckled. Which surprised me. I thought my story would have angered him enough to do some storming of his own, but he didn't. I figured it out. The headmaster knew exactly what had to be done, but he couldn't do it. Because of politics, because he had a bunch of government ministers' children in his school, he couldn't take action against his Religious Education teacher for politics in the classroom. Not being able to do what was right had to really hurt a good man like him. But I cut him zero slack. "If you're not going to kick that teacher out of your school, then I want Daniel excused from all Religious Education classes from here on," I told him.

"I fully understand, Mr de Jong and I am truly sorry."

Again, I cut him no slack. "I don't think you do understand. This is a Catholic school, over a hundred years old, built by the Jesuits to give boys a Catholic education. And you, the headmaster, have just excused Daniel from all his Religious Education classes going forward. The Pope is going to be properly bleak with you when he hears about this." I stormed out of the office. For the rest of the term, instead of going to RE, Dan went off on his own to do his homework.

A few weeks later, Jenny and I were invited to a Parent Teachers Consultation, where we could interact with Dan's teachers one on one, to find out how Dan was doing in class. I walked past Maths, Geography and the Sciences and headed straight for the short queue in front of the Religious Education teacher. I stared at him hard as I stood third in line. He was a big man, not far from running to fat and he looked at home and in his comfort zone behind his desk. But not for long. He felt my glare, and my hostility. He looked up at me and I gave him a full angry blast and he quickly went from comfortable to very uncomfortable. He had no idea who I was or why I was so pissed at him. Or maybe he did know. Whatever. Either way he twitched and squirmed while he went through the motions with the parents in front of me, continually flashing looks at me from the corner of his eye. Then it was my turn. He offered me up the parent's chair in front of his desk with a weak smile. I ignored both chair and smile and leant across his desk and poked him in his chest as hard as I could.

"My name is de Jong." I was talking loudly, very loudly. Around me the babble of many conservations died immediately, all eyes swivelled to the confrontation at the Religious Education desk, the headmaster included. "And if ever I hear that you've given my son a hard time, I will come here, and I will fuck you up!! In your classroom!! In fact, I will fuck you up if you just go anywhere near my son!!" He outweighed me almost two to one, but I was dying for him to start something. I was itching to climb over his desk and beat him, there and then. But he didn't. He just sat there and tried to disappear under his desk.

Eventually, Jenny pulled me away, and we went to meet Daniel's other teachers.

For the record, the rest of the consultation didn't go too good. The message back from all his teachers was that Dan was really struggling in all his classes, hopelessly out of his depth. Clearly, St George's was the wrong place for him. We needed to find a school where Dan would be with kids of his own ability. And every time I turned around to glare at the RE teacher, he all but crawled under his desk. I was sad when I drove out of St Georges. It wasn't such a beautiful school anymore. And it was wrong for Dan. I was also pissed off for not hitting the RE teacher. Not hitting him remains one of my regrets in life.

Late the next day, though, my fight instincts were replaced by my flight ones. I had just got back to the cottage after a day at my office when I got a phone call from the hotel receptionist. I could hardly hear him because he was whispering, scared witless about something. "I can't hear a word you are saying. Speak up, man," I told him.

"I can't, sir, otherwise they will hear me."

My hearing improved. Suddenly I could hear him perfectly. "Who? Who will hear you?"

"The people that are here, at the hotel, looking for you, sir."

"Who? Who's looking for me?"

"They are many, sir, at least more than twelve, or sixteen."

"But who? Who are they?"

"Comrade Hunzvi. And his men."

"Hitler Hunzvi is there? He's looking for me?"

"Yes, sir. He went up to your office. I told him that you weren't there. Now they are searching the bars for you, and the rest of the hotel. You mustn't come here tomorrow, sir, they are not good people, sir."

My legs all but collapsed. They knew all about Hitler Hunzvi, and his surgery come torture centre. And now he was at the George Hotel looking for me. I'm sure there wasn't any connection between Hunzvi looking for me and the confrontation at St Georges but either way my camel's back was well and truly broken through overload.

I gave into my flight instincts immediately. I absolutely wanted no part of Hunzvi.

We started packing up the cottage the next day. It didn't take long. Most of our stuff was still in boxes from when we ran away from the farm. The poor dogs went back into kennels. I had hurried meetings with Brian about the farm and with Nick Dickens about the hotels. I told them that I was leaving, sooner than later. I would head for South Africa to start with and then make up my mind from there. There were no arguments from Jenny, Veronica or Daniel. They were more than happy at the thought of living somewhere else, other than Zimbabwe. Dan had the most questions. He was excited about starting a new life, but he was also worried.

"How will Gary find us in our new home? Will he find us? And what about Nan and Pop? And can we get new cats?"

"For sure we'll tell Gary where his new home is going to be. And Nan and Pop. We'll stick together as a family, Dan, don't worry."

"Is my new school going to be like St Georges, Dad, or better?"

"I don't know, Dan."

"I hope better."

"Me too."

"Are we still going to live on a farm, Dad?"

"Maybe son, but one where we can plant trees."

"Why trees, Dad?"

"Because I want to live somewhere, Dan, where I can plant trees and know that I'm going to be around to watch them grow big."

"That sounds good, Dad."

"Sure does."

Chapter Thirty-Four

When first we ran away to South Africa, Jenny's sister Michelle and her husband Kevin put us up in their home in Kempton Park, even though we couldn't tell them how long we would be staying. I studiously avoided the use of the phrase 'maybe forever'.

I was the worst houseguest ever and don't know how they put up with me. I treated Kevin and Michelle's home as though it was my personal prison, pacing the boundaries of their small back yard morning, noon and night, dragging a black cloud of gloom behind me, with my cell phone glued to my ear, desperately seeking good news out of Zimbabwe, but finding none. Brian told me that Hunzvi's war vets had been back to the farm several times looking for me. He didn't think that it would be safe for me to come home anytime soon.

Reality sank in. I was forty-three years old and had absolutely no idea where in the world I was going to live and even less of an idea as to how I was going to provide for my family. I got more and more down on myself. I had zero skills, my curriculum vitae read like bad fiction. I'd be hard-pressed to find a job as a yard sweeper.

After two weeks of my misery, Kevin kicked me out. He had timeshare in a cottage in a wilderness area adjoining the Kruger National Park. He gave me the keys, directions and firm instructions to not come back until I'd pulled my head out of my arse. The last thing I wanted to do was go somewhere and have a good time, but the kids begged me to go and Jenny threatened me with death if we didn't. And so, we went. I think Kevin and Michelle threw a party as soon as we drove out of their driveway.

I grumped my way through the South African Highveld, a dreary place with old mine dumps, coal fields and not a tree in sight. And the endless maize fields that stretched out to the horizon and beyond were a salt in my wound reminder that others were farming, and I wasn't. But my mood lightened as we started to drop off the escarpment, down into the warmth of South African's Lowveld. Suddenly there was bush and trees all around, just like home. A mukwa tree jumped out at me and tugged at my heartstrings, reminding me of Zimbabwe. Before you start getting impressed, I need to point out that mukwa trees a.k.a. kiaat in South Africa, are about the only indigenous tree I can recognise, apart from baobabs.

I saw lots more farms, all busy, all productive. The soils looked good, deep and rich red. And everything was so green and growing. Which in the Lowveld heat, had to mean lots of water. I even saw some greenhouses down in a valley underneath the escarpment, which got me thinking and scheming for the final two hours of the trip.

Kevin's timeshare cottage was called Feather Lodge. It was delightful, neatly thatched and tucked away in the thick thorn bush adjoining the Kruger Park, thick bush full of shy little bushbuck, not so shy warthogs and a myriad of birdlife. Jenny and I stayed for just minutes, just long enough to dump the kids and our luggage before getting back in the car and driving an hour back to Nelspruit, the last big town that we had driven through. We were going farm shopping.

They say fools rush in where angels fear to tread. Well, I went in a whole lot quicker than the quickest fool. By the time we got into Nelspruit, I'd borrowed enough money over the phone from friends and family to give me nightmares, and hopefully enough to be able to put a deposit down on a farm and start farming again. Hopefully is the keyword here as I didn't have a clue what farms cost, I didn't know whether mortgages were available, I knew nothing. But just two hours and three very crappy little plots later, Jenny and I made an offer to buy the fourth farm we looked at. It was called Summerhill Farm, and it was near a little town called White River.

Summerhill was just forty hectares big but mostly all arable, with deep, well-drained soils courtesy of the big hill the farm was perched upon. It had an irrigation canal that ran right through the middle of the farm which fed off into two small storage dams. The top half of the farm was planted to avocado trees with a couple of hectares of ready to harvest ginger planted in the bottomlands. Included in the price was an old John Deere tractor, in working order, plus equipment and implements too numerous to mention. It was absolutely perfect. Oh. And it also had a big rambling thatched farmhouse that looked to be plenty big for all of us, plus two delightful little self-contained cottages overlooking the larger dam, perfect for Jenny's mom and dad. The views from the house went on forever, and the birdlife in the gardens and around the dams was prolific. Already I'd seen a bunch of birds I'd never seen before.

But most importantly of all, White River was by my reckoning about a thousand kilometres from Harare. I would be able to drive from farm to farm in a day. I'd already decided that I would carry on farming Running Dog from a distance.

I made the offer to buy Summerhill before setting foot in any of the houses. Mark Pearce, the very nice guy real estate agent who was looking after us, forced me into at least the main house for a look-see, just in case. As it turned out, the house was fine with two lounges, three bedrooms and three bathrooms, an adjoining office and a veranda that enjoyed therapeutic views of the valley and the hills behind it. Sure, the house would need a bit of TLC, but it was nothing that me and my trusty, almost brand-new Leatherman couldn't handle.

I was so excited. I'd never owned a farm with a dam before, or a John

Deere tractor or avocado trees. We went back to Feather Lodge, where I resumed my non-stop pacing, but now with mostly good stuff going on in my head. And when our offer was finally accepted, a couple of days later, Jenny and I popped a champagne cork before taking Daniel and Veronica to look at our new home. Both of them fell in love at first sight. The cancer of uncertainty that had been killing my family for three long years had been nipped in the bud by that most precious of commodities, hope. For now.

Moving to a new country involves a whole bunch of paperwork. First up, we had to apply for residency in South Africa. Which involved another medical but thankfully without any testicular connectivity tests. Whether or not my balls bounced when I coughed was of no concern to the South Africans, unlike the Australians. The Home Affairs official who processed our paperwork rolled his eyes at the prospect of yet more Zimbabweans joining his burgeoning fold. I say burgeoning because the huge waiting room was full of other Zimbabweans and Nigerians and Somalians and Pakistanis, also all looking to become South Africans. And after Home Affairs, it was registering companies and opening bank accounts. Left to my own devices, I would've fled. But Jenny wouldn't let me.

Once we'd signed every form in creation, we hot-footed back to Zimbabwe to wrap up and pack up our lives there, which didn't take long. Most of our furniture we decided to leave in the house on Running Dog and buy new in South Africa. We'd offered up our two Running Dog houses free, gratis and fully furnished to farmers who'd been kicked off their land and both had been snapped up by grateful refugees. It seemed weird that other farmers were allowed to live on our farm, but I wasn't. But then my problems weren't about my land and all about my politics.

Because I'd long ago handed the reins of the farm over to Brian, I was able to keep my final walk about Running Dog to under the prescribed ten minutes. The man with the gun who'd shot Terry Ford and who wanted to also shoot me still lived just down the road. I spent all ten of those minutes assuring members of my staff that I would be back, but not many of them believed me. Hardest of all was taking my leave of Raphael. The other workers I shook hands with but Raphael, I hugged. And I teared up while doing it. I couldn't help but feel I was abandoning him on the field of battle. Alas.

When we finally hit the road, we looked like a convoy of Vietnamese boat people. Both cars were full to overflowing with dogs, cats and crap, with pots, pans and yet more crap on the roof racks overhead. Including a full-length gun cabinet. I'd handed my shotgun in at the police station but decided to hang on to the gun cabinet. It was crazy. The gun cabinet, in full view on the Land Rover roof rack, passed through countless police roadblocks and two international borders, unopened and unchecked. The South African customs official who came out to search our vehicles pointed up at the gun cabinet and asked me what it was. I told him it was a gun cabinet.

"Oh," he said, "you can proceed."

If I come back as an international smuggler in my next life, that's how I'm going to roll. My Land Rover went past full to overflowing when my bulldog Waddle gave birth to three puppies just after we crossed the border. Oh, what fun we had!!

Summerhill Farm was in the middle of the Heidel Valley, a very productive farming community, mostly Afrikaners from what I could see from the farm signs on the roadside. I liked Afrikaners. Zimbabwe was full of them - all charming, friendly people who took hospitality to a whole other level. And at least now I had a chance to use my 'O' Level Afrikaans that I'd sweated through five years of school for. Ditto a headful of excellent Van der Merwe jokes I'd accumulated over the years. When we arrived at our new home, the dogs went crazy, exploring and christening their new lawn. While we were unloading the cars, I saw two of our new neighbours walking down our very steep driveway.

"Here comes some of that Afrikaans hospitality I was talking about," I told Jenny. "They're most probably bringing us a milk tart. Or some koeksisters." I love koeksisters.

"They're not carrying anything," Jenny said.

"Well, then they've most probably come to invite us back to their houses for dinner or something."

The driveway was long, so I had plenty of time to observe our new neighbours. They were obviously father and son, with the father in his mid-sixties and the son in his early forties. They were more obviously both farmers, wearing two-tone khaki shirts, veld shoes and hats with legs and arms burnt dark brown from the harsh Lowveld sun. When they got to where we were standing, they introduced themselves formally in strong, guttural accents and shook hands with huge hands calloused from no shortage of hard work. Introductions were followed by a horribly awkward drawn-out silence, which I tried to fill by inviting them inside our empty house for a cup of tea, assuming, of course, I could find the box with the crockery stuff in it. Thankfully, the son said no but not before Jenny gave me a vicious kick on the shin.

"Can we have a word with you, to one side?" the son asked. He spoke English well, but not comfortably.

"Sure." I followed them to the side of the driveway.

"Do you want to sell?"

"Huh," I said.

"Your property? Do you want to sell it?"

I stuttered and stammered through my reply. "Well, I've not really... um... given...um... much thought to selling seeing how we've ...um...only just bought the farm and just moving in for the ...um...first time."

"Oh." Another awkward silence. "Well when you do sell it, I want to buy your farm."

We had takeout pizza for dinner and spent the first night in our new home, sleeping on camping mattresses on the floor in amongst unopened boxes. The rambling thatched farmhouse had a good homely feel to it. I was sure we were going to be happy living on Summerhill. Dan and I went for a walk around our new garden before turning in. It was a bright night, full of stars and loud with the unfamiliar sounds of the chorus of frogs from the dam closest to the house. I decided to test Dan on the night sky above.

"Can you tell me where the Southern Cross is, Dan?"

"Sure, Dad, it's at home. On Running Dog, in the sky on top of your office between the two big trees." Which was where you saw the Southern Cross when standing in our garden in Zimbabwe. I laughed. But Dan's answer also dragged my thoughts back to my other home, my proper home.

Chapter Thirty-Five

Farming in South Africa was tough. Mostly because I didn't know how stuff worked. Back home in Zimbabwe, I knew loads of people who could and did help me before I cocked things up too badly. But in South Africa, I was on my own. And I found everything to be a challenge. I didn't know where to buy farm chemicals or fertilisers from. I couldn't find a set of labour regulations anywhere and remained completely in the dark about things like minimum wage levels, hours of work, annual leave. I didn't know the best place to buy electrical stuff or irrigation fittings. I didn't even know how my irrigation water on Summer Hill worked.

The business of irrigating on Summer Hill was easy as compared to Running Dog. On Running Dog, I pumped my irrigation water from nine boreholes, and that came with no end of headaches and hassles; submersible pumps and motors which burned out because of voltage fluctuations or single phasing or just because, boreholes that collapsed, falling water tables and the list went on. But irrigation on Summer Hill was too easy. Here, my irrigation water arrived in a concrete canal that snaked through the middle of the farm, delivering water via sluice gates into two holding dams that I pumped water out of. I didn't know where the water in the canal came from or where it went to after it left Summer Hill, it was just there. But not always, apparently. I went into a flat panic when I received a message from the Sand River Water Board, of which I was a member apparently, telling me that I would have to place orders fortnightly for irrigation water through my water bailiff because of the ongoing drought. What drought? I didn't even know we were having a drought. Everywhere I looked, all I saw was lush green bush.

There was a water meeting to discuss the restrictions. The meeting was held in my new neighbour's avocado pack shed. In Zimbabwe, I did my best to avoid farmers meetings, but this water meeting was important. And it would be a great opportunity to meet people and to build my network. It didn't help that my only almost khaki shirt was in the wash. I had to wear one of my normal loud, flower shirts instead. It was as if I'd walked into the crowded room with a social disease. People nodded at me, from a distance and reluctantly, only when I caught their eye. Quickly, I found the anonymity offered by a seat in the back of the room and sat and listened.

According to the farmer who served as Chairman of the Water Board, the drought was serious, the worst in fifteen years. And the Witklip Dam, where our irrigation water came from, had dropped below thirty percent and was falling fast. Farmers were urged to think of others when drawing down on their water allocations. Then the chairman opened the meeting to questions from the floor. My one and only question wasn't the most inspired. How could a person find out what their water allocation was? As one, the room turned to look at me. I guess it was a pretty stupid question. Apparently, my water rights were affixed to my title deeds, in amongst all the small print I make a habit of not reading.

On my way home after the meeting, I pulled over on the side of the road to get out and marvel at the ominously dark grey skies that hung low overhead. They were almost black and that low that I could practically reach up and touch them. There was a hell of a storm coming. I was still gawking upwards when a pick-up truck stopped. Two of my new neighbours who thought I'd broken down had stopped to help. I waved them on with a laugh. That sort of misunderstanding happens often when you drive a Land Rover. "I was just looking up at the storm coming and just wondering how much rain we're going to get."

They swopped long looks with each other. Then the farmer in the passenger seat told me in his guttural accent. "Those aren't storm clouds. That's smoke from the forest fires."

"Forest fires?"

"There are twenty thousand hectares of trees burning right now."

"Oh."

I read the small print affixed to my title deeds when I got home. Apparently, I had water rights for twenty hectares. They were expressed in cubic metres per season. According to my calculations, it was an impossible amount of water. I could drown the valley if I wanted to. Unless I got some extra noughts in there by mistake. It was extremely confusing. As were my calculations on how much water to order for my first draw down. I had absolutely no benchmark to base my order on. So, in the end, I came up with an eeny meeny miny moe number of cubic metres of water that I thought would get me through the fortnight and phoned it through to my water bailiff. I was off the farm when the bailiff came to adjust the two sluice gates on the canal. When I saw the pathetically small inflow trickle over the locked sluice gates, it was obvious I'd woefully under ordered. But I still wasn't worried. Both dams were full with plenty enough water in them for the two weeks ahead.

Alas. I've never seen anything drop so quickly as the levels of water in the dams. Other than my spirits. At the rate of I was pumping I would run out of dam sooner than later. The problem was it was so bloody hot. I'd never experienced heat like it before. The evaporation rates were through the roof. And all my newly planted seedlings were going to wither and die. And...

"Just phone the bloody water bailiff and order some more bloody water. Just tell him you made a mistake on your first order," Jenny snarled.

"I can't," I wailed. "I tried to phone, but he's on leave. He'll only be back next week."

"Well, then you'll just have to make a bloody plan." I think if the truth be known, I was getting on Jenny's nerves.

I hightailed it out of the house and pondered my woes next to one of my rapidly dropping dams. I eyed the sluice gate with its shiny new padlock. Curses. If only I'd done my bloody sums better. If only I had keys to the bloody padlock. If only... I tried to lift the sluice gate, more out of frustration than hope and there was some give, quite a lot actually. The gauge holes on the gate were quite a bit larger than the padlock, and straight away there was an increase of water into the dam. But I couldn't stand there and hold the sluice gate up for the next two weeks. I rushed off to find something I could use to jam under the gate to leverage it up and came back with a long thick branch of an avocado tree. It was a struggle to get the thick edge of the branch wedged under the gate, but I managed. And straight away the pathetic trickle of water grew to a torrent. I was sure that it would make all the difference. And next week I would treble my water order.

Two hours later, the pick-up that had stopped to help me after the meeting drove on to the farm, and the same two farmers got out. I went to greet them. It wasn't a social visit. They were from the bottom end of the canal. And they weren't getting any water. They just wanted to check my sluice gates, just to make sure I wasn't stealing water. The bald, bold accusation slapped me in the face like a shovel. Crap. Sure, I told them with my poker face down by ankles, they could check my sluice gates, no problem. I followed behind them reluctantly, with heavy legs. Maybe, just maybe they wouldn't pick-up on the half an avocado tree jammed under my sluice gate. Or maybe it wasn't there anymore, maybe it had been washed up by the strength of the current in the canal. Or maybe...

"Hey, look!! There's a huge big fucking log jammed under your sluice gate." one of my new neighbours pointed out helpfully.

"There is?" I asked miserably.

"Ya!! There is. I wonder how it got there." His voice dripped heavy with sarcasm.

I had my confession all lined up in my head. But it didn't come out. Alas. "I don't know. It wasn't there an hour ago."

"It wasn't?" More sarcasm.

"No. Maybe some kids stuck it there. Or a beaver." I burned red with embarrassment straight away. Not only was I the water thief who got caught red-handed by his neighbours, but I was also the water thief who blamed it on a fucking beaver. Good God. I was never going to be able to show my face in the district again.

I wasn't the only one in the family having problems fitting into our new home. In fact, my problems paled into insignificance as compared to poor Dan's. We booked Dan into a very nice private school called Penryn College, halfway between White River and Nelspruit. It was an easy commute from Summer Hill. We had no option but to go the private school route again because Dan's Afrikaans was non-existent to a point where he couldn't even ask his way to the toilets. There was no way he would cope in the mostly Afrikaans speaking public schools in the area.

Dan was over the moon happy with Penryn, not least of all because it was co-ed. He was just starting to notice girls as something other than a nuisance. And there were more girls in his class at Penryn than there were in the whole of Harare. Dan loved Penryn and everything about it. Even the uniform, which was long pants, no hat, no tie and no blazer. It's hard to pick up chicks in khaki shorts and a badly tied tie. Compared to St Georges, there were hardly any rules and hardly any pressure at Penryn. Dan didn't have to learn the names of every prefect and every senior in the school, he didn't have to learn the words to school war cries and anthems. Penryn was giving him a chance to start senior school all over again, a second chance most welcome after St Georges had gone so horribly wrong for him. Alas. In many ways, Penryn turned out even worse for Dan.

In the beginning, Dan found the schoolwork at Penryn easy, but only because the school adopted a weird group approach to learning. Kids got split up into learning groups and were given projects to complete. It was a new and progressive approach to education, and it worked. The Headmaster was proud of Penryn's academic achievements. But with regards Dan, the group approach didn't work so good. Within his group, he was a complete passenger. Not only was the syllabus absolutely foreign, Dan started Penryn in the middle of a school year, but he was just slower than the other kids, plain and simple.

Consequently, Dan didn't contribute to the group output. He couldn't. He just sat back and did nothing and learned nothing. Quickly resentment towards him built up in the group and Dan became an outsider. His new classmates excluded him, even before he got in in the first place.

Dan didn't just not fit because of his academic abilities, he didn't fit in, period. And I need to take more than a bit of blame for that. For the first time ever, Dan came home from school, asking for the most expensive name-brand clothing. And a cell phone. And he wanted hair gel, to make his hair stick up apparently. I very quickly slammed the door shut on all his requests not just because we couldn't afford it, but also because we didn't agree with it.

Coming from a country where you had a choice between Colgate and Colgate and thought nothing of it, I was appalled at how materialistic South Africans were. My first question at my first ever social function in White River was "What kind of car do you drive?"

"Why do you want to know?" I asked. "Have I blocked someone in? Or have I left my lights on?"

"No. I was just curious to find out what car you drive?" Before I could answer, my host went on to explain further. "I'm driving a new Audi. But I'm very disappointed in the gearbox. So, I'm thinking about upgrading to a new BMW."

"Oh," I said. "I drive an old and very fucked up Land Rover."

Which proved to be a bit of a conversation stopper. Eventually, he asked the question "But why?"

"Because that's all I can afford." Which really was the end of the conversation.

I was saddened by the peer pressure that Dan was being subjected to. The South African obsession with material things had been passed down from father to son. Dan didn't get his designer label blue jeans or the latest cell phone. Or his hair gel to make his hair stick up. And so, he improvised. He walked out to the car one morning for school with his hair all covered in some white gunk but fashionably standing on end, nonetheless. I touched it, and my hand nearly got stuck.

"What the hell have you got in your hair, Dan?" I asked.

'I found some hair gel stuff."

"Where?"

"In the toolbox in the storeroom."

"Get me the bottle."

As it turned out, Dan had emptied a bottle of wood glue on his head. We washed it out as best we could, but it was good glue, and much of it had already bonded. Jenny had to cut it out with a pair of scissors and a wood chisel.

To try and fit in, Dan even put up his hand for the Penryn athletics team trials.

"But you can't run fast, Dan," I pointed out helpfully.

"It's okay, Dad, I haven't volunteered for the sprint team. I've decided I'm going to be a fifteen hundred metre runner."

"Do you even know how far fifteen hundred metres is?"

As it turned out, Dan didn't have a clue. In his first fifteen hundred metre race, the look on Dan's face grew longer and longer every time they ran around the track without hearing the bell. But credit to him, Dan hung on grimly to finish fourth, albeit a good two hundred metres behind the kid who came third. Dan placed fourth only because every other kid in the race gave up when they saw they wouldn't place on the podium.

After he finally finished, I went up to pat a completely knackered Dan on the back for his valiant efforts. Which was when I noticed the completely white patches of skin the size of dinner plates, poking out of his running vest beneath both of his armpits. Against the dark brown of his tan, the contrast was stand-out massive. I lifted Dan's running vest and got a bigger fright. The white patch problem was even worse on his lower back and down into his waistline. The huge swathe of the white, almost translucent skin had all but taken over. It was like all his pigment had gone.

'Jesus, Dan. What's happened to your skin?"

"I don't know Dad. Remember it started behind my knee, that time when we were on holiday in Mozambique. Well, it sort of spread from there."

"But why didn't you say anything?"

"I was hoping that it would go away. But it hasn't."

When we got home, I made Dan strip to his underwear. The loss of skin pigmentation in places on his body was shocking, almost total, especially on his lower body, around his buttocks and his groin area. I was so ashamed. My son was clearly in the middle of some hugely gross medical disorder, and I'd been so wrapped up in my own problems, I hadn't noticed.

We took Dan in to see a doctor in White River who whistled when he saw the extent of pigmentation loss. Straight away, he referred us to a dermatologist in Nelspruit. Who also whistled when he saw the damage. He told us it was vitiligo, an autoimmune disorder. In layman's terms, Dan's body defence mechanism viewed his skin pigmentation as a threat and was now killing it. The skin doctor sent Dan off for a barrage of tests and whistled some more when he saw the antibody results. Normal was a reading of five or under. Dan's reading was nineteen hundred. He told us to come back in a month for another reading. He wanted to see if the condition was getting worse. It was. By the second test, Dan's antibody reading had soared to sixty thousand and climbing. The doctor said he'd never seen anything like it. He told Dan that if he lived in the United States, he'd be in a medical textbook. Poor Dan was quite proud of that distinction. Straight away, he asked if we could go and live in America.

The accelerated loss of skin pigment was remarkable. Within a few short months, Dan lost ninety percent of his skin pigment. The other kids at Penryn were cruel and started calling Dan 'The Albino Stalker' or 'Stalker' for short. And that was that, whatever self-confidence Dan had, went. The happy go lucky kid with the darkest of tans had quickly been replaced by a hugely unhappy albino, an albino hating life, with absolutely no idea what he'd done to piss God off so badly.

Chapter Thirty-Six

My new and specially imported section manager, John Mandavani arrived from Zimbabwe, all big-eyed and excited. John had a good college diploma and three years of post-grad experience behind him, mostly on Running Dog, but had never travelled outside of Zimbabwe before. He was like a kid at a new school, in a hurry to get stuck into Summer Hill and make a difference.

When he arrived, I moved John into the second cottage on the farm. The Summer Hill workers viewed him with great interest. He was a first for them, a black farm manager with a college qualification who lived in a white man's house with a view from the top of the farm, and not at the bottom of the hill in the compound with the workers.

Sure, there were language problems in the beginning. John was a Shona, and the workers were mostly Shangaans or Swatis. But African languages are all interconnected, and John was able to quickly find middle ground. He knew some Ndebele. Which was close to Zulu. Which was sort of close to Shangaan and Swati. And within the first week, John and the workers were communicating. He got more work out of them in the first few days than I'd got in three weeks. It looked like my experiment would work.

With John in the Summer Hill saddle, I was able to make my first working trip back to Zimbabwe. Brian sent me his Running Dog wish list of farm spares and chemicals. Zimbabwean shelves were running empty, and prices were rocketing. The difference in prices between Zimbabwe and South Africa was shocking, and savings made on Brian's wish list would cover the costs of my trip many times over.

I shopped hard for Running Dog. Land Rovers are the best smuggling vehicles ever with concealed compartments under the seats and a million nooks and crannies all hidden from view. I filled them to the brim with irrigation fittings, electrical spares, filters for tractors and trucks, herbicides and insecticides. I also bought a massive top of the range loudspeaker bullhorn megaphone for Morgan Tsvangirai.

MDC leader Eddie Cross asked me to buy the bullhorn megaphone because the MDC's public address system was broken. I was super impressed with my purchase. The megaphone was huge. People in Bulawayo would be able to hear Morgan in Harare. But huge was also a snag. The megaphone was way bigger than any hidey-hole in the Land Rover. In the end, I bolted it to the front grill of the Land Rover. Luckily the bullhorn housing was cream coloured, almost the same colour as the Land Rover. Unluckily, it stuck out past the grill a good four foot and looked like the prow of a Viking ship. I drove across the Beit Bridge with my heart in my mouth and the ridiculous megaphone in plain view.

Beitbridge border post has to be the most miserable place on earth. Empty supermarket shelves in Zimbabwe made for border queues longer and hotter than the queues into purgatory. And at the end of the queues, customs officials hovered like hungry hyenas waiting to pounce on smuggled contraband. The full vehicle searches - a mandatory prerequisite to getting an exit stamp on your gate pass - were a huge bottleneck and the queue moved at a snail's pace. Giving me all the time in the world to sweat bullets while practising my poker face and my bribe offer. Alas. My poker face was properly crap, ditto my bribe speech. And they got worse, the closer I got to the search teams at the front of the queue. Finally, it was my turn. I inched the Land Rover through the traffic control bollards and into an empty search bay. The customs official who walked up to the Land Rover was eagle-eyed and picked up on the ridiculous bullhorn megaphone straight away. "What is this thing?" he demanded; his voice heavily pregnant with suspicion.

My knees buckled under the pressure, and I had to grab at the rear-view mirror to stop myself from going down. Thankfully my mouth stepped in and took over. "It's a supplementary air intake valve control for the turbocharging fuel injection system thingy. It's very efficient, saves me a fortune in fuel. You should think about getting one for your car."

"No. It's too big. And it looks stupid." The customs official stamped my gate pass and waved me through. "You can proceed."

I drove through the border gates and into Zimbabwe with mixed feelings. I'd been gone just two months, but already I was looking at the potholes and littered verges with the eyes of a pampered foreigner. But the biggest thing that jumped out at me on the five-hundred kilometre drive through to Harare, apart from the suicidal donkeys, were the unproductive farms. A month ago, the empty farms had been the norm, but after a month in South Africa, they now jarred my senses. Where there should have been tractors swarming, busy, getting the lands ready for the season ahead, there was nothing, just empty lands, forlorn and unused. More commercial agricultural happened in the thirty kilometre stretch between White River and Nelspruit than in the five hundred kilometres between Beitbridge and Harare. It was criminal and stupid. And I was glad I wasn't caught up in it anymore. Apart from the big part of me, which was sad.

The first thing I did when I got into Harare was drop off the ridiculous bull horn megaphone before I impaled someone with it in traffic. Eddie Cross was thrilled and thanked me profusely. As always, Eddie's beer glass was one and a half times full, and he was bullish about the future. He told me the MDC was looking good for the 2005 elections. Preparations were coming along nicely; the MDC electoral team had identified the gaps in the system that had allowed the last elections to be rigged and were formulating a plan to shut them down. For sure an MDC government was on the cards. Eddie told me not to get too settled in South Africa, it wouldn't be long before I could come home. From your lips to God's ears, I told him and drove out to Running Dog with a smidgen of hope in my heart.

There were more mixed feelings when I drove onto Running Dog for the first time in two months. I was both hugely happy and hugely sad. The workers in the fields burst into song and loud ululation as soon as they saw the Land Rover driving in. Alerted by the noise, Brian and Raphael ran out of the grading shed with enormous grins on their faces. Straight away, my eyes teared up. Damn, but I loved these people. But I was also saddened by the signs of disrepair that I saw everywhere and angered. The light fittings in the fields, the plastic on the greenhouses, even the sign at the gate, it all looked beyond tatty and in need of some repair or replacement. Even the crops looked to be suffering, dwarfed in places by runaway flowering weeds, stunted in others by blocked irrigation drippers. In the recent past, that sort of stuff would have sent me off into an absolute rage. But I forced a lid on my anger. Staff morale on the farm was obviously at an all-time low and now wasn't the time to rant and rave. I had to make allowance for the Zim factor. Alas.

Brian was like a kid at the Christmas tree as we unpacked the contraband. Now he could get busy farming he told me. Raphael had more pressing matters on his mind. He and a few of the other main MDC supporters pulled me to one side for a political update. Raphael's version of events was at odds with the Eddie Cross version. On the ground in Zvimba, the MDC had lost huge ground. Running Dog was now an isolated island in a ZANU sea. Raphael said he could no longer enjoy the bottle store on the corner at night for fear of being beaten, or worse. Raphael foregoing the bottle store was like the Pope giving up on Sunday mass. The workers only ever left the farm in groups of four or more. But their spirit remained firmly undented. Clever told me proudly that he'd been elevated to MDC Security Officer for Zvimba South. Did I want to see his Party ID? When I told him sure, he rooted deep down into his underwear for what seemed like a good few minutes before pulling out a laminated and very official-looking identification card, complete with a scowling head and shoulders photograph. I was impressed. Despite the Zvimba Fear Factor, Clever had courage enough to walk around with a piece of plastic in his groin that would get him killed if found. And if the MDC were this organised countrywide, and this brave, maybe, just maybe.

Because the man with the gun who shot Terry Ford still lived just down the road, I cut my first visit home short after a whirlwind walk around the farm. I caught up with as many friends as possible. Most were in the process of leaving for pastures greener. The few that had made the decision to stay were calling themselves the Romanians, a play on the word remain. I was in both camps, but for sure, my heart was Romanian.

But my overriding memory from that first visit back to Zimbabwe was of the Anglican Archbishop in a field with children.

I spent my last night with friend Tony who'd once been threatened with the loss of his ears for driving my car. Tony grew roses, paprika, vegetables and sheep on a hundred-hectare farm in the district. It was good to catch up over a few beers. Tony told me about his new neighbour, the Anglican Archbishop no less, who'd recently stolen the massively productive and iconic St Marnock's farm. The Archbishop was thrilled with his new thousand-hectare farm which came complete with towering grain silos and impressive standing crops of maize and soya beans to fill them. The Archbishop's new farm even had a fully functional primary school on it. Apparently, he was less than happy when he found out that the school didn't pay him any rentals and operated free and gratis as a service to the community. How was a poor and simple farmer supposed to flourish if he had a bunch of free bloody loaders leeching off him, the Archbishop had fumed. And so he came up with a novel method of tithing the school kids who benefitted from his kindness and largesse with an hour a day of hard labour, to be spent weeding the Archbishop's maize and soya crops.

The next morning, I snuck down to Tony's boundary fence to film the Archbishop supervising the two hundred school kids as they weeded the bountiful lands that God and Mugabe had given him. Some of the kids were as young as five or six and were dwarfed by the badzas they wielded. The Archbishop wore his finest work clothes, a silk purple shirt with a white priest's collar, as he bossed up the children, exhorting them to work harder in their hour of labour before school. It was an absolutely disgusting display of petty power and greed. As I filmed, I was struck with the thought that God wasn't paying too much attention to his Zimbabwean flock these dark days. Alas. And more unfortunately, my efforts to film the Archbishop while farming came to nought. I should have used a better camera. The images I'd captured were too small and too grainy to be made out.

I arrived back on Summer Hill just in time for Daniel's birthday. He was turning thirteen. It was a milestone year, so we decided to do something special to celebrate. I told him we'd take him to Pretoria to watch the All Blacks versus the Springboks live at Loftus Versveld. Dan was thrilled. He was a huge Jonah Lomu fan and couldn't wait to see his hero in action. Veronica was less than thrilled at the prospect, but I told her tough luck for having a younger brother.

Loftus Versveld, the citadel of Afrikaner rugby, was pumping when we got there. It was a huge, forbidding stadium that sat fifty-five thousand plus. And it looked like every last seat had been sold. From what we could see, mostly to Springbok supporters. We stopped at one of the many roadside stalls to stock up on All Black regalia for the four of us. We bought black jerseys, black scarves and black beanies. Dan and Vee had white ferns on a black background painted on their faces. While the paint dried on his face, Dan eyed the sea of green around us nervously.

"Will there be other All Black supporters Dad, or just us?" Dan asked with a tinge of worry in his voice.

"Of course, yes," I said. "There will be loads of us wearing black inside."

Our seats were on the top tier, in line with the halfway line. They were great seats. I looked around for other friendly forces and spotted another group of at least two hundred All Black supporters and pointed them out to Dan. Unfortunately, they were on the far side of the massive stadium. On our side, it looked to be just us along with twenty-five thousand Springbok supporters, all wearing the green and gold. We hunkered down in our seats as low as we could. The barrage of abuse started in the celebrations that followed the first well-worked Springbok try. A half-empty plastic beer cup crashed into Jenny's back, showering us all with beer. Jenny leapt to her feet in anger and spun around, in search of the culprit. And straight away another dozen missiles rained down on us.

What followed was the longest game of rugby I've ever sat through. The Springboks played out of their socks to wallop the All Blacks 40 points to 24. Beer flowed mightily, ditto the abuse that rained down upon us. Jonah Lomu didn't score a bucket load of tries, and Dan got more and more miserable. At half time he turned to me asked me if maybe we should be Springbok supporters instead. I told him no ways, the All Blacks were our team, and we had to stand by them. The abuse got worse in the second half as the effects of the beer kicked in. An elderly lady, well oiled, bent over right into Daniel's face and screamed abuse at him in Afrikaans, non-stop for about thirty seconds. The veins on her neck were sticking out, flecks of spittle flew everywhere; the woman was clearly demented. I told her to leave Dan alone and told her that it was his birthday. She told me to fuck off. When they picked up on my local accent, the idiots behind me were even more incensed that we weren't supporting the Springboks. "Why are you supporting these fucking foreigners?" one of them demanded of me.

"I'm not a South African," I told him. "I'm a Zimbabwean. And what rugby team we support is of no concern to you. I'm a Zimbabwean farmer. And I've got bigger problems in my life than worrying about whether you approve of my choices." I threw the bit in about being a Zimbabwean farmer hoping for some empathy. No such luck. Not long after, one of the idiots stubbed his cigarette out on Jenny's back. She jumped up in pain, which got the whole row of idiots laughing. I stood up to tell them all to fuck off, but they were all big like mountains, so instead, I begged them to please leave us alone. It sort of worked. And I think maybe they realised that stubbing cigarettes out on women crossed the line of acceptable behaviour, even by Loftus Versveld standards.

The end of the game could not have come sooner. As we filed out of the stadium, a lady came up to us to apologise for the behaviour of her countrymen. She told us she'd watched the Springboks play in Auckland earlier in the year and the New Zealanders in the stadium had gone out of their way to make her feel welcome. It was a nice gesture on her part and repaired some of the damage done.

A few days later I answered the phone at Summerhill. It was the first incoming call I'd received. A man with a harsh guttural accent spoke. "Is that de Jong?" he asked.

"Yes. How can I help?"

"I'm phoning to give you some advice. You shouldn't have moved a kaffir into your cottage. So, I'm phoning you now to tell you to move him out of the house. And do not to let your kaffir walk on the road. Your kaffir must walk along the river with the other kaffirs."

I was shocked to my core. "Who is this?"

The man ignored my question. "And I'm also telling you don't wear your All Black shirt around town. Otherwise, there will be trouble." And then he hung up. The phone call made me feel drained, sad and weary, just like Burt Reynolds must have felt in Deliverance.

My cell phone rang not long after. I braced myself for another crank call, but it was Eddie Cross. I greeted him warmly. "Hold on the phone Eric, I've got someone here who wants a word with you." I recognised the voice straight away. "Hallo Eric. This is Morgan Tsvangirai speaking. I am phoning you to thank you for the splendid megaphone that you bought me. It is wonderful."

"Only a pleasure, Mr Tsvangirai, only a pleasure."

I walked around the rest of the day with the hugest smile on my heart. Morgan Tsvangirai was a busy man. For him to take the time out to thank me personally meant the world. I so badly wanted to go home.

Chapter Thirty-Seven

I knew that we'd jumped from the pan into the fire the night the
helicopter came to Summer Hill Farm. It was just after half-past six, we
were in the lounge watching television when the house filled with the loud
thump, thump noise of rotors. It sounded like something out of a Vietnam
war-movie soundtrack. The noise passed right over the house, very low
and very loud. Dan looked up into the rafters of the roof and asked in
wonderment "What's that noise, Dad?"

"Sounds like a helicopter."

As I spoke, the helicopter came into view, a dark shape against the
night sky, framed by the lounge window that looked out over the flower
field below the house. The four of us rushed to the window and plastered
our faces up against the glass. As the helicopter moved out across the
flower fields, an impossibly bright thick beam of light suddenly stabbed
out from the belly of the helicopter and pierced the dark. The helicopter
took up a station above the middle of the field and went into hover mode,
anchored to the ground by the broad probing searchlight beam.

"What's it doing, Dad?" Veronica asked. She had to shout to make
herself heard over the noise from the helicopter.

"I dunno. Having a good look at my flowers it looks like."

"But who are they?"

"I'm guessing some rich farmer with a helicopter who maybe heard that
we've started growing flowers and he wants to have a look."

"That's a bit rude," Jenny said.

"Very. Why don't we all go and wave at him?" The four of us stepped
out on the veranda and started waving up at the helicopter. The helicopter
shifted position slightly and carried on probing the shadows below with
the searchlight. Whoever was in the helicopter was obviously looking for
something. Or someone.

"Maybe it's not a farmer?" Suddenly, I didn't feel so safe standing out on
the veranda. Maybe it wasn't a farmer up in the helicopter. I pulled Jenny
and the kids back into the house and locked the glass door.

"Then who, Dad? Who do you think it is?" Dan asked, breathless with
excitement.

"I dunno. Maybe the police."

"I knew, I knew it. Just like in the movies." Dan rushed to the window
excitedly.

I pulled him back away from glass and hurriedly drew the curtains.

"But I want to watch, Dad."

"Well, you can't. If it is the police and they are looking for someone, then I'm guessing he's not a nice guy."

"What, like a robber? Or a murderer?"

"Shut up Daniel and watch television."

After ten minutes or so, the helicopter left. But instead of feeling relieved, I felt stressed and vulnerable.

We heard the next morning that a farmer four farms away had been murdered. The helicopter had been part of the police response team that had tracked the gang responsible into our flower field. They never caught them. Even worse than the knowledge that they were still out there was the fact that the incident only warranted a few column inches in the national newspaper. Life on South African farms was cheap.

The next evening, Jenny, Veronica, Dan and I were returning from a walk through the avocado orchards when we bumped into three black men in the farm workshops. It was dark, and they were carrying a torch. I shat myself. Presented with the fight or flight options, I went with the latter. "Run, run, run!!" I screamed to Jenny and the children behind me. Intent on following my own advice, I leapt up and did a mid-air one-eighty but landed heavily and badly on a piece of three-inch angle iron. The edge of the angle iron went deep into the soft bit below my ankle, down to the bone and I collapsed in a whimpering heap. One of the black intruders walked across and loomed over me large, pinning me to the floor with the beam of his torch. In pain and still firmly in flight mode, I used the muscles in my back to reverse away frantically, with both arms held above me to ward off his blows. Which didn't come. "What are you doing here? What do you want?" I asked, my voice frantic with fear and pain.

"I've come to fix the tractor" the intruder replied.

"Huh?"

"I'm fixing the link on the tractor, Boss. So I can be ploughing the field straight away tomorrow like you told me, Boss."

"Jesus, Shadreck, it's you." Relief flooded through me as I recognised the man. I'd just taken Shadreck on as a tractor driver a few days earlier. He was a huge, strong man. I'd hired him only because he could speak English and because he knew how to drive the tractor. But as he loomed above, it suddenly struck me that I knew absolutely nothing about the man. I didn't know him from a bar of soap. He could be a sociopathic murderer for all I knew.

"Yes, it is me," Shadreck spoke in a deep voice, big like him.

"Shit, you gave me a fright, man. Don't do that again."

"What, Boss?"

"Don't come up here at night, after work. And get that bloody torch out of my eyes."

"Yes, Boss." I thought I could hear amusement in his voice.

I started phoning around for security fence quotes the next morning, straight after I got anti-tetanus jabs and the gash in my ankle sewn up. I lined up three companies to ask for quotes, two were large name-brand fencing companies with national footprints and the third a small local fencing company. The small guys were called Robson Fencers and according to the punch line in their ad, their erections lasted longer.

The first national fencing company was super-efficient, and I had their quote by lunchtime. The quote was an arm and a leg expensive but impressive with three pages of detailed inputs. To compare apples and apples, I asked the small local guy, Patrick Robson, to base his quote on the same list of inputs. Patrick bluntly told me no. I was confused. What do you mean, no? He told me he couldn't quote for a fence based on the list of inputs I'd given him because he didn't erect bullshit fences. Everything in the big company quote that really mattered was undersized, and all the nonsense bullshit frills that counted for nothing were overstated. The end result would be I'd end up with a bullshit fence that kept nothing out. I asked Patrick what his fence would cost. He couldn't tell me there and then but said I'd get a better fence from him for way less. I liked the guy. I asked him to start on the fence straight away. He got busy the next morning.

The fence went up quickly. It was strong, straight and tall, with multiple strands of electrical wire spaced just eight inches apart that pulsed with current. The electrical strands were placed on the inside of the fence. Harder for intruders to interfere with, but easier for bulldogs on the inside to get zapped. Within the first five minutes of switching the hidey-hole on, Waddle christened it with her nose. I heard the vicious crack of the shock from inside the house. Neighbours kilometres away heard Waddle's subsequent squeals and yelps. The energiser that Patrick had put on the fence was oversized, big enough for a fence kilometres long. The shock it put out would make your eyes water and your hair curl. On the second day, a four-foot grass snake foolishly tried to slither up the fence and got fried stone dead. My fence was an absolute eyesore, and I loved it. It was stronger, taller and more vicious than any of my neighbour's fences. I lay in my bed at night, listening to the fence shorting and slept easier for it.

The next morning Daniel asked, "But what about a fence for around Nana and Poppa's cottage?" I couldn't answer him. Even with Patrick's generous discounts and extended terms, there was no way I could afford to fence off the cottages. The fact that I couldn't answer Dan's question really rankled me.

Crime in South Africa is in your face, all-day, every-day, especially on the farms. Only after we moved there, we found out that South Africa's murder rate was the highest in the world, outside of a war zone. I'm guessing it was higher than some war zones. It was especially bad on the farms. On the farms, people didn't just get murdered, they got tortured first with, with red hot irons and boiling water. And women got raped. Always, the women got raped.

We discovered our favourite restaurant in the world, just twenty kilometres from Summer Hill, in a disused, renovated railway siding on a mountain in the middle of nowhere on the way to a little town called Sabi. The restaurant called the Art Café was tiny, no more than twenty seats, run by the owner and his wife. Lunches in front of the roaring fire would drag out for hours, with too much food and too many Irish coffees. It was absolutely delightful and charming, and we loved it. But not for long. The owner and his wife were found one Monday morning, beaten and shot dead. I went and stuck flowers outside their restaurant. Which never re-opened.

I got mugged, delivering flowers in Nelspruit one day. Six men grabbed me, shoved me and pushed me around on a busy street, busy hands searching my pockets to see what I had. Then they found my cell phone, one of those ridiculously large Nokias with the flip-up screen and the qwerty keyboard. I clung on to it for my life. And then the knives came out. I scrambled in reverse up into the back of the Land Rover, kicking and fighting, but mostly screaming like a girl, at the top of my voice for help. And all the while, fifty people stood and watched, some as close as two metres away. And they did nothing. They didn't even walk away. They just stood and watched, silent and absolutely uncaring, because I was white. In the end, an old Afrikaans lady came out on to the street, told my attackers to fuck off because she'd called the police. I waited twenty minutes, but the police never came.

It was a small, petty crime. Shit like that happens the world over, every day. I'd been mugged before in Harare. But the reaction of the other people on the streets in Harare was the difference. You get mugged in Harare and you shout mbava, mbava a.k.a. thief, thief and the people around drop what they're doing, and they come running, from everywhere, to help catch the miscreants, and to beat them. When I got mugged in Harare, in the end, it actually turned out to be a heart-warming and uplifting experience. In Nelspruit, not so much. The only thing that I could read into the silence and non-reaction from the crowd who watched my attack was tacit approval. Maybe if I were black, maybe the reaction from the crowds watching would have been different. I don't know.

Rich Becks, a fellow Zimbabwean farmer bought a smallholding just outside Nelspruit next to the main Johannesburg highway. Rich and Lucy lived in a tiny cottage with their five-year-old son Rhys. The Crocodile River flowed along the bottom of their garden and hippos would sometimes come out at night to graze their lawn. It was lovely. In the eighteen months Rich and Lucy owned their smallholding, they got broken into eighteen times. The last thieves to break in left with nothing, mostly because there was nothing left to steal.

It didn't take long for violent crime to find us on Summer Hill. A gang arrived in the middle of the night, intent on stealing anything and everything. We had a young family staying with us in one of the cottages at the time. Their twelve-year-old son walked in on the thieves while they were busy disconnecting the television. Nine-millimetre pistols came out and started firing, blasting holes in the walls and in the roof but thankfully not into the boy. The thieves fled into the night to try their luck elsewhere.

I went into White River the very next day and bought a gun, the biggest I could find, a massive .375 magnum revolver. But before I could collect the weapon, first I had to pass an arms proficiency test. There was an examination testing centre in Nelspruit, next to an ever-busy gun-shop, where they trained you for a few hundred rand. I sat the tough, multiple guess exam in a crowded room with fifty others. We all got all one hundred questions right. Mostly because our examiner gave us all the answers, one by one. "The answer to Question one is A. Question two, also A," he told us. "But Question three is a tough one, the answer is E, all of the above." And so on and so on. In the end, we were all presented with certificates of firearm competency. At the time, I guessed that some of my fellow students would go out to earn livings with their guns. Alas.

Chapter Thirty-Eight

Roy Bennett is one of my heroes. A man of huge principles, he is strong, forthright and brave beyond belief. But he is also punchy and quick to anger.

When I was eleven, I joined the same boxing club as Roy. I wanted to learn how to defend myself. And I'd also just seen a movie about Rocky Marciano who looked like he had a pretty good life, courtesy of his fists. Roy was already a Rhodesian champion when I started boxing. Along with all the other younger kids at the club, I was in awe of his prowess in the ring. I quickly elevated him to hero status. I never spoke a word to Roy back then, in case I said something stupid, and he'd box me. Whenever he walked towards me, I was quick to give him all the room in the world. Mine was a short boxing career. I retired undefeated after just my second bout because my parents moved to Malawi and packed me off to boarding school.

Fast forward thirty years and I met Roy Bennett again, this time as a reluctant politician. Left to his own devices, I don't believe Roy would ever have left his beloved Charleswood farm. He got dragged into national politics because it was the right thing to do because evil flourishes when good men do nothing. His black constituents in Chimanimani called Roy 'Pachedu' which means together or one of us in Shona. They approached him and asked him to stand in the 2000 elections. Like me, all of them would have walked over broken glass for Roy. Roy won by a landslide and took up his seat as the Member of Parliament for Chimanimani.

And then the political persecution started. Vicious and unrelenting, it was directed at Roy, his family, his friends and his workers. Roy was arrested twice and assaulted three times. Two of Roy's workers were murdered, another shot and wounded. His female workers were raped. State agents killed and stole hundreds of Roy's cattle and over a hundred tons of coffee. Things came to a head when Roy's wife Heather suffered a miscarriage while she was forcibly evicted from their home by ZANU PF supporters. Throughout the attacks, Mugabe lauded the efforts of the ZANU PF supporters and publicly encouraged them to continue.

Roy looked to the courts for protection time and again. In the end, no fewer than six court orders were granted in his favour. But they counted for nothing. The Bennett's home was looted and vandalised. Eventually Roy and Heather moved to Harare where they leased another farm. The persecution followed them, and Roy and Heather got kicked out of their rented home too. All of this happened while Roy was an elected member of parliament. Throughout, Roy remained unbent, undaunted and steadfast. He carried on standing for what he knew to be right.

But then on the 18th of May 2004, during a rambling parliamentary debate on stock theft, the Minister of Justice Patrick Chinamasa singled Roy out on the backbenches and told him in Shona that his father was a thief and a murderer, ditto his grandfather, ditto all his other ancestors who stayed behind in England in 1890. (All this was fairly rich, coming from a man who'd just kicked Richard and Cally Yates and their young children out of their home on their Headlands farm.) I have already mentioned Roy is quick to anger. And he is all about family. You call his father a thief, and you will end up on your arse, double quick. Which is exactly where Chinamasa ended up. Ditto Didymus Mutasa, another ZANU PF heavyweight who tried to get a cheap shot in while Roy was busy with Chinamasa. And that was that. In two ticks it was over.

Parliamentary privilege exists in Zimbabwe. Members of parliament are immune from prosecution for things they do or say in parliament. But they went after Roy anyway. They formed a bullshit parliamentary committee, chaired by a ZANU PF Minister and made up mostly of ZANU PF MP's to investigate the assault incident. Roy admitted assaulting Chinamasa and Mutasa but raised the defence of provocation and self-defence. In further mitigation, Roy presented to the committee a detailed chronology of the more than three hundred attacks against him, committed by ZANU PF over the previous four years. The committee listened to Roy but heard nothing. They called just two witnesses, Chinamasa and Mutasa. In his testimony, Chinamasa, the incumbent Minister of Justice, dismissed the importance of the court orders that had been issued in favour of Bennett. After deliberating on the evidence presented for not very long, the committee found Roy guilty of causing a disturbance in parliament and sentenced him to fifteen months in prison, with hard labour. It was a complete bullshit sentence, unprecedented in Zimbabwean legal history and unprecedented in parliaments the world over.

Roy gave a final speech to parliament on the day he went to jail. "Everything I own has been taken. When I moved from Chimanimani and lived in Ruwa, the same thing happened. The army came, they beat the people and looted the homestead. They looted all the property from the farm. Two of my workers have been killed. Their perpetrators walk free. There has been no investigation. My female workers have been raped, and their homes burnt. What course of justice have I had? I have been to the courts. The courts granted me six court orders in my favour. Of which the Honourable Minister of Justice, sits in this house on top of these court orders and say Bennett will never set foot on his farm again when these court orders granted me permission to be back there.

Besides all this hatred, harassment and vitriol, have I ever taken the law into my own hands? I had approached the highest echelons of law to seek protection. I came to you, Mr Speaker, when the Chairman of your committee wanted to bring me to you and said please Mr Speaker, assist me, this what is happening. You were aware. What did you do Mr Speaker? What have I ever done to you or to anybody in this House?

I was in good books with the people of Zimbabwe, and I cannot allow your hatred to consume me. It is impossible. For those amongst you with whom we had friendship, I thank you for that friendship. To my colleagues who I shared with parliament, I have nothing but pride to have been able to serve the people of my country." Strong stuff indeed.

I was so pissed off with Roy's bullshit prison sentence. It was so unfair and so wrong on so many levels. I felt I had to do something to help, something to bring it attention of the world so that someone would step in and intervene. So, I built an ugly prison cell on Summer Hill farm out of scrap metal, just small enough to fit on the back of my farm pick-up. Every weekend, I loaded up my prison cell and delivered it to the car park of a busy shopping centre, climbed inside to spend a day in the boiling sun collecting signatures on a petition for Roy Bennett's release. When I had one million signatures on my petition, I'd hand it over to the South African President, and he would be moved to intervene.

I attracted a steady flow of signatures to my petition. On the bars of my prison, I hung a printed chronology detailing Roy's persecution. People were interested and keen to sign up. The South African Lowveld sun above me was harsh. Just twenty minutes into my sentence, I started thinking I should have put a roof on top of my prison cell. The heat off the black tarmac below was as harsh. I was getting cooked like a lobster from top and bottom. Luckily, I'd brought a big bottle of water along. Which I downed in one go. Fifty signatures down, just nine hundred and ninety-nine thousand and nine hundred and fifty and...alas. I couldn't do the sum. My brain was cooked. It didn't help that the litre bottle of water had gone straight to my bladder. I should have included a urinal in my cell design. I gritted my teeth and wrapped my leg around my other leg. Immediately my signature hit rate fell off dramatically with the punters worried about contracting St Vitus's dance or worse. Luckily, I'd prepared for every eventuality, and I called upon half my strategic reserve of fellow inmates who were sitting in the car for relief. Before Daniel climbed into prison, he made me cross my heart and promise that his sentence would only be as long as my toilet break.

"Thanks, Dan. And maybe Mom can also spell me a bit and..."

Jenny put the boot into my suggestions straight away. "What? And cook red like a lobster like you. There's no way I'm going into prison. Not without shade."

Dan staged a prison break as soon as I got back from the loo, never to be seen again. And Jenny refused to serve her sentence in the first place, so I was stuck inside on solitary confinement. I collected almost a thousand signatures that day. Unfortunately, I had to censor a bunch of them out because of the bad language in the comment column. I couldn't be handing a petition over to the South African President describing him as a useless fucking kaffir, over and over. Alas. Racial intolerance was alive and living in South Africa's carparks and shopping malls.

I sentenced myself to more prison time the following weekend, but this time outside a shopping mall with shade trees dotted around the car park. I was lucky enough to find an empty parking space beneath the leafiest tree I could find. I luxuriated in the shade, for about the first thirty minutes. Then the sun moved, and I was back in the boiling sun. Curses.

On the sixth weekend of my prison sentence, for something different, I positioned my prison cell at a busy bus stop in the black part of White River. To date, I'd focussed on the big shopping malls which attracted mostly white shoppers. I was interested to see what the black reaction would be to Roy's plight. I was hugely moved by the response I got. The blacks who stopped to find out what I was about were measured in their response, they read the paperwork carefully before signing the petition. The one supermarket worker was especially guarded. He spent a good ten minutes reading the Roy chronology from cover to cover. Before signing the petition, he quizzed me. Did I know Roy personally? Had Roy committed any other crimes not mentioned? Three hours later, during his tea break, the same guy brought along a dozen of his workmates to also sign.

Before my seventh weekend rolled around, I decided to apply for an early release from prison. I couldn't take the sun anymore. Some of my blisters had blisters. I had to up the ante. At the rate I was collecting signatures at, Roy would be free long before I got anywhere near my million signatures. When younger, Roy had played polocrosse for Zimbabwe, often against South Africa and was remembered fondly. I tracked down the head of the South African Polocrosse Association and told him about my prison cell and what I was trying to achieve. I asked him if he could get the South African polocrosse fraternity to rally behind Roy and show their solidarity by taking delivery of the prison cell for a bit, maybe move it around from tournament to tournament, collecting signatures and raising Roy's profile, just until my sunburn healed. I could almost hear the man's eyeballs rolling as he went through the motions of listening to my mad-hatter scheme. He told me he'd get back to me, real soon but I knew he wouldn't. Alas.

But I had a fall-back plan that was almost as good. I phoned the Confederation of South African Trade Unions and asked to speak to their General Secretary. I'd long regarded COSATU as key to getting the South African President to put pressure on Mugabe. Illegal Zimbabweans flooding into South Africa in their hundreds of thousands were taking away South

African jobs from South African workers. If I could get COSATU on board with my prison cell idea, if they'd take ownership of it for a bit, just until my sunburn healed, then Mbeki would have to intervene, and Roy would be released. After explaining myself to half a dozen people, eventually, I was put through to Patrick Craven. He was COSATU's national spokesman and a well-known figure on national television and radio. Not only was Craven an avowed communist, he was also English, and he was especially hated by Afrikaner conservatives who had him pegged him up alongside the anti-Christ. Over the phone, Craven sounded nice, with a plummy concise accent. He came across as a kindred spirit, someone who also liked to tilt at windmills. Craven got my hopes up.

I told him about Roy's imprisonment and about my prison cell. I wanted to send the prison cell to stand-outside the Government Union Buildings in Pretoria. Would Mr Craven consent to being locked up in it, to show his solidarity for Roy and for the people of Zimbabwe? Patrick Craven said he was following Roy's story closely. He said Roy's plight was close to his heart, as was the big picture Zimbabwean saga. He really felt for Roy and for the people of Zimbabwe. But he couldn't get into my prison cell. COSATU could not be seen to be taking sides. He told me it was complicated because of politics and because the ANC partnered COSATU in a tripartite alliance and blah blah blah. I stopped listening. In my book Craven was craven. I thanked him for his time and asked him for his direct line for future use, so I wouldn't have to waste my airtime with the COSATU switchboard. He gave it to me.

I used Craven's phone number straight away, on a flyer aimed at any and all Zimbabweans in South Africa looking for work. My flyer said that Patrick Craven was in a position to assist with work permits. Pass his phone number on, my flyer said. I printed one thousand copies and dished them out. I hope Craven's phone rang off the hook. Roy's prison cell project fizzled out a few weeks later from a general lack of interest. Alas.

As it happened, Roy ended up spending twelve months in prison. He got three months off for good behaviour. Roy came out of prison unbroken, with his hair long and his paunch gone, leaner, stronger and more resolute than ever.

Patrick Craven's attitude summed up South Africa's attitude to the Zimbabwean crisis playing out next door. Sympathetic, but not to a point where they would do anything to help. Zimbabwe wasn't South Africa's problem. It was for Zimbabweans to fix. Which was a fair comment I suppose. But it pissed me off. But it also galvanised me. I was a Zimbabwean. I didn't ever want to become a South African. I wanted to go home. So, I became an activist. I joined Sokwanele.

Sokwanele was a shadowy, underground Zimbabwean pressure-movement, prodemocracy and anti-ZANU PF. Their website and regular

IN WHICH ROY BENNETT GOES TO JAIL AND BORAT IS BORN

blogs challenged and confronted the ZANU government. The problem with shadowy, underground movements is that they are a bugger to contact and even harder to join, not surprising given the number of CIO informers out there lurking in the shadows. But I had a friend who I was sure might be a member. The last time I met him to drink beer and talk shit, he'd let something about Sokwanele slip after beer number six. I sent him an e-mail telling him I wanted to join. Obviously back in sober cagey mode, my friend wrote back and told me he didn't know what I was talking about. But he'd heard somewhere that a certain swallowsoaring@hushmail.com might possibly be able to assist me with my enquiries. But he told me I would need a Hushmail address first, before communicating with Swallow Soaring. Any and all open and non-encrypted e-mails with subject matter Sokwanele would be deleted.

I had no idea what a Hushmail address was, let alone how one would go about getting one. Thankfully Google did. Hushmail is a Canadian company offering secure, encrypted e-mail services and storage. Feeling very James Bond-like, I went online to Hushmail but stuttered when I got to the part where you had to register your e-mail address. For the life of I couldn't get swallows soaring out of my head. Think, think, think I told myself, but not about swallows. I'm guessing Borat must be diametrically opposed to swallows because that's the name I eventually came up with. And so borat@hushmail.com was born.

Borat, the activist, was welcomed into Sokwanele by Swallow Soaring, Dragon, Brunette, Amai, Hemingway, Oscar Golf and the other members of the group. There were about fifteen of them. First up, they gave me the rules of the group. No real names, no contact outside of Hushmail, and no promoting violence or partisan politics. The last bits took me by surprise. Dictators don't get voted out I told them; they get kicked out. And by its very nature, kicking would suggest a certain amount of violence. And furthermore, I pointed out, surely the easiest way to pull a dictator down, was to unite behind the main opposition and push like hell. No violence and no partisan politics, I was told. Donor's rules. And if you don't like them, don't join. I joined. No violence, no partisan politics, I told them with hand on heart and all my fingers and toes crossed.

Jenny walked in on me during a Hushmail session. Straight away my face burnt bright guilty red. I stood up and hurriedly slammed the screen down on my laptop, but not before she got a good look. "What's Hushmail?" Jenny asked me.

"It's just a search engine. I'd better go down to look at the flowers."

"What were you searching for on the computer?"

I lied through my teeth like a busted porn addict. "Nothing. Just checking out the news. And the cricket scores."

"Just as long as you're not doing politics, Eric. You promised me you'd give it up."

A footnote to this chapter. Apologies if my use of tenses are muddled when talking about Roy Bennett. I started writing this chapter early on a Thursday morning. Roy and Heather Bennett were killed later that same day, in a helicopter in New Mexico. It's very hard to attend to the correct use of grammar when you are crying on your keyboard. Alas.

IN WHICH ROY BENNETT GOES TO JAIL AND BORAT IS BORN

Chapter Thirty-Nine

My Sokwanele activist career got off an inauspicious start. I racked my brains. What could I do in South Africa to promote democracy in Zimbabwe and confront ZANU PF? I am embarrassed to say the first blow I struck for democracy on foreign soil came in the form of a piece of dog shit picked up off my lawn and wrapped up in gift paper and delivered in the guise of a Get Well present to a senior ZANU PF member recuperating in a private hospital in Johannesburg. I read about him in one of local papers. I picked out a Get Well Soon card with deep and meaningful words inside, crossed them out and scribbled the words 'I Hope You Die.' Wearing a cap pulled low over my face in case of cameras, I dropped the card and the dog shit gift off at the hospital reception counter. It was a crassly stupid and juvenile gesture that wouldn't bring about political change anytime soon but made me feel good, nonetheless.

While I was plotting with dog shit, my family were busy making White River home. Jenny was loving South Africa, mostly because of the no-politics rule that she thought I was adhering to. Alas. And even though she's not materialistic, she was also quite liking a supermarket full of choices. The toilet paper section was her best. Back home in Zimbabwe, loo paper choices were limited. Single-ply or twin ply, available in either white newsprint or white newsprint, both rough like sandpaper. In our South African supermarket, the toilet roll section went on forever, from single-ply right up to four-ply, embossed or plain and in a vast array of soft and soothing hues. Jenny zeroed in on a brand with a picture of Labrador puppies on the packaging. I failed to see the connection between seeing-eye puppies and bum wiping. And I winced at the price. "Just this once, Eric, we're going to spoil ourselves," she said.

After four long years at university, Gary came home to Summer Hill Farm River with a Bachelor of Arts degree and not too many ideas as to how to use it to make a living. He'd majored in photography. He told us he was thinking about maybe getting a job in advertising. As is my wont, I butted in. I think I might have been a sheepdog in a previous life. I have an overwhelming urge to herd the nearest and dearest in my flock to where I think they should go. I told Gary that if he went the ad agency route, all he'd do for twenty years is peanut butter adverts and toothpaste adverts and it would be a waste of his God-given talents. 'You love the bush, so why not become a wildlife artist rather?" I said.

"OK, I'll give it a go," he replied.

But first, he had to finish building a house to live in. Because I'd installed a manager in the second cottage, Gary had taken up residence behind the couch in the second lounge. He turned my bookshelf into a wardrobe and filed his underwear next to Terry Pratchett. I was flirting with being organised and had filed my books alphabetically by the name of the author. Jenny and I found a company that made wooden homes with a quality finish and had ordered a four-roomed unit for Gary. Left for Gary to do was to site it and install the plumbing and the electrics. He walked the bottom half of the farm and chose a site just below the avocado orchard, overlooking the dam. Gary would be able to sit on his veranda and paint, inspired by a view that stretched away forever. Don't you think you should move it back into the trees, Jenny asked. Your cottage has got a tin roof, and it will get hot inside under the full sun. I hushed her. Let Gary decide where his house is going to be.

Gary's little house on the hill went up in no time at all. Unlike me, Gary could spell DIY, and he did a great job installing the electrics and the plumbing double quick. Gary moved out of the lounge and into his new house. Armed with bottles of champagne, we crowded into Gary's little lounge for the house-warming celebrations. Given an ambient indoor temperature of plus forty degrees, the champagne lasted just minutes, and we had to move the festivities out on the tiny veranda to avoid heat exhaustion.

"Quite warm in there," said Gary.

"I told you so," said Jenny.

"It will be nice in winter," said I.

Gary's veranda was a productive studio, and it wasn't long before his little house on the hill was full to overflowing with finished canvases. Some of them were beautiful. Gary's art really had come on in his four years at University.

"Now I've got to try and sell them," Gary said with not a lot of confidence.

"Relax. With stuff this good, selling it will be too easy."

There was an artists' exhibition in Kaapse Hoop, a quaint turn-of-the-century mining town come tourist attraction perched on top of a mountain outside Nelspruit. I helped Gary load up his Mazda 323 with a table, deckchair and all the paintings he could fit inside and waved him off. He looked as happy and carefree as Vincent van Gogh just after he cut his ear off. He looked even more miserable when he drove back on to Summer Hill at the end of a long day, having sold not a single painting. There'd been more wannabe wildlife artists at the exhibition than members of the buying public he told us. And some of the work on show was really top-drawer stuff. And that didn't sell either. Gary was really down. "Relax," I told him, "you've just got to stick at it. Your work is good, and people will buy it. You just have to put it out there where people can see it." Gary put on a brave

OF DOG SHIT, NUDES AND DAN GETTING FRECKLES

face and trudged off back to his easel. I worried about his ears. I reckon Vincent might have done the damage to his ear after a failed art exhibition.

The next day Gary showed us a finished painting that was easily his best piece of work that I'd seen. It was a painting of a naked woman. He'd got her just right. Her breasts were full, and her tummy slightly rounded. She was both suggestive and seductive and shy and coy, all at the same time. I could have stared at her for hours, but that would have been weird, and Jenny would've hit me on the head. The next day Gary did another nude, just as good. And another, the day after. Gary had found his niche.

Along with some of his wildlife stuff, Gary took his bevvy of naked chicks into Nelspruit to an art gallery that he'd found. The art gallery owner liked them and put them up in his window. Where they very quickly attracted an audience of lewd old men, mostly wearing long raincoats. Gary and I watched one of his naked chicks' suitors fixating outside the gallery window. "None of them are going to buy any of them," Gary said miserably.

"They can't. Their wives would kill them. I think maybe Nelspruit is a bit too conservative."

"You think maybe I should put some clothes on my nudes?"

Veronica was loving South Africa. She was eighteen, she was pretty, and South Africa was wall-to-wall young men, all fawning upon her and showering her with attention. Everywhere you looked, rather everywhere I looked, and there were young beefcakes, asking her out. It was my worst nightmare come true. I interrogated one of her young suitors who was following us around a funfair in Nelspruit like a lovesick puppy dog. He was a good-looking young man, maybe nineteen or twenty, with lots of muscles and a pronounced Afrikaans accent. He worked in a local restaurant as a waiter. I interrogated him. What did he want to do when he grew up? He wanted to be a waiter, he told me. Damn. A boyfriend with zero prospects. I should've moved to the back of beyond in Zambia.

I don't know if the waiter with muscles had anything to do with it, but Veronica decided that she wanted to become a hotel manager. I tried to talk her out of it. The hours were long, you got to work weekends when all your friends were enjoying; it was a crappy job, especially for women. "But you studied hotel management," she told me. I should have studied reverse psychology because the more I tried to talk her out of it, the more she dug in. "You thought me going into hotel management was a good idea when we lived in Zimbabwe," she told me.

"Back in Zimbabwe was different, we owned two hotels there," I told her.

"I don't see the difference," she told me. "I want to study hotel management."

I caved in with extreme reluctance. "I'll have a look if there are any hotel schools around here."

"There aren't," she told me." I want to study in Johannesburg." Crap. My worst nightmare just got worse.

I think I've mentioned Dan's persistence in a previous chapter. Well, it was undimmed and still hard at work. Dan was determined to fit in, despite the Stalker tag he'd been given at Penryn and despite being shunned by all and sundry. Small wonder, he'd been shunned. Dan's vitiligo had savaged his skin pigment, leaving him ninety percent albino. And without skin pigment, Dan was hugely prone to sunburn and was forced to wear long sleeves and long trousers to protect him from the hot Lowveld sun. Dan was prepared to hang his unpopularity on his vitiligo. And he'd been thrown a lifeline by his dermatologist. Since taking on Dan as a patient, the dermatologist had been doing his homework on vitiligo. He told us he was certain that sooner or later, the disease would burn out, and the attack on Dan's skin pigment would stop. The skin pigment already destroyed by the vitiligo could not repair itself, but he thought he'd come up with a way to kick start the re-pigmentation process. The skin doctor got excited and animated as he talked us through his theory, dumbing it down for us laymen to follow. At the base of every hair follicle was a tiny pigment cell. It was unlikely the vitiligo had picked up on those little buggers. If he could stimulate those pigment cells with an intense blitz of UVB to get them busy talking to their neighbours, he could bring Dan's pigment back, bit by bit, hair follicle cell by hair follicle cell. I nodded my head knowingly throughout but didn't have a clue what UVB was. It sounded like an offshoot of a British reggae band. He backed up and told us UVB was radiation in the ultraviolet spectrum that caused sunburn and skin ageing and skin cancer. Ordinarily, UVB was bad but controlled intense bursts should serve to stimulate skin pigmentation.

The skin doctor put his money where his mouth was, big lots of money, and imported a UVB machine at a huge cost. There was only one other machine in the whole of South Africa he told us proudly, and that was in a university hospital in Johannesburg.

While we waited not so patiently for the machine to arrive, we continued with the monthly tests to peg Dan's antibody levels, to see if the vitiligo was slowing down. Normal was an antibody count of six or less. Impossibly Dan's count had further ballooned out to an impossible ninety thousand. At which point it levelled out. Maybe that was the maximum output a body could produce. Or maybe the disease was burning out. And then the next month, Dan's count dropped back down to sixty thousand. By the time the UVB machine finally arrived, Dan's antibody count was down to just twenty thousand, and it was time to get busy stimulating the hair follicle pigment cells.

The UVB machine would not have looked out of place on a Star Trek movie set. It was a glass cylinder with a bench seat and a mess of overhead

OF DOG SHIT, NUDES AND DAN GETTING FRECKLES

light beams. "Tell Scotty to beam you up," I said to Daniel when he climbed up inside the tube for his first UVB treatment.

"Who's Scotty, Dad?"

"Not to worry, Dan, just some guy in a television program a long time ago."

Dan was wearing only a pair of swimming goggles and his underpants, and he wasn't happy. 'Why can't I take my underpants off? I also want to be brown again on my bum, Dad."

The treatment lasted just three minutes. Dan was disappointed when he looked down at his body and still only saw the shocking bright white.

"Why hasn't it worked, Dad?"

"The doctor said it's going to take time, Dan, lots of time. But it will work. We just need patience. And faith in your doctor."

Patience and blind faith were qualities Dan had in spades. We took him into Nelspruit to climb into the UVB machine three times a week. Each visit cost us more than we could afford because of a tall shortfall on our medical aid cover. The doctor played the machine's complicated control panel like a concert piano, tweaking and fine-tuning, flirting on the edge of a vicious sunburn that was just another minute in the UVB machine away. The results were a long time coming. After twelve treatments in four long weeks, the first brown freckle appeared on Dan's forearm. It was tiny but stood out a country mile against the shocking white background that was the rest of Dan. A week later, the freckle had company. And the following week, even more, mostly on his arms and on the back of his hands.

"I'm just going to look spotty, aren't I?" Dan asked his doctor with more than a hint of disappointment in his voice.

"At first, Daniel. But then your freckles will start joining in the middle. It looks like your vitiligo has slowed right down and isn't attacking your new pigment. I think we're going to win this one, Daniel. It will take time, but I think we're going to win. And next week, I want you to go and see a colleague of mine, a thyroid specialist. Vitiligo is an autoimmune disorder, and I think my colleague will be better placed to help us to get to the bottom of your problems."

On the forty-minute drive back to Summer Hill Farm, Jenny watched Dan admiring his freckles. "You know we're in the right place," she said to me.

"What do you mean?"

"South Africa. It's the right place for Dan. If we were still living in Zimbabwe, Dan wouldn't be getting fancy UVB treatments. He'd be stuck an albino."

Jenny was right. Nelspruit wasn't a big city, but it boasted more specialist doctors than were left in the whole of Zimbabwe. And they were young and cutting edge, unlike those who'd who stayed behind in

Zimbabwe to switch the lights off. While that made me feel slightly better about living in South Africa, it didn't stop me from wanting to move back to Zimbabwe.

Chapter Forty

There are few places on earth as horrible as Zimbabwe in the run-up to an election. The Fear Factor is palpable and ever-present. Mugabe plays the Fear Factor like a maestro a violin. Sometimes his music is loud and in your face and other times his music is quiet and in the background. Going into the 2005 elections with the western world watching, Mugabe mostly played background Fear Factor music. But the threat of violence has just as much impact as actual violence, especially when your memories of your door being kicked open in the middle of the night by ZANU PF thugs there to beat and whip you because you'd been seen at an MDC rally are still so vivid that you can feel the pain of each and every blow.

The story goes that they played extra special Fear Factor music for Morgan Tsvangirai while he was in Harare Central Prison on trumped-up treason charges courtesy of bullshit allegations made by an Israeli political prostitute. The Powers That Be fast-forwarded five executions in a single night, just to send Morgan a chilling message that opposition politics could be bad for one's health. Morgan ignored the music and remained steadfast and resolute, but many of his supporters not so much.

As an election campaign strategy, Fear Factor is excellent value for money and gives you a return on your investment year after year after year. Small wonder poor Zimbabweans countdown to elections with absolute dread. Famine loomed large over the run-up to the 2005 elections, making things even worse. Five years of carnage on commercial farms had taken its toll, and there was no maize meal on the shelves, and precious little would be coming in off the empty fields. Government retained an iron grip on food relief distribution and squeezed hard. To get relief maize in the rural areas, you had to produce your ZANU PF membership card. No card, no food. Putting up election posters became an offence, punishable by arrest and beating unless of course, you were putting up ZANU PF posters. With just five weeks to go to the elections, the government announced with not so quiet fanfare the arrival of a massive shipment of Chinese small arms and anti-riot gear and recalled all recently retired military onto active duty, just in case.

Small wonder Jenny was less than thrilled when I told her I wanted to go back to Zimbabwe to help the MDC with their election preparations. Jenny said she would come with me, to catch up with old friends she said, but mostly to make sure I didn't do anything stupid that would get me into trouble. It was Jenny's first trip back. I was hoping that her absence from Zimbabwe had made her heart grow fonder. But all Jenny saw after crossing the border were the potholes and the poverty, the hopelessness and the squalor.

Despite the big black clouds hanging low overhead, there was some hope within the MDC Election Support Team, albeit of the long shot variety. Hendrik brought me up to speed on some important electoral reforms to which Mugabe had conceded. To bring Zimbabwe into line with SADC norms, Zimbabweans would now cast their votes into transparent, translucent ballot boxes. And the votes would be counted at the polling stations as opposed to being humped back to a central counting station. And as soon as the count was finished the results would be posted outside the polling stations for all to see. Which meant no more of my anti-rigging kits. And instead of voting over two days, there would now only be a single day of voting. Which would make logistics so much easier; food for just one day and polling agents didn't have pack overnight kit. And the mobile polling stations that had proved impossible to monitor in 2000 and 2002 had been replaced with fixed polling stations. And best of all, Hendrik said I was going to love the MDC candidates I'd be working with, compared to the likes of Titus Nheya who I'd worked with back in 2000, may he rest in peace. The MDC had been in parliament for almost five years, and the cream had risen to the top.

But there were also lots of big buts. Hendrik is a realist and calls a spade a spade. The all-important Voter's Roll was bullshit he said, not worth the paper the government refused to print it on. The MDC was supposed to have access to the Voter's Roll so they could audit it but all their efforts to do so came to nought. Overall, the Voter's Roll had increased to 5.8 million registered voters, but bizarrely within the MDC's power base in the cities, the number of registered voters had dropped. With run-away urban migration, how was a drop in town-based voters possible? And constituency boundaries had been further gerrymandered or re-jigged in ZANU PF's favour, diluting the urban vote with big chunks of the rural vote. The rural areas were still owned by ZANU PF. They had the traditional leaders in their pockets, courtesy of the government salaries they now all received. But easily the biggest problem was voting would continue to be ward-based and in the rural areas, villagers were told by their chiefs and headmen which polling stations they had to vote at. And before casting their votes, villagers would be lined up in alphabetical order. The chiefs would be there for the count and would be able to track voting patterns back to individuals.

All of which meant we would come horribly second in the rural constituencies in ZANU's heartlands - the three Mashonalands and the massive Midlands and Masvingo provinces Hendrik said. Which left us with the two Matabelelands, Manicaland and the urban centres. But if you did the sums and if we were super organised in those provinces and won all the seats on offer, maybe, just maybe we could pull off an MDC win.

Great, I said. Which constituency was I going to be given?
Constituencies, Hendrik said, as in plural, and all of them in Mashonaland
West. The number of support volunteers was way down, less than half
and those remaining would have to shoulder more responsibility. Hendrik
wanted me to provide support for a new constituency called Manyame, a
constituency called Mhondoro and my old stomping ground Zvimba South.
My candidates were a sitting Member of Parliament Hilda Mafudze, a new
high-flyer called Shakespeare Maya and one Emillie Masimba.

With just a week to go to elections, all the campaigning had already
happened. Hendrik told me there were no rallies to organise and all that
was left to focus on was polling agent logistics and the Parallel Vote Count.
Our six trained polling agents per polling station would track the number
of voters into the station, how many were turned away, spoiled papers, the
number of assisted voters and obviously the end count. It would be my
job to get the PVC numbers from polling agents at each station into MDC
Election HQ. From there, the information would be sent out for the world
to see. It would all be too easy, provided it didn't go wrong.

Hendrik also said the hawks within the MDC, who were fast running
out of patience with the notion of democratic change, were already starting
to make noises. If and when ZANU rigged the elections, the hawks wanted
to use the information from the PVC to fuel the fires of public anger and
stir up the people to march on State House and rip the walls down. Amen
to that I said. I was a hundred percent a hawk and had long held that
dictators weren't voted out of power.

Before meeting with my three candidates for the first time, I ran my
own background checks on them through a friend in the MDC. Hilda
Mafudze was good, my friend said, one of the MDC's go-getters who won
her seat in Mhondoro in the 2000 elections and had acquitted herself
well in parliament. Because they rated her and her chances, the MDC
was prepared to risk moving her from a safe seat to contest the new
constituency of Manyame, born out of ZANU PF gerrymandering. But
with regards Shakespeare Maya, the candidate contesting the Mhondoro
seat, my friend told me to watch out. Maya was a Doctor of something.
He'd contested the Presidential elections in 2002 as the leader of NAGG,
one of the crappiest political acronyms ever. He'd recently crossed over to
MDC, and they'd given him Mhondoro. But rumour and my friend had him
pegged as CIO operative tasked with infiltrating and disrupting opposition
politics. My friend wasn't a scaremonger, and I took what he said at face
value. He couldn't tell me anything about Emilie Masimba. Emilie had
to brave to be going up against Sabina Mugabe in Mugabe heartland. Or
stupid. But I left that unsaid.

My friend also brought me up to speed on the ZANU opposition. Sabina wasn't the only Mugabe I'd be butting heads with. Sabina was running in Zvimba South and her son, Patrick Zhuwao was the ZANU PF candidate in Manyame. I'd met Zhuwao before. He was young, trendy and wore his hair in dreadlocks. Because his uncle was Robert Mugabe, he was arrogant, spoiled and supremely certain of the fact he'd never have to work a day in his life. Me versus a pair of Mugabes. Oh, what fun!

I tracked my candidates down so I could offer up my services. Hilda Mafudze came across as happy to meet me. She presented really well and was bright and self-assured. And she was organised. She had prepared a list containing the names and cell phone numbers for all her polling agents. I looked forward to working with her.

I delayed meeting the possible CIO operative Dr Shakespeare Maya for as long as I could. And when I did meet him, I made sure my poker face was on. Alas. My poker face is crap, and I must have looked happy like a fat rat being introduced to a puff adder. If Maya picked up on my unease, he didn't let on. He was a slight man, well dressed and super confident. When I told him my job was to provide him with support, he told me he didn't think he'd need my help. He had everything covered. I heaved a huge sigh of relief. Unless.... Maya had the smallest of smiles on his face.... unless I could find him a few vehicles to use for the duration of the elections. Damn. Just when I thought I'd got away. For me, the toughest ask in election support was finding vehicles to borrow. People who knew me also knew my farm truck. Brand-new not so long ago, it was now a near write off, having been beaten up in the previous elections. Writing this years later, I'm embarrassed to say I cannot remember a single thing about Emilie Masimba, but I'm sure I met him, or her. Alas.

For our week in Zimbabwe, Jenny and I based up at best friend Gayle Arnold's house. I'd resolved to not go near Running Dog while in Zimbabwe. In an election week, my presence on the farm would attract trouble like shit attracts flies. Gayle's house in the suburbs was quiet with a decent internet connection. It was perfect. While Jenny and Gayle got busy with a catch up that would take all week, I commandeered a desk in Gayle's hallway and got busy. I loaded my phone with all the airtime I had and started contacting polling agents.

I started with Hilda's list of five hundred plus names. Her list was the most organised. She'd broken it down polling station by polling station, listing the names of the polling agents assigned to each station. Mostly her agents lived close to their polling stations, so there was no need to lay on any transport. I was lucky to get through to two out of five numbers I dialled. For the most part, the men and women I spoke with were primed and ready for Election Day. They'd been trained on the Parallel Vote Count and knew what was expected of them. We agreed that I'd contact them for updates during the Election Day, network permitting. If their polling stations did not have signal, they were to hotfoot it once the count was finished to a place that did have signal and send me a text with the final numbers. Ditto if there was any intimidation or violence in or around their polling stations. During the long day, I had brief reunions by phone with half the Running Dog staff who'd signed up to be polling agents.

My last two elections had been rock and roll exciting. When I wasn't scared to death, I'd had the time of my life. But without the campaigning and the rallies, the 2005 Election was mostly just slog and grind, on a phone, in a country where phones don't work properly. I hated it. But I stuck to my guns manfully and was rewarded with a crick in my neck from hell from cradling my cell phone and a telephonist's version of tennis elbow. But I got most of the job done. I even managed to briefly borrow a vehicle for Shakespeare Maya. I say briefly because the vehicle was captured by ZANU thugs on the way into Mhondoro and set alight. Alas. Which meant there was yet another person out there who would never again lend me a car.

Come vote day which fell on a Thursday, I was able to get out from behind my tiny desk and onto the ground, checking on polling stations. Because of the distances involved, I couldn't get around to all three constituencies, so I decided I'd focus my efforts on Manyame. Zvimba South was a no-hoper in my books, and I was petrified of Dr Maya. I'd spend the morning with Raphael visiting what polling stations I could in Manyame and then head back to Gayle's house to hit the phones, checking on all my other polling stations. Alas. The morning I spent driving around Manyame ended up hugely depressing.

Mostly we visited polling stations in the Norton and Darwendale farming areas that made up a big chunk of the Manyame constituency. Norton and Darwendale had once been amongst the top commercial farming districts in the country, but that was strictly past tense. Five years after the land grab, the stolen farms I'd spent the day driving through were now in various stages of ruin. The only crops I saw growing were the odd small blocks of maize, no more than a few hectares each and often badly. For the rest, the massive lands of fertile soils that stretched away towards distant horizons stood empty and unused, on the path back to being bush. On some farms, the homesteads still looked lived in, most probably on weekends only, other homesteads looked like they'd long been abandoned. And on the worst, the homesteads were all but gone with the walls only left standing after all the roofing sheets, door frames, window frames, wiring and fittings had been ripped out and sold off.

My drive down memory lane was made worse by the fact that I knew a lot of the farms from before. I drove past what used to be Joe and Wendy Whaley's farm. They had been hugely successful in growing tobacco and chickens. Their farm was a labour of love, and it showed. But the love was long gone, and the farm now looked buggered and forlorn. Alas.

The only good thing about my drive that morning was my polling stations visits. The vibe I got from all of them was good, and the polling agents Raphael and I spoke with were all quietly confident. From what I could see, Hilda had been effective in her campaigning and was in with a good chance of winning.

On the way back to town, I went to my local polling station in Mt Hampden to cast my vote. The queue was long and out the gate. I saw more than a few of my workers in the queue, but their greetings were muted like I had a contractible social disease. The fear factor was alive and well. It took me more than an hour to get to the front of the queue. Unfortunately, it was an hour wasted. I shuffled forward to present my ID to the Electoral Officer manning the Voter's Roll. He went through the motions and checked for my name. It wasn't under D where it should have been. Jenny's name was there, and Gary's but not mine. He checked under E and F for me but still no sign of an Eric George de Jong there either. Or under C. Alas. He gave me my ID back and told me sorry, better luck next time. I didn't even have it in me to argue.

Feeling down, I headed back to Gayle's house and started phoning polling agents. The rest of the Election Day was a blur. I worked my way through the dreaded lists from top to bottom, as best I could. The cell phone networks on the day were that useless, especially in the outlying areas, I was sure the government had pulled the plug on the network to mess with democracy. Any conspiracy theory will do me in a storm. Mhondoro was the worst. I wasn't able to get through to anyone and eventually gave up on the constituency completely. Dr Maya was on his own. Manyame and Zvimba South were only slightly better, and I was able to speak with less than half the polling stations and half those conversations were so broken they were worse than useless. I just hoped that the polling agents would stick to Plan B and report in as per plan.

Voting was steady at the polling stations I was able to get through to. The semi-urban stations close to large population centres were all reporting long queues. Which was all good news. Voter apathy would have been bad for the MDC, apparently. The number of voters being turned away was on the high side I thought, but I didn't have a benchmark to measure my numbers against. As compared to the 2000 and the 2002 elections, there weren't many reports of on the ground intimidation. A few polling stations complained about ZANU youth badgering people in the queues. And there were some reports of MDC polling agents being barred from entering their stations. I tried to phone the reports through to the observers but couldn't. Not that they would have done anything anyway. I sent my updated spreadsheets through to MDC Election HQ by e-mail on the hour, every hour, just like clockwork. Damn, but I was organised. I made a note to self to apply the same levels of organisation to my sock drawer when I got home.

I was on and off the phone with Hilda all day, fielding her reports and requests as best I could and feeding her the information I got from her polling agents. She was like a whirlwind, trying to be everywhere at once, and doing a pretty good job of it. From what I could see she was fearless, rushing in to shut down the campaigning ZANU youth, hurrying up slow voting where the queues had built up, taking the election officials to task.

All of a sudden, it was dark outside. I'd long ago lost track of time. I went through to the lounge in search of some coffee. Jenny asked me what time I thought I'd be finished by. I told her voting was supposed to stop at 19.00 and counting half an hour later. Working on an average of 600 voters or less per station, I figured the first results would start coming in by 21.00 and by midnight I'd either be popping champagne corks or sulking.

It didn't work out like that. At 19.30 some of my polling agents reported that as soon as their polling stations had started counting after closing, they received instructions to stop, until further notice. And furthermore, they had been told that when they'd finished the count, they weren't allowed to post the results on the wall outside. Apparently, the rules had been changed. Which didn't sound right. Something was stinking. I phoned the report through to MDC Election HQ. Apparently, the same instructions had gone out countrywide, and the MDC were completely in the dark as to why. And then at 22.00, an instruction went out to let the count resume. Shortly after that. I got my first final result by text message from a polling station in Zvimba South. Emilie Masimba had come second, by a bunch. Bummer. And then the next text in. Another second-place finish for Emilie. Bummer again. And so it went. And then in amongst the string of sorry Zvimba South results, Hilda's first result arrived. The polling station had finished the count and Hilda had won. I couldn't believe my eyes. So, I phoned the number and asked the polling agent to give me the count again, verbally. Hilda still won. I punched the numbers into my spreadsheet before I phoned Hilda to break the good news. Whoop, whoop, we were winning.

The rest of the night was a roller coaster of emotions, apart from the Zvimba South results where we didn't win a single polling station. But Manyame was a different story. I got another three final counts in, all of which had Hilda winning. And then two on the trot for Zhuwao. And then a win for Hilda, and another for Zhuwao. I celebrated the wins with Hilda and mourned the losses. Hilda wouldn't accept the losses. Every time she lost a station, she wanted to rush there and demand a recount.

Unfortunately, not all the results were quick in coming, most were long and dragged out like root canal procedure, even small stations that would poll just a hundred votes. I ranted at Gayle's cat. How long could it take a room full of people to count a hundred ballot papers? All bloody night would have been the correct answer. But as the hands on Gayle's clock inched their way past midnight and into the morning, more results dribbled in. Some wins, some losses. But definitely more wins. And according to my spreadsheet, Hilda was winning.

At three in the morning, I phoned Hilda to tell her I couldn't keep my eyes open. With final results in from two-thirds of the polling stations, I still had Hilda out in front. And the polling stations left to report were in wards where the MDC had strong bedrock support. Like Porta Farm, a massive squatter camp near Lake Chivero. Porta was one of Raphael's wards, and he said the MDC owned it, no ifs or buts. I was hopeful, but I was also dog tired. Was it okay with Hilda if I went to bed? Shame. Hilda sounded even more tired than I did. Which wasn't surprising, given that she'd been in the field all day and all night. She thanked me for my hard work and said that we'd pick things up first thing in the morning. I crept into bed next to Jenny and lay there for the next hour, absolutely knackered but wide awake with a head and a heart full of hope.

I must have only just fallen asleep when my phone woke me up. It was five o'clock. It was Hendrik phoning me to tell me Patrick Zhuwao had just been declared the winner in Manyame -by a big margin. I told him he had to be talking crap. When I'd gone to bed just a few hours earlier, Hilda had been well in front with only dead cert polling stations left to count. Rubbing what precious little sleep I had from my eyes, the only explanation I could come up with was that the numbers were made up bullshit, that the results had been cooked in favour of Zhuwao. Hendrik didn't sound convinced but asked me to collect Hilda and bring her into Harvest House. I hung up. The phone rang again, almost immediately. It was Hilda. She'd just heard the news and was absolutely distraught and beside herself. I told her I was on my way to Norton to pick her up. Harvest House wanted to see her.

When we got to Hilda's house, she was ready and waiting, dressed for business and good to go. On the way back into Harare, we stopped at Porta Farm. The squatter camp which was home to thousands was one of the polling stations that Raphael had assured me would vote MDC but had supposedly voted ZANU PF overwhelmingly. I wanted to have a look for myself, to assess the veracity of the ZANU victory, and the mood of the people who lived there. We got to Porta Farm just after first light, but already the place was buzzing, with hundreds of people milling around. There wasn't a lot of singing and dancing going on that I could see. The people I could see certainly weren't celebrating the ZANU victory. They were angry and sad. When Hilda got out the car to address the crowd, she was mobbed by people crying and weeping like mourners at a funeral. It was like she'd lost a loved one, not an election. There was absolutely no doubt that the people of Porta Farm revered and adored Hilda. They were one hundred percent her supporters. I stayed in the car because I'm scared of mobs. I phoned Hendrik and told him what I was watching. I told him there were hundreds of people at Porta, maybe even as many as a thousand, all of them fired up and angry enough to march on State House and pull the walls down. He told me to get Hilda into Harvest House as soon as I could.

I put my foot down on the way into Harare but very quickly got caught up in Friday morning rush hour traffic. The mood of the people stuck in the logjam around us was ugly, way more so than normal. We inched our way through a roadblock manned by policemen, quiet and subdued, awake to the anger around them. Hilda told the passengers in the cars and minibuses around us that she'd been robbed in the election. The policemen stood back and waved us through the roadblock.

When we got to the city centre, a crowd of thousands jammed the streets in front of Harvest House, the MDC Headquarters. We pushed our way through the throng and climbed the stairs to the fourth floor where Morgan Tsvangirai's offices were. As always, the lifts were out of order. The first three floors of the Harvest House were deserted and empty - long abandoned by tenants who'd learnt that having the MDC as landlords and neighbours was bad for business. When we got up to the President's floor, we got split up. Hilda was ushered through into Morgan's office, and I was shunted off to wait in a side office that belonged to Morgan's spokesman. I sat and watched a procession of the MDC leadership arrive, all serious and stern-faced; Welshman Ncube, Tendai Biti, Elias Mudzuri and others. They all looked through me like I wasn't there.

Morgan's spokesman was a nice guy, unlike the last one. He told me to make myself comfortable. Judging by the number of cigarettes he was smoking at once; he was clearly under a lot of pressure. Every time his phone rang, which was non-stop, he'd light up another cigarette, take a couple of deep drags to steady his nerves, put it down in the ashtray before taking the call. At one time, I counted five cigarettes burning and could hardly see him through the haze. Picking up on his side of the conversations only, I gathered the election results weren't going according to plan. The Manyame scenario was playing out in other constituencies across Zimbabwe.

The noises from the street below were getting louder. I got up to take a look. And also to get some fresh air. A recent non-smoker, the smoke cloud in the office was killing me. I whistled when I saw the size of the crowd outside. It had doubled. There had to be ten thousand or more. I was busy gawking and enjoying the spectacle when someone from Morgan's office stuck his head through the door and told me to get away from the window. The television cameras on the streets below were focused on Morgan's office windows and had picked up on me gawking. It wasn't a good thing for white men to be seen loitering in and around Morgan's office on national news, apparently.

I sat in the smoke-filled office for a couple of hours while the debate raged on in Morgan's office next door. I fished for the spokesman's opinion on what was going on behind closed doors, but he never bit. Jenny phoned. She wanted to know where I was and what I was doing. She also wanted to know when we were going to leave for South Africa. I'd promised her that we'd be in the car and our way down South as soon as the counts in my constituencies had finished. I could see the spokesman listening in on the conversation. I told Jenny I was caught up in something quite big and that we were going to be a bit delayed. No. I couldn't tell her where I was. I couldn't tell her what I was doing. She just had to please be patient. I hung up. From the look he flashed me, I could tell the spokesman was also a happily married man who hid stuff from his wife.

Eventually, the meeting next door broke up, and people started to leave. The first out was Elias Mudzuri. He had a face like thunder and stormed down the stairs. The others came out a while later, looking more worried than angry. I felt desperately sorry for Morgan. He looked absolutely exhausted, like he was carrying the weight of the world and then some on his shoulders.

After a short while, I escaped Harvest House and headed back to Gayle's house. On the way, I listened to the full election results on the news. ZANU PF had won 78 seats and MDC just 41. That was way down on the 59 seats they'd held going into the elections. Depression set in properly. All around me in the traffic I saw long and unhappy faces. Within an hour, I had Jenny in the car with me, and we were on the road to South Africa. Before I left Harare, I went to say goodbye to Hendrik at his temporary offices in Newlands. Hendrik also looked tired and weary. I apologised to him for my sudden departure. Hendrik thanked me for my hard work and told me I'd easily been his best support member. Hendrik didn't do praise easily, and his words made me feel a little bit better. I still felt like shit overall, but not quite as bad.

On the long drive back to South Africa, I had all the time to ponder long and hard about what had gone down. Without doubt, Mugabe had thieved the elections. He hadn't even bothered to stuff ballot boxes. In Manyame and I'm guessing a whole bunch of other constituencies, he'd just bullshitted the numbers, plain and simple. And when presented with the fact that Mugabe and ZANU had thieved yet another election, the hawks within MDC had pushed hard for Morgan to press the button on Plan B which called for him to stand up and declare the results null, void and nonsensical and to lead the people on to the streets to State House to claim what was rightly his. But I think the doves got in close to Morgan and whispered a reminder in his ear that hundreds of innocent people would be gunned down in the streets by Mugabe's army if they heeded Morgan's call to march on State House. And that their blood would be on Morgan's hands for the rest of forever. And because Morgan loved his people above all else, he pulled the plug on the Plan B that would've should've could've worked. And I reckon that judging by the look on his face when he stormed out of Morgan's offices that morning, Elias Mudzuri had been in charge of Plan B. Furthermore, I reckon the doves that had Morgan's ear read from a script that Mugabe had written. The theory of what happened, according to Eric. Alas.

Coincidentally the General Elections in South Africa took place a day after we got back to White River. A public holiday had been declared. We'd been invited to lunch in Nelspruit. But for a sea of Vote posters on every tree and every wall for thirty kilometres, you would never have known there was a general election on the go. From what I could see the two main parties, the DA and the ANC seemed to have shared the honours in the war for poster space. The voting queues we drove past were quiet and orderly and moving fast. No one looked to be on edge, people got on with their lives. The shopping centres were pumping as people made the most of an extra day off. The contrast with what we'd just experienced in Zimbabwe was staggering.

I said as much at the lunch. I said it was a pleasure to live in a country where elections were normal and not a war zone. There were five couples at the lunch, our hosts, another couple from Zimbabwe and two Afrikaans couples from Nelspruit. One of the Afrikaners sitting opposite me told me hadn't voted. He wasn't just making conversation. He was dropping a bomb in search of a reaction. He got one. I told him his attitude was short-sighted. To not vote in a functioning democracy was irresponsible and.... He held his hand up and cut my lecture short. He told me he hadn't voted because his choices were limited to voting for a Jew or for a stinking kaffir. I was staggered. The man had spat the words Jew and kaffir out with maximum venom and absolute hatred, enough to generate spittle. I eyed him out carefully before crafting my reply. Like most Afrikaners, he was a big guy. His Blue Bulls rugby supporter's jersey bulged ominously, all over. I told him that I wanted to tell him a story by way of reply. But because the story required some imagination, I was going to need him to concentrate real hard. His eyes squinted tight. I thought he was going to punch me there and then. But he didn't. So I carried on. "But before I tell you my story, you need to know my paternal grandfather died in the Second World War on his way to the concentration camps in Poland. He was Dutch. The Germans caught him hiding a Jewish family in his house. He'd been hiding them for over a year. My grandfather is one of my heroes."

'So what?" the Afrikaner spat at me.

"That's by the by. On to my story. I want you to imagine you are in a crowded room with a hundred people. Ninety-nine of those people are wearing Blue Bull rugby jerseys, and the other one is my stinking kaffir foreman from Zimbabwe. I've got one beer. Who do you think I'm going to share that beer with?"

"Huh?"

"Who am I going to drink my beer with, in that crowded room?" I didn't wait for him to answer. "I'm going to share it with my stinking kaffir foreman from Zimbabwe every time. Because he's my friend."

Jenny dragged me home before I got killed. I got it in the neck from her all the way home for spoiling the party. She was right to crap on me. In my previous life, I'd have ignored the Afrikaner and his comments. But that was before. I'd changed. I think all my politics had messed with my head.

Chapter Forty-One.

Even after the 2005 elections were thieved, I felt puffed up and bullish about the political outcome in Zimbabwe. Morgan was on the right track, and the economy was tightening like a noose around Mugabe's neck. Sooner or later, it would all came down to economics. And a million Mugabe spin doctors couldn't paper over empty supermarket shelves. Mugabe was on the ropes, reeling and we were lined up to deliver the knock-out punch.

But then Mugabe put the boot into all my feel good, pulling off two masterful dirty-poker political manoeuvres in quick succession. First up he launched Operation Murambatsvina - a military-style operation in which he sent bulldozers in to clear out slums countrywide, slums that had just overwhelmingly voted for the opposition. Murambatsvina is Shona for sweep out the rubbish. Huts, shacks and livelihoods belonging to an estimated 2.4 million people were reduced to nothing by big, yellow bulldozers that didn't give a shit. I was driving through Mbare, the teeming high-density suburb right next to Harare's city centre on the day the bulldozers came to level the shacks and captured the happenings on video, hoping to send the footage to Sky News but mostly I videoed my thumb. Alas.

Politically Murambatsvina was a Mugabe Fear Factor masterstroke. Under the guise of an urban cleanout and renewal, he issued the harshest retribution to the urban poor who'd just voted against him, forcing them out of their no longer existent shanty towns and back to their rural homes, where ZANU ruled the roost and all who lived there. And when the slums went back up, ZANU made sure that they were re-populated with ZANU supporters.

Sickened by photos of kids living like rats in amongst the ruins left behind by the bulldozers, the world cried out their shock and horror, but as usual, did nothing. Most probably, they were waiting for George W's point man to lead the way.

Next up, Mugabe proclaimed he was re-launching the Senate, the upper House of Parliament. Mugabe announced there would be 50 seats up for grabs in an election to be held before the end of the year, 10 seats reserved for traditional chiefs and 6 seats set aside for friends of Mugabe. Straight away Morgan Tsvangirai said the MDC would boycott the senate elections. Zimbabwe could ill afford another trough for fat-cat politicians to feed at. And why participate in another set of flawed elections? The last elections had been anything but free or fair, and nothing much had changed since then. I thought it was a good call. Finally, the MDC had woken up and seen the light.

Well, I got that all horribly wrong and just a few months after almost winning an election they should have won, the MDC split into two and opposition politics in Zimbabwe was irreconcilably knackered.

Apparently, not all of the MDC bought into the decision to boycott. The contingent from Matabeleland including Secretary General Welshman Ncube were bitterly opposed to the proposed boycott. As they saw it, Mugabe was creating another political space, a space they had to take up, otherwise, they risked letting ZANU get a foot back in the door in Matabeleland. It went to the vote, but the vote was deadlocked. In the end, Morgan Tsvangirai stood up and made an executive decision, the MDC would not contest another flawed election.

Quickly the deadlock got ugly and out of hand. Vicious arguments broke out between those in favour of contesting the Senate and those against. Accusations about spoiled papers and proxy votes that weren't counted properly flew. Fingers got pointed, tempers lost and the Press fed off it in a big way, especially the Herald who delighted in the MDC meltdown and fanned the flames mercilessly. Then the meltdown ramped up. Party Vice President Gibson Sibanda summoned his boss Morgan Tsvangirai to appear before the Party Disciplinary Committee on charges of violating the MDC's Code of Conduct and the Party Constitution. On the same day, the Disciplinary Committee served Morgan with a letter of suspension. Morgan responded by saying he was going nowhere. He said to participate in flawed elections that would have illegitimate outcomes, and predetermined results would signify yet another betrayal for the people of Matabeleland, just like the 'Unity Accord' Joshua Nkomo had signed up to after tens of thousands of Ndebele were slaughtered in the Gukurahundi. According to the mandate he'd been given by the people, Morgan's job was to confront Mugabe, not compromise with him. And in a tit for tat, he announced that he was going to expel pro-Senate faction from the MDC.

Whence upon things proceeded to get ugly. Lawyers and judges got busy washing the dirty MDC laundry in public for months. Nothing got resolved. The pro-Senate faction contested the Senate elections and won a whole 7 out of the 50 seats, vindicating Morgan's boycott decision.

And 3 months later the MDC split. As a party minion sitting in South Africa, I was horrified. But more than that, I was pissed off. Instead of focusing the fight on Mugabe, the MDC leaders were fighting each other like cats in a sack. I penned letters to both Morgan and Welshman Ncube, reminding them of the adage 'United We Stand, Divided We Fall'. But if either of them read my letters, neither paid attention. The split went ahead. Ridiculously, both factions kept the name MDC, leaving Party members, me included, to choose between belonging to the MDC N or the MDC T.

ONE STEP FORWARD AND A BUNCH OF STEPS BACK

N stood for Ncube and T for Tsvangirai. I quickly threw my lot in with Morgan. He'd had the right of it with the Senate being bullshit, and for sure the way forward was all about confronting Mugabe, not cosying up to him. Mostly all my friends thought like me but others, after agonising long and hard, opted to be Welshman Ncube men. Within Sokwanele, we were evenly split between the 2 factions. For the briefest of periods, the Ncube faction was the bigger party in terms of sitting Members of Parliament, but very quickly most of them crossed the floor to re-join Morgan.

On my next Harare trip, still pissed off with my political party for breaking in two, I visited Roy Bennett, recently released from prison, to get his take on things. Thankfully Roy had opted to stay with Tsvangirai. He told me his version of how the split had really happened, how it had been engineered by the CIO and Thabo Mbeki.

Thabo Mbeki had puffed his chest out and looked to be as proud as punch when George Bush appointed him as his point man in Africa in front of the world's cameras to protect and promote democracy, free trade and transparency, blah, blah, blah. It looked like George W had chosen wisely. In a continent blighted with corruption, turmoil and conflict, South Africa looked to be the standout, the shining example that countries to the North could look up to and emulate, starting with Mugabe's Zimbabwe across the river. Bummer for Zimbabwe that George W's point man was bent.

A liberation struggle cadre to his core, Thabo Mbeki's biggest fear for his beloved ANC was an opposition party born out of the labour movement. In Zambia, it was exactly that which had done for Kaunda and his liberation party that had delivered up freedom from the white bosses. And Zimbabwe looked to be shaping for more of the same. ZANU couldn't carry on blatantly stealing elections away from the MDC forever. And once Zimbabwe had fallen to the pesky winds of change, then next stop, South Africa. Unless someone stepped in and did something to stop the rot in Zimbabwe. Enter Thabo Mbeki.

With or without the connivance of the CIO, Mbeki saw the deadlocked MDC as the perfect opportunity to fracture the Zimbabwean opposition once for all. According to Roy, as soon as the MDC deadlocked, Morgan sent an emissary to the Executive Hotel where the pro- Senate faction leaders, all from Bulawayo, were staying, to look for middle ground. But by the time Morgan's man got there, just hours after the deadlocked vote, the South African Ambassador had already delivered up an offer from Mbeki to mediate in the dispute, plus 5 air tickets to Pretoria for Welshman and the other pro-Senate faction. And when Welshman arrived in Pretoria, Thabo rolled out the red carpet for him and offered up a peach of a deal. Ncube breaks away from Tsvangirai, taking his half of the MDC with him. Tsvangirai and his Trade Unionists become irrelevant, and Ncube and

Mugabe go onto to form a Government of National Unity with Ncube slotted in as Prime Minister and Mugabe as President and everyone lives happily after. Because Prime Minister Ncube rolled off the tongue quite nicely, Welshman went home and pushed hard for the split.

But alas for poor Mbeki the split didn't happen as planned. He was counting on Welshman taking half the MDC with him, as in all the academics, the lawyers and the liberals, leaving Morgan with the just the rabble-rousing unionists. But when the split happened, it followed strictly tribal lines, and only the Ndebele followed Welshman Ncube, all the rest staying behind with Morgan. Which for Mbeki was a real snag because in Zimbabwean politics the Ndebele counted for less than 20% of the vote, leaving Morgan still very relevant and still very in charge of the opposition. For his plan to work, Mbeki needed a Shona leader for his breakaway MDC in a hurry. But where to find one? Rats. All the good Shona guys had stayed behind with Morgan. What followed could have been scripted by the idiot who had Bobby Ewing waking up in the shower in Dallas a full season after he was killed in a car crash.

Mbeki with Ncube in tow quickly scoured the Zimbabwean diaspora and emerged with one Arthur Mutambara, who sort of ticked all the boxes. Arthur was undoubtedly Shona, he'd once led the Student Representative Council at the University of Zimbabwe so obviously had leadership skills in buckets and had once been arrested during anti-government riots, a must-have tick on an opposition leader's curriculum vitae. And the academics back in Zimbabwe were just going to love Arthur because he was a full-on Professor of Robotics and had studied in America. He'd even co-authored a paper called the Estimation and control for a modular wheeled mobile robot. And so, Thabo and Welshman parachuted Arthur Mutambara in from nowhere to take the lead of the other MDC, the pro-senate one. Both the leadership and the rank and file of that faction accepted him with open arms, proving that Zimbabweans make a flock of sheep look like independent thinkers. Arthur himself summed it up when, in one of his first interviews as the new Party President, he said "My position was that the MDC should have boycotted those Senate elections. I guess then that makes me the anti-Senate leader of the pro-Senate MDC faction. How ridiculous can we get? That debate is now in the past, let us move on and unite our people."

I stayed pissed off with Zim politics, especially the MDC now plural, for a long time. They'd let themselves and their egos be played like trout by CIO and or Mbeki. I and a million others deserved better of our leaders, If I could've found another movie to be in, I would've walked away from their sorry mess in a heartbeat. But alas, I couldn't.

ONE STEP FORWARD AND A BUNCH OF STEPS BACK

Chapter Forty-Two

We were lucky to live in one of the most beautiful parts of South Arica with stunning mountain vistas and the Kruger National Park right on our doorstep. But views are hard to enjoy when you have a son with what was starting to look like a runaway medical problem that doctors couldn't fix, the resultant medical bills you can't pay, debts you can't collect from little old ladies with blue hair, a job that required the use of the word gorgeous and a vivid imagination that amplified every night sound and forced you to sleep with a big gun next to your bed. Small wonder, I ran back to Zimbabwe at every opportunity.

I got a phone call out of the blue one day from Sylvia, a Dutch television journalist who'd been told I travelled back to Zimbabwe often. Sylvia wanted to do a story on Zimbabwe's land-grab and the impact it had on the lives of the affected farmers. Would I take her with me on my next trip she asked? Western journalists had long been persona non grata in Zimbabwe. The last thing Mugabe wanted was prying eyes while he and his thugs committed murder and mayhem, so he'd long ago booted them out his country. And because reporters are generally rather keen on the freedom of the Press, there weren't too many in a hurry to smuggle themselves into a country where the power of the pen would get you locked up in a hell hole or worse. But it was vitally important that the rest of the world know what havoc Mugabe was wreaking, so I told Sylvia no problem.

Sylvia arrived in White River, a tiny slip of a girl, all excited with her camera bags and lenses packed, ready for her big adventure. I went over the alibi I'd concocted for us. She was a family friend and keen on bird watching, and I was taking her to Zimbabwe to show her the wonderful birdlife. I gave her a couple of well-worn bird books and told her to leave her press cards and identification behind. She didn't seem worried at all about sneaking herself and her cameras into one of the most repressive regimes in the world. I worried enough for the both of us and tossed and turned all night, mostly picturing crocodile clips with lots of voltage being applied to my genitals by CIO agents wearing dark glasses. I woke up early and unrested with big black circles under my eyes and loaded more bird books into the Land Rover.

Thankfully our drive through South Africa and into Zimbabwe was uneventful. Sylvia interviewed me at length and on camera as I drove. White River to Harare is a fourteen-hour drive so I had all the time in the world to tell my story, about how painful it was to have your home, your livelihood and your dreams ripped away from you violently because of the colour of skin and your political persuasion, how hard it was to start over with a family of dependents in a foreign country at the age of forty with not a lot, blah, blah, blah. Cry me a river. It was like I was the first refugee ever.

As we drove across the Limpopo River, I put my heart in my mouth and sweated buckets while Sylvia captured her first sight of Zimbabwe on film. I wanted to tell her to hide her bloody camera under the back seat, but I forced myself to shut up. I couldn't have the world listening to the sheer panic in my voice. The Zimbabwean border officials were bored to tears and barely looked up from their picture magazines and last week's newspapers to stamp our passports, even though I walked up to them with guilt written all over my face like a shoplifter in a music store with a guitar hidden down the front of his t-shirt.

Then it was back to Sylvia's extended interview, given added impetus on the Zimbabwe side by the non-stop backdrop of empty farms and ranches, lying fallow and unproductive, all on their way back to being bush again. The contrast with the busy South African farms we'd driven past all morning could not have been starker. As always, there were lots of police roadblocks on the highway. Sylvia would scramble to get her camera out of sight, and I'd get my heart rate back up into high hundreds. In Harare, we stayed with friends who were clearly uncomfortable that one of their guests was a television journalist, in Zimbabwe illegally. I'd left that bit out when I'd invited myself to stay. The next day it was more of the same. I took Sylvia on an extended tour of empty farms and broken dreams. And we stopped at Running Dog unannounced so Sylvia could capture some hurried footage of me in the garden of the house I couldn't live in because of the man down the road with a gun who wanted to shoot me.

That night Sylvia and her cameras came with when I went to say goodbye to Eric and Fiona Dawson on their way to their new life in Thailand where Eric would be teaching Thai peasant farmers how to grow the type of tobacco that he and a thousand other ex-tobacco farmers were no longer growing in Zimbabwe. Eric and Fiona were my best friends. Their daughter Stacey was my goddaughter. I didn't know when I'd see them again, so the goodbye hugs Sylvia captured on film were long and emotional.

The standout memory though on that brief tour of Zimbabwe was my visit to Scratchy, one of Zimbabwe's most preeminent MDC activists. Sylvia and I were on the road headed back to South Africa when I took the call from Scratchy. He'd heard I was in the country and asked me to come and see him. So much for me keeping clandestine and under the radar. Scratchy had a parcel that he wanted me to take back to South Africa. He wouldn't tell me what it was over the phone but said it was important.

Scratchy lived in an upmarket complex of garden flats near the city centre. I left Sylvia in the car while I went in to collect the parcel. Scratchy met me at his front door looking like Hannibal Lecter, wearing long, bloodied rubber gloves and a white butcher's apron, also bloodied. He let me in and quickly closed the door behind me. Scratchy took his bloody glove off to shake hands briefly before taking me through to the kitchen. There was more blood on the counter. And a large cooler box, open and packed to the brim with ice. Through the ice, I could see plastic bags with what looked like meaty bits inside.

"I need to get the cooler box out the country, to South Africa." Scratchy always spoke very quickly, machine gun fast, like he was in a hurry to get the conversation out the way.

"What's in it?" I was scared to ask but had to know.

"Learnmore Jongwe" Scratchy said. Learnmore Jongwe was an MDC politician who'd been jailed for murdering his wife. "Well, not all of Learnmore, just his vital organs."

I almost upchucked there and then. Even though I'd heard Scratchy perfectly first up, I asked: "You've got Learnmore Jongwe's vital organs in your cooler box?"

"Yes."

"Why?"

"You know Learnmore died in prison. We think he was murdered, poisoned by CIO agents. So I got his vital organs. I need to get them to Johannesburg for a toxicology report. Can you take them? But you need to keep it top secret."

I heaved a silent sigh of relief. "Sorry Scratchy but I can't. I've got a Dutch journalist in the car with me. We're actually on our way back to SA now."

"Oh. Then you can't." Scratchy said goodbye to me and ushered me out the door, already busy in his head with Plan B.

Sylvia and I drove back to White River untroubled. She thanked me for all the help I'd given her and drove back to Joburg to edit her story. I sat glued to the television for that first week back in South Africa, waiting for breaking news on Learnmore Jongwe but there was nothing. After a week I figured it wasn't going to happen. Either Scratchy never got his grisly cooler box with Learnmore's bits out of Zimbabwe, or the toxicology results were inconclusive.

Sylvia sent me a video cassette with her mini documentary on it a few weeks later. She was happy with the way it had turned out and wanted me to have a copy. She'd submitted it to her bosses, and she was hoping that it would air on Dutch television in the near future. I watched the videotape on my own. Most of the Dutch monologue went over my head. My interviews came across okay, but I looked older than I did in the mirror, more drawn, and mostly I looked like I was nervous. A few weeks later my cousin Hanny phoned me from Holland to tell me I'd been on national television and please could she have my autograph?

It wasn't a month later before I got a phone call from another journalist. Crap. The word was obviously out that I was the go-to person for any journalists looking to sneak into Zimbabwe on the quiet. This time the reporter was from Sweden, and she wanted to do a story on Morgan Tsvangirai, and the MDC and someone had told her that I might be able to help get her into the country. I told her I could. Would I be able to get her in with Morgan Tsvangirai? And she wanted to meet with other MDC leaders and activists? I told her I'd do my best. I picked her up in Polokwane. She was Scandinavian blonde, very pretty and very quick to tell me she was happily married to another journalist. Compared to Sylvia, the Swedish journalist was way more hardened and street savvy. When I presented her with the birdwatching alibi and a bag full of birding books, she almost rolled her eyes but didn't. She was hardcore.

Because I like my friends, I never stayed with them on that trip. Instead, I arranged to stay with the activist acquaintance I'd approached for help in putting a program together for the Swedish journalist. I hated the whole trip and was on edge from the moment we crossed the border to when we left. The Swedish girl was so incredibly focused on her story and expected to be kept busy from the minute we got into Harare. My activist friend got us an appointment to see Morgan at his house in Strathaven on our first morning. There was a murder of CIO agents complete with dark glasses, posing as a municipal worker at the entrance to Morgan's road, scribbling down number plates in a notebook. (I don't know if murder is the correct collective noun for a group of CIO agents, but it seemed to fit.) At the sight of them, the squadron of butterflies in my tummy took flight. Crap. I just knew we were going to get busted.

Once inside Morgan's house, we parked by the garage and waited for someone to come and tell us where to go. There was the usual melee of hangers-on hanging about. They were clustered around Susan Tsvangirai who was in the garage behind the house, treating a little girl with her arms swathed in bandages. One of the hangers-on was Morgan's younger brother who broke away to greet us. He'd been an agronomist before his brother became important, so mostly we talked farming whenever we saw each other. He told us the little girl was Morgan's niece, from Susan's side of the family. She'd fallen into a fire at her rural home and was staying at Morgan's house while she received treatment. The Swede asked if she could take a photo. It would give her story a nice human touch. Morgan's brother told us no problem. On the floor next to where we were standing was a gas ring with a pot boiling away on top with a goat's head inside. The goat's eyes were open, and his tongue stuck out an inch. My stomach lurched while the butterfly squadron inside toyed with the idea of a mass exodus. Morgan's brother laughed. The goat's head was lunch. Quickly and before he could invite us, I told the brother we wouldn't be able to stay for lunch. Which got the brother laughing some more. He was still laughing as he led the journalist off to interview Morgan.

The interview lasted fifteen minutes. I enjoyed the warm sun next to my car and mostly watched the large group of hangers-on stand around and do nothing, other than talk. And laugh. They laughed a lot, so I don't think they were talking politics. It was amazing. You'd expect a group of people in the close orbit of a politician vying to be the next leader of the country to be busy, with a sense of purpose. But the people I was watching had nothing to do and all day to do it in. It was actually quite relaxing, and I could have watched them for longer, but my Swedish journalist emerged, in a hurry to be taken off to her next appointment.

We had to meet Iain Kay, an MDC legend from Marondera at a coffee shop in town. Iain was going to take her out into the districts for the rest of the day, leaving me free to do Running Dog business. On the way to the coffee shop, I asked the reporter what she'd thought of Morgan. She said he came across as a warm and caring person, but she didn't know if he was presidential material. It wasn't the answer I wanted to hear, and I wish I hadn't asked the question.

We were meeting Iain at a coffee shop on Samora Machel Avenue just opposite the Holiday Inn. It was a busy part of town, and I struggled to find a parking spot. We went inside and found a table. We were early, and I was hungry, despite the goat's head soup, so I asked the waiter if I could look at the menu. He bustled off to the back of the coffee shop and came back with two menus. Inside mine, there was a folded scrap of paper. I opened it up and nearly shat in my pants there and then. The note told me in not so neat capital letters THIS IS NOT A GOOD PLACE FOR YOU AND THE REPORTER. THERE ARE PEOPLE WATCHING YOU. LEAVE NOW.

With a bad case of the shakes, I pushed the slip of paper across to her. She read it, smiled at me sweetly and got up to leave, Scandinavian Ice personified. In a loud voice that every other table in the restaurant could hear, I told the waiter that we had another appointment elsewhere that I'd forgotten about and apologised for wasting his time. I followed the Swede out the coffee shop with my buttocks tightly clenched, doing my best not to break into a flat-out sprint. Once in the car, I phoned Iain and told him what had happened. I kept my eye on the door of the coffee shop to see if anyone followed us out but saw no one. I was fully expecting Iain to abort, but he was nonplussed and suggested another rendezvous point; at the back of the carpark outside the Red Lion Pub at Harare Sports Club. We'd meet there in five minutes.

On the drive to the Sports Club, I almost caused multiple accidents and the Swede to almost drop her icy veneer by driving with my eyes glued to the rear-view mirror, running robots and making sharp, sudden turns in front of oncoming traffic in a desperate attempt to lose anyone who might be trying to follow us. Not that I saw anyone suspicious. But just because I'm paranoid, doesn't mean there wasn't someone following us.

I heaved a huge sigh of relief when Iain drove away with the Swede in his car. Then I remembered I still had another two days in Zimbabwe with the Swede. Crap. I ended up spending the afternoon in the Red Lion catching up with old friends and stocking up on some badly needed fortitude. By the time Iain and the Swede got back in the late afternoon, I was full to overflowing with fortitude. Bring on the bad guys no problem, I told the Swede. My fortitude was all gone the next morning, eroded by a massive hangover and I spent the rest of that Zimbabwe trip back on the edge of my seat, hating every minute, Chicken Licken fully expecting the worst to happen. And there was every opportunity for the worst to happen. The Swedish journalist filled her diary to overflowing with clandestine meetings with opposition activists. I never sat in on any of the meetings. My job was to get her to them and then sit outside and stress, waiting for bad shit to happen. I hated every minute and vowed to never subject myself to that kind of pressure again ever. Until the next time. Alas.

Zimbabwe politics was a drug in my system that I couldn't kick. Indulging in it was bad for the health and brought me into conflict situations requiring a cool head and steady hands. It was a pity I didn't do cool heads and steady hands. And my over fertile imagination had me seeing bad guys in every shadow. But I couldn't give up politics. I hated living in South Africa. It was never going to be home. But home was never going to be like home used to be unless there was political change. And the only way that was going to happen was if people like me got involved. What a crappy Catch 22 for an avowed coward. Alas.

OF BLOODY BODY PARTS AND MURDERED MINERS

Chapter Forty-Three

Dan's headmaster summoned Jenny and me for a consultation. He told us Penryn wasn't working out for Daniel. The headmaster was the master of the understatement. He showed us Dan's recent test results. Dan had scored single figures only and was rock bottom in the class by a country mile. And he was quickly slipping further and further behind the other kids. I was shocked. We knew Dan was doing badly at school, but we didn't know how badly. The headmaster thought we should get Dan assessed again by experts who could advise on other more suitable forms of education. What did he mean by other more suitable forms of education, I asked? Like sheltered education, he said. Wham. All the air went out of me. The word sheltered when applied to your own child was like a kick in the nuts.

The headmaster offered up the names of two psychologists who'd be able to get a handle on Dan, so we could get more than one opinion. One of them worked out of White River and the other out of Barberton, a small mining town on the other side of Nelspruit. We made an appointment to see the White River psychologist first.

It all went so un-swimmingly well. First up, she told us on the phone that our medical aid wouldn't cover her consult. She was expensive. I was clueless as to how Jenny scraped the money together to pay her, but somehow she did. Dan was sulky in the car the whole way there. He didn't see why he had to go and have more stupid tests; he was normal and there was nothing wrong with him. He wasn't going to answer any stupid questions, he was just going to sit there and say nothing. I was in a foul mood by the time we got to the psychologist's rooms, which turned out to also be the lounge in her house. Dan's black sulk followed us in, and I got cross with him. I quickly endeared myself to the psychologist woman when I told Dan in front of her that his consultation was costing us a lot of money that we didn't have and that he'd better stop sulking and answer any questions she might have. The psychologist asked Dan very sweetly to wait in the waiting room outside, a.k.a. her hallway, and then crapped on me for being insensitive towards Dan's feelings, for putting a monetary value to his mental health and wellbeing. I almost told her fuck you because she had no idea how much pressure we were under as a family but didn't. Instead, I told her our story starting with the adoption. Then I told her about the trauma of the farm invasions and the death threats and how our family had been forced to flee in the middle of the night seventeen times in less than a year. I told her about how excited Dan had been about coming to

South Africa and getting a chance to start over but how that had also gone horribly wrong. I told her about the onset of his vitiligo and how the kids at Penryn teased and taunted him mercilessly. I told her Dan had struggled academically throughout but that he was now doing especially badly at Penryn and that the headmaster felt Dan would not be able to matriculate. I told her Jenny and I were at an absolute loss as to how to go forward. We didn't know how to parent Dan. Half of me said we should just accept that fact that Dan was slow and that he'd never cope in the mainstream and just love him. But the other half of me said that my job was to push Dan harder and to make sure he got an education, so he could look after himself in later life.

She was stone cold throughout. At a later consult that Jenny went to on her own, the psychologist woman told Jenny that she was sick and tired of all Zimbabweans who came into see her with their sob stories. But I digress. Back to Dan's first consult.

The psychologist woman called Dan back into the room and proceeded to tell him he could achieve anything he wanted, including top matric results, provided he set his mind to it. And by anything, she meant anything. If Dan wanted to become the best surgeon in the world, no problem. He just needed to need it badly enough to do it. To my credit, I didn't interrupt. I just sat there and got angrier and angrier, listening to her telling Dan it was all right to have false hopes. When she finished finally, I asked her if I could have a word alone with her. Dan left the room again, and it was my turn to crap on the psychologist woman. She knew nothing about Dan and his abilities. She hadn't seen his school marks, she hadn't looked at a single one of his books, she hadn't even engaged him in meaningful conversation before telling him he could pass his matric. I lived with Dan, and I knew his limitations. Not in a million years would he pass matric. He just wasn't bright enough. Alas. Her telling him he could pass his matric was like telling a man with no legs that he could win gold at the Olympic sprints, it was bullshit. Wham. Straight away, she hit me with the Oscar Pistorius story. Wham. Straight away, I hit back and told her that again she was talking crap. Oscar's personal best times put him right at the far back of every able-bodied hundred-metre race ever run.

Before we got into a pissing competition over Oscar, I changed tack. I told her about a friend who had a Down syndrome child. As compared to me, I told her my friend was lucky. My friend's only job was to love his kid, to hug her and look after her. He didn't have to try and push his daughter to get her ready for a life she would never be ready for. By telling Dan all kinds of bullshit that he could go out and do stuff he'd never be able to do, instead of helping us fix the problem, the psychologist woman was making it even worse. Thanks a lot for nothing, I told her. She looked at me with absolute disgust and told me I was the worse parent she'd ever met. Again, I wanted to tell her fuck you but didn't.

The next psychologist, also a woman, worked in Barberton. It was my first time being in Barberton, and I was excited. For those you haven't read and re-read The Power of One countless times, Barberton is the town where the hero of the book, Peekay grows up and learns to box. Barberton is a small mining town at the very bottom of the steep escarpment that falls away from Nelspruit. I don't think much mining goes on there anymore and the town was properly sleepy with not a lot of hustle and bustle to be seen. The psychologist's rooms were also in her home, a neat and tidy little bungalow in a neat and tidy little suburb on the edge of town, but at least her rooms were outside with a separate entrance. She had a wall full of certificates, and you felt like you were going in to see a proper doctor. She greeted us warmly and told us to call her by her first name, Alma. Before we got started, Alma took Dan off to a separate room to do some tests for her. The poor kid groaned out loud, and she gave him a hug.

Alma left Dan doing his thing and came back to talk to Jenny and I. But first, she asked Jenny for the file of reports and assessments on Dan that we'd collected over the years. Shame, it was a big fat file, and the kid wasn't even fifteen yet. Alma put the file to one side, to read and absorb later she told us and then we told her the story behind the reports. She was an easy listener. She made us both feel comfortable, and our sad story came gushing out. Alma didn't ask many questions but scribbled copious notes throughout. The one question she did ask was how Dan got on with his siblings. We told her he hero-worshipped Gary but fought bitterly with Veronica. When we got to the end of our story, I thought to myself, small wonder the poor kid was so mixed up. He really had been put through the mill properly.

After Jenny and I finished our story, we had to wait a bit for Dan to finish his tests, and then we could all head on home. Dan came out looking drained and nervous. He told Alma he'd tried his hardest and hoped he'd done well. Alma had a brief look at his work and said he'd done just fine. If Dan were a dog, he'd have wagged his tail. Alma allowed him to escape outside while she had a word with Mom and Dad. I braced myself for the worst. But it didn't come. Alma asked us to come back in a week. By then she would have analysed his test results and would be able to give us a clear picture of where we are at with Dan and the way forward with regards his education.

It was a long week. Mostly I stressed. I didn't have to stress about whether or not Dan had passed, that was already a foregone conclusion. The stressing was all about how badly he'd failed and the consequences thereof. If he didn't fail too badly, then he'd maybe be able to stay at Penryn, and we'd look for a remedial teacher to help him on the side. But if Dan had bombed badly, the prospect of sheltered education hung over us like an executioner's axe. I wasn't even sure what sheltered education entailed, but it sounded institutional, like something out of a Charles Dickens novel, or worse.

But even during that long stressed week, Dan continued to amuse. I was sitting in the lounge at Summer Hill, and I heard Jenny screaming in our bedroom. Snake, snake, snake. I leapt out of my chair and commenced to panic. Snakes have that effect on me. I ran off in two directions at once to look for a stick with which to beat the offending reptile to death. I grabbed Dan's hockey stick and bolted down the passage. I burst into the bedroom with the hockey stick at the ready and almost attacked Jenny's naked butt reversing out of our en suite bathroom, causing her to scream a second time. Automatically assuming she'd seen another snake behind me, I also screamed and leapt on the bed. Which got Jenny laughing, instead of screaming. She laughed until tears were rolling down her face, which was all rather annoying. I was there to save, not to amuse. Once she'd calmed down, she pointed me at the bathroom. The snake had ambushed her while getting into the shower. The snake was a big brown one, and it looked poisonous, and what was I waiting for?

"If it's poisonous, then I'm going to get my gun," I told her.

Jenny shoved me towards the bathroom. "You're not going to shoot up my bathroom. We've only just finished tiling it. You going to have to kill it with the hockey stick."

With the hockey stick held out in front, I inched through the curtains separating the bathroom from the bedroom, hesitant, miserable. It didn't help that Jenny was still laughing behind me. Where the hell was the fucking snake? I couldn't see it. The shower cubicle was recessed on my left and the toilet and the bath in front of me. Summer Hill was lousy with snakes. Please, God, don't let it be a puff adder. I especially hated puff adders. And don't let it be a cobra either, God, or a mamba. I especially hated them also. I still couldn't see the snake. Which meant it had to be hiding behind the toilet bowl in front of me. Which was good because if it could fit behind the toilet bowl, it was a small snake. Then I caught a flicker of movement out the corner of my eye. The snake was coiled up in the back left corner of the shower. Because it was still all curled up, I couldn't see what model it was. But I could see enough of the snake to know my hockey wasn't long enough. My golden rule in dealing with snakes is to always make sure the stick you're going to beat the snake to death with is longer than the snake. So I backed out the bathroom in a hurry, to look for a longer stick. At which point Dan arrived in the bedroom, causing more screams from the still naked Jenny.

'Dad, Dad, don't kill it, don't kill it. I want to catch it. You said I could keep snakes as a hobby. You said I could, you said I could."

Unfortunately, Dan was right. I had said he could collect snakes, provided they weren't poisonous. By this stage, courtesy of his vitiligo and his learning problems at school, Dan was the loneliest kid in White River. He had no friends, not a single one. He'd spend the whole day at school, and not one kid would talk to him, other than to taunt him and tease him and call him Stalker and or Albino. Kids are cruel, especially rich kids at fancy private schools. Which left Dan with zero self-esteem. Because of this, I spent an inordinate time telling Dan to get an interest in life. I told him he needed a hobby, something that he could be good at, something he could read about in books and get excited about. So, when Dan finally came to me to tell that he'd found a hobby, I was overjoyed. I told him to go out and grab his new hobby with both hands and embrace it. An unfortunate choice of phrases given that Dan's new hobby was collecting snakes.

We only found out about the snake part of Dan's new hobby when he walked through the front door with both hands full of what turned out to be little, writhing, baby Rhombic Night Adders. Jenny and I screamed like girls-even little baby snakes have that effect on us. Jenny wanted to dispatch the snakes there and then with the broomstick, but Dan wouldn't let her near them. 'You can't kill them, Mom, they're my new hobby."

"Nonsense. You're not allowed to collect snakes."

"But Dad said I could. He said I should grab them with both hands. And he said I should embrace them." I stepped in quickly and commuted the snakes' death sentence, and we got them safely into a shoebox. After fetching the snake book and positively identifying his Rhombic Night Adders as being properly venomous, the terms and conditions of Dan's new hobby were amended to specifically exclude any and all venomous snakes. Dan and I took the little Adders back to the spot where he'd found them and released them. Later I went back with a badza to look for them, but they'd slithered off to safety.

Fast forward back to the snake in the shower, Dan pleaded with me to not kill it. Please, could he collect it? So far, his snake collection had zero specimens. Reluctantly, I agreed, and Dan ran off to his bedroom and returned with his snake capturing equipment; a long wire thing to pin the snake down with and the pillowcase off his bed to put it in. I went off to my seldom-used workshop and came back with a stick longer than the snake and two workshop helmets with visors, for just in case. For just in case what, Dad? For just in case it's one of those spitting cobras, I told him. Dan's eyes got big. Dan's eyes looked even bigger once he'd put his helmet and slid the visor down. With his wire thing and my long stick at the ready, Dan and I advanced into the bathroom through the curtain. The Keystone Cops could not have done stealth and sneak better.

For starters, it didn't help that the insides of our visors fogged up almost immediately. And then the doorway wasn't wide enough to accommodate both of us. Being the adult, unfortunately, I got to go first.

The snake was still in the back left corner of the shower. Which meant we had to get past him and then turn to get a good look at him; a complicated manoeuvre in the narrow confines of the bathroom, especially with both of us trying to hug the wall as closely as possible so as to not piss the snake off. We successfully negotiated our way past the shower and turned to approach the snake front on. I wiped the inside of my visor so I could see. The snake stirred and flicked his tongue, once, twice, three times. I was mesmerised like a rat but snapped out of it.

I told Dan to get his snake catching wire thing ready. "Okay, Dad," he whispered loudly. He then added to the moment by spearing me in the soft bit of my neck behind my ear with the sharp end of his wire snake catching tool, causing me to squeal and jump, causing the snake to rear up high and flare its hood menacingly. Crap, it was a cobra. More crap followed when the cobra spat at us, splattering the front of our visors with venom. Snake lovers need to look away now. As soon as I felt some of the venom splash wet against my forearm, I leapt forward and quickly beat the poor snake to death with my long stick.

Afterwards, Dan sat on our bed, shaking, looking shell shocked.

"Sorry Dan that the snake didn't make it into your collection. But he was poisonous, so I had to kill him. Sorry."

"That's okay, Dad." There was a long silence. And then, "I was just thinking, Dad, that instead of snakes do you think I can maybe collect mammals instead?" I belly laughed and laughed. He was such an amusing child.

Dan might well have been amusing, but according to Alma, when we saw her the following week, he was also badly damaged. It was just Jenny and me meeting with Alma, she'd told us to leave Dan at home. She settled us down in her office with coffee and proceeded to tell us what she thought was wrong with Dan. She told us the human brain had a left side and a right side. The left-side controlled logic and the right-side emotions. For some reason, the left-side of Dan's brain wasn't working properly, which was why he was struggling so badly at school, especially in the sciences and maths. She boiled it down for us. Typically, Dan was capable of doing simple sums, like adding and subtraction and even multiplication. Jenny nodded in agreement. Dan was good at his times tables; way better than Veronica had been at the same age. Alma continued, prefixing her next sentence with an inevitable but. "But, presented with a formula with mixed functions, like 2 multiplied by 3 and then divided by 4, Dan cannot compute - the left side of his brain won't let him, it won't or can't mesh." Jenny carried on nodding. That was exactly Dan. And God only knew how many hours she'd spent trying to help Dan with his homework, trying to help Dan play catch up.

Alma told us that Dan's short-term memory was very good, probably compensatory, and that's what had got him through stuff like his times table. His above-average memory skills had allowed Dan to semi-cope at primary school, but secondary school was less about remembering and more about figuring stuff out. And that's what the bust side of Dan's brain wouldn't let him do. I teared up as it all came crashing home. Suddenly, so many incidents from Dan's troubled schooling were making sense, like how much he'd struggled with algebra during his brief stay at Saint George's College. And the six of the best caning I'd given Dan for failing his maths exam so spectacularly; he'd scored just 5%. Don't beat yourself up, Alma told me, I wasn't to know. But I was to know, I railed. I wasn't prepared to let myself off the hook so easily. How many supposed experts had Dan been assessed by? How come none of them had picked up on the problem? Alma shushed me and carried on. With regards Dan's relationship with his sister, it was classic tall poppy syndrome. Dan hated Veronica because compared to him, she was clever. And he would do what he could to pull her down to his level.

Going forward, Dan would require sheltered education, followed by sheltered employment. For example, she told us that Dan had opened up to her and he'd told her he wanted to be a mechanic when he finished school, mostly so he could buy a car and soup it up, with nitrous oxide and spoilers and a big, performance exhaust pipe. Which was all classic Dan. But she told us that would never happen. Dan might one day learn how to service a car, how to do basic oil and filter changes and the like, but he'd never be able to fix a car. He'd never be able to strip a gearbox or an engine, diagnose the problem and fix it and then put it all back together again. Because the left side of his brain could not and would not compute. Our house bore testimony to that, littered as it was with the carcasses of every toy car and boat and plane that Dan had ever had, mostly all working perfectly, up until the right side of his brain suggested his left side take them apart. That was the unfortunate part of it all; the right side of Dan's brain had him wanting to do all manner of cool things that the left side of his brain couldn't do.

But there was a way forward Alma told us. If we sent him to a school with a curriculum that would help Dan develop basic life skills and vocational training. There were two such schools that she knew of in the province which looked after children with special needs. That was the first time I'd heard the term special needs applied to Daniel, and it hurt me. Alma picked up on my reaction. She told me that Dan would benefit hugely from being with children with similar abilities, allowing him to develop friendships and the social skills that he so badly needed. And after school, if we managed his expectations, and if we provided him with sheltered employment, Dan would be able to contribute and learn how to one day stand on his own. There were a lot of ifs in there, but at least they threw up some light at the end of Dan's long dark tunnel. "What about farming?" I asked Alma. "Could we train Dan to work on the farm?"

'Perfect," she said. "Farming would be perfect for Dan, provided you give him dot to dot instructions. And you need to know he'd never be able to run the farm or make decisions like how much fertiliser to apply and when. He'd able to service your tractors, but he wouldn't be able to repair them." Him and me both. But I was so relieved that at long last, we had a way forward for Daniel. Alma promised us that she'd get the details of the two schools to us. We thanked her profusely for all her help.

Jenny and I had a real sob fest on the way home, we cried the whole way, mostly for Dan but we also felt very sorry for ourselves. And we also felt guilty. I couldn't stop thinking about caning Dan for failing his maths exam at St Georges. We phoned Veronica in Joburg and told her about Thelma's tall poppy theory. More tears. We also worked out our script, how we'd break the news to Dan that we were moving him from Penryn.

When we got home, we sat Dan down and told him that Alma had recommended he move schools, away from Penryn to another school with other kids like him, kids who also liked mechanics and working with their hands, other kids who weren't good at maths and science and normal school work. Dan took the news of his impending move away from Penryn more than well. He was thrilled, right up until I told him his new school would either be in Bethal, which was a three-hour drive from White River or in Belfast which was an hour away on the main Joburg highway. "So, I can't live at home anymore?" Dan had a tremble in his voice.

"Just during the week," I told him. "I'll pick you up every Friday and take you back to school on Mondays." I quickly did the commute sums in my head. Belfast would mean four hours of commute every weekend whereas the Bethal option would involve a massive twelve hours there and back, there and back. I offered up a quick, silent prayer to God. Please, please let it be Belfast God, not Bethal. Predictably, Bethal won in the end.

Jenny and I took a day off work and went to look at the two school options Alma had given us. It was school holidays, but both headmasters said they'd be available to meet with us. We left Dan behind, just in case. The phrase between a rock and a hard place was coined by a parent putting a child into a special needs school, in either Bethal or Belfast.

The school in Belfast was especially bleak, perched on top of a mountain, lashed non-stop by freezing cold gale-force winds, even in the middle of summer. What was it like in winter, I wondered out loud? The headmaster told me his school was very, very cold in winter, bitterly cold in fact. He rolled his r's as only an Afrikaner can and was seemingly proud of his school's bitter climatic conditions. The school was miserable with a harsh reformatory school feel to it, a place where hugging, loving and laughter were strictly verboden and against school rules. The word puritanical came to mind easily. The Headmaster told us the school offered education for children of mixed races with learning difficulties, mostly practical subjects including woodwork and engineering. He delivered the words mixed race with obvious distaste. He was cold and dispassionate with zero warmth, like the wind that howled outside. He had lots of vacancies at the school and would be able to accommodate Daniel. I told him we were also going to Bethal to look at a school there and would get back to him once we'd made a decision. I was glad to drive away from him and his school and got back on the phone to God. Please, please God let Bethal be better than Belfast.

Bethal is a farming town on the Highveld, surrounded by mealie fields and sunflower fields that stretch away as far as the eye could see. The town was bigger than I expected and, as is my wont, I managed to get lost and had to stop and ask a middle-aged lady for directions to Jan van Tonder School. She flashed up a quick look of pity, tempered with a mild touch of distaste as soon as I mentioned the name of the school. Jenny and I would get used to the pity look in the years ahead. Unfortunately, the lady didn't do English too good, so I had to repeat my request in my best mangled Afrikaans and she told me left, right, go straight and then left, left, right. Unfortunately, I don't do Afrikaans too good or directions, and so we got lost again. We ended up seeing most of Bethal, and it felt better than Belfast, at least it had some warmth.

Eventually, we found the Jan van Tonder School, the correct pronunciation of which offered up excellent throat-clearing opportunities. The Headmaster gave us the guided tour, almost reluctantly. He came across as being very tired. If ever a man was counting down to his pension and retirement, it was him. His school was almost as tired as he was. A lot of money had been spent on the school in years past, the metal workshop and the woodwork shop were especially well equipped, but like the headmaster, everything looked old, tired and past retirement date. The school boasted an agriculture department that looked to consist of a small dairy complete with a few black and white cows and a not so impressive vegetable garden, all run by the students. I liked the agricultural department. For me, it was the main point of difference between the two schools we'd looked at.

Jan van Tonder's boarding hostels were miserable though with a reformatory school décor and ambience. There was paint peeling everywhere you looked, and ten beds squeezed in per dorm, with mattresses on them so skinny and threadbare the kids might just as well have been sleeping on the cold, hard floor. The shared ablutions stank, not surprisingly because there was piss all over the floor. Picking up our looks of horror, the headmaster quickly told us there were some private rooms with their own bathrooms available, but they cost a few hundred rand extra per month. We had a look at one. The room was spartan, but it was clean.

And when eventually it did stink like piss, at least it would be Dan's piss.

Back in his office, the headmaster showed some animation for the first time when he showed us the school rules, all eight pages of them. He was very proud of them. There was even an English version, which I took to be a good sign. By this stage, I was trying very hard to look for positives. The set of rules were staunch and seemed to cover every possible transgression, including rape.

Jenny and I agonised about the decision about where to send Dan to school on the three-hour drive home. If the truth be known, both Bethal and Belfast were pretty crap, but they were our only options. We didn't have any others. Of the two, I preferred the Bethal option, mostly because of the agricultural department with its built-in dairy. Jenny said she was happy with the private room we'd seen in Bethal and said she'd be able to sew up some curtains and make it a home from home. Both of us studiously ignored the inclusion of rape in the school rules. In the end, we wimped out and said we'd leave the final decision with Dan. At the start of the school term, we'd take him to both schools, and he'd get to say yes or no.

School started the following week. We were rooting for Bethal, so we took Dan there first. He was very nervous and chewed his lip non-stop in the back of the car on the three-hour drive. I was even more nervous than Dan and badgered God the whole way there. Please, please God, let Dan like Jan van Tonder. The school hostel was a hive of activity when we got there, with cars and pick-up trucks parked two deep, busy offloading kids and their regulation black school trunks for the first day of term. There was lots of noise, parents shouting at their kids, kids shouting at other kids, teachers shouting at everyone, all of it in Afrikaans. But in amongst all the shouting, I was happy to hear laughing. Dan heard it too. And straight away, even before getting out the car, he told us that he liked Jan van Tonder, that he wanted to go to school there. Shame, poor kid. Only then did we get a glimpse of how desperately unhappy and how desperately lonely Dan had become at Penryn.

Chapter Forty-Four

Roy Bennett was released from prison in 2005 three months early, for good behaviour according to the newspapers. I think it was more of a case of them hurrying to get him out of their prison system before he took it over. When first they threw him in prison after he was found guilty by the bullshit parliamentary committee, to try and break him they forced him into a stinking, lice-infested, shit encrusted prison uniform. Roy told them Fuck You in perfect Shona and ripped the filthy uniform off, telling them he'd rather walk naked and keep his dignity. Throughout the prison, thousands of other prisoners followed suit, ripping their uniforms off and stripping naked in solidarity. The prison warders tried everything to break Roy but couldn't. While inside prison, Roy won the hearts and minds of his fellow prisoners and, I'm guessing, more than a few of his wardens. At a press conference after his release, Roy was unbowed and unrepentant and told the world that he'd carry on fighting for a better Zimbabwe for all Zimbabweans.

It wasn't long before Roy was in trouble again, his name was linked to an arms cache in Mutare, supposedly linked to a plot to assassinate Mugabe. It was all smoke, mirrors and bullshit. The truth of it was ZANU was scared of Roy. He'd just been elevated to the position of Treasurer General within Morgan's MDC and was now in a position to shape policy and bring some order to the ranks. But more than that, they were scared of Roy's connection to the people of Zimbabwe. It was strong, both ways. Roy would walk across broken glass for the people of Zimbabwe, and vice versa. And then when Roy got out of prison and immediately started exploring the military's Achilles Heel, the massive chasm that existed between the lower to middle officer ranks and the corrupt fat cat Generals way up high, the Generals hatched the arms cache plot. Roy knew that coups were carried out by the Lieutenants and the Captains and the Majors that occupied that chasm. This time the Generals wanted Roy locked up for good so they could kill him.

But Roy was a step ahead of them and skipped the border into South Africa and went into exile. He arrived in South Africa with nothing more than the clothes on his back and a mandate from the MDC to organise the Party's external fundraising and membership structures. In the first week that he was there, I tracked Roy down in Johannesburg and offered up my help. Roy needed bank accounts opened yesterday, but because he'd entered South Africa illegally, he didn't have the resident permits as required by the banks. I told him no problem and got busy opening bank accounts for the MDC in my name. Roy needed offices and somewhere to live. So, I put him in touch my best friend and fellow activist who I will call Baldric. Baldric's speciality in life is giving people in need the shirt off his back. And Baldric knew Johannesburg and everyone in it. Quickly Roy got settled in his new home. Which he hated. Roy hated the hustle, bustle and the impersonality of big city life. He yearned for his beloved Zimbabwe, but he put all of that aside and got on with the job.

Roy came to see me in White River with his brand-new, never been used laptop computer. He told me he needed help. Before he could get busy fundraising, he needed proper budgets in place and financial targets to aim for. Could I help him with those? I was drinking a cup of coffee at the time and choked on it. I told him asking me for help with budgets, and financial forecasts was like asking a blind man for help crossing a busy road. Roy was embarrassed.

"But you know how to use Excel?" he asked me.

"Of course I do.'

"Well, I don't," he said. "And I need you to teach me quickly."

We got busy setting out budgets for the MDC.

I ambushed Roy that first night he spent at Summer Hill Farm. By then, White River and surrounds had attracted lots of Zimbabwean refugees, mostly farmer types looking to start over after losing their homes and livelihoods in the land-grab. And most of them were bitter and twisted about Zimbabwe and what had happened to them and their families there and had no intentions of ever returning home. Which pained me hugely. Once we'd won the politics, I wanted all of them to also move back to Zim, so we could go back to how things had been before, so we could live happily ever after. So, I invited a cross section of my ex-countrymen to dinner that night and asked Roy if he'd share his vision for Zimbabwe with them. I asked him to turn a light on for them. Roy wasn't the most polished public speaker I'd ever heard, but he was easily one of the most compelling. On my back veranda, Roy spoke from the heart and told my friends about his experiences while in prison and how the rapists and murderers and the lowest of the low had helped him survive hell on earth, about how colour blind those Zimbabweans had been. They didn't see Roy as a white farmer, they saw him as one of them, just another poor Zimbabwean suffering at the hands of Mugabe. Like something out of Desiderata, Roy belonged. We all did, he told us.

Not everyone listening bought into Roy's vision. Robs Richards, a daughter of best friends Marco and Judy, refused to believe. Their workers on their farm had shown their true colours when they'd turned on the family, choosing to side with the land invaders, There was no place in Zimbabwe for whites anymore, she told Roy. Roy was pained to his heart by her comments. Alas. Robs now lives in Prague.

Roy didn't have it easy in South Africa. One of his main objectives was to mobilise and organise illegal Zimbabweans living in South Africa into MDC party structures, complete with chairmen and vice-chairmen and organising secretaries ad infinitum. Personally, I thought it sounded like a waste of time but went with Roy to one of his first meetings with the Zim illegals in Braamfontein. Braamfontein, along with Hillbrow next door, was home to about a million illegal Zimbabweans. The meeting was held in a huge church hall and was an unmitigated disaster. As soon as Roy called the crowded hall to order, members of a large Ndebele contingent stood up, cussed Roy and all the other Shona at length and then stormed out. I was aghast. The hatred was naked and in your face and from what I could see, completely unresolvable. Not surprising. Twenty thousand Ndebele murdered is not an easy thing to move on from. But just as well the Ndebele contingent exited the building because had they stayed; the meeting would have ended in bloodshed. Roy tried hard to get his meeting back on track but failed, and it ended in shambles.

I drove back to White River hugely down. I'd never seen such out in the open hatred before. But even worse, I reckoned that more than a few of the malcontents who'd taken charge at the end were CIO operatives sent out into the diaspora to sow hatred and division. I never went to another MDC party meeting in South Africa again. Roy battled on resolutely, but he never won. And years later, I still maintain a long list of Zimbabwean exiles that I don't trust and won't be in the same room with.

I much preferred activisiming, which I defined as free-wheeling politics as opposed to organised stodge. Roy phoned me up and asked Baldric and me to meet him in Johannesburg. We went out to a self-storage yard somewhere on the East Rand. Roy had the keys to one of the units. We opened it up. Inside were tons and tons of political paraphernalia-playing cards with derisive caricatures on them that pulled the piss out of the ZANU higher echelon, including Grace, the Generals and Mugabe himself. There were Mugabe condoms and best of all, toilet paper with a picture of Mugabe on each sheet so you could wipe your arse with his face, I let out a whistle. Someone with a lot of money-as in millions- and a lot of imagination had been extremely busy. Roy told me the shipment had been the brainchild of a fringe Sokwanele member who went by the name of Hemingway.

"What does he want us to do with it?"

"Flood Zimbabwe."

Baldric and I loaded up the truck. On my way back to Nelspruit I had to stop for an emergency roadside crap. Luckily, I had a truck full of Mugabe toilet paper.

Baldric set up a distribution point at the busy Park Station in downtown Johannesburg. He had around the clock volunteers dishing out free packs of playing cards and toilet paper to anyone and everyone climbing on to a Zimbabwe bound bus. Because we had tons and tons of stuff to move, I took a load up to the busy border town of Musina and hired a young Zimbabwean exile called Victor to handle distribution. I told Victor my name was Eric with no surname. Victor worked at a busy bakery for not a lot and jumped at the chance to earn a couple of hundred bucks extra per month. He liked the product, especially the playing cards but didn't know how many he'd be able to move. It would all depend on the price. I told him there was no price, he'd be giving it away for free. His eyes rolled. Clearly, he thought I was mental. I told him to be careful not to attract too much attention to himself, Musina was lousy with CIO operatives. Victor just laughed. Musina was his town, and he knew how it worked.

I was pretty sure he was going to be selling the stuff but didn't have a problem with that, as long as he moved it. And move it, he did. Quickly, Victor started moving big loads of the merchandise. I had to resupply him within the first week. White River to Musina was a bum numbing 10-hour round trip. I gave Victor another bakkie load, but straight away, he told me it wouldn't be enough. And sure enough, I'd only just driven back on to Summer Hill when I got another call from him. I groaned. Running to and from Musina every second day was going to cost me a fortune. I was going to have to find another way of getting the merchandise up there.

I answered the phone. "Yes, Victor. What do you want?"

But it wasn't Victor on the other end of the line. A harsh voice demanded "Who are you? And, where are you?"

The voice sent a right chill through me. I knew exactly who the voice belonged to, someone who wore dark glasses for a living. Victor had been grabbed by the CIO. "Where's Victor?" I asked.

The harsh voice demanded "Who are you? Where are you?"

"And I asked you where Victor is? What have you done with him? Let me talk to him."

The voice changed tack and tone, harsh was gone, replaced by wheedling. "I'm a good friend of Victor. And I like your playing cards too much. I want to know where I can get some more for my friends. And also your condoms."

"I don't know what you're talking about."

Dark glasses on the other side of the phone went back to harsh. It suited him better. "Tell me your name."

"Fuck you." My hands were shaking as I hung up the phone.

I never heard from or saw Victor again. I drove up to Zimbabwe three weeks later and asked after him at the bakery where Victor had worked, but they said they hadn't seen him in over a month. He'd just stopped coming to work. Because the labour in Musina was so transitory, they'd automatically assumed he'd gone back to Zimbabwe. Which is what I was also thinking but just not of his own free will. Alas. Poor Victor. But the show went on. With more than a quarter of Zimbabwe in South Africa illegally, looking for jobs, it didn't take me long to find another Victor to carry on with distribution. I told the new Victor what had happened to the old Victor and to be extra careful. He told me no worries.

It took Baldric and me and others the best part of a year to empty the storage unit in Johannesburg. And whether or not our efforts and all those playing cards, condoms and toilet paper made one iota of difference to the Zimbabwean political landscape is subject to debate. Over the years, I've thought about Victor often, with more than a twinge of guilt. Alas.

Someone up top in Sokwanele secured funding for a billboard campaign to reach out to and influence Zimbabweans. With so many Zimbabweans streaming through them every day, Musina and Johannesburg Park Station were the logical focal points. While other more talented Sokwanele activists worked on the artwork, Baldric and I went billboard site hunting. Baldric nailed down a perfect site at Park Station- on the side of the building that overlooked the bus terminus. I got lucky in Musina and found a vacant billboard up for rent between Musina and the border. Small wonder it was vacant- I could have rented a 4 bedroomed house for less -but I snapped it up for 6 months.

The artwork options, all incredibly hard-hitting and punchy with an election theme, were sent out via Hushmail. We agonised over them for a week, but there was one clear winner when put to the vote, Sokwanele was a very democratic organisation. Against a background of flames and stark barbed wire, the message read in big, bold font 'We Know Why You Are in South Africa, Life in Zimbabwe Is Murder These Days'.

Along with his pointing index finger, we cribbed the smaller pay offline at the bottom from Lord Kitchener. It read 'Remember Your Country Needs You. Come Home at Election Time and Vote for Freedom'.

I drove up to Musina on the day the billboard went up and marvelled at the power of the message. The billboard was a showstopper, literally. The very first car that drove passed the finished article slowed down, stopped and then backed up for a long, proper look. To bump into freedom of speech less than a kilometre from the Zimbabwean border was obviously hugely profound. I was thrilled. We were going to get huge value for money from our investment. But not for long. Alas. Less than a week after going up, CIO sent a team over from Zimbabwe in the dark of night to rip the billboard down.

We had enough money in the Sokwanele account-but only just- to replace the damaged billboard. I gave the billboard company the order for fresh artwork, and they dispatched a team. To maximise exposure, we put a story out about how the billboard's message had struck a nerve and about how Mugabe's regime had sent a team across an international border to deface it. Luckily, we hit pay dirt. On what was obviously a quiet news day, one of the big American newspapers sent their Africa correspondent up to Musina to cover our billboard story. And while he was taking photos of the replacement artwork going back up, the billboard workers were arrested by the South African soldiers, under the supervision of the Mayor of Musina. The reporter snapped away, merrily, and the story went viral. They take things like Workers Rights and Freedom of Speech seriously in South Africa. Opposition parties entered the fray, ditto the billboard company and their army of lawyers and after much ado, our billboard which now had international celebrity status went back up, and stayed up. It was money well spent.

Afterwards, we were able to piece together what had happened. Long story short; apparently a high-up in the Mayor of Musina's office was having an affair with her Zimbabwe counterpart and had promised him that she'd stop the billboard from going back up after Zimbabwean agents ripped it down in the first place.

Musina was fertile ground for my activisiming. In early February of that year I picked up on a small news item on the internet announcing that Mugabe had chosen Beitbridge as the venue for his annual birthday celebrations. Every year, taxpayers and ZANU sycophants spent huge money the country didn't have throwing Mugabe a birthday bash so they could fawn over him. And this year, lucky Beitbridge was it. I punched the air and gave a jump for joy. We'd give the old fucker a birthday party that he wished he could forget.

Birthday parties need money for party decorations, and to bus party goers in from Joburg and other parts. They also need police permission, especially if you want the party a.k.a. demonstration to be held right on Beit bridge over the Limpopo river. I went to Sokwanele for the money. They loved my idea of a Mugabe birthday bash demo at the border and told me to push the button. For the South African police permission, I went to a staunch activist friend of mine called Simon Mudekwa a.k.a. Simon Dread. Simon was the President of the Zimbabwe Revolutionary Youth movement. He'd fled Zimbabwe for fear of his life just after the 2000 elections and, along with hundreds of other refugees, now called the Methodist Cathedral in the heart of Hillbrow home. Simon Dread was born to stand in front of a crowd and whip them up into frenzy. He absolutely loved it. Almost as much as he loved my Beitbridge idea. He told me "If you find the money to hire busses Mr Eric, I can fill a hundred of them with demonstrators and youth members."

"I'll find the money to hire the busses but first we have to get police permission."

"Don't you worry about that, Mr Eric, my friend in the SAP can organize, no problem." I had serious doubts but Simon's friend in the

SAP came through for him, in a morning. Incredibly, we'd been given permission to hold our demonstration on the side of highway right outside the South African border post. It was game on.

With just fourteen days until the big day, preparations were frenzied. I asked Roy Bennett if he would make a birthday speech for Mugabe at the party and lead the after-party rally and he told yes me in a heartbeat. Baldric was in charge of Bob's party decorations including balloons and cakes. He pulled out all the stops. Bob's birthday balloon was the best, a helium filled Zeppelin over thirty metres long with heart felt birthday messages for Mugabe inscribed on both sides. The plan was we'd winch the Zeppelin up hundreds of metres into the sky so that it would be clearly visible from Beitbridge stadium where Mugabe's other party was happening. I wanted to go with obscenities instead of happy birthday wishes on the balloon but got shot down on account of the fact that women and children would also see it. In the end we went with "Free and Fair or Just Hot Air?" on the one side, in reference to the next elections and 'Have Your Cake and Beat it Bob" on the other. The cake in question was also a beauty. Made out of plastic, the cake was five meters in diameter and two meters high. After the speeches, the plan would be for Roy Bennett to cut the cake whence upon activists wearing skeleton costumes would jump out symbolising masses who would be starving in Zimbabwe whilst Mugabe enjoyed birthday cake. The skeletons all had names of people murdered by Mugabe like Josiah Tongogara and Herbert Chitepo. I was impressed. I had no idea Baldric could even spell symbolism, let alone do it.

Our plan came together like clockwork. Baldric, Roy and I drove up to Musina the night before the birthday party with the balloon and the cake and the costumes. We'd booked in at a guest lodge near the border where we were joined by Hendrik O'Neill and Mike Mason who'd driven through from Zimbabwe for the party. I hadn't seen Hendrick or Mike in months, and we caught up over beers until late in the night.

Early in the morning on February the Twenty First we drove through to the South African border control to set up the cake and Baldric's helium zeppelin. And then we had to wait for Simon Dread and his birthday party activists. We heard the birthday party activists long before we saw them. Simon and his Revolutionary Youth Movement had departed Joburg's Park Station at ten o'clock the night before and I think more than a bit of the food money I'd given Simon had been invested in beer and booze.

Mostly political rallies are ten percent wow and ninety percent yawn. The rally on the Beitbridge was all wow. Roy Bennett in front of a crowd of Zimbabweans was beyond electric. Because he spoke in Shona, I didn't have a clue what Roy said but whatever it was, the crowd loved it and went crazy. I stood right at the back of the crowd next to a group of South African police observers. They were bowled over by at the genuine love, warmth and affection that the big black crowd showed Roy. And the crowd got bigger and bigger, swelled by a steady stream of Zimbabweans from Beitbridge who'd heard by about the 'other' Birthday party on the go. By the end, I think we had more Zimbabweans at our party than Bob had at his. There was a large contingent of men in dark glasses moving in amongst the crowd, maybe twenty or more, obviously CIO. Ordinarily, I'd have been shit scared of them but I got caught up in the moment and hit them with big MDC chinja salutes every time one of them looked at me.

When Baldric winched Bob's birthday balloon high up into the air, the crowd went crazy. Baldric had two hundred metres of cable on his winch and he let out every last meter. And still the Zeppelin was huge. There was no way that the people gathered at the Beitbridge stadium across the river couldn't not see it. The zeppelin hadn't been up for more than fifteen minutes when a small flight of light military aircraft appeared in the sky over Beitbridge, approaching from the north. They circled the Beitbridge stadium once, twice and then a third time, just beyond our zeppelin. It had to be Mugabe, arriving for his birthday party. Our zeppelin stuck out in the sky like a pair of dog's balls. There was no way Mugabe could miss the big balloon and its birthday messages. The crowd went crazy again. I could hear the one guy near me shouting "Fuck you Mugabe, Fuck You." I joined in, as loud as I could, hoping the old bastard in the plane on the other side of the Limpopo River could hear me. I saw one of the CIO watching me and shouted even louder. And then it was time for Roy to cut Mugabe's birthday cake. As the skeletons climbed up out of the cake and on to the road, the crowd surged forward and hoisted Tongogara and Chitepo up on to their shoulders and paraded them around.

All in all, it was my best birthday party ever. For the first time ever, I'm guessing Zimbabweans got right in Mugabe's face and showed him exactly what they thought of him. We were told afterwards that Mugabe was apparently so incensed by our birthday balloon that he'd given orders for it to be shot down out of the sky. But his senior commanders talked him out of it, knowing full well the aggression would trigger an international tsunami of massive proportions. Whether it was true of not, I seized on the story as being gospel.

I drove back to White River on an absolute high, shouting 'Fuck You Mugabe' every few minutes. I was still fully excited when I got home hours later and tried to re-capture the moment for Jenny but failed. She shook her head sadly and told me well done for trying but told me I'd achieved not a lot, other than to waste a lot of money. I didn't care though. I knew that I'd gotten in right under Mugabe's skin.

Not long afterwards, I had another opportunity to poke Mugabe again, but this time properly. I was working behind the counter in our flower shop in Nelspruit, peddling carnations and chrysanthemums when a small, compact man walked in and asked for me by name. The small in stature guy asked if we could talk in private. Great, another top-secret Nelspruit wedding, I grumped under my breath. I took him through to my little office in the back of the shop. He eyed the thin chipboard walls critically. They weren't up to keeping secrets. Could we rather have the conversation on the street outside the shop? Thinking I had a proper nutter on my hands, I traipsed back through the shop with him and out onto the privacy of the noisy street.

"So how can I help you?" I asked.

"Mutual friends told me you were involved with the MDC. I'm from Zimbabwe a long time ago and don't like what's happened there. So, I've come to offer my services."

"With what?'

"I'll go in there and kill anyone you want me to kill. I'll take out whoever." He smiled as he said it, but his smile didn't go anywhere near his eyes. The guy was deadly serious. He might have been small in stature but what there was of him looked to be all steel. I'd hate to come up against him in a dark alley.

I'd stepped outside fully expecting to haggle over the price of carnations, but here I was talking to a hitman. It was surreal. And having never had a discussion that centred on assassination before, I was clearly struggling. The hitman offered to fill in some gaps for me. He'd lived in Zimbabwe as a child but had emigrated with his parents after independence. He'd joined the British Army and had spent twenty years with their Special Forces. After leaving the army, he was now working in Iraq and Afghanistan as a private security contractor. He had a hankering to go home to Zimbabwe but didn't like what Mugabe had done to the place. And doing what he'd been doing for the last twenty years, he didn't think the MDC was on track to change anything. Dictators like Mugabe didn't get voted out, they get taken out forcibly, with the emphasis on force. And killing someone up close to Mugabe would help hurry that process along. So what did I think?

I badly wanted to say something deep and meaningful, but nothing came out. My mouth was more intent on goldfish out of water impressions. I decided to come clean with him, but it came out a babble. His friends had sent him to the wrong person, they'd sent him to a political lightweight who'd be out of his depth in a carpark puddle. If he was looking for some Mugabe toilet paper or condoms, no problem but assassinations were out of my area of expertise. He cut me off. "They told me you can me put in contact with Roy Bennett."

"That I can do."

"So, tell him what I said."

"Okay."

And then come back to me."

"But I don't have your number."

"No, you don't," he agreed. "You can contact me on Hushmail only." His Hushmail address was as innocuous as the first impressions of the man himself.

I went to Johannesburg to see Roy the next day, all excited to tell him about the hitman. I'd tossed and turned all night, playing the conversation over and over in my head. I couldn't but think the guy had it spot on. Democracy didn't work with dictators like Mugabe. Roy shook his head and marvelled at my capacity to end up in the wrong places with the wrong people. Some people always landed with their arses in butter, but mine always went for thorns. But with his poker face firmly in place, he took the hitman's Hushmail address. He told me he'd send someone to meet the guy and hear him out.

What followed was dreadful. I sat on edge and in the dark for weeks and heard nothing back from Roy. I waited with fingers crossed and bated breath for the most dramatic of headlines, but they never came. Alas. And I grew more and more frustrated. From what I could see, the MDC was getting nowhere fast, due in no small part to Mbeki's machinations. I went to meet Roy a month later to ask him if he'd met with my assassin. Roy was more than an hour late for our meeting. He was in Pretoria meeting with Mbeki. Eventually, Roy stormed in with a face like thunder. His security adviser, Pete Cutting, edged in after him. Which was a bad sign. Pete, ex-Special Branch, had been round the block more than once and was easily the most cynical man I'd ever met. And when Pete felt the need to tiptoe around Roy, it was time to take cover.

Unfortunately, there weren't too many cover options in the foyer of Roy's office. I put my happy face on and greeted Roy warmly and asked him how it was going. Clearly not well. Roy shouted his answer as he stormed past me to his inner office. "Mbeki is a duplicitous cunt." He slammed the door shut and that was the last I saw of him that morning.

I was desperate for details of the Roy Mbeki meeting and tried to wheedle them out of Pete Cutting, but that was like trying to move the unmoveable. Pete could keep secrets, no problem. But he let vent on other growing frustrations. Pete was the original call a spade a fucking shovel man, and he let rip. He described the MDC as a shower of shit without a plan. "We should have gone with your little hitman."

"Why didn't you?"

"We pushed it up to Morgan's office, I'm not sure why. Half of them in there are fucking CIO and the other half are soft cock liberals, so it died a quick death. That's the problem with this Democracy bullshit. Too many egos, too many other agendas and no decisions. We should be running this like a military operation. Send in people like your little man to take the bad fuckers out. That's the only way we'll dislodge them."

"Do you think he was the real deal? That hitman guy?"

"Oh yeah. Stone cold killer."

"Did you get back to him? To tell him no."

"No."

I hatched a plan on the drive back to Nelspruit. I sent the hitman a Hushmail apologising. I told him that Roy and Pete had been stonewalled by Harare. But I had an idea for another project that he might be interested in. Could he come and see me in the flower shop the next time he was near Nelspruit? He walked in two days later. Again, we met in my office on the busy street, and I told him what Pete had told me.

"He's right. They should be running this like a military operation. But they're not. Shit happens. So, tell me about your idea."

"The way I see it, South Africa is the problem. Mbeki could fix Zimbabwe in a heartbeat. But he doesn't want to. He'd rather things carried on like they are. Zimbabwe's industry has collapsed, and instead of being competitors in Africa, Zim is now a customer for South African products. Business has never been better for South African exporters into Zim. And a failed MDC isn't going to inspire South African Unions to rush out and form their own political party."

"Correct." He was a man of few words, which was quite disconcerting. "What's your idea?"

"We film a video. Black guys in like urban camouflage, with rifles and stuff. They call themselves the Zimbabwe Freedom Front, based in South Africa and angry that the South African government is doing nothing to stop Mugabe. And the Zimbabwe Freedom Front tell the world that the South Africans aren't doing anything to stop Mugabe because they're profiting from the situation. Zimbabwean industry collapses and all the while South African trucks are shipping South African products up to fill Zimbabwean supermarket shelves."

"Ok."

"The Zimbabwe Freedom Front says they'll target South African trucks, on both sides of the border. They'll stop them and burn them."

"Ok."

"Then we send the video into the television stations. And then maybe Mbeki will do something."

"Ok." He had a glint in his eye that scared me.

"But we're not actually going to do any of that," I said hurriedly. "We're not going to burn any trucks. We're just going to say we're going to, on the video."

"Ok. Let's do it. Where? And when?"

"Where what?

"Where are we going to film it?"

"I suppose we can do it here, in my flower shop. But we'll have to do it after hours. And don't tell my wife."

We agreed to meet at the flower shop three nights later. The hitman said he could bring a rifle plus other props and the video camera. I'd bring the actors and the script. I worked on my script long and hard, and I thought it was perfect. It spoke from the heart and was full of fire and brimstone, menace tempered with regret, sincere but also no-nonsense. We told the world we would target South African trucks full of South African goods, Zimbabwe bound, and we'd blow them up. We'd come across as good men with our backs to the wall, doing bad things but only because we had no choice.

My cast, on the other hand, was less than perfect, but then I wasn't exactly spoiled for choices. My screenplay called for a cast of two, the fearsome front guy who'd deliver the script with menace and his number two who'd skulk threateningly in the background. My actors were Zimbabwean refugees, both staunch MDC members and both working on farms in White River. The one was a huge strong man who was clever and articulate and but for his voice, would've been perfect for playing the fearsome frontman. His voice was high pitched with a slight lisp. I was going to have to go with him skulking threateningly at the back of the set and have the other guy play the Zimbabwe Freedom Front frontman. Which was a snag. Because the other guy should've been born a Buddhist monk. He was a small gentle man with a happy face that absolutely radiated gentleness like a lighthouse throws out light on a dark night. Even when he frowned, he looked happy. I figured maybe I'd be able to hide his happy face behind a full-face balaclava. Both actors had signed up to the job in a heartbeat when first I'd spoken to them about the project. Both had families at home and wanted nothing more than to be able to go home to them.

Once I had the actors in the car, I went over the script with them. We were going to shoot a movie with them cast as urban terrorists. Unfortunately, the words shoot and urban terrorist set the little one off. I thought he was going to throw himself out the door of the car. I calmed him down and reassured him we were just play-acting, for the camera. And they weren't terrorists, they could be freedom fighters instead. But not proper ones, just pretend ones because we weren't really going to blow-up any trucks like in the script. The phrase blow-up set off a nervous tic in the little guy's face so violent it almost put his neck out. To calm him down, I got him started on reading the script. I say started because he never got anywhere past the first sentence. His nervous tic stormed his voice box and manifested itself as a vicious stammer. Crap. With him reading, we'd be shooting the video all night. I went back to a variation on Plan A; a ZFF Commander in Chief with a high pitched, lisp. Maybe he'd come across as sinister.

The hitman was at the shop waiting for us with a bulging kit bag. He rolled his eyes when he saw I was wearing my squash kit. I explained that I'd told Jenny I was playing a grudge match. More eye-rolling. Keeping a close eye on my little urban terrorist to make sure he didn't do a runner, I let us all into the shop. I gave myself full marks for remembering to turn the shop's alarm off. I introduced everyone to everyone. The actors were nervous and said little. We got busy transforming the back of a flower shop into the ZFF HQ. The hitman set up his camera equipment and the lighting, and I turned the florist's worktable into the Commander in Chief's operations desk. I dug out a hessian overlay that we used for weddings and threw it over the desk. Then I draped a Zimbabwe flag over the hessian, for patriotic effect. I took a step back for a critical look and pronounced it perfect. The hitman disagreed and removed from the wall behind the war desk two posters, one promoting a new range of cut flower roses and another a range of florist's foam. But then the wall was too white and empty, and it would look stark on camera. We needed to create the right mood. I filled the gap with a large motorist's map of Southern Africa that I had on my office wall. The map had little gold and silver stars stuck all over Mpumalanga.

I explained to the hitman that the stars denoted florists in the province. The gold stars were florists that bought their flowers from us and the silver stars were florists that didn't. Embarrassingly there were way more silver stars than gold ones. Alas. The hitman rolled his eyes. He asked if he could pull the stars off the map. He said when military intelligence analysed our video footage, better they not see all the gold and silver stars clustered around Nelspruit. He stuck them back on the map, all along the main Johannesburg Zimbabwe highway. In the context of the video, the stars would look ominous. It was just a pity they weren't a more military colour.

We were good to go the hitman said, it was time for the actors to take up their positions and for the camera to roll. But when he pulled an AK47, a pistol and some hand grenades out of his kitbag to use as props, he triggered off the nervous twitch in the little terrorist's face again. It looked like the little guy's face had been plugged into the mains. And when he handed the rifle to the little guy to hold menacingly, impossibly the twitch stepped up a notch, like a facial version of St Vitus's dance. The hitman looked alarmed and stepped back. On film, the twitch would look especially horrible and off-putting, so I quickly hid it with a full-face balaclava. That was much better. The little freedom fighter looked okay, a bit on the small side and not very menacing, but at least the twitch was hidden from view.

The commander-in-chief, on the other hand, was perfect. In his full-face balaclava and with his muscles all big and bulging under his black jacket, he looked properly threatening. Until he opened his mouth and the squeaky lisp came out. The hitman stopped filming. He played back the tape to listen and shook his head. It wasn't going to work, he said. No disrespect he said, but no one was going to take the tape seriously if the C-in-C sounded like a girl. Couldn't we use the other terrorist as the spokesman? I explained about the stammer, and we stuck with Plan A, the big guy with the slight lisp. After two and three takes, I had a brain wave. If we pulled the balaclava mouthpiece over his mouth, thus forcing the C-in-C to talk loudly through the wool, maybe the worst of his lisp would be muffled. It sort of worked. In takes four through to fourteen, the C-in-C struggled with the worst bundle of nerves imaginable and kept fluffing his lines. I thought the hitman was going to grab the pistol off the table and shoot him. Evidently, so did the C-in-C, because take fifteen was near perfect, and near-perfect was good enough. That was a wrap, the hitman told us.

It had to be close to fifty degrees plus under their woollen balaclavas, so the actors ripped them off in a hurry. I told them well done. If the South Africans heeded the warnings on our tape and started exerting pressure on Mugabe, then they'd have done a good thing for their country. And if nothing changed, then at least they'd tried. The little ex-terrorist clearly wasn't happy, though. His bottom lip was trembling, on the edge of an emotional melt-down. "But if they catch us, sir, won't we be tried as terrorists, won't we be hung?" he asked miserably.

I jumped in quickly to reassure him. "No, no, they don't hang people here anymore. South Africa abolished the death sentence in 1994, I think."

My reassurances didn't work too good. "So instead we'll just go to prison forever, for being terrorists?" he asked even more miserably. I thought he'd burst into tears.

"No, no, no. Of course not. Because you're not terrorists remember, you're freedom fighters, and besides, it's all pretend."

"But how will they know that? When they catch us?"

"They're not going to catch you."

"But what if they do?" His tears weren't far off.

"I'll tell them. I'll tell them you were just acting. In fact, I'll tell them now, on camera. I'll confess that it was all my idea and that you were just acting and if ever they catch us, I'll give them the tape."

"OK."

Clearly thinking I was mental, the hitman recorded my confession. I told the camera my name, what we were doing, and why we were doing it? There was no such thing as the Zimbabwe Freedom Front. We didn't even know how to make bombs, let alone blow trucks up. We were staging a publicity stunt that would allow us to go home to Zimbabwe. But we couldn't because the South African government was on Mugabe's side and were helping him hang onto power. It wasn't fair. So to shock them into action, we'd filmed our protest film. But it was all make-believe, and no trucks were actually going to get blown up and...I was starting to ramble, so the hitman cameraman said cut, and stopped filming.

When I got home, I told Jenny I'd played good squash and was exhausted and ready for bed. I hid both tapes in the back of sock drawer and tossed and turned all night, playing the tapes back in my head, but mostly my confession tape.

The following week I went to Joburg to deliver the Freedom Front communiqué. Figuring they had more experience with terrorist communiqués, I decided that I'd deliver it to Al Jazeera instead of Sky. Their bureau was in a big building in Auckland Park. I walked into the foyer of the building sweating profusely, with my heart hammering and the brown envelope containing the tape clutched tightly. I told the security desk that I wanted to deliver a parcel.

"Can I see your ID?" the security officer said.

"Why? Why do you want to see my ID? I just want to drop a parcel off?"

"I need to see your ID because the rules say I need to look at your ID," the security officer told me with more than a hint of suspicion in his voice.

"Sure then, I'll just go get it from the car then." I fled the building with my sweaty envelope. I tracked down a Post Office and posted the envelope to the Al Jazeera Bureau Chief. Only after I'd dropped the envelope in the post box, I remembered I should've wiped it clean of prints. Crap.

Back on Summer Hill Farm, I watched Al Jazeera non-stop for two weeks waiting for my bombshell story to break, but alas, it never did. Something had obviously gone wrong. Most probably the postal service. Or maybe, if Al Jazeera got the tape, they'd played it and seen straight away that it was bullshit. Crap. I should've gone with Sky instead. They were more sympathetic to Zimbabwe's plight. After burning my confession tape, I beat myself up long and hard. All our hard work and efforts had been for nought. I sent a sorry for screwing things up apology Hushmail to the hitman. He sent me back a nice reply telling me that at least I'd tried. I never spoke to him again after that.

Years later, after he'd pulled out of politics, Roy Bennett told me over a beer that he had hired an assassin in 2009 to take out one of Zimbabwe's top security chiefs. Roy's hired assassin was to have pulled up next to the security chief's car in Harare traffic and put a round through his head. It would've worked, Roy told me but for the intervention of the British. They uncovered the details of the plot and fed it into Downing Street just hours before the trigger was due to be pulled. Tony Blair called Morgan Tsvangirai and told him what Roy was planning and told Morgan to pull back on Roy's leash, or else. And so it came to nothing. Roy told me that the plot had been leaked to the Brits by one of my Sokwanele comrades who'd been on the MI6 payroll all along. He told me to never to trust the man. But he wouldn't tell me who his assassin was. Maybe it was my little guy.

Chapter Forty-Five

The grin on Dan's face was that wide he was going to have problems getting it into the car. I hadn't seen him happy like this since forever. And the reason for the grin was a boy called Billy. Billy was Dan's first friend in years. He was also Dan's only friend in years.

Billy was a good-looking kid, maybe a year younger than Dan, with bright eyes and a happy smile. From the outside, he didn't look like he should be at a special needs school. In fact, none of the kids I'd seen so far at Jan van Tonder looked anything but normal. They all looked like Dan. Billy had an English surname but spoke with a slight Afrikaans accent. And boy did he speak. He'd followed Dan out to the car and standing in the car park, he'd opened up to me like a book. Billy told me he lived in Barberton, where his dad worked for an engineering company. He'd been at Jan van Tonder School for a year and was very happy now that Dan was also coming to Jan van Tonder because Dan was his new best friend ever.

I'd driven the 300 kilometres to Bethal to pick Dan up after his first week at Jan van Tonder School on the edge of my seat, praying to God the whole way, pleading for a happy Dan. Jen and I had what little hope we had left all pinned on Jan van Tonder being the right fit for Dan. It had to be because we'd run out of other options. And it looked like God had listened to my prayers. Dan asked me could he stay at school for the weekend instead of coming home with me. Billy was going to stay because he was playing rugby on the Saturday. And then they were all going to watch movies in the hostel, and please, please, please could he stay at school for the weekend? I told Dan no problem and turned around and drove the three hours home a happy man.

But on the outskirts of Nelspruit, a racial brawl at a set of traffic lights involving thirty or more whites and blacks took the shine off my happy. It was dreadful. With all four lanes blocked, I had no option but to lock my doors and watch what had obviously started as a minor fender bender between a black motorist and a white motorist, quickly spiral into a full-on, no holds barred racial street brawl. There were maybe ten whites and twice as many blacks, all slugging away at each other in the middle of the intersection. Even though they were outnumbered two to one, my money was on the whites. They were all huge men, I was guessing Afrikaners, standing back to back in the middle of the intersection, all with their shirts ripped off, whaling away at the nearest black man. The mindless violence carried on for a good ten minutes before a convoy of police vehicles came barrelling in with sirens wailing, to put an end to proceedings. It was horrible, the harshest starkest reminder that I was stuck living in the middle of a cauldron of absolute, racial hatred.

Billy turned out to be a nice kid. A couple of weeks into the term, we picked Dan up for a long weekend and Billy tagged along. Instead of going back to the farm, we booked in at a Hot Springs resort, complete with water slides and the two boys ran riot for three days. Dan was fairly active, but by comparison, Billy was a Duracell bunny. He just did not stop. And Dan tagged along behind him, faithfully. Jen and I were happy. Billy was going to be good for Dan.

And then Billy came to stay with us on the farm for a weekend. He loved the farm and told Dan that he was very lucky. We hardly saw the two boys, they spent most of the weekend at the top of the farm in the avocado orchard hunting with Dan's pellet gun. We met Billy's parents when they came to pick him up on the Sunday morning. They'd been at church. The father and mother were slightly younger than Jenny and me. They were both quite reserved and turned down my offer of tea, coffee or a beer. The father told me he was a Rhodesian and had moved to South Africa as a boy and was glad that his parents had made the move. He'd never been back to Rhodesia and had no intention of ever doing so. I told him the country was called Zimbabwe now. Jenny shot daggers at me with her eyes, but it was too late, and our driveway conversation came to an abrupt halt, and Billy's family left. I told Jenny that I was guessing that me and Billy's dad would never become best friends. And alas, that came to pass sooner than later.

An hour later, I asked Dan where his pellet gun was. I was hoping he hadn't left it up in the avocados. It was a good pellet gun, a Bruno. We'd bought it for Dan's last birthday, and I was determined that he'd look after the thing. The pellet gun was nowhere to be found, and Dan had guilt written all over his face. Eventually, and only after I threatened to call the police to investigate the theft of a pellet gun, Dan told me he'd swopped his pellet gun for Billy's plastic water pistol. I couldn't believe it and went the ballistic route as was my want. I ranted and raved at Dan. His pellet gun had cost us an arm and a leg. I'd worked hard to buy it for him. And he'd gone and swopped it for a cheap piece of Chinese shit water pistol that leaked. I told Dan that we were going to un-swop the water pistol and get his pellet gun back.

I calmed down to a fit before phoning the father. I apologised for phoning him on a Sunday night but needed to tell him that Billy had Dan's pellet gun.

"He told me he'd swopped it," the father said.

"Yeah. For a plastic water pistol." I couldn't believe that he knew.

"And so?" he asked with some bristle in his voice.

"And so, I want it back."

"But a deal's a deal."

"What? But we're talking about an expensive pellet gun here. We'd just bought it for Dan for his birthday. And your kid swopped it for a plastic water pistol."

"That also costs money."

"Listen. I want that pellet gun back. No ifs, no buts. I'm going to drive to Barberton, and I want that pellet gun."

"I have to ask my other son."

"What do you mean you have to ask your other son? What other son?"

"Alan. He's my oldest. He bought it off Billy. When we got home."

I couldn't believe it. And I couldn't hold the expletives in anymore either. "For fuck's sake. You've only been home for a few hours, and already the thing's been fucking bought and sold."

"Don't swear at me."

"Look. Like I said, I'm coming to Barberton tomorrow to collect that pellet gun." I slammed the phone down. And then I had to phone him back promptly for directions. I had no idea where in Barberton he lived. After telling me turn left and then right and then left again, he told me I should phone him first before leaving, in case Alan didn't want to give up the pellet gun. Mindful of his don't swear request, I slammed the phone down again.

The next morning, I calmed myself down before phoning the man. I didn't want to get into another blazing row with the father of Dan's one and only friend. Alas. It was to no avail. I phoned him up to ask what time I could collect the pellet gun and where, he told me I was going to have to pay Alan first, for re-blueing the pellet gun.

"What re-blueing?"

"He had to take it into the gun shop to have the barrel re-blued. You son didn't look after his pellet gun very well."

"But when did he do that?"

"First thing this morning. Alan is very particular about his guns." He sounded very proud of his eldest son.

"But didn't you tell him that I was coming to get it back."

"Only after he took it in. Anyway, it's going to cost you three hundred."

"Three hundred? But the pellet gun only cost me five hundred new."

"Well three hundred is what it's going to cost you now. Your son should look after his things better. And it will only be ready on Thursday." I slammed my long-suffering phone down yet again. If Dan stayed friends with Billy for any length of time, I was going to have get a new phone.

On the Thursday afternoon after work, I drove down to Barberton and found Billy's house on my third attempt. Rather than let me into the house, Billy's father came out onto the street to meet me. I paid over the three hundred rand with extreme reluctance, and he handed over the pellet gun. Which looked exactly the same as it had before. I squinted at the barrel in the later afternoon sun with suspicion. "They did a real good job on that re-blueing, don't you think?" Billy's father asked with a smirk. "Looks like brand-new." If I'd been on the phone with the man, I would have slammed it down real hard.

The next day I drove to Bethal to pick Dan up from school day. Dan was waiting for me in the hostel car park. Billy was conspicuous by his absence. Normally, he'd have been underfoot like a Labrador puppy. I asked after him. Dan shrugged. He told me that he and Billy weren't really friends anymore, they'd grown apart in the week. Shame. I wanted to cry for the kid. It was hugely tragic. Dan had made his first friend in literally years, but now he'd lost him. I suppose I should've leapt at the opportunity to give Dan the Hallmark 'If you love something and let it free, blah blah blah' lecture, but couldn't see how poetic nausea would help so we drove back to White River mostly in silence. When we got home, I gave Dan his pellet gun back plus a stern lecture on the need to look after his belongings. Given the choice, I think Dan would rather have Billy back than his pellet gun.

After that, Jan van Tonder went downhill very quickly. The following Friday, when I picked Dan up, he was sporting a massive black eye already a few days old. It wasn't your run of the mill schoolboy bruise; it was an ugly thing that fully enveloped half his face. In my eyes, the bruise was go and see a doctor bad, but Dan said only the hostel matron had looked at it and she'd told him it was just a black eye and would clear up soon enough. Sitting in the school carpark, Dan pleaded with me to start the car and move on, but I told him I wasn't going anywhere, not until I'd found out more about what had happened. I wanted to know who'd punched Dan and more importantly, why. Reluctantly, Dan told me he'd got into a fight with one of the older black kids. It was just a dumb fight over not a lot, and now it was over and please, please could we go home. How old, I wanted to know? Dan said twenty three. I couldn't believe it. Twenty three? Twenty three wasn't a kid, twenty-three was a man. What the hell was a twenty three year old man doing at a high school in the first place, let alone beating up on kids much younger than him? I exploded out of the car and stormed off to the headmaster's office to get some answers.

Predictably, the headmaster was holed up behind his desk in his office, counting down to his retirement. Looking wearier than when last I'd seen him, he allowed me to take up one of his visitor's chairs with extreme reluctance. How could he assist me, he asked? He spoke with the voice of a busy man being asked to jump through meaningless hoops. Absolutely seething on the inside, I told him I was there to find out more about the attack on Dan. I wanted to know who did it and what he'd done about it. The headmaster quickly parked his busy, officious tone of voice, in favour of his best conciliatory one. Yes, yes, he knew all about the regrettable incident involving Daniel and the other learner, and he'd spoken to both sternly, and in his heart, he was sure the incident would not be repeated. And that was that. He sat back behind his empty desk with fingers steepled, looking for all the world like he was waiting for me to thank him before taking my leave. But I was going nowhere. I wanted to know if he'd reported the attack to the police. The mere mention of the word police had him sitting bolt upright in his chair. He told me he'd seen no reason to get the police involved. It was just a fight between two schoolboys. I came back at him. Twenty three wasn't a schoolboy, twenty three was a man. And what the hell was a twenty three year old man doing at school anyway? He explained that was how things were in the new South Africa. In the old South Africa, blacks had often been denied the chance of getting an education and now they were playing catch up. And Jan van Tonder was especially attractive to blacks in that it offered skills training, like woodwork and engineering and agriculture. He's not even special needs is he, I asked? This is supposed to be a school for special needs kids, and you've enrolled adults looking for job training, adults who beat up on the special needs kids. He shot straight back at me. Your son hit the black boy with a chair after the black boy punched him. And he broke the chair too, on the black boy's head. I was horrified. Dan was a gentle kid; he didn't have it within him to go around breaking chairs on people's heads. This place was turning him into something he wasn't.

Looking back, I should have pulled Dan out of the Bethal school right there and then. But I didn't. Jenny and I had run out of options for Dan. We were down to Jan van Tonder or Jan van Tonder. So instead of doing the right thing by pulling him out, I bought into the Headmaster's bullshit assurances that the incident was over, that there wouldn't be any further attacks or bullying, blah, blah, blah. I drove Dan home for the weekend where Jenny fussed over him, rubbing healing balm on his facial bruises, baking him a batch of biscuits to take back to Bethal with him while I went out and spent money we didn't have to buy Dan a guilt present -a new entertainment centre so he could listen to music in his room at school. And then on Monday, I delivered him back to Jan van Tonder with promises that everything was going to work out just fine.

But alas, things didn't work out fine. After dropping Dan off, I was only an hour into the three-hour drive back to White River when my cell phone rang. It was Dan. He was phoning from the headmaster's office. Through a flood of tears, he told me that someone had hacked through his cupboard door with an axe and had stolen his new entertainment centre, and the biscuits Jenny had baked him. After I'd dropped him off at school, he'd locked his things away. But while he was at breakfast, someone had bust into his room and chopped their way through his cupboard door and had stolen all his stuff. And the poor kid asked me to please, please not be angry with him for losing everything.

I pulled off the road. I told Dan to put the headmaster on the phone. He came on to the line and told me Good Morning. I cut him short. I wanted to know had the police been called in. Someone had walked into his boarding hostel with an axe and had walked out again minutes later with a brand-new music centre, in broad daylight, on a Monday morning, for Christ's sake. Someone had to have seen him. The headmaster cut me off hurriedly. Seeing that it was my property that had been stolen, it was up to me to report the theft he told me, maybe when I got back to White River. I spun my car around before he'd finished. The hour drive back to Bethal only took thirty minutes. Dan was big-eyed sitting in front of his wrecked cupboard door. In less than five minutes, I'd loaded Dan and his remaining belongings into the car, and we were driving out of Bethal. I didn't even bother with the headmaster. Let him find out that Dan was no longer a learner at his school on his own. Where are we going, Dad, he asked? We're going home Dan, we're going home. To do what with you, I do not know. I left that part unsaid.

Back in White River, Jenny and I scrambled to find a stopgap Dan solution. I bought him overalls and safety boots and enrolled him on an extended welding training course. He was very proud of his graduation certificate and stuck it up on his bedroom wall with sticky stuff. As a reward for passing, I bought him his very own welding machine complete with goggles and gloves and welding rods enough to build another Titanic. Jenny found him a DIY book on welding projects for the home, full of burglar bars and plant stands and other things he could make and sell for money. Jen and I had this quaint theory that one day, Dan could maybe get a job as a welder or maybe even make a living out of welding when we were no longer around to support him. Dan went through the motions of being excited for about ten minutes. He made a pot plant stand that couldn't stand and then just stopped. He switched off his welding machine and hung up his goggles and gloves and never took them down again.

I lost my temper properly with him, ranted and raved about how ungrateful he was and told him he'd never amount to anything if he didn't get off his arse and try. In no time at all, I managed to scuttle what little self-esteem Dan had. He fled in a flood of tears, slamming his bedroom door shut behind him. Well done Eric and way to go, I congratulated myself bitterly. Dan working for me or with me on the farm was supposed to be our fall-back position for when Dan got older, but I just couldn't even see myself having the patience. Morning, noon and night, I couldn't stop stressing about who the hell would look after Dan when Jenny and I were gone?

While I was busy messing things up, Jenny found Dan a desk at a tiny special needs school in Nelspruit. Based in a room in a church in the

Nelspruit suburbs, the school's curriculum combined academics, mostly writing and arithmetic with life skills training. The school would find work placements for their students in businesses in and around Nelspruit. It sounded perfect for Dan. We went to go and have a look. The school had a headmistress, a teacher and a student body of about twenty kids, ranging in age from twelve to eighteen. Some of the kids looked normal, but some shouted out special needs loud. For me, lumping Dan with them was a big and dreadful step to take. It was like putting up a big sign telling the world my son isn't normal. But we didn't have any other options.

We met the lady who would hopefully be Dan's teacher. She came across real good. Her empathy for the children she taught shone bright. We met the headmistress, who was less good. She wielded her title like a club, and she talked a lot. She was intense but all over the place. Like some of the children she taught, she lacked focus. She'd start a sentence about one thing and finish it off on another. It was most disconcerting. But her heart was in the right place, and beggars can't be choosers. The headmistress' little school for special needs children was her stated mission in life. Not that it was going to be little for much longer. She told us rather proudly that she was in the progress of registering her school with the Ministry of Social Welfare, hoping to tap into state funding and then she'd really make things happen. She'd buy a permanent home for the school, she'd get in extra trained staff, enrol more kids, do specialised testing and...I dragged her back to the here and now. What about Dan? Did she have a place for Dan now? Could she take him or did she need to do some tests? She told us she could take Dan no problem. I breathed a huge sigh of relief. We'd found a stopgap home for Dan that would do until we figured out what we were going to do with him for the rest of his life.

We settled into some sort of a routine quickly. Dan's new school was within walking distance of our Flower Shop. He'd walk to school in the mornings, come back to the shop for lunch, do his homework and then he was supposed to help out around the shop. Just as quickly, the wheels came off our brand-new routine. Dan hated helping around the shop and would do less than a half job on any and every task given. Jenny was of the firm opinion that he was messing up on purpose in the hope that we'd eventually stop giving him stuff to do whereas I was keen to cut Dan a whole bunch of slack on account of the fact he was now officially special needs. It was a recipe for disaster. Alas. And if Dan hated working in the shop, he hated doing his homework under supervision even more. And small wonder. His academic standards had regressed unbelievably. I was shocked. Everything Dan had learnt at school growing up, had now been un-learnt. His handwriting had been reduced to an unreadable scrawl, the most basic of words he now spelt incorrectly and any and all sums were now beyond him.

But the real shit storm came when Jenny caught Dan smoking on his way back from school. Again, I was ready to cut Dan some slack. I'd been a fifteen-year-old boy previously, looking to experiment with cigarettes and booze and worse, but for Jenny, smoking was the ultimate sin. It was a dirty, disgusting habit that caused cancer that would eventually kill you. As well we knew. The children's birth mother had died of cancer, and my father was down to just one lung because he'd smoked. She whaled into Dan and boxed his ears all the way back to the shop. Oh, what fun we all had.

And then just when things couldn't get worse, they did. After one of Dan's monthly consults with his dermatologist, we ended up at a thyroid specialist. The skin doctor was still determined to get to the root cause of Dan's prolonged vitiligo attack and wanted a reading of Dan's anti-thyroid antibody count. When the numbers came back, they were scary. A normal antibody count was under five, Dan's was tracking at over sixty thousand. The thyroid doctor whistled. He'd never seen such high numbers before. He told us to come back in a month for another antibody count. The thyroid doctor whistled longer and louder the following month. Dan's count had jumped to ninety thousand. Having paid little or no attention during biology lessons at school, I was completely in the dark. What did a high antibody count mean for Dan? And what the hell was a thyroid? The thyroid doctor dumbed it down for us as much as he could. Your thyroid is a gland that produces hormones that regulate all manner of things inside you, your metabolism rate, brain development, digestion, etc. Dan's thyroid was now under attack from his auto-immune system, chances were he had something called Hashimoto's thyroiditis. Dan's eyes went big. It sounded like he had a whole Japanese Star Wars thing going on inside him.

Looking for some reassurance, I asked the doctor what would happen next. Which was a bad move. The doctor said Dan's thyroid would eventually be destroyed. Dan looked like he wanted to bolt. Shame. The first he knew about his thyroid was that it was important and that his was in the process of being killed. But why he asked of the thyroid doctor, why is mine being killed? I don't know was the doctor's reply. Hashimoto's thyroiditis was fairly common in middle-aged women but rare in boys of Dan's age. And he'd never seen such high antibody numbers before. The thyroid doctor told us that Dan's autoimmune system would stop the attack once the thyroid was dead. And then Dan would have to be on hormone replacement medicine for the rest of his life, but otherwise, he'd be just fine.

The changes to Dan's body came quick. His hair coarsened almost overnight and went from a wavy blond to dirty brown and curly. And his body was hot to touch, as though he was running a permanent temperature and the palms of his hands sweated non-stop. And then there was his appetite. It had always been growing boy healthy, but it kicked into overdrive with a vengeance. All of a sudden Dan had no brakes on his appetite, whatsoever. If we left the coffee out, Dan would binge drink it, cup after cup, until the whole big tin was gone. He'd drink twenty cups of coffee in a morning. Loaves of bread were the same, biscuits, pockets of potatoes, anything and everything left out, got eaten. Dan put on some weight, but not a lot. His metabolism just burnt it all up. Just as quickly, our kitchen turned into a Fort Knox. Oh, what fun we had.

Chapter Forty-Six

One of my few stand-out regrets in life is not buying a pair of the coolest leather shoes ever made that I once saw in a roadside curio shop in Zimbabwe. The leather shoes were almost as cool as the leather poncho in Amsterdam that I'd once admired when I was a kid but never bought. I blame my granny for missing out on the poncho. When I told her I was going to use all my pocket money to buy the poncho, she told me I'd look stupid in it. When I argued the point, she boxed my ears and dragged me out of the department store squealing. For missing out on the shoes, I blame Robert Mugabe and his right-hand idiot in charge of all things monetary, Gideon Gono.

I tried to buy the shoes four times in eight months but got thwarted by noughts every time. The first time was in May 2007. I was driving up to Zimbabwe on one of my monthly trips. I stopped at a roadside stall just outside Umvuma that sold cold cokes and curios. I walked in to buy a coke, saw the shoes and fell right in love with them. They were handcrafted leather moccasins with two-tone uppers, and they were just beautiful. I'd never such beautiful shoes since my life. I had to have them. Sensing blood, the store clerk rushed over and urged me to try them on. I still had a wallet full of cash leftover from my last trip a few months earlier...a happy man, I sat down to try them on. Then I saw the price. They cost three thousand dollars. The number blew my mind- for a pair of shoes. I told the clerk sorry, but there was no way on earth that I was going to spend three thousand dollars on a pair of shoes, even if they were handcrafted leather. The clerk burst out laughing. Which was not quite the reaction I was expecting. When he came up for air, he told me I'd missed a nought. The shoes were thirty thousand, not three.

I spent the rest of the drive to Harare in shock and horror. Thirty thousand dollars for a pair of shoes? What the hell had happened in the few short months since last I'd visited? I was staying with Mitch and Lulu Whaley in Harare. Mitch was running Running Dog at the time. With four teenage sons, the Whaley house was like a noisy railway station, and I absolutely loved staying there. I told Mitch about the shoes, and he said I should have bought them. When I wasn't watching, apparently the black-market US Dollar rate had impossibly jumped to twenty-six thousand to one. I'm not geared up to track that many noughts, but I did the sums as best I could in my head. And immediately rejected the results. Surely not. I did the sums again, but this time on paper, to make sure. And I still came up with the same answer. My handcrafted leather shoes were going to cost me just over one dollar. I did a little celebratory jig in my head. I was going to look so fine in those shoes. I decided that I wouldn't buy just the one pair, I'd buy four.

At the end of the week, when it was time to go back to South Africa, I drew two hundred thousand dollars from the farm safe, in crisp ten thousand dollar notes. The denominations were crazy big. Mitch told me to take more, just in case, but I was loathed to. Already I was feeling guilty blowing two hundred thousand just on shoes. I felt like Imelda Marcos all the way to Umvuma, but alas, when I got to the curio shop, it was closed. A scribbled note in the window told me the salesclerk had gone to a funeral. Damn. What kind of a stupid way was that to run a business? I cursed and swore for a bit, but the shop stayed closed. I was going to have to wait a month to buy the shoes.

Events conspired against me, and it was the end of August before I could escape South Africa for another Zimbabwe visit. It was more than just a farm visit. I had Jenny with me, and we had bookings for five days in Mana Pools followed by five on a houseboat in Kariba. It was Jenny's first visit back to Zim, and I was pulling out all the stops, hoping to rekindle her love for Zimbabwe.

All the way from the border to Umvuma, I hoped and prayed that the curio shop was open and that the shoes were still there. God came through for me on both counts. I rushed into the shop with Jenny in tow and with the cash burning a hole in my pocket. I headed straight for the shoes. The salesclerk recognised me from months before.

"Ah. You are back for your shoes?"

"How many pairs have you got in a size ten? Chances are I'll take the lot."

"Just this one pair only."

"Shame. I'll take them."

"OK. That will be three hundred thousand dollars."

"Huh?" I could not believe it. In a little over three months, the price of my shoes had gone up ten-fold.

Jenny laughed at the look on my face all the way to Harare. Mitch also quite enjoyed the story. He put things into perspective for me. While I'd been away, the black-market rate for the dollar had climbed from twenty-six thousand to over three hundred thousand. Mitch said that the wheels were coming off everything in a big way. Prices were doubling overnight, and supermarket shelves in town emptied faster than they could be restocked with people prepared to buy anything and everything at any price rather than hang onto money that lost value overnight. Jenny was horrified and told all our friends she was glad she was out of it. Alas. I should have left Jenny at home that trip. Not even the magic of Mana and Kariba could compete with the shock trauma of the empty supermarkets, with aisle upon aisle and shelf after shelf of nothing for sale. I don't know why the supermarket owners didn't just give up and lock up for good.

Our Romanian friends who'd opted to stay in Zimbabwe were wonderfully resilient. They made a plan. A wonderful trading network was quickly born. Impossibly someone would hear of butter for sale, and they'd snap up the lot then swop it for eggs or meat or flour or anything and everything else that was short. People looked out for friends, and their friends looked out for them. And incredibly there was still more laughter in Zimbabwe than bitching. I was very jealous of my Romanian friends and wished I was part of them.

But back to the coolest pair of handmade leather shoes ever made. Come time to go back to South Africa at the end of our holiday, I drew two million dollars out of the farm safe, this time in crisp new two hundred thousand dollar notes. I marvelled at how they'd got so many noughts on a single banknote. Jenny and I drove out of Harare in the dark to arrive in Umvuma just after the curio shop opened. In my worst nightmare, I arrived in Umvuma late and just in time to watch someone else buying my shoes. The clerk greeted me warmly and with a big smile on his face. By now, we were nearly good friends. "Ah, the owner of my shoes. I hope you have brought enough money with you this time."

"Absolutely. I've got two million on me.' I couldn't but sound smug.

His smile fell away. "Sorry for that," he said. "Since yesterday, the shoes are now costing three million dollars."

I stopped at the curio shop only once after that, more out of curiosity than out of desire. It was about a year later, and by then, it was a curio shop in the name only, with empty shelves and only cool drinks for sale. I greeted the salesclerk. He recognised me immediately. "Ah, sorry, my friend, your shoes are not here anymore. We are not selling curios anymore because the tourists, they are not coming to Zimbabwe these days."

"What happened to my shoes that I wanted to buy?"

"They were bought by the other man about six months ago."

"How much for?"

"I think they sold for some trillions of dollars, in the end, I can't remember exactly."

Alas. Only in Zimbabwe could a pair of shoes soar from thirty thousand to some trillions, in less than a year. And only in Zimbabwe could a lowly salesclerk talk about price of some trillions with near boredom in his voice. And small wonder because at the time, an egg cost fifty billion. That's a number with nine noughts on the end, for an egg.

Zimbabwe became world-famous as the home of the hundred trillion dollar banknote, the world's largest ever denominated banknote. We also owned bragging rights to the highest ever rate of inflation. One search engine offered up 89,000,000,000,000,000,000,000 percent as the rate of inflation that Zimbabwe peaked at- a number with so many noughts I don't think they've even thought up a name for it yet. Another search engine talks about an annual rate of inflation in December 2008 estimated at 650 million googol percent, apparently 6.5×10 percent. I don't even know if that number is higher or lower than the 89 followed by the 21 noughts?

Years later, even just writing about the hyperinflation years of 2007 and 2008 makes my head hurt. Living through it at the time, or even worse trying to work through it, was worse. It was like sticking your head in a high-speed washing machine every day, just one big chaotic blur. In amongst the blur, there were some standout memories.

Like when I paid a street kid ten billion for looking after my car in the middle of town. The street kid swore at me, threw my offerings into the gutter and walked away. I was shocked and deeply offended. And worse still, mine wasn't the only banknote in the gutter. I badly wanted to get out and pick them all up but was worried the army of street kids would throw rocks at me and beat me up. If you were clever, you made sure you paid all your utility bills and taxes by cheque because, by the time the cheque cleared, the cost to you in real money would have more than halved. But if you tried to pay by cheque in a shop, back when shops still had goods on their shelves to buy, the shopkeeper would ask you to write out your cheque for double so that he didn't lose on the transaction. I remember taking my dad to Llew Hughes's restaurant in Borrowdale to join a table of friends for dinner, carrying my money for the night in a big black dustbin. Everyone carried their money in big black dustbin bags. We looked like a convention of dustbin men. And at the end of the meal come time to pay, the pile of money in the middle of the table was high like a mountain, you had to stand up to look over it. And just as our long-suffering waiter had finishing counted out the money, best friend Phil Weller couldn't resist the urge and grabbed armfuls of cash and threw them up into the overhead fan above and billion and trillion-dollar banknotes were flying all over the place. My dad said that night was up there with the most fun he'd ever had.

Shame, but there wasn't a whole bunch of fun going on at the bottom of the food chain. Which was where my farmworkers lived, even though every month end they were trillionaires and billionaires a few times over, briefly. I remember towards the end of 2008, we had over two hundred workers on the books at the time, and their combined minimum wages came to the grand total of five US dollars. Two hundred men and women had worked for twenty-six days in the month, for eight hours a day, to earn just five American dollars, to be shared amongst the entire workforce. And our workers counted themselves lucky. In a farming district where for miles around us, the farms were all fallow and derelict, they still had jobs. But only because over and above the absolute pittance that was their salary, we paid them in cooking oil and maize meal and candles and soap and cans of sardines and tins of corned beef and toothpaste and the list went on and on, all imported from South Africa. Mitch and Brian worked out an elaborate pay scale in groceries for all the various pay grades and every month I'd drive from White River to Johannesburg to shop hard for two hundred people at the Makro in Woodmead.

But the people who had the worst of the hyperinflation were the old-age pensioners. They were a generation of bankers and doctors, builders and engineers who knew how to build a country but who knew precious little about how to duck and dive to survive in the land of noughts. After investing thirty or forty years of their lives in their careers and their pension schemes, after they spent their entire working careers saving for their retirements, they lost everything, their wealth, their pensions and their dignity, almost overnight. Because they saved. Every spare cent they had, they squirrelled away in the bank and in their retirement policies. And once their children had flown the nest, they downsized. They sold off their three or four bedroomed homes for something smaller and banked the difference so they could live off the interest. In a normal world, savings and positive interest and all that other sound economic stuff might work, but in the land of the One Hundred Trillion Dollar note, not so much. Banks collapsed, and pensioners became paupers overnight. Ordinarily, old folk would have the safety net of their children beneath them, but in Zimbabwe, most often those children were now in England or New Zealand or Australia, starting over and struggling and in no position to help. Alas.

The man who pushed out the hyperinflation envelope like it had never been pushed out before was a man called Gideon Gono. I met him in the early nineties when Jenny sold him membership in a timeshare resort we were running. He came across as a nice man but quite full of himself. He very proudly told Jenny that he'd worked his way up from being a teaboy to being the managing director of one of the largest banks in Zimbabwe in just fifteen years. Ten years after we met him, Mugabe made him the Governor of the Reserve Bank. Whence upon all hell broke loose.

Gideon's first move as Zimbabwe's boss banker was to boldly axe three noughts from the Zimbabwe dollar and to roll out a shiny new dollar, worth a thousand of the old dollars. With a flair for drama, Gideon codenamed his currency reform as Operation Sunrise, complete with the catchphrase, From Zero to Hero. To give himself lots of wiggle room, Gideon had fourteen denominations in his range of new banknotes which ran from a One Cent note all the way up to a Hundred Thousand Dollar note. That was in August 2006. But alas, not even six months later, the three noughts were back. By August 2007, Gideon had pressed the button on a Seven Hundred and Fifty Thousand Dollar note.

But still, the noughts came fast and furiously. In January 2008, Gideon went through the six nought barrier with a Ten Million Dollar bill. And by

May of that year, there was a Five Hundred Million Dollar bill. And from there it was a just a hop and skip to Billions and Trillions. And on the 30th of July 2008, Gideon desperately lopped off yet another ten noughts and rolled out yet another new, improved Dollar, worth Ten Billion of the old ones. But the ten noughts he disappeared were back on the banknotes by January 2009. A great proponent of the 'If At First You Don't Succeed, Try, Try, Try Again' school of thought, Gideon reacted to their reappearance with his third re-denomination of the Zimbabwe dollar, axing a further twelve noughts. In total and in the space of just two and a half years, Gideon Gono disappeared a staggering twenty-four noughts from the Zimbabwean currency.

I am suggesting that Gideon should have stayed a teaboy. He was probably better at making tea that he was at governing Reserve Banks. But then if he's stayed a teaboy, I doubt he'd have built himself a 112 roomed palace. Gideon built his palace behind Mugabe's palace. Rumour had it there was a pedestrian gate linking the two properties. Rumour also had it that Mugabe was irked that Gideon's palace was bigger than his. Gideon's palace had an Olympic sized swimming pool, more than one helipad and the entire building was lined with granite tiles, each hand-carved with the face of either Gideon, his wife or his two children. A friend of mine won the contract to put in a paved driveway for Gideon, over ten thousand square metres of paving. When he presented an invoice with many, many noughts on it, he was told to drive his pick- up truck down into the basement of Gideon's new Reserve Bank building in the centre of town where he was loaded up to the hilt with bundles of hot off the press Hundred Trillion dollar bills. Gideon's driveway was that big, it took more than one pick-up truckload to pick-up the payment.

In his spare time, Gideon was a farmer. He ended up owning one of the largest flower farms in Zimbabwe. I think Gideon ended up owning a lot of farms but this particular one was his flagship farm. A friend of mine was running the farm for a corporate at the time Gideon gobbled it up. The farm was on a stunning hundred plus hectares right on the City boundary, at the start of the Enterprise Valley. Because it was such a standout property, come the land-grab, it attracted the attention of a whole posse of high up, greedy war veterans. Out of desperation, my friend's boss, the Managing Director of the corporate, went to see Gideon in his capacity as Reserve Bank Governor with a reasoned appeal to intervene on account of the fact the farm generated lots of valuable foreign currency for the fiscus, employed hundreds of workers, blah, blah, blah. Gideon was so moved, I'm thinking more by the property than the appeal, he agreed to intervene. But to scare off the wannabe land thieves, it would be best if the farm had a black shareholder, preferably a person of consequence, like say a Governor of a Reserve Bank. And once he had his foot in the door, it was a hop and a skip before Gideon gobbled up the whole farm.

At his first management meeting, Gideon openly boasted to my friend how he'd first become a US dollar millionaire in just three and a bit transactions, starting with just 1000 US dollars in seed money. You sell your 1000 US on the black-market for 1.6 million Zimbabwe dollars. With your Governor of the Reserve Bank hat on and using the official exchange rate of fifty-five to one, you use your 1.6 million Zim dollars to buy 29000 US dollars. Which you then sell for 46 million Zimbabwe money. Which you then use to buy 846,000 American. Which you then sell for the number greater than my calculator is able to cope with and hey presto, you're US Dollar millionaire many times over. And next stop, a billionaire. All too easy.

The friend of mine who worked for Gideon Gono is one of the most industrious and productive men I know. He is never happier than when building new greenhouses. To start off with, he was very happy working for Gideon. Because he had the keys to the Reserve Bank, Gideon threw pots and pots of money at his flower farm, and my friend was able to build endless greenhouses, all planted to roses. Driving past the farm on the Enterprise Road, it really was most impressive. After the land-grab, Gideon's flower farm became the face of Zimbabwe's Land Reform Programme, headlining on every visiting Head of State's itinerary. Their oohs, ahs and wows filled the farm's leather-bound visitor's book. I read the book and found their comments to be very racist. One of the hard to spell Nigerians wrote something about how Gideon's farm was a shining light for black agricultural achievement, proof that blacks could farm just as well as whites. On the days when a V.I.P. was visiting, my friend was given the day off and strict instructions to not show his white face around the farm.

Life in Zimbabwe can wear you down, even if your boss has the keys to the Reserve Bank, and eventually, my friend tendered his resignation. He gave Gideon three months of notice. He also offered to help him find a suitable replacement. To cope with a workforce of over two hundred workers and ten or more different varieties of cut roses, the incoming general manager would have to be very experienced. And cutting edge as well, because my friend had taken the farm very high tech with all the bells and whistles, like a state-of -the-art computerised irrigation scheme that he drove from his laptop, etc., etc. Gideon told him there'd be no need for him to get involved in the recruitment process. He'd decided his nephew, aged under twenty-five with less than two years work experience, would take over the running of the farm. Alas. It took the nephew less than six months to kill every last rosebush on the farm. The empty greenhouses remained standing and empty for over a year, with the plastic ripped, tatty and blowing in the wind, towering monuments to the destructive power of incompetence Eventually Gideon had them ripped down. In their place, he built row upon row of state-of-the-art chicken houses, huge, shiny ones, and the best that money could buy. I drove past Gono's chicken farm a couple of years later. His state-of-the-art chicken houses all stood empty. They have been empty for years. Apparently, Gideon built his chicken houses too close together, and because of that, his flock was wiped out time and again by disease. Alas. Like I said, he should have stuck to making tea.

Chapter Forty-Seven

Of silver linings and dark clouds

A cynic once pointed out that behind every silver lining, lurked a big dark storm cloud. And our South Africa storm cloud was particularly virulent.

Things all started going horribly wrong just when they started going right. I should have taken that as a sign and fled. Incredibly and despite my unfocused inattentions, or more likely because of them, we started making money in South Africa, not lots, but some. The first time we had money left over at the end of the month, Jenny did her sums again, thinking there must have been some bills that she'd left out. But she'd paid the lot. Which meant we'd posted a profit. And not just in the shop but also on both farms. My strategy of growing our own flowers to give us competitive edge was working. Because my arms aren't long enough for me to be able to pat myself on the back properly, I walked around for days asking other people to do it for me. I am unbearable that way.

I say both farms because by then, we'd invested in a rose farm in White River. The farm had been set up by ex-Zimbabweans as an export farm with all the greenhouses planted out to sweetheart rose varieties suited to the European market, but despite their best efforts, the farm had bellied up under the strain of the appreciating Rand. I lured best friend Etienne Engelbrecht down from Zimbabwe, and we replaced the sweetheart rose varieties with large-headed rose varieties, and we took the local market by storm. I say we, but it was all Etienne's hard work. He had the greenest of fingers, and he knew roses inside out, and it showed in the quality of the roses he was producing.

And much the same was happening on Summer Hill with Colin Fletcher in charge. When I was running Summer Hill, it had lurched from one financial crisis to the next, mostly because my heart and more than half my attentions were still in Zimbabwe. But that all changed when I was able to headhunt Colin Fletcher to join me. Colin had just been violently booted from his farm in Bromley, Zimbabwe. He had a young family and was desperate. He was also a hugely talented, hard-working farmer and he was able to stop the haemorrhaging on Summer Hill. And then when we put in a half hectare of Chrysanthemums for me to sell through Flowers R Us, we were away. The farm started posting decent profits, ditto the shop.

Chrysanthemums and roses were the two top varieties in terms of demand. The fact that we grew both on our own farms gave us a huge competitive edge on the local market. I was able to sell flowers that were fresher, cheaper and better, and we dominated. It was all going swimmingly well to a point where Jenny and I stopped dreading month-end. We were even able to upgrade back to four-ply toilet paper.

But then I cocked things up by expanding the retail side of the business. It was a Catch 22. Under proper management, the farms were producing more than I could sell through Flowers R Us with the excess going on to the Flower Auction where it fetched a pittance. With the Rand trading at seven to the dollar, South Africa was an attractive export destination, and the Joburg Auctions were overtraded with asters and roses out of Zimbabwe, Zambia and Kenya. Local growers came second. Which was sort of why we set up Flowers R Us in the first place. If only Nelspruit were bigger. It might be the perfect sized town to live in, but it was way too small to be able to sell lots of flowers into. I started looking further afield for bigger markets. And Johannesburg was the logical start point.

I trolled Joburg's leafy suburbs for a few weeks, sussing out other flower markets that wholesaled to the public and marvelled at their prices and how much stock they seemed to move. From what I could see, they were all printing money. I went back to them week after week after week, posing as a customer, plotting prices, counting buckets of flowers. And I got excited. I got especially excited at the sheer volume of people in Joburg. There was a shopping centre on every corner, full to the brim with housewives shopping and spending money. All I had to do to get them spending their money on my flowers was to find premises for the flower market I was going to open.

And then I hit pay dirt. One of the opposition markets I'd been tracking was in a shiny upmarket shopping mall tucked away in the middle of Fourways, smack dab in the middle of Joburg's affluent northern suburbs. I'd been to check out that particular flower market often and it was always busy with lots of flowers and lots of customers. But on this particular day, the flower market was all locked up with a For Rent sign on the window. I rushed off to the Mall Management offices to enquire and was told that the previous tenants had been kicked out following a turnover dispute with the owners of the Mall. Apparently, their lease fee was a percentage of turnover, and they'd been caught fiddling. And now the Mall owners were looking for someone to take over. I quickly got very excited. The premises were perfect. So, I made an appointment to meet the Mall owners.

The owners, three Greek brothers with offices that were over the top opulent, impressed the hell out of me. I met the youngest brother, who was brash with swagger to burn. Everything about him shouted wealth, especially his Rolex and his Bentley. I'd never met anyone who owned a Bentley before. And even though he had a Bentley, he invited me to join him at a swanky coffee shop for a coffee and a lecture on how successful his family was, and why.

The family owned several prestigious shopping malls in Johannesburg's affluent north. They also owned the Kyalami racetrack, but that was by the by. The brothers were successful in retail because they understood that within a successful and affluent family, it was the mother who spent the money. The husbands were too busy working to make money to keep their wives' credit cards charged. And so the brothers set up their malls with women in mind and loaded them with jewellery shops and top-end grocery stores, fashion boutiques, beauty parlours and trendy coffee shops, and for the younger moms, toy stores and baby stores. He told me that within their malls, there was not a hardware store or a paint shop to be seen.

Flower markets were entirely in keeping with this formula, so they found someone to open one at their flagship mall. To help get it up and running, the brothers paid for all the shop equipment and fittings, at great expense, which they'd recoup through a reasonable share of the turnover. But then the tenant got greedy and started skimming the turnovers. Until he got caught....The pause that followed was dramatic and heavily pregnant with threat. The brother never told me what happened to the errant tenant, but all I could picture was dead racehorses' heads in bed. After the long, hanging silence, the brother asked if I'd like to take up the lease on his flower market. My heart hammered, unused to lucky breaks. I looked around me for inspiration, and everywhere I looked, all I saw was money. Shiny marble floors and fountains with shiny chandeliers overhead, housewives draped in jewellery on their way to the gym and the Greek brother with the Bentley outside. He looked at his Rolex pointedly while he waited for my answer. I drank in the Rolex and thought of the Bentley, and I badly wanted to be a part of all of that. I don't normally lust after money, but I was also sick and tired of being poor and on the bones of my bottom. So, I told him yes. Not so fast, he told me. Part of the deal on offer was that I had to open other flower markets in his other malls. No problem I told him. The more flower markets, the merrier.

I rushed home to White River to spread the good news. Which went down like a lead balloon. Colin Fletcher was worried about opening more than one new business at a time in a city far away. And he expressed his reserves about opening in the other malls, none of which we'd seen yet. Etienne shared his concerns. Piffle, I told them, the guy had a Bentley, and the malls had marble fountains. What could go wrong? Plenty, they suggested. And if the flower shops were slow to get to break even, both farms were on such thin ice in terms of cash flows, they wouldn't be able to prop the shops up. No problem, I told them, I had some rainy-day money tucked away for emergencies. And from my perspective, opening the shops was an emergency. Both farms were on a crash course. It was just a matter of time before we hit the financial wall hard. Alas. After much earnest pleading, I was able to win Jenny over and access our precious reserves.

And so, I leapt into the complex Johannesburg retail market boots and all. As it turned out, I would have saved time, pain, angst and heartache if

I'd walked out into the garden and burnt boxes of cash on the braai.

I didn't cock things up all on my own, I had help. The month we opened our first two shops, South Africa's power utility ESKOM introduced rolling blackouts in Johannesburg as a measure to cut back on power consumption before their thermal power stations ran out of coal. Not that there was a potential shortage of coal in the country. South Africa had coal reserves to burn for hundreds of years to come. It was just that some fucking idiot had cocked up his planning and the coal was still in the ground and not in a pile waiting to be fed into a furnace. But whatever the reason, the rolling blackouts caused chaos and bedlam on a massive scale. Typically, the blackouts would last for three or four hours, but often longer. In Zimbabwe, four-hour power outages happen that often, they're not even worthy of comment. But when you are stuck in hopelessly gridlocked, ill-tempered Joburg traffic, three or four hours is a lifetime. Joburg motorists aren't the most patient of people at the best of times. Jam them in traffic that isn't moving anywhere soon, and tempers boil over quickly.

The mood in the traffic wasn't the only thing to get heated. Inside our shiny malls, temperatures soared. The only thing that got powered up by the not big enough standby generators was the emergency lighting. Which allowed me to watch my flowers wilt and die when the air conditioners and cold rooms stopped working. Along with everything else in the mall; cash registers, computers, credit card swipe machines, nothing worked. So the few shoppers who weren't stuck in the traffic outside couldn't shop anyway because no one in Johannesburg shops with cash anymore. The rolling blackouts happened nearly every day for months. Looking back, I should have shut up shops and waited for the fucking idiot at ESKOM to order more coal. But I didn't. Instead, every day I bought in more fresh flowers so they could look pretty until they wilted and died in my shops, by the truckload.

My worst performing shop by a country mile was in a swanky new mall in Randburg. It should have been the best. It was in the heart of row upon row of swanky townhouses, all with shiny cars parked outside, all with equally shiny housewives looking to buy flowers. Swank and shine were the operative words. The Mall was brand-new when we moved in, it was a thing of absolute beauty with wide sweeping marble floors and fountains and the cleanest of lines. We were allowed to display our flowers on the mall floor, right next to a cascading marble fountain. Our shop was tiny, less than thirty metres of floor space but that still cost us a staggering forty thousand rand in rent every month. But I guessed that was the price you paid for prime retail space. Alas.

The place turned out to be an absolute dud. Even when there weren't any power cuts to blame, the mall was empty and entirely bereft of passing feet, even though I'd flooded the townhouse complexes for miles around with advertising flyers. The place stubbornly remained like a shiny morgue. After a particularly bad day, mostly spent watching my flowers die on the shop floor, I went next door to commiserate with the manager of a countrywide name brand convenience store. I had to wait for the manager to complete his end of day cash up. As it happened, I didn't have to wait long. In a full day of trading, across five till points, the name brand store had turned over just one hundred rand. And the saddest thing was I could count him lucky. At least at the end of a bad day, he didn't have to throw away most of his old stock and refresh with new.

I'd headhunted a retail specialist with bags of relevant experience to open and manage the Johannesburg shops. He was a big, burly man with a calm and reassuring manner about him. Which in amidst the looming crash and financial burn was anything but calmly reassuring. I didn't want to be the only one doing all the panicking. I asked him where we were going wrong. ESKOM blackouts aside, he told me that in his considered opinion, our flower markets were in bad locations and would never work. And he had serious doubts about the malls' women-only formula. According to him, the malls' tenant lists were flawed. No hardware shops or paint shops, no sports shops, no golf shops all meant fewer feet. Better we move to other more balanced malls he said. Which is not want you to hear when you've just spent a fortune opening them and signed up to long and expensive leases. So, I fired him. And then I commenced to panic even more because I didn't have anyone to replace him. And if I didn't find someone real soon, I'd have to move to Johannesburg myself and fail first-hand. And I didn't want to do that on two counts. Failing first-hand sucks but above that, I hated Johannesburg. And it scared me. It was way too big and way too fast. I'd drown there if I lived there. Unfortunately, the last place on earth that I wanted to be in was also the same place I'd just opened three businesses. In itself, that was a recipe for failure.

As a stopgap, I found a displaced Zimbabwean acquaintance, newly stranded in Johannesburg, desperate to earn some money and willing to try anything after his business plans to import and sell high-end teak furniture out of Zimbabwe had failed. We had a semi-interview. Older than me, he'd had spent most of his career working either with thoroughbred horses or selling furniture. He didn't know the difference between a rose and a foxglove. Slightly disconcerting during the interview was a violent twitch that grabbed hold of the entire side of his face every one or two minutes and gave it a good shaking. It was as if there was something inside his face fighting to get out, like the alien in Sigourney Weaver's tummy in the movie Alien. Whenever the twitch happened, I had to fight the urge to run away in case the something got out. I couldn't remember him having the twitch when I knew him in Zimbabwe and said as much. He told me his twitch was brand-new, a nervous reaction to Joburg traffic. But the desperate and

OF SILVER LININGS AND DARK CLOUDS

willing to try anything bits shone through in his interview, and I snapped him up. The job was his for as long as he could stand the traffic, or until I found a replacement who knew the flower business.

My Zimbabwean stopgap manager's wardrobe was one hundred percent khaki, more befitting a safari guide than a flower shop manager and he looked horribly out of place in amongst roses, foxgloves and other flowers on the shop floors. But he had bags of confidence, customers liked him, and most importantly, he got stuff done. He was no-nonsense and worked his way steadfastly through long To-Do lists. Under his guidance, our third branch took shape quickly. I called it Fat Boys Flower Market and shamelessly cribbed the little round guys from Southpark in my logo. My son, Gary, designed it and it was the coolest logo ever.

Fat Boys Flower Market was in a small shopping centre, near the middle of Sandton, just off the busy M1 highway. Sick and tired of throwing flowers away, I spent a lot of money I didn't have on a massive cold room that took up most of the Fat Boys floor space. To avoid frostbite, any customers looking at the merchandise would have to wear jerseys. I planned to hold the stock at Fat Boys and resupply the other two retail branches on a just-in-time basis. Whence upon I'd throw the flowers away anyway, because we still weren't attracting the customers to the retail branches, despite the ongoing flood of advertising flyers. And all the while, I was burning money, trying to keep the shops open and fully stocked.

Impossibly things took a turn for the worse when my stopgap manager detached a retina while twitching in heavy traffic. His eye practically fell out of his face. He was in the Fat Frank delivery van at the time and pulled out of traffic and phoned me. Luckily, I was in Johannesburg and was able to rush him to a nearby eye hospital for emergency surgery. With the blood streaming down his face, he told me that he was sorry and that he didn't think he'd be able to carry on working. Crap. And then I did something that I still hugely regret to this day. It was stand-out bad, stand-out wrong on so many levels, and it still shames me to this day. I asked son Gary to come down to South Africa to help me run the family business.

At the time Gary was happy like the proverbial pig in shit, filming wildlife, mostly in Tanzania, Zambia and Botswana, spending up to six months of the year in some of the most beautiful bush in Africa with cameras wrapped around his neck, enjoying. The rest of the year he lived in Bulawayo, editing the footage he'd shot, turning it into movies. He was wonderfully talented at editing and loved it. Until I came along and ripped him out of his happy, comfort zone.

I should've been a second-hand car salesman because I sure can talk up a big piece of crap into something nice and sweet-smelling. I sucked Gary into sharing my vision for the Johannesburg shops. There was no denying the potential and the massive positive knock-on effect they'd have on the farming side of our family business, but only if someone with passion and a vested interest came and grabbed them by the scruff of the neck and made them work. I reminded Gary of the burden that his younger brother was fast becoming, and the need to share the load, not so much now but later when Jenny and I were old and doddery or gone. And then there were his grandparents, also living on Summerhill, also dependent on the family business surviving.

Gary was born to help carry heavy loads. He is dutiful and loyal. Helping others is part of his make-up, and it defines him as a man. He said yes on the turn, he'd love to move to Johannesburg to run the flower shops. For my sake, he even managed to mask the reluctance in his voice. Which must have been tough because there were bucket loads of it. From the word go, Gary in Johannesburg was the quintessential square peg in a round hole.

The week before he was due to arrive in Johannesburg, I rented him a two bedroomed townhouse, in a huge sprawling complex complete with sparkling communal pool, just a two-minute drive from our flagship flower market. Taking the sting out of Gary's daily commute in Johannesburg would add years onto his life. And to help him navigate Joburg's tangle of busy streets, I borrowed a GPS from John Stanton and entered in the co-ordinates for the Flower Auction and all three flower shops. Gary was good to go.

On day one, I took him on a tour of his new world. First thing in the morning, as in just before sunrise, we visited the busy Flower Auction floors where Gary's working days would start, going forward. Gary would be in charge of buying flowers not just for the three Joburg flower shops, but also for the Nelspruit shop, and our biggest customer in Maputo. Gary took screeds of notes and asked a million good questions. Then we spent time at each of the three flower markets, going over problems and possible solutions. Halfway through the day, Gary's eyes started to glass over, but I pressed on valiantly. It was a lot to take in all at once, but Gary was young and bright. We finished off at the flagship market mid-afternoon. After an hour or two there, I told Gary we'd wrap it up. He told me he had a few things he still wanted to do. He gave me the keys to his apartment and told me he'd see me in thirty minutes.

It took me just five minutes to get to Gary's apartment. I squeezed out on to his postage stamp balcony, opened a beer and almost put my neck out trying to enjoy the sunset. But for half of built-up Johannesburg in the way, it would've been quite spectacular. After another two beers and forty minutes, there was still no sign of Gary. I phoned him up to tell him work was over for the day. He told me he was in the car and on his way home. I opened him a beer. After fifteen minutes, still no Gary. I was starting to worry, not about Gary but about dwindling beer stocks, so I phoned him again. "I'm on the highway, Dad. According to the GPS, I should be there in

OF SILVER LININGS AND DARK CLOUDS

forty minutes. But I don't know so much because the traffic is real bad."

"Forty minutes? And what highway, Gary?"

"I don't know what it's called Dad, but it's real big, five lanes, all full of cars."

"How did you end up on a highway? There isn't a highway between the shop and your apartment. It's a five-minute drive."

"I don't know Dad." Gary was sounding flustered. "After I locked the shop up, I got in the car and pressed home on the GPS, and it brought me this way."

"You silly boy. That's John's GPS, so I guess you're on your way to his home." Gary was completely knackered when he eventually got home, after three hours spent getting off the highway, getting lost trying to get back on the highway, etc. It didn't help that I laughed and laughed.

We'd only just fallen asleep when all hell broke loose outside Gary's apartment. My tiny first-floor bedroom was awash with screaming and shouting, searchlights and flashing blue lights. What the hell was going on? I stuck my head out the window for a look-see. Straight away a Robocop in uniform with muscles and a weapon of mass destruction screamed at me to get my head back in. I did so with alacrity. There was more screaming, followed by gunshots. What the hell was going on? I inched my head up over the windowsill. The apartment directly opposite Gary's, just twenty feet away because the complex architect sure had crammed them in, was lit up bright by the brightest of searchlights operating from the first floor somewhere to my right. It swept across the apartment opposite from left to right and back again, making a nonsense of the flimsy lace curtains. Beyond the curtains, I could see four or five black men, all in a panic, all rushing from room to room trying to evade the glare of scrutiny. They were carrying guns and plastic bags.

"Shit. It's the Nigerians." Gary had joined me on his hands and knees at the bedroom window. "It must be a drug bust."

The excitement went on for what seemed like hours. And it wasn't just limited to the apartment directly opposite us. It spread across the complex, to other Nigerians, in other apartments. By night the place was like downtown Lagos. Lying next to Gary on the floor of his tiny apartment, bathed in searchlight and gunfire, I felt desperately sorry for him. A month earlier, he'd been in the Selous Game Reserve in Tanzania filming animals. He'd gone from that to living on the set of a real-life gangster movie. And it was all my doing. What had I done? Alas.

Chapter Forty-Eight

There are many four-letter words in use in Zimbabwe, but hope is the one that Zimbabweans seek out and feed off at every opportunity. Without hope, every decent Zimbabwean would either be in Perth or Birmingham or Braamfontein, starting over. It was exactly hope that allowed us to forget about every stolen election that had gone before so we could look ahead to the 2008 elections without fear and trepidation. With his economy in full million, billion and trillion dollar meltdown, Mugabe had absolutely nowhere to hide. Bar his generals, and a select few ZANU sycophants, no one in Zimbabwe wasn't bleeding because of gross economic stupidity. And having had their wealth and their worldly possessions reduced to nothing, there was no way on earth the people were going to vote Mugabe. The MDC's prospects had never been brighter.

The elections were scheduled for the end of March 2008. With my best happy, smiley face firmly in place to hide my terrified face, I sidled up to Jenny in the flower shop and broke the news that I'd volunteered to go back and help the MDC with the elections. I told her I'd only be gone for a week, maybe ten days at the most. Jenny rounded on me. If she'd been holding a broom or a club with a nail through it, she would've smacked me with it, no doubt. She told me that I couldn't have chosen a worse time to run away and shirk my responsibilities. She reminded me that with only six weeks left to Mother's Day, our second biggest day of the year where we could do a month's turnover in a day, I should be nowhere else other than in the shops, driving things. God knew we needed the revenue boost. Gary was in Joburg struggling with the new shops that I'd started, the same shops that were dragging both the farms and the Nelspruit shop down with them. And to top it all off, Daniel's illness was getting worse, Veronica had just had a baby, and here I was swanning off to tilt at windmills in Zimbabwe, so I could lose yet another election.

Everything that Jenny said was right, but alas, I couldn't not go. I had to go back to Zimbabwe to help win the elections. If the MDC won, we could go home, and our lives could go back to the normal. In my heart of hearts, I knew I was doing the right thing. But it didn't stop me from feeling inadequate, a shirker, like I was running out on Jenny and my responsibilities. The word shirk resonated in my head for days. Come the day to leave, Jenny thawed and gave me a hug and a kiss and told me to stay safe and to not do anything stupid.

I was driving up to Zimbabwe for the first time in my brand-new Tata pick-up truck, a downgrade from my beloved Land Rover. I don't do status symbols, but I couldn't but cringe every time I got into the Tata. Even though the thing had started first time every time so far and hadn't broken down in the first thousand kilometres, for me it was the automotive equivalent of single-ply toilet paper, a shout out to the world that I wasn't doing very well financially. And unlike my beloved Land Rover, the Tata didn't have a million hidey-holes in which to smuggle stuff through borders. Alas. And it was a very big alas because the Sokwanele activist Hemingway, he of Mugabe toilet paper fame, had asked me to pick up some election contraband in Louis Trichardt on my way through to Zimbabwe. Hemingway wouldn't go into the specifics of what he wanted me to pick-up over the phone, in case someone was listening in, but I knew full well that he was talking about stuff for his Plan B. Which made me beyond super nervous.

Hemingway was a hawk. In fact, he made hawks look like doves. According to him, dictators didn't get voted out, they got booted out, violently. He despaired that the MDC under Tsvangirai was too peaceful, too soft to grab power and would always, as a result, come second. Hemingway had developed a Plan B which was all about fanning the flames of public anger on the streets of Zimbabwe if and when the elections were stolen, building up to full-on civil-disobedience campaign and beyond. Plan B wasn't new, but Hemingway was the first person I'd met who was actually going to do something about it. Hemingway had recruited and trained up a band of agitators and smuggled them into the country, but now he needed me to get vital inputs to them so they could stir shit. Nothing that would kill, he reassured me, no guns, no bombs or grenades, just tear gas canisters and tazers and flash-bang fireworks. Non-lethal ordnance he called it.

Hemingway couldn't take them in himself because he had a high-profile day job, so he wanted me to deliver the shit-stirring equipment. I was his only delivery option. Mostly Sokwanele was full of doves that didn't do violence, in accordance with the wishes of their precious donors, so Hemingway's Plan B was strictly off the books. Personally, I liked Plan B but was less than thrilled at the prospect of being personally involved in the rollout and would've much rather spectated from the safety of distant bleachers.

Reluctantly and only because there were no other mules, I met Hemingway outside a shopping centre in Louis Trichardt as per plan. He issued me with two cheap burn phones, pre-loaded with Zimbabwean sim cards and airtime, one for me and one for Baldric. I was picking Baldric up at the airport in Harare. Hemingway gave me phone numbers for his men on the ground. They'd travelled to Harare the previous week and were expecting my call. Hemingway also gave me his lecture on the cell phone security, no real names to be used, check-in twice per day, etc.

And then we started transferring boxes and boxes of non-lethal ordnance from his car to the Tata. There were six boxes in all. The space behind the seats in the Tata was already full of billions and trillions of Zimbabwe dollars; bribe money for the trip. Which left only the space beneath the seats and the cubbyhole. We filled those with the contents of the first box and then proceeded to fill the back of the Tata with the other five, where they stuck out like dogs' balls. I rearranged a too small tarpaulin to no avail. "How the hell am I get all of this through the border? And then through all the roadblocks?" I whined. Going into an election, police roadblocks would be thick like hairs on a dog's back.

"Bribery and corruption, my good man, bribery and corruption. I hope you brought lots of cash like I told you to." Hemingway laughed heartily. It was all right for him, I thought bitterly as I headed towards my hell on earth a.k.a. the Beitbridge border post, he wasn't going to be the one sweating bullets in the search queue.

To this day, I have absolutely no idea how I got through the border search unscathed. Vehicle search is mandatory at the Beitbridge border post, carried out by customs officials permanently stationed in the car park. Unless they'd stamped your gate pass, you didn't get out the gates. And worse luck, the border post was all but empty when I drove up. I'd been hoping and praying for a scrum of buses, trucks and cars to distract attention away from my illicit load. I shuffled through the border clearance process slowly and miserably, with the word guilt etched across my face for all to see, absolutely dreading the search, trying to figure out the protocol for paying a bribe surreptitiously when the bribe money, bricks and bricks of billions and trillions, took up all the space behind both seats of the Tata. I shuffled up to the two customs officials behind the desk in the carpark like the dead man I was soon-to-be. They asked me which car was mine. I pointed to the Tata. The two officials shared a quick look of pity that Tata owners quickly become attuned to. And then they stamped my exit pass. I was free to go. I thanked them profusely, over and over. Which straight away, I regretted. I should've gone with nonchalance instead. And then for added effect, I managed to stall the Tata right under the noses of the customs officials. Who laughed and laughed. "You should've bought a Toyota instead," they told me. I heaved twenty sighs of relief and had to make an emergency stop to jettison the contents of my bladder at the first available bush. One hurdle down, only twelve hurdles left to go.

As it turned out, twelve was the number of police roadblocks on the road between Beitbridge and Harare. Again, with guilt written all over my face, I sweated bullets at each and every one of them, praying to God to not let the cops check under the tarpaulin in the back, or under the seats, or in the cubbyhole, or in my holdall bag. God came through for me at the first seven roadblocks where I wasn't even asked to stop but just got waved through by policemen too bored to even go through the motions. But at the

WHERE HOPE SPRINGS ETERNAL BUT NOT FOR LONG

Featherstone roadblock, a hundred kilometres from Harare, my good luck ran out, and a keen-eyed policeman waved me to a halt. I forced an inane grin onto my face and greeted the policeman warmly as he walked up to the driver's window. "Hallo, Officer, how are you? Thirty years ago, I could've been you at this roadblock."

"What do you mean?" he asked suspiciously.

"I mean I used to be stationed here, thirty years ago, as a policeman. That was my house over there, back then it was the single quarters."

"It is still the single quarters, Sir. I am living there now." There was an almost tentative smile

"Like I said, you could be me."

"I think that back then the Police Force was far much better than now." He looked down at my SA number plates. "What are you doing these days?"

"I am a farmer. In South Africa. I used to be a farmer here until..."

He moved to the back of the truck and lifted up the tarpaulin and took in all the pepper sprays and tazers. "Why are you here now?"

I took the hugest of gambles. "I'm back to help with the elections."

"You can proceed."

To this day I like to think the policeman in Featherstone was one of us.

When eventually I got into Harare in the late afternoon, I was bathed in sweat with nerve ends twanging loud like Jimi Hendrix guitar strings. In my rear-view mirror, every car was suspicious and poised to swoop. I drove to the airport to pick up Baldric. We were both staying with Bob and Julie Hamill. But there was no way I could pitch up there with a car full of teargas, tazers and flashbangs. Julie would use them to kill me. Before we left the airport carpark, I used my burn phone to call Hemingway's man on the ground. I felt very like a spy. He didn't answer. I phoned again. Still no answer. Crap. On the third attempt, the man answered eventually. There was a whole party of loud music on his side of the line, and I had to shout to be heard. "This is Borat. Where can I..."

"Who?"

"Borat. I can't hear with all that music. Can't you..."

"Who is that? I can't hear you because of the loud music."

"For fuck's sake, can't you move away from the music?"

"I can't hear you, so I am going to move away from the music." After forever, he came back. "Who is this?"

"Borat. I've got your..."

"Ahhh! Borat. And my tear gas. And my tazers. And my bang flashes. This is excellent. "

"Shhh! For fuck's sake, don't shout man. Where can we meet?"

We agreed to meet in the carpark at Newlands shopping centre in thirty minutes. I'd met Hemingway's man before so knew what he looked like. Baldric and I got to the shopping centre five minutes early and drove around looking for anything or anyone suspicious. There was a hell of a party going on in the car park with a half dozen of more taxi minibuses parked together, playing loud blaring music and all covered in MDC election posters, thronged by revellers, again all wearing MDC t-shirts and party regalia. While we watched from the corner of the car park, Hemingway's man peeled off from the party on a resupply run to the supermarket's bottle store section. When he was well away from the music and just about to enter the supermarket, I phoned him from my burn phone.

"Borat, Borat, where are you?" I cringed. I could almost hear him from my side of the carpark.

"Shhh! Not so loud. I'm in a white pick-up truck near the north side of the car park."

"Huh?"

"I'm outside the paint shop."

"I see you Borat, I see you." He rushed across the carpark, surreptitious in his bright red 'Vote for Morgan Tsvangirai' t-shirt, with his arms in the hug position. To dispel any doubts as to who he was meeting, he shouted Borat out very loudly every few metres. We could tell he was liquored up when his booze breath reached the Tata well before the rest of him. And then he recognised Baldric trying to cringe away beneath the dashboard next me. "Ah, Baldric also. Hallo Baldric, hallo." Baldric, ever polite, raised his head up from his hiding spot and waved weakly. I was less polite and told Hemingway's man to shut the fuck up before every CIO operative in creation came down on us like a ton of bricks. For a minute, I thought he would break down in tears. "OK, Borat" he sniffed, "it's just that I am happy to see you."

"I'm also happy to see you. But I just want to give you your stuff so we can get the hell out of here."

"Ok."

"But we need to do it quietly, where no-one is watching..."

Too late. He'd already turned and wolf-whistled loudly for his motley and extremely merry crew to come across and offload the ordnance. I tried to distance myself from the exercise by feigning interest in the paint shop window but had to abort that plan when I saw a pissed Hemingway minion making off with my kitbag.

It took just minutes to transfer all the boxes across to the minibuses, but they were the longest minutes of my life. Throughout, all I could see were the barbed wire fences and whitewashed walls and towers of Harare's remand prison across the road, a harsh, stark reminder of where I was going to end up if the farce I was playing a starring role in continued to play out for much longer. How we didn't get busted, I do not know. When finally we arrived at Bob Hamill's house, drained and still shaking, it took more than a few beers to calm my nerves.

The next day I reported to MDC Support HQ for duty. Not surprisingly, HQ was at Hendrik O'Neill's house in Newlands. I don't think there is a man out there who has given more for the cause than Hendrik. An army of volunteers had taken over his house and garden, apart from the part of the garden where Hendrik's pet crocodile lurked. Hendrik had brought the crocodile and a young Kudu and some carnivorous Crowned Cranes into town with him when he got kicked off his farm. Hendrik's volunteers were busy preparing polling agent packs for the more than ten thousand polling stations countrywide. Hendrik had put months of effort into improving the Parallel Vote Count system that hadn't worked too well last elections. He told me he had it sorted this time round. There was a lot of paperwork, an A4 envelope bulging per polling station. Times ten thousand. I almost broke out in hives. Paperwork has that effect on me.

Before throwing me into the deep end, Hendrik gave me a final briefing on the big picture. There were three elections on the go- Presidential, Parliamentary and Local Government. The big wahoonie and the one that we had to focus on winning was the Presidential race. There were just three horses in that race- Morgan, Mugabe and Simba Makoni – ex-ZANU PF but now a moderate with a new no-name brand political party. Welshman Ncube's MDC faction wasn't fielding a presidential candidate, choosing to rather focus their energy on the Parliamentary elections only. Churlishly, Ncube had urged his faction members to vote for Makoni instead of Morgan. Morgan was fielding Parliamentary and Local Government candidates in all the constituencies. I'd be running support for three of them, all in Mashonaland West.

I tracked down the tables that were looking after my three constituencies- Zvimba East, Zvimba West and Norton so I could get busy planning my polling agent deployments. But alas, they weren't ready. The harassed envelope stuffers were concentrating on the more distant constituencies first, to allow for transport time. Hendrik worried that it would be touch and go as to whether they got the job done in time so asked me to try and round up more volunteers. I told him no problem and headed to Mitch and Lulu Whaley's house and returned with their second son Stephen, and his best friend Miles. Aged just fifteen and fourteen, Stephen and Miles had already nagged me non-stop by e-mail to find them election jobs. They were over the moon happy to be contributing until they saw the mountain of envelopes that they had to stuff. Their faces dropped. "But we want to do something exciting, Eric, and dangerous," Stephen sniffed.

"This stuff is important, Stevie. And your mom will kill me if I get you caught up in something exciting and dangerous." I had no desire to ever meet an angry Lulu.

I left them to it to go to a meeting with my constituency candidates.

Some things in Zimbabwe never change. Knox Danda, the candidate for Zvimba West, couldn't make the meeting. He sent three of his supporters instead. The supporters told me Knox had been placed under house arrest by his opponent, a former Mashonaland West Governor. Who further told Knox he would be beaten and or killed if he left his house to campaign – or rather what remained of his house. Half of Knox's house had been burnt down two weeks earlier by ZANU thugs in an attack that followed an MDC rally. In the same attack, Knox's supporters, including the three emissaries standing in front of me, had been badly, badly beaten. Both the attack and the subsequent death threats had been reported to a police station just fifteen kilometres away, but the police said they didn't have a vehicle and couldn't investigate. Through his supporters, Knox was asking if I could bring his plight to the attention of the election observers.

I drove to the Meikles Hotel there and then with one of the supporters to track down an elusive Election Observer. I chose the Knox supporter with the most visible damage. Eventually, after waiting what seemed like hours, I bullied my way into the offices of the Pan African Parliament Observer team and met with their head of delegation, the Honourable Khumalo from South Africa, who was very puffed up with self-importance and lunch, lots of lunch. Knox's supporter told his story about how Knox couldn't campaign for fear of death. He spoke well and convincingly but judging by the look on his face, the Honourable Khumalo remained unconvinced. I told the supporter to lift his shirt and show the Honourable Khumalo the injuries he'd sustained during the attack on Knox's house two weeks earlier. The injuries were horrific and moved the Honourable Khumalo to tut, tut, tut. He said that if the incidents were true, they were most unfortunate. If they were true? I offered to drive the Honourable Khumalo out to Zvimba there and then but regrettably he was too busy. I pushed him. When could he come? At his earliest opportunity, he told me. Which was when? He considered an empty diary and told me that unfortunately, his earliest opportunity was only going to be on the Sunday, the day after the elections. I was incensed. So how the hell were the elections in the meantime going to be free and fair if Knox Danda was locked up in the remaining half of his house, unable to campaign, for fear of death? The Honourable Khumalo signalled that our meeting had unfortunately come to an end. I told him I'd see him on the Sunday, bright and early. He looked less than thrilled at the prospect.

The saddest thing about the whole incident was how many times Knox's supporter thanked me for taking him to see the Honourable Khumalo and for forcing the Election Observer into making a promise to go to Zvimba the day after the elections to make everything right. I gave him bus fare money and sent him on his way, a happy man.

Next up, I had to rush out to Running Dog to start planning polling agent deployments with Mitch and Willie Viljoen. I hadn't been on Running Dog for close on two months and felt my heartstrings twang as I drove through the main gates, especially when a group of workers working in a field recognised me from afar and dropped their tools to run and greet me. I hugged it up especially big with Raphael. He was looking old and tired but still had a sparkle in his eye. He told me he had lots to discuss, both politics and production. I told him I had to take a rain check and got straight into planning the deployments. Mitch and Willie, both displaced farmers who'd long been kicked off their own farms and were now running Running Dog, had put their hands up to help with polling agent deployment. Thank God, because there was no way I was going to be able to transport seven hundred polling agents on my own. The meeting wasn't an hour old when Hendrik phoned me. Something had come up. He needed me back in town to do a job for him. I left Mitch and Willie to do the planning and hot-footed it back into town, getting caught up in the afternoon rush hour traffic in the process.

As soon as I walked in to Support HQ, Hendrik asked me if I'd drive to Bulawayo quickly to pick-up a load of satellite phones, one hundred of them, just in from South Africa. I told him no problem. I'd drive to Bulawayo first thing in the morning, collect the phones and turn around. Hendrik told me no, he needed me to drive through the night. He needed the phones back in Harare by first light so he could get them set up and working in time to deploy them to the districts. Because Hendrik was a man you didn't say no to, I told him yes, I'd leave in the hour. All I had to do was to figure out how I was going to drive through the night without killing myself. I was still knackered from my drive up. I needed a co-driver. But who to ask? I played a conversation in my head in which I asked Bob Hamill if he'd help me drive, but Bob told me to fuck off. And Baldric couldn't help because he was going to be working through the night setting up internet links for the support office and would be the one to commission the phones. And Mitch was going to be even busier deploying the polling agents that I was supposed to deploy. Then in a stroke of genius, I thought of young Joe X, son of a best friend and the same age as Veronica. I phoned Joe up and asked if he fancied a drive through the night. Feeling like Tom Cruise, I told him I couldn't tell him what our mission was, because it was top secret, but it was for the good of the country. Joe said no problem.

I picked him up from the farm where he worked. I told Joe we'd take it in turns to drive, two hours on, two hours off. We hit the main Bulawayo road just in time to catch the setting sun. It was right in my eyes, and the glare was vicious. I slowed right down. I'm a nervous driver at the best times, and even worse when I can't see anything. Joe looked at the speedometer, looked at his watch, did the sums and then asked me if I wanted him to drive. "Because it's going to take us until next Wednesday to get to Bulawayo and back if we drive at forty kilometres an hour."

"OK, Joe, you drive, and I'll catch up on some sleep. Wake me up when you want me to take over."

I would have bet good money that there was no way my Tata pick-up truck could do one hundred sixty kilometres an hour. Had I made the bet, I would have lost. Just minutes after taking the wheel, Joe had nudged the speed up and over one hundred sixty. There was a neat handrail on the dashboard above the cubbyhole, purpose-made for nervous passengers. I grabbed it and held on to it for all my worth, white knuckles the whole way, until we got to Bulawayo. I gave up on the idea of trying to sleep in the first minutes and instead, helped Joe stay awake by whimpering loudly every thirty seconds or so, with intermittent screams, especially when there was oncoming traffic with headlights on bright, of which there was a lot. I have never been so terrified for so long in all my life. Joe remained unflustered throughout. He told me he'd learnt how to drive fast on a video game. At least he slowed down going through towns and police roadblocks. Again, the police roadblocks were mostly disinterested in our stories about who we were and where we were going.

We drove into Bulawayo just after midnight. We picked up the shipment of satellite phones and a badly needed full tank of diesel from a Sokwanele activist code-named Soaring Swallow. Where these people got their codenames from, I do not know? While Joe and I loaded the back of Tata full of satellite phones, Soaring Swallow told me the phones were a gift from the Americans. They'd been smuggled across the border in a plastic water tank. He asked me to sign for the phones. There were more than a hundred of them, each costing three thousand US and the Americans wanted them back after the elections, apparently. I signed as Borat, just in case. If the Americans didn't get their phones back, they could take it up with Sacha Baron Cohen.

Fortified with coffee and sandwiches provided by Mrs Soaring Swallow, Joe and I got back on the road just after one o'clock. It was more white knuckles the whole way home, and we drove into Harare as the sun was getting out of bed, just in time to drop Joe off at work. He looked fresh as a daisy and good for a day's work, but I was beyond knackered. I delivered the phones to a grateful Hendrik and then went home for a quick three hours sleep. Which made me feel guilty as hell when eventually I made it out to Running Dog to help with the polling agent deployments.

Both Mitch and Willie had also driven right through the night, without any rest, dropping polling agent teams off at their polling stations. Mitch was looking especially worse for wear, with lumps, bumps and bruises, courtesy of a beating he'd received at the hands of a notorious CIO thug who went by the name Gushous and whose main claim to fame was that he was one of Mugabe's nephews. Mitch had bumped into the man in

WHERE HOPE SPRINGS ETERNAL BUT NOT FOR LONG

the small hours of the morning while deploying polling agents. Gushous had chased Mitch in his Isuzu twin-cab, trying to run him off the road repeatedly. When eventually he cut Mitch off, forcing him to stop, Gushous leapt out and gave him a beating, for being white and for supporting the MDC. Mitch went through the motions and reported the incident to the police. And then he went back to deploying polling agents. Mitch is one of the softest men I know, but also one of the strongest, especially inside, where strength really counts.

I spent the rest of the day driving around Zvimba Communal Lands, visiting remote schools and clinics in the back of beyond, deploying polling teams. I was on edge the whole day, waiting for bad stuff to happen, but it didn't. Traditionally the areas I was driving through were considered to be the heart of ZANU heartland, but no longer. Things had changed from five years earlier. The people I saw were clearly sick and tired of Mugabe and the poverty he'd brought along with his millions, billions and trillions. Old men with grey peppercorns in their hair, standing outside the walls of Mugabe's Kutama home, saluted me openly with the MDC's open hand and they didn't care who was watching. It was momentous. There'd been a seismic shift in the attitudes of the people on the ground, the people who'd be voting come Election Day. This time round the MDC had a very real chance of winning.

I got home to the Hamill house exhausted, but also fired up and excited. Baldric was jealous. He'd signed up to do exciting but had been trapped all day, bored to tears, capturing serial numbers and commissioning the one hundred satellite phones before deploying them. But it was job done, and he'd be joining me for a day in the field on Election Day. I was more than happy for the company. I slept the sleep of the dead. But not for long. A phone call from Hendrik ripped me out of my slumber. It was almost midnight. I'd been asleep for less than two hours. Hendrik sounded twitchy. He was looking for his mother-in-law's Mercedes Benz. I rubbed precious little sleep from my eyes and asked him why he was asking me?

"Because those two kids you brought to my house yesterday have got it. And I don't know their names. How do I get hold of them?"

"How come they're driving your mom in law's Benz? They're only kids, one fourteen and the other fifteen. They haven't even got driving licences."

"Shit. They didn't tell me that."

"What did they tell you?"

"I asked for volunteers to drive the satellite phones down to Mutare. And those two kids volunteered. But they said they didn't have a vehicle. So I gave them the keys to my mother-in-law's Benz. That was first thing this morning. Now it's midnight, and my mother-in-law wants to know where her car is. Shit. Can you help me find it? And them, I suppose?"

I allowed myself five minutes of stressing before I phoned Mitch and Lulu to tell them their fifteen-year-old son and friend had driven across the country and through a million police roadblocks in a Mercedes Benz and were now missing in action, presumed arrested. Ominously, Mitch answered on the first ring. He allowed me to stumble and stutter through the intro to my story but then cut me short. "Don't worry, Stephen and Miles are fine. And so is the car. Lulu's with them. They're almost home."

"How did Lulu come to be with them?"

"When she heard what they were planning, she made them come and pick her up."

Hendrik was hugely relieved when I phoned him back to tell him his mother-in-law's Benz was safe, ditto the boys.

In a small footnote to the story, Hendrik told me that when the car was dropped off the next morning, you couldn't see the paintwork for all the Vote Morgan posters stuck on it.

Chapter Forty-Nine

Election Day dawned, complete with singing birds and full of endless possibilities. I woke up, leapt out of bed, ready for anything. Today was the day when good things would happen. Accordingly, my coffee tasted perfect, and my cornflakes crispy. Baldric and I set sail in the Tata early. We were going to try to cover all three constituencies, so we had a full day in front of us. Baldric was excited like a kid on holiday. He'd never worked an election before. "So what are we going to be doing?" he asked.

"We'll start in Zvimba West. We'll spend a few hours visiting polling stations, checking for any anomalies, checking with polling agents, making sure they're doing their paperwork, that sort of stuff. And then we'll move onto the next constituency and do the same there."

"Oh." He sounded less excited.

On our way to Zvimba West, we picked up Nixon, the Constituency Election Agent, a bright and eager young man plus two MDC supporters, Shepherd, who worked for me and Jericho, the guy who'd had the Party initials carved into his back with an Okapi knife in the 2000 elections. Jericho lifted his shirt to show Baldric his scars. Baldric was impressed.

It didn't take us long to find our first electoral anomaly. Our second stop of the day was the polling station at the Gwebi Agricultural College. Half the Assembly Hall had been screened off to accommodate the polling station, and the other half was being used as the venue for a premature celebratory victory party hosted by the local ZANU PF councillor. We got there just after eight in the morning, and already the beer was flowing and the music blaring and everywhere you looked, there were local ZANU PF heavyweights in their full regalia, enjoying, right next to the polling station and in full view of the long queue of voters waiting to cast their votes. Nixon was incensed. The beer drink broke every electoral law in the book. He stormed up to the Presiding Officer to complain. The Presiding Officer, a civil servant, drafted in for the day, was eyeing out the party next door rather wistfully and said he couldn't see where the problem was. Nixon waved a copy of the Electoral Act in his face, but still, he couldn't see the problem. He told Nixon the party was just a social gathering and the room had been hired and paid for months earlier.

Nixon stormed out of the confrontation and asked if we could search out an Election Observer team. There was supposed to be one team per constituency. The Observer Team proved to be extremely elusive, but eventually we found them, or rather him, hours later at a polling station on

Royden Farm, not far from Lilfordia School.

I hadn't been on Royden in years. It had once been a model farm, owned by Alastair Smith, up until he got violently booted in the land-grab. Alastair's family had helped shape commercial agriculture in the country and in the district and his uncle David had been Ian Smith's Minister of Agriculture for years. In the early years of Zimbabwe, Smith family farms had headlined on every visiting dignitary's tour itinerary, a shop front for Mugabe to showcase his country's vast agricultural potential. But that was back when Mugabe didn't hate white farmers. Fast forward twenty-plus years and Royden had been destroyed. Pastures and fields had gone back to bush, houses and buildings now derelict with every window frame, door frame and roofing sheet long stolen. I tried to tell Baldric how good the farm had once been, but I failed.

The one-man Election Observer team, visible in his high visibility vest, was standing outside the tent that was the Royden Farm polling station, talking to a young dreadlocked man wearing tight designer jeans, shiny pointy shoes and a crocodile smile. Nixon groaned. The man was Patrick Zhuwao, incumbent Member of Parliament, son of Sabina Mugabe, and nephew to Robert Mugabe. His crocodile smile firmly in place, Zhuwao asked me why I'd driven all the way from South Africa to support a losing party. Around him, a bunch of his adoring groupies laughed to order. I suggested to Zhuwao that given the fact the votes hadn't been counted yet, perhaps his observations were premature, unless of course, he knew something I didn't. The Zhuwao groupies sneered.

We left Zhuwao and pulled the one-man Observer team to one side to complain about the ZANU PF beer drink at the Gwebi Polling Station. The observer, a young Zimbabwean and clearly petrified, made all the right noises when he heard our story but unfortunately, due to a lack of transport, he wasn't going to be able to react. I offered him a lift to Gwebi. Unfortunately, he had his hands full observing the nearly empty Royden tent. But he did offer to write up our complaint in his notebook.

Listening in, Zhuwao laughed. Then he and his groupies swaggered off to a brand-new shiny twin-cab and drove off in a cloud of dust. With Zhuwao gone, Nixon asked the observer again if he'd come with us to Gwebi to shut down the beer drink, but the answer stayed no. Alas. Before we left, Nixon went into the tent to check on his polling agents and their paperwork. Which didn't take him long. In the five hours it had been open, less than fifty voters had passed through the tent to cast their votes.

As we were driving out of Royden on a rutted road through bush that had once been a field, a group of very excited young children rushed into the road and waved us down. In a flurry of high-speed Shona, they warned Nixon that the road ahead was blocked. And it was, by Zhuwao, in his twin-cab.

"What's he doing? Why's he stopped? What are we going to do?" Baldric asked.

I couldn't answer because my heart was in my mouth. And I couldn't pass because the bush was thick on both sides of the narrow road. And then Zhuwao started driving again, oh so slowly, at just twenty kilometres an hour. Ominous music played loud in my head as I followed reluctantly.

"How about we go back to Royden and look for another way out?" Baldric asked.

I assured him that Zhuwao wouldn't try anything on polling day, it was obvious the ZANU PF man was just nursing his new car on the bad roads. My sphincter wasn't so sure and urged me to consider Baldric's suggestion. And then when we were just three hundred metres from the Lilfordia road ahead, Zhuwao and his crocodile smile pulled off and waved us through. I accelerated past him with a huge sense of relief.

The relief lasted not even a minute. As I pulled on to the tar road, Jericho stuck his head through the back window and screamed loud in my ear, "Go, Go, Go!" My sphincter thought Jericho was talking to it and I nearly shat my pants. I almost stalled. What the hell was going on? I looked in the rear-view mirror and found it full of angry faces in a silver Isuzu. The twin-cab with ten or more men on board all but crashed into me. My first instinct was to slow down. Which got Nixon also screaming in my ear. "Don't slow down, Eric, don't slow down!"

"Who is he, Nixon? And what does he want?"

"It's Gushous. He's bad. He'll kill us if he catches us!"

I knew the name straight away. Gushous was the thug who'd beaten Mitch up two nights earlier. I jammed my foot flat on the accelerator and the Tata surged forward, pulling away from the Isuzu.

I rammed the pick-up through the gears with engine screaming and the next time I looked down at the speedo, we were nudging one hundred sixty k.p.h. Which on the Lilfordia road was a snag. Technically, it was still a tar road, but only in places. Erosion and a complete lack of maintenance had reduced the tar to a narrow and erratic strip barely one wheel wide, with vicious drop-offs a metre deep or more on both sides and I ended up careering along at a crazy forty-five-degree angle. Every now and then the narrow tar strip in front would disappear completely, swallowed by huge potholes. But there was nowhere to hide, and I hit the first one so hard my front wheels came off the ground, and the top of my head smacked into the roof of the cab. It didn't help that I hadn't put my seatbelt on. Somehow, I managed to hang onto the steering wheel throughout and kept the Tata sort of on course. I risked a quick look in the rear-view mirror. I still had three bodies in the back, hanging on for dear life. And more importantly, the Tata had pulled away from the Isuzu, opening up a fifty-metre gap.

Gushous had a bigger, more powerful car, but he also had ten or more bodies on board. And he was a shit driver. I let out a quick whoop of triumph and then went back to trying to dodge the potholes in front, mostly failing. Spurred on by my whoop, Jericho let out a whoop of his own and grabbed a fist full of MDC election flyers from the box and flung them up into the air, back into the Gushous vehicle. I could almost see the veins in the necks of the men in the Isuzu behind us bulge even more ominously. The coward in me of whom there is a lot almost told Jericho to stop. But we were pulling away from them, so fuck it, throw more.

The distance from Lilfordia School to the main Harare-Chirundu highway is about fifteen kilometres. How we didn't die on that stretch of road, I have no idea. After smacking my head up against the ceiling four or five times, I shouted at Baldric to grab my seatbelt and jam into the clasp. During that drive, I fell in love with my Tata. I promoted it from the Piece of Shit Tata to the Mighty Tata. It was pig ugly and drove even worse, but man, it flew through ruts and potholes that would have broken my Land Rover into little bits.

By the time we got into Nyabira, a tiny village where the Lilfordia road met the Harare- Chirundu highway, we were three hundred metres plus ahead of the Isuzu full of bad guys. The Nyabira Police Station was right on the road. I screamed to Nixon through the back window. "Shall I stop at the Police Station?"

There was no hesitation from Nixon. "No, no, don't stop. The police will just give us to Gushous."

Alas. So I hit the highway with engine screaming and foot flat and tried to put my foot flatter. It was about thirty kilometres into Harare City Centre. The speedo needle inched up to one seventy but no further. Baldric and I strategized as we flew. On good tar, Gushous would start gaining on us. It was going to be tight, very tight but I was sure we'd make it. We decided to push on into town and head for the Meikles Hotel, which would be full of international Election observers observing the elections from the safety of the cocktail bar and the lounge. Once we got to the Meikles, there was no way Gushous would follow us in.

Our escape plan went swimmingly well, right up until the police roadblock on the edge of the city limits. The black and white barriers stretched across both lanes had long stops with rifles deployed before and after. I pounded the steering wheel in frustration and started to slow down. "Fuck, fuck, fuck it."

"Just run it, mate, foot down flat and bust through it," Baldric said from the passenger seat. "They haven't got a vehicle, so they'll never catch us."

"But what about the long stop with the FN? He'll shoot us."

"He'll miss. Do it. Bust through."

I should've listened to Baldric but chose to dither instead. "I can't do it, Baldric. Up to now, we haven't broken any laws. And maybe he won't stop us, and if he does, maybe we'll be through before Gushous gets here."

Looking out the back window, Baldric said "I'm thinking maybe we won't. Here comes Gushous. And he's coming fast."

By then, we'd inched up to the barriers. I prayed to God furiously, asking him to make the policeman let us through the roadblock. But God must have been busy elsewhere because the policeman, a Sergeant, held his hand up, signalling me to stop. I forced a smile onto my face, but it didn't stay there long. Behind us in the distance, Gushous started flashing his headlights at the policemen and sounding his hooter. Straightway the policeman's demeanour changed. He went from bored to alert. I took a gamble and told him. "He's CIO. He's chasing us because we're MDC. We think he wants to kill us. Please let us go."

My gamble almost worked. For sure, the Sergeant had empathy. I could see that deep inside, he wanted to wave us through. But he didn't have the balls. He apologised. "I'm sorry. You need to turn your car off."

My mind was racing, almost as fast as Gushous behind us. "OK. But I want you to arrest us, not him. Don't let him take us. If he takes us away, he'll kill us."

"Why?"

"Because we're MDC."

"No, I mean, why am I going to arrest you?"

"I don't know. Tell him you're arresting us for a traffic offence. But don't let him take us. Stand up to him and tell him you know that CIO haven't got powers of arrest."

That was all I had time for. The Isuzu screamed to a halt and Gushous, and his thugs leapt out. There were ten of them. They swarmed towards us, headed up by Gushous.

Gushous was a short, squat man with a weightlifter's build. He stormed up to the policeman, radiating anger and authority. The young Sergeant visibly quailed. Gushous introduced himself as being with the President's Office and said that he was arresting us.

Somewhere deep inside me, I found the balls to speak out. "You can't arrest us. You're CIO. And CIO haven't got powers of arrest. And we're foreign passport holders. I'm Dutch, he's British. And our embassies know exactly where we are."

With a face like thunder, Gushous told me to shut up. But I didn't. I told the young policeman. "You arrest us. Take us to the police station if you think we've done something wrong. But don't let this man take us. He'll kill us."

Gushous quickly switched to Shona. I don't do Shona, but I could follow the conversation. Gushous was insistent with his demands, remonstrating with both hands, the veins in his bull neck bulging. I was sure the Sergeant was going to buckle under the pressure. But he didn't. Instead, he shook his head at Gushous and reverting to English, told him that if anyone were going to arrest us, it would be him. But he needed Gushous to tell him what crimes we'd committed. Gushous exploded, almost losing the top of his head in the process. And still, the sergeant stood firm.

Gushous changed tack. He told the policeman to hold us while he went into town to consult his superiors. The Sergeant told him no problem. For good measure, before he left, Gushous stormed across to the Tata and ripped out the keys, breaking the steering lock in the process.

As soon as Gushous was gone, I went to work on the policeman, pleading with him to let us go. No, he told us. He was going to hold us at the roadblock until the CIO man got back. Then he'd take us to Harare Central Police Station and hand us over to his superiors. It wasn't first prize, but it was a hell of a lot better than Gushous dragging us off. Baldric and I retreated to the Tata to strategize again. After pondering for a minute, Baldric came up with a great idea." Let's tell the cop we need to have a shit. Then we go into the mealies, and we leg it for the hills. They'll never catch us."

"And leave the Tata?"

"I'll buy you a new one."

"We can't run. Up to now, we've done nothing wrong. We've broken no laws. But that all changes if we run."

Quickly five minutes turned into fifteen, then thirty. While we waited, Baldric got busy on his phone to Roy Bennett in South Africa, telling him what had happened and where we were. Roy said he'd get the best lawyers onto our case straight away. He told Baldric to keep him fully informed throughout. The policeman asked me who we were talking to. When I told him Roy Bennett, he was suitably impressed. Then in a hushed voice, he told me that he was related to Nelson Chamisa, the firebrand MDC youth leader. I told him that ever since the 2000 elections, Nelson was one of my best friends in the MDC. We all but hugged.

After an hour of waiting and still no sign of Gushous, I went back to work on the policeman. It was starting to get dark. Why didn't he just let us go? We'd broken no laws. And clearly, the CIO wasn't coming back. The policeman thought long and hard and then agreed. We could go. Baldric, Nixon and I high fived each other. We were free. Then I remembered that Gushous had the Tata keys. Fuck. No problem, said Baldric, he should be able to hotwire the Tata. Predictably, just as Baldric got his head under the ignition, Gushous came speeding around the corner. He got out, glared at us and the policemen and told us to get in his car. He was taking us to Police Central where the Law and Order Maintenance, the ZRP's feared political section, would deal with us. I told him no, I wasn't getting in any car with him. CIO didn't have powers of arrest. We were just getting into that argument when the sergeant said he'd arrest us. He'd follow Gushous into Central in the Tata and then hand us over to his superiors in the Traffic section. They could decide whether or not Law and Order Maintenance got us. Gushous, less than happy having his authority trod upon by a lowly Sergeant, enjoyed a minor but memorable thrombosis. But the Sergeant stuck to his guns and minutes later, we were following Gushous in the Tata.

While the Sergeant drove, Baldric updated Roy Bennett on where we were being taken while I set about sanitising the Tata. First out the window were our burn phones, closely followed by the half dozen pepper sprays, tazers and flashbangs that I found under the passenger seats. Before we got to Harare Central, I phoned Jenny to tell her I was being arrested but that she wasn't to worry and that everything would work out just fine. I told her Roy was going to help us with lawyers and that she should keep in touch with him.

Harare Central Police Central is a huge, square edifice, utterly cheerless and clearly designed by an architect suffering haemorrhoids, toothache and irritable bowel syndrome. Now dirty and unkempt, the building radiated misery and suffering. Which perked Gushous up no end. He was all over the Sergeant, crowing and laughing at our misery, all but dancing on the balls of his feet. The Sergeant ignored Gushous as best he could as he led us down grey corridors with peeling paint through to the Traffic Section where he handed us over to his Commanding Officer, a Chief Superintendent with shoulder epaulettes full of gold pips and a serious face. The Chief Supt listened to the Sergeant's story, looked across at the glowering Gushous, took a deep breath and then quickly collapsed to jelly. We were out of Traffic and on our way to the Law and Order Maintenance faster than the hottest potato. Alas.

Fittingly, the Law and Order Maintenance offices were in the basement of the building, deep down where the sun didn't shine. The only thing missing from the dark and dingy subterranean entrance was the 'Abandon Hope All Ye Who Enter' sign. The place stank of piss, fear and faeces, literally. You didn't have to try hard to hear long ago screams. Gushous herded us down a long dark corridor to an empty interrogation room with a desk and a hard-wooden bench. My balls all but retreated up into my body cavity when they saw a car battery complete with crocodile clips on charge in the corner. They knew exactly what car batteries complete with crocodile clips were for. And it was a big battery like you'd find on a thirty-ton rig. Gushous told us to sit down and shut up. The five of us squeezed on to the hard, uncomfortable bench, but only just. Gushous picked up a rubber baton off the desk and smacked his hand with a few times. Inside me, my balls clambered up even higher, but not before telling the soles of my feet that they were in for a beating. In my mind, I'd been inside this interrogation room a million times and knew exactly what was coming. But it didn't. Gushous enjoyed the fear and terror on our faces and then stalked out the room with baton in hand, closing the door behind him. We heard his footsteps walk away outside.

After a long pause, Baldric broke the silence. "Fuck it. We should've run away in the mealie field."

"Yeah." I couldn't but agree.

"Did anyone make out the number on the door outside? So I can tell Roy where we are." Incredibly, Baldric still had his cell phone.

Nixon answered. "I saw the number. This is room seventy-seven."

"You sure."

"I'm sure." Nixon was a resolute young man.

"OK. Here goes." Baldric pressed the send button.

And seconds later Roy Bennett sitting in Joburg replied. Baldric read Roy's reply. "Good. Keep me informed. Your lawyer at the cop shop now. But they are hiding you. Will tell him room 77. Hang tough. Fuck the bad guys."

Straight away, our dark and dingy prison got a whole lot less dark. But not long after, the battery on Baldric's cell phone died, ditto our link with the outside world.

They left us in room seventy-seven for hours without coming near us. I took that to be a good sign. They had us, but they didn't know what to do with us. And now that there was a lawyer in the building who knew exactly where we were meant they couldn't be plugging our genitals into the mains or beating the soles of our feet with batons. Which served to make me very combative when eventually they did come for us.

It was close to midnight when we were taken to see the Law and Order Maintenance big cheese, Superintendent Makandenga. He was seated behind his desk, which was big, like a football field and raised on a dais. His uniform still looked starched, but the man himself looked bone tired, even more tired than I felt. Makandenga didn't even look up at us as we filed into his office but carried on working away at an in-basket that was full to overflowing. I watched him work. Makandenga had bossed up the persecution of the MDC for the last eight years. Ordinarily, the mere mention of his name would have struck fear in my heart. But not tonight. When eventually he deigned to look down at us, like we were pieces of dog shit stuck to the bottom of his shoe, I attacked him. "Why've you arrested us? We've committed no crimes. And why haven't we been given access to our lawyer? He's been here looking for us for hours, but you haven't given him access to us. I want to see him now. And my Embassy."

Makandenga looked taken aback. Normally the dog shit in his office didn't talk to him like I was talking.

"Who are you?" he asked.

"Ask our lawyer. He's at your front desk. He'll tell you exactly who we are."

"Why are you in Zimbabwe?"

"I came here to help the MDC win the election."

"Why did you hand out MDC election material within twenty metres of a polling station?"

"I didn't."

"You did."

"I didn't. And if I did, why didn't the policeman at the polling station arrest me?"

Makandenga couldn't answer. But it didn't stop him from asking the same questions, over and over, for the next twenty minutes. And over and over, he got the same response, from all five of us. We hadn't handed out any election materials, at any polling stations. Eventually, the headache going on inside Makandenga's head got the better of him, and he stabbed at the intercom on his desk and barked orders for us to be removed from his office. But he did it reluctantly. I could tell that what he really wanted to do was wipe the cocksure grins from our faces. But he couldn't. Not with two embassies watching on.

We were collected by a young plainclothes policeman and taken down the corridor to a room with a gaggle of desks in it, like a group office. The young policeman looked tired and old. He told us to sit on the floor up against the wall and wait for morning when his colleagues would come in to start our interrogations. Then he left us to it, locking the door behind him. I checked the office out for car batteries with crocodile clips, but there weren't any. But there was a skylight window high up on the one wall. The bright moonlight struggled through the dirt. I was drawn to the window like a moth to a candle. By standing on the desk, I was able to reach up to the windowsill above and pull myself up to stare out onto Inez Terrace outside. If anyone had been walking past on the normally busy pavement outside, I'd have been staring up at their ankles. But at three in the morning, the pavements were empty. The walls on the building directly opposite the police station were covered wall to wall in election posters. I did a quick stocktake before my arms gave in. By my reckoning, the MDC won that election battle, hands down.

Nixon, Shepherd and Jericho fell asleep on the hard office floor no problem, but Baldric and I struggled. I was past exhausted, but I had the busiest of heads and sleep just wouldn't come. Instead, we ended up talking right the way through the night, sorting out all the problems of the world in the process, especially Zimbabwe's. Unfortunately, we also talked about the food we were going to eat when finally we got out of the mess we were in. We hadn't eaten a thing in almost twenty-four hours. But talking about cheeseburgers and thick chocolate milkshakes on the emptiest of stomachs was a silly idea and got me to salivating and thinking about nothing else.

At seven o'clock the first office dwellers, two men and a woman, unlocked the door and got busy at their desks. They paid us little or no attention. My bladder was bursting. I asked one of the men if I could go to the toilet. He told me down the passage, third door to the right, barely looking up from his paperwork. The toilets were filthy and stank of old shit and piss. After adding to the odour, I reckon I could've just walked out the building but didn't. When I got back to the group office, I asked the same man who'd let me go to the toilet if we could have something to eat. He told me later after he'd taken our fingerprints and warned and cautioned statements. I asked him what we were being charged with, but he couldn't tell me, yet. He was waiting on his bosses for that information.

By eight o'clock, all eight desks in the room were occupied, seven men and the one woman, all in plain clothes. They were slow to get busy and spent most of their first half an hour at work, talking amongst themselves, studiously ignoring us five criminals camped on the floor in the corner of their office. The plainclothes policemen all spoke Shona, but I heard Morgan Tsvangirai's name over and over, so I was guessing the elections were the main topic of conversation. But because they all had their poker faces on, I couldn't tell whether they were happy, sad or indifferent. At eight-thirty, an older, more serious policeman with gold on his epaulettes stalked into the room, glared at us in the corner with maximum venom and barked instructions. The plainclothes officers jumped. Two of them whisked us off for fingerprinting.

Fingerprinting is quite an interactive event, especially if you are printing a suspect with wonky, unreliable ring fingers like the ones I've got. The officer told me to roll my fingers from left to right across the fingerprint pad, starting with my left hand. I did good until I got to my ring finger which ignored my instructions and smudged, rendering all the previous and successful prints on the form null and void apparently. As soon as I'd smudged, in an attempt to fend off the bollocking that had to be coming, I apologised profusely. But the bollocking didn't come. Incredibly, the cop was human. He told me don't sweat it, lots of people smudged first time round. I asked him what we were being charged with. He told me they'd been told to charge us under the Electoral Act for distributing electoral material at a polling station. I told him the charges were bollocks and incredibly, he apologised. He was just following orders he told me.

When we got back to the group office, we had our statements taken. I ended up at desk between Jericho and Shepherd and answered the questions put to me by the lady policeman loudly and clearly, so both Shepherd and Jericho next to me could hear my answers. I had travelled to Zimbabwe to help the MDC win the elections. As a member of MDC Support, I was within my rights to enter into the polling stations to speak with MDC polling agents. No, I hadn't distributed any electoral material near a polling station. The charges against us were trumped up, by Zhuwao and the CIO. The woman cop wrote down my responses in longhand, neatly and methodically. She remained poker-faced throughout. Her cell phone rang mid-question. She looked down at her screen and told me sorry, she had to take the call. At the end of the short, one-sided conversation, her poker face fell away and was replaced by a huge, beaming, ear to ear grin. "We've won," she told me.

"Beg your pardon."

"I said we've won. The MDC has won."

"Huh?" was the best I could come up with.

"That call was from my friend at the Zimbabwe Electoral Commission." By now, the policewoman was talking to the room at large. "He just told me that Morgan Tsvangirai has won the Presidential Election. By sixty percent." A cheer went up from every policeman in the room. I couldn't believe it. I was in a room full of Law and Order Maintenance policemen, and the lot of them were closet MDC supporters. Opposite me, the policewoman stood up from her chair with tears in her eyes, walked around her desk and gave me the biggest hug. Her tears were contagious. My eyes sprung the biggest leak. My tears were all joy and no sorrow. After hugging the policewoman, I rushed across to hug Baldric. We'd been through so much together, and now it had finally paid off. Then I hugged Nixon. And Shepherd and Jericho. And then all the other cops in the room. I sobbed throughout the hug-fest. It was like all my Christmases had come at once. I'd never, ever been so happy in all my life. And everyone in the room was exactly the same. One of the Law and Order Maintenance policemen summed it perfectly. "We've been in the darkness," he told me. "But now we are in the light."

But alas, not for long. The senior policeman stormed into the room, looking absolutely distraught like he'd just lost a relative, or worse still, an election. On his face, distraught was quickly replaced with anger when he saw all the happy, smiley faces. Spittle flew from his lips as he tore into the cops with the most vicious of tongue lashings. The policemen stood bolt upright to attention and let his anger wash over them. It was a full-on rant that went on for minutes. It was all in Shona so I couldn't pick up on specifics, but he was that pissed off, I thought he was actually going to hit someone. And that someone was going to be me if he picked up on my happy smiley face that flat out refused to disappear. So I stared down at my feet throughout. All the while the senior cop was ranting and raving, inside all I wanted to do, was to tell him it was game over and better he shut the fuck up. He was a bad guy, and the bad guys had lost. Better he run away because for sure we were going to come after him. He and his had caused so much hurt and pain for so many in the last eight years and more. But at long last, the shoe was on the other foot, and it was payback time.

Thankfully though my little speech stayed inside and remained unsaid.

Eventually, the senior cop ran out of vitriol and stormed out the room. My policewoman flashed me the smallest of smiles before motioning for me to take up my seat at her desk again. And then it was back to taking my statement. Which against the backdrop of an MDC win was absolutely meaningless and inane. But we went through the motions, lest the boss cop pop his head around the corner again.

I can only liken the mood in the room to the last day of school when teachers tried their hardest to put the lid down on all the holiday feel good but failed. I was the worst. I sat with the biggest broadest grin on my face and every time I was able to catch anyone's eye, I flashed the open-handed MDC Chinja salute. Ten minutes into the resumption of statement taking, our lawyer came into the room. He was a power hitter by the name of Alex Muchadehama. I'd never met him, but straight away, I knew who he was. Alex Muchadehama was a top human rights lawyer and given the political state of affairs in Zimbabwe, he'd quickly become a household name, especially if your house were like mine. I'm guessing Roy pulled strings to get Alex on to our case.

Alex greeted the policemen first, one by one, and then came across to introduce himself. He had a worried look on his face which I guessed was an almost permanent fixture, given his line of work. I'd never been so pleased to make anyone's acquaintance, and I gave him the biggest grin and an even bigger MDC Chinja salute. Alex's worried look got a lot more worried, and he told me to hush up. "And don't do the political slogans in here, and especially not now."

"You obviously haven't heard, Alex, Morgan's won. One of the cops just told us."

"Shhh. You need to keep quiet. Let me get you out of here first."

"But we won."

"I don't know if we have. A big something is going on, and it's not good. Until I get you out, just sit here quietly. And no more Chinja stuff." The last comment he directed at me. Alex disappeared out the door, leaving us huddled in the corner.

In the next thirty minutes, the corridor outside was very busy, with a never-ending procession of very senior Army, Air Force and Police Officers walking past. There were lots of them, Generals and Colonels and Senior Commissioners, all in uniforms and all with faces like thunder. They looked like men on a mission, and the mood in the room grew more and more sombre every time another one of them passed. As per instruction, we sat huddled in the corner, saying and doing nothing. It was horrible. I tried to ask my policewoman what was going on. But the woman who'd hugged me not so long ago was gone. With her Law and Order Maintenance face back on, she told me to get back to the corner, sit and keep quiet.

After about two hours which seemed like forever, Alex bustled back into the room, holding our release order in his hands but with the worried look on his face still firmly in place. "OK, we can get you guys out of here. But we need to move quickly. Let's go, let's go, let's go." He spoke like the building was on fire. It worked for me. I wanted to say goodbye to my comrade policewoman but didn't. We exited Harare Central out the front door. I've never felt so happy to leave a building before. The fresh air outside felt especially good. I started heading for the carpark where the Tata was parked before realising I didn't have the keys. I told Alex that I had to go back inside. He told me no, better I leave the Tata and arrange for someone else to collect the vehicle another time. "But how am I going to get back to SA? I drove up."

"Fly. Preferably on the first plane. Before those people in there to change their minds."

"That works for me," said Baldric. "I can organise you a ticket no problem."

And so, Baldric and I flew out of Zimbabwe. We said goodbye to Nixon, Shepherd and Jericho in the carpark. I couldn't but feel like I was deserting them. Nixon especially looked like he wanted to come with us. Alex drove us home to Bob's house. On the way, I asked what he thought was going down. He told us that he'd heard that Mugabe wanted to concede defeat, but the Generals and Mnangagwa wouldn't let him.

"But they can't do that."

"They just have."

"But what's going to happen?"

"I don't know." I think by then Alex had had enough of us.

Bob gave us a lift to the airport. He got us there early, so we didn't miss our plane. I think Bob had also had enough of us. After clearing customs and immigration, Baldric and I drank a lot of beer in the departure lounge waiting for our flight. We weren't the only ones drinking lots. Around us, there was a party going on, with people celebrating Morgan's victory. But we didn't join in. And we didn't have the heart to tell them that chances were Morgan wasn't going to win. Alas.

Chapter Fifty

Our plane took forever to take off from Harare airport. It was one of those watched pots never boiling sort of things. Baldric and I sat in the departure lounge quaffing copious quantities of beer, fully expecting the Gestapo to come boiling in through the doors to drag us back to prison. My imagination gets heightened when there is beer about. When eventually the boarding call came, I was well on my way to being pissed. As our plane climbed up into the night skies over Harare, I looked down on the sprawl of lights below with the hugest sense of relief. I'd never been so happy to leave anywhere in my life. Or so sad. From high above, Harare almost looked normal, pretty even. But I knew that down on the ground, it was anything but. I spared a quick thought for the poor bastards I'd left behind and then it was back to the beer, all the way to Joburg. When they poured me off the plane in Harare, it was sans my phone. By the time I noticed my phone was still on the plane, I was halfway to Nelspruit. Jenny met me with a hug, a kiss and a ringing slap around the ears for putting her through hell. Never again, she told me. Never again, I told her back, but with all my fingers and toes cunningly crossed.

The parliamentary results were announced a few days later. It was a resounding victory with ZANU losing control of parliament for the first time ever. Morgan's MDC won ninety-nine seats, including some big rural constituencies in the middle of Mugabe heartland, the other MDC won ten, all in and around Bulawayo, and ZANU PF won just ninety-seven. But the gloss was taken off the win by the non-announcement of the Presidential results. In Mugabe's Zimbabwe where Presidential powers rule, parliamentary majorities count for not a lot.

The country, already on a knife's edge, was told the Presidential count was still being verified, apparently. They'd counted the parliamentary ballot papers in no time flat, but apparently, the Presidential ballots took a lot more counting. The verification count dragged on for a week and still no result. To test the temperature, the sycophantic Herald ran a piece on the probable need for a runoff. Apparently, according to them, Zimbabwe's electoral small print clearly stated that a simple majority wasn't enough to win the Presidency. To win, you needed fifty percent of the vote plus one. Failing that, the constitution called for a second round of voting.

I fumed. What a load of bollocks. And back in Zimbabwe, the whole country fumed along with me. I harangued Hemingway on Hushmail. Where the hell was his Plan B? Why the hell weren't they pressing the button on it? Plan B was scripted exactly for a scenario like this. I didn't get an answer. Tendai Biti almost got things going by jumping the gun and declaring Morgan, the winner. But the Generals' response was lightning fast. They told the world that a premature victory declaration would be looked upon by the army as a Coup d'état and they'd crush it. The verification count dragged into its second week. And then into its third. And then into the fourth.

And while the world watched on, confused and befuddled, the Army took charge. Uniformed soldiers targeting anywhere and everywhere that voted MDC commenced a reign of terror that was likened to the start of the Rwandan genocide. White farmers still on the land were especially targeted with one hundred and thirty-four violent invasions reported in just four days in early April. In Gokwe, soldiers shot an MDC supporter through both legs in public, just because. MDC supporter Tabitha Marume was captured by soldiers in Makoni West and dragged off to the Chiwetu Rest torture camp where she was shot and killed. In Magunje, the soldiers were more subtle in the way in which they went about their torture. They lined villagers up, gave them bullets to hold while contemplating the follies of voting for anyone other than Mugabe come the run-offs. In Mutasa South, the soldiers opted for less subtle. They ransacked and burnt the homes of five hundred villagers accused of voting MDC. The soldiers were ably assisted in their beating, burning, raping and pillaging duties countrywide by squads of ZANU PF youth militias. In Mutoko, twenty homes were burnt, in Murehwa five homes. In Uzumba, five-year-old Brighton Mberwa burnt to death when his parents' huts were torched because they voted MDC. Not even sick people in their hospital beds were excused. Patients at a rural hospital in Murehwa were dragged out of their beds by armed militiamen and herded to an all-night rally where they forced to sing liberation songs and shout Mugabe slogans. To make up the numbers, passing motorists were flagged down on the main highway and dragged out of their cars. Anyone lacking enthusiasm or not singing loudly enough received a thorough beating.

In the first month of Mugabe's yet to be announced run-off campaign, the Army killed fifteen MDC supporters, with more deaths likely, pending the arrival of an arms shipment from China.

Tucked away safe in South Africa, I lived in front of my television and on my computer screen, prisoner to Zimbabwe bad news sites. I watched them morning, noon and night. I was so glad I wasn't in Zimbabwe. But I also so badly wanted to be there. Sitting safe in South Africa, I felt like a coward. I'd already told Jenny that I had to go back for the run-off election, whenever it was. Jenny told me that this time she was coming with me.

I wasn't the only person watching Zimbabwe burn with bated breath. Britain was sufficiently moved to sneak Zimbabwe on the U.N. Security Council agenda under any other business. Joined by the other Western nations, they wanted the UN to send a Special Envoy to Zimbabwe plus a moratorium on arms sales. But South Africa, together with those other bastions of democracy, China, Russia and Libya, spoke out against any further Security Council action. Mbeki, Bush's impartial mediator on the Zimbabwe crisis, flew up to Harare, held pinkies with Mugabe at the airport in front of the cameras and told the world at large that there was no crisis in Zimbabwe. That I was living in South Africa at the time, served to make Mbeki's treachery all the more personal. If he'd walked in front of me in the carpark, I'd have run him over.

On the second of May, fully five weeks after the election, ZEC finally announced their cooked version of the results of the March Presidential ballot- Morgan forty-seven percent, Mugabe forty-three percent and Simba Makoni eight percent. As per the constitution and because Tsvangirai didn't win by fifty percent plus one, a second-round run-off election would be held, supposedly within three weeks. Even though I'd known that the results would be bullshit made-up ones, I was that pissed off my poor cat had to hide for a month. I was especially pissed off that all Makoni's votes came from the Matabeleland provinces, provinces where Mugabe was hated more than the anti-Christ. But for Welshman Ncube urging his supporters to vote Makoni in the absence of their own Presidential candidate, those votes would have gone to Tsvangirai, pushing him past the fifty percent plus one mark needed to win.

Mugabe, ZANU PF and maybe even Makoni himself, had played the breakaway faction like a fiddle, splitting the opposition vote. I cussed my Bulawayo based Sokwanele comrades and their fair play insistent donors soundly. What didn't they understand about united we stand, divided we fall?

On the ground, the violence continued unabated. People were beaten and killed countrywide, and quickly; the death toll jumped to fifty. And then to sixty. And then, seventy. And every time another death was announced, I felt more scared about going back for the run-offs and more uneasy about Jenny coming with me. But she remained adamant. So I booked one-way air tickets for two because my Tata was still stuck up in Harare.

Mostly the police did absolutely nothing about the rapidly rising death toll although they were moved to arrest Tsvangirai and his top leadership for eleven hours after they had reason to believe a vehicle in the Tsvangirai motorcade did not have a valid registration. And a day later and on the other side of the country, the police were also moved to run a convoy of British and American diplomats off the road at gunpoint after the diplomats refused to accompany them back to the police station to answer questions on why they were asking questions of victims of political violence. The police were further moved to beat up the Zimbabwean driver

SWEATING IN THE POT AND ABSOLUTELY DREADING THE FIRE

of one of the diplomatic vehicles and to slash his tyres. The US government were reportedly outraged by the incident and told the Zimbabwean government they were going to tell on them at the United Nations. The British government equally outraged, went a step further and summoned Zimbabwe's ambassador and gave him a stern talking to.

Meanwhile back on the ranch, the Zimbabweans sentenced three South Africans working for SKY News to six months in prison for illegal possession of broadcasting equipment and told three of the biggest international NGOs in the country to shut down and desist.

South Africa's Foreign Minister weighed in on matters. Apart from one hundred plus dead, the two hundred plus abducted and missing, the hundreds of MDC members jailed on spurious charges, the tens of thousands beaten and the tens of thousands forced from their homes, Nkosazana Dlamini-Zuma opinioned that Zimbabwe's first round of voting had been largely free and fair and hoped that the second round run-off, just a few weeks away-would likewise be free, fair and peaceful. The sick feeling in my stomach at the thought of having to go back for the second round of voting was pretty sure Dlamini-Zuma was talking shit and or on drugs. And worse still, Jenny remained adamant that she was coming back with me. I wanted to remind her about the honour and obey small print in our wedding vows but was scared of her right cross.

And then at the eleventh hour, at a press conference on 22nd of June in Harare, Morgan Tsvangirai announced that because of the ongoing state-sponsored violence, he was left with no choice but to withdraw from the run-off election. He said that his supporters faced being killed for supporting him and he couldn't put them at risk. Watching on the television at home, I shouted Amen to that and thank you, thank, thank you, Morgan Tsvangirai. I didn't have to go back to Zimbabwe. I've never been so relieved in all my life, even if it meant I was out of pocket two air tickets to Harare.

Morgan explained his decision. He said the police had been reduced to bystanders while ZANU PF militia committed crimes against humanity including rape, murder, abduction, arson and other atrocities. The state-sponsored violence, the ongoing harassment of the MDC leadership including Tendai Biti's arrest for charges of treason, no foreign press, no access to the media-Tsvangirai's long list of reasons why free and fair elections in Zimbabwe were impossible went on and on. Tsvangirai's sought refuge in the Dutch Embassy later that day, obviously fearing for his life. In New York, the UN Secretary-General said he fully understood Tsvangirai's decision to withdraw and suggested the run-off be postponed until conditions were conducive to free and fair. Both the African Union and SADC concurred, but South Africa's ruling ANC came in on cue and rejected the idea of foreign intervention into Zimbabwean affairs, especially by former colonial powers.

Mugabe was incensed by Tsvangirai's withdrawal. It would piss on his parade and take the shine off his election run-off victory. In a rambling monologue, Mugabe said that because Tsvangirai hadn't given the required notice, tough luck, the run-off election would go ahead with his name on the ballot, whether he liked it or not. Mugabe and his Ministers belittled Tsvangirai, calling him a chicken for pulling out of a contest he knew he couldn't win. He said the Zimbabwean people's right to choose their President in the run-off was sovereign and could not be interfered with. And besides, he pointed out, other elections in other African countries had racked up greater death tolls but hadn't received nearly as much criticism from the West. Which obviously meant Tsvangirai and his MDC were puppets of the West.

The run-off election happened on June 27th. The thing was a sham from start to finish. By accident, I watched Mugabe vote on television. He was unbearable, describing himself as being optimistic and upbeat. Zimbabwe state media described voter turnout as huge. The Pan African Parliament observer team's observations were less glowing, describing the turnout as very, very low and saying the situation was not normal and things were tense. The BBC reported people in townships around Harare being forced to vote. As per normal for Zimbabwe at election time, there was no shortage of people getting beaten. But this time they got beaten for not having ink on their fingers. Who'd want to be a poor bloody Zimbabwean voter? Cry the beloved country.

Counting the Presidential votes in the first round took five weeks but the second time round the count took just two days. On the 29th of June Mugabe was declared the winner with eighty-five percent of the vote. In his victory speech, Mugabe said he was humbled and honoured and singled out Mbeki for praise, saying that Zimbabwe was indebted to him for his untiring efforts to promote harmony and peace, quote unquote. Fucking bastard more like, I railed. My television came oh so close to getting a rock through it.

Secure in the knowledge that all they had to look forward to was another five years of Mugabe misrule, the flood of Zimbabweans fleeing the country quickly turned into a tsunami. Some estimates put the number of Zimbabweans refugees as high as four million, a staggering one-third of the total population. That had to be a record for any country outside of a war zone. Johannesburg, South Africa was the first port of call for many of them. Sandton became known as Borrowdale South, and the Zimbabweans poured in. They had a reputation as being hard-working, well-educated and desperate to earn a living, and most were able to find jobs easily. Because they could read and write, Zimbabweans were especially sought after in the hospitality industry as waiters and front of house staff. Sit in any restaurant in Johannesburg and listen and you'd hear Shona being spoken by the workers.

From when first we'd arrived in South Africa, I put it out that I was available to help Zimbabweans where I could, especially political refugees. Since then, we'd had a steady stream of MDC waifs, and strays passing through Summer Hill, Morgan and Susan Tsvangirai included. Some were with us for just days, others for longer. Post the war that was the 2008 elections, we got swamped. Some political refugees, but most economic-normal folk just looking for normal.

Like husband and wife, Enoch and Matilda, who arrived at Summer Hill within a week of Mugabe's re-inauguration, looking for jobs and a new place to call home. Back in Zimbabwe, Enoch and Matilda had both worked for Mike Carter, one of the founding members of MDC Support. Mike asked me if I could help Enoch and Matilda. He said they were salt of the earth, nice people and deserving of a break. I told him no problem, send them down. Helping Enoch and Matilda was win-win. My labour force on Summer Hill was mostly made up of Mozambiqueans, Swazis and South Africans and they were making me pull out what little hair I had left. It would be bliss to have Zimbabwean workers. A week later Enoch and Matilda were joined by another ex-Zim farmworker called Leverson who'd followed his boss to South Africa a few years earlier after their farm had been grabbed early in the land-grab. Leverson's boss had tried to start up anew in SA but had failed and had moved onto a job in the Far East, leaving a floundering Leverson in his wake. Leverson was an experienced cut flower foreman, so I thought better he come flounder on Summer Hill.

Black Zimbabweans did the whole emigration thing tough. Most of them left their wives and or kids behind in Zimbabwe while they looked to earn a living outside the country. They'd enter South Africa often illegally or on a holiday visa and then once in the country and sorted with a job, they'd apply for a Special Dispensation Permit under a blanket scheme hurriedly cobbled together by the South Africans to deal with the flood of incoming Zimbabweans. But the permits were at best, temporary. At least once a year, rumours would swirl that the South Africans were about to abandon the Dispensation Permit scheme and all Zimbabweans on it would be herded back home. There was no way I could live like that, separated from my family and living from year to year on a temporary arrangement. But Zimbabweans were past masters at living for the moment.

I took Enoch and Matilda into Nelspruit to the Home Affairs office to apply for their permits. When they came out successful, they were happy like they'd just won the lottery. A month or so later, we all watched Leverson suffer through his permit renewal, stoic and pokerfaced on the outside but sweating on the inside. Leverson said that even if his permit were revoked, he'd never go back to Zimbabwe. He had no intention of ever setting foot in Zimbabwe while Mugabe ran the country, let alone going back to live. As it happened, Leverson's permit got renewed without any problems.

A week later, conversationally I told him it was a pity he wasn't from Mozambique. One of the farmers in the district told me the special dispensation thing going for Mozambiqueans was a permanent arrangement. If you were from Mozambique and you found a job, pretty much you got permanent residency. I think it was an Ubuntu thing linked to Mandela having married former Mozambiquean President Samora Machel's widow. Leverson's ears pricked up. Despite the fact that neither he nor Enoch had ever been to Mozambique, they trotted off to see a Mozambiquean labour broker in Nelspruit with a story about how they were Mozambiqueans who'd lost their worldly possessions including documents in some disaster or other. They filled in some forms, paid some money for replacement documents and within three months, they were both Mozambiqueans, complete with Mozambiquean names, places of birth, birth certificates and passports. Jason Bourne would have been hugely proud of them. According to his new passport, Leverson was now Fernando while Enoch was Samora, which was handy because he even looked like Samora Machel. Enoch a.k.a. Samora was especially happy because according to his new passport, he was ten years younger.

I was impressed and amazed, but Matilda was jealous and angry she'd been left out. She made Enoch a.k.a. Samora take her to the same labour broker where she rolled out the same lost property story. But the labour broker smelled a rat. He didn't think she was a Mozambiquean. Matilda crossed her heart and hoped to die if she lied. So the broker asked her some trick questions. What is the capital city of Mozambique? What is another city in Mozambique? Who is the President of Mozambique? Alas. No Mozambiquean passport for Matilda. She went home and swotted up on her Mozambiquean general knowledge, but the labour broker wouldn't give her a second shot.

Within the Summer Hill labour force, my three Zimbabweans remained an island, apart and different from the other workers. Even though they picked up the local language Swati quickly enough, they were never accepted by the other workers. The Zimbabweans were stand-out different. Their work ethics were good, both in the workplace and at home. For instance, the Zimbabweans were the only ones in the compound with vegetable gardens planted outside their houses. They saved every cent earned, rather than convert them into booze and or dagga every month end. And they didn't eat monkeys. Troops of vervet monkeys would traverse the farm from time to time. If the monkeys strayed too close to the compound, the men, women and children in the compound would be overcome by blood lust. They'd corner the poor monkeys and beat and hack them to death. The noise of screaming monkeys was dreadful and could be heard up at the house. Whenever we heard the noise, we'd rush down to the compound to try and save the poor things, but invariably, we'd get there too late. Enoch, who was a very gentle man, was especially traumatised by his barbaric workmates. "They've killed the monkeys to eat," he told me "Even though the monkeys have got hands just like us. How can you eat something with hands?"

I tried to promote both Enoch and Leverson to supervisory positions, but that never worked out. They had all the knowledge needed but were too scared to discipline, and the other workers just walked all over them. Alas.

My Zimbabweans were lucky that the xenophobic attacks that swept through South Africa never made it out on to the farms. Xenophobia was easily Black South Africa's longest and most favourite word. They embraced the word and practised it periodically to great effect. There was no shortage of refugees in South Africa sheltering from all the crap going on in their own countries- Zimbabweans, Somalians, Congolese, Nigerians, and the list went on and on and on. By comparison to where they came from, South Africa was the land of plenty. Including hate, unfortunately. Periodically and usually set off by a successful Somalian tuck shop owner or some hard-working Zimbabwean waiter, black South Africans would get all riled up at all the foreigners working hard in their midst, and they'd rush out and murder them. They'd hunt them down in packs and beat them or burn them or worse.

Nesbit, one of the Zimbabweans we tried to help in 2008, told me about xenophobia. Back in Zimbabwe Nesbit had worked for the export company that I'd shipped my flowers through. But he fled Zimbabwe to look for work to feed his family after the export company fell on hard times when farmers stopped farming because of the land-grab. Nesbit arrived in Johannesburg and phoned me to ask for help. He was a clever guy, way better than me with numbers on computers, so I couldn't offer him up a farm job. I told Nesbit I'd ask my friends in Johannesburg for help finding him a permanent job, but in the meantime, we could try him out as a flower buyer on the auctions in Johannesburg. I took Nesbit to the auctions to show them how they worked.

For a first timer, the auctions were mind-boggling. Buyers sat behind tiny desks in an auditorium looking at three auction clocks, each of which had a steady stream of flowers on trolleys flowing beneath them. The hand on the clocks would start at a high price and fall away until one of the buyers pressed his button and registered a buy. To be good at it, buyers had to be nimble of mind and fleet of finger. With the hand-eye co-ords of a dead spaniel, I was really crap at buying and showed Nesbit how not to.

I told him that the key to being successful was knowing what flowers were on the floors. To do that, you had to get to floors early so you could walk the lines of trolleys with your list of orders for the day and check out what there was lots of and what was in short supply. The auctions started at seven in the morning, but the good buyers got there as early as five. Nesbit had found lodgings in Tembisa, one of the big townships on the East Rand. To get to auctions by five, he would have to leave home at four. But the upside was he'd be finished work for the day by eleven in the morning. We couldn't pay much, but Nesbit grabbed the job with both hands because beggars can't be choosers.

Nesbit's first day was a disaster. He got to the auctions only after half-past seven and spent what little was left of the auction in a muddle trying to catch up. His second day was even worse. He only got there after eight by which time half the flowers had been sold. And his third day wasn't any better. I had no option but to crap on him. I was angry that Nesbit was taking advantage of my good nature, so I gave him a stern lecture laced with expletives about the need to be punctual. You need to get up earlier I told him. He told me he'd set out from his home at three-thirty that morning.

"So why so late? It shouldn't take you more than an hour from Tembisa on a minibus."

"Because I keep having to get off the bus. Every time one of the other passengers picks up from my accent that I'm a foreigner. Once they know you're foreign, they beat you, or worse." And then it all came pouring out. His landlord had hidden him from a mob that were searching for foreigners just the previous day. Two Zimbabweans not so lucky had been killed by the same mob. I felt so bad. I had absolutely no idea how bad it was for my fellow Zimbabweans out there. Alas.

Not long after the Mugabe's re-inauguration, I took Leverson home to Zimbabwe, even though he'd said loud and proud that he'd never go back to Zimbabwe. But that was before he got full-blown AIDS. Leverson went from healthy to skin and bones shockingly quickly. After he'd been off sick for a week, I went to see him in his house and was staggered at the change in the man. He lay in his bed, too weak to get up and with his eyes huge in his head. The room stank like he was dead already. His bedclothes were wet from where he'd shat in them, repeatedly.

I wanted to heave. Leverson told me he wanted to go back to Zimbabwe. Could I take him? Better to get better first before he travelled, I told him. He told me he wasn't going to get better. He said he knew he didn't have much time left. And he didn't want to die in South Africa. He wanted to die in Zimbabwe. Could I take him? I got a big lump in my throat, and I told him yes. Thank you, he told me. And could I look after his money for him? He knew that the other workers knew that he had money in his house and now that he was too weak, they'd come and steal it from

SWEATING IN THE POT AND ABSOLUTELY DREADING THE FIRE

him. I told him that I'd lock it up in the farm safe for him.

The money was in a plastic shopping bag under his pillow he told me. He was too weak to even lift his head. Could I get it for him? The bag of cash was almost as big as the pillow. Leverson told me there was forty one thousand one hundred rand in the bag. I couldn't but whistle. I couldn't remember when last I'd had that much money in my bank account, let alone in cash. Looking around his room, Leverson owned nothing other than the clothing that he wore day in and day out, and the sack of cash. Leverson must have saved every cent he'd ever earned in the years he'd worked in South Africa.

I took Leverson to the Musina border post in the farm pickup truck. Gary offered to come with to keep me company. We laid Leverson out in the back, all rolled up warm in clean blankets with plenty of cushioning under him. I felt guilty that I was taking Leverson loaded in the back of a pickup instead of in the car but was vindicated after Leverson shat in his blankets almost immediately. The plan was we'd meet one of Leverson's sons on the South African side of the border post, and he'd help his dad through customs and immigration. Summer Hill to the border was a seven-hour drive in the pickup. After the first hour, we stopped to see if Leverson wanted for anything. He was still alive but only just. I poured some fruit juice into his mouth and then we carried on.

It was a long weekend and the queue to get to the border was miles long. I inched the pickup through the throng of traffic, attracting no small amount of hooting and shouting. The world loves a queue jumper, especially in forty-degree heat. Eventually, a policeman stopped me and asked where the hell I thought I was going. I told him we had a very sick person in the back. He took a look at Leverson and then waved us through. It took us thirty minutes to ease our way to the boom gates. I tracked Leverson's son down in amongst the crowds. He was in his late twenties, smartly dressed and well-spoken and unable to hide his shock when he saw his father. I handed him his father's bag of belongings, unzipped the zip and showed him the A4 envelopes stuffed with the cash beneath the layers of clothing, I gave him a piece of paper with the cash breakdown and told him to be careful with it. And then it was time to say goodbye to Leverson. At which point we hit a major snag. Leverson was too weak to stand, let alone walk. Neither Gary nor I had passports with us, so we couldn't drive him through the border and across the bridge. No problem, the son told me, he'd make a plan. He came back ten minutes later with a man and a wheelbarrow and loaded up his dad like a very sick sack of potatoes. I told the son I'd pay for the wheelbarrow hire. It was the least I could do for his father. The wheelbarrow man told me he wanted a thousand rand. I told him bollocks. I'd bought a brand-new wheelbarrow in White River just a week ago for eight hundred rand. The wheelbarrow entrepreneur told me better I go back to White River and fetch my new wheelbarrow and walked away. I chased after him and handed over the thousand with not a lot of good grace.

We manhandled Leverson out of the pick-up and into the wheelbarrow gingerly. I tucked him up in his blankets as best I could, and with a frog in my throat, I told him to get better soon and hurry back to work. I had to bend down low to hear his reply. He told me he'd be back for next season. But both of us knew he wouldn't be coming back to South Africa ever. And then he managed the weakest of waves before being pushed across the border in his wheelbarrow.

The son phoned me less than a week later to tell me that his father had just passed away and to thank me for looking after him. He also told me he'd counted the cash and it was correct to the last rand.

Chapter Fifty-One

Towards the end of 2007, Mitch Whaley dropped a bomb on me from Harare.

"NECCI have just hit the farm with a search warrant. They've taken away all the computers and a bunch of files."

"Fuck." Apologies for the language but when I'm scared the Raphael in me comes out.

"And they want to talk to you," Mitch said.

The flight over fight instinct is very strong within me. I was over a thousand kilometres away from Harare, I didn't know who or what NECCI was and all I wanted to do was run away further. "Tell them you don't where I am, Mitch. Tell them you can't get through to me. And who the hell are NECCI?"

"National Economic Crimes Investigations. And I can't tell them I don't where you are. They know I work for you."

"Fuck. What do they want with me?" I wailed.

"They saying you committed economic crimes between 2003 and 2006."

"Fuck. What do they mean economic crimes?"

"Forex. They're saying you sold forex illegally. And that you got money out the country illegally. Like I said, they want to talk to you."

"But that's bullshit. Everyone in Zimbabwe breaks every forex law every fucking day just to survive. Without the black-market, the place would curl up and die."

"I know that. And they know that. But that doesn't mean you're allowed to do it."

"The computers they took from the farm, are they clean?"

"All the computers are clean. There's nothing on them to find."

"Thank fuck for that." I breathed a sigh of relief, but just a small one. "2003 is a fucking long time ago. I can't even remember last week. Do you know if they have anything on me, anything specific?"

"The warrant had your name on it so I think they must have something on you."

"Fuck. I wonder what it is."

"I don't know. So, can I give them your number? I have to go and see them at their offices tomorrow."

"Fuck. I suppose so. And I'm sorry Mitch, to put you through all this bullshit."

"No problem." The phrase no problem was coined with Mitch in mind. He is just the nicest guy and would give you the shirt off his back if asked.

I spent the next three days waiting, dreading a phone call from Zimbabwe. And when finally it came, I had to fight the urge to throw my cell phone away.

I was all nerves, shakes and stammers as I answered. "H...H...Hallo."

"Is this Eric de Jong?"

"Yes."

"My name is Moyo. I am from NECCI, and I want to interview you about..."

I couldn't help myself and cut him off. "Sorry. This is a really bad line. You're breaking up." I shouted down the phone all the while moving it away from my mouth and back again. "I'm afraid I'm only picking up every second word you're saying."

Jenny walked in on my theatrics. "Who you talking to?"

"Shhhh!!!" I hissed at her furiously.

On the other side of the phone conversation, Moyo ran out of patience. "When are you next coming back to Zimbabwe? So, I can interview you. About economic crimes committed between 2003 and ...."

"I'm not."

"What?"

"Coming back to Zimbabwe anytime soon. But not because I'm guilty, but because my car's broken."

"I don't believe you."

"Tell you what. Send me your questions by e-mail, and I'll answer them honestly. Promise. And sorry, I can't talk anymore because I'm in a Doctor's surgery and it's my turn to get anaesthetised. Bye." I killed the conversation and collapsed in my chair, absolutely drained and shaking. Then I saved Moyo's number so I could dodge his next call.

Moyo took to harassing me daily, always calling from a different number. He was like a stuck record, on at me about economic crimes allegedly committed between 2003 to 2006 and the need to interview me in Harare as a matter of urgency. More like he wanted to plug my genitals into the electricity mains. I told him my doctor had grounded me from travelling, because of high blood pressure, caused by his continual harassment. Not being able to go back to Zimbabwe weighed heavily on me. The thought of what would happen if I did go back weighed even more heavily. I went back to living on Zimbabwean news internet sites morning, noon and night. It was a horrible time, and I had no idea what to do.

I was moved to ask God for help. I'd always got on pretty good with God. Other than lots of deceit relating to secret smoking, dodgy tax returns, and a bunch of cool stuff that I'd coveted that I shouldn't have coveted, like the small change in my mom's handbag, I was one of the good guys. And I'd never bothered God with frivolous requests for divine intervention, apart from the once when I asked Him to smite down a teacher who'd repeatedly molested me with homework and exams. And because He hadn't blitzed the teacher as per request, I figured God owed me. So, I asked Him to intervene in Zimbabwe and put an end to all the misery, suffering and evil goings-on, like for instance NECCI witch hunts.

It was a formal request, tendered at a 'Pray for Zimbabwe' session at the Methodist Church in White River that I'd organised. We attracted a decent congregation for a weekday morning. The priest had grown up in Zimbabwe and was strong and forceful in the pulpit and delivered up a stirring, fire and brimstone condemnation of Mugabe's evils. Because I'd organised the Prayer session, he called me up to give a reading from the Bible. I stammered my way through the reading. The priest then moved everyone to tears by playing Henry Olonga's "My Zimbabwe" on the Church sound system. It was a wonderful prayer session, and I was sure we'd grabbed God's attention.

The timing for some divine intervention was perfect. Mugabe had to be at his lowest ebb and on the ropes, just waiting for the knock-out punch to come along. He was printing an absolute flood of worthless millions, billions and trillions morning, noon and night to keep Zimbabwe afloat but was failing badly. And outside the country, he was running out of friends. Apart from sycophantic South Africa and a few others, world pressure on Zimbabwe was steadily mounting. But alas, God sure does move in mysterious ways. Instead of the requested knock-out blow, Mugabe got gifted two huge Get out of Jail cards; a Government of National Unity and the Marange diamond fields.

The idea of a GNU as a way out for Zimbabwe was born amongst the wreckage of Zimbabwe's economy which had totally collapsed, triggering one of the world's largest refugee crises outside of a war zone. On paper, the GNU looked to be the perfect pressure release. Cabinet seats within the transitional government would be parcelled out between ZANU PF and the two MDC parties. Differences would be set aside so that energies could be focused on fixing the broken economy. Also on the To-Do list was a raft of electoral reforms needed for free and fair elections to be held in five years. Mugabe would be President, but beneath him, Tsvangirai would be the executive Prime Minister actually running the show. The International community loved the idea and gave it their blessing and promises of support. I thought it was the crappiest idea I'd ever heard. Any process in which Mugabe was involved in would be flawed. Mugabe was a dirty poker player, and he'd lie, cheat, subvert and murder to win. He'd eat Morgan like a green mealie. I thought a better plan would be to let the system crash, burn and collapse completely and then start over, without Mugabe.

I made the long trek to Joburg to ask Roy Bennett where he stood on the whole GNU thing. When I got there, Roy was packing up his house and his office. He was going home, back to Zimbabwe to participate in the

GNU and to make sure it worked. He said the GNU would be the perfect opportunity for the MDC to show Zimbabwe and the world they had the nous to govern a country. They'd push to get the important ministries, like Finance and Health where they'd be able to make a tangible difference to peoples' lives. And as members of government, the MDC would be able to take their brand out into the rural areas, the bedrock of Mugabe's power. As a party, the MDC was less than ten years old, and no one took them seriously. The GNU would be the perfect opportunity to learn the business of running a country. For sure Mugabe would play dirty poker but they the MDC would have to be on their toes and stay a step ahead of him. There was more good than bad in the GNU. Roy was my absolute guru. If he told me the sun would rise in the west and set in the east, I'd rearrange my garden furniture. But that didn't stop me from driving back to White River with a troubled heart. In my limited experience, dirty poker players generally won.

And especially if the dirty poker player had all the money in the world behind him. Proof that fate is the cruellest of bitches, the Marange diamond fields that Mugabe had stolen in 2007 started producing in earnest. Between 2010 and 2013, forty-one million carats came out of the ground in Marange, with the promise of plenty more to come. Some estimated that Marange had diamonds enough to supply up to 25% of the world's diamonds.

The Marange diamonds were discovered in 2006 on claims owned by ARC, a Zimbabwean owned company listed on the London Stock Exchange. Amidst the Zimbabwe doom, gloom and poverty, diamonds were especially shiny, and as soon as news of ARC's good fortune got out, their claim was overrun by thousands of desperate and illegal miners, all looking to get rich. Not surprisingly, ARC called the cops. The cops responded, bust some few heads and arrested some illegal miners for illegal possession of big shiny diamonds and went back to the cop shop, job done. But it wasn't long before the cops were back at Marange. This time though, they were there to kick ARC off their claim, on orders from the very top. ARC filed an urgent application in the High Court and won, but to no avail. They got kicked off the Marange claim.

Marange quickly turned into the Wild West. As many as thirty five thousand illegal miners poured into the vacuum left by ARC's forced eviction, looking to turn the seven hundred square kilometres of Marange bush into a big hole as they scrabbled in the dirt, looking to get rich. They found diamonds by the bucket load. Marange's alluvial deposits were close to the surface and more than abundant.

Mugabe had kicked ARC off their claim because he wanted the diamonds for himself, not for the people. So he acted quickly and decisively. He launched Operation Hukodzokwe a.k.a. Operation No

OF ERIC THE ECONOMIC CRIMINAL AND 'GET OF JAIL' CARDS

Return, a brutal military operation to drive the illegal miners out of the area and to keep them out. He used helicopter gunships and troops on the ground, and in just one day, two hundred illegal miners were shot.

I was in Zimbabwe just after the two hundred miners got shot, on a reluctant flying visit at Mitch Whaley's behest. Mitch needed me to go to the bank with him to sign a power of attorney so he could get on with running Running Dog while I hid in South Africa from Moyo and NECCI. Looking to spend as little time as I could in Harare, I booked on same day flights in and out. My radar started pinging as soon as I stepped down off the plane and onto the tarmac at Harare International Airport. Welcome home. I'd never wanted to be anywhere less in my whole life.

My day in Zimbabwe was the longest ever. Technically now under the GNU, Zimbabwe should have already started a new lease on life, but there was precious little sign of any change on the ground. I was a bundle of nerves from when I got there to when I left, imagining Moyo from NECCI behind every bush. Somehow I was able to keep a lid on my flight instincts long enough to get the bank documents signed, the briefest of visits to the farm for a walk around and to collect some soil samples that Mitch wanted analysed in SA and then it was back to the airport so I could get out of Dodge.

I was on the way to the airport when Scratchy phoned. I hadn't spoken to him since the incident with Learnmore Jongwe's body parts. I don't know how he did it, but somehow Scratchy had heard I was in Zimbabwe. He had yet another parcel that had to be in South Africa yesterday. I diverted to his flat with extreme reluctance. Scratchy met me at the front door with a smile. It was a small parcel this time, he told me, no body parts, just a computer memory stick. He needed me to drop it off at the Sky News offices in Johannesburg. What was on the stick I asked? Scratchy powered up his laptop and showed me.

It was video footage of what looked like a mortuary, a mortuary full to overflowing with dead bodies. They were on the slabs and on the floor, some lying on top of each other. The camera zoomed in on the first corpse, a black guy who had a big hole where the back of his head used to be. The cause of death was a no brainer, pardon the pun. He'd been shot with something big. The camera panned down to the dead guy's gumboots which still had mud on them before moving on to the next body, and the next, and the next. All the corpses were black and dead from gunshot wounds. Who were they? I asked Scratchy. They were illegal diamond miners from Marange, shot from above like fish in a barrel by helicopter gunships. Mike Mason had risked life and limb to shoot the footage in the mortuary and Scratchy needed me to get the footage to Sky, so they could break the story world-wide. I slipped the memory stick into my pocket and told Scratchy consider it done.

I was ten minutes late getting to the airport, so I had to hurry. I checked my suitcase in at check-in counter and then headed to the first passport control. Because Big Brother in Zimbabwe takes his job seriously, your passport gets checked three times before you get on the plane. I was walking away from the first passport control desk when a man in the dreaded dark glasses and a suit combo ran up to the desk to ask if Passenger de Jong, Eric George had been through yet. My sphincter muscle clenched tight. It had to be NECCI. Somehow Moyo had found out I was in the country. I practically ran to the next set of control desks, Reserve Bank and Immigration. First up was Reserve Bank. No, I wasn't smuggling any Zimbabwe dollars out of the country. Yes, I had enjoyed my visit. There was a queue of other passengers building up behind me. My heart was hammering away as I answered the Reserve Bank guy's inane questions. All the while, my eyes were locked on Dark Glasses and a Suit still busy talking to the first passport control desk. Then he finished up there and headed towards the Reserve Bank and Immigration desks. He got to the Reserve Bank as I fled the Immigration desk. My next obstacle was the radar machine. I jumped the queue, rammed my cell phone and briefcase into one of the trays and hopped through the x-ray machine. Which complained bitterly. Crap. Something in my pocket had set it off. Car keys, pen and Scratchy's fucking memory stick. Crap. I'd forgotten about the bloody memory stick. Shit. Maybe it wasn't Moyo, maybe it was CIO. Maybe they had Scratchy's flat bugged and knew what was on the stick and were trying to stop it from getting out. That had to be it.

I looked across back to Dark Glasses and a Suit. He was now at Immigration, desperately seeking Passenger de Jong, Eric George. I flung the bloody memory stick and my car keys and pen into another tray and stepped back through the radar machine. All clear. Not all clear, the security detail holding the scanner told me. I had to go back and take off my shoes. In case there was a bomb inside them. Crap. Damn Richard Reid the shoe bomber. Behind me, a crowd of passengers had built up again, not so patiently waiting their turn to be searched. Through them, I could see Dark Glasses and a Suit headed towards me with purpose. I ripped my shoes off, flung them into yet another tray, and threw it on the conveyor belt. My big toe poked out through a hole in my sock. Crap. I was going to go to jail with a hole in my sock. How embarrassing. I jumped back through the x-ray, got scanned and then grabbed my shoes and other belongings and bolted for the sanctuary of the nearest Duty Free shop just metres away. I pulled my shoes back on, jammed my keys, pen and the bloody memory stick in my pocket and rushed to the queue of passengers waiting at the boarding gate.

Two queues were shuffling forwards oh so slowly towards the airline ground staff checking passports and boarding passes. I joined the shorter queue. Behind me, I could see Dark glasses and a Suit bearing down on me. The memory stick burned in my pocket. It felt big, like a brick. I was standing next to a dustbin come ashtray. Somehow, I resisted the urge to bin the memory stick. Then my queue stopped. In front of me, an old Indian lady couldn't find her boarding pass in amongst all the crap in her handbag. Fuck. She had everything but the fucking kitchen sink in her bag. I jumped across to the other queue and pushed in. "Sorry, sorry, sorry", I apologised to the people behind me. I lied through my teeth. "My elderly mom is in front of me, and I have to help her get her luggage into the overhead locker." As I got to the airline check-in girl, Dark Glasses and a Suit arrived at the first queue, the one the old Indian lady was still clogging up. He pushed in front of her and asked if Passenger de Jong, Eric George had checked in yet? The old Indian lady interjected. Couldn't Dark glasses and a Suit see that the airline clerk was still busy with her? How dare he push in front of her so rudely?

Thanking God for little old Indian ladies and their huge fucking handbags, I left the confrontation behind me and fled for the sanctuary of the bus parked outside the terminal doors, waiting to take another batch of passengers out to the plane. I was going to make it. C'mon, c'mon, c'mon, get the show on the road, I urged the bus driver silently. He must have heard my silent prayers. The doors of the bus closed and slowly we pulled away from the terminal building and headed across the apron towards our waiting plane. I'd made it. Whoop, whoop!! I looked back at the terminal. Dark glasses and a Suit burst out the doors and started running after the bus, waving his arms frantically. Crap. The bus slowed down.

What the fuck was the driver stopping for? Didn't he know that there was a whole fucking plane full of people waiting for him? Completely ignoring all my silent pleas, the driver stopped the bus, and the doors whooshed open and Dark Glasses, and a Suit stepped on. He stood there, gasping for air like a fish out of water. Was Passenger de Jong, Eric George on the bus, he finally asked when he got his breath back. Reluctantly and with heavy, heavy feet and with the memory stick big like a brick in my pocket, I stepped forward. What had I done wrong, I asked? Dark Glasses and a Suit asked me to follow him back to the terminal. But what had I done wrong I asked for the second time? Still no answer. He looked like he was keen to drag me off the bus, kicking and screaming, so I followed him. All the way to the terminal, I could feel the eyes of my fellow passengers burning in my back. I felt like the shoe bomber.

I slowed down a bit as we entered the terminal building, allowing Dark Glasses and a Suit through the door first. I pulled the memory stick out of my pocket and dropped it deftly into a tall ashtray as I walked past. Normally I don't do deftly, but this was neatly done, just like Tom Cruise. I felt very proud of myself. I pulled level with Dark Glasses and a Suit and asked him again, but this time with a renewed sense of innocence, what I'd done wrong. He said they'd found something in my luggage and needed me to explain it if I could. Straight away, I dropped innocent and went back to looking guilty. Crap. What had they found in my suitcase?

Dark Glasses and a Suit ignored a whole bunch of Do Not Enter signs as he led me off deep into the bowels of the terminal. What the hell had they found in my suitcase? I was about to find out. He pushed through a last set of swing doors, and there was my suitcase, opened up on a stainless-steel work counter and emptied. It looked forlorn, in amongst a cluster of grim men staring down at it. Looking even more forlorn was the small pile of my clothes next to it, all mostly dirty. Suddenly I panicked. Please, please don't let there be skid stains on my underpants. And I could feel the hole in my sock with my big toe poking out. Crap. I was going to be arrested with a hole in my sock and dirty underpants. But what for? What the hell had they found in my luggage? As one, the grim men turned to stare at me as I was escorted up to the table. I felt the word guilt written all over my face, in capital letters. And then I looked down onto the table. Next to my pile of dirty clothes were five brown paper bags, all bulging, all stapled shut. Bar the one they'd opened up for a look-see. There was a pile of soil next to it. A huge sense of relief rushed through me like a runaway freight train. They were the soil samples Mitch had given me for analysis in South Africa. I'd forgotten all about them. "What are they?" Dark Glasses and a Suit asked me.

My explanation gushed out in a hurry. "They're soil samples. From my farm. I'm a farmer. I'm taking them down to South Africa for analysis. So I know how much fertiliser to apply next season. I get it done in South Africa because it's much cheaper. And more accurate. Because the soil lab I used to use closed down. And now there's only really the government lab, and they're bloody ..." I stopped short before I talked myself into more shit.

"Are you sure it's just soil and not gold or diamonds?"

"Promise, promise. And look I've even got a soil sample request form here in my briefcase. Look, look, five samples listed for five different sections on the farm."

The laboratory request for analysis form that I'd filled out on the farm got passed around, and they all took turns to scrutinise it closely. They dragged it out just in case I felt a compelling urge to confess. But when I didn't, they handed me the form back and told me I was free to go back to the plane.

Dark Glasses and a Suit escorted me back as far as the first Do Not Enter sign. On the way, we chatted and laughed and commiserated about how tough things were, and he actually turned out to be human. When we got to the public area, I offered up my hand, and he shook it. On my way back to the boarding gate, I stopped at the ashtray. After looking around

OF ERIC THE ECONOMIC CRIMINAL AND 'GET OF JAIL' CARDS

to make sure no one was watching, I pulled the lid off and dived down in amongst all the stompies and detritus to recover Scratchy's memory stick.

The story of the diamond miners murdered by Mugabe's soldiers was huge when it broke. The world sat up and noticed the blood on Mugabe's hands, but only for a brief while. Then they went back to not giving a shit. Alas.

Back on the ground in Marange, once the illegals had been driven out to never come back, Mugabe parcelled out the diamond fields to his nearest and dearest like Father Christmas. What do you give a woman like Grace, who had everything? Too easy, you give her a diamond mine. There was a mine each for the Army, the Air Force, the CIO, the Police, and even the Prison Services got one. As did the ubiquitous Chinese. On paper, the MMCZ, government's mining regulatory body retained a fifty percent shareholding in all the Marange mining operations, but off paper and on the ground, they counted for nothing and saw precious little of what came out of the ground. The Chinese went so far as to build a landing strip in the bush that could take wide-bodied jets right outside their mine. Less than ten years later, Mugabe himself estimated that fifteen billion dollars of diamonds were disappeared out of the system.

Looking back, I can't but think that but for the Government of National Unity and but for the diamonds of Marange, Mugabe and ZANU wouldn't have seen out the end of 2008. Alas.

Chapter Fifty-Two

By 2009, my life in South Africa was unravelling that quickly on all fronts, I became a Chana owner. For those not in the know, a Chana is a Chinese pick- up truck, and it is about as low as you can go without being an actual pedestrian. Although Chana owners normally end up as pedestrians sooner than later. And that the Chana wasn't the worst thing that happened to me that year, shows how bad things got.

First up, Jenny's dad went out and got himself diagnosed with an aggressive form of lung cancer. Which truly, truly sucked. Tony didn't do cigarettes, he didn't do booze, he didn't anything bad that warranted a cancerous death sentence. He was the one of cleanest living, most harmless men I knew, one of life's nice guys who'd never looked for anything more from life than peace and quiet. But just when he finally got to an age where he could enjoy being a Grandpa full time, some hard-boiled oncologist told him very matter of factly, that he was going to be dead, most probably within the year. The whole family had assembled in the doctor's rooms in the hospital in Nelspruit to hear the shocking news. Tony hung tough. He didn't say anything, but I could tell from his eyes that he was hurting and aggrieved and more than a bit pissed off.

They kept Tony in the hospital for two weeks to drain a build-up of fluid from his lungs. When eventually they discharged him to let him go home to his little cottage overlooking the dam at Summer Hill, Tony knew he was going home to die. There weren't any faint glimmers of hope, no miracle cures in the wings by way of chemotherapy and or radiation. All he had to look forward to was maybe a year at the most, a year of pain and of not getting better.

I hated that year. Even the sunny days on Summer Hill were grey. But the year also brought out the best in those closest to Tony, especially Jenny and Hester. Hester kept herself busy loving Tony and fussing over him, cleaning and tidying. And I watched Jenny pull her family together, in close around Tony, week in, week out. Every single Saturday for a year, Jenny organised a braai at Tony's cottage. We'd take over the braai and the chairs and all the meat from our house, and the dogs and even the bloody parrot. When Tony was well enough, and if the weather was okay, we'd carry him outside to sit on a comfortable armchair under the trees next to the braai to listen to a family trying their hardest to not be sad. If there was a rugby match on, Tony and I would watch the game on the television inside his bedroom. If there were more than four of us watching the game, it would be a real squeeze in the tiny room. Tony and I always supported opposing teams, especially if it was Springboks against the All Blacks or his beloved Natal Sharks against whoever. When it came to rugby, Tony wore his heart on his sleeve, especially if his team was losing and the air in the lounge would be blue. After every braai, Jenny would cry a bit when we got home because she'd seen her dad a bit worse than he'd been the weekend before. It was a long, crappy year but there was a lot of love in it.

One of the worst incidents during Tony's long drawn out illness involved Hester's adopted dog, Boy and a woman who lived down the road, who shall remain nameless. Boy was a big brute of Staffordshire Bull Terrier, over the top friendly and with way more brawn than brain. He'd come barrelling up to Hester and Tony's cottage one morning, looking for food and or affection. He got both in spades, and so come time to leave, he didn't. Hester put out a blanket for him, and he became part of the family. Hester called him Boy. Boy seemed to like his new name and his new life. As soon as he was called, he'd come bounding up with tail wagging. He'd hang around for maybe ten minutes max, and then he'd be gone again, exploring. Boy was a busy dog, too busy to stay at home. As much as he liked his new life, Boy also liked the freedom of his old one, and he quickly settled into a new pattern; home in the evenings for dinner and out and about, all day, every day. Short of chaining him up, Hester wasn't going to change Boy, so she turned a blind eye to his wandering and welcomed him home every evening with love and a bowl of food and everyone was happy; apart from the woman who lived down the road.

The woman had recently married the son of a wealthy farming family. I had met the son and liked him a lot. I hadn't yet met his new wife but knew what she looked like from afar. Alas. Boy took to calling on the new bride daily, mostly to sniff her dogs' bums and to eat their food. Because the family was wealthy, I'm guessing her dogs' menu ran to salmon flavoured cubes and the like. Boy had boundless energy and an appetite to match and would happily lay claim to any and all food not yet eaten, which outraged the new lady of the house. To the point where she chased Boy away with rocks and sticks. For Boy, her stick and stones were water off a duck's back, and he'd return every morning to enjoy her offerings. So the woman decided to follow Boy home. She followed him up Hester's driveway and all the way to the front gate.

Hester was inside the cottage tending to Tony when she heard the car and went outside to see who was visiting. Hester was old enough to be the woman's granny, but that didn't stop the woman from going purple in the face and turning the air around her blue, with her swearing and cursing. She stood at Hester's gate and told her to chain her fucking dog up; otherwise, she'd shoot the fucking thing the next time it came onto her property. But it was her parting shot that hurt the most. She looked down her pert little nose at Hester's modest little cottage, distaste all over her pretty, made-up face and told Hester she was just another poor fucking white from Zimbabwe and why didn't we all fuck off back where we came from.

When I heard what had happened, I hated that woman. She was the epitome of everything I hated about South Africa personified; brash, materialistic, hard outside, even harder inside with nothing soft. I wanted to rush over to her big, fancy farmhouse mansion and tell her that Hester was the nicest person she'd ever meet, with a heart of gold and never a bad thought in her head. I wanted to tell her that Tony on his deathbed inside had listened to every swear word and curse word thrown at Hester and that he'd wanted to get up and defend her but couldn't because he was too weak. I wanted to tell the woman that sure Hester and Tony were poor, we all were, but that wasn't of our making. And it didn't stop us from being decent folk. I wanted to tell her that I wished to God that sometime in the future when South Africa also got stupid about whites owning land, the woman would also get kicked off her farm with fuck all and just because she was white, so she could see what it was like to start over again in a new country with nothing, like a poor white. But Hester wouldn't let me. She reminded me that the woman's mother-in-law had done me a kindness when first we'd moved to White River. Hester told me to forgive, forget and move on. Only because it was Hester asking, I did.

That was also the year Dan finished with school. Dan's education had been a long haul with very little reward. In terms of literacy, Dan had gone backwards quickly. Aged almost eighteen, his handwriting had regressed to an illegible scrawl, and he'd be hard pushed to read the back of a cereal box. The small special needs school that we enrolled Dan into after Jan van Tonder started out fine but had fallen apart quickly.

When he started at the special needs school, it was housed in a hall adjoining a church and had a proper school feel to it with a notice board and proper school desks and stuff on the wall. And Dan's teacher was trained and committed to her job. Academically, Dan wasn't playing catch up, but at least he stopped backsliding and at least he was happy. And he looked forward to going to school and came home every day with a bit of self-esteem. But then Dan's teacher fell out with the headmistress and stormed out. It was a disaster, but hardly surprising. The teacher was as good at her job as the headmistress was bad at hers. Which made for lots of friction. One confrontation too many and the teacher was out of there, headed for greener pastures. The headmistress, all puffed up with self-importance, said she would fill the gap herself, in addition to all of her headmistress duties, on account of the fact the school couldn't afford a replacement just yet. Straight away, Dan stopped even going through the motions.

Not long after losing the teacher, the headmistress also fell out with her landlord a.k.a.the church and the next thing, we were told the school was moving somewhere better and more affordable. The headmistress jumped around and quickly found an abandoned shed on a beat-up smallholding on the road to Barberton that they could rent for a little more than they'd been paying for the hall adjoining the church. With just an enormous amount of work and money, they could get the shed habitable to a point where it would be a super little school, the headmistress enthused. Alas without us, I told her. Dan was almost eighteen, and he'd reached the end of his school road. It was time for us to try him on another path.

Sheltered employment on the family farm had long been on Dan's cards but to make him want it, I made him go through a formal interview process. It was a short interview, and it did not go swimmingly well. Seated behind the desk with my stern face in place, I told Dan that because he was the boss's son, he had to be the hardest worker on the farm. He'd start off at the very bottom, weeding, then he'd learn how to pick flowers, he'd learn how to grade them and box them and then we'd teach him how to spray and how to scout for pests and diseases and... Dan butted in. "I want to drive the tractor, Dad. I don't want to do any of that other stupid boring stuff, I just want to drive the tractor. And maybe the truck." My head threatened to boil. I didn't have the patience to deal with Dan. But I put a lid on my temper and forced myself to stay calm. I dumbed it down for Dan. "Well that other stuff, the boring stuff, is the important stuff. If you don't do that stuff right, then your flowers won't sell on the market, and then we'll be out of business."

Dan had heard variations of the same lecture a million times. And it was once too many. "But I hate weeding. And all that other stuff. And I hate you. All you want to do is control me. Well, fuck you, Dad, you can't control me because I'm almost eighteen." And he stormed out. By then, Dan was bigger and heavier than me, so I didn't storm out after him.

The next day I went and asked my rose farm business partner Etienne if Dan could serve an apprenticeship there. It was an unfair request. As a thirty-three percent partner in the business, I knew that the rose farm was struggling and the last thing it needed was deadwood to carry. But Etienne was a friend, and he had a soft spot for Daniel and the patience of Job. Etienne said sure, Dan could start tomorrow. I thanked Etienne and told him that I'd cover Dan's minimum wage every month so that he wouldn't be a burden on the rose farm. I rushed home to tell Dan the good news. He was really excited that he was finally going somewhere with his life, he was going to be a rose farmer. We bought him a new work suit and work boots and delivered him to work on time the next morning, spic, span and feeling good.

Etienne put a huge effort into drawing up a two-year training program for Dan that would expose him to all aspects of the farm, including menial stuff like weeding, harvesting and grading. Standing on the side lines, I waited for the explosion, but it didn't come. Coming from Etienne, menial instructions were all right apparently. Next up, Etienne gave Dan his first Swati phrase to swot up and learn. 'I-hallo, igama yami u Daniel. Hallo, my name is Daniel.' Every morning, Dan would get a new Swati phrase to learn. Dan's workmates were all black, and Dan needed to be able to communicate with them in their own language. Dan nodded earnestly and went off to start out on his new direction in life, practising his introduction furiously under his breath, over and over. I-hallo, igama yami u Daniel. I-hallo, igama yami u Daniel.

Dan, the learner rose farmer started off as keen as mustard, but that wore off pretty quickly. He hated weeding roses as much as he hated weeding flowers at Summer Hill and picking them was worse, because of the thorns. He hated most jobs on the rose farm, apart from the maintenance department which he quite liked, until he found out that hard work was involved. Somewhere along the way, within Dan the line between inability and lazy had become very blurred. His Swati vocabulary didn't progress much beyond Hallo, my name is Daniel. I think Dan was lonely at work. Etienne aside, his workmates were all black, and ninety percent were older women who either ignored Daniel completely or were vaguely amused by his inability to pick up even the most basic of tasks. They weren't horrible to him, though, which surprised me. My own experiences with black female South African farmworkers were less than stellar but more of that later.

Stand-out in Dan's first year post-school was his first argument with one of his co-workers. Etienne overheard the argument with the woman in the grading shed which culminated in Dan telling her to go fuck a snake. But all in all, Dan was happy enough with where he was in life. He didn't have to write anything or read anything. No one was shouting at him, he got to wear overalls and big boots which made him look qualified and come month-end, his minimum wage made him feel like a millionaire, for a short while. Mostly he blew his salary on cheap Chinese shit, quickly, before Jenny made him save it.

Alas. My good intentions of paying Dan's salary came to nought in the first month when we couldn't afford even that. I felt hugely embarrassed that I'd dumped dead wood on the partnership, but I was even more thankful that I'd found somewhere to park Dan while we figured out the next step. Etienne told me not to sweat it. I promised him that Dan's employment was temporary, I'd move him elsewhere after a year, when things got better in 2010. Things had to get better because they couldn't get much worse. But I told Jenny not to worry because I had a plan.

Along with most of the rest of South Africa, I was gambling on the

World Cup in 2010 as being the stimulus for my business recovery, replacing a winning ticket in the Lotto which had previously underpinned my business turnaround strategy. I admit that pinning my hopes on a winning lottery ticket was a tad pie in the sky, but in the doom and gloom that followed the collapse of the Joburg flower shops in Johannesburg and the disastrous Zimbabwe elections, it was the best I could come up with. And so when something tangible like the 2010 FIFA Football World Cup came along as a survival option, I grabbed it with both hands.

My new turn-around strategy was simple. Nelspruit had been named as one of the World Cup host cities. Workers worked morning, noon and night to finish the huge purpose-built stadium on the outskirts of town on time ready for kick-off, ditto the brand-new Urban Transport System, ditto the Fan Park in the middle of town, ditto the multitude of hotels and guest lodges springing up all over to accommodate the incoming flood of millions and millions of football fans. And all of whom would obviously need flowers. Which I would supply. 2010 would be too easy, like shooting fish in a barrel. I'd make a bunch of money, enough to build a flower empire that would guarantee Dan sheltered employment forever and tide us over until Mugabe was finally gone, at which point we could go back to Zimbabwe and live happily ever after. However, to take advantage of 2010, I first had to make it through 2009.

Someone had recently told me that in business, you need to either go big, or go home. With 2010 looming, it sounded like sage advice with a bit of devil may care sexy thrown in, sort of like the advice Donald Trump might give himself in the mirror. Steadfastly ignoring the fact that the guy who'd given me the sage advice didn't have two pennies to rub together, stupidly I went big again for the second time and opened more flowers shops. Bummer. I should have gone with option B and gone home instead.

First up, though, I had to get my business decision to go big past, Jenny. Which given my recent run of extremely shitty business decisions, was going to be tough. Before dropping the bomb on her that we were set to become the largest purveyors of fresh flowers in all of Mpumalanga, I lined up a whole bunch of extenuating circumstances as back-up. For starters, we were going to have more mouths that needed feeding, three of them. Already we had Gary. Following the collapse of the Joburg flower shops, I'd brought him back to White River to help run things. And now I was also going to bring Veronica, her partner Arnold and their two-year-old daughter Jocelyn to join us. Vero and Arnold had been struggling hugely in Pretoria, and I couldn't be watching loved ones struggling from afar, especially if Jocelyn was involved. It was amazing how a little thing like Jocelyn had very quickly become the biggest thing in our lives.

In our family, it always falls to Jenny to ask the difficult questions. "So how we going to pay two extra salaries when already we're struggling to just pay Gary? We can't even pay Dan like you promised Etienne you would. And that was before we lost Sarah's business."

Sarah was a big snag. She used to be our biggest customer until she opened up in opposition. Sarah was a South African florist living in Maputo in Mozambique. For years, she'd been our biggest customer, accounting for almost half our turnover. She was happy with our service and bought tons of flowers from us every month. But now her eldest child had reached school-going age, suddenly everything had changed. Maputo was short on English speaking schools. Rather than send the child to boarding school, she'd decided to relocate to White River where she was going to open a flower shop, to keep herself busy, but mostly to source the flowers for her Maputo operation, which she'd now manage from a distance. Wham, in one foul swoop we'd lost our biggest customer and picked up serious opposition on our doorstep. I used to like Sarah, but now I hated her.

"Don't worry about Sarah. And don't worry about the extra salaries. We're going to need extra staff because we're going to expand the retail side of the business."

Jenny fought the urge to hit me on the head with something heavy and hard, she went with sarcasm instead. "You didn't get the memo on the Joburg shops collapsing?"

"Those shops collapsed because they were so far away. And we didn't know the city. This will be different. We're going to expand locally. We're going to open a small retail shop in the Mall for Veronica to run. And we're going to go into the supermarkets as well with mixed bunches. Arnold can run that."

"That's going to piss Petro off."

"Tough. Maybe if she paid her bill, we wouldn't compete."

Petro also used to be one of our biggest customers, putting mixed bunches into supermarkets across the province with some success. She was also our second biggest debtor and owed us over a hundred thousand rand. She hadn't paid a cent towards her debt in months and now bought all her flowers from the opposition. Because she was a little old lady complete with a hearing aid, I didn't have it in me to sue her. And she knew it and played me like a fish. Petro could've paid her bills at the drop of a hat. Putting flowers into mixed bunches to sell into supermarkets gave her seriously good margins. But she'd worked out that her margins would be even better if she didn't pay for her flowers in the first place. Now that Petro had stopped playing the game, I decided to rip up my non-compete policy and declare open season.

I could see that Jenny was teetering on the edge of buying into my expansion plan. So I quickly dropped my biggest bomb. "And we're also going to open in Maputo." I did my best to camouflage my plans to become a multi-national with a mumble and a cough.

"What did you just say?"

"We're going to open a Flower Market in Maputo. Because we've got the cold room and all the equipment left over from Joburg shops. It won't cost us anything to open."

"Let me get this straight. You want to open a flower business in another country, where no one speaks English because you've got all the equipment left over from the flower shops that failed in Joburg, mostly because Joburg is so far away?" Jenny was getting the hang of sarcasm.

"Yes. Sort of. But it's not as stupid a plan as you make it sound."

"Pray, tell."

"Maputo has been our biggest market for years. That's where we sell most of our flowers. But that was before Sarah decided to open up here in opposition to us." Jenny nodded reluctantly. She was almost hooked. "So to hang onto our Maputo market share, we've got no choice but to open up there in opposition to Sarah. We'll have the biggest cold room in Maputo, and all the other florists will flock to us, never mind the public. We grow our own roses, we grow our own chrysanthemums, and we grow our own greens and our own fillers, all just two hundred kilometres from Maputo. All that plus the biggest cold room in town, and we'll own the place."

"Didn't you just tell me the Joburg shops collapsed because they were so far away? And now you want to open up in another fucking country?"

"It's different, Jenny. We know the Maputo market well. And if we don't compete with Sarah, we might as well shut up shop now."

"I suppose."

I suppose was almost as good as a yes, so I went in for the kill. "It will work, Jenny, I know it will. And then one day you and I can retire, and Gary and Veronica can look after Dan between them." Playing the 'What happens to Daniel after we were gone' card was a masterstroke, and Jenny capitulated. I got the green light to go ahead with my expansions. Alas.

Veronica's little flower shop was phase one of the expansion. Because rentals in the mall were an arm and a leg expensive, we sub-let floor space from an upmarket Belgium Chocolatier. The shop turned out way better than I expected and our flowers on the shop floor looked like a million bucks. And I thought the mix of fancy chocolates and fresh flowers to be really good. Husbands and boyfriends would flock to shop for their loved ones under the one roof. Or not, as it happened.

The first day's turnovers were hugely disappointing. I forced myself to not be despondent. Rome wasn't built in a day, I told Veronica cheerfully as we binned the flowers that weren't looking too cheerful at the close of business. The aircon units in the mall weren't doing a very good job of keeping our fresh flowers fresh. Alas, it turned out Rome wasn't built on the second day either, or the third, the fourth or the fifth. And worse still, because the mall management had this quaint rule that all tenants had to be open seven days a week, from nine in the morning to six at night, we had days six and seven to contend with as well. Come the end of our first week of being open, despondent was my default emotion. Ditto poor Veronica, just from looking at my long face a couple of times a day. Jenny's 'I Told You So' rang loud in my ears, especially when she found out I'd signed the sub-lease for a year. Crap, it was like the worst of Johannesburg revisited. Just as well the mall was a single storey building. Had it been multi-storied, for sure I would have jumped off it.

Thankfully and because my expansion was multi-facetted, my eggs weren't all in the one basket. If we lost money to start with in Veronica's little shop, at least we'd make money on the mixed bunches on the supermarkets. First up we had to get Arnold on the road and mobile. Which meant I had to go car shopping. Given my very limited budget, buying new was out of the question. Buying second hand in South Africa is fraught with danger, especially with my technical expertise as smooth-talking con artists abound. I enlisted the help of a mechanically savvy friend. I trawled the second-hand car lots in Nelspruit and found many must-have bargains, all of which my friend shot down in flames as being crap. I was starting to run out of time. Then driving out of Johannesburg one day, a roadside billboard grabbed my attention. Apparently, I could buy a brand-new 1000 cc Chana pick-up truck for a price even I could afford. Apparently, again according to the billboard, Chanas were reliable, tough and economical to boot. I thought long and hard, for about two minutes and then went into the lot to have a look. The salesman was a friendly chap with a permanent smile and a thick Afrikaans accent that explored all the throat-clearing opportunities offered up by the word Chana. He told me I had a choice between white and white, so I went with white. Sitting behind the steering wheel in the sales lot, I quite liked the Chana. It had everything you wanted in a delivery vehicle; central locking in that both doors were well within reach, even if you had short arms, an adjustable rear-view mirror, handbrake, all the normal pedals, a sun-visor on the driver's side and a space in the dashboard for a car radio. It even had a new car smell. On the downside, the Chana's cab interior was a bit pokey- even with the seat adjusted back as far as it would go, my kneecaps pressed up firm against the dashboard. Then I remembered that Arnold was shorter than me, so for him, the cab of the Chana would most probably be quite roomy. So, I bought it.

Alas. Arnold was less than thrilled with his new company car. And after driving the Chana back from Joburg, I could see why. Only after driving it for an extended period of time, like more than twenty minutes, did you realise how small the thing was. It was tiny, inside the cab, on the road, all-round, it was all just minuscule. In it and next to normal cars, you just felt so vulnerable, especially with both knees resting up against the metal dashboard. And worse, there was nothing between the dashboard and the open road outside where other much larger cars and trucks ruled because the Chinese had stuck the engine under the driver's seat. How they could stick a whole engine under the driver's seat was beyond me, until I looked. The Chana's engine made the rest of the car look big. According to the logbook, it was supposed to be a thousand cc's, but I think some of them got lost in translation, that or they'd forgotten to put some of the engine bits on.

Suffice to say the Chana was woefully underpowered, even though it was only a bit bigger than a wheelbarrow. It could do nought to sixty eventually, but only on the steepest of downhills. And you didn't want to go there because sixty in the Chana, felt like a hundred. The whole thing started shaking alarmingly, noxious fumes, noises and vibrations emerged from the engine just below your bottom. But worse than all of the above, was the reaction you got from the rest of the motoring public. I've never felt quite as poor as I did, driving along the busy highway in the Chana, with traffic whizzing past at speeds above forty kilometres per hour. And because you were going oh so slow, roadside children were able to laugh and sneer at you for extended periods of time. South Africa has to be one of the most materialistic societies on earth, and nothing drives that home more than driving a Chana. When eventually I arrived in Nelspruit after the longest day on the open road ever, I tossed the keys across to Arnold and told him, "She actually handles quite well."

As a 'Get out of Jail' card, our brand-new supermarket bunching division sucked. We picked up service contracts with a dozen supermarkets, six in town and the others spread across the province, all on a consignment basis, which meant we only got paid for the bunches that sold. We shared all of our supermarkets with Petro, but I wasn't scared of the competition. Our bunches looked like a million bucks as compared to Petro's. Gary was in charge of mixed bunch design and had an artist's eye for colour, and our bouquets were stand-out good. And because we grew half the flowers in the bunch, they cost us less, and we were able to put out bigger bunches than Petro, and fresher. And our display stands were bigger, better and more imaginative. We should have won the battle of the mixed bunch hands down, but we didn't. Petro was outselling us in each and every store. Something was going horribly wrong. And it didn't take me long to find out what.

I went into what should have been our busiest supermarket to do an off the cuff inspection and phoned Arnold in a panic. "Arnold, we've got a problem. I'm standing in the store, and I'm looking at thirty of our bunches on the display stand, and not a single one of them is in water. They look wilted and half dead."

"Impossible. I re-stocked that store yesterday and replaced all the water in all the vases." There was a prickle in his voice.

"I'm not saying there's no water in the vases. But what I am saying is the flowers aren't in the water. Not a single one of them. All the bunches are bone dry."

"Shit. Shit. Shit. It's Petro. I swear to God, she's sending someone into the stores after I've restocked them to pull our flowers out the water."

"Surely not. Surely the store management would stop them."

"Not if they don't know it's happening, not if Petro's girl goes in pretending to be a customer. She pulls our bunches out to smell them or to take a closer look, and when she sticks them back into the vase, she makes sure the bunches are out of the water, job done."

I was shocked and horrified and went to complain to the store manager, a big Afrikaner who also happened to be a big Petro fan from way back. He looked at me like I was a whiner. "You can't be coming into my office making false accusations about Petro just because her flower bunches are nicer than your bunches. I've known Petro for many years and know her to be a nice woman."

"But..."

"No buts. Now just please leave my office." He had some growl in his voice, and because he outweighed me two to one, I left.

The next day our flower display stand had been moved to the very back of the fruit and veg section, right next to the bananas. It took me most of that year to learn a valuable life lesson; little old ladies with purple hair and hearing aids are killer at dirty poker.

With two of the three new enterprises struggling, it was left to the Maputo branch office to save us. To make sure I didn't cock it up, I spent weeks trawling Maputo, learning the town, looking for the right partners, looking for the right address. Maputo had a huge, vibrant population that liked flowers. Flowers were a part of their make-up and not just for weddings, funerals and Valentine's Day. Even the poor parts of Maputo had flower vendors on every corner, selling what passed for fresh flowers in Mozambique. Our cold room would give us such a competitive edge. Combing the yellow pages, I found out that Sarah was just one small fish in a huge pond. There were more than twenty florists advertised. But best of all were the weddings in Maputo. Jenny and I visited Maputo on a weekend and counted forty white wedding bridal parties in the one park overlooking the bay at the same time, all holding bridal bouquets, queueing for bridal photo shoots next to an ornate fountain that hadn't worked since the Portuguese fled Maputo more than thirty years earlier. Forty white weddings in one park on one day. We were so going to clean up in Maputo.

But Mozambique was all about overcoming language barriers, bureaucracy and officialdom. If we didn't have the right partners to guide us, we wouldn't get past go. By chance, I met a businessman of Portuguese Mozambiquean extraction who said he might be keen on investing in a flower market. He had a pest control business with contracts with most of the big hotels, and one of his customers was looking for a new supplier of flowers. He spoke excellent English, drove a variety of big, fancy cars and had a partner who was a banker. With partners like that, there was no way I could go wrong. Now if I only I could find some decent premises. The very next day I happened upon an empty house up for rent, in exactly the right part of town, around the corner from the Embassies and the Polana Hotel. It had four rooms we could use as offices and a cement slab for a backyard that would be just big enough for the cold room, all at a price that I could almost afford. I signed the lease. And how I laughed when I saw that my new business address, my bastion of free enterprise, was on the corner of Mao Tse Tung Avenue and Vladimir Lenin Avenue. Looking back, I should have cried instead.

Chapter Fifty-Three

I started writing a best-selling novel in January 2009, both as a form of escape but also for cash flow purposes. My hopes of winning the Lotto were dwindling faster than my business empire was floundering across three countries. At the rate it was going, my business empire was going to make minus money. Before I started writing page one, I googled Wilbur Smith's net worth next, to make sure I wasn't chasing down dead ends and whistled when I saw all his noughts. Big fat books were obviously good business. Damn, I should have started writing years earlier. Straight away, I bumped up the target length of my best-selling novel from two hundred pages to six hundred.

My first day as an author was tough. I got up at four in the morning, made a bucket of coffee and drank it in front of an empty computer screen in my wooden office at the bottom of the garden. After an hour, the only thing I'd come up with was the working title 'Eric's Best Seller.' I googled Writer's Block in the hope of finding a cure, but there were no quick fixes on offer. I drank another bucket of coffee, staring at my empty computer screen.

I decided my novel would be set in Zimbabwe. I'd have a good guy farmer as my hero up against an evil regime, led by an evil president. Because I figured defamation of character could be an expensive pastime, I called the president in my book Gamube. And having changed Mugabe's name, even just slightly, I was free to make up stuff that wasn't true. For example, the president in my book wouldn't just be a murderous old bastard, he'd also have a boatload of foul perversions to boot. The President's second wife a.k.a. the Second First Lady would be called Virtue instead of Grace, and she'd be a pig-shit-thick nymphomaniac, fucking bodyguards and pool boys left, right and centre. Although that was most probably cutting it close to the bone. My best seller was going to be pay-back time, and I was going to so enjoy writing it, provided of course I got past Page One.

Two hours into my career as an author, my computer screen remained stubbornly blank. But cooped up in my little wooden office at the bottom of the garden staring at an empty screen was infinitely better than going to work.

I was absolutely hating the business of selling flowers in South Africa. I hated it before because it was so boring with zero excitement, but now with so many family members involved and huge financial pressures, I was hating it even more. Gary was okay because he was easy to get on with, and he did all the stuff that I didn't like doing, and he did it well, way better than me. But working with my son-in-law was proving to be a different story. Alas. He and I were very prone to clashing, mostly because I micro-managed him. The problem was I had no idea as to his capabilities and didn't have the time or the money to find out. So, I told him what to do, when to do it, and how. Which caused tension, not just in the business but also in the family. To try and ease that tension, I took to walking on eggshells around him, which in turn caused even more tension. It was horrible. Alas.

If the truth be known, Arnold and I didn't know each other from bars of soap. If I added up all the time I'd ever spent talking to him or with him, I'd be hard pressed to get past twenty minutes. Outside of the fact that he was married to my daughter and the father of my granddaughter, we had absolutely nothing in common. We couldn't even talk rugby or cricket because he followed neither. He was now not only my son-in-law, but he was also my employee, and a reluctant one to boot. I often got the impression that the last place on earth that Arnold wanted to be was at work with me, or Jenny. He and Jenny especially clashed. In the clashes, poor Veronica had no choice but to side with her new husband. A few years ago, I would've struggled to spell dysfunctional, and now I was living the word. It was crap, and I hated it.

Before I would have run away to Zimbabwe on the spur of the moment business trip at the first sign of tension, but with Moyo and NECCI on my case, Zimbabwe trips had lost their appeal. Moyo was still hounding me by phone and e-mail wanting to know when I'd be back in Zimbabwe to answer his questions, of which there were many. I'd already given him many plausible bullshit answers, all of which he'd rejected outright. He also rejected my many and varied excuses as to why I couldn't travel back to Zimbabwe to prove my innocence –my car was broken, I had medical issues, and my doctor said I shouldn't travel, my mom was very ill and I had to look after her, etc. Moyo was like a pit bull terrier. I figured he had to be on some sort of a commission. If he kept it up, he was going to end up in my book, albeit with his name spelt slightly different.

My Maputo Flower Market project should have provided me with the escape I needed. Mozambique was hugely foreign. With coconut trees and raucous seagulls and the smell of the ocean as you got closer to Maputo, going there even for just a day was like a holiday. Maputo itself a vibrant city, big, foreign and full of cosmopolitan hustle and bustle, anchored by third-world squalor. Business-wise, the project had huge potential. There was the promise of enough noughts to get us out of the shit financially. I invested heavily in a copy of the 'Dummies Guide to Project Management', read it from cover to cover and absolutely buried everyone in colour coded Gant charts and Flow charts.

The Maputo Flower Market should've, would've, could've worked but alas, didn't. Things started going wrong at my very first board meeting with my new partners. The first thirty minutes were fine, mostly spent admiring my charts, budgets and projections. The business was looking good going into the future. Then my partners inexplicably switched to Portuguese. I sat there, helpless like a goldfish. My Portuguese didn't extend much beyond asking if there would be a frost tonight or ordering ice-cold beer. Neither subject though featured in the heated debate that flowed around me like I wasn't there. After ten minutes of foreign babble, I got pissed off. My partners were playing me like a trout. I interrupted them and asked them what they were talking about. The alpha-male Portuguese partner told me they were discussing how best to overcome some banking challenges. "But why discuss in Portuguese, why not in English?" I asked.

"Because our English isn't good enough to cover the technical banking terms."

"Ah, okay," I said. But it wasn't okay. I didn't trust them. But I had no choice other than to trust them because they were the local partners and they were handling the company formation and all the administrative and confusing bullshit that I'd be dead in the water with. Alas. "What challenges?" I asked. Apparently, we were experiencing unexpected delays in forming the company. Which was a snag because that meant we couldn't open a bank account. Which meant we couldn't start trading. But not to worry, they had a Plan B. They could offer up another bank account into which the Flower Market could deposit funds received but the extra costs incurred would obviously have to be recovered. And there might be some short delays in clearing cheques and paying foreign invoices, i.e. mine, but that shouldn't be too much of a problem. At least the Flower Market could start trading. I heaved a sigh of relief, but only a small one.

The first truckload of flowers that went into the Maputo Flower Market was nerve-wracking and took years off my life. Having loaded the truck in Nelspruit, I decided I'd drive the truck myself, through the border and all the way to Maputo, to make sure everything happened like clockwork. We'd sent hundreds of shipments into Mozambique for Sarah over the years, and there'd never been any problems because Sarah had a guy who handled all the customs clearing and import procedures and it all just happened. But now, we were the importers. To learn the ropes, I decided that I'd be the guy. Which was a bad mistake. I drove into the border post at around midday- the queues were miles long, and it was forty degrees plus in the shade, but alas there was no shade to be had for love nor money. If it was forty degrees outside, it was sixty inside the truck where my poor long-suffering flowers were packed. Fuck. At this rate, they would be compost by the time I got them to Maputo.

It took me hours and more money than I had to get through the South

African border, the corrupt officials feasted on me and sucked me dry like big fat ticks. And that was quick and cheap as compared to the carnage on the Mozambique side of the border. The Mozambiquean customs officials gathered like clouds of vultures on a kill. They couldn't believe I wasn't using a guy. At least that's what I thought they were saying. There wasn't a smidgen of English to be had between the lot of them. I offered up my commercial invoice and packing list hesitantly. It was a long list, itemised stem by stem, box by box. The customs officials and others, including a couple of bored loiterers, poured over the invoice intently with lots of debate, head shaking and vigorous gesticulating. I kept a vacuous grin on my face throughout. Until the boss customs guy gesticulated at me to unpack the truck.

Whence upon my grin slipped off my face to not be seen again. The boss customs guy gesticulated further, not only did they want me to unpack the truck, but they also wanted me to open up every single box so they could count each and every stem. Surely, he had to be fucking joking. I think up until then they were just joshing with me, enjoying the panic on my face. But then I used the F word. I'm pretty sure that it was the only English word the boss customs guy knew, and it was a red rag to the bull inside him. The next thing I knew, I was unpacking flowers boxes on the hot tarmac outside the customs building so that one of his minions could count them one by one. I left hours later, only after paying out every cent I had in unforeseen duties. Crap. There was no way I was going to come even close to breaking even on my first shipment.

It was late at night by the time I got into Maputo with a truck full of hot flowers. It took me another hour to unpack the flowers into water in the cold room. I climbed into bed a.k.a. a sleeping bag on the floor in one of the offices, just in time to welcome an incoming cloud of mosquitos, looking to suck out any remaining blood. I tried to hide my head in the sleeping bag, but it was seventy degrees centigrade inside the bag, and I lasted not even two minutes. Just as I pulled my head out, the disco next door fired up Mozambiquean house music at volume ten. Oh, how I was enjoying being a multinational corporate.

I hadn't got over my business trip to Maputo when Baldric phoned. "Did I want to go on a flying visit to Zimbabwe?"

'I can't, Baldric, I got this NECCI investigation thing hanging over my head."

"Don't worry about that because Prime Minister trumps NECCI."

"What are you talking about?"

"A guy I know has chartered a plane to fly to Harare for Morgan Tsvangirai's inauguration as Prime Minister. There are just nine seats up for grabs, for people who've helped the cause. Do you want one?"

"Hell yes. When do we go?"

"We fly up on Thursday the 12th and out again on Saturday the 14th."

"That's Valentine's Day."

"So?" Baldric was long married, and Valentine's Day wasn't on his radar anymore. Whereas it was huge on mine. Valentine's Day was the day of the year in which we could do one month of flower shop turnover in a single day.

"I can't do that to Jenny, not on Valentine's Day, not again."

"After all you've done for Morgan, you got to be there for his inauguration. And did I tell you we're flying up on a private jet? With leather seats and champagne I expect."

With the mention of a private jet, all resistance crumbled. "Okay, I'm in. Unless Jenny kills me when I tell her."

"What you meant to say was when you beg her." Baldric knew me too well.

Valentine's Day was such a schlep in our lives, a day full of red rose acrimony and anger, death threats and worse from florists if you didn't deliver on the promise of red roses. And this Valentines was especially important. Things were that tight for us, this one was literally make or break. If we had a good Valentine's, we'd survive to see another. And if we didn't, we wouldn't. And here I was looking to flit off on a private jet while the rest of the family bust their balls. It was like Father Christmas asking for December 25th off. It took days on my knees, begging and pleading before Jenny relented. But she was pissed off and rightly so. It was not exactly my finest moment. But what a trip. The whole thing was too good from the start to almost the finish.

Private business jets are just the coolest things out, and I wouldn't be surprised if they catch on real quick. The one we were flying on was a Pilatus PC12, shiny and sexy. But I'm embarrassed to admit I was slightly disappointed when I found out it was actually a turboprop as opposed to a jet. Flying up in on one's private turboprop isn't quite as cool as flying up in one's private jet. But it was cool nonetheless, way cooler than anything I'd ever flown on before. Also cool was our host for the day, a wealthy young activist based out of Dubai who'd been working closely with Roy Bennett on fundraising for the MDC. There were nine of us on board, mostly fellow Zimbabwean activists plus a journalist, all kindred spirits who'd been involved in the struggle that was now culminating in Morgan's inauguration as Prime Minister. For me, Morgan's inauguration as Prime Minister, as opposed to President, had a slightly hollow ring to it, sort of like the turboprop versus jet, but those on the plane more in the know said that as executive Prime Minister, Morgan would have control over the Government of National Unity with Mugabe reduced to a figurehead President, on his way out. I'm always easily swayed by those more in the know and parked my misgivings and got caught up in the celebratory party mood on board the plane.

Our pilot was a young slip of a girl with red hair who looked far too young to be piloting planes. But she got us off the ground and into the air, no problem. The cooler boxes on the plane were full when we took off but empty when we landed at Charles Prince airport. Our final approach took us in over Running Dog. Because I was quite pissed by then, I shouted and waved at the workers in the flower fields below me, but they never heard. We poured off the Pilatus and carried on the party in the Flying Club pub which had been my local for years. I had a reunion with barmen Jimmy and Pious. I phoned Mitch and Brian at the Running Dog and told them to down tools for the day and to come next door to join in the party.

As it turned out, the whole of Harare was in a party mood. Change had finally come about; Morgan was now the man and Mugabe was all but gone. I was booked in to stay with Bob and Julie at the Hotel Hamill. Bob and I went to a huge gathering of MDC Support members from across the country. It was a wonderful gathering of like-minded souls. All of us had put our heads on the chopping block and had stood up to be counted, and now we all had a very real sense of achievement. I hugged it up with old friends and new, including Eddie Cross. Eddie, who'd narrowly missed out on a Ministerial position in Morgan's Cabinet, was able to bring us up to speed on the Government of National Unity and the manner in which the Ministries had been parcelled out between ZANU PF and the two MDC factions. The MDC parties had taken control of strategically important Ministries that really mattered like Finance, Health, Education and Energy while ZANU had grabbed the more political Ministries like Defence, Justice and Information. Not surprisingly, ZANU had hung onto to the Lands and Agriculture Portfolio, but this would be offset by Roy Bennett's appointment as Deputy Minister.

As is his wont, Eddie was very upbeat and bullish about Zimbabwe's prospects for the future. It belonged to us MDC activists he told us. He paid tribute to our efforts and the sacrifices we'd made and said that it was now payback time for those of us in business, one of those 'To the victors, the spoils' sort of thing. As members of the MDC Support, we now had friends in government, friends who now counted. If we were clever, Eddie told us we could take advantage of those relationships to make sure we were in poll position and on the inside track of Zimbabwe's recovery, before the rest of the world came pouring in to invest billions and trillions. Eddie is a wonderful speaker and swept me up in his feel good.

The only downer in the whole night came about when I phoned Roy after noticing he wasn't at the festivities. "Where you, Roy? I've got a beer here with your name on it." Roy managed a laugh but only just. He told me he was in hiding at an Embassy because Mugabe was refusing point blank to swear him in as Deputy Minister and wanted him arrested instead, on charges of treason and sedition. Roy sounded very alone. I didn't know what to say, other than to wish him luck. After I hung up the phone, I opened yet another beer and went back to the party, but my sad lingered.

The next day at the inauguration proper, the party continued. We didn't crack the nod to the actual inauguration event, a sterile ceremony at State House where Mugabe, looking like he'd stepped in fresh dog shit, reluctantly swore Tsvangirai in as executive Prime Minister. Instead, we went to the inauguration that counted, the peoples' one at Glamis Stadium in the Show Grounds in front of tens of thousands. Bob Hamill and I got there early, and already the centre field in front of the podium where Morgan would be standing was full to overflowing. We wangled our way into the VIP section where the podium was situated. It didn't take us long to find a bar, and it took us even less time to get back to where we'd happily left off the night before, with happy being the operative word. There were thousands of people at the stadium, lots of them old friends and all of them kindred spirits. I don't think I've hugged as many people as I did on that day.

Around us, the excitement built and built and built. Predictably Morgan was late in arriving, but there was no shortage of speakers keen and eager to get behind the microphone and in front of the crowd. The crowd was very generous and gave each and every one of them a rapturous welcome, even the no-name brands. Most of the speeches were in Shona and lost on me, but I enjoyed them nonetheless, courtesy of a bunch of beer. When Tendai Biti took the microphone, he got the hugest welcome. Tendai was the Minister of Finance in the new cabinet. He cut to the chase and told the crowd that first thing he was going to do when he got into his office was to get rid of the Zimbabwe Dollar and replace it with the US Dollar. Government payday was in just two weeks, and all civil servants would be paid in US Dollars, he said. The crowd went absolutely crazy. I watched one guy near the front of the crowd rip up some billion dollar notes into shreds and fling the worthless confetti up into the air. The crowd around him followed suit, and suddenly the air was full of bits of billions and trillions.

Finally, Morgan arrived and screams of Chinja, Chinja Chinja lifted the roof, and I got goose pimples all over. I don't think I've ever been that happy, before or after. I'd given up a big chunk of the last ten years of my life for Morgan and the MDC and standing in Glamis Stadium surrounded by tens of thousands, watching Morgan swear his Oath of Office, it was all absolutely worth it. Standing in that crowd, I quickly worked out that I was where I belonged. I resolved there and then to come back home to Zimbabwe to live. I would return to South Africa and get my business down there tidied up, hand it over to Gary and then come home.

The next day my hangover and I headed back to Charles Prince Airport for the trip back to SA. We all met in the Flying Club pub yet again while we waited for the plane to be readied. I was happy to see that Baldric looked tattier than I did. The guy who was chartering the plane told us that there'd be a slight delay as we were being joined by an extra mystery passenger on the leg to Joburg. Ten minutes later, Roy Bennett walked through the door with his son Charles. Roy was the mystery passenger, kept under wraps because he was a hunted man. I rushed up to Roy and gave him a big hug. Roy said he was still on Mugabe's shit list but rather than carry on hiding in the German Embassy, he'd decided to go back to Joburg to help Heather pack up their house while pressure was applied to Mugabe to swear him into the government. When Roy walked in an excitement swept through the place. Behind the bar, Jimmy called Pious from out back to come ogle Roy. Pious was closely followed by the kitchen staff and then by the airport staff. Even the Immigration Officer came to gawk. Roy had rock and roll star status.

Finally, it was time to board the plane. One of our party gathered up all the passports and took them through to the Immigration Officer to be stamped while we finished our drinks. Charles gave his dad a farewell hug before we filed out onto the tarmac to board the plane. But as we were boarding, the pilot told us there was a slight technical problem with the turboprop and asked us to go back inside while it was being sorted out. After 30 minutes of yet more drinks, the plane was pronounced ready, and it was time for us to leave. Charles gave his dad another goodbye hug and headed back into town. Roy grabbed the first seat on the right behind the pilot. I sat in the seat behind him so we could carry on our conversation. The pilot asked for and received permission for take-off, and we taxied out onto Runway One Four, the runway that would take us out over Running Dog. It struck me then that I hadn't even set foot on the farm all weekend. Plenty of time for that after I moved back.

The pilot gunned the engines, but as we started rolling forward, a white Isuzu twin-cab screeched out onto the tarmac with lights and indicators flashing. As it powered towards us, the radio in the cockpit squawked loudly. Even two seats back, I could hear the instructions from the Control Tower clearly. The Tower was revoking our clearance for take-off. Our pilot got flustered. She didn't know what to do. The Pilatus carried on rolling forward while she dithered. The Control Tower squawked even louder. "Papa Sierra, you are not cleared for take-off, I repeat you are not cleared for take-off."

"What do I do, what do I do?" the pilot asked, sounding impossibly young. "They're telling me to abort take-off."

Roy leant forward out of his seat and told her to hit full throttle. While he sounded calm, there was an edge to his voice. "Take off. Ignore them and get this thing in the air. Tell the Control Tower they're breaking up and you can't hear them properly. And that you're proceeding with take-off. And then get this thing up in the air."

But the pilot had hesitated too long, and the Isuzu was now directly in front of the plane, rushing towards us headlong, just like in an adventure movie. The pilot powered the plane down. She obviously she didn't do adventure movies. She apologised to Roy. "I'm sorry, I'm really, really sorry. But I'd lose my licence. And we don't know what they want with us."

"I do," said Roy. "They want me." I couldn't get over how steady his voice was. He turned back to the pilot. "Okay, open the door, so I can get out." While he waited, he turned and gave me his laptop and his cell phone and a scrap of paper with two phone numbers scribbled on it. "Hide these for me Eric and keep them safe. Give them to Heather. Just make sure you don't let these bastards get them. And phone this number, speak to someone called the General and tell him what's happened. I'm going to get out the plane and talk with them. Follow me to see what happens. If they put me in a car, I need you to give the General the details of the vehicle and tell him the direction they've taken me in. And also tell Charles, my son." And then Roy stepped down off the plane and walked towards the twin-cab now parked beneath the nose of the Pilatus.

I gave Roy's laptop and phone to Baldric to guard while I followed Roy out the plane. He was talking to the men in the twin-cab. I hung around the bottom of the stairs, awkward like a voyeur, waiting and watching to see what they did with Roy. Instead of bundling him into the twin-cab, the details of which I'd commenced memorising, the two grey suits frogmarched Roy around to front of the Flying Club to the tiny Customs and Immigration building. I followed at a distance. Every time one of the suits turned around to glare at me, I stopped and resumed my awkward voyeur stance. Surreptitiously, I inched my phone out of my pocket and punched in the General's number. He was busy on another call. I tried him again. He was still busy. I hung back even further and tried Charles's number. That also just rang. I wasn't doing well.

Things got busy when a posse of other twin-cabs barrelled in, and the scrum of people around Roy grew larger. I could only just see Roy in the middle with the two original suits and the Immigration guy who'd stamped our passports. Roy was very animated with his voice raised. I inched closer to hear what I could hear, but the debate was all in Shona. Some uniformed police arrived and milled around uncertainly. I had no idea what was going on. The brave part of me wanted to push through the scrum and demand Roy's release on the grounds that he'd done nothing wrong but the rest of me insisted on hanging out at the back. Then the debate ended abruptly, and Roy was quickly bundled into the backseat of a newly arrived silver Toyota twin-cab, and he was gone.

Crap. I was caught flat-footed and only managed to get half the number plate in my head. Silver Toyota twin-cab AEV 4 plus three numbers. Silver Toyota twin-cab AEV4 plus three numbers. Silver Toyota twin-cab AEV4 plus three numbers. Frantically, I tried the General again. It rang, rang, rang ...and then he answered. "Who is this?" The General's voice was black, calm and collected.

I was anything but. "My name's Eric. I'm with Roy Bennett, in Harare, on a plane, at Charles Prince Airport, well I was up until just now, but now Roy's been grabbed and..."

"Who's got him?"

"CIO. At least I think they're CIO. They took him away in a silver Toyota Hilux twin-cab reg number AEV 4 and...and that's all I got. I think they're headed into Harare, but I couldn't see. And..."

"Thank you. If you hear anymore, let me know." Then he hung up. Next, I phoned Charles to tell him his dad had been grabbed off the plane. Somehow, I felt responsible, guilty for not having stopped Roy from getting grabbed. I also gave Charles the description of the vehicle and felt guilty some more, for not having captured the whole registration number.

After my conversation with Charles, I went back to the other passengers now standing in a forlorn huddle outside the plane, looking shocked and stunned like mourners at a funeral, to tell them what had happened to Roy. After a weekend of feel-good, Zimbabwe was back to being a black, dark, horrible place. I realised there and then that nothing had changed in Zimbabwe and that nothing ever would, not until Mugabe was gone. While he was still alive, Zimbabwe would always be dark and horrible.

Left to my own devices, I would have gone off and sat in a corner somewhere and cried. But credit to Baldric, he told me to pull myself together. He told all of us to get busy on our phones. We had to tell the world what had just happened to Roy, reporters, activists, the MDC, lawyers, embassies, anyone and everyone. We had to turn it into an international incident; otherwise, Roy would disappear. I started working through my contacts list which was full of journalists and reporters. But first up, I phoned Jenny to tell her I was going to be late because I'd been arrested, again. It was my hardest call. Peter Godwin, the author and reporter, arrived with his sister and lots of questions, closely followed by other reporters and even more questions. But after an hour, they all left.

By then, we'd run out people to phone, so we just sat and stressed. The Immigration Officer who'd stamped our passports came through to commiserate. He zeroed in on Baldric and pulled him to one side. He told Baldric his name was Danny and that because he'd try to help Roy, he now had reason to fear for his life and it was important that he get out the country. Could Baldric help him? I'd decided that at best the guy was a bull shitter looking for free drinks, at worst he was part of the system that had just fucked Roy. I didn't like him, I didn't trust him, and so I left him and

Baldric to it.

After another hour of just sitting and stressing in the Flying Club pub, not drinking and hardly talking, the Air Traffic Controller came into the room and told us we'd been cleared for take-off and were now free to go. For the second time that day, we trooped aboard the Pilatus and took our seats. The second time round there were no dramas, and we took off into the night skies and headed south. A part of me felt nothing but relief, but a bigger part of me felt like it was running out on a friend. I looked down into black nothingness below and couldn't but think about where Roy was, and about what they were doing to him. Alas.

Chapter Fifty-Four

I arrived back in White River after my Harare misadventures in the small hours the day after Valentine's Day, drained and exhausted, looking for sympathy and support from my wife and family. But sympathy and support were in short supply in our house the day after Valentine's, especially for a delivery driver who'd abandoned his post on the biggest day of the year to swan off on a private jet junket. Jenny, Gary, Veronica and Arnold were all recuperating from Valentine's Day deliveries, and residual red rose recriminations from angry florists feeling short-changed on quality, quantity or both and were too knackered to give a shit about what I'd been through. As it happened, we actually made money enough that Valentine's Day to limp on for another few months to come. Yippee.

And then rather than help with the post Valentine fall-out and chaos, I dropped myself further in the shit with Jenny by driving back to Joburg pretty much straight away to see Heather Bennett to offer her my help. I felt guilty about leaving Roy in the lurch. I met with Heather and Aussie Stu, Roy's right hand man and closest adviser. Heather looked vulnerable, but she was strong, like her husband. Heather brought me up to speed on the happenings in Zimbabwe and on the Roy Bennett vigil was playing out in Mutare. The Roy Bennett vigil was a wonderful thing that gave you goose bumps, a stand-out example of what being a Zimbabwean was all about.

As it turned out, the flurry of phone calls we'd made from Charles Prince Airport after Roy's abduction had triggered off an amazing chain reaction. Armed with my description of the vehicle that Roy had been bundled into, friends of Roy had staked out all major roads in and out of Harare. They picked up the Toyota Hilux exiting Harare on the Mutare Road and followed it without being spotted, first to the infamous Goromonzi torture camp and then after a few hours, onto Marondera and finally through to the Mutare police station where Roy was positively identified as he was bundled out of the vehicle and into the police station.

I don't know why the bad guys chose Mutare as an incarceration destination for Roy, but it was a bad move on their part because Mutare was Roy Bennett heartland. Within hours, a group of MDC supporters a hundred strong or more, mounted a vigil outside the police station. In the morning, a member of the vigil entered the police station to hand over a food parcel for Roy. The cops went into full lockdown and refused to let them inside. They told the MDC supporters to disperse. But Roy's vigil went nowhere. When the Hilux that had delivered Roy tried to leave the Police Station, Roy's supporters blocked the road and wouldn't let the vehicle pass, not without searching it first to make sure Roy wasn't being disappeared. They told the police they would not allow Bennett to be taken away to be murdered or dragged off to a nearby torture centre, like so many other activists before him. The police tried to disperse the crowd with riot squads and dogs but failed. If anything, the crowd grew. By the Sunday morning, the vigil had doubled in size. Reluctantly the police allowed food parcels for Roy in, plus two lawyers and two members of the MDC Provincial leadership. The lawyers were told that Roy was being charged with treason. On the Sunday, the lawyers were told the charges against Roy were being reduced to lesser arms charges. The lawyers told the cops that they had until Monday to formally charge Roy; otherwise, they'd be holding him illegally. Come Monday, the first day of the working week, the vigil numbers stayed steady waiting for Roy to be taken to court. It didn't happen. Inside the Police Station when the members of the vigil gave Roy his food parcel, he asked them to bring more the next day, for the other prisoners who were starving. Later that week, Roy was formally charged and moved to Mutare Prison. The vigil moved with him.

After my meeting with Heather, I drove back to White River with a heavy heart. I hit the phones hard, trying to raise money to keep Roy's vigil on the streets outside the prison. Raising money to help was easy, like shooting fish in a barrel. It took huge logistics of keeping a crowd of people in place outside a prison twenty-four seven but Roy's vigil was unwavering.

Before the end of the first week, the members of the vigil were wearing Free Roy t-shirts. Inside the prison, the conditions were abominable with twelve prisoners or more crammed into a two-man lice-infested, excrement strewn cell. One of Roy's cellmates died overnight. Looking to break Roy, the prison warders left the body inside the cell for days before removing it. In the four weeks that Roy spent in Mutare prison, a total of five fellow prisoners died inside Roy's cell.

Roy stayed strong throughout and got busy working on improving conditions in the prison. He put in an order for Jeyes Fluid to be included in his next food parcel and with the help of his fellow prisoners, he scrubbed his cell from top to bottom. By the end of the first week, the guards were helping with clean-up operations. After three weeks, one of the prison guards put in an order for eighteen Free Roy t-shirts, eight for the night guards and ten for the day shift.

I was consumed by Roy's vigil. I wanted to be there, but I couldn't. Instead, I fundraised hard to help keep the vigil going, and when I wasn't fundraising, I was on the internet looking for updates. Jenny got very grumpy with me, so I decided I'd take her away for the weekend to celebrate her birthday. Very grumpy is when Jenny prefixes Zimbabwe or the MDC with the word fucking. We booked into a guest lodge up in the mountains near Lydenburg. After a day spent holding hands while marvelling at forever views at God's Window and similar, we tracked down a quaint little restaurant for dinner. Having not mentioned fucking Zimbabwe or the fucking MDC all day, I was doing well and inching my way back into Jenny's good books up until the television on the wall in the restaurant Jenny announced the death in a car accident of Susan Tsvangirai, the wife of Zimbabwe's Prime Minister. There was speculation that the accident wasn't an accident, that it had actually been an attempt on Morgan's life. Morgan had been seated next to Susan in the car at the time but sustained only minor injuries. I was more than happy to join the dots and jump to the murder conclusion. In Zimbabwe, cars and trucks were the assassination weapon of choice. You just had to ask Josiah Tongogara and countless others since, now all dead traffic statistics.

That was the end of our quiet, romantic dinner. I'd met Susan Tsvangirai and liked her. I had to get on the phone to Baldric to find out what had happened. In Roy's absence, Baldric was my go-to guy for Zimbabwean updates. He had an amazing network of contacts in dark places and always knew what had really happened. Baldric told me his contacts were calling the accident murder. Morgan was on his way to Buhera for a rally, travelling in his official vehicle in convoy with his security details when they got sideswiped by a truck. The thing stank to high heaven. First up the truck that hit Morgan belonged to Saviour Kasukuwere, former CIO operative and current Mugabe strongman and enforcer. Ironically the truck had been on lease to a US AID affiliate delivering AIDS medicines. Normally the truck should have been driven by US AID driver but wasn't. Baldric's contacts said the driver was ex-military. And then there was the matter of Morgan's lead-out vehicle. The lead-out vehicle was supposed to stay close enough to the principal's vehicle to be able to prevent attack by vehicle, but Morgan's hadn't. Inexplicably the front-lead-out vehicle had opened up a large enough gap to allow the truck that killed Susan Tsvangirai in. And Baldric said that cell phone records had the driver of the truck and the lead-out vehicle talking to each other more than once in the lead up to the accident.

I was angry and horrified but not in the least bit surprised. For the rest of the weekend, I went through the motions for Jenny's sake but inside I was sad, for Morgan and for the rest of Zimbabwe. Mugabe was a murderer who would stop at nothing to hang onto power forever, and no one was lifting a finger to stop him. As soon as I got home, I wrote a murder by truck scene into my book and changed the working title to 'God doesn't work here anymore.' Alas.

Business-wise, I continued to flounder on all fronts. Mozambique especially was turning into a four-letter word. The only glimmer of hope on my horizon was the 2010 Football World Cup, now just months away. It was all go. Workers swarmed over the purpose-built Nelspruit stadium twenty-four seven in a frantic effort to finish it on time. The stadium was huge but would only be used to host four preliminary round matches, all involving minnow teams. And after the tournament, the stadium would undoubtedly morph into a White Elephant. I don't know who did the cost and return sums, but I was pretty sure he wasn't a South African taxpayer. In the middle of Nelspruit at a central high school, work on the official Fan Park was equally frantic. The biggest show on Earth was coming to town and man were they going to use up a whole bunch of flowers.

Using all my sleuthing skills, I eventually tracked down the offices of the FIFA Organizing Committee in Joburg. I drove to their offices wearing my best long pants and offered up my purpose printed business card to an impossibly young and efficient German and asked to be considered for the position of Official Flower Supplier to the 2010 World Cup. Because I was a flower farmer in my own right and a flower wholesaler with a full-time buyer on the Auction Floors blah blah blah, I was happy to be FIFA's man on the ground, and they need not look any further. The young German apologetically told me I was two years too late but gave me the name of the sub-contractor in charge of arranging flowers in all the stadiums and venues countrywide because they would need to sub-sub-contract a florist to put flower arrangements into the Nelspruit venue. While standing in front of the young German, my ego deflated like a sad balloon. I hugely hated being tagged a florist, now I was going to be a sub-sub-contracted one. But I had bills to pay, and the World Cup gig was the only potential money maker on my radar. "Did I tell you that I employ some of the best award-winning florists in the whole of Nelspruit?" I asked the young German.

The only person in the family who was impressed with our new sub-sub-contracted florist status was Dan. He was infected with Soccer World Cup fever in a big way. Dan's chosen team was England, mostly because they'd won the cup in 1966 and it was obviously their turn to win again, and because of David Beckham. Dan had a David Beckham poster up on his bedroom wall and even briefly considered buying a Spice Girls poster when he heard that one of them was actually Mrs Beckham. It fell to me to tell Dan that Beckham hadn't been picked for the English World Cup squad. Major depression set in. "But how're we supposed to win without David Beckham?" he asked.

I tried to cheer him up. "But England are still a good team, even without him."

"Who's the new guy that they've picked instead?"

"His name is Rooney, I think."

We looked Rooney up on the internet, and Dan's depression ramped up a notch. "But look at him, he's not even good looking" Dan wailed. "How are England going to win with an ugly captain?"

Dan's career as a trainee rose farm manager had come to an end. After almost eighteen months and despite Etienne's close attentions and infinite patience, Dan had learnt not a thing. He was dead weight just going through the motions. And the rose farm finances were such that they couldn't afford any dead weight whatsoever. Etienne told me that he was more than happy to keep Dan on the books because he was that sort of guy, but I told him thanks but no thanks. It was time to make a Plan C for Dan to prepare him for life after Jenny and me. It was going to have to be a robust plan because Dan wasn't in a good place. Alas.

By then, Dan's vitiligo had come and gone but had left him without pigment around his eyes and neck and on his hands and joints. Ditto on his torso beneath his shirt. Dan never took his shirt off with others watching. And inside Dan wasn't doing so good either. His thyroid was now officially dead, killed by Hashimoto's Thyroiditis. Without a thyroid, Dan's metabolism was run away fast. The palms of his hands sweated constantly, and his appetite knew no bounds. Dan could put away a loaf of bread an hour after a big breakfast and still be hungry at lunchtime. If we left a kilo tin of instant coffee out, Dan would drink it, cup after cup non-stop. He didn't put on any weight because his body just burnt it up. His appetite caused ructions in the family and led to countless screaming matches that left everyone feeling bad. Shouting at Dan was like shouting at a child who'd done wrong but didn't know better. Mentally, Dan seemed duller than before and without spark, but I put most of that down to a huge lack of self-esteem. I did what I could to boost that but didn't do too good.

A couple of times a month, I'd take Dan to a pub in town where we'd play bad pool for a couple of hours. Dan especially played bad pool. He knew nothing about angles and thought there was a direct link between the force applied and the number of balls that disappeared down into pockets. Every single shot, he'd hammer the white ball has hard as he could and would stand back expectantly, waiting for the table to clear. To give him an interest, any interest, I bought him another dreaded model aeroplane, a Red Baron World War One biplane, but not a Fokker. We found a model aeroplane club on a farm not too far from Summerhill, and I took him there most weekends in the hope that he'd make friends with someone, anyone but alas, that never happened. Mostly the club members were all adults and other than his red biplane, Dan had nothing in common with them. As far as I know, Dan's biplane never flew. I should've taken up the sport myself but didn't. I had even less in common with the model aircraft club members.

It was all very wearying, and I started looking at Dan as more of a burden than a son. When Gary moved back to White River from Joburg, he took over a lot of my Dan duties and lightened my load hugely. Dan worshipped the ground Gary walked on. Gary was good with Dan. He had time and patience for his younger brother and took over beating him at pool and added fishing badly to Dan's curriculum. Like pool, Dan equated force applied while casting and striking to the size of the fish he was going to catch, ditto the size of hooks used and weight of the weights on the end of his line. Dan should've caught whales.

But without Gary and me, Dan would have nothing. And we weren't always going to be there for him. I had to work towards getting Dan ready for when we weren't, I had to get him a life and a career.

I decided that helping Dan get his driving licence would be a good start point to kicking him out of the family nest, this even though I was still emotionally scarred and vulnerable from my exposure to Veronica as a learner driver. Gary, the learner driver, had been easy, Veronica had been a shocker. I had an inkling that Dan would be the worst by far. Before we got him behind a steering wheel, he had to pass his Learner's Licence. Which unfortunately for Dan involved learning the Rules of the Road, which involved reading, which for Dan was hugely tough. By then, Dan had almost forgotten how to read and almost gave up before he started. The only thing that pulled him through was the fact that the exam was in a multiple guess format, A through to E. Which technically meant he had a one in five chance of answering every question correctly. And unlike in Zimbabwe, in South Africa, learner drivers didn't have to get 100 % right. To pass, they just had to answer twenty four of the thirty questions correctly.

For Dan, those were great odds, and he set about learning the answers that I'd ringed in his Rules of the Road book, parrot-fashion. 1-A, 2-D, 3-C, 4-E, 5- also E, 6-B and so on all the way through to 30, over and over, again. He had no idea why the answer to Question 1 was A, it just was.

Dan flunked his first test handsomely, guessing less than 10 % of the answers correctly. But he was undeterred. He told me he'd just got horribly out of sync on his A.D.C.E.E.B sequence of answers and just had to practice them harder next time. Dan went around all day, muttering his long list of letters over and over. His short-term memory was surprisingly good, and he made excellent recital progress, by his standards. On his second exam, Dan came home over the moon happy with his much-improved results, he'd got just 70% wrong. He was on a roll. It was just a matter of time before he passed. And so it came to pass. On his tenth attempt, Dan got the requisite twenty-four out of the thirty questions right. Whoop whoop. Next stop was his driving test, and he'd be home and dry, a licenced driver.

Neither Dan nor I were worried about the actual driving part of the test. Already, he was a better driver than Veronica and knew his brake pedal from his clutch and his first gear from his reverse gear and could use them without having to look down at them while eeny, meeny, miny moeing under his breath. Unfortunately, he also knew what the accelerator was for. Man, but the kid liked to drive flat out fast, and it was a constant battle to get him to keep it under a hundred, even in reverse. Armed with his 80% pass mark, Jenny and I took him to the Test Centre to register for his driving test. I sent Dan in on his own to fill out the forms. "Shouldn't you go in with him to help fill in the forms?" Jenny asked me.

"No. It's his driving test, not mine. He's got to learn how to do stuff like filling out forms for himself."

Dan came out five minutes later pleased as punch, waving his learner driver registration about excitedly. "Can I book for lessons, Dad? Can I, can I? I want to book my test next week, but first I've got to do lessons."

"Whoa, slow down, Dan. Let me take you for a few lessons first, then when we think you're good enough, we can book you in for some finishing lessons with a Driving School."

"But I can't learn in Mom's car because I'm booked to do a Code Ten licence, for heavy-duty trucks, Dad, big thirty-ton ones."

I choked on a jumble of four-letter words all trying to get out of my mouth at the same time. Eventually, I came up spluttering for breath. "What?"

"I said I got to go for lessons at a driving school, so I can learn how to drive a heavy-duty truck for my Code Ten licence."

I forced myself to be calm. It took some doing. Eventually, I asked Dan, "Why? Why? Why did you register for a Heavy-Duty licence, Dan?"

"Because big trucks don't have to know how to parallel park, Dad. Parallel parking is really hard. This way, I don't have to learn how."

"Oh."

"And also, so I can get a job as a truck driver and drive across America."

Even though the idea of Dan driving off across America in a big truck seemed like a very good one, I went into the Test Centre to get Dan re-registered for a normal driving licence. The hundred kilo woman in the too-tight uniform behind the desk shook her sadly. "Sorry for that. If the learner driver wants to also register for also a Code Eight, the learner driver would have to re-sit the Learner's Test. He cannot be sitting behind two different steering wheels at the same time." Because the chances of Dan getting twenty-four questions right out of thirty a second time were very slim, we booked him into a Driving School for heavy-duty driving lessons. Alas.

The next step towards Dan's independence was choosing a career path for him. I didn't involve Dan is the selection process because I knew we wouldn't get past racing car driver or similar. I scoured all the trade options looking for one that didn't require secondary education qualifications. Which ruled out mechanics, electrician, auto electrician and even carpenter. Jesus would've been appalled. Eventually, I hit pay dirt with plumbing. Apparently, plumbers didn't have to be clever, they just had to be able to put up with the smell of shit. Plumbing would be perfect for Dan. All I had to do was find a plumbing firm locally that offered up apprenticeships. But first I had to sell the idea to Dan.

I told him he was leaving the rose farm to start an apprenticeship in Nelspruit, so he could learn how to stand on his feet. Dan quite liked the idea of moving on from the rose farm and standing on his own feet but wanted to know what an apprenticeship was. I told Dan that Leonardo da Vinci had started out as an apprentice and had gone on to achieve great things as a painter. "But I don't know how to paint nicely like Gary, Dad?"

"No. You're not going to be an artist; you're going to be an apprentice plumber."

"A plumber? But that's a shit job, Dad. I remember when that plumber came to the farm to fix the toilet, and he ended up covered in my shit."

"Well, that wasn't supposed to happen. But you want to know how much he charged me in the end to fix the toilet."

"How much?"

"A lot of money, Dan, a big lot of money."

"So are plumbers rich?"

"Yes. Filthy rich, the lot of them."

"O.K. I'll become a plumber then."

Nelspruit's yellow pages were full of plumbers. I started phoning them one by one, working my way through the alphabet. A few of them spoke Afrikaans only, and I didn't get past "Hallo, my name is Eric". Most of the others were one-man bands, in no need of assistants or apprentices. It was only towards the end of my list; I got my one and only bite. A Mr Quick from Quick Plumbers said he would be prepared to consider Daniel as an apprentice, but only if he worked hard and if he wasn't scared of getting his hands dirty. Mr Quick, who was Afrikaans, asked if Daniel had his driving licence.

I was able to tell him that Dan was a qualified Learner Driver and well on the way to getting his licence to drive, including heavy-duty trucks. Mr Quick was impressed. He had an eight-ton truck in his fleet, and it would be a great help if he had another licenced driver to call on. Mr Quick edged towards the subject of remuneration, nervous like a Form One boy at his first high school dance. He told me that I had to appreciate a first-year apprentice would add zero value to his business and as such, apprentice plumbers got paid very little in their first year. No problem, I told him. Or in their second year, he said. Again, no problem with peanuts for pay in Dan's second year or third year even, I told Mr Quick. That sealed the deal. Dan was now a fully-fledged first-year apprentice plumber. We bought Dan new overalls and work boots and booked him into a boarding house in Nelspruit within easy walking distance of Quick Plumbing. Dan would spend Monday through to Friday in town at his boarding house and come home for weekends.

It sounds like horrible parenting, but Jenny and I had a party the first night Dan was away in Nelspruit. The house was empty of children, and it felt good. Finally, finally, we had light at the end of our tunnel. We just had to get Dan through three years of being an apprentice plumber, and we'd have our lives back. And if in that time we made bucket loads of World Cup money, we could get the South African farm and the flower shop standing back up on their feet and then we could go back to Zimbabwe and live happily ever after. By then, Morgan would have consigned ZANU PF to the shit heap, and NECCI and the like could all fuck off. Whoop, whoop. I shared my vision of the future with Jenny, but she told me we'd have to wait and see. A lot of water had to go under a lot of bridges before we could start planning moves back home. Jenny is a lot more cynical than me.

The Football World Cup got bigger and bigger, the closer it got. Nelspruit would host four preliminary round matches, and everyone involved was going to make millions. Months out from kick-off, FIFA block booked out every hotel and guest lodge room in a 50-kilometre radius of Nelspruit. White River was going to be right in the thick of things with the Chilean national team based at the Ingwenyama Lodge on the outskirts of town there for the duration of the tournament. We drove past the Ingwenyama every day on our way to and from Flowers R Us and watched as it was all but gutted and rebuilt, complete with practice football fields. Dan was quite taken with the Chile strip and seriously considered a defection away from Beckham-less England but changed his mind when he found out that Chile didn't speak English. Jenny bought a Brazilian flag, and I invested heavily in the orange of Holland. Gary didn't have time for football, he was too busy planning a million flower arrangements.

Gary and I had driven through to Joburg to meet the FIFA sub-contractor in charge of flowers and décor and had come away with the Nelspruit contract. I came away staggered by the level of organisation that was going into the World Cup. As the official sub-sub-contractor in charge of Nelspruit floral arrangements, we were given detailed site plans of the stadium, highlighting all the public areas and private suites and where the flower arrangements were to be placed and by when. I got caught up in the moment and rushed out and bought a clipboard. We were also given precise dot to dot instructions on the five different arrangements that we'd be arranging. I'd salivated when I saw the list of flowers and floral requisites required and offered my new boss sizeable discounts from Summer Hill and Flowers R Us. The smug bastard laughed at me and my naivety. Supply contracts had been buttoned down more than a year ago, and World Cup flowers already paid for were being purpose grown in fields across the country. As sub-sub-contractors, the only thing that Flowers R Us would be able to charge out for was our labour- Florist Class A at X per hour and Assistant Florists Class B at Y per hour. I went back to salivating. The X and Y labour rates were based on European standards and were very generous with lots of room for margins. And we'd need a veritable army of Florists and Assistant Florists. We'd charge Jenny, Veronica and even Gary out at Class A rates and every farmworker on Summer Hill would be Assistant Florists for the duration. I whoop whooped all the way back from Joburg, doing the money sums in my head. I don't normally get excited about the prospect of money, but after months and years of doom and gloom, a silver lining on the horizon was exciting.

A month out from the tournament kick-off, a veritable army of cloned versions of the young efficient German that I'd first met at the FIFA offices bustled into town and started putting the finishing touches to the organising. There were Italians and Austrians and South Americans, all impossibly young with not a South African that I could see amongst them. They might have been young and unable to shave but damn they were efficient. There were bets all over town that the Nelspruit's stadium wouldn't be ready on time. And with a week to go, it was still an unfinished bloody mess. But as the first Match Day neared, Honduras vs Chile, somehow the stadium all came together.

Our flowers and vases arrived two days before Match Day, truckloads of them, and then it was a crazy race to get them arranged. We shipped in farmworkers from Summer Hill and under supervision from Jenny and Gary, worked like crazy to put the arrangements together. The farm girls caught on quick, and the end results looked just like the diagrams we'd been given, apart from the arrangements that I did which looked different. I quickly got kicked off the production line and was demoted to putting the arrangements into the private hospitality suites overlooking the pitch. There were about fifty suites dotted about the stadium, and I had a good snoop to see how other half lived while watching football. They lived really well. The suites were well-appointed with huge flat-screen televisions on the walls, Sony were headline sponsors, and private fridges full of fancy French wines and booze from all over the world. The main course meals on the menus were to be flown in on match day from Cape Town and the puddings from Germany. Rumour had it that Sepp Blatter's daughter had the contract to supply the puddings. I don't know what they charged the hospitality suites out for, but even if it was two arms and two legs, they weren't going to break even. As it turned out, it was a moot point. Ninety percent of the suites were unsold on match day.

We finished arranging the flowers just in time, went home, showered, got dressed and went back to the stadium to watch the game- New Zealand v Honduras. Normally I wouldn't walk across the street to watch a game of football, but World Cup football was different. The noise from the vuvuzelas was deafening, especially the vuvuzelas just inches from the back of my head, but they added to the atmosphere. I shouted for Honduras, but they were crap and lost one nil. But it didn't matter. It was the best fun ever.

After the game, while waiting for the crowds to die down a bit before attempting the escape home, we watched the private suites being looted, of everything, from fancy wines to the television sets off the walls. They were stripped clean in minutes, mostly by the security guards from what I could see. After the tournament, everyone queued up to give the South Africans kudos for putting such an excellent World Cup together. The only thing that I saw that the South Africans were in charge of was television set removal after the matches. And wine and booze and anything else that wasn't bolted down. Alas.

We didn't make the million bucks I was needing to make from the first match, but it gave us all a huge positivity boost nonetheless and lots of feel-good to go forward with. With the four Nelspruit matches crammed into just nine days, it was all pretty frantic. And we actually made some money for a change. Jenny and I watched Italy vs New Zealand, and again I shouted for the losing team. We gave our tickets for the other two games to Gary, Veronica, Arnold and Dan. All in all, we had such fun for the whole tournament, apart from the last game, North Korea vs Ivory Coast. Tony died the morning before that game.

After a year of pain, suffering and great fortitude, Tony slipped away just before first light. We'd all known that Tony was nearing the end. We'd carried on with the braais every Saturday at Tony and Hester's cottage, but Tony hadn't been able to make it outside for the last six or seven. The visits from the Hospice team of carers had increased in frequency, and they told Hester to start preparing for the end. Even so, though I was still gutted when he finally went. I was also hugely pissed off with myself. Hester had asked me if I would spend the night at the cottage so that there'd be someone with her when Tony finally passed. I'd told her sure no problem but got too busy and didn't go across as promised. Hester woke me up out of a deep sleep. She was crying. She told me that Tony was dying and please, please would I hurry so I could be with her when he went. I jumped out of bed, pulled on a t-shirt and a pair of track shoes and ran as fast as I could. It was just two hundred metres from our house across the dam wall to the cottages. I ran like the wind, but it felt like slow motion, and I got there seconds too late. Tony was gone, and I hadn't been there for him. I closed Tony's eyes and hugged Hester tight and told her how sorry I was that I hadn't been there for her when she needed me.

I felt even more like crap when we had to leave Hester behind later that morning to go work at the stadium. Hester and Tony had been married for more than fifty years. Tony was everything to Hester, and now she had nothing, just a huge hole in her life where he used to be.

Working at the stadium that day was dreadful. We worked with a dark cloud hanging over us. There's nothing like a death in the family to get rid of any light-hearted banter. Jenny absolutely immersed herself in getting the job done, alone with her thoughts, drowning out all else. I blamed and hated Mugabe all day long. All Tony ever wanted out of life was to retire on his railway pension to his happy home in Bulawayo home with daughters and grandchildren close by. Thanks to Mugabe, he got to enjoy none of that. Alas.

Chapter Fifty-Five

To pay me back for renaming my yet to be finished best-selling novel 'God Doesn't Work Here Anymore', God sucker-punched me post World Cup with a three-month lull before the mother of all storms smashed down all over us. For that short time, all was good in our world.

Dan, the plumber, seemed to be happily apprenticed and enjoying life on his own in Nelspruit. I called in on Mr Quick in Dan's first week to see if our apprentice plumber was behaving. Mr Quick told me he was happy enough with Dan's performance so far, this even though both he and Dan were covered head to toe in shit at the time. They were just back from cleaning out someone's septic tank. Unfortunately, instead of hitting the Suck button on the pump as per instructions, Dan had pushed the Blow button. Instead of being furious, Mr Quick was calm and collected. In his laboured English, Mr Quick was very Afrikaans, he told me "For Dan, it is good to make mistakes in the beginning. That is how he will learn. And in this job, it is also good that Dan doesn't mind getting dirty." Dan took this as high praise and grinned like a Cheshire cat, albeit a very smelly one.

Jenny and I also called in at Dan's boarding house, to check that he was also behaving himself after hours. So far, sort of good the boarding house owner said, although he'd had to speak to Dan a few times about keeping the noise down late at night. Dan had discovered Rocco's Night Club just around the corner and was working towards becoming a regular. Jenny wanted to box Dan around his ears there and then, but I told her to cut him some slack. It was all part of growing up. Gary had more than enjoyed his time at university, as had Veronica at hotel school. And now it was Dan's turn. And on the pittance we gave him as pocket money, he wasn't going to be able to do any lasting damage. As parents, we had to let him get on with growing up and hope and pray that he emerged on the other side, unscathed. My parenting speech impressed Jenny, not a jot, and she still wanted to box Dan's ears. She told him no nightclubbing during the week. And why was his room such a bloody mess? He was brought up better than that. A seasoned pro at being shat upon, Dan replied dutifully. "Yes, Mom, sorry, Mom and yes, Mom."

To develop his social network, Dan decided he'd take up rugby as a sport and joined the Nelspruit Rugby Club, aged eighteen. I tried to reason with him. He hadn't played rugby since he was eight and even then, he hadn't enjoyed it. He didn't know the rules, he didn't even know how many players made up a rugby team. And not being able to speak Afrikaans, maybe he should reconsider joining an Afrikaans club. He told me, "I can

run fast Dad, and I'll learn the rules as I go along. And I'll make friends."
Alas, none of that came to pass. At Dan's first practice, it turned out that
every other player on the pitch could run faster than him. And when they
caught him, they all but buried him. I saw Dan a day after his practice. He
was bruised and battered but mostly hurt inside. He said the worst was
when a few of his own teammates tackled him, hard, really hard. "Why did
they do that, Dan?" I asked.

"Because I kept passing the ball forward. I didn't know that was one of
the rules. Did you know that, Dad?"

"Yeah, kind of."

"Anyway, they didn't like it when I kept doing that. But I think mostly
they tackled me because I can't speak Afrikaans, only English. They called
me a bloody rooinek. What's a rooinek, Dad?"

"It's a stupid name Afrikaners call Englishmen. Sorry for that all of that,
Dan, but I did try to warn you. Are you going to go back?"

"I think I'll play American football instead. Because you're allowed to
pass the ball forward in American football. Do you know where they play
that in Nelspruit, Dad?"

Even business-wise, things went smoothly for us during the lull. In
South Africa, we made enough from the World Cup to be back in the black
briefly. And it led to us being awarded other contracts or sub-contracts.
We were sub-contracted to do the flowers for a seventy million rand mega
wedding for a black South African billionaire. It was ridiculously glitzy, to
the point of nausea. Clearly, the groom, who was getting married for the
second time, had watched far too much celebrity television. But it was good
money for us.

In Zimbabwe, NECCI's interest in me seemed to have waned. It had
been months since Moyo last hassled me. Provided I didn't advertise my
presence while there, I felt comfortable enough sneaking in and out of
Zimbabwe regularly. And best of all, I had had another Eureka moment,
possibly my finest yet.

Normally my Eureka moments hit me at three in the morning, but this
one struck in broad daylight while driving the fifty-odd kilometres between
Bushbuck Ridge and Acornhoek, two little towns north of White River.
The area was a huge black homeland, densely populated with millions.
It was always slow driving between the two towns. because the road was
thick with donkeys, cattle, taxis and pedestrians but on that day, it was
even slower than normal because I got stuck behind a funeral procession
kilometres long.

Funerals in black South Africa are big business. Blacks don't do small,
polite funerals. They do huge, all-day affairs with stretch hearses and
hundreds of mourners, sometimes thousands, all looking to be fed in return
for being sad. To pay for their funerals, most black South Africans start

OF FAKE FLOWERS AND SCHIZOPHRENIA

saving up for them as soon they start working, paying into comprehensive funeral insurance policies every month of their whole working lives. I'd long tried to get a piece of the black funeral trade but was told by the funeral insurance companies that they hardly ever used fresh flowers at their funerals, only fake ones, either silk or plastic depending on whether the dead guy was rich or not. Their dead policyholders wanted the flowers on their graves to last, apparently.

Anyway, back to my Eureka moment. It hit me like a shovel in the face while I was tucked in amongst the funeral procession, driving along at a sedate 30 k.p.h. I'd import fake flowers and get into the funeral wreath business and make millions. Whoop whoop. Sensitive to the others in the procession around me, I resisted the urge to hit my hooter in celebration.

I got to work on my idea straight away. When I arrived back in White River, I drove home via the cemetery to check out the competition. There were fake flower arrangements on every grave, little round arrangements, big round ones, long ones like coffins, all of them covered in crap plastic flowers that didn't even come close to looking real. And the arrangements themselves were also crap with no artistic style at all, this coming from a man who could only draw stickmen badly. I decided that competing in the fake flower arrangement business would be easy, like falling off a bicycle. I'd import the best fake flowers in China, lilies and roses and orchids that at least looked real. I'd get Gary to colour co-ordinate designs for the different arrangements, and then I'd get the florists in the shop to mass-produce them, millions and millions and millions of them. I'd call the company Sympathy Flowers with a simple yet elegant logo with white doves fluttering sadly above a stylish font, tugging at heartstrings. I'd get Sympathy Flowers on every grave into the country. It would be huge.

Embarrassingly, I have to admit to borrowing a sample arrangement from a grave, so I could take it home and break it down so I could cost the inputs. Considerately, I borrowed the sample from an old grave where the cooking pots on top had long rusted, figuring the dead guy who technically owned the funeral wreath had long ago got bored with them. And I did take the flowers back as soon as I'd finished cribbing them and mumbled a thank you to the dead guy for letting me borrow them.

And then it was all systems go. I spent days and days on the internet hurting my head, looking at endless photos of silk and plastic flowers, mostly plastic though because the silk ones were bloody expensive. After narrowing my choices down to a top one thousand, I eeny meeny miny moed my final selection. Which Jenny quickly rejected and replaced with nice flowers. Then taking the money we didn't have, I invested in a forty-foot container of beautifully gaudy, crappy plastic flowers and Sympathy Flowers, purveyors of the finest kind plastic flowers to discerning dead people all over South Africa and beyond, was born. I was really, really pleased with my business acumen. The addition of Sympathy Flowers would round out my portfolio of businesses nicely, reducing my dependence on perishables and taking me into what had to be one of the biggest growth industries in Africa, burying dead people. I was soon-to-be on the way up. Alas. I should have braced myself for things to start going wrong, as soon as it looked like everything was going right.

First up, I got a phone call from Mr Quick, Daniel was acting very strangely.

"What's he been doing?" I asked.

"Can you come and see me, Mr de Jong? I'd rather tell you face to face. And besides, I think he might be listening."

My blood started boiling on the short drive to Quick Plumbers. I'd really struggled to find Daniel an apprenticeship, and if he screwed it up, I decided I was going to kill him. Mr Quick was almost apologetic when I got there. He motioned me through to his office and sat me down in front of his busy desk. I couldn't wait for him to organise himself on the other side of the desk. "What's Daniel done, Mr Quick? And whatever it is, I'm really sorry, and he won't do it again, I promise."

"Daniel is eavesdropping, on me, on my workers, on everyone."

"Huh?"

"I first caught him this morning, outside my office window hiding while he was trying to listen to me on the phone, I was talking with my wife. And then the workers also caught him sneaking outside where they have their tea, trying to listen in on what they were talking about. And then they complained to me. And when I told Daniel he mustn't do it anymore, then he told me the workers were plotting to kill him. He said they are working for Mugabe. And he was really scared, Mr de Jong, really scared. So, I sent him back to his boarding house."

"Huh?"

"He was really, really scared Mr de Jong. I think you need to take him to see a doctor."

"He'll need a doctor when I'm finished him. I'm really sorry, Mr Quick. I'll speak to him, and I'll make sure he cuts it out."

"I don't think he should be working."

"It won't happen again, Mr Quick, I promise you. Please give him another chance."

"All right," Mr Quick said, oh so reluctantly.

I went straight to Dan's boarding house. His room was open but empty. It was also a bloody mess even by Daniel standards, with a week's worth of dirty clothes strewn all over. There was no sign of Dan. I found the boarding house manager in his office playing games on his computer. He looked less than happy to see me.

"Dan was here just now. Until I told him to bugger off. I came in from town just now and caught him hiding by my office window, listening, trying to peep in through the window."

"Shit. Look I'm really sorry and..."

"And it's not the first time. Some of the other residents have also complained about Daniel. He's always sneaking around, listening in on people, like he's a secret agent or something. And he keeps going on about some black SUV that's following him, he says they want to kill him."

"Huh?"

"He's like crazy. And he's frightened the whole time, like really, really frightened."

"Look, I'm sorry, but I've no idea what's going on. He's never done anything like this before. When he gets back, can you send him to see me at the flower shop straight away?"

I seethed, all the way to Flowers R Us, but I also started panicking. Something was wrong with Dan, and I didn't know what.

Back at the shop, I told Jenny what I'd been told. We put two and two together and came up with drugs. We had zero experience with drugs but had heard all the stories about how big the drug problem was in schools in South Africa and in all the night clubs, including Nelspruit. Drugs were the only explanation that we could come up with for Dan's behaviour. Dan must have taken some sort of hallucinatory drug that was making him act all weird. We decided that we'd send him for blood tests so we could get a full toxicology report so we could find out what they hell was going on. Jenny and I sat in the flower shop waiting for Dan, mostly angry but also frightened. Toxicology was a word straight out of a crime show on television and not one that you wanted to associate your eighteen-year-old son with. When eventually Dan walked into the shop, he looked like absolute shit with the biggest black circles under his eyes like he hadn't slept in a week. Concern won out over anger, until he started talking. "Dad, Dad, a black SUV followed here with men inside who want to kill me. I think Mugabe sent them to look for me, to kill me."

Jenny and I lost it straight away. We rounded on him and dragged him into the back of the shop, away from the customers' ears and eyes. I pinned him up against the cold room wall. "What drugs are you taking, Daniel? What have you been smoking?"

"What do you mean, Dad?"

"You smoking something that's making you talk all this shit about men in black SUV's."

Dan came back at me with a babble. "I promise you, Dad, I saw them, I promise you, on my bible, Dad. They were there, in the black SUV, following me, waiting to get me. They're always there." Dan had a hunted look about him and cowered in the corner. I wanted to smack him around his ears but restrained myself. "Do you know how hard I worked to find you an apprenticeship? Bloody hard. You were lucky to get in with Mr Quick. No one else wanted to touch you because you've got no school qualifications, you can't speak Afrikaans, and you haven't got your driving licence. But I managed to persuade Mr Quick to give you a chance. He didn't want to, but I persuaded him. Well, now you're fucking it all up, acting weird, because you're smoking fuck only knows what. Well it's going to stop. You're going to do a blood test, and it's going to tell us what drugs you're on. And you're going to stop taking them. Because you owe me and you owe Mr Quick."

"I didn't smoke anything, Dad, I promise you. I don't do drugs. And I did see the black SUV. And the men in it want to kill me."

I dragged Dan into the car and drove to Dr Malan's rooms to ask him to give Dan a blood test. Dr Malan was Dan's thyroid specialist. I left Dan in the waiting room while I filled Dr Malan in on what had been happening. "It doesn't sound like drugs to me, but these days you never know," he said. "I'll give him the test, and if there is something, we'll know."

There were more dramas from Dan in the doctor's rooms. Dan had had a million blood tests but didn't want this one. "Why you doing this to me, Dad? He's going to inject something into me, something that will kill me. Why you making me do this?" he wailed. For a while, I thought we were going to have to hold him down. But Dr Malan was able to calm Dan down. He'd been treating Dan for years for his Hashimoto's Thyroiditis and had a good rapport with him. After he'd finished drawing blood, he shook Dan by the hand warmly and told him not to worry because everything was going to work out just fine. He told me that the blood tests would be back in a few days and that he'd phone me when the results were ready. Dr Malan held me back in his rooms while Dan went out to the car and told me to go easy on the kid.

I wish I'd listened, but I didn't. Instead, I dragged Dan back to his boarding house. He was going back to work, whether he liked it or not. Dan begged and pleaded. He didn't want to go to the boarding house, he didn't want to go to work - he was scared and just wanted to go home. Tough shit I told him. He had a responsibility to Mr Quick, and he was going to go to work, end of story. But first, he had to apologise to the manager at the boarding house. And he had to tidy up his room. It was like a bloody pigsty.

The next day Jenny and I had to go to Joburg for the day. We left at four in the morning and talked Dan and his drug problem all the way, commiserating with each other, wondering what we'd done so wrong to have God to punish us like he was. Man, but we were miserable. We were even more miserable when Dan started phoning us. Not once, not twice but a dozen times. He hadn't gone to work because he was too frightened. The black SUV was back again. Couldn't he come with us to Joburg? Couldn't we turn around and pick him up from Nelspruit? Or could Gary come and pick him up from the boarding house and take him back to Summer Hill? Or maybe he could go sit in the shop with Gary and then go home to Summer Hill after work? Had we heard from Dr Malan? Did I think there was something seriously wrong with him? Was he going to be all right, or was he going to die? Eventually and thankfully, Dan ran out of airtime. Thank God for that. Then the Please Call Me messages started. We studiously ignored the first one. And the second one just seconds later. But I couldn't let the third one go unanswered.

With blood boiling, I stabbed Dan's number on speed dial. I was going to let Dan have both barrels, as soon as he answered. But I never got the chance. As soon as he answered, Dan, started sobbing, heart-wrenching sobs that came from deep down inside him. He was really, really frightened and please, please could we come and pick him up? I could hear the terror in the kid's voice, and I couldn't be angry with him. Instead, I felt hugely sad. Whatever dreadful drug he'd been taking had really messed him up inside. Fucking Nigerians. Those dealing drugs should be lined up against the nearest wall and shot and the rest of them that weren't, deported back to the shithole they came from. Dan's sobbing dragged me back to the moment. I told him that I'd get Gary to pick him up and take him to Summer Hill. I also told him that everything would be all right. But deep down inside, I knew it wouldn't.

When we got back from Joburg that night, Dan rushed out and hugged us in the driveway. He looked dreadful with black circles under his eyes that deep you could practically fall into them. The kid hadn't slept in a week. Jenny quickly made him some soup and bundled him off to bed. We weren't far behind him, exhausted from Joburg and even more exhausted, stressing about Dan. I'd just fallen into the deepest of sleeps when Dan burst through our bedroom door. I nearly shat myself. Dan's eyes were huge in his face, and he struggled to get words out through his sobbing. "Dad, Dad, there's a helicopter outside, coming to get me. They're coming to take me away. Please, please can you hide me? Don't let them take me, Dad, promise me, promise me." The kid was shaking and trembling, his terror absolutely stark bollock naked. I rushed to our full-length curtains and ripped them aside to show Dan that there was nothing outside in the night; no noise, no lights, no helicopters, no nothing. Dan, hugging the bottom of our bed tightly with both arms, wouldn't go near the window. But at least he stopped sobbing. I talked him down gently. "There's nothing out there that's going to hurt you, Dan, you're safe. Come. Let's get you back to bed."

The heart-wrenching sobs fired up again. "I don't want to go back to my bedroom, Dad. Please, please can I sleep in here with you and Mom, please, please?"

Jesus. I didn't know what to do. Thankfully Jenny took over. While Dan cowered at the bottom of our bed, she went through to his bedroom and came back with blankets and a camping mattress and made up a bed for Dan at the foot of our bed. It was war veterans in Zimbabwe revisited. We coaxed Dan into his bed on the floor, turned out the lights and lay there rigid, like ironing boards, waiting, waiting, waiting. Nothing. I could hear Dan sleeping. Thank God for that. And just as I closed my eyes in search of sleep, Dan's scream ripped through the darkness. Jesus. Again, I nearly shat in the sheets. It sounded like the kid was having both his arms cut off with a blunt saw. I fumbled for the lights. "What the fuck, Dan?"

"It's the helicopter again, Dad, it's right here, above the roof. Can't you hear it, Dad?"

Suffice to say, it was a long night. Dan never slept a wink, and neither did we. After the helicopter, it was bats, spiders on the wall, men in the black SUV, all night long, and all scaring the crap out of Dan.

Halfway through the night, I fled to the lounge in search of a sentence buried in a book on thyroid disorders that I remembered reading long back, when Dan first got Hashimoto's. It took me forever to find the book and then another forever to find the sentence, because my bookshelf is worse than my sock drawer and thyroid books are very long and very boring. But when I found it, I punched the air, more in hope than in triumph. 'Sub-acute thyroiditis could sometimes present as acute psychosis.' Maybe Dan's thyroiditis was to blame. And maybe, maybe, hopefully, Dr Malan would be able to fix Dan in the morning.

First thing in the morning, we gate crashed Dr Malan. I told the receptionist that it was an emergency. Which got her eyebrows up and all excited. Clearly, thyroid emergencies didn't happen too often. Dan sat right next to us in the waiting room, right next to us as in practically on our laps. Daylight had done little or nothing to ease his fears. As soon as he had a gap, Dr Malan called the three of us into his office. Before I even sat down, I started telling Dr Malan about Dan's behaviour, the endless phone calls, the long night of helicopters, bats and spiders. And then quickly I hit him with my sub-acute thyroiditis diagnosis. "Do you think it could be that, Doc, Dan's thyroid again? Maybe we just need to up his Eltroxin dosage or maybe change it for another drug, something stronger?"

"No." Dr Malan punctured my hopes. "This is not thyroiditis. And it's not drugs either. Dan's blood tests came back clean. I'm sorry to tell you that I'm almost certain Daniel is paranoid schizophrenic."

Fuck. Fuck. Fuck. Tears welled up in my eyes, and I grabbed Jenny's hand and squeezed it tight. I wasn't even sure what exactly paranoid schizophrenia was, but I was pretty sure it was bad, real bad.

"Does that mean I'm going to die?" Dan asked, terror, dripping from every word. On top of helicopters and black SUVs, the poor kid could now add schizophrenia to his list of fears.

"No, Daniel, it doesn't mean you're going to die. Schizophrenia is manageable. But first, we need to make sure my diagnosis is correct. We are lucky in Nelspruit to have one of the country's finest psychiatrists now living here. His name is Dr Braunstein, and he operates a clinic close by, just around the corner. If anyone is able to help Daniel, it is Dr Braunstein. I will phone him and make arrangements."

Fifteen minutes later, we were in Dr Braunstein's rooms. He was a big man, tall and strong and he towered over me but with a kindness in his eyes and a sadness. He told me he'd recently moved his practice to Nelspruit from Johannesburg after he and his wife were nearly beaten to death in an armed robbery at their home. Over and above his private practice, he was heading up the mental health unit in the local government hospital. Dr Braunstein told me better to register Daniel as a patient with the government hospital rather than with his private practice because he was very expensive and he'd cost me a fortune. "Better the government pays me rather than you," he said. Finally, a doctor who'd read the small print at the bottom of the Hippocratic Oath. Then he asked us to tell him all about Daniel. He sat with fingers steepled and listened to our sorry story. "OK. Do you know what schizophrenia is?"

"No."

"OK. There are four types, disorganised, catatonic, childhood and paranoid. Most probably Dan has paranoid schizophrenia, which is a long-term, mental illness where Dan's body is churning out excess dopamine, a neurotransmitter typically produced when you're scared." Sitting in front of Dr Braunstein's desk, I teared up as soon as I heard the words Dan and long-term mental illness in the same sentence. Dr Braunstein carried on, dumbing it down for us. "And because he's got too much dopamine going on inside his head, Dan's most probably hearing voices the whole time, telling him about bad stuff that's happening. For Dan, the voices and the warnings are very, very real." Next to me, Dan never said a word, he just sat there with huge, sad eyes. "OK. So here's what we're going to do. We're going to book Dan into the clinic for observations, for a couple of weeks." I gulped. From what little I'd seen, the clinic looked fancy, and expensive. Dr Braunstein picked up on my panic. "Don't worry about your medical aid, I'll make sure they play ball. During his time here, we'll work out how best to medicate Dan's condition so that going forward, he can have quality of life and function relatively normally. We'll try him out on various antipsychotic drugs, mood stabilisers and the like, looking to block out the effects of the excess dopamine, so that Dan doesn't hear the voices anymore. OK. Dan, I'm going to ask one of the nursing sisters to book you into the clinic while I talk with your mom and dad." Dan looked small, lost, sad and scared as he followed the sister out. Dr Braunstein waited until Dan had left the room before carrying on. "Any questions?"

I had a big one. "Why? Why Dan"

"The exact causes of Schizophrenia are unknown. It could be genetics, it could be triggered by trauma, sometimes by recreational drugs. Looking at your history here, in Dan's case, it could be all of the above."

"How do we fix it?"

"In Dan's case, we won't. Both you and your wife will have your work cut out caring for Dan. The medications will curb his paranoia and his psychosis, but he will be dependent on them for the rest of his life. It is unlikely that he'll ever be able to go out and get a normal job and will most probably continue to be dependent on you. But I also need to tell you that I'm here to help you."

By now, Jenny was sobbing silently. I could do little else other than sit next to her, holding her hand tightly while I struggled to process what Dr Braunstein had just said. Dan had just gone from being a son to being a burden, a forever burden who was never going to go away. Fuck, fuck, fuck. And then as soon as I'd thought that, I thought what an absolutely dreadful thing for a parent to think, so I tried desperately hard to un-think it. But life doesn't let you un-think stuff. Once a thought is out there, you can't cancel it out and stick it back in the box, pretending it didn't happen. Dan was my son, and I loved him hugely, more than life itself maybe. But I still didn't want to look after him, forever. Alas. Fuck, fuck, fuck.

It was while Dan was in the clinic that things really started to go wrong. The farm got a final warning from the taxman asking us to pay back three hundred thousand rand of VAT, by the end of the month. My partner Colin trudged up to the house with the weight of the world on his shoulders to show me the letter. He looked like he was walking to a funeral. Colin, one of the nicest men ever, was hugely apologetic. He told me the farm had been struggling to pay bills for a couple of years, let alone the VAT. Colin could have tracked the VAT debt back to Flowers R Us not paying the farm, ditto the Maputo shop, ditto the Joburg flower shops when they crashed and burnt without paying the farm, but he didn't, because he was one of life's gentleman. I eyed up the number at the bottom of the tersely worded letter dumbly. I couldn't get my head around it. In the context of where we were at, three hundred thousand rand was a massively huge number. "Fuck. What are we going to do?"

"If we liquidate all the farm assets, the cold room and the vehicles and all the equipment, we'll put a dent in the three hundred K, then we can work out how we sort out the rest."

"But, but, but...can't we trade our way out of the shit?"

"No. The wheels came off long ago. We've tried to trade our way out of trouble for the last few years, and we've only ended up deeper in the shit."

"How about we liquidate Summer Hill and tell the taxman he can whistle for his VAT money?"

"The Vat number is registered in your personal name, not Summer

OF FAKE FLOWERS AND SCHIZOPHRENIA

Hill."

"Fuck."

"I'm going to get out of South Africa. I've been offered a job in Zambia, and I'm going to go up there and start over."

I quickly weighed up my options. The prospect of starting over fresh, somewhere new and unsullied, flashed before me, bright and shiny like a new day. But it took just seconds for reality to come crashing down on me like a ton of bricks. I was already smack dab in the middle of my new start, and I wasn't going to get another one. If it was just Jenny and me, maybe. But it wasn't. It was very crowded and cramped in the house of cards I'd built. We had Dan in the mental hospital in Nelspruit, going nowhere for the rest of his life. And Hester lived on the farm with us and didn't have anywhere else to go. And then there was Gary and Veronica, Arnold and Jocelyn, all dependent on the Summer Hill and the flower shop. I had no option but to make it work.

In the end, I bought Colin out of the partnership for the proverbial dollar and took over his share of the debt. I put on my one and only suit and a winning smile and went off to charm the taxman. Which didn't go too well. The taxman, actually a Rottweiler wearing woman's clothing, got angry when I asked her for a discount and to be let off with just a warning. She told me by rights she should have me thrown in jail for theft. Vat money wasn't mine to use and to squander at the end of every month, it belonged to the government. I was no better than a common thief. And then with a face like thunder and a stroke of her pen, the woman taxman doubled my debt from three hundred thousand to six hundred thousand - penalties and interest. Fuck. I but...but...butted a few times and then fled before the Rottweiler's pen got busy again.

Jenny and I weighed up our options, which didn't take long. We were fucked. The only thing we could do was sell up, settle what we could of our debts and go back to Zimbabwe. I went into Nelspruit to break the news to my parents. Who offered to lend us money to pay the taxman. My mom and dad were very happy in Nelspruit, mostly because me, Jenny and the kids were so close. Without us around, Nelspruit lost its attraction.

Jenny and I went back to weighing up our options. Again, it didn't take too long. We'd just picked Dan up from the clinic, drugged up to the eyeballs and petrified, of his shadow, of sudden noises and above all, petrified of Zimbabwe. Mugabe and his evil minions were the root cause of all Dan's fears, a shitty souvenir from my adventures in politics. We needed to keep Dan unstressed and unexcited. The lid on top of Dan's paranoid schizophrenia was sort of kept in place by bucket loads of pills, anti-psychotics, anti-depressants, anti-epilepsy, anti-pretty much everything. Dr Braunstein said the voices in Dan's head were still there but were now very muted, because of all the drugs. Going forward, the doctor wanted to see Dan twice monthly, to tweak the regimes and see what was working for Dan and what wasn't. If we moved back to Zimbabwe, we would blow the lid right off Dan's treatment, and he would go back to being crazy. So we quickly accepted my parent's offer to lend us the money. We had no option but to make Summer Hill work.

Chapter Fifty-Six

Colin was one of the best farmers I'd ever met. On top of his university degree, he had green fingers and a way about him that made the people under him want to work, South African farmworkers included. Despite the ugly black clouds hanging over it, Summer Hill looked ship-shape and in order. In pride of place was a field of Crocosmia, a bulb crop that was six weeks from harvest and that had 'Get out of Jail' written all over it. If we got it to market, maybe, maybe we'd laugh all the way to the bank. But in the context of things, six weeks away was a lifetime.

Colin and I did a very brief hand-over take-over, which filled me with so much self-doubt, I had the stuff pouring out of my ears. But I forced myself to knuckle down to the task at hand, which was to get Summer Hill back on its feet and in a position where I could to pay back my parents. Alas. I was fucked before I even started. I had way too many other distractions going on; the farm in Zimbabwe, Flowers R Us, the Mozambique shop, Sympathy Flowers, and now Summer Hill. And all of them, could've, would've should've worked, but they weren't. They were in all in the shit financially and going under.

Summer Hill's problems had started with Flowers R Us. Back when the flower shop had paid Summer Hill, the farm had been profitable, mostly because of Flowers R Us. It was a vicious Catch 22. The farm needed the flower shop, but it was also going under because of the flower shop. I was sitting at my desk in the flower shop, arriving at the conclusion for the umpteenth time that the florists who owed me close on a million rand were the root cause of my problem when I heard one of them talking in the front of the shop. It was the worst of the lot, the serial debtor with the splendid tits who owed me four hundred thousand rand. I'd started legal proceedings against her a year ago, but the case hadn't made into court yet. Justice moved slowly in South Africa.

I walked through to the front of the shop and watched her pick out half the flowers on the shop floor. She was putting together a huge order, she obviously had a big wedding or function on the go. Only once the salesclerk had finished totalling the florist's invoice, I stepped forward. "Cancel the sale. Put the flowers back. The lady is taking nothing."

"But I'm paying cash, Eric," she told me. I'd cancelled the woman's account when I started legal proceedings against her. She still bought from me, but only when her account with the other flower market was maxed out. She hadn't paid back a cent of what she owed me in over a year.

"I don't want your cash today. I want the four hundred thousand rand that you owe me, the four hundred thousand that's making me go under. Pay that back, and you can walk in here and buy flowers. But until you pay it back, I won't sell you a single stem."

The woman started to tear up, and her bottom lip wobbled, along with her surgically enhanced tits. That she was wearing a designer outfit that cost thousands suddenly pissed me off hugely, ditto her brand-new out-the-box BMW parked outside. "Because of you, I can't pay my wages on time, I can't pay my rent. Because of you, I'm going bust. Now get out. And don't come back."

I felt good for about five minutes. Then I went back to stressing.

A month later, after more than a year of waiting, I finally had my day in court with her. Flowers R Us v the florist with the surgically improved bosom. Walking into the courtroom, my lawyer was confidence personified. Backed up by boxes and boxes of our copies of her invoices, all with her signature on them, the lawyer said we had a slam dunk case. I held off celebrating when the florist started fluttering and flashing her long-lashed Bambi eyes and splendid bosom at the Magistrate, who positively leered, the lecherous bastard. Crap. We were dead in the water, even before our opening argument. But I was pleasantly surprised. The Magistrate found in our favour, for the full four hundred thousand rand, in double quick time. Whoop, whoop, I celebrated silently.

The Magistrate then asked the florist if she wanted to say anything. She stood up, managing to look lost and forlorn in the process, bar her bosom which continued magnificent and addressed the Magistrate in a voice all wobbly with emotion. She started with a contrite apology. She was very sorry Your Worship, that she'd fallen behind in her payments. I fumed silently. Fallen behind? More like never fucking started in the first place. But, Your Worship, she was a single mother looking after two precious children, and she wanted to ask for leniency with regards the payment plan, to allow her to continue to honour a list of unavoidable monthly expenses. The Magistrate leered for a bit and then agreed to her request. He asked for her list of unavoidables. It was a long list. A thousand rand for horse riding lessons, the same again for piano lessons, private school fees times two, ballet lessons for the girl and tennis for them both, an arm and a leg for orthodontist's braces for the daughter and adding insult to injury right at the end, fifteen hundred rand a month for fucking bikini waxing. Leaving her just seven hundred rand to go towards her debt. The Magistrate stopped leering, looked stern and with a bang of his gavel, okayed her repayment plan. Seven hundred rand per month. On a four hundred thousand rand debt.

On the way out the courtroom, somehow my lawyer still managed to look smug. We'd won, he told me. Some victory I told him, it was going to take the bitch five hundred and seventy-one fucking months to pay me back, just the principle, let alone interest. He said we could lodge an appeal against the payment plan, but only after I'd settled his fee. The florist paid me the seven hundred for just the first two months and then stopped, to never pay another cent again. Maybe the cost of her bikini waxing went up. Alas.

Over the next few months, the financial noose around my neck tightened as we careered towards a looming precipice, hopelessly out of control. But for the first time in forever, I was fully focused on the job at hand. For the sake of pretty much everyone in my life, I had to make Summer Hill work. I called a meeting with all the farm workers and told them tough times were on us and to survive, we had to all become more productive. Going forward, I was going to be pushing everyone hard. It was a wonderfully rousing speech, but all I got back was quiet sullen. I was very disappointed. Maybe they hadn't understood what I'd been saying, maybe the language gap was bigger than I thought. Alas. Because it really had been a wonderfully rousing speech.

The labour force was up to about forty, which was about thirty-nine more than I could afford, but there was a lot of work on the go. The foreman was a Mozambiquean called Johannes. He was bright, spoke good English and had lots of confidence and lots of energy. I was sure I'd be able to work fine with him. I wasn't so sure about a big hulking ugly brute of a woman, erroneously called Beauty. Beauty outweighed me by at least seventy kilos, all of it muscle. Colin had used her as a team leader, but I had her pegged as a potential troublemaker. On my first morning as big boss, I called her out about her team's weeding performance, and she told me to fuck off, in front of her workmates. I didn't have a clue what to do. So, I did nothing and pretended I hadn't heard. As I walked away, the laughter behind me was loud in my ears which burnt bright red. The next day I cut her from the team and made her weed on her own, as far away from the other women as possible. Problem solved for now, until the next time.

The next time turned out to be the next day. I was admiring my Crocosmia, it was easily the most-watched field of flowers in the world, when I saw Beauty rip one of them out instead of a weed. Now you need to know there is nothing remotely weedy about Crocosmia plants, they're that stand-out different not even a blind man could mistake them for weeds. And while I was trying to process the shock and horror, Beauty ripped out another one, and then another one. I looked back down the row she was weeding, and it was full of huge gaping gaps. The woman was a plague of locusts, destroying all before her. I called her out. "What the hell are you doing, Beauty? You've just pulled out three Crocosmias. How the hell are we going to pay wages if you pull out all the flowers?"

She looked up and told me, "Fuck you."

I waited for Johannes the foreman next to me to enter the fray, but he stood quiet, saying nothing, doing nothing. I dragged him into it. "Jesus, Johannes, don't just stand there, man. You're the foreman. Do your job. The woman is fucking up a field of perfectly good flowers. And she told me fuck you. She can't do that."

Johannes told her sternly "Beauty, you mustn't tell the Boss to fuck you." Which came out sounding horribly wrong.

I looked around to see if any of the other workers were listening and they were, all of them. Laughter couldn't be far away. Fuck. I had to get some control back. "Look Johannes tell her that I'm going to have no option but to give her a written warning. And three written warnings and she's gone." Again, she told me fuck you. That was it. I was a patient man, but the woman had overstepped all the boundaries. I marched her up out the fields and to my office with Johannes trailing behind me reluctantly. I was sure I had a template for a written warning on my computer somewhere.

The office on Summer Hill was a delightful building with big glass French doors, built by Colin under the shade of a huge willow tree, right on the edge of the dam, so he could cast a rod into the water from his desk. I'd tried that but kept getting hooked up in the tree, or in the curtains. Beauty stomped into the office behind me, followed by Johannes. I started rooting around in my computer, looking for written warning forms, all the while talking to Beauty through Johannes, telling her what was going to happen. "I'm giving Beauty a final written warning, Johannes, for Gross Insubordination, for doing her job badly and also for swearing at me. The final written warning will last six months. If she transgresses again in the period, I'll dismiss her."

Johannes nodded dutifully. "Yes, Boss. But what is transgresses?"

"It means if she fucks up again."

"Oh."

"Well, tell her, man. In case she didn't understand me properly.

"Yes, Boss. "He turned to look up at Beauty standing next to him. "Beauty, the Boss is giving you a written warning for Gross Insubordination, for doing the job badly and for telling him to fuck you." Again, that came out sounding wrong. "And you can't tell him to fuck you again for six more months or..."

Beauty snapped. Her neck veins bulged, and her eyes nearly popped, and spittle flew from her lips. It wasn't pretty. "Fuck you too, Johannes. I don't care what the Boss says or does, I just don't care. And I can also fuck you up, Johannes."

Johannes reacted to her threat by trying to leg it out of the office. He only got as far as Beauty's brawny arm. She all but decked him with a clothes-hanger. While he was making awful choking noises on his hands and knees, she slid the French door shut and locked it. And then she grabbed a screwdriver off the desk, grabbed Johannes by his skinny neck, hauled him up and pinned him up against the wall, the screwdriver jammed into his throat. She told him she would kill him if he talked more shit. It was like watching an action movie playing out in real life. Johannes opened his mouth but then wisely closed it again. I gathered myself as best I could, very thankful for the desk between Beauty and me. "Tsk, tsk, tsk Beauty. Threatening to kill your supervisor with a weapon is yet another dismissible offence. As is actually killing him. And I can't be writing you another final final warning, so why don't you just let Johannes go?"

Johannes whimpered, Beauty said fuck you, Boss, again. And it was back to stalemate.

I changed tack. I pulled my cell phone out. "Look Beauty, if you don't let Johannes go, I'll phone the security company." My finger hovered above the speed dial threateningly. "I'm going to, I promise." No response, other than another whimper from Johannes. So I hit the button.

The security company switchboard lady answered promptly. "Alpha Security, how may I help?"

"Roger Alpha, this is Summer Hill Farm here, phoning to report a life-threatening situation, over."

"Say again Summer Hill. Confirm you have a life-threatening situation in progress?"

"Roger that Alpha. I have a hostage situation ongoing, with a member of staff threatening another member of staff with a deadly weapon, over." I don't know why, but I couldn't speak to the security company without rogers and over and outs all over the place. It sounded so Hollywood, but I just couldn't help myself.

"Ok, Summer Hill, reaction vehicles are rolling now, ETA ten minutes." Her voice was deadpan, excited like she was ordering milk.

"Ok, roger that and thanks. Over. And out." I hung up.

And then we waited. With Beauty and me saying nothing and with Johannes whimpering every now and then, it was one of the longest ten minutes I'd ever endured. Mostly I looked at my computer screen trying to pretend I was busy with e-mails and stuff, mostly Beauty just glared. And then finally the SWAT team arrived, in a cloud of dust with blue lights flashing, engines roaring and tyres squealing. As a show of force, it was impressive. I couldn't count the number of vehicles involved, ten, maybe fifteen, pick-up trucks and SUVs'. They screeched to a halt in the yard between the office and the house and commenced disgorging heavily armed men, who milled around threateningly with fingers on triggers, looking for the life-threatening situation. Eventually, one of them walked over to the office. He was a small, angry-looking man wearing black overalls, military-style webbing and a scowl, carrying a stubby automatic M14 look-alike rifle. Even his muscles looked to have muscles. He tried to open the door, but it was locked. So he knocked. Beauty unlocked the door with her free hand.

She still had Johannes pinned up against the wall with the screwdriver. The security man stepped around her. "Are you Mr de Jong? Did you phone to report a hostage situation?" he demanded in his harsh Afrikaans accent?

"Um... roger that, I mean yes, I'm de Jong and yes I did phone in the report."

"Where is the life-threatening situation?"

"It's um...there, by the wall, right behind you there."

He turned to look at Beauty and Johannes. "What, these two kaffirs?"

"Yes. The big one, the woman, threatened to kill the other one with the screwdriver. And she locked the door."

"Is that little screwdriver the weapon that you reported?" He almost laughed. And as he asked the question, the screwdriver shrunk in size, down from scary and life-threatening to just four inches and stubby.

"Um yes. Yes, the screwdriver is the weapon, but it did...um...look to be longer, when she was holding it up against Johannes's throat, and sharper, it looked much sharper."

"But why didn't you just stop her?"

"I did tell her to um...stop um...to stop threatening him but um...she wouldn't listen to me."

"So why didn't you just give her a good smack. Like this." He spun around quickly and punched Beauty on the side of her head. The punch was delivered with appalling force, and it dropped Beauty like a shot giraffe. Johannes whimpered some more. Beauty was out cold. The hard as nails security guy shouted out the door to his men. "You guys can stand down. False alarm. And drag this fucking bitch into the truck and take her to the cop shop."

At the police station, Beauty, Johannes and I were all called upon to give statements. Beauty gave hers first, which I thought was odd. And I couldn't but notice that the policeman who took Beauty's statement shared her surname. Come time for my statement, the policeman all but yawned all the way through my factual recount, most of which he ignored. In the end, he let Beauty off with just a warning. He also gave her a lift back to the farm, overtaking me on the road so that Beauty got home before me. The long arm of the law in South Africa is sometimes very short. Alas.

After the Beauty and the screwdriver incident, staff relations on Summer Hill went downhill quick. Just before the next payday, Enoch, my remaining Zimbabwean worker, called me to the homestead gate after hours. Standing in the shadows to avoid the security light, he was all nerves and obviously shit scared of being seen talking to me. Things were not good in the compound he told me. Johannes was stirring trouble amongst the other workers, telling them that it was wrong that they weren't getting paid on time and that the workers should either go slow or down the tools completely, to force my hand. Fuck. "But Johannes knows that I won't be able to pay anyone if we don't send flowers to market. And the Crocosmia is almost ready. Once that's in, hopefully we'll be okay. Thanks for warning me though. I'll sit down with Johannes again and explain how important each and every stem is. He'll understand. He's not a fool, and he knows...."

Enoch cut me off. "You must be very careful of Johannes, Boss. He is bad. I saw him talking with tsotsi gangsters early today, by the road, and one of them even had a gun. I am sure he's organising with them to rob you when you are on your way back from the bank."

Fuck. I all but went to pieces in front of Enoch as every bad news farm murder story I'd ever read or heard about played out loud in my head. All I wanted to do was get back inside the security gate and back inside the house quickly. With my mouth all dry, I struggled to thank Enoch for warning me. I told him it would all work out all right, but I could tell he didn't believe me.

Jenny wanted me to go to the police with the story. "What will they do?" I wailed. "They'll accuse Johannes, and he'll just deny it. Or they'll do nothing." Instead, I organised with Alpha Security to give me an armed escort when I drove back from the bank with the month-end wages. Well, with half of the month-end wages. Half was as far as my overdraft would stretch. I braced myself for the worst when I convened the workers for pay parade. I told them that because our production figures had dipped, I wasn't going to be able to pay them everything I owed them. But they mustn't worry because I'd be able to catch up in the middle of the month when we were paid again by the auctions, after the Crocosmia kicked in. There were some more angry murmurings, but for the most part, the workers seemed stoic and accepting. One of them even offered to lend me money to help pay wages. I watched Johannes carefully throughout, but he kept his poker face firmly in place. I called him up to the front of the meeting to talk to the workers, to tell them that everything would work out fine if we pulled together and worked hard. He said all the right things. But for Enoch's warnings, I would have believed him.

The next day not a single worker reported for duty. Six-thirty came and went. Seven o'clock also came and went, still no workers. At eight, I walked down to the compound, past the field of Crocosmia, wincing at the overblown flowers in the field. Johannes and two of the other supervisors were seated in the sun, next to the path that led down from the offices, manning the picket line. They stood up and greeted me.

"Where is everyone, Johannes? Why is no one at work? Already there are flowers that overblown."

The gloves came off straight away. Johannes looked me fair-square in the eye and said: "No one is going to go to work today, not until you pay us."

In the background, I could see Enoch, Maria and most of the grading shed girls gathered, dressed and ready for work. "Who said that, Johannes? You? Or the other workers?"

"We have decided. No one will work, not until you go to the bank and get the rest of the money to pay us."

"I told you I have to wait until the middle of the month when the next auction payment comes is."

"Then no one will work, and your flowers will rot in the field."

At eight-thirty, we started picking flowers. But instead of forty harvesters, there was only me, Jenny, Gary, his girlfriend, Veronica, Arnold, Hester, my mom, my dad, and even Dan, who at first was too scared to step out the house. By nine o'clock, the sun was hot in the sky, and we'd made not even a dent in the Crocosmia in the field. My dad with just half of his one lung was wheezing like he'd run a marathon. I made him go and sit down in the shade.

And all the while, Johannes and his flunkies watched, to make sure none of the other workers came and helped. Enoch sent me a text message to apologise. He told me Johannes had threatened him with death if he crossed the picket line. By ten o'clock, we were all completely knackered, and already the grading shed was full of flowers waiting to be graded. But all the graders were seated in the compound behind the picket line. We were running out of buckets. And the flowers that hadn't made it into the cold room were already spoiling. It was an unmitigated fuck up. So, I called time on one of the worst days of my life. Jenny and my dad didn't want to give up, but I told them it was useless. I was going to have to make another plan to get the flowers picked. I thanked everyone for their efforts and sent them home. In the background, I could hear Johannes laughing. I've never hated anyone so much in all my life.

It was late that afternoon when Johannes and a large group of workers, thirty or more, arrived at the office door. I looked up at them and then ignored them. Fuck Johannes. I wasn't interested in talking to him anymore. I'd spent the rest of the day trying desperately to find casual workers to come and pick flowers. With help from a friend, I'd organised to send a truck up into Bushbuck Ridge the next day to recruit labour enough to get the job done. Johannes slid open the door, stepped into the office, followed by a flood of other workers. Very quickly the office filled to overflowing. The last worker in, closed the door behind him and locked it. All of a sudden, I got real scared. "What do you want, Johannes?"

"We want our money."

"I told you already that the farm will only get paid next by the auction on the 14th of the month."

"We want our money."

"I haven't got it to give to you. You'll have to wait."

"We are going nowhere, not until you pay us the money. And neither are you."

Jenny phoned me when it got dark. She wanted to know when I was coming into the house. I told her I wasn't. With Johannes seated on the corner of the desk listening, I told her I was being held in the office by the workers. She asked me did I want her to phone the security company. I told her no, not yet. The stalemate dragged out past eight o'clock, then nine o'clock, then ten. By then, my headache was all-consuming. My mouth had dried out hours earlier, and suddenly I was absolutely exhausted. I just wanted the worst fucking day ever to be over. So, I phoned my immediate neighbour. I apologised for waking him up so late, but I needed to ask him if he wanted to buy my tractor, the green John Deere. How much did I want for it? I told him I needed fifteen thousand five hundred and fifty rand, coincidentally the exact amount outstanding on the previous month's wages. The tractor was worth a lot more than that, so my neighbour said yes, for sure he'd buy the tractor. I said there was one condition. Please, could he come to give me the cheque now, as in tonight? It took the neighbour ten minutes to get dressed and to drive over with the cheque. I pushed my way through the scrum of workers to shake hands on the deal. "Jesus, Eric, what's going on here? Do you want me to phone the cops for you?"

"No worries, Fanie, you've already solved my problem for me."

Johannes checked the cheque carefully to make sure it was signed and legit before letting me out the office. I could hear him and the other workers laughing all the way down to the compound.

The next morning the full labour force arrived for work, bright and early.

"What do you want, Johannes?"

"We've come for work, Boss."

"Sorry. There's no more work. Summer Hill is closed for business. We don't have a tractor anymore. You can't farm without a tractor. Come back at ten o'clock, all of you, and I'll pay you off."

"But what are you going to do?"

"I'm going home." Johannes looked confused. My house was only fifty metres away. I spelt it out for him. "I'm not talking about that house. I'm talking about my home in Zimbabwe. I don't want to live here anymore."

Chapter Fifty-Seven

Of Alzheimer's and ashes in the wind and going home with cat crap in the laundry basket

Our last few months in South Africa flew past. We packed up and sold what was left of our South African lives. And my mom got Alzheimer's, and my dad died.

My mom had always had a memory like a sieve, especially when it came to names of places and people. So, when she started telling the same story once, twice, three times in a day, none of us took too much notice. It was just Bets getting a little more dippy. Then one day she arrived home with her car all smashed up in front. It was way more than just a dent in the fender. She'd hit something hard, another car, judging by the paint marks. She was very flustered and got even more so when I asked her what had happened. "Jesus, Mom, who did you hit?"

"I don't know."

"Did you hit another car?'

"I don't know."

"Where did the accident happen, Mom? And was anyone hurt?"

"I don't know."

"Jesus, Mom, you can't not know. Think. Where've you just come from?"

"Eric, I don't know." She burst into tears and fled into her bedroom.

"Shit, Dad, you'd better take her to the doctor."

"Of course, I'll take her first thing tomorrow" But alas, he never did.

One of the problems was my mom didn't do sick. I couldn't remember a single day where she'd been sick in bed, ever. And as for her not knowing where she'd had her accident that was entirely in keeping with Bets. She'd been living in Nelspruit for over four years and did not know the name of a single street, other than the one that she lived on. Before that, she'd lived in Cape Town for ten years, and she hadn't known any street names there either. Ditto Pietermaritzburg, ditto Salisbury now Harare.

But then two weeks later, my mom went to visit the neighbours, at two in the morning, wearing a skimpy nightie and nothing else. Not surprisingly, the neighbours had been fast asleep. Eventually, they woke up with Bets hollering and banging on their front door. Bets told them she'd popped in for a chat and a cup of tea because they were neighbours and it was bad that they saw so little of each other. The neighbours walked her home, woke my dad up and handed her over. I went to the doctor with my dad, just to make sure he actually took her this time. The doctor told us that there were seven stages of Alzheimer's and in his opinion, my mom had just moved from stage three to four, possibly even five. As he talked us through the various stages, especially the early ones, it was like he was describing my mom; struggling to communicate because she couldn't find words, losing her focus and her concentration along with her keys and or her purse, and or handbag, and or pretty much anything and everything. Shit, my mom had Alzheimer's, and I hadn't even picked up on it.

"What comes next, Doc?" I asked. The doctor told us that Alzheimer's was a degenerative disease and there was no reversing it. With medication, we could slow the disease down, but we couldn't stop it. And if my mom was stage four going into five, she wasn't far away from needing full-time care. Obviously, she wouldn't be able to drive anymore. And her walkabouts would only get worse. Maybe she'd be better off in my home if my dad couldn't cope.

Fuck. In my parent's home, my mom did everything, and my dad did nothing. He didn't know how to turn the washing machine on, ditto the vacuum cleaner. And the only time I'd ever seen him cook anything was when my mom was in hospital giving birth to my sister, and he'd boiled us eggs in the kettle for breakfast, lunch and dinner. The man couldn't even make a sandwich. There was no way he was ever going to be able to look after my mom, especially with Jenny and I back in Zimbabwe. We were going to have to put my mom into a home, God forbid. My mom made our decision for us by going walkabout again in the early hours of the morning, but this time without her panties on. When my dad phoned to tell me, I rushed into town to see what I could do to help. It was horrible. My mom was in her bed, still without panties and talking the biggest load of nonsense out, to the point where I had absolutely no idea what she was talking about. I fled the room after two minutes and told my dad better we press the button on moving her to a home sooner than later.

There were several old-age nursing home options in Nelspruit, but only one with a specialised Alzheimer's unit attached. The main part of the old age home looked fine, nothing fancy but it was clean, well laid out with friendly staff and the old folk who lived there looked happy enough. There was a bingo game on the go in the main hall when we arrived, and everyone seemed to be having fun. Then we went to look at the Alzheimer's unit. It was easily the most depressing places I'd ever been into. It was a full lock-down facility with floor to ceiling bars and an armoured gate. And once under lock-down, from what I could see the Alzheimer residents did nothing, others sit and stare, either at a big television on the wall, at each other or at nothing. They didn't talk, they just sat, just stared. But easily the worst, it was a mixed unit with the merely forgetful Stage Three patients mixed in amongst the nearly comatose and drooling Stage Sevens, so the Stage Threes knew exactly what was headed their way.

Holding my mom by the hand, I led her down the passage to the tiny bedsit she would now call home. To add to the moment, two old ladies had at a proper go at each other with their walking sticks right outside my mom's room, screaming and screeching at each other like harridans in some sort of turf war. The nurse escorting us ignored the fight completely and opened my mom's bedroom with a bright and breezy" There you go, all ready for you, Mrs de Jong." The room was dreadful, stark and austere, painted out in institutional grey with room only for the hard hospital bed, and even harder visitor's chair and a set of tiny bedside drawers. "Very nice, Mom and very compact. I think you'll be very happy here." I had to fight away the tears as I lied through my teeth.

My mom looked confused and lost. Thankfully she didn't have a clue as to what was going on. I laid out the family photos that I'd brought on her bedside drawers. There was a photo of me, Jenny and our kids, one of my dad when he was young and handsome, a photo of brother Kees when he was young, irresponsible and still alive, and a photo of each his daughters, my mom's granddaughters. The matron had told me to bring the photos. Apparently, they'd help anchor my mom to reality. But as soon as I'd laid them out, I wished I hadn't. In that horrible little hospital room that was now my mom's home, the photos were a cruel reminder of the life that she used to have, the life that her illness had taken from her. I fled the room and my mom before my tears got the better of me. And to make dreadful even worse, lucid paid my mom the briefest of visits. "Why are you leaving me here, Eric? Take me home" she called out after me.

"I can't take you with, Mom, I have to leave you here."

"But why?"

"Because you're sick, Mom."

She got angry. "Nonsense. I'm not sick. You're talking crap, man. Take me to your father now."

I ran away, leaving the nurse to try and calm my mom down.

My dad and I agonised over our decision. What the hell had we done? The matron came and gave my dad a hug and told him that he'd made the right decision. She told us that as the disease progressed, Bets would be able to do less and less for herself. It was better that she was in a place where professionals could nurse her and look after her. Looking back now as I write, and being harsh, I think the matron was just making a sales pitch, chasing down another seventeen thousand rand a month patient, to help her reach her financial targets. But at the time, the matron's advice seemed sound. Jenny and I were headed back to Zimbabwe, and there was no way on earth my dad would ever cope looking after my mom. My dad proved the point by dying exactly one week later.

Dad decided to move out of their very nice retirement home up on top of the hill and move into the same old age home that my mom was in, but only he'd live upstairs, in the normal part where they played Bingo.

That way he'd be able to visit my mom all day, every day. It was also very much a money decision. After paying the seventeen thousand rand that my mom's lock-down cost every month, there wouldn't be enough money left over from their pensions to pay for the retirement house on top of the hill. Once he'd made the decision to move, my dad rushed at the logistics like a bull in a china shop. Because the new bedsit that he was going to move into was tiny, he sold up all their furniture and belongings in a morning, for an absolute pittance. He practically gave the stuff away, mostly to neighbours. And because he no longer had any lounge furniture to sit on of an evening, and he because he didn't have a wife to nag at him to come in from the cold after the sun had gone down, he sat outside on his beloved patio, overlooking the lights of Nelspruit, reading his book, sipping brandy and coke, catching a chest cold. And because my dad only had half a lung left after his prolonged fight with cancer, chest colds were serious shit. On the day that he moved into the old age home, I helped him to move his few remaining boxes of belongings. I picked up on his hacking cough, but alas, thought nothing of it. The next day it was worse, and the day after that he was dead, just like that.

I got the call from the nursing home to tell me my dad had died. They said he died in hospital just an hour after he'd been admitted for observation after complaining in the morning that he was feeling dreadful. We later found out that his chest cold had fast-forwarded to pneumonia overnight and he died of respiratory problems. Fuck. I was shocked to my core, numbed and clueless as to how to process the information that a man who'd survived lung cancer for over twenty years was dead, because of a chest cold. First, I phoned my sister Irene in Holland. She'd been out to visit just a few months earlier. Then I had to go and tell my mom that my dad was dead. How the hell was I going to do that? I sprung my mom from her maximum-security prison and told her on the way to the hospital. I got zero reaction from her, not even when we went into the room where he'd died to say goodbye. My mom just stood there looking down at him. I teared up as I bent over and kissed my dad goodbye on his forehead. Under my breath, I told him that I'd look after my mom for him.

We organised my dad's funeral service under the thatched gazebo in the retirement village up on the hill. My dad would have approved because he'd been real happy living there. We organised rows of plastic chairs for mourners. Ironically, the lounge suit my dad had sold was in storage in the gazebo and got press-ganged into service. I sprung my mom out of maximum-security again and told her we were going to Dad's funeral. She kept her poker face firmly in place. I watched her carefully, looking for a reaction from her as we drove into the retirement home that had been her home for five years but again got nothing. She was wrapped up warm in her little cocoon. As we filed into the gazebo, the place was already full of her former neighbours and mourners. My dad had been a popular member of the community, and everyone from the village had come to say goodbye and to pay their last respects. My mom said hallo to anyone and everyone that came up and hugged her, but there wasn't any recognition. The only upside of her Alzheimer's was that it was shielding her from the pain of losing the biggest and most important thing in her life. I led my mom to the centre of the first row and sat her down on one of her old armchairs.

Predictably the funeral service got all cocked up. My dad's favourite singer in the whole world had been Susan Boyle. He'd sit and listen to her songs over and over again. Arnold very kindly tracked down a recording of Susan Boyle singing Amazing Grace, the cornerstone hymn of my dad's funeral service. Come the time for the hymn, Arnold would play the Susan Boyle recording and the mourners would sing along with Susan from the hymn sheets the funeral home had printed for us. It all went swimmingly well, Susan's strong, powerful voice rang out loud and clear, while we mumbled along with her. Until the second verse, at which point Susan went off on own her tangent, with completely different lyrics to those printed in the hymn sheet. A ripple of uncertainty swept through the congregation.

Some bolder congregants stepped up their volume, trying their best to drown Susan out while others less bold stopped singing and lip-synced instead. There was brief convergence in lyrics and a massive surge in volume when we got to the chorus bit, and Susan was back in step again. But only briefly. Come to the third verse, Susan buggered off course again, with her own version of the hymn. Jenny looked at me and started laughing. It was that or cry. By the end of the third verse, the whole front row was laughing, even my dad I reckon, up in heaven. But not my mom. She looked wooden throughout. Until suddenly she looked down at the armchair she was seated on, gripped my arm hard and demanded loudly. "Hey, Eric, this is my chair. This is my lounge suite. And that's my carpet. Why's all my furniture in here? Who's pinched my stuff?"

I shushed her up as best I could.

Later that week, I collected my dad's ashes from the crematorium. They were in a square wooden box, rather than an urn, with his initials and his date of birth handwritten on a sticker. Rather than have him clutter up our mantelpiece, or worse still, get lost on our move back to Zimbabwe, I decided I'd scatter his ashes straightaway. I chose the escarpment at Kaapse Hoop, a rugged granite outcrop high above Nelspruit which had a stark almost lunar landscape strewn with massive boulders and a magnificent view that stretched away forever. My dad had told me often it was one of his favourite places on Earth. To get to the escarpment from the car park was quite a hike, so I decided against taking my mom. Because it was the last time I'd be with my dad, I only invited Jenny and Jocelyn to go with me. I don't do heights too good, a legacy passed down to me by my dad who got white knuckles on the shortest ladder, but I forced myself to clamber up on the huge granite outcrop overhanging a sheer drop of a thousand metres or more. I got double nagging from Jenny and Jocelyn to be careful, while I struggled to get the lid of the box open. When I finally got it open, I mumbled my last goodbyes and repeated my promise to look after my mom, and then I flung the ashes out into the void. It was a wonderfully dramatic moment, spoilt entirely by the massive gust of wind that blew my dad's ashes back into my eyes, my face and my mouth.

From there, it was a crazy mad rush to pack up our lives. I moved my mom out of the maximum-security prison into a much nicer and more gentle care facility that I'd found on the outskirts of Nelspruit, while I searched for an Alzheimer's facility in Johannesburg where my mom would live, until we were ready to move her back to join us in Zimbabwe. Gary fled back to Zimbabwe to restart his wildlife photography business, relieved that he'd done everything he could and more to help us win in South Africa, and even more relieved that it was finally over and he could pick up doing what he loved and what he should have stuck with all along.

It had taken me eight years and more money than I had to build up a portfolio of businesses in South Africa and Mozambique. I took me just two months to wind them all down. I exited the rose farm with nothing. A friend took over Sympathy Flowers, which was already showing signs of not becoming the huge runaway success that I'd envisaged. I closed the Maputo Flower Market down with alacrity and zero regrets. A black Mozambiquean businessman who I'd befriended took over the assets and the debt, apart from the three hundred thousand rand that I owed myself. Alas. I drove away from the corner of Mao Tse Tung Avenue and Vladimir Lenin Avenue, with the hugest sense of relief and release. I liked Maputo, but if I never went back there again, it would be too soon.

Arnold and Veronica told us they would stay on in Nelspruit and battle on in the flower business. Arnold wanted to carry on with selling mixed bunches and bouquets into the supermarkets, so we separated that part of the business from the rest of Flowers R Us and handed it over to Arnold with fervent wishes of good luck.

What remained of Flowers R Us, I sold to one of our nicer customers, a handsome young man who I'll call Juan. Juan had the whitest of teeth and a smile that made Jenny swoon every time he came into the shop. Juan used his smile to great effect to build up a successful business organising conference, weddings and events in Nelspruit and across the province. He and I agreed on a price that was win-win and which would allow me to settle some of our debts. We'd built Flowers R Us into a good little business and somehow it had survived all my attempts to expand it into a huge, multi-national conglomerate. Juan swept into Flowers R Us like a breath of fresh air and gave it a massive facelift, transforming it from a bland but functional flower wholesaler into a very tasteful, high-end emporium selling flowers, décor and wedding finery. I marvelled at what Juan had achieved in such a short time and wished him all the very best going forward. Alas. Juan defaulted on his deposit payment and never paid me a single red cent. I thought about suing him but didn't. Juan looked like he also bikini waxed often, and expensively.

Which left just Summer Hill. Which I managed to sell to the neighbour who'd bought the tractor for a song, also for a song, and just a week before the bank foreclosed. The neighbour paid us out what we owed the bank plus some very small change. And that was that our South African business empire all wrapped up. We had to use the inheritance that Jenny got from Tony to pay for half a removal truck to move half our household of furniture back to Zimbabwe. It would have been nice to take the whole household, but Jenny's inheritance wouldn't stretch that far. Alas.

In between all of the above, I was able to squeeze in a full-on mental breakdown and ended up joining Daniel under the care of Dr Braunstein who put me onto a healthy daily dosage of Sulpiride to cushion me from the rigours of our South African extraction. Good stuff, Sulpiride.

Once I'd semi-recovered from my mental wobble, I went up to Zimbabwe to tell the farm I was coming home, and to find Daniel, a psychiatrist. I signed Daniel up as a patient with a very capable and competent psychiatrist who I'd known as a schoolboy. He told me that he'd be able to shield Daniel from the worst of his fears and phobias. While in Zimbabwe, I found us a home to rent in Harare. Brian warned me about moving back into our house on the farm straight away because of local politics on the ground. He said the neighbourhood war veterans including the man who'd murdered Terry Ford and the district ZANU PF would be less than enamoured with my decision to come home. I also managed to get import permits for 3 dogs and two cats.

Our migration north got slightly more complicated when at the eleventh hour, Arnold and Veronica asked if they could also move back to Zimbabwe with us. Without subsidised flowers from Summer Hill, Arnold's supermarket venture wasn't going at all well. I was overjoyed. Jocelyn was easily the brightest thing in our lives and Jenny and I had been hugely saddened at the prospect of leaving her and Veronica behind in South Africa. But it also meant we'd have to try to smuggle another two dogs and one cat in with us, plus whatever of their household furniture that we could manage.

We spent the last week camping in the half-empty house at Summer Hill, amongst the furniture and bits and pieces of our lives that weren't coming back to Zimbabwe with us. We practised packed and ran out of room way too early and had to jettison a whole bunch more of our belongings. We dumped them with best friends Jackie and Patrick Robson with a promise to collect all our junk later, but we never did. It was easily one of the worst weeks of our lives, and it put a cap on the South African chapter of our lives.

We'd fled to South Africa in fear of our lives eight years earlier, and it had offered us a port in the storm, somewhere to regroup and re-gather and start again. But almost from the beginning, it had gone very horribly wrong for us, mostly because of me and my belief that handshake deals counted. Alas. Jenny had been happy in South Africa despite the lumps and bumps and was sad to leave. But I wasn't.

We drove out of Summer Hill in two cars an hour before midnight, on our long trek home to Zimbabwe, looking like Vietnamese boat people loaded to the hilt and beyond. To add to the moment, as I drove out of the Summer Hill gate one of the cats in the laundry basket just behind my seat, shat. Zimbabwe, here we come.

Printed in Great Britain
by Amazon